YALE LAW LIBRARY SERIES
IN LEGAL HISTORY AND REFERENCE

# AGAINST THE
# PROFIT MOTIVE

*The Salary Revolution in American Government, 1780–1940*

Nicholas R. Parrillo

Yale

UNIVERSITY PRESS

*New Haven & London*

Published with support from the Lillian Goldman Law Library, Yale Law School, and with assistance from the Mary Cady Tew Memorial Fund.

Yale University Press books may be purchased in quantity for educational, business, or promotional use. For information, please e-mail sales.press@yale.edu (U.S. office) or sales@yaleup.co.uk (U.K. office).

Set in Electra type by Newgen.
Printed in the United States of America.

Library of Congress Cataloging-in-Publication Data

Parrillo, Nicholas R.
Against the profit motive : the salary revolution in American government, 1780–1940 / Nicholas R. Parrillo.
pages cm. — (Yale Law Library series in legal history and reference)
Includes bibliographical references and index.
ISBN 978-0-300-17658-2 (hardcover : alk. paper) — ISBN 978-0-300-19475-3 (paperback: alk. paper)   1. United States—Officials and employees—Salaries, etc.—History.
2. Fees, Administrative—United States—History.   I. Title.
JK776.P37 2013
331.2'813517309034—dc23
2012051295

A catalogue record for this book is available from the British Library.

This paper meets the requirements of ANSI/NISO Z39.48–1992 (Permanence of Paper).

10 9 8 7 6 5 4 3 2 1

To my mother and father,
Gale and Joseph Parrillo

# CONTENTS

# ACKNOWLEDGMENTS

I could never have written this book without the advice, generosity, scrutiny, and support of a great many teachers, fellow scholars, friends, and institutions. I owe so many debts, and such great ones, that I can never repay them.

First, my graduate school advisers. Jean-Christophe Agnew was a formative teacher, particularly on the book's fundamental issue of how to understand money and human motivation. Bob Gordon was the perfect interlocutor for a young legal historian—and that goes not only for me but also for a generation's worth of people in the field. Jerry Mashaw inspired me to study the administrative state and showed me that the subject, dry to some, implicates the most profound questions of human behavior. Stephen Skowronek deepened and transformed my interest in history by showing me its importance for understanding politics.

The Yale law faculty has provided a wonderfully stimulating setting in which to write the book. The two deans with whom I have served, Harold Koh and Robert Post, have been generous and supportive. John Langbein, Claire Priest, Jim Whitman, and John Witt have made Yale a terrific place to write legal history. I have benefited immensely from conversations about the book with them and with Bruce Ackerman, Akhil Amar, Ian Ayres, Rick Brooks, Jules Coleman, Bob Ellickson, Bill Eskridge, Heather Gerken, Michael Graetz, Henry Hansmann, Oona Hathaway, Christine Jolls, Tony Kronman, Yair Listokin, Jonathan Macey, Daniel Markovits, Tracey Meares, Judith Resnik, Susan Rose-Ackerman, Alan Schwartz, Scott Shapiro, Kate Stith, and Tom Tyler.

Further, I am deeply grateful for the insights I gained from discussions with Brian Balogh, Joseph Bankman, Christopher Beauchamp, Susannah Blumenthal, Andrew Cohen, Charlotte Crane, Daniel Ernst, George Fisher, Barbara Fried, Ron Harriss, Dirk Hartog, Jill Hasday, Kristin Hickman, Daniel Ho,

Daniel Hulsebosch, Richard John, Amalia Kessler, Naomi Lamoreaux, Assaf Likhovski, Peter Lindseth, Deborah Malamud, Ajay Mehrotra, Bill Novak, Karen Orren, James Pfander, Jed Purdy, Gautham Rao, Kim Scheppele, Jed Shugerman, Patrick Weil, Barry Weingast, Barbara Welke, Michael Willrich, and Viviana Zelizer, as well as participants in workshops at the American Society for Legal History conferences, the University of Michigan, the University of Minnesota, New York University, Harvard University, Stanford University, and Tel Aviv University. All errors are, of course, my own.

I especially thank Bill Nelson, for his extraordinary mentorship and wisdom, and Stephen F. Williams, for his example of how to live the life of the mind.

I have been fortunate to work with several excellent student research assistants: Allyson Bennett, Glenn Bridgman, Miles Farmer, Beth Foster, James Fowkes, Benjamin Gross, Tian Huang, Danielle Jackson, Alexia Koritz, Sergio Perez, Stephanie Reichelderfer, Clare Ryan, Trevor Sutton, and Julio Vasquez.

Much-appreciated financial support was provided by Yale Law School, the William Nelson Cromwell Foundation, the Golieb Fellowship in Legal History at New York University, the Whiting Fellowship in the Humanities in the Yale Graduate School, the Oscar M. Ruebhausen Fund at Yale Law School, and the Esther Guthery and Robert Barbeau Mautz Fund for Distinguished Younger Faculty at Yale Law School.

Historians are nothing without librarians. I am delighted to acknowledge the aid of Blair Kauffman, John Nann, Mike Widener, and the staff of the Yale Law Library; of Gregory Eow and the Yale University Library; of Susan Strange; of the staff of the U.S. National Archives in College Park, Maryland; of Rosalie Spire; of the National Archives of the United Kingdom; and of Clements Library at the University of Michigan.

At Yale University Press, I have been very lucky to work with Mike O'Malley, who expressed an early interest in the book, and with Bill Frucht, who has shepherded it (and me) through the whole process. I benefited from thorough readings by the press's anonymous referees. And I thank Jaya Chatterjee, Mary Pasti, and Jay Harward for their work on the manuscript.

Last, my greatest debts. It is due to the example, guidance, and loving encouragement of my parents, Gale and Joseph Parrillo, that I have become a scholar and teacher. This book is for them. Through many years of writing this book, my dear wife, Jenny Chou, has been my steadfast companion and partner in everything.

———————————•●•———————————

In quotations from primary sources, I have silently modernized spelling and capitalization (but not in titles).

Material in Chapter 9 originally appeared as "The De-Privatization of American Warfare: How the U.S. Government Used, Regulated, and Ultimately Abandoned Privateering in the Nineteenth Century," *Yale Journal of Law & the Humanities*, vol. 19, pp. 1–96. I appreciate the journal's permission to use it here.

# INTRODUCTION

## THE ARGUMENT IN BRIEF

In America today, the lawful income of a public official consists of a salary. However, in the eighteenth century and often far into the nineteenth and early twentieth centuries, American law authorized a wider variety of ways for officials to make money. Judges charged fees for transactions in the cases they heard. District attorneys won a fee for each criminal they convicted. Tax investigators received a percentage of the evasions they discovered. Naval officers were awarded a percentage of the value of the ships they captured, plus bounties for the enemy sailors on board ships they sank. Militiamen enjoyed rewards for capturing Indians or taking their scalps. Policemen were allowed rewards for recovering stolen property or arresting suspects. Jailors collected fees from inmates for permitting them various privileges, and the managers of penitentiaries had a share of the product of inmates' labor. Clerks deciding immigrants' applications for citizenship took a fee for every application. Government doctors deciding veterans' applications for benefits did the same, as did federal land officers deciding settlers' applications for homesteads. Even diplomats could lawfully accept a "gift" from a foreign government upon finalizing a treaty.

What these arrangements had in common was that the officers' incomes depended, immediately and objectively, on the delivery of services and the achievement of outputs. By a gradual yet profound transformation extending from the late eighteenth century through the early twentieth century, American lawmakers abolished all these forms of income and replaced them with the fixed salaries that we now take for granted in government service, thus attenuating the relationship of officials' income to their conduct. In so doing, they made the absence of the profit motive a defining feature of government.[1]

1

The key to comprehending this transformation is to understand the non-salary forms of pay that initially predominated. There were two basic types, which I term *facilitative payments* and *bounties*. A facilitative payment was a sum that an officer received for performing a service that the affected person wanted or needed, such as processing an application or issuing a permit.[2] A bounty was a sum that an officer received for performing a task that the affected person did not want and might resist, such as arresting a suspect, discovering tax delinquencies, or forcing an inmate to do hard labor.[3]

The two forms of payment tended to give rise to two very different social relationships between officials and the people with whom they dealt. The facilitative payment tended to promote reciprocal exchange between the officer and the recipient of the service, working to the benefit of both. It fostered mutual accommodation. The officer viewed service recipients as "customers" to be attracted, and service recipients viewed officers as vendors offering valuable benefits to be purchased. In contrast, the bounty tended to promote adversarialism. The officer gained by the affected person's loss—by taking state-mandated action that the affected person wanted left undone. Affected persons typically found this an alienating experience: they were subject to the coercive power of a person whose interests were directly adverse to their own.

The two different social dynamics generated by facilitative payments and bounties inspired, respectively, two different arguments for why officials' profit-seeking was incompatible with the needs and values of a liberal-democratic republic and therefore had to be abolished. The critique of facilitative payments was essentially that customer-seller accommodation no longer had a rightful place in government. At first, this critique aimed not at facilitative payments per se but at their relatively unregulated status. For centuries, the law had authorized a substantial amount of bargaining between individual officers and those who received their services. But lawmakers of the late 1700s and early 1800s, influenced by republican and liberal ideologies, came to believe that officers were not quasi-independent vendors entitled to strike variable and individualized bargains, but instead were creatures of a democratic legislature obligated to serve citizens equally—and to charge them prices that were uniform and reasonable. Thus, lawmakers and judges by the mid-1800s came to the conclusion that officers could legally take facilitative payments only when authorized and fixed by an act of the legislature. But officers and recipients often refused to get with the program. True to the essence of the facilitative payment, they continued to engage in reciprocal negotiation in ways that departed from the fixed prices. Judged against the new dogma that facilitative payments required legislative authorization, such negotiations were defined as "corrupt," and lawmakers reacted by banning facilitative payments altogether and replacing them with salaries, as a prophylactic against corruption.

Meanwhile, even in areas where officers and recipients conformed to the fixed uniform prices, facilitative payments still caused officers to view recipients, as a class, as their "customer base" and to focus on meeting the wishes of that base in handling public business. As a result, the critique of facilitative payments expanded by the late 1800s to condemn not merely unregulated exchange but also customer-oriented exchange of any kind, regulated or not. Treating public services as customer-seller transactions, said critics, harmed interests that were not represented in those transactions (much as economists today worry about externalities). For example, letting naturalization officers "sell" citizenship rights to immigrants harmed native-born Americans by diluting their voting power. Letting public-land officers "sell" homestead rights to settlers harmed future generations by depleting the public domain. Critiques like these came to the fore because, as mass democratic politics became more sophisticated and organized, relatively diffuse interest groups, such as nativists and conservationists, increasingly acquired the capacity to assert their claims. Thus arose the mass interest-group rivalry of modern politics. Government could no longer simply distribute resources to a customer class but had to balance rival mass claims to those resources. This required the replacement of facilitative payments with salaries, to sever the customer-seller bond between officialdom and service recipients. Severing this bond was a major step in the differentiation of the state from the persons with whom its officers dealt.

The critique of bounties was quite different. This is because bounties had far different implications for modern government than facilitative payments did. The clash between facilitative payments and the modern state was intuitive, even obvious: the will of a democratic government could not have much independent meaning if the officers charged with implementing it aimed primarily to meet the "customer preferences" of the particular individual or interest group immediately affected. But the clash between bounties and the modern state was not intuitive or obvious. On the contrary, bounties, ever since the Middle Ages, had held great promise as instruments to vindicate the directives of the sovereign, for they incentivized officers to enforce those directives in the face of the contrary preferences of those affected. After the age of revolution, with sovereignty vested in democratically representative legislators, the promise of bounties grew even brighter, for such legislators proved far more ambitious than the kings and oligarchs who preceded them in seeking to reform and improve society in novel, aggressive, and intrusive ways, and the bounty could motivate officials to do their duty in the face of resistance from particular communities or individuals who resented the legislature's reforms and improvements. What better motivational fuel than a bounty to ensure that officers would faithfully carry out the great positivist endeavors of nineteenth-century lawmakers—to impose taxes at higher rates on novel bases to finance new public projects, to suppress drinking and gambling, to forcibly transform prisoners into productive workers, and so forth? As legislation reached new heights of ambition in the mid- to late 1800s, lawmakers experimented with using bounties more intensely than ever before.

But the very intensity of the experiment was the bounty's undoing: it led to such disappointing and perverse results that lawmakers soured on bounties and rejected them altogether. Yes, such payments instigated the aggressive exercise of coercive power. But the construction of a workable state (as lawmakers now concluded from experience) could not rest upon coercion alone, for it was impossible to deploy enough enforcers to achieve the requisite deterrence. The effective implementation of legislative will depended (and still depends) on a large degree of mass voluntary cooperation by the affected individuals, and bounties turned out to undermine such cooperation. The officer's monetary incentive to impose sanctions on laypersons placed him in such an adversarial posture toward them as to vitiate their trust in government and elicit from them a mirror-image adversarial response. In addition, officers' profit motive discouraged them from making the kind of subjective and discretionary decisions *not* to enforce the law that were (and are) necessary to sand off the hard edges of modern state power so it can win acceptance by the population. As lawmakers vested officials with more power and charged them with more ambitious missions, selflessness and forbearance became necessary to vest the officialdom with legitimacy and to foster the essential minimum of lay cooperation that makes the modern state workable.

Taken together, lawmakers' disillusionment with facilitative payments and with bounties resulted in a convergence upon the solution of paying officials by salary. The salary embodied a new state-society relationship, one that distanced the official from the wishes of the layperson (in contrast to the facilitative payment) without radically alienating the two from each other (in contrast to the bounty). Compared with the two old forms of compensation, the salary placed the official in a middle distance vis-à-vis the population.

## PREVIOUS SCHOLARSHIP AND UNDERSTANDINGS

That American government made a transition from profit-seeking toward salaries is a story largely untold and unknown.[4] There has never been a

comprehensive treatment of the transformation. Although Max Weber identified the move toward salaries as an aspect of the rise of modern government, he
said nothing particular about the matter in the United States.[5] Scholars have
done some synthetic work on the old profit-seeking regime in English officialdom,[6] but there is nothing comparable on the American side.[7] Merely to realize
the magnitude of the change (to say nothing of understanding it), one must
consult numerous scattered monographs on particular American government
functions in particular times and contexts. These works usually treat the subject of official income briefly and as a peripheral issue. A handful of function-
specific studies go into somewhat greater depth, but very few give the matter
the attention it deserves in its own right.[8] The deepest function-specific histories
are those by Allen Steinberg, on police magistrates and prosecutors in Philadelphia, which has helped inspire my analysis of facilitative payments,[9] and by
Rebecca McLennan, on Northern state penitentiaries, which forms the basis
for one of my case studies of bounties.[10] In addition, there are some important
studies that, though mainly concerned with other subjects, shed light on the
law and regulation of facilitative payments.[11]

American government's transition from profit-seeking to salary calls not only
for a synthesis of the scattered and mostly superficial secondary works but also
for new primary research to produce a critical mass of new case studies geared
directly toward the matter of compensation and its effect on how officers interacted with laypersons. Those are the tasks of this book.

On the basis of the secondary works and especially the new primary research,
I depart from the common view of today's scholars (following Weber) that the
"salarization" of modern government was all of a piece, consisting of the rejection of a single type of premodern official profit-seeking (or, alternately, of an
undifferentiated hodgepodge of such profit-seeking).[12] On the contrary, there
were two distinct though simultaneous transitions, each with its own inner
meaning, that ended up in the same place: one rejecting the facilitative payment, which drew officials too close to the layperson, and the other rejecting
the bounty, which alienated them too far from the layperson. It should be noted
that, although modern scholars have ignored the distinction between facilitative payments and bounties, at least some contemporaries recognized it (if not
in exactly the same terms). Among these was Jeremy Bentham, circa 1780, who
denounced as bad policy the receipt of money by officers "from those who
require their services" but who praised as good policy such practices as tax-
farming and naval prize-hunting.[13]

My interpretation of the salary also departs from another common scholarly view: that premodern governments paid non-salary forms of compensation

mainly because they lacked the strong taxation and disbursement mechanisms necessary for salaries, so the shift toward salaries can be explained by the strengthening of those mechanisms.[14] It is true that the weakness of taxation and disbursement mechanisms in Anglo-American government during the early modern period rendered the payment of salaries logistically difficult. It is also true that facilitative payments and bounties avoided the need for such mechanisms: the former could be paid from the pockets of the service recipients, and the latter could be extracted from the persons targeted (for example, a convicted defendant could be forced to labor to pay the bounty of the officer who arrested him).[15] But while the strengthening of taxation and disbursement mechanisms during the nineteenth century may have been a necessary condition for the shift toward salaries,[16] it certainly was not a sufficient one. This is evident from the fact that the U.S. government and many state governments assumed responsibility for paying facilitative payments and bounties to their officers out of general public revenue (mainly from taxes), often maintaining such arrangements for many decades and sometimes for more than a century.[17] In other words, a government can make the leap to paying its officers out of general public revenue, yet still pay them by the task. The imperative to alter the format of compensation, rather than merely its source, arose from factors outside the history of governmental fiscal capacity. (Note that, even when the government assumed responsibility to pay facilitative payments and bounties out of general public revenue, the incentive properties and social dynamics associated with those payments could remain largely unchanged. For example, an officer entitled to a fee for providing a service at the request of a citizen would view that citizen as a customer regardless of whether the fee came from the citizen's pocket or from the government's coffers.)

Further, my story departs from two assumptions, common among social scientists, about the kind of organization in which salaried jobs tend to exist. The first of these two assumptions is that a salaried job is associated with secure tenure and career stability. This connection is prominent in Weber's ideal type of bureaucracy, which he describes as a hierarchical organization of salaried offices, with people in the higher offices directing those in the lower ones. Each office's salary matches its rank in the hierarchy, and incumbents are protected against firing so long as they fulfill their duties. Under these conditions, people enter the organization early in life and can expect to spend their whole careers there, working their way up toward more responsible and higher-salaried positions, by seniority, merit promotion, or both. Weber concludes that an organization's best strategy for being effective is to offer people "an assured salary connected with the opportunity of a career." In his ideal bureaucracy, an office is not "exploited for rents or emoluments in exchange for the rendering of certain services," but instead entails "a specific duty of fealty to the purpose of the office . . . in return for the grant of a secure existence."[18] The secure tenure and career stability emphasized by Weber have been central to the historiography of American public administration, which has devoted great attention to the rise of civil service protection.[19]

The second of the two assumptions is that a salaried officer is typically subject to top-down control by a supervisor. This assumption, too, has it origin in Weber's ideal type of bureaucracy, in which officers follow strict rules under the watchful eye of their boss. Salary reinforces top-down control, for it keeps the officer dependent upon the organization's favor and ensures that the officer's earnings are less than those of the boss or of any other superior.[20] Today's institutional economists likewise view the salary as distinctly appropriate for agents under top-down control (as opposed to contractors paid by the task). The reasoning of these economists varies somewhat from Weber's. They see the issue in terms of limits on the boss's knowledge. Say an organization finds it hard to specify in advance the tasks it needs its agents to do, or to verify (after the fact) whether its agents have accomplished the needed tasks. In situations like these, argue the economists, the organization will typically address the problem by paying its agents a fixed sum to place themselves at its disposal for a set period of time, during which the agents follow whatever commands the organization gives, ad hoc, and submit to its constant supervision.[21]

Although these two assumptions might suggest that lawmakers converted officials to salaries as part of a program to provide them with secure tenure and career stability and place them under top-down control, the history of America does not really bear that out. On reflection, this mismatch is not very surprising. In comparison to the officialdoms of other developed nations, it has been (and remains) much less common for American officials to have stable, lifelong careers within an agency or to be situated in clear top-down hierarchies. In America, the public officialdom has more of a revolving door with the private sector, is less insulated from electoral politics, and is more decentralized and localized, with more entry points for disparate and clashing influences.[22]

Historically, although some instances of American salarization did coincide with the advent of career stability and top-down control, this was far from the universal pattern. In many instances, career stability and top-down control never came at all, or they came by a gradual and halting process that only got going well after salarization had already occurred for independent reasons.[23]

Relatedly, American civil service reform was not coextensive with the move-ment for salarization, and the two certainly cannot be understood as a single phenomenon. Civil service reformers usually supported salarization, but the movement for salarization was broader, and often advanced on an earlier time-line, than the one for civil service.[24] (Conversely, some eminent advocates for bounties during the Gilded Age were supporters of civil service reform,[25] which confirms that bounties for a time held promise as instruments to build a mod-ern, effective, and efficient state.)

Nevertheless, Weber was absolutely right that Western governments shifted toward salaries in the course of the nineteenth and twentieth centuries, and the bare fact of salarization was as real in America as in any other Western nation. But we cannot adequately explain salarization (at least in America) as part of a package with the other aspects of bureaucratization to which Weber connected it, that is, career stability and top-down control. Rather, salarization arose (at least in America) mainly from causes independent of bureaucratization, which I stated at the outset of this Introduction. To repeat: as to facilitative payments, the causes were (1) the aversion to officer-layperson bargaining that arose from republican and liberal principles and (2) the aversion to "customer-serving" government that arose from the mass interest-group rivalry of modern demo-cratic politics. As to bounties, the cause was the aspiration of lawmakers to foster mass lay cooperation with their increasingly ambitious and intrusive programs, coupled with their realization that the bounty placed laypersons and officials in an adversarial relation, which crippled any effort to build up the legitimacy of the state and the public's trust in it.

In my analysis of bounties, I am invoking and extending another of Weber's ideas: his insight that a government cannot rule by force alone but must find a way to elicit the voluntary compliance of its population—that is, to achieve legitimacy.[26] Although Weber identified salary as an element of modern govern-ment and legitimacy as an element of many kinds of government, he did not link the two. Instead, he connected salary only with intragovernmental orga-nizational features like secure tenure and top-down control. One of my aims, therefore, is to demonstrate historically that these two Weberian themes—salary and legitimacy—are profoundly connected in a way that Weber did not discuss (or perhaps even notice). In that sense, this book is an effort to elaborate, refine, and deepen Weber's ideas through empirical investigation. More broadly, the book seeks to further our understanding of how the modern state has sought and acquired legitimacy—a subject on which there is a burgeoning literature, but one that pays very little attention to the monetary incentives of the officials who make up the state.[27]

## THE ARGUMENT IN DETAIL

In the remainder of this Introduction, I set forth the argument of the book in detail. Some of the reasoning and evidence composing the argument only appears here in the Introduction, although most of it appears in the book's subsequent chapters. This Introduction includes summaries of those chapters and explains how each fits into the book's argument. Readers who absorb this Introduction will be able to delve into any chapter of the book, follow what is being said, and see how it figures in the story as a whole.

The book's argument consists of two parts, of which Part One covers the transition from facilitative payments to salaries (Chapters 1–4) and Part Two from bounties to salaries (Chapters 5–9). Though I think it best to treat each of the two forms of payment in its own separate part, I should note that the forms could sometimes overlap in certain ways. First, a single officer could receive facilitative payments for some acts and bounties for others. For instance, a customs official could take bounties for catching merchants who tried to circumvent the customhouse as well as facilitative payments from merchants who, submitting to the government's authority and passing their goods through the customhouse, wanted their goods processed in a prompt and friendly manner. Second, a single payment to a single official could simultaneously operate as both a facilitative payment (vis-à-vis one layperson) and a bounty (vis-à-vis a different layperson). For example, where the victim of a crime offered money to a constable for apprehending the perpetrator, that payment both encouraged the officer to accommodate the victim and spurred the officer to take an adversarial stance toward the suspect. In these overlap situations, facilitative payments and bounties were each still subject to their distinctive critiques, which might be leveled simultaneously at a single officer or single payment.

### A Prefatory Note: The Utopian Ideal of Honorary Service

As Americans struggled with the choices among facilitative payments, bounties, and salaries, they often had in the back of their minds an unattainable ideal that officials should do their jobs for no pay at all. The civic republican dream of the revolutionary era was to divorce governmental power from individual self-interest, including pecuniary self-interest.[28] This meant that official service should ideally be honorary. Men should fill offices out of a sense of disinterested obligation toward the citizenry. They should receive no compensation, or so little as not to influence their desire for office or behavior in it. Said Montesquieu, "[I]n a republic under the reign of virtue, a motive that suffices in itself and excludes all others, the state rewards only with testimonies to that virtue."[29] In England, the honorary ideal resonated with a tradition, dating to the Middle Ages, under which local administrative power in the countryside resided mainly in the landed gentlemen of the locality, who performed offices like county sheriff or justice of the peace for no pay or little pay.[30] The tradition had analogues in some of the localities in the American colonies, where wealthy gentlemen filled offices out of noblesse oblige, or middling folk were required to serve on a short-term, rotating basis with little to no pay, under penalty of a fine.[31] The Revolution itself further elevated honorary service as an ideal. George Washington, with his huge private fortune, pointedly refused all pay as commander of the Continental Army.[32] At the Constitutional Convention in 1787, Benjamin Franklin, who like Washington possessed great private wealth, proposed that federal officers "receive no salary, stipend, fee, or reward whatsoever for their services." If government offices were remunerative, warned Franklin, the public service would select for selfish and intemperate persons who would skew their decisions to serve themselves and engage in destructive factional rivalries to keep and accumulate power.[33]

Beautiful though it was, the ideal of honorary service was not a practical plan for government as a whole. Even in Britain, the honorary ideal came near realization only in the local government of the countryside, not of the cities,[34] nor in national institutions like the customhouses, excise service, royal courts, army, navy, Treasury, Exchequer, and so on.[35] It was even further from realization in America, which did not have as many financially secure gentlemen as the mother country.[36] When Franklin made his proposal, the members of the Constitutional Convention, embarrassed at the practical difficulty of following their professed principles, deferred consideration of it and quietly refrained from ever taking it up.[37]

But while the honorary ideal could not be directly implemented on a wide scale, it did, at times, exert a kind of gravitational pull on the debate over how best to structure compensation. As we will see in Chapter 2, the civic republican notion of official disinterestedness helped fuel the campaign in the late 1700s and early 1800s to ensure that facilitative payments be regulated. And, as we will see in Chapter 3, republicanism was the intellectual parent of nineteenth-century populist and reformist sentiments against official incomes becoming too high. These sentiments proved significant in the late 1800s, as rising business swelled the total sum that an officer could earn from facilitative payments. Official fortune-making became an argument in favor of the salary, which was a sure means to keep an officer's income limited.

## Part One: Facilitative Payments to Salaries

Part One tells the story of facilitative payments. These arose when individuals gave money to officers in exchange for their services. They were essentially the prices in a customer-seller relationship, with its attendant sense of reciprocity and mutual benefit. From the Middle Ages to the 1800s, the terms of these exchanges were often set without the involvement of the legislature. The common law—the body of legal principles that applied by default in the absence of a legislative act (statute)—effectively permitted officers and service recipients to make interchanges by agreement, much like bargains in the private economy. In this way, facilitative payments could "bubble up" organically from numerous decentralized negotiations between officers and the parties with whom they respectively dealt. Officers were quasi-independent vendors, as connected to their customers as to anybody else. They were not yet the creatures and dependents of a lawmaking body.

Chapter 1 identifies the common-law bases for negotiation between officers and service recipients in Britain and North America in the 1700s and early 1800s. We begin with the doctrine of extortion, which prohibited any officer from "tak[ing] unlawfully" a payment that was "not due." Originally, a payment was "due" only if it was authorized by statute or by immemorial custom and usage. An undue payment was "taken unlawfully" if (1) the officer coerced the payor to make it, (2) he lied to the payor about the amount due, or (3) the payor intended the payment to induce the officer to breach his duty—what we today call bribery. But if none of these elements was present, the payment was lawful, even if undue. In other words, if an officer did his duty, and the service recipient, knowing that he or she owed nothing, voluntarily gave an unsolicited "gratuity" or "tip" for it, that was fine. Compared with us, people in the eighteenth century had a looser understanding of the scope of official duty and the meaning of voluntary action. If an officer offered to do his duty faster or more diligently in exchange for money, that was not a breach of his trust. And if a service recipient found it necessary to tip an officer to make him do his duty vigorously, the recipient was still said to pay "voluntarily."

The lawfulness of gratuities opened the way for a good deal of negotiation between officers and recipients. Furthermore, if several recipients paid a gratuity at the same rate for a while, it could acquire the sanction of custom and usage. This meant that the payment became legally "due," and the officer had a right to demand it. Gratuities were constantly evolving into customary fees. New gratuities would then arise on top of them and go through the same process. To be sure, the doctrine of "immemorial" custom and usage, if applied strictly, meant that a payment was not lawfully "due" if anybody could prove that it had not been taken continuously since the beginning of legal memory (in the year 1189!). But practically, everybody realized that such strictness would be disruptive and unreasonable. Inquiries into the historical pedigree of fees, if made, usually went back only a few decades, if that. Thus, the doctrine of custom provided legal cover for the continuing evolution of payments through officer-recipient negotiation.

In addition to lawful gratuities and immemorial custom, there was another doctrine that helped justify negotiation: *quantum meruit*, the principle that any person who performs a valuable service for somebody else is entitled to reasonable recompense for it. If an officer provided a service to a recipient and there was no customary fee, he could still sue in *quantum meruit* for the service's value. And, of course, he and the recipient could agree to settle the claim without litigation—to bargain in the shadow of the law.

To be sure, the British Parliament and colonial legislatures often enacted statutes to regulate the payments that officers could take for their services. But these statutes operated against the rich background of common-law doctrines that authorized bargaining as a default matter. In the same way that people today speak of statutory economic regulation "intervening" in a preexisting market constituted by common-law rules of property and contract, so were statutes regulating official fees in the eighteenth and early nineteenth centuries "intervening" in a preexisting universe of exchanges that were not established by statute yet were still lawful. Public offices were independent of legislative power in a way that seems strange to us today. They were freestanding vendors that the legislature might regulate but sometimes did not, just as it might or might not regulate a business today.

Prior to the early nineteenth century, statutory interventions in officer-recipient exchange were limited. It was difficult to enumerate officers' services and fix prices for them in advance. Services often were idiosyncratic, required variable amounts of labor or speed depending on the circumstances, or reflected unanticipated changes in administrative methods or in the needs of service recipients. And even if a service were long-standing, stable, and familiar to officers and recipients, the legislature might accidentally forget to include it. (There is an analogy here to what economists call the incompleteness of contracts.) In several instances, lawmakers acknowledged these limitations by enacting statutes that fixed the fees for certain named services but left the pricing of all other services to the common law. Even when the wording of a statute did not clearly indicate such a limitation, officers and courts often interpreted it that way. The assumption that statutes left common-law negotiation to thrive with respect to unenumerated services preserved a relatively unregulated "market" not only for truly unnamed services but also for named services that, because of circumstance, required more work than usual and could therefore be viewed (by some stretch of the imagination) as unnamed. The unusual aspect of the service could be hived off as a freestanding unenumerated item deserving extrastatutory compensation. In certain jurisdictions, the doctrines supporting negotiation proved so robust—and the regulatory efforts of legislators so imprecise, crude, and poorly updated—that regulatory statutes became dead letters whose obsolescence officers and courts openly proclaimed.

The practice of letting service recipients pay officers for their services, observed a parliamentary commission in 1787, brought the two "into a mutual relation," promoting "habits of pecuniary obligation or exchange of private interest."[38] To many, this seemed a good thing: as with any seller-customer relationship, the promise of payment induced prompt, attentive, and faithful service. And it was not just that the recipient paid the officer, but especially that the two could negotiate the transaction. The recipient's freedom to adjust the price and the officer's freedom to adjust the service opened the way for mutual benefit. In the eyes of many, bargaining between officers and recipients was not only convenient but also necessary to the continued functioning of government as the needs of service recipients evolved. This reasoning resonates with modern arguments that corrupt (that is, illegal) payoffs in developing countries may furnish a valuable and efficient degree of flexibility.[39] The key difference, of course, is that during the eighteenth century such payments frequently were legal, unhindered by the handicap of secrecy that comes with illegality.[40]

But then things changed. As Chapter 2 demonstrates, the American regime of negotiation was outlawed through an ideological and political transformation that had precursors in the 1600s, gained ground in the 1700s, and greatly accelerated and culminated in the early 1800s. Up to the American Revolution, critics of negotiation made three arguments against the prevailing regime and in favor of tight statutory regulation. First was the idea that negotiation too often deteriorated into monopoly price-gouging. Though negotiation's defenders believed that rising fees and extra charges resulted in faster or new-and-improved services, its critics insisted that such "adjustments" in price arose merely from the officer's abuse of his monopoly over the service (or from the superior information that he enjoyed about the sum for which he was willing, or obligated by custom, to do the job).

The second argument for statutory control rested on legislative supremacy. Parliament in the 1600s and the colonial assemblies in the 1700s were on a quest to set themselves up as the gatekeepers for all sources of funding by which the king might run the government. Negotiated fees threatened legislative power because they allowed the officialdom to support itself without the legislature's approval. Even more dangerous than negotiated fees—which arose organically from numerous decentralized officer-recipient relations—were fees that the king himself (or the royal governor) purported to authorize his officers to take by unilateral ordinance. Edward Coke argued in the early 1600s that such royally enacted fees were tallages (nonparliamentary taxes) and therefore unconstitutional. Colonists in the 1700s would stretch this argument to criticize all fees unregulated by statute, even if the king or governor had said nothing about them.

The third argument for statutory control arose from civic republican views of official duty and citizenship. The negotiation of fees meant that official service was a reciprocal exchange between officer and recipient. But civic republicans thought this was evil. To them, the recipient was a citizen enjoying a right to the service, and the officer was, ideally, a disinterested person whose sheer virtue motivated him to fulfill the service obligations of his position. The officer should, if possible, receive no compensation at all, thereby guaranteeing that his action arose from duty and not reciprocity. But if compensation were necessary, then it should be regulated rather than negotiated, since regulation provided less leeway for reciprocity.

All three arguments—anti-monopoly, legislative supremacy, and official disinterest—were associated with the strain of English political culture that originated with the opposition to the early Stuarts and briefly came to power under the English Commonwealth (1649–53), which, not coincidentally, saw valiant attempts to regulate fees, though these faded after the Restoration in 1660. Still, commonwealth ideology sprang up again repeatedly, most strongly in the assemblies of the American colonies in the 1700s, where it became the mainstream discourse, strengthening those elected bodies and pushing them to revolt in 1776. This radical Whig ideology manifested itself in the different colonial assemblies in different ways. In a few—those of Maryland, Virginia, and North Carolina—it took form in (among other things) a strong aspiration for legislative control of official fees. These three assemblies made the first concerted attempts to prohibit all negotiation and assert that fee-taking depended on statute alone. This view, complete with denunciations of nonstatutory fees as "taxation without representation," became established in the revolutionary victory of 1783 in those new states.

This might imply that the positivist concept of fees—that officers could lawfully charge fees only with specific statutory authorization—arose automatically from the radical Whig ideology that fueled the Revolution. But it is not that simple. Radical Whiggery happened to get coupled with fee regulation in the Upper South colonies, but in many others it did not, and in those other places, the nonpositivist concept of fees survived for longer. To wit, nonstatutory fees remained lawful, or at least legally ambiguous, until the 1810s in Pennsylvania, until the 1820s in Massachusetts and South Carolina, until the 1830s in New York, and until the 1840s in Louisiana and New Hampshire. Still, by about 1850, lawmakers and judges in all those states, indeed everywhere in the nation, came to embrace the same positivist view of official income as the Upper South had in the 1700s. The old doctrines of *quantum meruit* and custom lost their hold. Lawmakers rewrote statutes to prohibit charges for unenumerated services. And even when the text was not so clear, judges developed a general presumption that officers could charge money only when expressly authorized by statute.

The transformation of the 1810s to the 1840s arose from certain interrelated trends in the postrevolutionary development of American republicanism, liberalism, and democracy. We can identify these trends by considering the common themes that appear in the relevant statutes and cases: a distrust of officers and anxiety about their monopolistic and coercive powers; a strong preference for legislative authorization over official discretion; and an objectified understanding of official duty, in which the incumbent had little freedom in deciding what efforts to make when asked to perform a service. These themes resonate with larger changes in American political culture during the period. First, offices once held by aristocrats, who had ties to the community and enjoyed deference from their inferiors, now went to persons of lower status, with fewer such ties, less capacity to elicit deference, and time horizons shortened by the principle of rotation in office—changes that all made the new incumbents seem less trustworthy. Second, elite definition of the "rule of law" shifted from the participatory self-governance of local communities toward a more positivist view centered on the state legislature and on relatively objective, rule-bound claims to rights on the part of white male citizens. Third, lawmakers and judges became obsessed with imposing uniformity—a formal and legalistic equality—on all interactions between white male citizens and the government. Fourth, the old Anglo-American anxiety about monopoly reached unprecedented intensity, pushing lawmakers to guarantee open and equal access to all resources that were inherently monopolistic, including official services. These four factors all counseled in favor of a more objectified concept of office, one that had uniform, equal, and rule-bound relations with all service recipients, with no room for bargaining or ad hoc adjustment. The nineteenth century is remembered for its ideology of laissez-faire, but it would be more accurate to say that Americans of the period favored a sharpened public-private distinction, gravitating toward the market on the private side but toward regulation on the public side. Officers had once been quasi-independent vendors who *could* be regulated by the legislature, but they were now reconceived as *creations* of the legislature, who had no lawful rights except those that the legislature established. Thus was born the foundational idea of today's administrative law: that administration is subsequent to legislation.

By reducing all facilitative payments to statutory schedules, Americans sought to preserve a mode of compensation that was pre-positivist in its history and essence but to regulate it and thereby render it compatible with a more modern institutional world. Interestingly, this program resonates with suggestions that are sometimes made, as in developing countries today, that certain payoffs should be legalized, regulated, and made transparent.[41]

That makes it all the more important for us to consider why American lawmakers ultimately found facilitative payments (even when regulated) to be so problematic that they had to be replaced by salaries. Nineteenth-century Americans hoped and expected that facilitative payments would continue their age-old function of motivating officers to render prompt and attentive service. But, as Chapter 3 demonstrates, the rigidity and clumsiness of the new statutory regulations became a major obstacle to their doing so. Statutory fee regulation compiled a sorry record from the mid-1800s (when it became established as a legal ideal) through the early 1900s. Lawmakers writing fee schedules too often forgot to price certain services, or crudely imposed a single price on a service that varied greatly in effort from case to case, or failed to anticipate new services that arose after enactment. Such mismatches between lawful prices and actual business generated two distinct dangers. First, the officer might conform to the statute but also to the irrational incentives that it created, allocating his effort disproportionately toward the subset of services that happened to be in the schedule. Alternately, the officer and the person seeking a service, in cases where the statute did not allow the latter to pay the former, might engage in extrastatutory negotiation to ensure the job got done, resulting in a payment that was now viewed as "corrupt." Such exchanges proved very common: after all, they had been the legal way of doing things for centuries prior to the novel aspiration for absolute statutory control. Such control became the stated ideal of lawmakers, judges, and the bien-pensant middle class, but in the workaday world, old habits died hard.[42] The ancient legal justifications for nonstatutory charges—voluntariness, custom, just recompense, and statutory obsolescence— survived in the folk understandings of many officers and recipients. Plus, the officer and recipient could often cloak a negotiated payment by claiming that it comported with the schedule through some stretched interpretation whose bad faith was not obvious to the casual observer. The legislature might play cat and mouse with the officers, monitoring their stretched constructions and amending the statute to close the loopholes. But it was a fool's game. The officers were always a step ahead.

Such dynamics fueled the perception, which became widespread by the late 1800s, that fee-based compensation of officers, even when formally regulated by a statute, led unavoidably to fee-taking that evaded the statute, which was now defined as "corruption." Reformers argued that, to stop officers from taking unlawful fees, one must prohibit them from taking *any* fees, placing them on salary instead. This argument came up again and again in the period circa 1870–1920.

To be sure, the substitution of salaries for statutory fees was not a panacea to the problem of unlawful fee-taking, since it was possible for a salaried officer to demand illegal payments for services. But salarization did remove a major aggravating factor. The statutory fee system had invited officers and recipients to agree upon unlawful charges because it created a particularized class of services that needed to be performed yet were uncompensated (or inadequately compensated) by law. It also signaled a generalized moral approval of exchange between officer and recipient, and it established, as a matter of office practice, a cash nexus between the two, which could be used as a cover for charges that pushed the edge of the law or went beyond it. It was much easier for enforcers, recipients, and officers themselves to recognize the illegality of exchanges when they were not allowed at all, as opposed to being allowed restrictively. Negotiation was the essence of the facilitative payment. It could not be eradicated unless the facilitative payment itself was eliminated.

In other words, facilitative payments proved fatally incapable of meeting Americans' aspirations for the subjection of government to law. The flight to salaries was an admission of law's weakness and failure. Statute drafters sought to enumerate and price services to provide fair compensation and to make things so transparent as to eliminate ingenious manipulations, but drafting was not precise enough to contain the wishes of officers and recipients to go their own way. Weber characterized modern government as both rule bound and salaried. But salaries, at least in the American story, are actually a concession to the inadequacy of rules to constrain self-interested human behavior, unless they are relatively crude and simple—"you can take nothing from the people you serve."

The effort to prevent corrupt exchange was not the only regulatory challenge that pushed lawmakers to give up on facilitative payments. There was the further challenge—also recounted in Chapter 3—of preventing each individual officer from earning too high an income in the aggregate, which became more pressing in the second half of the 1800s as increases in population and improvements in office technology allowed many an officer to provide far more services than ever before, thereby earning a much greater total of facilitative payments. As these totals came to light, lawmakers came under pressure to regulate them, for they sparked populist resentment and excited fear that lucrative offices would attract unscrupulous candidates and corrupt the political process. Theoretically, lawmakers might have regulated each officer's total income by amending the statutory prices the officer could charge for individual services, but that proved unworkable, for reasons similar to those that hobbled the effort to regulate corrupt individual transactions: unforeseeable changes in business might swell the total once again, or the officer might stretch the meaning of the items in the amended schedule to swell the total himself. As with the regulation of corrupt individual transactions, the regulation of total incomes ultimately required salarization, a crude but sure solution to the problem.

In addition to the terrible difficulty of regulating individual facilitative payments (and the total incomes from them), there was one other reason that lawmakers rejected such payments in favor of salaries: they soured on the very idea that "customer service" was an appropriate paradigm for governance. That is the subject of Chapter 4. Although positive regulation constricted the legal space for reciprocity between officer and recipient, it did not eliminate it. Even after the law confined monetary exchange between officer and recipient to regular payments authorized by positive authority (by circa 1850), it was still possible for those legally authorized payments to foster a dynamic of mutual benefit between the two, particularly when the service was relatively familiar, standardized, and unchanging. The officer still had an interest in attracting as many customers as possible, which he could do by making his service as attractive to prospective claimants as possible. Thus, facilitative payments continued to imbue many officers with a customer service mentality, even when they obeyed the laws that told them not to create new charges or increase old ones. This dynamic was evident through the second half of the 1800s and sometimes into the early 1900s. Facilitative payments continued to facilitate.

Chapter 4 shows that fee-driven customer service flourished in several contexts from the mid-1800s onward, even within the bounds of positive regulation. It also shows why lawmakers reacted against it by the early 1900s. They came to condemn not merely unregulated payments but also reciprocity per se. Facilitative payments imbued officials with a narrow view of their jobs, in which they focused on meeting the needs of service recipients but paid comparatively little attention to other interests that were less immediate and more diffuse. Increasingly, however, this style of administration ran up against the mass interest-group rivalry of modern politics. An increasing number of groups and movements were organizing themselves and entering the electoral and legislative arena to advocate for interests that had once been diffuse. These groups and movements criticized the narrow customer orientation of facilitative payments. Customer service, they said, came at the expense of other worthy interests. The solution was to embrace salaries, thus severing the bond of customer-seller reciprocity between the officer and the people who sought his services, providing the officer with the financial independence to say no. This opened the way for the officer to balance more diffuse interests against recipients' immediate wishes. This is not to say that salarization promoted an especially precise, careful, or sophisticated balancing of interests. At the very least, however, there was more attention to a wider range of interests than in the pre-salary era. In this respect, salarization reflected the rising complexity and multi-dimensionality of mass electoral politics. For the recipients themselves, the severing of the reciprocal bond was a profound loss. It psychologically estranged them from officials they had once viewed as solicitous and friendly.

To demonstrate how facilitative payments continued to promote a customer service ethos—and how lawmakers ultimately reacted against that ethos—Chapter 4 relies upon three case studies. They concern three of the most important federal decision-making systems of the nineteenth century. The first is the adjudication of immigrants' applications to become naturalized citizens, which were decided by federal and state judges and court clerks. I trace this system from the explosion of immigration in about the 1830s through the nativist reforms of the early 1900s. The second is the adjudication of veterans' claims for disability benefits by federal examining surgeons. I trace this system from its massive growth during and after the Civil War to its replacement by a more restrictive system during and after World War I. The third is the adjudication of Western settlers' claims for land under the Homestead Act and similar "settlement laws" by the registers and receivers of the federal land offices. I trace this system from the rise of the settlement laws in the 1840s through the conservationist reforms that took off in the early 1900s.

In each of the chapter's three case studies, I make the same four points, pegged to each case study's four numbered sections. First, I show that, in all three schemes in the pre-salary period, the law vested adjudicators with discretion to treat applicants stringently or liberally and that, in fact, they treated applicants liberally. The wideness of the adjudicators' discretion arose from a couple of factors. For one, the statutory criteria for whether to confer the benefit (e.g., citizenship, pension, land) were vague. Also, proceedings in each of the three systems were one-sided: there was nobody to oppose the applicant's claim, so the outcome depended largely on whether the adjudicator chose to believe the applicant's story. In practice, officers in all three systems became famous (or notorious) for indulging applicants. Judges and court clerks gave Irish and Germans the benefit of every doubt as to whether they had lived in the United States for the requisite period, were attached to the U.S. Constitution, and so on. Examining surgeons gave Civil War veterans the benefit of every doubt as to whether they were truly "disabled" and how badly. Land-office registers and receivers gave homestead applicants the benefit of every doubt as to whether they were really working the land.

Second, I argue that a major factor motivating the liberality of adjudicators in all three systems during the pre-salary period was their desire to maximize their facilitative payments. Court clerks (and sometimes judges) were entitled to a fee every time they granted citizenship to an immigrant, and registers and receivers enjoyed a fee every time they granted a settlement-law application. The incentive for these officers to grant applicants' claims was obvious, and contemporary observers confirmed it. Examining surgeons had a somewhat different pay structure: they received a fee for every veteran who came to them seeking a pension (or a pension increase), regardless of how they decided the veteran's application. Nevertheless, the surgeons had a pecuniary stake in encouraging veterans to seek them out and (therefore) in maintaining a reputation for generosity, as contemporaries confirmed. Further, in all three systems, competition increased the pressure on adjudicators to meet the wishes of "customers." It was common for multiple naturalizing courts to be located near one another, and immigrants could decide where to take their business. Examining surgeons, likewise, were often only a short distance apart, and veterans had much freedom in deciding whom to patronize. In the case of land offices, competition was less direct, since each office was a monopolist within its own geographic area, yet competition probably still existed, for Western migrants were mobile and could choose between districts in deciding where to make claims. In addition, adjudicators in all three systems had their liberality monitored and encouraged by private intermediaries who made it their business to drum up applicants and channel them toward adjudicators.

Third, I note that, throughout the pre-salary era in each of the three systems, congressmen were aware of the system's liberality and rejected administrative reforms that would make it operate less liberally. This explains why fee-driven liberality lasted for so long. It also helps us assess the ethical status of fee-driven liberality. It is tempting to dismiss such liberality as corrupt, as moralistic contemporaries sometimes did. But how do we define "corruption"? Obviously, corruption involves the exercise of public power for a private interest, but that is too broad as a definition, since almost nobody expects public servants to act completely without reward. We might attempt a definition by saying that the exercise of public power for private interest is corrupt when it violates the public interest or violates public sentiment, but those concepts are too vague. Alternately, we might adopt a definition used by many scholars: that the exercise of public power for private interest is corrupt when it violates applicable law.[43] But by that standard, much of the liberality in naturalization, pensions, and homestead claims was not corrupt, since fee incentives simply channeled the discretion that adjudicators exercised by virtue of vague laws. One might argue that adjudicators somehow violated the law by allowing their statutory discretion to be influenced by pecuniary considerations, but that argument is weak, for (1) the fees were instituted by law and (2) lawmakers knew of, and acquiesced in, the liberality of the three systems, which predictably resulted from the fees. Yet another possibility is to characterize the fees as corrupt according to the definition set forth by James C. Scott, who describes corruption as a variety of influence over policy outcomes that postdates the enactment of the relevant legislation—an influence that tends to be particularist, adjusting general statutory mandates to the peculiar needs of individuals or local groups.[44] But again, this does not quite fit. The effect of facilitative payments on naturalization, pensions, and land claims was to *systemically* shift policy outcomes *nationwide*, generally in a single direction (favorably toward applicants as a class), in a way that members of Congress understood.

In my view, fee-driven liberality should not be understood as corrupt at all, but as an example of what Terry Moe calls "the politics of structural choice"—a feature of a statute's implementation scheme that is mandated by the legislature and can channel policy outcomes just as strongly and systemically as the substantive terms of the statute do.[45] We cannot understand facilitative payments, at least in the mid-1800s and later, as a primitive phenomenon that predates the generality of modern legislative policy-making. On the contrary, facilitative payments in the 1800s became instruments of that kind of modern policy-making, insofar as the legislature wanted to shift outcomes systemically in favor of service recipients. (It is only the earlier variety of facilitative payments—those negotiated ad hoc at common law in the 1600s and 1700s between an individual officer and a few service recipients—that we can justly understand as particularist and premodern.)

That lawmakers systematically channeled outcomes in favor of the recipient class reflects the importance, during the mid- to late 1800s, of what Theodore Lowi calls "distributive policy." This is policy that "in the short run . . . can be made without regard to limited resources," so that "the indulged and the

deprived, the loser and the recipient, need never come into direct confronta-
tion."[46] Distributive policy was unusually prominent (though not, of course,
exclusively dominant) in America during this period.[47] In many major areas,
lawmakers perceived the age as one of inexhaustible resources, so government
could afford to be generous. Policies in naturalization and veterans' benefits fit
the distributive definition well. Liberality to the recipient class came at a cost,
but that cost was so diffuse that the millions of people who bore it were unconscious of their burden. To wit: the cost of easy naturalization was the dilution
of native-born Americans' votes. The cost of generous veterans' benefits was a
heightened federal tax burden, in the form of the tariff—invisible to the consumers on whom it fell. For the settlement laws, the distributive designation also
fits well, insofar as we focus on the federal district land offices and their fee-paid
personnel, whose job was to decide rights to federally owned land as between
the U.S. government and prospective white users. The cost of indulgence toward white settlers' claims to federally owned land was the depletion of that
land for future generations—a very diffuse and unconscious interest through
the late nineteenth century. Of course, if we widen our focus to consider how
land entered the federally owned category to begin with, the distributive designation does not fit, for then we confront the work of separate agencies—the
military and the Bureau of Indian Affairs—tasked with expropriating land from
Indians. That task imposed very concentrated costs. Consistent with this, officers in the military and the bureau did not live by facilitative payments and did
not treat Indians as customers. Still, the accomplishment of Indian expropriation created a widespread perception of open land among white politicians,
which inclined them toward liberality in settlement-law administration.[48]

We come last to the fourth point in each of the three case studies: the reaction against customer service and the abolition of facilitative payments. Legislative decision-making in the early 1900s saw intensified interest-group rivalry, an
increasing sense of scarcity, and a decline of free-and-easy distributive policy in
many areas where it once prevailed.[49] More than before, politicians saw the disbursement of every government benefit as coming at the expense of some other
value or interest. In the realm of naturalization, nativists gained more clout
and exerted unprecedented pushback against the easy admission of foreigners
to the polity, which they insisted was degrading the electorate. In the realm
of veterans' benefits, the fiscal challenge of World War I and the replacement
of the (nearly invisible) tariff by the (highly visible and concentrated) income
tax made tax dollars seem scarcer. Taxpayers and budget-conscious lawmakers
therefore demanded closer scrutiny of claims on the Treasury. In the realm of

land policy, the newly ascendant conservation movement warned that land was not inexhaustible. Distribution to settlers had to be more closely scrutinized and targeted—and in some cases stopped altogether, to let the government manage land for sustainable use.

Congress proved very responsive to these three movements in the early 1900s. It put the brakes on the distribution of public largesse. Some of the response came in the form of changes to substantive law, though these were relatively minor.[50] The main thing Congress did was to revamp the administrative machinery for deciding claims, to make it less claimant-friendly. Lawmakers transferred (or encouraged agencies to transfer) real power away from fee-paid officers and toward salaried ones. Applicants for citizenship, benefits, and lands now faced gatekeepers who had no pecuniary interest in letting them through the gate. Congress thereby established a government capable of saying no to service recipients in a way that acknowledged (if crudely) rival mass claims to public resources—nativism, fiscal conservatism, and conservationism.

Service recipients who lived through this transition felt profoundly estranged. They had once been treated as customers, with courtesy, solicitude, and expedition. Now they increasingly faced indifference, suspicion, and delay. It is tempting to think that salaries gave officers the independence to evaluate every application objectively and impartially, thus guaranteeing faithful execution of the law. But that is naive. The statutory criteria for naturalization remained vague, and officers in the first several years after salarization did little to fill them in with uniform guidelines. The same is true of World War I disability determinations, which remained quite subjective, especially given the uncertainty of newly discovered neurological disorders. Also, the disappearance of customer service incentives for naturalization and veterans' benefits subjected applicants to long delays that caused many of them to give up, regardless of the merits of their claims. Adjudications under the settlement laws probably saw a greater increase in objectivity, but they still involved subjective judgments of "good faith." In all three systems, the most verifiable effect of salarization was not to make decisions more accurate but to make them less generous. That is no surprise, for salarization in each case arose from the demands of newly ascendant interest groups that wanted the government to be stingier. Salarization may have brought administration nearer to Weber's ideal of being a "precision instrument" for the accurate implementation of policy,[51] but it is more certain that it symbolized the government's acknowledgment of the ever-stronger tug of rival interest groups that came with modern legislative politics. Customer service was too simple and narrow a paradigm for the modern political world.[52]

## Part Two: Bounties to Salaries

Facilitative payments encouraged officers to perform acts that recipients wanted. By contrast, bounties—the subject of Part Two—encouraged them to perform acts that the affected persons did not want and were likely to resist. Going back to the Middle Ages and through the early modern period, such rewards held a special attraction for lawmakers, for they could provide the motivational fuel to enforce novel, ambitious, and intrusive legislative programs that sought to override and change the existing norms and preferences of the population. As such ambitious legislative endeavors reached unprecedented heights between about the mid-1800s and the early 1900s, American lawmakers experimented with using bounties more intensely than ever before. But the very intensity of the experiment was the bounty's undoing: it led to such disappointing and perverse results that lawmakers soured on bounties and rejected them altogether, concluding that such rewards undermined the legitimacy, trust, and cooperation that were necessary for a workable modern state.

*Familiar Imposition, Alien Imposition, and Motivational Fuel.*    To understand bounties, we must begin by thinking through the different ways in which a government may impose its will. It helps to think in terms of two ideal types: (1) familiar imposition, which was characteristic of early modern governance, and (2) alien imposition, which arose in many isolated pockets during the early modern period and then spread dramatically in the nineteenth century to become the overriding mode of governance in modern life.

The defining feature of familiar imposition was that the enforcer, the enforcee, and the norm being imposed all had reference to a single face-to-face community and its shared set of social expectations (or, at least, to the ongoing compromises and accommodations its inhabitants made, avoiding disruption in their shared social life). The enforcer and the person he targeted usually knew each other, as they lived in a community where everybody knew just about everybody else. High-level enforcers, such as justices of the peace, were leading gentlemen of the locality ("local notables," as Weber called them). Low-level enforcers, such as the town constable or town assessor, were middling persons who took turns filling the office when pressured to do so by their neighbors. The norm enforced often took the form of custom or common law (or, if reduced to an enacted text, was vague), thus allowing the enforcer to adjust it according to the individuals involved, the community's attitude toward them, and the possible need to soften enforcement to accommodate any potential divisions in the community. Responsibility for initiating enforcement and providing the information on which to base it rested largely with lay community members themselves, either when they personally suffered a wrong and came forward to air their grievance or when they served in short-term, rotating bodies like the grand jury, whose members kept an ear open to the troubles of their neighbors, sorted through them, and together "presented" the transgressions that they felt demanded admonition or reprimand. Under these conditions, the exercise of official power was generally in equilibrium with the expectations of the local polity. An officer was disinclined to take coercive action unless it was against no more than a few recognizable deviants, to avoid the resentment of any significant part of the community in which he was so enmeshed.[53]

Though familiar imposition predominated in Anglo-American governance during the early modern period, there were also many instances of alien imposition, which appeared episodically and in isolated pockets. (Alien imposition would later proliferate dramatically in the nineteenth century—the concept is largely synonymous with modernity—but we shall defer that part of the story till a bit later.) Imposition was alien when a sovereign external to the community demanded compliance with directives that violated the social expectations of the people governed. The sovereign might be a monarch, or a legislature representing an electorate larger and more diverse than any individual community. The sovereign could also be a local government, if the locality's population had grown large and diverse enough to encompass distinct communities. The sovereign's command characteristically took the form of an enacted text, lacking the built-in adjustability of custom and common law. To do the work of enforcement, local-resident officers with ties to the community were unpromising candidates, for they would be disinclined to force alien directives on their friends and neighbors. Outsiders lacking social ties were better suited to the job. And given the foreign nature of the demands, it was hard to rely upon community members to initiate enforcement and provide information about violations. In fact, violations of many sovereign directives were "victimless." They harmed no particular individual but instead some abstract sovereign interest, like the public revenue, or national economic policy, or a certain concept of public morality. The initiative for enforcement—and the gathering of information about violations—would have to come from the sovereign's agents themselves, since neighbors were not going to come forward.[54]

Familiar and alien imposition are ideal types, not exclusive categories. Although the distinctive features of each type reinforced one another, it was possible for a regime of governance to include some elements fitting one type and some the other. Thus, it was possible for a formally alien law—that is, a text enacted by a faraway sovereign—to be implemented by local-resident officers, enmeshed in the community, who would interpret it loosely to accommodate their neighbors' views of what was reasonable. Such a law would therefore seem familiar to the people who lived under it.[55]

With our concepts defined, let us now consider enforcers' motivations and incentives. To a large degree, familiar governance provided its own motivational fuel. Members of the community, whether playing the role of officers, grand jurors, or individual complainants, were engaged in the common project of running their local affairs as they believed they ought to be run. This helps explain why rural justices of the peace, constables, grand jurors, and other such actors often did their jobs for little or no pay.[56] Men served in these offices to meet the expectations of their neighbors and to have their "say" in how their community was governed. Indeed, one reason for the prestige of honorary service was its association with participatory communal self-governance and therefore with English liberty or, in postrevolutionary America, republican liberty.

By contrast, alien governance did not provide its own motivational fuel. Whereas enforcers under the familiar regime went after isolated deviants and enjoyed the backing of their neighbors, enforcers under the alien regime faced a community in which most or all of the inhabitants were violators or sympathetic to violators. Indeed, the population might not even recognize the sovereign demand as "law."[57] Facing such intransigence, it was natural and common for kings and legislatures to adopt a strategy of coercion—the detection and punishment of noncompliance. But they realized that the enforcer under these circumstances would need some external motivation to do the detecting and punishing. They often found this external motivation in the bounty. Cash would guarantee the alignment of enforcer incentives with sovereign interests that community self-government failed to deliver.

The peculiar attraction of bounties for sovereigns making alien impositions is evident in the many *qui tam* statutes, stretching from the Middle Ages through the early modern period, in which Parliament and later the colonial legislatures banned certain conduct and offered a share of the penalty to any individual (the "informer") who successfully prosecuted a violator. Take, for example, the regulation of wool, then England's principal commodity, in the 1500s. Originally, wool made its way from landlords to cloth makers via dealers, most of whom were small time. But a sudden contraction in the export market for cloth prompted Parliament, in 1552, to restrict the purchasing of wool to a national cartel of big dealers (or to the few additional dealers who obtained a license directly from the crown) and to cloth makers themselves, of whom only the big ones had the capacity to buy without the aid of dealers. The idea was to prop up the strongest segments of the cloth-making and wool-buying industries.

This highly innovative legislation threatened not only the small dealers but also the landlords and small cloth makers who used them, plus all communities that depended on such economic actors.[58] Many landlords and small dealers ignored the law and went on with their accustomed transactions.[59] The statute included an informer provision, which proved to be commonly invoked over the rest of the century.[60] The government had to rely on informers to prosecute small dealers who bought from landlords, for it could not rely on the local justices of the peace to do so, seeing as how justices in the wool-selling areas were themselves landlords and therefore sympathetic to business practices in which their neighbors (or they themselves) had long engaged.[61]

For another example in the same period, consider the regulation of skilled trades. Initially, it was customary in many trades for a person to serve an apprenticeship of some years, but the terms were a matter of familiar governance, decided by the local tradespeople or commercial town. But in 1563, Parliament—anxious about industrial growth, poverty, vagrancy, and labor unrest—imposed a "one-size-fits-all" term of seven years on all trades, unprecedented in its uniformity and inflexibility.[62] As with wool-dealing, the statute's provision for informers resulted in far more prosecutions than came from local officers like justices of the peace.[63]

The same pattern obtained in the administration of royal customs duties and the regulation of foreign trade during the 1500s. Officials in that context, though appointed by the king, were drawn from the very merchant communities they were supposed to police, and they were complicit in local cultures of smuggling and evasion. Informers provided one of the few promising avenues for replacing local-official accommodation with an incentive to vindicate the crown's revenue interest.[64] (A later one, tried intermittently from the 1570s to the 1670s, was tax-farming.)[65]

The alien cast of regulation in wool-dealing, apprenticeship, and foreign trade extended to *qui tam* statutes pretty broadly, it seems. Through the 1600s, these enactments generally focused on business regulation and taxation, areas in which the prohibitions were likely to be *malum prohibitum*, that is, premised on sovereign edicts unrooted in the moral views of the community where violators lived. Some proscribed nonestablished religious worship, which might be considered morally right in some communities. Informer provisions in the 1700s covered many of the same subjects but also expanded to victimless "vice" offenses like selling gin, running a gambling house, and so on.[66] Many of these statutes were likewise at odds with the social expectations of local communities, as evidenced by popular riots in London against informers operating under the unprecedentedly strict Gin Act of 1736.[67] A sampling of informer provisions enacted by the Virginia legislature in the 1740s and by the U.S. Congress in the 1790s indicates a similar focus on business regulation and taxation.[68] In the early 1800s, the Boston district attorney John T. Austin (later attorney general of Massachusetts) characterized informers' bounties as especially linked to the "multitude" of offenses "which regard the peace, comfort, and good morals of society, without being particularly injurious to any one [person] more than another, and those acts which become criminal only by positive prohibitions," such as market regulations, road regulations, liquor regulations, or gambling regulations, in contrast to "cases in which public opinion, or individual interest is excited," such as murder or other violent crimes, when "there is generally an alacrity of pursuit after the offender" without any governmental inducement.[69]

The English government also offered bounties, at times, for the private prosecution of certain crimes that were, admittedly, *malum in se* (proscribed by morality, not merely by sovereign edict). These English rewards took off in the 1690s and were made by statute and royal proclamations; they lasted until the government ended the proclamation rewards in the 1740s and repealed the statutes in the 1810s. Note, however, that the rewards, far from covering all *malum in se* crimes, focused on a selected set of newly prevalent property offenses, particularly highway robbery and burglary.[70] And they aimed mainly at such conduct in and around London,[71] which was an extremely unusual place. In the 1690s, London was far more populous than any city in the Western world except Paris, which was nearly as big, though London was growing much faster, because of record immigration,[72] which coincided with never-before-seen unemployment, thus undermining familiar patterns of community and governance and demanding radical measures to fill the vacuum.[73] The rewards aimed to govern a social world so disintegrated that any peacekeeping would have to be alien. Coupled with a radical expansion of capital punishment, the rewards were an innovative and positivist response of a central state facing an unprecedented challenge.[74]

Though bounties offered by the *qui tam* statutes and reward statutes were formally available to all individuals, ordinary people did not go around seeking them casually. They were often the preserve of enforcers who, though private, were specialized and invested in their roles. On this point, we observe two mutually reinforcing dynamics: (1) enforcers of alien impositions tended to elicit the distrust, resentment, scorn, and violent resistance of the communities in which they operated; and (2) social outsiders to a community were more effective at imposing alien law than were social insiders, since they had no friends or reputation to lose, meaning that they could focus coldly on the money.

Informing meant risking one's social ties and respectability in exchange for cash. To make that investment pay, it was best to go whole hog, committing oneself to an outsider status that provided the perfect launching point for profitable operations. This helps explain why the English *qui tam* statutes gave rise to the "professional informer," who often brought cases across multiple localities,[75] achieving social distance on his targets. It also helps explain why the rewards gave rise to London's specialized "thief-takers."[76] Occupying the role of bounty seeker might be remunerative, but it invited social odium. These enforcers suffered physical attacks by riotous mobs and epithets such as "base," "lewd," or "viperous vermin"—and those were only the epithets used by judges![77]

As in England, so in America. A scholar of colonial New England concludes that informing "fell into equally low repute" there as in the mother country.[78] Legislators did sometimes try to integrate bounties into regimes of familiar governance and thereby render those regimes more exacting, as when the Massachusetts legislature offered an informer's share to every "tythingman" (neighborhood liquor watchman) who prosecuted a seller of alcohol not licensed by the local justices of the peace. In Boston and other towns, however, it proved impossible to find community members willing to serve on a rotating basis in neighborhood posts where they would be identified as bounty-seeking enforcers.[79] This is not to say there was no enforcement, only that it likely took different forms, such as grand jury presentment, or prosecutions by more "professional" informers, such as the colony's excise commissioners, each of whom worked a whole county, not just a town or neighborhood. But even these "professionals" had to struggle with local social constraints: in the 1760s, one ceased his enforcement campaign during his later years in office, "perhaps as a concession to opposition," and left the colony a few years after that.[80]

Social suspicion of bounty-seeking persisted in postrevolutionary America. When the New York City Council in 1817 resolved to stamp out the old and pervasive custom of keeping pigs in the streets, it repeatedly offered bounties for catching them, but "[n]eighborhood solidarity almost certainly made the risks of pignapping far higher than the rewards."[81] In 1830, Austin, the Boston district attorney, observed that in areas like liquor regulation, reward-seeking informers often suffered "something like public indignation," and their work "most commonly raises a question in the public mind, whether it be not better that an offender should escape, than that an informer make money by telling of his crime."[82] The illustrious law reformer Edward Livingston, discussing the code he drafted for Louisiana in 1833, urged rewards for exposing certain offenses (including giving or accepting a challenge to duel, which many people thought the state had no business regulating), but he worried about whether the bounty would "attach any odium to the performance of the duty" and admitted that "[p]ublic prejudice is against it: this cannot be denied."[83]

Bounty-driven enforcement of alien law, if taken to its logical extreme, could be so adversarial that it might seem like a kind of war between the sovereign and the populace. Not coincidentally, the other realm where bounties were most prominent, apart from domestic law enforcement, was in actual war against foreign countries, in which alienation between the sovereign's agents and the targets was taken for granted—hence the Anglo-American law of "prize," in which a ship capturing an enemy vessel could keep a percentage of the proceeds.[84] On land, colonial governments fighting Indians offered bounties for prisoners and scalps.[85]

Bounty-seeking had a complex and changing relationship with officeholder status. As already noted, bounty offers were often the sovereign's response to the unreliability of officers who were enmeshed in local patterns of familiar governance and therefore reluctant to enforce alien law. At the same time, however, it was common for public officeholders to be included within the larger universe of individuals who were lawfully eligible to win bounties. Bounty eligibility could even be specifically or exclusively coupled with officeholder status—a linkage that appears to have become more common over time. For example, when colonial governments fighting Indians made offers of bounty to all comers, many of those seeking the rewards were part of special public militia units known as "rangers."[86] At sea, proceeds of prizes were actively sought by the crews not only of privateers but also of public naval ships,[87] and, seeing as how Britain and the United States licensed no privateers after 1815, the rewards went exclusively to public naval personnel from that date onward. The English government's offer of cash for catching and prosecuting perpetrators of certain crimes in the 1700s was open to everybody, including constables, and while most of them sought to serve out their brief terms "as quietly as possible," a few decided to make a living of the post, served repeatedly, and aggressively sought rewards, often in cooperation with professional thief-takers.[88] Legislatures of the early American republic went further in this direction, establishing fees for arrests for constables exclusively.[89] In the realm of the customs, shares of forfeitures were initially available to everybody, including customs officers. Then in 1662, Parliament declared that, in English ports, only customs officers could make the requisite seizures (though officers could make side payments to informers),[90] whereas in the colonies it seems that rewards remained directly available to officers and laypeople alike.[91] When the new U.S. Congress took over the customhouses in 1789, it strengthened the officers' bounty rights, making those in charge of a port the default claimants for all forfeitures and granting them a substantial automatic share even when some other informer was involved.[92]

As a matter of state-building, it made sense to focus bounty eligibility on officeholders: bounty-seeking tended to estrange the enforcer from the community of targets, so a bounty-seeking officialdom would tend to be more separated from society and faithful to the sovereign's alien commands. But while monetary incentives had the potential to drive official behavior, they did not determine it automatically all by themselves. For example, it appears that, throughout the colonial era and into the early national period, bounty offers to customs officials were feeble counterweights to the persistently strong pressure that local port communities exerted on officials to refrain from strict enforcement.[93]

*The Modern Spread of Alien Imposition and the Promise of Bounties.* Now that we have a sense of bounties' place in early modern governance, we shall consider their role amid the vastly accelerated changes that occurred in governance between about the mid-1800s and the early 1900s. Whereas alien impositions had once occurred in isolated pockets of public policy, they now proliferated dramatically, dominating American government as never before.[94] The main cause of this spread was the rising ambition of lawmakers, emboldened by new ideas of mass democracy and Promethean progress, to legislate in ways that would deliberately change the societies they governed. Their positivist aspirations covered both the direct regulation of people's behavior (e.g., to stamp out drinking and gambling, to mandate new health precautions, to make convicts into useful workers), as well as taxation at higher rates and on novel bases, to finance larger public projects (e.g., bigger wars, better roads, universal schools, and the like). Innovative regulations and taxes meant that a growing percentage of proscribed conduct was *malum prohibitum* and that a growing percentage of law was textual and rigid, rather than customary and adjustable, thus pushing law further out of phase with everyday morality. As challenges seemed bigger, lawmaking gravitated toward higher and more distant levels of government—town to county to state to Congress. And even when local bodies acted, they represented larger and more diverse populations and therefore were more socially distant from the persons they oversaw.

Lawmakers' unprecedented aspiration to impose alien law, starting in about the mid-1800s, created a greater demand than ever before for officers to violate the social expectations of the persons with whom they dealt. Historically, the bounty had been a common way of meeting this kind of demand. Yet it had always been somewhat difficult to find agents who would respond to the bounty, for anyone who did so risked losing social ties. However, the nineteenth century also witnessed several trends—rising population, the growth of cities, and increases in geographic mobility—which meant that officers were more likely than ever before to be strangers to those with whom they dealt. In other words, offices were increasingly filled by the very types of people who were historically most susceptible to bounty incentives. An additional trend that sometimes converted officers into strangers was the decline of the "local notable" and the rise of the "spoils system," in which persons won offices not by virtue of their privileged positions in the community's organic social hierarchy but instead by virtue of their positions in a rationalized party organization that might transcend the community (particularly in federal offices).[95]

Not only were officers increasingly strangers, but the information on which to base enforcement increasingly manifested itself in forms that were legible to strangers.[96] In the eighteenth century, familiar institutions like the grand jury were relatively well suited to law enforcement, since neighborly gossip was among the best available sources of information about deviancy. During the nineteenth century, however, ever more data about people's conduct and property took written form and were centrally stored, meaning that those data could be discovered, communicated, and used by less-personal enforcers of the type attracted to bounties. For example, the surveillance of taxpayers became a very different game as businesses engaged in more elaborate and standardized record-keeping and as wealth migrated from real estate toward bank deposits, stocks, bonds, and other institutional forms.

In light of these factors, the bounty held great promise as an instrument to effectuate the rise of alien imposition—and therefore of positivist governance, state-building, and modernity itself. In 1848, a federal judge, interpreting an ambiguous statute to offer bounties to a wide range of customs officers, explained that "the enforcing of fines and forfeitures is always attended with more or less odium, and sometimes with danger, and . . . the legislature has thought it expedient to stimulate the activity and quicken the diligence of the revenue officers in doing what is sometimes an ungrateful service, by offering them a share in the forfeitures."[97] In 1887, U.S. Representative Thomas Brackett Reed, the House Republican leader and one of the era's most formidable lawmakers, endorsed the award of bounties to customs officers, federal prosecutors, and federal marshals and their deputies. He powerfully articulated bounties' potential as offsets to social pressure:

> [I]n order to prevent [crimes] the United States must make it for the interests of its officials to look them up and to destroy them.

... [T]he crimes against the State and the crimes against the United States are entirely different in their character. Crimes against the State are crimes which are under the common law, and every lawyer knows that crimes which are punished by the common law have in their punishment and in their detection the support of every individual in the community. The officers of the law are there sustained by a vigorous and healthy sentiment, whereas the crimes against the United States are not those which are universally recognized as moral criminalities.

The whole community is awake to detect murder and to punish theft. But what community ever bestirred itself against frauds on the internal revenue, against moonshine distilleries, against smuggling, against a hundred things which are crimes against the United States? What, then, do you need in order to bring your criminals against the United States laws to detection? You need to have the officials stimulated by a similar self-interest to that which excites and supports and sustains the criminal.[98]

Reed identified state law with familiar imposition and federal law with alien imposition, and that identification was surely exaggerated. But Reed perfectly captured the peculiar importance of bounties for alien imposition. To engage in alien imposition was anti-social behavior, and bounties were rewards for being anti-social.

*The Intense Modern Experiment with Bounties and Its Negative Conclusion: Lawmakers' Realization of the Need for Legitimacy.* Amid the unprecedented escalation of alien imposition that began in the mid-1800s, lawmakers in numerous instances relied on bounties to effectuate their novel demands upon society—as previous sovereigns had done, but on a larger scale. Yet the very intensity of this experiment led to bounties' demise: the results left lawmakers so disappointed, disillusioned, and disturbed that they rejected bounties altogether. In particular, lawmakers banished bounties completely from the all-important realms of taxation and criminal justice, where they had episodically played a role for hundreds of years and seemed—for a few climactic decades in the late 1800s—to be playing a bigger role than ever.

What did lawmakers discover to be wrong with bounties? Recall that bounties were offered for the enforcer's success in detecting a violation and imposing a sanction for it. If you make the Benthamite assumption that people obey the law only insofar as they fear detection and punishment, then incentivizing enforcers to detect and punish is all the state can do to elicit mass compliance. That was the theory of bounty-based enforcement. But American lawmakers of the late 1800s and early 1900s concluded—sometimes through dumb trial and error but sometimes articulately—that they had to bolster their new demands with something more than coercion in order to achieve mass compliance. They needed what we today call legitimacy.

Legitimacy, as one study aptly defines it, "is a quality possessed by an authority, a law, or an institution that leads others to feel obligated to obey its decisions and directives voluntarily," that is, above and beyond their fear of detection and punishment.[99] Obviously, some directives are legitimate because they match moral precepts that people would generally obey even if the directive were suddenly repealed, like the taboo against incest. But the legitimacy of many other directives depends on their status as enacted law. An example is the U.S. income tax today. It enjoys legitimacy, in the sense that people comply with it at a substantially higher rate than can be explained by the probability that the government will detect and punish their evasion.[100] But if the tax were repealed, people would not generally continue to pay it. That kind of legitimacy— premised on positive enactment yet not dependent solely on state deterrence— is our particular concern here. Crucially, an imposition can acquire this kind of legitimacy yet still be alien. Such is the case with the income tax. Its rates and base are defined by exact and uniform rules. They do not arise from any organic face-to-face community but from the enactments of a Congress that is far away from the typical taxpayer and well beyond his or her influence or meaningful participation. The tax is administered by a centralized group of strangers who possess the independent capacity and motivation to surveil the population. Yet the tax still enjoys a degree of legitimacy, in the sense of compliance above the level explicable by state deterrence. Alien impositions are illegitimate if they operate solely by fear of punishment but legitimate insofar as they operate by more than that.[101]

How does an alien imposition attain legitimacy? This is an important question, for the process is critical to state-building, because the state cannot practically rely on coercion as the sole means to vindicate its positivist demands. It cannot put a police officer on every corner.[102] But the question is also a difficult one, for the process depends on numerous factors that are partly contingent on historical and cultural context. Some of the potential sources of legitimacy have to do with the structures of the state itself, including its macrostructures like democratic elections, as well as microstructures, such as how officers treat individual laypersons.[103] My aim in Part Two is to analyze one particular source of legitimacy in the American story: lawmakers' decisive turn in favor of "not-for-profit" enforcers. Legislators seeking legitimacy for their unprecedented alien impositions decided, after much experimentation, that bounties were not good instruments to achieve legitimacy for such impositions, that the rewards might well be sapping legitimacy, and that the state's agents needed to be deprived of any pecuniary benefit from detection and punishment if things were to improve. I do not claim that lawmakers were necessarily correct in their understanding of how bounties affected legitimacy; the correctness of a view like that is probably unknowable. But I do believe their view was plausible.

It was plausible in part because it resonates with two insights of present-day social science. The first of these comes from the psychologists Tom Tyler and Yuen Huo. In a study of American policing and criminal courts (which they argue is applicable to frontline public officers more broadly),[104] Tyler and Huo find that individuals are more likely to comply voluntarily with the law when they have "motive-based trust" in those who enforce it. Motive-based trust is "trust in the benevolence of the motives and intentions of the person with whom one is dealing."[105] Tyler and Huo distinguish this variety of trust from other kinds, such as confidence that the authorities possess technical competence, that they will make objectively correct decisions, or that each specific action they take will be predictable. Motive-based trust, by contrast, involves the citizen's perception of the enforcer's subjective aim or desire, and especially whether that aim or desire is to do what is best for the citizen, as a trustee would. We have motive-based trust in an enforcer when we expect that the enforcer "will act out of goodwill and do those things that he or she thinks would benefit us"—that enforcers are "motivated by the desire to do what is right for the people with whom they are dealing and whose interests they represent." "An inference of trustworthiness, in the motive-based sense," explain Tyler and Huo, "always reflects the belief that a particular authority . . . is not using his or her authority for personal gain."[106] Tyler and Huo say very little about authorities' monetary compensation.[107] But it is fair to assume that, if citizens are facing alien impositions of uncertain legitimacy, the knowledge that authorities stand to profit personally from punishing noncompliance with those impositions would undermine the citizens' motive-based trust in the authorities.[108] Citizens would therefore be less inclined to comply voluntarily.[109]

The second of the two insights comes from the economist Ian Ayres and the sociologist John Braithwaite, in a study of business regulation, primarily in America and Australia. Ayres and Braithwaite start from the notion that every person has "multiple selves." Laypersons who are subject to regulation, such as corporate executives or other businesspeople, "are not just value maximizers—of profits or of reputation. They are also often concerned to do what is right, to be faithful to their identity as a law abiding citizen, and to sustain a self-concept of social responsibility."[110] Which of the layperson's "selves" comes to the fore depends in part on the attitude that regulators take. If the regulators are quick to attribute bad conduct to laypeople and to resolve doubts in favor of maximal punishment or the threat of it, this dissipates the layperson's intrinsic motivation to abide by the law for its own sake, and the adversarial attitude elicits an adversarial response, in which the layperson no longer views the enforcers as purveyors of shared norms but simply as opponents to be outwitted and defeated, often through a game of "cat-and-mouse,"[111] in which the layperson has many informational advantages. For the regulator, the key to greater compliance is not to be adversarial but to nurture the law-abiding and cooperative identities of laypersons, which the regulator can do by starting from a presumption of their good faith, finding bad motives and imposing punishments only in measured fashion, and constantly seeking to return to the cooperative equilibrium.[112] This model is applicable to many areas of government beyond business regulation.[113] Though Ayres and Braithwaite say nothing about the compensation of enforcers, it is obvious that bounties—which reward the finding of a violation and the imposition of a punishment for it—would not only push enforcers toward excessively punitive and therefore counterproductive behavior but also send a signal to the population that the officialdom is eager for citizens to violate the law and be punished. This is not a recipe for mass cooperation.

Consistent with these present-day studies, the bounty in the centuries leading up to the 1800s had always been a double-edged sword. It could spur the courageous enforcement of law in the face of community hostility, yet bounty-paid enforcers were usually distrusted, scorned, and despised. Edward Coke encapsulated this tension. On the one hand, he said of informers, "Their office, I confess, is necessary."[114] Yet on another occasion he coined the phrase "viperous vermin" to condemn them.[115] Bentham, the prince of positivists, recognized the "prejudice which condemns mercenary informers" and deeply regretted the way that it undermined their obvious potential to vindicate positive legislation: the prejudice was "an evil" and "a consequence of the inattention of the public to their true interests, and of the general ignorance in matters of legislation."[116] To be sure, some degree of distaste for bounty seekers was inevitable, because the bounty's purpose was so often to effectuate laws that were unpopular to begin with. But the works of Tyler, Huo, Ayres, and Braithwaite suggest that the enforcers' profit-seeking status—by undermining motive-based trust and eliciting an adversarial response—*aggravated* the preexisting legitimacy deficit of alien law. This is consistent with the pervasive social hostility (noted earlier) that greeted professional informers from the 1500s through the 1800s. In her book on English apprenticeship regulation in the period 1563–1642, Margaret Davies briefly but incisively touches on this point: "The informer was not a good advertisement for his wares; contempt for the individual was transferred to the function." Thus, "distaste for a principal method of enforcement came to taint the whole concept of regulation by the state."[117] In 1830, Austin, the Boston district attorney, warned that the employment of bounty-seeking informers "brings on the law itself the stigma of a mercenary spirit, discreditable to its character, and, in a free state, unfriendly to its influence."[118]

The tension between the bounty's good tendency (to motivate enforcers) and its bad tendency (to undermine legitimacy) reached a crisis amid the dramatic rise of alien impositions between about the mid-1800s and early 1900s. A short-lived but spectacular example of the tension arose when Congress, as part of the Compromise of 1850, attempted to effectuate the right of Southern masters to take back fugitive slaves in the Northern states. Northern communities were content to let masters own slaves within the South, but they objected to the intrusion of slave catchers in their midst—an objection reflected in Northern state laws that erected various legal obstacles to the fundamentally alien process of slave-catching, including a role for local juries (well known as guarantors of familiar governance). In 1850, however, Congress imposed on the Northern states a new corps of federal fugitive-slave commissioners, aiming to make slave rendition independent of local actors.[119] Bounty-seeking formed part of the scheme: the commissioners were to receive double the ordinary fee in cases where they decided that the person in custody was a fugitive.[120] The extra cash may have encouraged the commissioner to stand up against community hostility. Yet, as so often, it was a double-edged sword, making the commissioner seem more illegitimate and untrustworthy in the eyes of Northerners than he otherwise would have.[121] That illegitimacy was a problem for effective enforcement, for slave catchers needed the cooperation of local deputies,[122] and they could be deterred by local hostility.[123]

Though the Civil War mooted the question of how to return fugitive slaves, alien imposition in most areas of life kept growing inexorably. The unprecedented prevalence of such impositions meant that bounties were more important and more salient than ever, yet the threat they inherently posed for legitimacy—combined with the fact that lawmakers' positivist ambitions made the need for legitimacy more urgent than ever—ultimately led to their demise.

Chapter 5 presents a case study of this dynamic in operation. It focuses on taxation at the state and local level, and particularly on the most important levy at those levels during the nineteenth century: the property tax. In the early 1800s, the administration of this tax was a familiar imposition. In each locality, people's tax liabilities (for both state and local purposes) were decided by a single assessor who was elected by the locality and served part-time for a small daily wage. This officer was closely enmeshed in the social and political life of the local community. The people he assessed were his neighbors and his constituents. Assessing them was a matter of face-to-face accommodation and compromise. This consensualist approach to taxation worked fine, because, at the time, the financial needs of states and localities were small, and because most people's property took the form of land and livestock, which was plainly visible to everybody in the community, so there was a focal point to foster agreement about each person's share of the burden. Intangible assets like bank accounts and securities were comparatively rare and much harder for the assessor to find, and a social expectation developed that (practically) they would not be taxed at all.

But starting in the mid-1800s, taxation went from familiar to alien. State legislators and local lawmakers became far more aggressive in their tax demands. They felt the need for much bigger sums of revenue, to pay for new initiatives in sanitation, public health, policing, schooling, and highways. And as agriculture and rural life gave way to industry and cities, intangibles overtook land as the primary form of wealth. Now that intangible property was so prevalent, lawmakers decided they had to tax it. But the new imperative to reach intangibles ran up against the expectation of its owners, built up over the preceding years, that their wealth was protected by a tax-free zone of privacy. Thus, by about the 1860s, lawmakers were demanding more taxes than ever before, and especially from owners who expected that they did not have to pay at all. This was taxation as alien imposition.

These novel attempts at alien imposition initially met such widespread resistance that they were, for their first several years, a dead letter. Lawmakers' campaign to tax intangibles could not get off the ground because they continued to rely on the local assessors, whose offices had been structured to engage in familiar imposition, not the intrusive and feather-ruffling investigations that lawmakers now wanted. Local assessors were accountable to the taxpayers who elected them, through a neighborly hand-shaking politics. Such officers were reluctant to draw the ire of any of their constituents, and so they refused to upset the settled expectation of intangibles owners that their property was tax-free. Thus evasion remained rife.

Bent on making the owners of intangibles pay, lawmakers resorted to bounty-seeking as a promising means. Starting in the 1870s, legislatures in ten states— plus localities (often large cities) in ten others—hired "tax ferrets," that is, agents with the mission to discover tax liabilities that the ordinary assessors had missed, in exchange for a share of the proceeds. The tax ferrets were generally persons from outside the localities to be investigated, thus replacing familiar neighborly accommodation with the coldhearted maximization of profit (and revenue). Accordingly, the tax ferrets devised innovative and intrusive methods of surveillance against the owners of intangibles, aggressively searching various sources of personal financial data.

But lawmakers' intense experiment with bounty-seeking ultimately led to their disillusionment with it. They learned from experience that the tax ferrets, in seeking to achieve compliance through coercion and deterrence, in fact yielded at best a modest increase in compliance and perhaps even a reduction. Lawmakers thus came to believe that a sound tax system depended on a high degree of voluntary taxpayer compliance—legitimacy—which the ferrets did not foster and might well undermine. Because the owners of intangible assets could easily conceal or move their property, taxing such property was impossible without a substantial amount of taxpayer goodwill. Starting around 1900, reformers proposed a method for winning that goodwill: to "classify" intangible property as a special category enjoying a lower rate that would "coax" its owners to pay tax on it. In the reformers' view, laypersons were not narrowly selfish tax minimizers but instead had some intrinsic desire to be law-abiding, so long as the law seemed reasonable and worthy of cooperation. By this thinking, bounty-seeking enforcement was counterproductive. It meant that state agents benefited when citizens violated the law and were then forced to comply. This placed state and citizen in an adversarial relation and alienated them from each other, sapping the intrinsic desire of citizens to comply with law for its own sake and undermining their trust in the state. From the 1910s onward, in state after state, lawmakers embraced this program to elicit taxpayer cooperation, rejecting the tax ferrets and classifying intangibles at a lower rate.

Chapter 6 addresses similar themes in a case study of taxation at the federal level, and Chapter 7 does the same for criminal prosecution at both the federal and state levels. Besides elaborating on the problems of motive-based trust and adversarialism initially raised in Chapter 5, Chapters 6 and 7 introduce an additional and related issue: the tension between bounty-seeking and the exercise of enforcement discretion.

Before I summarize Chapters 6 and 7, I must say a word about discretion as a general matter. As noted already, the rise of alien imposition meant that lawmakers subjected people's behavior to ever more specific regulation through more elaborate written rules. One might assume (following Weber) that, concurrent with this trend, official behavior became ever more exact and rule bound.[124] Ironically, the truth is nearer the opposite: the proliferation of elaborate restrictions on conduct required those who administered such restrictions to exercise ever-greater subjective judgment, discretion, and forbearance in imposing—or, more accurately, refraining from imposing—the sanctions for such conduct. As early as the seventeenth century, a member of Parliament warned that, if regulatory statutes were enforced "to the utmost, it would be unsufferable."[125] Then, as now, no rule could describe with perfect accuracy the conduct that lawmakers intended to proscribe, so lawmakers commonly wrote an overly broad rule whose sharp edges could be "sanded off" through selective nonenforcement.[126] And even if lawmakers intended a prohibition to be as broad as they wrote it, a good deal of "sanding off" might be necessary as a concession to the brute political preferences of the affected population.[127] Without these kinds of forbearance, alien governance could become so radically divorced from prevailing moral sentiment or so practically unbearable that it would lose even the grudging cooperation of the populace. (It could also become fiscally burdensome, insofar as the state picked up the costs of enforcement or punishment.)[128] The exercise of judgment to temper harsh rules took at least two forms: (1) the rules themselves might say that the proscribed conduct was punishable only if the person engaging in it did so with bad intent, so the officials had to make an inherently subjective judgment as to the inner thoughts of the accused; or (2) the rules might contain no intent requirement, so the officials had to exercise "raw" prosecutorial discretion, that is, judge which legally guilty persons did not deserve punishment as a matter of policy and morals, irrespective of the letter of the law.[129] In either case, bounty-seeking rendered it very difficult for enforcers to make subjective judgments in a sound way. The profit motive pushed them, consciously or not, to resolve doubt in favor of punishment.[130] Bounties' tendency toward untempered enforcement—plus their apparent potential to vitiate motive-based trust and to elicit adversarial responses—made them dangerous to legitimacy. Weber viewed rule-boundedness and salarization as twin pillars of modern government, but it would be more accurate to say that salarization fostered the necessary softening of rule-boundedness that has made it bearable.[131]

Chapter 6 explores the subject of bounties—with emphasis on the problems of discretion and subjective judgment just discussed—through a case study of federal taxation, particularly the most important federal tax of the nineteenth century: the customs duty. Customs officers were entitled to a share (moiety) of all goods that were forfeited for intentional evasion. The 1860s and 1870s saw an unprecedented spike in forfeitures and moieties, and there was a sudden flood of complaints that these incentives were pushing officers to construe every mistaken underpayment as intentional, thereby putting officers and merchants in an adversarial posture toward each other and destroying the trust and confidence between them. At first glance, the timing of these events presents a puzzle, for customs officers had been eligible for moieties since colonial times. Why did persistent problems arise only in the 1860s and 1870s?

The reason is that moieties' effect depended on the larger governance structure of which they were a part, and that structure changed over time. Recall (as noted earlier) that customhouse moieties for most of their history had been a feeble counterweight to a regime of imposition that was familiar, not alien. During the eighteenth century and into the early nineteenth, the typical customs officer was appointed from the ranks of local notables who lived at the port and had strong social connections to the port's merchants—ties the officer was not about to jeopardize to earn a quick buck. Furthermore, customs law itself was not at all harsh: rates of duty were generally low, the legal formula for calculating a forfeiture was forgiving toward the merchant, and the officers had almost no legal power to force the merchants to cough up the kind of information that would help build a case. Under these conditions, officers administered the law in a mild and indulgent manner, and merchants, thinking the government's demands were reasonable, complied willingly, if loosely.

But then, between the 1820s and 1860s, familiar imposition gave way to alien imposition. The rise of nationally organized political parties in the 1820s and 1830s meant that customs officers came to be appointed not from the social network of the port but from the ranks of the party machine, thereby weakening the social ties between merchants and officers that had constrained bounty-seeking. Then, in the 1860s, Congress acquired a ferocious new appetite for high tariffs (these were initially to meet the Civil War emergency, but the ascendancy of protectionist Republicans ensured that rates would remain high even when peace returned). To make the high rates stick, congressmen imposed more draconian forfeiture rules and empowered customs officers to search merchants' books and papers, thus opening up vast new stores of information in which to find accusatory evidence. As the government made unprecedented pecuniary demands on the merchants and peered more intrusively into their affairs, it enthusiastically embraced bounties as a promising means to ensure that the new demands would be met and the new powers exploited to their potential. Thus, Congress in 1867 reaffirmed and expanded the moiety incentive system, and in 1869 the Treasury Department began hiring full-time customs detectives, nicknamed "moiety men." The bounty was no longer a feeble counterweight to a regime of familiar governance. It had instead become the motivational engine for a new regime of alien governance.

Integrated into this more modern regime, the bounty proved terrifyingly effective at motivating enforcement. Seeking profit, officers went after the merchants as never before, pressing them to agree to harsh settlements, quite often in cases in which the underpayments turned out to be innocent mistakes.

As these results became clear in the early 1870s, congressmen concluded that they had created a monster. The bounty had come to seem dangerous not just to the merchants but also to the workability of modern government. Congressmen very much wanted to maintain the protective tariff, and they knew that high rates, serious punishments, and intrusive surveillance would be necessary to do that. Yet Congress feared that, if officers continued to operate the ambitious new revenue system in such an adversarial and narrowly self-interested manner, they would make it impossible for the merchants to maintain trust and confidence in the government. The merchants' trust and confidence, as congressmen came to believe, were necessary for the system to work. There were too many imports and not enough officers for the government to rely on coercion alone. Mass compliance required the merchants' voluntary cooperation and goodwill. To foster that, congressmen in 1874 abolished moieties, believing that nonprofit officers would be more likely to exercise forbearance in making the delicate, subjective judgment of whether an underpayment was an innocent mistake or a fraud. By making such judgments with care and good faith, officers would be more likely to elicit the trust of the merchants, and the government would have the benefit of a more cooperative taxpaying population. In other words, it would acquire legitimacy.

Chapter 7 is a case study of bounties for another important class of officers: public prosecutors, at the federal and state levels. When these officers first emerged at the state level in the late 1700s and early 1800s, they inhabited a regime of familiar imposition. Typically, they received a fee for every case they brought to trial, regardless of whether the defendant was convicted or not. Laypersons would come forward claiming to be victims of crime, and the district attorney maximized his fees by bringing all their accusations to trial without much scrutiny, essentially holding the courthouse door open for them and allowing them to tell their stories to the jury. This arrangement motivated the public prosecutor to impose *some* hardship on defendants, in that he forced them to go through the hassle of a trial, but he had no incentive to convict them. Defendants experienced prosecutions not as governmental attacks but as complaints of fellow laypersons in their neighborhood (whom they could prosecute right back, if they wished). This effectively allowed the lay inhabitants of a neighborhood to control the machinery of criminal justice and collectively define "crime" for themselves. It was familiar imposition.

But then, in the decades leading up to the 1860s, more than half the states changed public prosecutors' fees so that they were available only if the officer won a conviction (or were much higher if he won a conviction). Instead of holding open the courthouse door for anybody who wanted to accuse, the district attorney now had an incentive to scrutinize private accusations, concentrate his efforts on cases that he judged to be winners, and shut the door to the accusers whose cases looked like losers. And once the officer picked a case as a winner, he had the incentive to win it—to get the defendant convicted and punished. Thus, the conviction fee was a bounty. The district attorney was no longer a conduit for the aggregate complaints of the community, but a proactive gatekeeper. Defendants experienced prosecution not as a neighbor-to-neighbor dispute but as an intervention by a more independent and external force—alien imposition. In addition to this, legislatures by the 1860s moved toward alien imposition in another way: they enacted more aggressive laws criminalizing victimless conduct and pushing against the norms and expectations of certain communities, especially stricter laws about liquor, gambling, taxes, concealed weapons, and business regulation. To punish these victimless *malum prohibitum* crimes, legislatures had to rely on public officers, and they often granted public prosecutors the very highest fees for winning such convictions.

To illustrate how lawmakers initially put their faith in bounties but ultimately became disillusioned with them, the chapter culminates with a case study of federal prosecutors. Like many states, the federal government in the 1850s began offering conviction fees. Commentators considered the rewards especially promising as motivators for the enforcement of *federal* criminal law, which was almost always alien, cutting against local communities' norms and wishes. This federal-local tension was most intense in the case of the new excise tax of the 1860s that imposed draconian anti-evasion regulations on the folk practice of making and selling whisky in the South and West. Yet after a few decades of experience under this regime, Congress concluded that it was backfiring and converted the U.S. attorneys to salaries in 1896, much as legislators did with the tax ferrets and the moiety men. Conviction fees, concluded congressmen, pushed prosecutors to focus too much on piling up convictions for extremely minor and technical offenses, since the perpetrators were easy to round up and convict, given the overly broad nature of the law. The defendants were guilty, yes, but usually of violations so picayune that punishing them only increased local contempt for federal law. As statutes got harsher, they had to be tempered with a less adversarial mode of enforcement, including a good deal of discretionary nonenforcement. So long as people who lived in "moonshine country" could cynically attribute all enforcement to the narrow self-interest of the officers, it would not be possible for federal law to achieve legitimacy, for the officialdom to win the trust of the population, or for community sentiment

to develop in favor of voluntary cooperation. For these things to happen, bounties had to go.

The tension between bounties and enforcement discretion ranged well
beyond the tax investigators and public prosecutors discussed in Chapters 6
and 7. For example, in far-flung states, one finds complaints about the unwarranted pursuit of "trivial" or "technical" offenses by police and other law enforcement officers who made (or approved) arrests and received fees for doing
so.[132] In that vein, let me here briefly discuss a variation on the theme of Chapters 6 and 7, using as an example the abolition of arrest fees in Birmingham,
Alabama, which occurred in 1919, as explained in Carl V. Harris's insightful
history of the city. This story is of interest because of the radical alienation
between the white power holders and the black labor force in the Jim Crow
South. Under such a regime, it would be impossible for the state to get black
workers to "trust" its motives, or to convince them of its legitimacy, in Tyler
and Huo's sense. Yet even so, Birmingham's power holders sought to reform
the incentives and actions of their agents in the hope of inducing compliance
that was voluntary in a weaker sense. The aim of Birmingham's businessmen
was to ensure that African Americans lived in the area and provided labor. To
this end, businessmen pressed for enforcement of the vagrancy statute, but the
typical deputy instead focused his attention on *employed* African Americans,
who congregated near the industrial sites where they worked, hoping to catch
them in "trivial" or "petty" offenses—often customary but illegal acts like crapshooting. Focusing on work sites made it possible to arrest several men (and accrue several bounties) in one trip, and it meant that the bounties would be paid
instantly by the employer, so the officer did not have to wait for the arrested
man to earn cash through convict labor. This maximized income for the officers, but it caused free black workers to leave Birmingham in search of locales
where they could avoid fee-driven arrests, and it lowered the morale of workers who stayed. To make officers forbear in their policing of employed African
Americans, the business community mounted a successful campaign to replace
officers' fees with salaries. The purpose of salarization was to provide these employees with assurances against at least some forms of state molestation, in hope
of inducing them to stay in the area.[133] While the Jim Crow state would never
win the motive-based trust of its black inhabitants, it could at least temper its
adversarialism so as to appeal to them at the level of expediency—"stay and
work, you won't be harassed."[134] Implicit in this appeal was a grudging recognition of the autonomy of the black population: despite employers' vocal support
for vagrancy enforcement, they knew such coercion was useless against African

Americans who departed the city altogether, so they banished the profit motive to make governance bearable enough that more (so they hoped) would stay.

Thus far, my discussion of bounties has focused on their power to incentivize the aggressive enforcement of alien laws and their consequent tendency to promote adversarialism between officialdom and population. Under certain circumstances, however, it was possible for bounties to have the opposite effect, that is, to promote cooperation between officers and the affected population, but in a perverse way that turned the intent of the legislature on its head.[135] The pattern went like this: in a community where violations of law were rife, an enforcer would periodically round up small-time violators to win bounties, but he would not dare take action that would permanently suppress violations (for example, by prosecuting ringleaders instead of small fry), since the pervasiveness of violations was a steady source of income for him. This pattern could be the result of explicit collusion between enforcers and violators, or it might be a tacit understanding. When perverse cooperation arose in bounty schemes, it provided yet another argument in favor of salaries, since such cooperation obviously went against any plausible public-regarding legislative purpose, and it did nothing to legitimate alien governance, which the affected population came to view merely as a racket.

Such perversions became more likely when (1) the punishment was mild, or could be rendered mild with the enforcer's help; (2) the amount of the bounty stayed flat as the severity of the violation increased, so that enforcers, to maximize their profits, wanted violations to be numerous; and (3) the enforcer was elected by a polity that included prospective violators or their sympathizers, thus giving him an incentive to figure out a way to make money from bounties without alienating that section of the electorate. There is very little evidence of such perversities in the cases of tax ferrets and moiety men, likely because, in those cases, punishments and rewards rose with the size of the evasion (at least roughly), and the enforcers were not elected. There is more evidence of such perversities among some U.S. attorneys and state-level district attorneys (as Chapter 7 discusses), likely because punishments were light, rewards consisted of flat fees, and the enforcers (at the state level) were elected. Conversely, it seems likely that bounties drove Birmingham deputies toward true adversarialism in part because their African American targets were disenfranchised, just as other bounty-seeking enforcers notoriously selected nonvoting immigrants as their prey.[136]

The essential pattern that we observe in Chapters 5, 6, and 7—that lawmakers strove for alien imposition, experimented intensely with the bounty, and then were disillusioned by experience—also obtained in the realm of incarceration, as Chapter 8 documents. The principal eighteenth-century carceral institution was the local jail. Typically, jail time was not itself a punishment, for the jail was a holding area for people awaiting trial or corporal punishment, or unable to pay debts. Confinement in this holding area was familiar imposition, for the jail was remarkably open to the surrounding community and to inmate preferences. The inmates effectively governed the place, asserted customary rights, and took advantage of a free flow of resources from persons on the outside. In keeping with this, the jailor routinely sold inmates a variety of privileges (e.g., nicer beds, glasses of beer) in exchange for facilitative payments. But around the turn of the nineteenth century, American states undertook a major experiment in alien imposition: they imposed confinement itself as a punishment, for long terms at hard labor, aiming to reform the convicts. The managers of the new "penitentiaries" were not to cater to inmates' wishes but instead force them to work. Hence lawmakers banned facilitative payments and adopted various combinations of salaries and bounties, often salarizing the warden and guards while inviting contractors inside the prison walls to extract the inmates' labor, sell what they produced, and take the profit. This mixed regime of salaries and bounties had become well established by the 1850s, and its operation was fairly stable.

But in the 1870s, state governments—swayed by the promise of for-profit contractors to keep inmates disciplined and productive—hired bigger contractors and gave them more complete power over the management of the penitentiary, including corporal punishment. It was now the profit-seeking extractors of labor, not the salaried warden and guards, who controlled inmates' lives. Given this extreme convergence of power and profit motive, the penitentiary became a kind of dystopia in which the contractor relied almost exclusively on naked threats of physical pain to squeeze the last ounce of labor from inmates. This was alien imposition of the most extreme and adversarial kind, virtually denying the humanity of the governed. In reaction to this, inmates rioted in unprecedented numbers. The riots contributed powerfully to legislative decisions starting in the 1880s to expel the contractors from the prisons and rely solely on salaried staff. Lawmakers and officials came to realize they could not maintain order within the prisons through simple coercion and fear but instead needed to adopt less adversarial methods that would elicit inmate cooperation. Thus, the "managerial penology" of the early twentieth century would seek to accommodate and win over the inmate population through recreational activities, "good time" credits, and the like. Even in prison, power needed legitimacy and voluntary cooperation, which required banishing the profit motive.

Finally, in Chapter 9, we close Part Two with a discussion of alien imposition, bounty-seeking, and legitimacy in the context of naval warfare. To see the commonality between the navy's story and those of the preceding case studies of bounties, we must appreciate a peculiar aspect of military power in American political culture. From the revolutionary period through most of the nineteenth century, Americans were terrified of alien imposition by the military—not only foreign militaries but also their own military. They therefore emphatically rejected the buildup of a European-style permanent military establishment, fearing that such an institution would be fatal to their republican ideal of self-government by local communities. A permanent military establishment would demand high taxes by the most distant level of government; raise up a quasi-aristocratic officer class alienated from civil society; and subject the American people to the alliances and rivalries of the European powers, thus dragging them into frequent and costly wars. To avoid these horrors, Americans kept their permanent army and navy small. Still, within its confined institutional space, it was fine for the U.S. Navy to imitate the other navies of the world. Thus, the U.S. Navy—following the universal practice of its bigger European counterparts—motivated its officers and seamen by offering a percentage of the value of merchant ships they captured (prize money), plus rewards for every sailor on board an enemy warship they sank (head money, nicknamed "blood money"). In the nation's infrequent naval conflicts—the War of 1812 and the Civil War—naval personnel won very large sums. But the navy remained very small in peacetime (after the Civil War, it shrank dramatically), so nobody thought much of it. Congressmen in the Civil War era were well aware of prize money and head money and generally considered them just rewards for fine patriotic work.

Yet in 1899, immediately after the navy's signal victory in the Spanish-American War, Congress suddenly and unanimously abolished prize money and head money. So far as U.S. lawmakers knew, their country was the first in the world to do so. (The British—the world's experts at naval war—reaffirmed naval profit-seeking in 1900 and abolished it only gradually between the 1910s and 1940s.) Congressmen in 1899 were responding to a sudden wave of popular American revulsion against naval profit-seeking. This wave arose because the victory against Spain had given the United States an overseas empire that everybody realized would require a huge permanent navy to maintain. This was an exciting change, but a wrenching and alarming one, for it portended the dangers of a permanent military establishment. To allay these anxieties and legitimate the new imperial navy—both for the public and for themselves—the hawks focused on the purity of the navy's motives. They trumpeted the humanitarian justification for the war with Spain (to save Cuba from oppression) and cast the navy as an instrument of selfless humanitarianism and civilization. In this quest to build up the mass public's trust in an alien institution, naval profit-seeking was a major embarrassment, and it had to go. Nonprofit status meant that newly empowered naval personnel would have no monetary incentive to start wars, and it also fit with a simultaneous U.S. initiative to immunize civilian ships from capture on the high seas, thereby promising an apprehensive public that war would become less destructive even as the United States became a more engaged global actor. Lawmakers thus invoked official selflessness as a means to win trust for the officialdom and legitimate its unprecedented power.

*Part One*

## FACILITATIVE PAYMENTS TO SALARIES

# THE OLD REGIME

*Lawful Bargaining for Public Services*

Part One of this book tells the story of facilitative payments—the moneys that public officials received for providing services to "customers" who wanted them. From the Middle Ages up to the late 1700s and early 1800s, these payments were, to a significant degree, unregulated. That is, officers and the recipients of their services could engage in a fair amount of bargaining. In this chapter, I begin by explaining the doctrines of Anglo-American common law that made such bargaining legal. Next, I show that, while Parliament and American legislatures often enacted statutes to fix the prices of officers' services, these laws had exceptions and limits that allowed for a good deal of lawful negotiation to continue. Finally, I consider how all this bargaining imbued government itself with an ethos of customer-seller reciprocity.

## COMMON-LAW BASES FOR NEGOTIATION IN ENGLAND

In reconstructing the legal regime that governed exchanges between officers and service recipients in early modern England and colonial America, one might assume that we should begin with the doctrine on bribery. But that is not so: bribery at common law was a narrow offense with little or no application beyond judges.[1] However, much behavior that we today would label "bribery" was still criminal for any public officer. It was punished under the broad umbrella offense known as extortion, "the main offense used to combat public corruption" in late medieval and early modern England.[2] Our inquiry must, therefore, center on extortion. Largely following Coke,[3] Blackstone in 1769 defined extortion as "any officer's unlawfully taking, by color of his office, from any man, any money or thing of value, that is not due to him, or more than is due, or before it is due."[4] For our purposes, the definition raises two questions. How did one tell what payment was "due"? And what did it mean to "take unlawfully"?

As for the question of what payment was due, the answer was straightforward: any payment established (1) by statute or (2) by immemorial custom, that is, by a usage that stretched back to "time out of mind." The officer had a right to demand such payments. As the chief justice of the Common Pleas said in 1793, an officer could claim a fee "by ancient usage or act of Parliament."[5] Through the 1600s and 1700s, the point appeared in multiple legal abridgments,[6] plus the leading justice-of-the-peace manuals.[7]

Thus, an officer taking a statutory payment, or a customary payment, was not guilty of extortion. But the reverse was not necessarily true. In other words, there were some nonstatutory, noncustomary payments that were still lawful. How could this be? This brings us to the other key element of the offense: that the payment be "unlawfully taken." The meaning of this phrase is not obvious on its face. Fortunately James Lindgren, in his immensely valuable doctrinal history of extortion, describes the facts of more than one hundred English cases on the subject from before the nineteenth century. As to the "mode of taking,"[8] the payments held to be extortionary overwhelmingly involved at least one of three elements: (1) the officer engaged in some kind of coercion, such as threatening to withhold a service the payor needed or to take action the payor wished to avoid;[9] (2) the officer deceived the payor, say, by lying about the amount due;[10] or (3) the payor intended to induce the officer to betray his duty, for example, by getting the officer to let the payor escape jury service, or let a suspect out of custody, or grant a license regardless of the applicant's qualifications—that is, what we today call "bribery."[11]

But what did English law say about payments to officers that involved neither coercion nor deception nor bribery? In other words, what if an officer did his duty and the recipient of the service, knowing that he legally owed nothing, voluntarily gave him an unsolicited "tip" for it?

Such tips were, in fact, legal at common law. To be sure, Lindgren's work does not provide affirmative support for making this conclusion, but neither does it stand in the way. Such tips are peripheral to Lindgren's research agenda, and he is not explicit about their legal status.[12] Certain narrow categories of such payments, he rightly notes, were criminalized by specific statutes: there were several legislative acts, in England and the American colonies or states, that (1) fixed or banned payments for certain named officers or named services and (2) criminalized the mere receipt of any payment for official service in violation of those regulations, even without coercion, deception, or bribery.[13] Some of Lindgren's commentary on these anti-receipt statutes might be taken to mean that they declared the common law—that mere receipt was always criminal unless affirmatively authorized by statute (or, perhaps, by custom). But Lindgren is not very explicit about the declaratory reading and certainly does not emphasize it.[14] On the contrary, for offices or services not covered by statute, Lindgren centers his description of extortion not on mere receipt but instead on the unholy trinity of coercion, deception, and bribery.[15] Further, his numerous discussions of individual cases prior to 1800 almost invariably mention coercion, deception, bribery, or violation of an anti-receipt statute. I have researched the only three cases of official extortion with no such mentions and have found that they, too, involved officers subject to anti-receipt statutes.[16] Thus, Lindgren's work does not foreclose the idea that tips were lawful.

Plus, there is affirmative support for the legality of tips at common law in the work of G. E. Aylmer. In the second edition of *The King's Servants*, which he published after more than twenty years of archival research on seventeenth-century English administration, Aylmer describes a common type of payment to officials known as the gratuity. "[G]ratuities," explains Aylmer, were "*not* illegal."[17] Using the term *bribe* in the colloquial sense of an inducement to breach official trust, he elaborates: "Today tipping a public servant . . . smacks of impropriety. But it would be a great mistake to equate tips [i.e., gratuities] with bribes in seventeenth-century England. At that time bribery implied an attempt to persuade an official to follow a course of action other than that which he knew he ought to have followed. It implied the acceptance of a present or gratuity by an official, knowing that its purpose was to influence his decision improperly."[18] Aylmer speaks of the 1600s, but the principle survived through the following century. Thus a pair of parliamentary commissions in the 1780s, cataloging the frequent receipt of "gratuities" by numerous officers in various parts of the government, warned that such payments might easily be abused so as to induce officers to betray their duty, but—crucially—the commissioners did not suggest that such payments were unlawful per se.[19] In the case of one office, they were careful to note: "We do not say, or mean to insinuate, that we have discovered any instance of such abuse" among the officers who were receiving gratuities.[20]

A strong affirmation of the legality of gratuities at common law appeared in the third volume of Matthew Bacon's *A New Abridgment of the Law* (1740), a leading reference. In a passage that remained intact through four subsequent editions during the 1700s,[21] and was reproduced in the authoritative 1819 treatise on criminal law by William Oldnall Russell,[22] Bacon said of extortion: "[A]n officer, who takes a reward which is voluntarily given to him, and which has been usual in certain cases for the more diligent or expeditious performance of his duty, cannot be said to be guilty of extortion; for without such a *praemium* it would be impossible in many cases to have the laws executed with vigor and success."[23] It is evident from these words that lawyers of the period understood coercion and bribery more loosely than we moderns do. To them, an officer who offered "more diligent or expeditious performance of his duty" in exchange for more money was not (within limits) committing a breach of official trust. Conversely, a citizen who found it otherwise "impossible in many cases to have the laws executed with vigor and success" could still be said to pay the necessary premium "voluntarily." No doubt this looseness provided cover for some exchanges that we (and even people at the time) would say involved coercion or breach of official duty.

But this did not stop eighteenth-century lawyers from believing that some category of lawful gratuities existed. Consider a 1796 case in the King's Bench, where one man usurped the office of another, performed an official service, and received money from the recipient of the service. The justices held that the wronged officer could not recover the money from the usurper if it were "a gratuity" that the service recipient might "have refused to give if he had pleased," as distinct from the "regular fees due" by custom or statute. The justices spoke of gratuities as perfectly ordinary things and did not intimate they were illegal; on the contrary, one justice pointed out that they depended "entirely on the behavior and civility" of the officer.[24] Consider also the testimony of Thomas Davies, one of the highest civilian administrators in the Royal Navy,[25] before a parliamentary commission in 1787. Informing the commission of the gratuities he received for processing the accounts of contractors and naval officers (which added up to big sums), he frankly admitted that there was "no positive authority for receiving them" but also "no prohibition to receiving them." With apparent appreciation of the link between voluntariness and lawfulness, he emphasized that the "whole" of the "gifts" was "voluntary," that "they are never demanded," and that he "never intimated to the party" that a payment was "too small, or less than usually given by others."[26] Many other administrators reported and justified their gratuities along the same lines.[27]

Tipping and "gift-giving" were familiar practices in early modern English administration, particularly when an officer provided quick or extraordinary service: gratuities were optional for the donor, and they were most likely to be given when the officer was providing some new or special service that was optional for him, too.[28] "It is very natural," wrote Jeremy Bentham circa 1780, "that an individual who has been served with an extraordinary expedition [by an officer], should add something to the accustomed fee."[29] Tipping was especially accepted for services during off-hours. In a case before the Common Pleas in 1778, a sealer of writs offered to open his office and provide service on a holiday (the Feast of St. Barnabas), but only for 10s., far more than the usual fee of seven pence. The man seeking the service paid but then sued to get his money back. The chief justice explained that the sealer's "claim must be to keep the office shut, if any thing; and if the officer has a right so to do, he may set his own price on opening it." (The court decided against the sealer, but only because the Feast of St. Barnabas was not a legal holiday.)[30]

The permissibility of gratuities allowed officer and citizen to engage in a degree of negotiation beyond the constraints of statutory and customary fee levels. But there was more to gratuities than that. A gratuity could *become* a customary fee, thereby altering the baseline of what payments were "due," such that the officer had a right to demand them. "If a gratuity is taken, at a more or less standard rate, for the rendering of the same service over a long enough time," explains Aylmer, "it can sometimes become a fee without anyone being aware of the transition, at least not until after it has happened." The evolution of gratuities into fees, he says, was a "constant process" in the 1400s and 1500s.[31] And it was still going strong in the late 1700s: as the parliamentary commissioners wrote in 1782, a gratuity "very soon assumes the name of custom, and becomes a claim."[32] The commissioners' data on various offices offered snapshots of gratuities at various stages on this evolutionary path. One top administrator said that the "greatest part" of the payors of "gratuities" gave at one particular rate but that "some give more, some less, some differently at different times, and some never give any thing."[33] In several other cases, an officer's "gratuities" were so regular that he kept a written schedule of what amounts were typically paid for what transactions.[34]

Thus, although the notion of immemorial custom and usage might suggest, at first blush, that customary fee schedules dated back for centuries and were extremely stable, they were in fact the result of an ongoing and decentralized process of bargaining between individual officers and the citizens with whom they dealt. The doctrine of "immemorial" usage had the practical effect of providing legal cover for these organically negotiated increases. To be sure, the doctrine on its face might seem strict: by the most extreme definition, an English custom lost its immemorial status if anybody could prove that it had not been continuously in place since the start of legal memory—the year 1189! But as a practical matter, notes one historian of the jurisprudence of custom, inquiries seldom went back farther than sixty or seventy years.[35] Further, officers' assertions regarding customary fees could be difficult to refute. This was because, in any dispute over fees, the fee-taking officers themselves enjoyed an informational advantage: they knew the office's practices, its history, and its records as nobody else did. While customary fees were sometimes ascertained in a relatively official and accessible schedule,[36] in many other cases the most authoritative sources were the interested officers' personal memories, or lists that they drew up and kept. The "distinction between what [payment] is permitted and what [payment] is prohibited," wrote Bentham circa 1780, "in many cases, is exceedingly minute," giving rise to "many temptations" to exploit "the ignorance of strangers" to the office.[37]

A good illustration is the failed royal investigation of alleged fee increases that occurred in the early seventeenth century. James I in 1623 ordered his investigators to gather information "by examination of any person or persons, and by view of any rolls, books, orders, privy seals, certificates, and other records, memorandums, and things whatsoever."[38] When Charles I acceded, he soon made a similar order. It was no accident that under both monarchs, throughout the eighteen years during which the inquiries dragged on, the most active investigator was a career historian, Sir Henry Spelman. The task of discerning lawful fees, when taken seriously, required arduous historical research: "Officials sent in lists of the fees they claimed; in the central courts juries of underclerks, solicitors, and attorneys commented on the officers' statements; in the Court of Common Pleas officials made rejoinders to the jury's report explaining at length the nature of the work of each office. Where increase of fees was suspected, records were searched, orders of the court were collected, and witnesses were examined." Apparently worried that turnover among the offices' clients had made it difficult to find citizens who could remember paying lower fees, Spelman advised his associates to "enquire for old men"—track down elderly witnesses who could remember the fee levels of past decades.[39]

A similar pattern can be seen in several offices in later years. For example, Parliament in 1691 ordered the Barons of the Exchequer to investigate the "ancient legal fees" of the officers in the financial branch of the Exchequer and to reduce those fees to a single accessible schedule.[40] In carrying out this task, the Barons took testimony and did documentary research. They managed to determine some fees on the basis of an official table from the year 1558, but others came from a less formal source—a list of fees that the current officers testified had been passed down to them in 1676 by one William Burges, "a long time clerk in the said office."[41] At the Treasury, up till its salarization in 1782, the customary fee levels were not recorded in any more official source than a list that each clerk kept of the fees he individually took.[42] Things were the same among the dozens of clerks who managed the Royal Navy in the 1780s.[43] Over at the Navy Pay Office, the fees were simply those "usually" taken, "as far back as the memory of the oldest officers now employed in [the] office reaches."[44] At the common-law courts in 1818, according to a parliamentary commission, the "grounds" upon which the clerks and other officers took their fees were, "for the most part," mere "[c]onstant receipt by the present officers and the information as to a similar receipt by their predecessors, derived either verbally or from books of accounts or written memoranda."[45]

Faced with these informational difficulties, the authorities were modest in their efforts to "turn back the clock" on the evolutionary growth in fees. At various times in the 1620s and 1630s, monarchs and members of Parliament proposed to figure out the level at which fees had stood at some point in the past and to fix them there; the dates considered were 1558, 1568, 1587–88, 1598, 1603, and 1608.[46] None of the proposed dates was terribly far in the past. This was partly because of the concern that evidence became less plentiful as one looked farther back: one member of Parliament in 1621 warned that 1558 was so far distant that the fees taken at that time could not "certainly be known."[47] (In the end, no turn-back-the-clock measure was adopted at all.)[48] Similarly, the anonymous but apparently well-informed author of a 1736 London pamphlet titled *A Discourse on Fees of Office in Courts of Justice* explained that, while most fees could not pass the strict test of immemorial usage (that there be no evidence of contrary practice after 1189), everybody realized that strict application of the test would be unreasonable and disruptive. Though suitors and officers believed that usage imposed some constraint upon the demand for fees, they did not define it strictly or exactly: on the question of "what is the length of time necessary to render them legal fees," the period was "by some confined to sixty, by others to forty, and some to thirty years."[49]

And when the fees of a particular office or service lacked the sanction of even brief usage, the law was still flexible, for one could claim a fee for an office or service by analogizing it to some other office or service that did have a customary fee.[50] As late as 1845, a judge of the Queen's Bench noted that the office of a clerk to a justice of the peace was "analogous to that of the clerk of assize, which is an immemorial . . . office," such that the justice of the peace's clerk was "entitled to fees of the same sort as had been paid to the analogous officer of the old and immemorial court."[51]

Besides the linked doctrines of lawful gratuity and immemorial custom, there was yet another—and perhaps more important—legal basis for the negotiation of payments. This was *quantum meruit*, the principle that any person who performed a valuable service for somebody else was entitled to reasonable compensation for it. This doctrine was first held applicable to public officers in

*Veale v. Priour*, decided by the Court of Exchequer in 1666.[52] The case involved the London register of marine insurance policies, an office dating to the 1570s. A statute of 1601 required merchants to enter their policies with the officer in order to enjoy access to a specialized tribunal for dispute resolution.[53] Though the statute authorized London's mayor to fix the fee for entering policies, he apparently never did so. Nevertheless, an informal practice arose whereby merchants paid the register for the service. In deciding whether the incumbent had a right to this money, Sir Matthew Hale, the court's top judge, sidestepped the doctrine of immemorial usage but still concluded that the officer was entitled to the money, simply because he "must have what he reasonably deserves, as every one must, that does any thing for another at his request." The policies had to be entered under the statute of 1601, "and the law will allow a reasonable matter for entering them." The "usage since the [passage of the] statute hath now settled [the payment], if not as a fee, yet as a competent recompense for [the officer's] labor; as laborers' rates, though certain, yet are not fees, but *quantum meruits.*"[54] The usage in itself established no right, but the principle of *quantum meruit* established the right to a reasonable payment, and the usage was evidence of what payment was reasonable. Hale's reasoning was cited and confirmed in *Ballard v. Gerard*, decided by the King's Bench in 1702, in which Chief Justice Holt noted that the jury was the final arbiter of the amount that constituted reasonable compensation for an official service.[55] When a payment was too novel to be sanctioned even by the loosest definition of immemorial custom, noted the *Discourse on Fees* in 1736, it could still be upheld as reasonable by a jury. The *Discourse* further noted that, for services involving "extraordinary" labor, officers had "an equitable right to a suitable recompense, which is extremely difficult, if not . . . impossible to reduce to certain and fixed fees [in advance]. . . . In these cases there is seldom any difference with suitors"; that is, the officer and citizen simply negotiated a payment on the spot. But if any dispute "should arise," it could be "settled" by "*quantum meruit.*"[56] Thus *quantum meruit*, as interpreted by Hale and Holt, provided additional legal support for the informal, on-the-street negotiation that had already long taken place under the cover of gratuities and immemorial custom.

## COMMON-LAW BASES FOR NEGOTIATION
## IN COLONIAL AMERICA AND THE EARLY REPUBLIC

The common law of gratuities in early America was much the same as in England. In an era during which most American lawyers relied on imported treatises, Bacon's *Abridgment*, with its strong articulation of gratuities' lawfulness, was tied for being the second most widely available general treatise in eighteenth-century American libraries.[57] And Bacon's analysis of gratuities continued to be widely disseminated in the early republic. The *Abridgment* went through the first of its several American editions in 1811.[58] Its passage on gratuities appeared at length in a major new justice-of-the-peace manual published at Albany in 1803; in Nathan Dane's *General Abridgment* of 1824 (the first major reference work on American law); and in the first American edition of Russell's classic treatise on crimes, in 1824.[59]

American officers themselves frequently affirmed the legality of receiving a voluntary payment to do one's duty. In several colonies during the eighteenth century, there was no statute regulating the fees of customhouse officers, but those officers still received regular payments, arising from "informal consultations between the collectors and various merchants."[60] When the imperial reforms of the 1760s sparked controversy about fees, the customs commissioners instructed one officer "not to take any fees unless the merchants voluntarily granted them."[61] When the Board of Trade in 1764 conducted a survey of all officers in the royal colonies, asking what payments they took and by what authority, one Massachusetts customs officer reported and justified several payments on the ground that they were "with the consent of the merchants and trading people."[62] Responding to a similar survey in 1771, other customs officers claimed regular payments "by consent of the trade,"[63] or the like.[64] Such reasoning ranged beyond the customhouse. In New Hampshire, the recorder reported that one of his regular payments came "by indulgence";[65] the admiralty judge took money "by agreement" for the rare and extraordinary service of condemning a vessel;[66] and the governor received, for land grants, "what the grantees thought proper to pay," with "many" giving "no fee."[67]

The doctrine of gratuities also appeared in reports of American cases. Consider *Kilty v. Hammond*, a 1793 case in Maryland's central statewide trial court. The governor issued a proclamation exhorting all "officers of the peace" to apprehend a named criminal suspect. One Hammond offered $400 "for apprehending" the suspect "agreeably to the . . . proclamation." One Kilty captured the suspect, but Hammond refused to pay, and Kilty sued him. Hammond asked the judge to instruct the jurors that Kilty "could not recover [the reward] in this suit, unless he proved" that he was a peace officer, or acting pursuant to an officer's instruction or with a warrant. Only by proving one of those things could he show that he acted "agreeably to the . . . proclamation." The judge gave the instruction. Neither Hammond's defense strategy nor the judge's instruction would make any sense unless officers could lawfully receive voluntary rewards for doing their duty.[68]

Gratuity doctrine also arose in the 1821 impeachment trial of the Massachusetts probate judge James Prescott on charges of extortion. Daniel Webster defended the judge before the state senate by quoting Bacon's analysis of gratuities
and contending that the sums at issue "were paid voluntarily. [The accused] in
no proper sense demanded them. He did not refuse to do his official duty till
they were paid."[69] (Prescott was acquitted on some counts but convicted on others, and the senators gave no reasons for their decision, so the case likely turned
on the rather complex facts, not on a question of law.)

As with gratuities, so with customary fees: Americans followed English precedent, repeatedly recognizing that custom furnished officers a legal basis to
charge money. In 1737, the South Carolina assembly appointed a committee
to find out "what fees are taken or claimed by the respective officers," whether
under an old fee statute "or by virtue of any other laws, custom, or usage."[70]
In 1779, the Pennsylvania assembly, faced with wartime inflation, pegged all
fees to the price of wheat, and when it identified the payments that were to be
escalated in this fashion, it referred to them thus: "the said fees as they were
regulated by law *or practice* under the late government of Pennsylvania" prior
to 1776.[71] As the state's high court later said, the legislature had thereby "recognized the propriety of receiving fees due by custom and practice."[72]

Similarly, the British Parliament and imperial authorities, in administering
the colonies, assumed that fees could rest upon custom. Up to the 1760s, as
noted earlier, customhouse officers in several colonies had taken fees through
informal understandings with the merchants, without the colony's assembly enacting a statute on the matter. When Whitehall tightened tariff enforcement in
1764, many colonial assemblies resisted by enacting statutes to prohibit the customhouse officers from taking fees. Parliament countered with multiple statutes aimed at preserving the officers' pre-1764 fees. Acknowledging that many
such fees had been customary, Parliament in one such act declared that officers
were "entitled to . . . such fees, as they and their predecessors respectively . . .
had been generally and *usually accustomed* to demand" prior to 1764.[73]

In their responses to imperial surveys in 1764 and 1771 and in other statements, officers in the American colonies frequently relied upon custom and
usage in claiming rights to the fees they reported. The register of the Boston
vice-admiralty court suggested that his customary fees were very old, at least
by colonial standards: they had been taken "since the court was established"
in 1702, though he hedged by adding, "[S]o far as I know."[74] But suggestions of
such antiquity were rare. In all other instances where surveyed officers stated
the age of their customary fees, the periods were much shorter and reflected no
uniform assumption about the time necessary to establish a right: one customs

officer claimed a fee as having been taken for at least "thirty four years";[75] a governor, for "more than twenty years";[76] other customs officers, for "twenty years" (in two ports),[77] for "12 or 14 years,"[78] or for "three years" (in two ports).[79] In fact, it was unusual for officers to pin themselves down to any number whatever. The more common pattern was for the incumbent to say the current fees had been usual when he first entered the office;[80] or to say that his immediate predecessor had taken them;[81] or to state (more amorphously) that his predecessors (plural) had taken them, without saying which predecessors or for how long;[82] or—the most common response—to speak the magic word *custom* or *usage* or a similar term with no details at all.[83] The collector at Salem, whose most important fees were "customary," admitted he was "ignorant how long" they had been "established before he was in office."[84] The officers generally volunteered no documentation for their responses.

Leading minds of the colonies made clear that customary fees could be lawful, even if short lived and not immemorial. In a controversy over Virginia court fees in 1774, Edmund Pendleton, perhaps the most respected lawyer in that colony and soon to be the new state's chief justice, acknowledged the argument that "we [Americans] are not ancient enough to establish any point upon custom, as that must be time immemorial," but retorted that "various kinds of customs have different modes and terms of acquiring the force of laws or regulations according to the nature of the subject to which they are applied," and fee levels did not need to be immemorial.[85] The longtime New York politician and administrator Cadwallader Colden, during one of his several terms as acting governor in 1764, claimed fees on the ground that his predecessors had taken them "above forty years," adding that "few fees in the public offices of Great Britain are upon a better establishment."[86]

Custom, as it was invoked to justify fees, was so short term, and so nonspecific as to the payments' origin, that it could retroactively legitimize, at any particular point in time, an ongoing process of change, cloaking uncertainty in a fiction of stability. As an illustration, consider the case of Benjamin Pemberton, who served as the naval officer of the Boston customhouse, one of the top jobs in that institution. (The title was a misnomer; it had nothing to do with the navy.) In an unusually detailed report to the Board of Trade in 1764, Pemberton explained that he had been in the job from 1733 to 1741 and again from 1749 to the present. There had never been a statute regulating the naval officer's fees, and so, upon first taking over in 1733, he determined—"by what verbal information, certificates, and other evidence I could obtain" and also by "my own experience . . . as a merchant"—that it "had been customary ever since the year 1722 or 1723 for said officer . . . to take *nearly* the same fees" as were fixed by a 1716 Massachusetts statute for another official (the collector), insofar as the naval officer and collector did the same tasks. (The practice prior to 1722–23, he admitted, "cannot now be well ascertained for want of certificates or other evidence.") Since there had been no further statutory enactments during the intervening years, Pemberton had "continued the former practice" to the present time, "with the implied consent of the merchants and traders."[87] At a glance, it might seem that his claims in 1764 rested simply upon a custom predating his tenure.

But in fact, the story of Pemberton's fees involved more give-and-take between himself and the merchants than he let on. First, not all the fees he claimed for services overlapping with the collector's services in the 1716 statute actually matched the sums in that statute; two were the same, but one was higher, and another was omitted.[88] His statement that the custom "nearly" conformed to the statute seemed to acknowledge this mismatch. But on top of that, his claims in 1764 covered at least three services that were not in the statute at all.[89] Such fees still might, of course, have been part of the custom that prevailed since 1722–23, ten years before he came on the scene. Yet in an inquiry into the naval office by an assembly committee back in 1735—shortly after Pemberton first took office and supposedly twelve years into the duration of an unchanging practice—he had named several services "for which he thinks he ought to be entitled" to certain stated amounts, but (said the committee) "for which no fee is allowed by law." The merchants complained to the committee that several of these services were needless and "a great imposition on them, especially his exacting money therefor" (the one exception being his deciding applications for passes to trade in the Mediterranean, which they considered valuable).[90] Pemberton's enumeration of nonstatutory fees in 1764 still included one of the supposedly needless services, but apparently at a lower price,[91] as well as the Mediterranean passes, also at a lower price.[92] It thus appears that, between 1735 and 1764, he had continued some of his novel demands but moderated the prices in light of the merchants' wishes, which suggests that he was more accurate when he said his receipts came "with the implied consent of the merchants" than when he asserted an unbroken usage of forty-one years.

Pemberton's story reveals the evolving process of give-and-take that presumably underlay many "customary" fees. Indeed, when Parliament in 1764 legislated to preserve customhouse fees as they had been paid up to that time, this offered little practical help to the officers, since the fuzziness and dynamism of the fees made it easy for the rebellious merchants "to question the claims of the customs officers as to what was the established rate."[93]

PARRILLO, NICHOLAS R.


AGAINST THE PROFIT MOTIVE: THE SALARY REVOLUTION
IN AMERICAN GOVERNMENT, 1780-1940.
                                  Paper     568 P.
NEW HAVEN: YALE UNIVERSITY PRESS, 2013
SER: YALE LAW LIBRARY SERIES IN LEGAL HISTORY
AND REFERENCE.
AUTH: YALE UNIV., LAW. REVISED DISSERTATION ON
HOW LAWMAKERS BANISHED PROFIT MOTIVE FOR SALARY.
LCCN 2012-51295
  **ISBN** 0300194757     **Library PO#**  GENERAL APPROVAL

|  |  |  |  |
|---|---|---|---|
|  | **List** | 55.00 | USD |
| 5461 UNIV OF TEXAS/SAN ANTONIO | **Disc** | 10.0% | |
| **App. Date** 12/18/13  PAD.APR  6108-11 | **Net** | 49.50 | USD |


SUBJ: UNITED STATES--OFFICIALS & EMPLOYEES--
SALARIES, ETC.--HIST.


CLASS JK776         DEWEY# 331.28135173 LEVEL ADV-AC

---

**YBP Library Services**

PARRILLO, NICHOLAS R.


AGAINST THE PROFIT MOTIVE: THE SALARY REVOLUTION
IN AMERICAN GOVERNMENT, 1780-1940.
                                  Paper     568 P.
NEW HAVEN: YALE UNIVERSITY PRESS, 2013
SER: YALE LAW LIBRARY SERIES IN LEGAL HISTORY
AND REFERENCE.
AUTH: YALE UNIV., LAW. REVISED DISSERTATION ON
HOW LAWMAKERS BANISHED PROFIT MOTIVE FOR SALARY.
 LCCN 2012-51295
  **ISBN** 0300194757     **Library PO#**  GENERAL APPROVAL

|  |  |  |  |
|---|---|---|---|
|  | **List** | 55.00 | USD |
| 5461 UNIV OF TEXAS/SAN ANTONIO | **Disc** | 10.0% | |
| **App. Date** 12/18/13  PAD.APR  6108-11 | **Net** | 49.50 | USD |


SUBJ: UNITED STATES--OFFICIALS & EMPLOYEES--
SALARIES, ETC.--HIST.


CLASS JK776         DEWEY# 331.28135173 LEVEL ADV-AC

Early American law and practice followed that of England not only in the area of gratuities and customary fees but also *quantum meruit.* By the early 1700s, as noted already, the right of public officers to reasonable compensation for services rendered was established by Hale's opinion in *Veale* and Holt's in *Ballard.* This reasoning was well known in the colonies. The upper house of the Maryland assembly affirmed it in 1755: "Each officer by the common law," if no statute or other regulatory ordinance applied, "would be entitled in compensation of his service to *quantum meruit.*"[94] Many American officers invoked *quantum meruit* in response to the Board of Trade survey in 1764, typically coupling it with some mention of usage (as had been the case in *Veale*).[95] But *quantum meruit* could also be invoked independent of usage, when new labors arose. The master in chancery of South Carolina reported that he was charging a fee "of new creation" for a new duty imposed on him by the court: "I thought it but just and reasonable compensation for my trouble and as such have taken it."[96] It was common for officers who had many of their fees taxed by a judge (such as sheriffs or constables) to be rewarded by *quantum meruit.*[97] But *quantum meruit* could also open the way for direct officer-citizen bargaining outside the immediate supervision of a judge, as had occurred in *Veale* itself. Thus New York's top executive officers, charging for land grants in the 1760s, invoked the doctrine as a basis for their claims.[98]

*Quantum meruit* had no more effective expositor than Webster. At Prescott's 1821 impeachment trial, he declared that "the right" of an officer "to receive fees, is the general right to receive reasonable compensation for services rendered, and labor performed." The fees of many judges in England, Webster pointed out, "were of an earlier date than any statute respecting them," meaning that, even in the absence of statutory authorization, a judge could ask a fee for any service he did for a suitor. "[I]f the reasonableness of the fee be disputed," continued Webster, citing *Ballard,* "it may be tried by jury." He then cited *Veale* and went on to declare that "[a]lmost every officer in the Commonwealth [of Massachusetts], whose compensation consists in fees of office, renders services not enumerated in the fee [statute], and is paid for those services; and this through no indulgence or abuse, but with great propriety and justice."[99] Webster's opposing counsel was Lemuel Shaw, another leading attorney, soon to be one of the nation's most revered judges. Though Shaw initially suggested that the relevant statute should perhaps be presumed to negate such common-law rights, he ultimately backtracked from this position, conceding that "the officer" could "demand a reasonable fee," but adding that such demand was "at his peril" if it were unreasonable.[100]

American officers often ran together the legal bases of voluntary gratuity, custom, and *quantum meruit*. A collector in Massachusetts said one fee was "by consent of the trade as a reasonable compensation for the trouble."[101] The South Carolina master in chancery described a long list of items as "established by long usage and custom and I have followed the steps of my predecessors in office and have always taken and been allowed them as a *quantum meruit* for my trouble."[102] In addition to the usual three justifications, officers could also claim fees on the ground that their services were analogous to those provided by other officers who claimed fees by custom or some other legal basis.[103]

These doctrines of negotiation were so familiar and so flexible that colonial elites sometimes spoke as if an exchange between officer and citizen, in the absence of a statute fixing the price, had the unrestrained quality of the market. Take Maryland in the 1720s and 1730s. Prices for many official services were set by a 1719 statute, due to expire in 1725.[104] As expiration approached, it looked as if the lower house of the assembly, the upper house, and the proprietor might be unable to agree on a new tariff of fees. The upper house—which was allied with the proprietor and probably included several officeholders—warned the lower house to "consider the evil consequences" of expiration, "for then there will be no rule between the officers and the people, what charges shall be made for the services done by the several officers, but they will be left to their own discretion to charge what they please which will lay a foundation for endless disputes between them and the people and produce innumerable lawsuits to the great prejudice of the people and much to the advantage of the officers who will thereby increase their fees."[105] The lower house passed a new fee bill, but with much-reduced prices. Though the upper house assented, it asked the proprietor to veto it, which he did.[106] By this point, the 1719 statute had expired, and therefore the officers' fees—in the words of an eminent London lawyer retained by the proprietor—were no longer "ascertained by any act or other fixed regulation."[107]

The result was a free-for-all, not unlike the market for some unregulated commodity. Early in 1726, the lower house began trumpeting the complaints of various colonists that officers were raising their charges. The upper house acknowledged their "hardship" but concluded that, without a statute, it was "in the option of the officers to demand what fees they please."[108] Taking a different view of who was bearing the brunt of the unregulated market, the governor wrote to the proprietor that officers were "very ill paid," for "every insolent fellow [receiving services] thought himself free to refuse payment, and browbeat . . . the officers."[109] But still a legislative agreement proved impossible. "[W]e think it better," pleaded the upper house in 1728, "to regulate [officers'] fees by a law than leave them at liberty to charge what they please for the services to be done by them."[110] As of 1732, several officers were charging fees according to the high levels of the expired 1719 statute.[111] That year, a committee of the lower house condemned such charges as unjust, invoking—as the standard of just fees—the vetoed statute of 1725, as well as a "resolve" later passed by the lower house declaring that the vetoed statute had offered "a sufficient satisfaction."[112] Stability returned, at least temporarily, in 1733, when the proprietor himself proclaimed a new fee schedule for all officers.[113] Though the lower and upper houses had previously discussed the possibility of refunds of excessive fees taken during the statuteless years (albeit without agreement on the criteria for excessiveness),[114] the proclamation made no mention of refunds, and it appears that none were ever given.[115] The officers kept whatever money the laypersons had been willing to pay.[116]

## THE LIMITED NATURE OF STATUTORY REGULATION UP TO THE EARLY NINETEENTH CENTURY

Thus far, I have focused on the common law of exchanges between officers and the recipients of their services, though I have also mentioned statutes regulating those exchanges, insofar as these happened to be necessary for understanding the common-law examples. Let me now focus on fee-regulation statutes in their own right. Such laws were passed by Parliament to cover certain offices in England and by nearly all the American colonial legislatures to cover many and sometimes all of the offices within their respective bounds.

When legislators set out to regulate officer-recipient exchanges by statute, they did so against a rich background of common-law doctrines (voluntary gratuity, custom and usage, and *quantum meruit*) that authorized numerous exchanges as a default matter. Today, people speak of statutory economic regulation "intervening" in a preexisting market constituted by common-law rules of property and contract. In the same way, fee-regulation statutes in the 1700s and early 1800s were "intervening" in a preexisting universe of exchanges that were not established by statute yet were still lawful. Public offices were independent of legislative power in a way that seems strange to us today. They were freestanding vendors whom the legislature *might* regulate (in the same way it *might* regulate a business today) but sometimes did not. Webster said it best. The fees of judges in English probate cases, he explained at Prescott's trial in 1821, "were, from early times, in most cases regulated by custom and the authority and direction of the courts themselves, without statute provisions." These fees "did not originate in the grant or provision of any act of Parliament." Statutes were later passed, but "only to restrain and limit the amount" of the preexisting fees. Similarly, the fee-regulation statute that Prescott was accused of violating—which set prices for numerous services by Massachusetts officers—"is simply a *restraining* statute. It fixes the amount in the *cases* [*i.e., services*] *mentioned*, leaving every thing else as it stood before" (emphasis in original).[117]

### The Survival of Negotiation for Services Unenumerated by Statute

Fee regulation was a daunting challenge for legislators. Statutes could regulate payments for official services most effectively when, as a New Hampshire court aptly phrased it in 1820, they focused on services that "were common, well known, of an uniform value, and whose nature was such that a fair price could be put upon them before they were performed."[118] But many services did not fit this description. That is, many services were idiosyncratic, required variable amounts of labor or speed depending on the circumstances, or reflected unanticipated changes in administrative methods or in the needs and wishes of service recipients. "[T]he quantum and instances of fees," explained the *Discourse on Fees* in 1736, "are in their own nature variable in different times, and as the methods and manner of business vary and alter." "[A]ncient methods of business" would "grow out of use," and officers needed a "reasonable recompense" for "new methods of business, or for additional business, or duty laid on" them.[119] Even if a service were long-standing, stable, and familiar to officers and recipients, there was still the possibility that the legislature might accidentally ignore it, or price it in a manner not proportioned to the work and responsibility involved. After all, lawmakers of the eighteenth and early nineteenth centuries were casual part-timers, without staff or professional drafters, and could not be expected to understand and anticipate the exact operations of law courts, equity courts, admiralty courts, probate courts, justices of the peace, customhouses, sheriff's offices, the constabulary, coroners, land-grant officers, surveyors, product inspectors, and all the other officers of their time.

In several instances, lawmakers acknowledged these limitations by enacting statutes that fixed the fees for certain named services but left the pricing of all other services to the default common-law regime of gratuity, custom, and *quantum meruit*. Even when the wording of a statute did not clearly indicate such a limitation of scope, officers and courts often interpreted it that way. The assumption that statutes left common-law negotiation to thrive with respect to services unenumerated in the text preserved a relatively unregulated "market" for those services.

Some examples will flesh out the point. The New Hampshire assembly in 1718 enacted a table of fees for several officers and declared that any officers who took "any greater or other fees than are mentioned" in the table *"for the particular matters [i.e., services] therein mentioned"* would be punished.[120] The table covered only a fraction of the services actually provided, and officers felt themselves free to charge for unenumerated services on a common-law basis. Hence, when the judge and register of the colony's probate court reported their fees to the Board of Trade in 1764, they explained that the statutory table was "so imperfect that half the articles and services are omitted," and they proceeded to list the payments they regularly took, designating several as "not in the table" or the like.[121]

Another example comes from New York, where in 1710 the governor, advised by the council, had issued a statutelike ordinance regulating fees. The text of the ordinance was self-contradictory: at one point, it suggested that officers could take no fee for any service unless it were authorized in the list, but at another point, it seemed to leave officers unregulated as to unenumerated services.[122] The colony's chief justice, reporting to the Board of Trade in 1764, took the ordinance to mean that charges for unenumerated services were permitted. Noting that the ordinance's schedule was "imperfect in omitting many necessary services," he provided one schedule of judges' fees (thirteen items) fixed by the ordinance, plus a second schedule of judges' fees (nineteen items) "for services not specified in the ordinance, . . . all usual and customary fees, as never have been to our knowledge complained of as immoderate." The judges allowed themselves such fees as "a *quantum meruit*," at a level "*nearly* in the proportion fixed by the ordinance for services in some respect similar."[123]

The same pattern prevailed in Pennsylvania, where the legislature in 1752 enacted an elaborate fee schedule but identified as violators only those who took "any more, greater or other fees than is hereinbefore appointed" for "*any of the matters or things hereinbefore enumerated.*"[124] The legislature returned to the subject in 1779, declaring that all fees, "as they were regulated by law *or practice*" prior to 1776, were to be pegged to the price of wheat, apparently preserving the permissibility of charges for unenumerated services.[125] The point was tested in 1780, in the impeachment trial of Francis Hopkinson, the judge of the Pennsylvania state admiralty court, on several charges, the most serious being extortion. This trial warrants close attention, for it illuminates the dynamics of fee-taking in a context where statutes played some role but did not occupy the field. The charges were brought by Hopkinson's enemies in a political rivalry that had nothing to do with the admiralty business.[126] The facts were not in dispute: Hopkinson clearly took a fee not authorized by the fee statute for a service not enumerated in the fee statute. He had ascended to the bench only recently, in 1779. A case soon arose with services not covered in the statute.

According to Hopkinson, he approached the court's register, a twenty-seven-year-old named Andrew Robeson who had been on the job since 1776, and asked him "[h]ow the fees were to be adjudged in such a case." Robeson answered that "for services not referred to in the Act, the custom was to charge the fees according to the ancient rates." To this, Hopkinson "gave his assent." Thereafter, in making charges in all cases (including the one at issue), Hopkinson deferred to Robeson, who "charged the former customary fees."[127] Among the many customary fees that Robeson had charged was one for "holding court," at the rate of £1 and 4s., at least some of which went to the judge. When the prosecution demanded to know whether a fee for "holding court" was really customary, Robeson answered, "Yes, it is according to the practice by Mr. Ross [who had presided as judge in 1779] and Mr. Shippen [who had presided from 1755 to 1776], as far back as I know any thing of it."[128] Robeson's testimony perfectly followed the English definition of an immemorial fee: he knew of no time when it had not been charged—though he had only been register since 1776.

The state's executive council, which tried the impeachment, voted unanimously to acquit. Its president, Joseph Reed, a highly respected lawyer and a conciliator of the state's warring factions, delivered the opinion. Referring to fees enumerated in the statute as "specific" and fees for services unenumerated in the statute as "compensatory," he defended the latter as perfectly normal: "There are in almost all offices compensatory as well as specific fees.—In fee laws, . . . it is very difficult to enumerate all the services. In such cases compensatory fees must be allowed, or the necessary business will not be done."[129] But even as Reed approved of compensatory fees in principle, he added: "[W]e take this opportunity to say, that the fees of the court of Admiralty have increased lately extremely." The rising rates, Reed was careful to note, were not Hopkinson's doing. On the contrary, Hopkinson had merely taken "things as he found them." Rather, the increases had crept in "within [the past] four or five years."[130] Responsibility may have rested particularly with George Ross, who presided briefly in 1779 and, according to Robeson, "frequently looked at the bills, and where a [customary] charge for holding court was omitted, he directed me to make it."[131] Reed cautioned that the register should itemize all charges going forward and, "if on complaint made, errors are not rectified, there will be a proper ground for criminal prosecution."[132] But distinguishing erroneous "customary" charges from valid ones would require a complainant with historical proof of how the court's rates had changed. And nobody had effectually complained through "four or five years" of rising rates. Even Hopkinson's enemies, in pushing his impeachment, had not attempted to demonstrate changes in customary rates. Rather, they had simply argued that all fees for services unmentioned in the statute were unlawful—an argument that did not require an arduous inquiry into historical facts.

The lawfulness of payments for unenumerated services extended below the Mason-Dixon Line, where the South Carolina legislature, enacting a fee schedule in 1791, mandated that the amounts therein be "paid . . . in the respective public offices in this state, . . . for the different services in the respective suits in this act specified and contained, in lieu of all other demands whatever *for said services*."[133] In a major insurance case before the state's high court of chancery in 1802, which had been "solemnly argued," the judges confirmed that "there were some services which might be performed, for which the register might demand fees, though not enumerated in the lists in the act."[134]

Charges for unenumerated services were lawful in Massachusetts as late as Prescott's impeachment trial in 1821. The relevant statute, passed in 1795, listed several services and fees and then warned that, if any officer "shall willfully and corruptly demand and receive any greater fee or fees *for any of the services aforesaid*, than are by this act allowed and provided," the officer would be liable to punishment.[135] Although none of the lawyers on either side directly cited this statutory text,[136] they ultimately agreed that the act permitted charges for unenumerated services. Initially, it looked as if the prosecution might contest the point, when Shaw floated a theory that (as I discuss in Chapter 2) was gaining currency in other states. In response to the argument of Prescott's counsel "that where there are certain services necessary, which are not provided for by the statute, the judge may lawfully take a reasonable compensation for performing them," Shaw stated: "But there is another view of the case. If to some service the statute has affixed fees, and for others which are necessary, no fees are provided, it may well be supposed that the legislature intended that these services should be performed without particular compensation." The theory that Shaw was floating did not rest on the statute's text, which (if anything) was against him. Rather, he was urging that judges, when interpreting fee statutes, should follow a background value judgment—what lawyers call a substantive canon of construction—in favor of absolute legislative control of fees. Aware that he was out on a limb, Shaw hedged: he argued in the alternative that Prescott's charges for unenumerated services, even if lawful in principle, were of unreasonable amounts and therefore in violation of common law.[137]

The theory of absolute legislative control, tentatively floated by Shaw, elicited a dire warning from Webster, who emphasized how much it would disrupt government in Massachusetts, where fees for unenumerated services were familiar and essential to everyday public business. "It is certain," pronounced Webster, "that Judges of Probate, in this state are required to perform many acts

. . . for which no fees are specifically established by the statute." Charging fees for such business was the "universal practice" of the state: "Almost every officer in the Commonwealth, whose compensation consists in fees of office, renders services not enumerated in the fee [statute], and is paid for those services; and this, through no indulgence or abuse, but with great propriety and justice."[138]

After hearing this, Shaw lost his nerve and retreated: "I am not disposed to contend" against the proposition that, "when new and distinct services are required of an officer, . . . to which services no fee is annexed, such officer may lawfully claim and receive a reasonable fee." The contrary "remark, which I made on a former occasion[,] I apprehend has been somewhat over-stated." For a fee statute to preclude payment of unenumerated services, concluded Shaw, there would have to be very strong indicators that the legislature wanted it that way.[139] The senators convicted Prescott on one extortion charge but not others; though they gave no reasons, the outcome suggests they agreed with Webster (and the chastened Shaw) that charges for unenumerated services could be lawful in principle.

### Expansive Understandings of "Unenumerated Services"

It was also possible for the doctrine of unenumerated services to soften a fee statute's regulation of the *enumerated* services that were supposedly at the core of its regulatory purpose. If a particular instance of an enumerated service called for unusual labor, the unusual aspect of it could be hived off as a free-standing, unenumerated service deserving of extrastatutory compensation.

This idea was well articulated by the New Hampshire supreme court. Recall that New Hampshire's fee statute enumerated some services and allowed extrastatutory payment for the rest. One of the enumerated services was "the service of a writ" of execution by a sheriff, with a small fee attached. The court in 1820 held that this regulation applied only to *ordinary* instances of the service. Additional "labor and expense may, on particular occasions, become indispensable to the due service of a writ, and from their very nature, no just average price for them can be fixed before they are performed"—for example, "the removal and care of a great amount of property attached, or the employment of assistants, and the delay in making difficult arrests and commitments." On a strict reading, admitted the court, such efforts might be understood as part of "'the service of the writ[';] yet they are not a part of the ordinary service, [and] could not have any just average estimate previously placed on their value." "For these reasons," concluded the court, "we deem it highly improbable, that the legislature, by the word 'service,' . . . intended to include and compensate all such incidental duties of an officer in all cases." Thus, the court permitted officers to split up enumerated services into ordinary labor and extra labor and to make nonstatutory charges for the latter.[140]

The high court in Massachusetts, drawing upon a similar statute and adopting a similar interpretation, illustrated in 1804 how this approach could foster mutually beneficial exchange. The Massachusetts statute fixed the fee of a deputy sheriff for levying an execution, collectible from the debtor. In the particular case, the deputy was about to arrest a debtor, but the debtor beseeched the deputy "to allow him time to procure money to satisfy the execution, or such security" as would satisfy the creditor. The deputy decided to give the debtor a break and allowed him "time for that purpose," but he "was put to extra trouble and expense thereby," since it was necessary for him to "procure keepers" to ensure that the debtor would not skip town during the grace period. For accommodating the debtor in this way, the deputy charged him extra. The deputy was then prosecuted for extortion, on the ground that his charge exceeded that fixed for levying execution, but Justice Samuel Sewall instructed the jurors that "if they believed the [extra charge] was taken for extra trouble and expense, they must acquit," which they did.[141]

This approach fostered mutually beneficial exchange between officer and citizen. But it could potentially render hollow the regulation of fees even for enumerated services: if "extra trouble" were interpreted broadly enough, the regulations might be overridden by case-specific recompense in most or all cases. When Prescott defended himself against extortion charges in 1821, he attempted to slice and dice the enumerated services in just this way. The exasperated prosecutors responded by insisting that the services claimed as extra were in fact "only *parts of* the same services for which compensation is allowed by the fee [statute]."[142]

Slicing each enumerated service into "ordinary" and "extraordinary" parts was not the only way to soften fee statutes within their area of supposed application. It was also possible that, if a usage grew up whereby a higher fee were taken for a service than allowed by a statute, the officer could be acquitted of extortion, for guilt required the officer to know that his charge was unlawful, and usage might negate that knowledge. Hence, even though fee statutes were supposed to kill off custom for enumerated services, custom could rise from the grave to keep officers from being punished. An example of this reasoning arose in a different portion of the 1804 Massachusetts case discussed earlier. The fee statute, for a deputy sheriff levying execution, capped the fee at a certain percentage of the judgment. The deputy, besides his charge for extra labor, had made a second extra charge, this one simply a customary sum that officers in his county always added to the percentage on executions. The court "doubted" that this surcharge "was authorized by the statute," but since all parties agreed that the extra charge was usual in the county, it "would not evince a corrupt intention, and therefore would not bring [the] case within the [extortion] statute."[143]

## Obsolescence of Statutes

The Anglo-American doctrines supporting negotiation were so robust—and the attempts of legislators to impose regulation so imprecise, crude, and liable to go out of date—that it was possible for a regulatory statute to become obsolete, so that officers and even high courts openly proclaimed it a dead letter, even if the legislature did not repeal it.

Such obsolescence occurred on both sides of the Atlantic. One striking example involved the fees of customhouse officers on England's coast. These had rested on custom up to the Restoration in 1660, when Parliament—in contrast to most of the colonial legislatures—sought to take absolute control of the customhouse officers' receipts. A regulation appended to a 1660 statute declared that no officer of an English customhouse "shall . . . receive any other or greater fee . . . than such as are or shall be established by the Commons in Parliament assembled."[144] Accordingly, the Commons in 1662 and 1670 issued fee tables for the principal officers at London and all other major English ports (known as "head ports"), with the understanding that the table for each head port was to govern the smaller ports near it (known as "member ports" of the head port).[145]

But this experiment in absolute legislative control soon collapsed, and the old doctrines of negotiation reasserted themselves. The lists of fees were problematic from the beginning. Despite the 1660 statute's mandate that no customs officer could take an unenumerated payment, the tables of 1662 and 1670 covered only the principal officers, despite the fact that many ports had numerous additional officers. Worse, Parliament after 1670 completely failed to make the updates that would have been necessary to keep the fee tables workable. There were no significant revisions for the following 115 years![146] While Parliament slept, English oceanic trade expanded tremendously, causing the business of the customhouses to grow much bigger and more complex. Total personnel nearly doubled between 1690 and 1763.[147] By the time a parliamentary commission investigated the customhouses in the 1780s, it was insane to think their operations could continue if the officers' income were confined to the old tables.[148] The "contents" of the tables, announced the commissioners, were "very limited" and "totally inapplicable to [i.e., unsuitable for] the business and officers of this time."[149] Rather than let oceanic trade grind to a halt, officers had naturally ignored the increasingly unrealistic statutes and fallen back on common-law negotiation. At London, "the business of the customs and the number of officers are greatly increased" since 1660, and "consequently many other fees are paid at the custom-house, . . . than are to be found" in the table of 1662.[150] The commissioners solicited, from the numerous officers at the London customhouse, tables of the fees they claimed as of 1785. These tables added up to more than fifty pages of transactions, whereas the 1662 table had been less than seven pages.[151] In contrast to the 1662 table of "fees established by the legislature," these additional fees—the overwhelming majority of all that were charged—were "grounded upon usage, or the discretion of the officer."[152] In the ports beyond London, where the tables had been "framed at a time when the business of the customs, and the extent of that department, had little resemblance to their actual state at this day,"[153] negotiation had made a similar comeback.[154] The fees taken in all ports of the realm—apart from the small minority that appeared in the old parliamentary tables—rested "solely on ground of usage."[155]

Officers in the 1780s clearly believed themselves lawfully entitled to these nonstatutory fees. They listed and claimed them in sworn statements, invoking "usage" as a mantra to support their claims.[156] In the commissioners' catalog of the tables of actual fees that officers had hung up in their respective buildings, under the query "authority by which the fees are taken," officers at forty-nine ports answered (at least in part) "ancient usage."[157] Parliament's failure to update the regulations in a way that would have stemmed the tide of negotiation demonstrates that English lawmakers were not really committed, in the seventeenth and eighteenth centuries, to the project of regulating officer-recipient exchange.

Jumping across the Atlantic, we encounter a similar story in colonial New York, except that here the breakdown of positive regulation extended to all offices, not merely the customhouses. As noted earlier, in 1710 the governor of the colony, advised by the council, had promulgated a statutelike ordinance regulating fees. Its wording was inconsistent on the status of unenumerated services, and the colony's chief justice construed it, in stating his own fees and those of the other judges in 1764, to permit charges for services not listed. Apparently, however, the chief justice did not feel himself bound to obey the ordinance at all, even as to the prices of enumerated services, and he was following it, to that extent, only by choice. In the very same letter in which he reported taking fees according to the ordinance for tasks enumerated therein, he added that the whole ordinance had "long since been considered not of force." The whole blasted document, he noted, was "not only imperfect in omitting many necessary services, but exceptional in not assigning a reasonable allowance for such services as are therein enumerated."[158] Rather than seek to have it revised, officers had gradually come to ignore it and negotiate different payments with their customers. Colden, the acting governor and a major player in New York politics, explained that the colony's lawyers generally believed the ordinance was "not now in force and that the officers are at liberty to take such reasonable fees, for their services, as the nature of their service deserve"; that the judges frequently taxed fees "without strict regard for the ordinance"; and that the view taken by the judges and lawyers "may perhaps have had some influence on other officers in taking fees due for their services."[159] Attorney General John Tabor Kempe concurred, adding that the judges, even for enumerated services, awarded sums exceeding those in the ordinance.[160] The assembly in 1761 had confirmed that the ordinance was a dead letter, noting the "want of a legal es-tablishment of fees."[161]

To get a sense of how the ordinance faded away, let us focus on the fees taken for one especially important service: land grants, in which the governor, attorney general, and colonial secretary all participated. The ordinance of 1710 allowed the governor 10s. per hundred acres, the attorney general £2 per grant, and the secretary £5 per grant.[162] Sometime after 1710, it became common for investors to seek a grant as a group. This could be a perfectly legitimate invest-ment strategy, though it could also be used to circumvent the standing royal instruction that no person receive more than two thousand acres or, after 1753, one thousand acres. (The instruction arose from the crown's fear that land held for speculation was less likely to be improved and produce revenue.)[163] Investors seeking a large acreage would assemble a group of buyers (so that the acres per buyer did not exceed the cap) and obtain the grant, but some of the buyers would be "dummy partners" who had agreed to sell their shares to the true investors for a side payment.[164] There was just one obstacle to this maneuver: the land-granting officers had to agree to the group format, but group grants were bad for the attorney general and surveyor, since those of-ficers were paid per grant. Sometime after 1710, investors reached a mutually beneficial accommodation with the officers, whereby they paid fees not per grant, but instead (1) in the case of the attorney general, per grantee, at a rate of £3,[165] and (2) in the case of the secretary, per thousand acres, at a rate of £4.[166] The governor was paid per hundred acres as before, though the investors upped his rate from 10s. to 25s.[167]

These became the standing arrangements, which the officers claimed as their lawful entitlements when reporting to the Board of Trade in 1764 and again in 1767. Arguing for the lawfulness of the higher fees, Attorney General Kempe, in each report, invoked all three of the great common-law doctrines:

custom, *quantum meruit*, and voluntariness on the part of the payors. He attested that the increased fees had been in place when he started the job in 1759, having "been so taken I am informed [for] above forty years," and "upon the authority of such long usage I have also taken them." He assumed they had initially arisen because "the ordinance was esteemed invalid, and the fee not a *quantum meruit* for the service." The increases were "for the emolument [i.e., benefit] of the grantees," in that they allowed for grants to be made in group format, and he claimed, "I never heard it was complained of" by those who paid.[168] The secretary echoed these arguments, emphasizing that the "alteration" permitting group grants had been "for the convenience of the grantee."[169]

It was not only English customhouse officers and New York colonial officers who made arguments for recognizing the obsolescence of outdated enactments, but also the British Privy Council itself. On this point, consider the council's treatment of Jamaica in the 1760s. Back in 1711, the Jamaican assembly had passed a statute regulating fees, but officers nevertheless continued to raise their charges, even for enumerated services.[170] The increases, as an assembly committee would later note, were at first "so small, as not to deserve opposition, and so modestly demanded as not to provoke it,"[171] but gradually they built up. The Privy Council in 1764 ordered a crackdown on extortion, and while it proved to be short lived, the Jamaican governor, allied with the assembly, took the order seriously and moved to enforce the 1711 statute. But the fee-taking officers had enough pull in London that, in 1765, the Privy Council reversed itself and issued an order declaring the suprastatutory payments lawful. It scolded the assembly for "arraign[ing] the conduct and justice of the [officers], to condemn the practice of taking fees established by custom and long usage." The 1711 act, it concluded, was "obsolete." The governor was to permit the officers to take "such fees, as have by long usage been taken by them, or their predecessors in office, although the same have exceeded the rates settled by the said act of 1711."[172] Now the officers, lamented a committee of the assembly in 1766, were "at liberty . . . to continue as they have done for some time past, to impose what burdens and taxes they think fit upon the commerce of his Majesty's subjects."[173]

The Privy Council's behavior in this instance was not unusual. Though the imperial authorities since the 1600s had officially required the governor or assembly of each colony to regulate all officers' fees,[174] they had never seriously tried to stamp out officer-recipient negotiation.[175] The Jamaican controversy of 1765 was one of multiple instances in which Whitehall confirmed the continuing vitality of the old common-law regime.[176]

## THE SOCIAL MEANING OF NEGOTIATION:
## RECIPROCITY, FLEXIBILITY, AND CUSTOMER SERVICE

Monetary negotiation between officers and the public informed the very nature of government services. Reflecting on the English customhouses, the parliamentary commissioners observed in 1786: "The practice of allowing the officer to be paid by the merchant, for the performance of official business," brought the two "into a mutual relation," thus promoting "habits of pecuniary obligation or exchange of private interest."[177]

To many, this seemed a good thing: as with any seller-customer relationship, the fee was the recipient's guarantee of prompt, attentive, and faithful service. As the English jurist William Hawkins wrote in 1716, it was "vain to expect that any officers who depend upon a known fixed salary, without having any immediate benefit from any particular instances of their duty, should be so ready in undertaking, or diligent in executing [their duties,] as they would be, if they were to have a present advantage from them."[178] Bacon feared that, without tips, "it would be impossible in many cases to have the laws executed with vigor and success."[179] The Maryland assembly in 1770 rejected a proposal to place major officers on salary, since they "would not perform their duties with as much diligence when paid a fixed salary as when paid for each particular service."[180] The Pennsylvania Executive Council in 1780 recognized that payments had to be made for services that the statute did not anticipate, "or the necessary business will not be done."[181]

It was not just fees for service that mattered, but especially the capacity of the two parties to *negotiate* the transaction. The recipient's freedom to adjust the price and the officer's freedom to adjust the service opened the way for mutual benefit. In 1784, Richard Champion, a leading Bristol manufacturer and merchant, published a tract advocating liberal trade policy, which included this vivid description of reciprocity in English customhouses:

> It was always a known and well understood indulgence to the merchant, to have the power of facilitating the dispatch of his vessels, or of any goods on board them, though it was not exactly conformable to the regular hours, or the precise forms of custom-house business. Whenever any goods were landed, and in general when shipped, the officer was gratified by a present, according to the trouble he had been at; in some cases at the pleasure of the merchant, in others a customary fee. But this was chiefly optional, and according to the attention shown, and facility given to the business. All these transactions, which have been mentioned or alluded to, were of such a public nature, as

not to admit of any impropriety of conduct in the officer to the prejudice of the revenue. It was a known and established custom, with which the officer was indulged for attention, civility, and dispatch of business.[182]

Note how Champion checked off the legal bases of voluntary gratuity, custom, and reasonable recompense while simultaneously emphasizing the flexibility, reciprocity, and mutual benefit that, in his view, characterized the whole system. Similarly, New York's top executive officers, as noted above, reached an accommodation with real estate investors whereby such investors could acquire land jointly in a single grant by paying fees that escalated with the size of the transaction. These mutual adjustments, as Kempe explained, were to "the emolument [i.e., benefit] of the grantees,"[183] or as the secretary phrased it, "for the convenience of the grantee."[184] Later New York officers, acting under the same incentives, continued to attract plentiful land-grant business by accommodating the wishes of investors in ways that circumvented the crown's instructions. (Their actions cannot be dismissed as merely "corrupt." The governor in 1772 made clear that he viewed the crown's acreage cap not as a hard-and-fast prohibition but simply as the crown's statement of its view in an unsettled dispute with the New York assembly, and he openly made policy arguments to the crown in favor of large grants.)[185] The same pattern, on a much smaller scale, was evident in the 1804 Massachusetts supreme court case discussed above: a man facing debtor's prison begged the deputy sheriff to allow him a few days of grace to gather the funds to pay his creditor, which the deputy was willing to do, because (as the court confirmed) he could charge extra for the trouble of imposing special safeguards on the free debtor.[186]

In the eyes of many, ongoing negotiation between officers and recipients was not merely convenient but also absolutely necessary to the continued functioning of government as the needs of service recipients evolved. The *Discourse on Fees* put this point forcefully: "[T]he quantum and instances of fees are in their own nature variable in different times, and as the methods and manner of business vary and alter," and if the fees could not vary according to such changes, "the consequences might be terrible and cruel."[187]

The tendency of fee-paid officers to adjust the nature of their services to customer wishes could be couched in highbrow terms, as when Adam Smith in *The Wealth of Nations* (1776) praised the influence of fee-seeking judges on the development of English law. Each of the rival courts at Westminster, said Smith, "endeavored, by superior dispatch and impartiality, to draw to itself as many cases as it could." Elsewhere in the passage, however, Smith made clear that "impartiality" was not really the basis of the judges' marketing strategies.

What they were selling was not impartial application of fixed law, but instead plaintiff-friendly reinterpretations of law, particularly in the area of jurisdiction and remedies. Because each court wanted more business, it "was, upon that account, willing to take cognizance of many suits which were not originally intended to fall under its jurisdiction," and "each judge" sought to "give, in his own court, the speediest and most effectual remedy, which the law would admit, for every sort of injustice." Smith believed that the remedies at English law had originally been inefficiently narrow, so the fee-driven expansion of remedies was, in his view, an improvement.[188]

This same customer-soliciting mentality could also be couched in lowbrow terms. Consider this 1732 report, signed by the North Carolina attorney general, regarding the grant of marriage licenses by Governor George Burrington: "[W]ithout consulting who takes [the licenses] or directing any security to be taken on delivering them out," Burrington "makes merchandises of them, exposing them to sale to any purchaser at ordinaries [i.e., inns], ale houses, or public taverns, employing people keeping such houses as his brokers to dispose of [the licenses] through the province; by which means any young persons may and many actually are married without and even contrary to the consent of their parents or guardians." This practice "entirely defeated" the usefulness of marriage-licensing for "the preventing of clandestine" unions. Notably, Burrington had recently raised the fee for a license.[189] Presumably, his alteration of the standards made it possible for him to ask more.

Highbrow or lowbrow, the ethos of seller and customer was pervasive in eighteenth-century government. It even permeated public functions in which, for us today, a customer-seller relationship seems inconceivable. The most astonishing example of this is the case of international diplomacy, with which I shall close this chapter.

Throughout the early modern period, it was lawful and expected for a European diplomat to receive "gifts" from the foreign sovereign with whom he dealt. The usual occasion for a gift was the end of the diplomat's tenure at the sovereign's court or the successful negotiation of a treaty between the foreign sovereign and the diplomat's own sovereign.[190] As one contemporary explained in 1790, "when an ambassador or other public minister leaves a court, where he has given satisfaction by his conduct, he receives a testimony thereof at his departure," with the amount "according to the estimation he is in, or the consideration entertained for his sovereign, and sometimes also according to the importance of the business that has been the object of his embassy."[191] "[S]ince most governments based the value of their presents upon the degree of favor held by the recipient minister at court," writes one historian, "diplomats would endeavor to do their very best to secure and maintain a favored position."[192] On "rare" occasions when a diplomat "had particularly displeased a foreign power," he "might receive no gift or a gift designed to show displeasure," as when the British minister to Sweden received, upon his departure in 1794, "a very lewd painting."[193] For successful diplomats, gifts could be significant financially. Upon concluding the peace treaty of 1763, the French government gave the British minister a gift worth about £1,500,[194] and for that of 1783, about £1,000.[195]

These presents were part of a larger practice of gift-giving that typified the culture of European diplomacy at this time—a culture of exchanges, reciprocities, alliances, and intrigues. Thus, diplomats might themselves give presents to influential persons at court. With reference to this practice, the era's leading manual on the "diplomatic art" noted that "a gift presented in the right spirit, at the right moment, by the right person, may act with tenfold power upon him who receives it"—indeed, "the manner in which this little custom is carried out may have an important bearing upon high policy."[196]

Early U.S. diplomats partook of these rewards. When Benjamin Franklin, Arthur Lee, and Silas Deane successfully negotiated the U.S. military alliance with France in 1778, Louis XVI gave Franklin, "who was in favor," a gift worth £1,500 and the two other men gifts worth £300 each.[197] Lee asked the Continental Congress if it was acceptable for him to keep the gift, and in 1780 they decided it was.[198] Franklin initially kept his without asking,[199] then asked and received permission in 1786.[200] Although the Articles of Confederation in 1781 prohibited U.S. officers from accepting presents from foreign states,[201] this prohibition—like so many positive enactments regulating official income in this era—had no effect. U.S. diplomats took gifts at least five times during the 1780s. John Adams received one of about £225 on departing Britain in 1788, and Jefferson one of about £280 on leaving France in 1789.[202] The exact rationale for ignoring the Articles of Confederation is murky. Jefferson, without referencing the Articles, wrote circa 1791 that congressional approval of Lee's gift in 1780 had "formed the subsequent rule."[203] A congressman in 1798 said the receipts had been justified on the ground that they occurred immediately after each man left office and was technically no longer a U.S. officer.[204] Whatever the legal argument, another congressman in 1798 made the important point that the diplomats of the 1780s ignored the Articles "for a good reason, because they could not refuse [the gifts] without giving umbrage to the courts which presented them."[205] So pervasive was reciprocity in eighteenth-century government that it was difficult to forswear.

# BARGAINING OUTLAWED

This chapter tells the story of how American lawmakers and judges outlawed the bargaining described in Chapter 1. Since the 1600s, adherents of the Anglo-American republican and Whig traditions had identified certain evils of unregulated negotiation between officers and laypersons. Negotiation gave officers the opportunity to exploit their monopoly power, it allowed the government to "tax" the people without the consent of their elected representatives, and it violated the ideal that officers should act from virtue and that citizens should receive services as a matter of right. In the mid-1700s, colonial lawmakers in the Upper South, motivated by the Whig ideas that underlay the American Revolution, used these arguments to assert complete legislative regulation of officers' fees. That is, no officer could take a fee unless it was established and fixed by a legislative act.

Outside the Upper South, however, negotiation survived beyond the Revolution. Lawmakers and judges across the rest of the nation repudiated negotiation only in the first half of the 1800s. In so doing, they were acting on several rising trends in the development of the new republic: the democratic opening of public office to lower-status people and the related loss of trust and deference toward officers, a more positivist and objective understanding of the "rule of law," a commitment to formal legal equality for all white men who sought public services, and an intensified hatred of monopoly. Driven by these ideas, the lawmakers and judges who repudiated negotiation effectively decided that officers were no longer quasi-independent vendors whom the legislature could regulate but sometimes did not. Instead officers had no lawful existence whatever apart form legislative will. This principle is universally accepted by American lawyers today and is crucial to the doctrine of legislative supremacy in a democracy. In this chapter we see how the idea was born.

## THE ARGUMENTS FOR SUPPRESSING NEGOTIATION
## IN THE PREREVOLUTIONARY ERA

Statutory fee regulation could be strong or weak in many different ways. It was possible to have a statute or not, to construe a statute to permit or prohibit payments for unenumerated services, to construe the enumerated services narrowly or expansively, and to find that usage could (or could not) negate corrupt intent. A legislature could be more or less serious about updating the statute to reflect the necessary business. Judges and officers could be more or less eager to conclude that an old statute was obsolete.

We have already considered the arguments in favor of weak (or nonexistent) statutory regulation: that freedom to bargain made officials attentive to recipients' particularized needs and ensured that officers' pay would remain flexible and realistic in light of the business that needed to be done. On the opposite side, the prerevolutionary period saw three interrelated arguments for strong statutory regulation, including the extreme view that officers should take no payments at all except those fixed by statute.

The first argument centered on the danger of monopoly power. To the defenders of negotiation, the freedom to bargain resulted in mutually beneficial accommodations between officer and recipient. But in the view of others, higher prices and extra charges resulted not from commensurate benefits to the payor but from the officer's exploitation of his monopoly over the service. Extortionate fee-taking officers incurred the same odium as price-gouging monopolies. Adherents of the English proto-opposition that emerged under James I attacked the evils of monopolies and excessive fees together.[1] The Parliaments of 1621 and 1624 viewed monopolies and official extortion as two of their most pressing grievances. That of 1624 passed major legislation to restrict the former and was planning to address the latter but was dissolved.[2] The economist William Petty argued in 1662 that fee-taking offices "are of parallel nature to monopolies" and "have the same to be said for and against them as monopolies have," noting that officers could keep the prices of their services high despite low costs.[3] The "chief danger of oppression," commented the jurist William Hawkins in 1716, "is from officers being left at their liberty to set their own rates on their labor, and make their own demands."[4] It was not only the officers' monopoly of the service that drew criticism but also their monopoly of information about the prices for which they were willing (or obligated by custom) to provide the service. "The distinction between what [payment] is permitted and what [payment] is prohibited, in many cases, is exceedingly minute," complained Bentham circa 1780, "and how many temptations may occur of profiting by the ignorance of strangers, when circumstances will insure impunity!"[5] Reformers frequently urged that fee schedules be posted to prevent officers from taking advantage of ignorant persons seeking services.[6] The surest way to do this—and to prevent the list from being manipulated—was to enact a schedule by statute.

The second argument for statutory regulation was legislative supremacy. As the feudal bases of English royal income broke down, the Tudors and Stuarts searched for new sources of money to keep the government running.[7] Parliament wanted to be the gatekeeper for those funding sources, both to protect the property of its constituents and to maintain leverage over the monarch. Negotiated fees threatened Parliament's role because they allowed for the financing of the officialdom without parliamentary approval.[8] Even more dangerous than negotiated fees—which arose organically and informally from numerous decentralized officer-recipient relations—were fees that the king himself purported to authorize his officers to take, by unilateral royal ordinance. The anti-absolutist Edward Coke, in his *Institutes* (written circa 1630), argued that such royally enacted fees violated the English constitution, for they were nonparliamentary taxes (tallages).[9] Later the colonial assemblies stretched this principle to cover not only royally enacted fees (which were clearly Coke's target) but also fees that arose organically from officer-recipient negotiation. In 1708, for instance, a committee of the New York assembly announced that "for any officer whatsoever, to extort from the people extravagant and unlimited fees . . . not positively established and regulated, by consent in general assembly, is . . . unlawful, a great grievance, and tending to the utter destruction of all property in this plantation."[10] The assembly declared that no fee or tax should be imposed "unless by the consent of the people convened in general assembly and some positive law or statute so enacted . . . to justify and authorize the same."[11] The assembly therefore enacted a regulatory statute, but the crown disallowed it as too stingy.[12] The governor issued a regulatory ordinance in 1710, which, as we have seen, became obsolete and gave way to the common law. Up to at least the 1730s, the New York assembly continued its attempts to regulate fees, but they could enact nothing without the governor and council.[13]

The third argument in favor of statutory regulation rested on civic republican views of official duty and citizenship. The eighteenth-century British empire was a monarchy, to be sure, but a "republicanized" one, as Gordon Wood says.[14] And whereas negotiated fees defined official service as reciprocal exchange

between officer and recipient, republicanism conceived of the recipient as a citizen enjoying a right to the service and of the officer as, ideally, a disinterested
man whose sheer virtue motivated him to fulfill the service obligations of his
position. As I noted in the Introduction, civic republicans thought that officers
ideally should receive no monetary compensation at all, guaranteeing that their
action would arise from duty and not reciprocity. Montesquieu condemned
money-based reciprocity as anti-republican: "In despotic countries the usage is
that one does not approach a superior, even a king, without giving him a present," which made sense "in a government where no man is a citizen," and "the
superior owes nothing to an inferior." But such presents "are an odious thing in
a republic because virtue has no need of them."[15] In a free government, it was
best that officers be unpaid. But if they must be paid, then *negotiated* fees were
especially pernicious, since they were especially susceptible to reciprocity, thus
allowing citizens to make particularized "deals" instead of relying simply on
their rights qua citizens. In 1783, Andrew Kippis, an English dissenter associated
with the "commonwealth-men," ticked off a list of republican bogeymen—
monopolies, sinecures, placemen, public debt—in which he also included the
evil notion that "fees are to be upheld as a necessary incentive to the relaxed
state of office, and one merchant is to bid against another, for having that business expedited which the smallest, as well as the greatest, by every rule of law as
well as policy, are entitled to have dispatched without perquisite or gratuity of
any kind." If these abuses continued, "Actum est de Republica"—it was all over
for the commonwealth.[16]

## TIGHTENING OF REGULATION IN THE UPPER SOUTH
## DURING THE REVOLUTIONARY ERA

All three arguments for statutory fee regulation—protection of subjects'
property from monopolistic power, supremacy of elected legislators, and official disinterestedness—were associated with the strain of English politics that
originated with the opposition to the early Stuarts and briefly took power under
the Commonwealth (1649–53). Though the Commonwealth "failed to abolish
fees," it made "almost continuous" attempts "to restrict them and to stamp out
exactions," and also to curtail gratuities.[17] A republican pamphlet in 1651 urged
that "the fees, and allowances of all officers . . . depending upon any courts
of justice" ought to "be settled, and made known" and "published in print,"
and that officers taking "greater fees, or rewards than shall be allowed them by
the appointment of the state" be "severely punished."[18] Though the commonwealth ideology faded (along with fee regulation) at the Restoration in 1660,[19]

it sprang up again in the Exclusion Crisis of 1679 and the Revolution of 1688, lived on among the radical Whigs of Hanoverian England, and became the mainstream discourse in the assemblies of the American colonies in the 1700s, strengthening the assertiveness of those elected bodies and contributing power- fully to the revolt of 1776.[20]

This radical Whig ideology manifested itself in the different colonial assem- blies in different ways, depending on which concerns happened to be most pressing for the members. In a few assemblies—those of North Carolina, Vir- ginia, and Maryland—it manifested itself in a strong aspiration for legislative regulation of official fees, just as under the English Commonwealth. Assem- blies in these colonies approached (if they did not achieve) absolute legal power over fees by the mid-1700s.

The North Carolina assembly passed increasingly comprehensive fee stat- utes in the early eighteenth century.[21] By 1731, its members stretched English constitutional restrictions on taxes to condemn nonstatutory fees, asserting what they called "the undoubted right and privilege of the people of England that they shall not be taxed or made liable to pay any sum or sums of money or fees, other than such as are by law established."[22] Their efforts reached a high point in 1748, when they persuaded the governor and council to approve a bill by which "no new or other fees shall . . . be demanded, taken, or received, other- wise than such as shall be established by the authority of the governor, council, and general assembly, any law, custom, or usage, to the contrary, notwithstand- ing."[23] The words strongly indicate a repudiation of custom and of charges for unenumerated services. Governor Arthur Dobbs apparently viewed the statute as a genuine constraint: he complained to the Board of Trade in 1761 that "there are many cases where no fees are paid for services done and no other fees dare be taken."[24] Still, the legislature's assertion of power was so unfamiliar against the background of Anglo-American law that later governors apparently refused to read it literally. Governor William Tryon made a formal report to the impe- rial secretary of state in 1767 that official fees in the colony were *"for the most part if not altogether* regulated by statute and particularly by the act of assem- bly" of 1748.[25] His successor, Josiah Martin, revealed in a similar report in 1772 that North Carolinians had been paying fees to Tryon himself for performing "services not provided for by former [fee] laws." Martin came to an agreement with the assembly whereby the fees that Tryon had been taking informally were now ratified by statute, but he couched this more as an effort to avoid a political headache than as necessary to legality. He had asked for the revised statute sim- ply "to obviate every possible ground of complaint" while insisting that Tryon had governed his charges by "very moderate and reasonable rules," that nobody could doubt "the equity of Mr. Tryon's conduct," and that the "clamors" against Tryon had been "unjust."[26] But then came the Revolution, which confirmed legislative supremacy, and the maximalist view of statutory fee regulation won out. At North Carolina's first ratifying convention for the U.S. Constitution in 1788, the members demanded a federal guarantee that "no aid, charge, tax, *or fee*, can be set, rated, or levied, upon the people without their own consent, or that of their representatives so elected."[27]

Another colony that moved toward complete statutory regulation in this period was Virginia. As in North Carolina, Virginia's fee statutes had become gradually more ambitious since the first English settlement.[28] A Virginia act of 1745 ordered officers to take the stated fees "for *any business* by them respectively done, *by virtue of their several offices*, and *no other fees whatsoever*." This seemed to prohibit money for unenumerated services and was probably intended to, though the statute's penalty clause perhaps introduced some confusion by saying that no officer could "take, any more or greater fees, for any writing, or other business by him done, *within the purview of this act*, than herein before set down and ascertained."[29] Despite this ambiguity, the importance of fee control to the House of Burgesses was quite evident during a controversy in 1752, in which the burgesses resolved that anybody who paid a new fee instituted by the governor-in-council "shall be deemed a betrayer of the rights and privileges of the people,"[30] and a leading burgess insisted that governors taking fees without statutory authorization "demand that which the law does not give them and therefore are guilty of taking from the subjects without legal authority."[31] In their responses to the Board of Trade inquiry in 1764, Virginia officers asserted their entitlement to fees overwhelmingly by statute, occasionally by statutelike gubernatorial ordinances, and never by custom or *quantum meruit* (though one officer noted he regularly received a gratuity, which was "never compelled").[32] This was in contrast to the more frequent assertions of custom and *quantum meruit* in the reports of several other royal colonies under inquiry (New Hampshire, Massachusetts, New York, and South Carolina), as well as the contemporaneous acknowledgment of nonstatutory rights by the Pennsylvania Executive Council.[33] That said, regulation was not easy to sustain across the board: surveyed in 1771, officers at the colony's customhouses did assert rights to customary fees, perhaps because of the confusion that had ensued in tariff administration after the attempted crackdown of the 1760s.[34]

The Virginia assembly's commitment to statutory fees faced a test in the revolutionary crisis. The colony's comprehensive fee statute of 1745 was actually a temporary act that the legislature renewed, for a certain period, every few years. In 1773–74, the governor was violently at odds with the House of Burgesses and dissolved it before there was a chance to renew the fee statute, which then expired. This came to the attention of the General Court, the colonywide trial court for major cases. Following the old idea that the fee statute merely regulated a preexisting entitlement that continued to exist in its absence, the General Court issued an order that all its officers should continue to take payments according to the rates of the expired law (using that old law as a benchmark for reasonableness), unless and until the legislature reconvened and said otherwise. It remained to be seen what the county courts (which handled minor cases) would do. Meanwhile, the House of Burgesses reassembled, but the governor quickly dissolved it again, with no resolution on fees.[35]

Angry Whigs considered their options. Some of them had come to believe, contrary to the General Court's order, that legislative affirmation was necessary for officers to charge fees. In this view, fees were illegal at common law and could be made lawful only by legislation. (To be sure, not every Whig felt this way: the renowned Edmund Pendleton circulated an opinion upholding the old doctrines of custom and *quantum meruit*.)[36] If legislation was indeed necessary for fee-taking, then Virginia's court officers could not lawfully take any pay, and the courts would have to shut down. Was that an outcome the Whigs should hope for? In some ways, it was: it would cause disruption, draw attention to the Whigs' grievances, give fee-taking royal officers an incentive to pressure Whitehall to compromise, and help Virginian debtors escape English creditors. But in other ways, shutting down the courts seemed like a bad thing to do. The courts performed services that Whigs felt squeamish about shutting down, such as the prosecution of criminals and the administration of estates. Ultimately, the Whigs succeeded in pressuring the courts to shut down partially, refusing ordinary civil litigation but continuing to provide other services considered essential. Legally, this made no sense: if the absence of a fee statute negated the entitlement to fees in any cases, it ought to negate it in all cases. But the partial shutdown was just what the Whigs wanted from a tactical and political perspective.[37] Pendleton remained unimpressed by any of the arguments for complete or partial closing, but, seeing that his Whig allies were adamant, he refrained from openly opposing them.[38]

Thomas Jefferson, then a relatively unknown thirty-one-year-old lawyer, sent a memo to Pendleton arguing (at least implicitly) that the statute's expiration negated all fees and that the courts had to close for all business, even prosecuting crimes. In particular, the memo argued for a strict application of the test for "immemorial" custom.[39] Pendleton was unconvinced, and the other Whigs had no stomach for Jefferson's too-perfect logic, heedless of consequences.

But once the Whigs overthrew the crown, they could impose their vision without having to worry about a government shutdown. Virginia's revolutionary constitution, after establishing several statewide and local offices, mandated that "all fees of the aforesaid officers be regulated by law."[40] Further, the assembly set up a committee to revise the state's laws, which drafted a new extortion statute, probably Jefferson's handiwork,[41] prohibiting payment for unenumerated services even more clearly than had the 1745 act. No officer could "take, in any form, any manner of gift, brocage, or reward *for doing his office*, other than is or shall be allowed by some act of general assembly" passed after independence.[42] It became law in 1786.[43]

The third major colony in which statutory fee regulation triumphed in the revolutionary era was Maryland. As we have seen, the colony went through a turbulent period of unregulated exchange in the 1720s and 1730s, ending with the proprietor's regulatory ordinance of 1733. This was followed by a statute of 1747, with strong wording that appeared to cut off payment for unenumerated services: no officer or officers, *"by reason or color of his or their office or offices,* shall have, receive, or take, . . . any other or greater fees, . . . than by this act are hereafter limited."[44] Since Maryland did not participate in the Board of Trade's 1764 survey, it is hard to know whether Maryland officers took this wording as strictly as their Virginian neighbors.

In any event, the right of officers to take money in the absence of a statute remained a subject of controversy on the eve of the Revolution. Like its Virginia counterpart, the Maryland statute was temporary. When it expired in 1770,[45] the land-grant officers ordered their clerk to continue taking fees according to the rates in the expired act, insisting that they were "not bound to perform services, without receiving or securing a reward for them, and in settling our demands, we thought the regulation established by" the former "act of assembly, . . . would be a proper rule."[46] In other words, they believed themselves entitled to *quantum meruit* and took the expired statute as a benchmark for reasonableness, even though (one might argue) this defeated the purpose of making the statute temporary. The royal governor, Robert Eden, backed the officers.[47] But the House of Delegates was outraged and jailed the fee-taking clerk.[48] To justify this action, the delegates issued a series of messages, which were not entirely coherent. On the one hand, the delegates seemed to argue that a nonstatutory fee charged by an individual officer was just as evil — and just as unlawful — as the better-known Whig bogeyman of a nonstatutory fee imposed by the king (or by his stand-in, the proprietor).[49] On the other hand, the delegates seemed to recognize the legitimacy of *quantum meruit*, which was the very doctrine that the land officers professed to be following. In particular, the delegates said "that in all cases where no fees are established by law for services done by officers[,] the power of ascertaining the quantum of the reward for such services is constitutionally in a jury upon an action of the party."[50] By this, the delegates perhaps meant that it was extortion for an officer to take money under the doctrine of *quantum meruit* unless he went to the trouble of bringing an actual lawsuit and obtained an actual jury determination of the fair price. That is, it was illegal for the officer and recipient to settle instead of going to trial. If that is what the delegates believed, it would be a bizarre theory, inconsistent with Hale's opinion in *Veale* and Webster and Shaw's arguments in Prescott's later trial. Alternately, it may be that the delegates, by insisting on a jury proceeding rather than a nonjury one, were making a clever gambit to undermine *quantum meruit* from a practical perspective: most Maryland fees fell below the minimum sum required to obtain jury trial in Maryland courts.[51]

Whatever the delegates believed, their imprisonment of the clerk provoked Governor Eden to dissolve the legislature and, a few days later, to issue an ordinance regulating fees, solely on his own power.[52] At last, the battle lines were clear. Eden was the stand-in for the proprietor, who was the stand-in for the king. Therefore, Eden's creation of fees was legally equivalent to the king creating fees—exactly the practice Coke had branded unconstitutional. Upon reconvening in 1771,[53] the lower house invoked Coke, concluding that "the fees of office are a tax upon the subject."[54] On this basis, the lawmakers integrated the fee fight into the biggest controversy of the Revolution, crying "taxation and representation are inseparable."[55]

Eden was not persuaded. For one thing, he pointed out that taxes and fees were not generally equivalent in English law, observing (correctly) that the judges and officers of the courts at Westminster took numerous fees without statutory authorization.[56] But the lower house's argument for the tax-fee analogy was not legal or historical so much as functional. Requests for official services, they believed, were "not of choice but necessity," adding the example that "[r]edress cannot be had for the smallest or most atrocious injuries, but in the courts of justice."[57] They were arguing for regulation on the ground that officers were monopolists, who controlled a service to which citizens had a right.

As a further response to the tallage argument, Eden—clearly assuming that officers were entitled to fees at common law—insisted that, if the legislature and governor could not agree on a statute to regulate fees, it was better to have regulation by the governor than no regulation at all. He clearly believed that officers had the right to bring actions for *quantum meruit* and that, in an ideal world, officers would ask only reasonable sums and service recipients would pay those sums without forcing the officer to sue. But the world was not ideal, and so Eden feared that, "without some rule to control the demands of officers, there would be great danger of extortion, and of perpetual contest" — "the timid might submit to the most grievous oppression, and the turbulent refuse to pay the most reasonable demand." It was absurd for the House of Delegates to say that the governor was "not authorized to prevent the mischiefs of extortion and litigation, by restraining the officers' demands." If lawsuits "should be brought for the establishment of each fee," or officers "be prosecuted [on complaint of recipients] for extortion," the result would be "litigation" that would not benefit "the community in general."[58] At one level, Eden's argument was eminently reasonable: he was not creating the fees but instead was regulating preexisting, common-law fee rights — rights that were recognized in England, in other colonies, and in Maryland's earlier history. At the same time, however, his analysis revealed the implicit tension between Coke's proscription of crown-imposed fees, on the one hand, and the common-law doctrines that permitted officers to negotiate fees individually, on the other. Conceptually, the real underlying threat to legislative control of officers was the officers' common-law right to bargain for fees as individuals. Regulation of that right by a king or governor did not create that threat; it merely concentrated the threat in the executive and rendered it more salient. Marylanders were confronting implicit tensions that had long lurked beneath the surface of English law.[59]

In Maryland, as in Virginia and North Carolina, the Revolution's verdict was for complete legislative regulation. Marylanders wrote in their Declaration of Rights that "no aid, charge, tax, *fee, or fees*, ought to be set, rated, or levied, under any pretence, without consent of the Legislature."[60] A statute of 1779 basically repeated the strong extortion language of 1747.[61]

A case decided after the Revolution confirmed that the common-law bases for negotiation were dead. The case arose when a juror failed to show up at the General Court in 1778. Luther Martin, the state's attorney general and later a top anti-Federalist, made the routine move of asking for an attachment of contempt against the missing juror. He billed for the service and was paid, by one or by both of the parties. He was indicted for extortion in 1783 and convicted in 1788, paying a fine of £5 but keeping his office.[62] After a long delay, the case ended up in the state's high court in 1805. Martin, still the state's attorney general, stepped out of his public role to represent himself. The relevant statute fixed fees for various services, including for an "action,"[63] and Martin argued that the attachment of contempt fell within the definition of that word.[64]

Likely sensing that this argument was a loser, he relied in the alternative on the common-law bases for official compensation. He began with custom.

In the court's "dockets of 1779," he pointed out, "there are a number of attachments against jurymen," and "in all such cases the fee of the attorney-general" appeared. The same pattern could be found in "[o]ther dockets before and since 1779" during the tenure of then chief justice William Paca, who had long practiced in the court and knew its ways, so the fee was unlikely to be a recent usurpation. When Martin was indicted in 1783 and convicted in 1788, there had been a new chief justice, who "had never practiced in the provincial or general court, and could not be supposed to know the practice of either of those courts previous to his appointment."[65] Then, moving from custom to his second common-law argument, Martin attested that the "attorney is entitled to a *quantum meruit.*" He cited *Veale* and *Ballard*, paraphrasing Hale with the words, "Where there are no fees limited [by statute], the person must have what he reasonably deserves."[66]

Since Martin himself was attorney general, a lawyer had to be specially appointed to argue for upholding his conviction. That man was William Pinkney, another leading member of the bar, who would become U.S. attorney general in 1811. (Martin and Pinkney later had a rematch in *McCulloch v. Maryland.*) Defending Martin's conviction, Pinkney did not even argue that statutory law was the exclusive basis for official fees. He felt quite comfortable asserting it. If Martin "has a right to charge a fee in [this] case," Pinkney began, the "act . . . must give it to him. It is in vain to talk of usage." Unless Martin "can produce a law justifying the demand, he is guilty of extortion." Pinkney repudiated *Veale*, contending that *quantum meruit* did not apply to public officers. It might apply to private attorneys, but the "case of a public officer is very different, and he must show an express law to authorize his demand."[67] Interestingly, Pinkney did not cite the text of the extortion statute as the basis for his arguments; he appeared to rely simply on a transformed understanding of the common law, or perhaps on a general presumption about the comprehensiveness of fee statutes. The justices, without opinion, sided with Pinkney.[68] Custom and *quantum meruit* had been submerged by legislation.

### TIGHTENING OF REGULATION NATIONWIDE IN THE EARLY 1800s: OFFICE AS A CREATURE OF THE LEGISLATURE

In light of the developments in North Carolina, Virginia, and Maryland, it is tempting to think that the positivist concept of fees—that officers could lawfully charge them only with specific statutory authorization—arose automatically from the radical Whig ideology that fueled the Revolution. But it is not that simple. Radical Whiggery played itself out in each colony through a series of particular issues, usually involving taxes but also (depending on local circumstances) land policy, church matters, fee regulation, and others. Radical Whiggery happened to get coupled with fee regulation in the Upper South colonies, but in many others it did not, and in those other places, the nonpositivist concept of fees survived for longer. Nonstatutory fees remained lawful, or at least legally ambiguous, until the 1810s in Pennsylvania, until the 1820s in Massachusetts and South Carolina, until the 1830s in New York, and until the 1840s in Louisiana and New Hampshire.

Still, by the middle of the nineteenth century, lawmakers and judges in all those states, indeed everywhere in the nation, came to embrace the same positivist view of official income as the Upper South had in the 1700s. Why? Unfortunately, the sources (mostly statutes and cases) do not contain much explicit discussion of the basis for the new thinking. (It cannot be explained as the program of one political party or the other. It was a shift in the entire zeitgeist, supported by aging Federalists and Whigs as well as Jacksonians.)[69]

Still, the cases and other sources do exhibit certain common themes: (1) suspicion and distrust of officers and anxiety about the monopolistic and coercive powers they wielded; (2) a strong preference for positive legislative authorization over official discretion and sometimes an almost-perverse pleasure in the enforcement of rigid legislative dictates; and (3) an objectified understanding of official duty, in which the official had little to no freedom in deciding what efforts to make (and therefore little to no freedom to bargain over those efforts). There are obvious links between these themes and larger trends in the political culture of the burgeoning republic.

Begin with distrust of officers. In the eighteenth century, officers were typically members of the same social community as the service recipients, joined by ties of kinship, neighborhood, business, and so on. Also, officers tended to be men of wealth and high social standing, who enjoyed the deference of their social inferiors.[70] In the generations after the Revolution, these two things became ever less true. Some of the causes were demographic: as the population grew larger, more urban, and more mobile, social hierarchies were less stable and people who encountered one another were more likely to be strangers. Other causes were political: suffrage and office-holding became open to all self-supporting white men, electoral politics became more of a full-time specialty, and incumbents rotated rapidly through offices instead of staying for life. The new class of men filling the offices—with their reduced social status, loss of deference from the citizenry, weakened social ties to their surroundings, and short time horizons—could not be trusted as easily to bargain with their constituents. In that respect, the tightening of fee regulation was in keeping with

Jacksonian-era reforms by which the government sought to rely less upon incumbents' personal probity and more upon rigid institutional safeguards to cabin discretion and prevent overreaching.[71]

As to the sources' emphasis on legislative authority, this can be linked with the contemporaneous rise of a more objectified and positivist concept of law. To be sure, Americans of the revolutionary period had a concept of the rule of law. But practically this meant empowering the assembly to protect local communities—with their internal authority structures and face-to-face cultures of legal and political participation—against outside intrusion by royal officers, crown, or Parliament. It did not mean that the assembly should itself make rules that would penetrate those communities.[72] But in the seventy-five years after the Revolution, the rule of law was increasingly operationalized in the form of positive legislative governance that originated in the state capital and broke down the varied, discretionary, personalized justice arrangements of the localities. The old regime's sensitivity to local norms and individual problems was now denounced as favoritism or corruption, to be replaced by more exact and equal rules. Human beings were no longer members of an organic local hierarchy and participants in its informal give-and-take. Instead, they were reconceived as falling into two categories. Self-supporting white men were individuals with claims of right upon the protection of an abstract government, and everybody else was a dependent or marginal person whose claims were conditional or nonexistent.[73] Because most persons asking for official services *were* self-supporting white men, it now seemed proper that service recipients should face officers as claimants of rights, one equal to the next, all paying the same rate for what the public owed its constituents.

Relatedly but more broadly, Americans of this era exhibited an obsession with imposing uniformity—a formal and legalistic equality between persons— on every interface between the government and the self-supporting white male population. This manifested itself in myriad ways: constitutional provisions to suppress private laws and local laws, the strengthening of judicial review to eliminate "class legislation" favoring one group over another, the replacement of special corporate charters by general incorporation, and the shift in public finance from ad hoc levies and favoritism-ridden public enterprises toward a general property tax.[74] Uniform fee schedules for official services, allowing no adjustments, exceptions, or special treatment, fit perfectly with this aesthetic.

The nemesis of uniformity was privilege, and the worst form of privilege was monopoly, a longtime bogeyman of Anglo-American political discourse that Americans in the first half of the nineteenth century elevated to satanic status. Where monopoly could be avoided, it was to be abolished. But where it could not, it was to be controlled and regulated, to prevent exploitation and to ensure open and equal access for all citizens, or at least as many as possible. Thus, the policy of rotation ameliorated the inherently monopolistic nature of public office. This brings us back to the anxiety in the fee cases regarding officers' exploitation of their monopoly power: fee regulation was yet another way of mitigating the inherent dangers of office's monopolistic nature and its consequent coercive power over service recipients.

Taken together, these trends established a new way for lawyers, lawmakers, and judges to think about "offices," one that was more separated from the personality of the incumbent, less independent of legislative sovereignty, and more objective and defined in its obligations to service recipients. Though Americans of the first half of the nineteenth century are rightly remembered for fashioning the first iteration of a recognizable American libertarianism in the private economy—abolishing state enterprises and cutting back certain kinds of regulation[75]—they were simultaneously the first great regulators of public offices. They stood not for laissez-faire in general but for a sharpening of the public-private distinction, lionizing market exchange on the private side while suppressing it more completely than ever before on the public side. Though offices and their pecuniary basis historically predated the legislature, that history was now erased. Offices (including their incomes) were reconceived as logically subsequent to legislation, existing only by legislative authorization and sufferance.

### Repudiating *Quantum Meruit*: No More Negotiation for Extra Services

As we have seen, one of the most important principles underlying the old regime was that officers could still negotiate payments according to the common law for services not enumerated in the statute. Under this heading, officers and recipients could bargain for payments for services that the legislature forgot to price or that arose after the statute was passed. Further, it was possible for an enumerated service to be sliced into its ordinary and extraordinary aspects, thus allowing for negotiation over the extraordinary aspect, which further expanded the sphere of bargaining.

This approach survived in several major jurisdictions well past the Revolution, but lawmakers and judges ultimately repudiated it. The first big state where they did so during the nineteenth century was Pennsylvania. The statute of 1752 had prohibited nonstatutory fees only for "matters or things hereinbefore enumerated,"[76] and the executive council in 1780 had declared that, for unenumerated services, "compensatory fees must be allowed."[77] In 1795, however, the legislature subtly altered the statute, prohibiting every officer from taking "greater fees than is hereinbefore expressed and limited, *for any service to be done by him.*"[78] Yet fees for unenumerated services were so familiar that neither the officers, nor the judges who approved many officers' fee bills, understood this as making any change.[79] In 1814, however, the legislature unmistakably asserted exclusive control, warning that "if the judges . . . shall allow any officer under any pretense whatsoever, any fees under the denomination of compensatory fees for any services not specified in this act or some other act of assembly, it shall be considered a misdemeanor in office."[80]

Judges on the state's high court got the message. Indeed, they embraced the reform. In an 1815 case, arising under the old 1795 statute, they looked with disfavor on the old common-law doctrine, even though they were still supposed to apply it in that particular case. A sheriff who provided a service unmentioned in the statute sought to recover on an implied promise to pay by the recipient, arguing that "the custom of the courts, to allow fees for services not specified in the act, proves the law to be, that the officers are entitled to a reasonable compensation," meaning that "the right of the officers is *independent of the courts*, the law raising an implied promise of payment for every service performed."[81] Indeed, Pennsylvania officers in preceding generations *had* taken fees for unenumerated services independently of the courts. The Philadelphia customhouse officers—none of whose fees were charged through a judicial proceeding—reported in 1771 that they "generally and usually" charged fees for many tasks not in the statute.[82] This was perfectly consistent with *Veale*. But the Pennsylvania justices in 1815 felt embarrassed about the old doctrine, and they construed it with a novel narrowness, rejecting the sheriff's claim. Their reasoning was not a fair reflection of legal thinking during negotiation's heyday, but it did fit the views of the legislators who passed the 1814 reform.

Chief Justice William Tilghman, a Federalist,[83] argued that it was appropriate to sacrifice the flexibility of ad hoc bargaining to protect service recipients against the power and monopoly position that were peculiar to public officers. In "the usual transactions of life," he acknowledged, "when one man performs services for another, at his request, the law implies a promise to pay as much money as they are reasonably worth." But "there is a very imperfect analogy between [private] services and such as are performed by public officers." Public services were special, for it usually was not "in the power of the party to employ any other [person] than the officer to whom the law has committed the performance of the service." It was "of very great importance . . . that every man should know what he has to pay; for if it is left to the parties to agree upon the compensation, . . . there is great danger of oppression to the lower and more ignorant people." As a protection against such exploitation, "the compensation [of officers] is fixed by positive law." To this last sentence, Tilghman appended the qualifying phrase "in *most* cases," but of course, after the 1814 statute took effect, it was to be all cases. Significantly, Tilghman was perfectly aware that exclusive positive control of fees was a clunky and clumsy way of doing business, since it was "impossible for human wisdom to foresee every service which will arise." This was "known to the legislature, and therefore, in framing the [fee] table, they have taken care to allow what [fees], *on the whole*, will render offices sufficiently lucrative, although for many services there may be no compensation at all." The regulatory system would be inevitably rigid and crude: "If the fixed compensation is more than the service is worth, the party must pay it; if less, the officer must be content with it; neither can resort to any other rule than the written law."[84] Such rigidity was necessary to protect citizens against monopolistic official power.

Having explained the reform's rationale, the Pennsylvania justices in later cases elaborated on its profound implications. The abolition of *quantum meruit* reflected a new concept of office as the creature of legislation: "Where a positive law prescribes the manner and nature of the payment to be made to an officer, the directions of the law are, and ought to be, the only rule. . . . An officer derives equally his authority and his compensation from the law, and where both are defined in the law, he can no more enlarge the one than the other."[85]

Similar thinking spread to Massachusetts. The statute in place seemed to permit *quantum meruit*: officers could take no more than the fixed fees "for any of the services aforesaid."[86] At Prescott's impeachment trial in 1821, Webster attested that officers throughout the state understood the statute to allow them payments for unenumerated services. For his part, Shaw floated the idea of interpreting it, despite its text, to outlaw such payments, but he then retreated, arguing that Prescott's receipts, even if they could in principle be taken on the basis of *quantum meruit*, were of unreasonable amounts. The senate's verdict—convicting Prescott on one of several counts of extortion—was hard to interpret, given the absence of an opinion and the factual complexity of each charge. Still, the fact that the senate removed and disgraced an otherwise respected judge for taking rather small sums appeared to suggest a rising anxiety about the dangers of negotiation, similar to that in Pennsylvania. It is therefore no surprise that, when the opportunity arose in an 1822 case, the Massachusetts supreme court distanced itself from its prior case law, which had stretched the concept of unenumerated services to include "extra trouble" in performing enumerated services. In the 1822 case, a deputy sheriff was prosecuted after he took the statutory sum for levying execution and then extra money for the trouble of selling the goods seized. The statute, held the court, "gives no such [extra] compensation, but limits the officer to a fee for levying." As in Pennsylvania, the justices admitted that the fee schedule was crude: the stated sum might be "an inadequate compensation in some cases," but it was "a liberal one in others," so that, "upon the whole, it would afford a sufficient reward." The officer could "receive nothing for extra trouble, his compensation being provided for by the fee [statute]."[87] Along the same lines, the legislature, revising the statutes in 1836, added a provision to outlaw the receipt *"for any official duty or service,"* of "any greater fee than is allowed by law."[88]

Other states moved in the same direction. Whereas Connecticut statutes had initially been silent on pay for unenumerated services,[89] the legislature in 1816 provided that, "in civil cases," no officer "shall add or make any other items of fees, not specified in this act . . . but shall be wholly confined to the fees in this act specified."[90] In an 1823 case where the efforts of a deputy sheriff clearly helped a creditor collect his debt but slightly departed from the prescribed acts in the fee schedule, the state supreme court permitted no recovery and condemned the deputy's demand as extortion, for it would "be in the face" of the statute to "remunerate an officer for meritorious service, . . . or by reason of his having been the remote cause of an important benefit to the creditor."[91] In South Carolina, where courts had held in 1802 that officers might receive fees for unenumerated services,[92] the legislature in 1827 changed course by adding a new preface to the fee schedule: "for all services not hereinafter specifically recited, the said officers shall not be entitled to any fee, but the said services so omitted in this act, shall be taken and understood as incidental to others for which fees are charged."[93] And in New Hampshire, where the courts had defended *quantum meruit* at length in the 1820s,[94] it seems that the legislature halted the practice with a new statute by the 1840s.[95]

The same transformation was evident in New York during the 1830s, where it was the subject of an especially robust debate. After the breakdown of positive fee regulation during the colonial period, the postrevolutionary legislature passed fee statutes that seemed to permit charges for unenumerated services, though they were so confusingly drafted that it is hard to tell.[96] This left the matter to the courts, which apparently considered fees for unenumerated services lawful in the 1810s.[97] And two decisions of the early 1830s suggested wide judicial tolerance for negotiation.

The first was *Hatch v. Mann*, decided in 1832 by the New York Supreme Court (the state's second-highest court, reviewable only by the special Court of Errors). In that case, Gallup owed a debt to Hatch, who asked a constable (Mann) to arrest Gallup. Hatch promised Mann that he would *"pay him well for"* making the arrest. Mann and his helper staked out Gallup's house at 3:00 a.m. and waited until dawn, when at last they caught him. But Hatch failed to pay, and Mann sued him. A jury awarded what it considered the reasonable value of the service, which exceeded the statutory fee for an arrest. Hatch wanted to tell the jury that Mann was a constable, but the trial judge would not let him. Reviewing the case, the Supreme Court held unanimously that Mann's official status did not matter, since officers could lawfully take these kinds of extra rewards. "The evidence shows," concluded the court, "that the arrest of Gallup was understood by both parties to require extraordinary efforts beyond those which an officer was strictly bound to make, or which could legally be required from him," which constituted "a good and legal consideration for a promise to pay what the extra service was worth."[98]

The second big decision approving negotiation came in 1833, from the vice chancellor in New York City, William T. McCoun, a Jacksonian appointee.[99] In the case, a bank was robbed and offered a reward for recovery of the cash. The stolen money was discovered, and the robber captured, by the joint efforts of some police officers and private citizens. The question was whether the police officers should be barred from sharing in the reward by reason of their official status, since they were already "entitled to a stated compensation or to certain fees allowed by law," of which the reward was not one. McCoun decided that the police officers were eligible to share. He cited *Hatch* as precedent. Further, he argued that officer-recipient negotiation was good because it adapted official efforts to the individualized and varying needs of service recipients: "Rewards are offered [by citizens] only when it is supposed the ordinary means of discovery and detection would prove ineffectual. They are voluntary offerings and *adapted to what the party making the offer deems to be the necessity and urgency of the occasion.*" Negotiation also promoted the just reward of services well done: "The object is to awaken public attention to the subject, excite vigilance, and call forth extraordinary individual efforts for the accomplishment of the end proposed to be gained," and "he who succeeds becomes entitled to the reward, upon the ground of his superior vigilance or sagacity, or of his having used greater exertions, or encountered dangers which others were disinclined or not in a situation to hazard."[100] New York jurists appeared to be staking out a position independent of Pennsylvania and Massachusetts, one that would find a place for negotiation in nineteenth-century officialdom.

But there soon came a backlash. In 1835, *Hatch* came up for review before the state's highest tribunal, the Court of Errors, consisting of all the state senators, the chancellor, and the Supreme Court justices (though the latter recused themselves, since they had decided the case below). The Court of Errors reversed the decision by a vote of 18–5.[101] There was no opinion for the whole court, but two of the men deciding the case chose to issue opinions for themselves, both favoring reversal. One was Chancellor Reuben Walworth, a Democrat; the other, Senator Albert Tracy, a Whig.[102] In the view of both men, the Court of Errors' decision covered all public officers,[103] and it was meant to settle the extra-services issue not only for the purpose of officers' capacity to contract and sue in *quantum meruit* but also for the purpose of their criminal liability for extortion.[104]

Walworth admitted the possibility that extra money might be permissible for truly unenumerated services,[105] but he signaled that the definition of each service in the statute was to be interpreted broadly, to encompass any special efforts or tasks that might be related to it, thereby keeping nonstatutory charges to a minimum. The service Mann performed was "that of arresting a party on a warrant," as listed in the statute, "and although he went in the night time, it was still a part of the same services for which a specific allowance is made by law. The fact, therefore, that it was done at an unusual hour, cannot authorize the constable to receive an extra compensation."[106] Walworth conceded that this interpretation tended to decouple the level of pay from the needs of the recipient and the efforts of the officer in each particular case. Yet the legislature had countervailing reasons to prescribe "a fixed allowance" for each service: "to prevent extortion and oppression on the part of public officers, and the interminable litigation which must necessarily arise if the amount of their compensation or the value of their services was dependent upon the circumstances of each case." In instances where "this fixed compensation is an inadequate allowance for the service performed," it was nevertheless "reasonable that the officer should sustain the loss," for the fixed price would likely be "more than the service is worth" in other instances.[107]

Tracy similarly rejected the notion of slicing an enumerated service into its ordinary and extraordinary aspects, making clear that his aim was to suppress negotiation between officers and recipients. "The pretence that [the extra sum] is for extra services," he feared, "would cover any conceivable corruption or extortion. What are extra services in the performance of a defined official duty?" Noting that the Supreme Court, in its opinion below, had defined them as "extraordinary efforts, beyond what an officer is strictly bound to make," Tracy asked: "What are the 'extraordinary efforts' which an officer can make to discharge his official duty, which he is not strictly bound to make? When he takes upon himself the office, he solemnly swears to discharge the duties of it 'according to the best of his ability.' Has he then an extraordinary ability beyond his best ability, for the exertion of which he may legally demand extra pay?"[108] Tracy's aim was to make objective and uniform the efforts required of officers, to prevent ad hoc negotiation with those with whom they dealt.[109] If extra pay were permitted for extra service, then "sheriffs, legislators and judges might and soon would put their 'extraordinary efforts' in the market, to be had by the highest bidder."[110]

Once *Hatch* stigmatized pay for unenumerated service as a dangerous thing to be construed narrowly, New Yorkers apparently came to conclude that such pay was not lawful at all. By the 1870s, the state's high court took it as conventional wisdom that no officer could take a fee for an official service unless fixed by statute.[111] When the legislature adopted a new penal code in 1881, it affirmed this understanding, deleting the confusing language of the early nineteenth century and defining extortion as the officer's receipt of compensation "for his official service," either "in excess" of the statutory amount or "[w]here no fee . . . is allowed [the officer] by statute."[112]

Thus, by the second half of the nineteenth century, it was the reigning assumption throughout America that officers' lawful monetary claims were creatures of statute, attached to their various acts by arbitrary legislative will and not by any kind of consensual bargain reflecting the wishes and needs of the individual officer and his customers.[113] So dedicated were some courts to enforcing the command of the sovereign that they punished the receipt of money even when the fee statute's omission of the service was clearly a drafting error. Consider an example from Tennessee. Historically, the state's statutes had allowed fees to sheriffs and constables for each of the routine services involved in executing a judgment. In one revision of the act, however, the legislature accidentally deleted one of the services in the constable's schedule. A constable took the usual fee and was convicted of extortion. The state's high court in 1857 affirmed the conviction, candidly admitting that the legislature "surely should have allowed a constable a fee" for the service at issue and that "[t]his will, doubtless, be done when the defect or omission is discovered, and brought to the attention of the Legislature." Further, it was clear that the poor constable "honestly believed he was entitled to the fee charged." Still, the court insisted that it was "beyond our power to add to or detract from what [the lawmakers] have enacted," though "we very much regret the necessity we are under to declare the law in this case to be against [the constable]." Nevertheless, "the principle that it is extortion to exact fees not allowed by law is indispensable for the protection of the people, and cannot be relaxed." "Every officer must beware that he takes no compensation for services not sanctioned by some law on the subject. He collects costs at his peril; and for each and every item must be able to put his finger upon some particular act."[114]

The exclusively statutory basis of official charges—originating in the mid-1700s and spreading through the first half of the 1800s—was a piety of the second half of the nineteenth century.[115] Judge Hamilton Robinson of the New York Court of Common Pleas proclaimed the now-dominant vision in a much-cited 1874 decision:

> The right of an officer to his fees, emoluments or salary is such only as is prescribed by statute. . . . The compensations for official services are not fixed upon any mere principle of a "*quantum meruit*," but upon the judgment and consideration of the Legislature as a *just medium,* for the services which the officer may be called upon to perform. These may in some cases be extravagant for the specific services, while in others they may furnish a remuneration that is wholly inadequate. The time and occasion may, from change of circumstances, render the services onerous and oppressive, and the Legislature may also increase the duties to any extent it chooses, yet nothing additional to the statutory reward can be claimed by the officer. He accepts the office "for better or for worse," and whether oppressed with constant and overburdening cares, or enabled from absence of claims upon his services to devote himself to his own pursuits, his fees, salary, or statutory compensation constitutes what he can claim therefor.[116]

This passage veritably revels in the positivist rigidity of the statute-based regime. Historically, fees had grown up organically through thousands of diffuse and particularized reciprocities between officers and service recipients, achieving regularity through informal patterns of mass social coordination. Now they were reconceived as creations of top-down legislative authority. In their theoretical and legal nature, they were as tied to the sovereign as a salary paid from the fisc.

The new theory manifested itself in a new maxim of statutory interpretation, put succinctly by the U.S. Supreme Court in 1894: "Fees allowed to public officers are matters of strict law, depending upon the very provisions of the statute. They are not open to equitable construction by the courts, nor to any discretionary action on the part of the officials."[117] In many areas of American law, courts during the late nineteenth century actively sought to preserve common law in the face of ever-growing numbers of statutes.[118] In the realm of official fee-taking, however, this did not happen: the common law had been buried and forgotten. Statutory construction in this area remained unrelentingly positivist. The reconceptualization of officials as creatures of the legislature was complete.

Rigid positive control of fees was a blow to customer service. If a service recipient wanted to pay for some harmless and helpful extra service, and the officer was willing to perform the service for the payment, the two could no longer make the exchange without breaking the law. In the West, for example, settlers applying for homesteads offered money to the federal district land officers in exchange for help in filling out their forms—a service not enumerated in the fee statute. The land officers in 1881 asked the commissioner of the General Land Office if they could take this money. In a wonderfully candid response, the commissioner admitted that settlers needed help filling out their forms and that the land officers were well suited to do it: "It is doubtless true that settlers would often prefer that the papers . . . should be prepared by the land officers and that those officers could do this work at less cost to the settler than would be entailed upon him by employment of an attorney." Yet positivism reigned, customers be damned. The commissioner told the officers that it would be praiseworthy for them to help the settlers, but they could take no money for it. "Whatever gratuitous assistance your time, official duties and facilities may enable you to extend to settlers may properly and meritoriously be so extended," he explained, "but the charges for extra service or the receipt of unauthorized compensation in any form or under any pretence, cannot and will not be tolerated."[119]

## Repudiating Custom and Usage

Apart from *quantum meruit*, another basis for negotiated fees at common law had been custom. This, too, met its demise in the first half of the nineteenth century. Much of the evidence for that demise can be found in the preceding section, in judges' strong pronouncements that statutes were the exclusive lawful basis for fee-taking. Such statements were so universal as to negate not only *quantum meruit* but also custom.[120]

But, as we have seen, there was another way that custom might provide cover for negotiation, apart from furnishing a direct legal basis. If an officer took a customary fee without statutory authorization, the officer could invoke custom to help prove that he had not acted with corrupt intent, thus shielding himself from the criminal charge of extortion. The Massachusetts supreme court had allowed usage to negate intent in an 1804 case. But in 1821—possibly in response to the spectacle of Prescott's impeachment earlier that year—the court reversed itself. The case concerned a justice of the peace who took a fee higher than what the statute allowed for a particular service. When tried, he sought to prove "that certain other public officers in [his] county of Bristol, whose fees are regulated by the same law, have been in the habit of receiving greater fees than the law allows." But the judge refused to admit the evidence. When the justice of the peace appealed his conviction, citing the 1804 case, the high court pulled the rug out from under him. It held that evidence of usage "had no tendency to justify or excuse the defendant. If it were to be otherwise held, the consequence might be a combination of officers; and the illegal acts of each would always be excused by the illegal acts of the rest."[121] A year later, the court elaborated that an "unlawful act cannot become lawful by usage; and it cannot be known whether the defendant may not himself have contributed to establish the practice under which he would defend himself."[122] The Connecticut high court reached the same conclusion, almost simultaneously.[123] Custom for centuries had served to cloak the organic renegotiation of fees, and now, for that very reason, it was condemned.

Another case illustrating the repudiation of custom—and of mutually beneficial negotiation—was *Ogden v. Maxwell,* decided by the U.S. Circuit Court in New York City in 1855. By a federal statute dating to 1799, passengers landing at a U.S. port had to list their personal property on forms provided by the customhouse. The statute provided that the collector was then to grant a "permit . . . for landing the said articles."[124] For each permit, he was entitled, by another statute of 1799, to a fee of twenty cents.[125] But the statutes did not specify whether a permit was to be granted for each passenger, for each ship, or by some other method. The collector presumably could have construed the statute to require a permit for each passenger, but that would involve enormous paperwork and delay. It was more convenient for the shipowners if he issued a permit for each ship, but that would cut his fee income to almost nothing. At some point, the collector apparently reached an accommodation with shipowners whereby he issued a permit for each ship but charged the twenty-cent fee for every *five* passengers. The compromise was reminiscent of the New York land-grant officers' deal with real-estate investors back in the 1700s.

But such arrangements had become much harder to justify. In the mid-1850s, certain shipowners who had paid the collector twenty cents for every five passengers apparently soured on the arrangement and sued the collector, arguing that the payments, insofar as they exceeded twenty cents for each actual permit, were unlawful and should be given back. The collector contended that the arrangement had been the "uniform practice" for "more than ten years" and defended it as "a long-continued usage and practice in the collector's office." But the court rejected this argument. It construed the statute to prohibit any payments for any official service not expressly provided for by statute, even if backed by custom. There was "no warrant in law, except under the statute, for imposing any charge or fee for that official act. The [officer] would, without the aid of the statute, be guilty of extortion, in levying fees of any kind for his official services." And the "statute gives no reward except for doing the individual act named," that is, twenty cents for actually granting a permit. "No equity or usage in respect of these rates or compensation can be appealed to, as a sanction for a departure from the terms of the act." Importantly, the judge was well aware that the collector and shipowners had developed the arrangement for their mutual convenience, but he insisted that "no consideration of convenience to either or both of the parties, or saving of expense, by substituting another practice in place of that directed by law, will authorize the collector . . . to charge and receive compensation for a service differing from that appointed by positive law."[126]

By 1892, it was easy for a treatise writer to speak of a distinctly American rule regarding customary fees. Though "in England" the "immemorial existence of fees" could establish title to them, "in the United States, there can be no usage, which of itself will entitle an officer to fees, where they are not expressly allowed by law."[127] What the writer did not say, and probably did not even realize, was that this transatlantic distinction had not always been in place but resulted from a shift on American soil between the mid-eighteenth and mid-nineteenth centuries.

### Negotiation's Last Stand: Unofficial Services

As lawmakers and courts increasingly concluded that officers could take no money without statutory warrant for any official service, the last remaining excuse for such takings was to argue that the service for which the recipient paid was unofficial.[128] There had been intimations of this argument in New York in the cases of *Bangs v. City Bank* and *Hatch v. Mann*, where pro-negotiation judges argued that the extra money was for efforts beyond what the officer was bound to make,[129] though they were ultimately rebuffed by the Court of Errors' conclusion that officers were always obligated to perform every official service to the best of their ability. But if the service itself were unofficial, things would be different. The expansiveness or narrowness of an officer's duty therefore became significant. Technically, this issue could never go away, and it still has not: unless people who fill public offices are barred from any outside income, there will always be moonlighting. Generally, however, judges of the mid- to late nineteenth century erred on the expansive side, realizing (correctly) that a narrower view would subvert the larger project of subjecting officer-citizen exchange to statutory control.

We can best appreciate the victory of pro-regulatory forces in the controversy over unofficial services by examining a pair of archetypal cases, decided by the high court of Louisiana, which powerfully illuminate the opposing arguments for negotiation and regulation. The two cases were captioned *Hills v. Kernion*, decided in 1844,[130] and *Kernion v. Hills*, decided in 1846.[131] They involved the same parties, the same facts, and the same question of law. But the two cases were decided immediately before and after the state's new constitution of 1845, which abolished and reestablished the high court, replacing all the judges.

The old court, dominated by Whigs, endorsed negotiation. The new court, dominated by Jacksonians, endorsed regulation, reversing the view of their pre-decessors.[132] Taken together, the two cases vividly illustrate the robust debate over official compensation that occurred in this period—and the pro-regulatory thinking that won the day.

The two cases concerned the tobacco market at New Orleans. Tobacco planters sent their product to the city in barrels, which dealers offered for sale to buyers. A Louisiana statute required that a barrel of tobacco, before it was of-fered for sale, be examined by one of several public inspectors. There were four quality grades for tobacco. Under the statute, the inspector was to determine the grade, brand the barrel accordingly, and provide the dealer with a certifi-cate stating the grade. For these services—branding and certifying—the statute granted the inspector a total fee of sixty cents.

But the statutory scheme did not meet the needs of the market. Buyers—and the dealers who sought to attract buyers—wanted more information than was reflected in the grade. They wanted inspectors to provide (1) a sample of the ac-tual tobacco from the barrel and (2) a label, attached to the sample, specifying any concerns the inspector had about the barrel, such as whether the product was damaged, whether the barrel included additional packaging or was of un-usual dimensions, and so on. But the statute was vague as to whether it required those services—known as sampling and labeling—and it surely did not specifi-cally enumerate them, or any fees specifically for them.[133]

The case reports are not entirely consistent on whether the inspectors had been willing to engage in sampling and labeling up to the mid-1830s.[134] What seems most likely is that the inspectors did perform these tasks, but not thor-oughly,[135] because they were paid nothing for them. It is certain, however, that in 1836 the corps of inspectors exchanged a series of public notices with a "large meeting of the dealers" whereby the two groups agreed that the dealers would pay the inspectors a fee of forty cents per barrel for sampling and labeling, on top of the statutory fee of sixty cents for grading and certifying.[136]

Many and perhaps all dealers paid the forty-cent fee starting in 1836. But in 1842, some or all of them questioned its legality, announced they would pay only under protest from that point forward, and in fact ceased paying. Still, the inspectors continued to sample and label, pending resolution of the dispute. The 1844 case in the Louisiana high court concerned the claims of dealers to recover the forty-cent fees that they had paid up till 1842.[137] The court approved of the negotiation that had resulted in the fee. The dealers lost. The inspectors then sued the dealers to recover the forty-cent fees that the dealers had refused to pay them after 1842, resulting in the 1846 case before the new, Democrat-dominated court,[138] which repudiated their predecessors' legal analysis and denied recovery to the inspectors. Thus, the two cases concerned separate sets of transactions, but practically there was no difference between them in terms of the facts and the legal questions.

Upholding the inspectors' right to the forty-cent fee in 1844, the old court's opinion centered on the idea that sampling and labeling were unofficial services, "beyond those specified in the law," which the inspectors were "not bound, as inspectors, to furnish."[139] Since sampling and labeling were done "extra-officially," compensation for those tasks was not constrained by the statute: the inspectors could take the forty-cent fee as an "*extra-charge*, distinct from the [sixty-cent] charge made under the inspection laws."[140]

The old court probably viewed the "unofficial services" argument as its only option for justifying negotiation, given the rising tide of opinion that nonstatutory payments were illegal for any official services. And yet, in the judges' opinion, there are strong overtones of the older justifications for officer-recipient negotiation: that payment was originally voluntary on the part of the service recipients, that it constituted reasonable recompense for services that benefited them, and that it now enjoyed the sanction of usage. Unofficial service, it seems, was a cover for smuggling the old justifications of negotiation back into a legal system that had supposedly expelled them. Thus, as to voluntariness, the judges noted that the extra fee had initially "been paid without complaint on the part of any one,"[141] that the dealers "*consented to pay*" the charge,[142] that "[n]o one ever complained of the charge, nor were any persons ever vexed or harassed by the inspectors," and that one dealer-witness testified he "always paid his [extra fee] very cheerfully."[143] As to reasonable recompense, the judges proclaimed that "equity forbids that [the dealers] should profit by the labor of others without a fair remuneration," that "the services rendered . . . were greatly beneficial to the [dealers],"[144] and that the dealers had "always considered the [extra] charge as a fair one, and that it was just remuneration for the services . . . rendered." As to usage, the extra fee was obviously not immemorial by any strict test, but the court did believe that its eight-year run further justified it. The dealers had "submitted for a long space of time to the charge of forty cents, to which they now give the epithet *extortion*." The charge had "constituted the usage and mode of trade until now."[145]

Most significant, the old court emphasized that the nonstatutory fee — whether couched as unofficial service, voluntary payment, reasonable recompense, or custom — redounded to the mutual benefit of the officers and the service recipients. This, deep down, had always been what justified negotiation, and here the judges made it explicit. Buyers and dealers wanted better information about the product, but information was costly for the inspectors to obtain and convey, and the extra fee solved the problem by inducing them to do this valuable work. Everybody was better off. "By the adoption" of the extra fee, said the court, "the tobacco trade has been put on a better footing than it ever was before; it has better secured the interest of the buyer and seller, and facilitated the operations of the trade." Dealers, buyers, and tobacco planters had all "been benefited by the imposition of the charge of forty cents," which constituted "a kind of compromise between the [dealer], seller, purchaser and inspector."[146] Now that inspectors were being paid to produce the information, dealers had more confidence in the information produced.[147] The judges believed that sampling and labeling, induced by the extra fee, had caused the price of tobacco to rise,[148] since buyers no longer had to bear as much risk.

This happy view of officer-recipient negotiation was not shared by the complaining dealers. Rejecting the judges' characterization of the transaction as voluntary, they insisted that they were "necessitated to submit to the charge, to avoid the delay and injury which would have resulted from resistance thereto."[149] Furthermore, the complaining dealers adopted an objectified and expansive view of the inspectors' duty, one that encompassed sampling and labeling and allowed for no dickering over the matter: though defenders of extra fees stressed "the fact, that the public has been better served since the extra-allowance has been paid," it was outrageous to argue that, "where a charge is not authorized by law, an officer may exact it provided he be more attentive to his duties."[150]

Nor was the happy view of the extra fee shared by the new judges who took over the Louisiana high court after the constitution of 1845. Evaluating the extra fee's legality in the inspectors' suit against the dealers in 1846, the new judges departed from their predecessors and credited the complaining dealers' contention that they were forced to pay by reason of the monopolistic power which the statute conferred upon the officers. The dealers, said the court, "were compelled by law to employ the [inspectors] to inspect their tobacco," and they submitted to the extra fee "in order not to be delayed in their business." And while the judges conceded their predecessors' point that usage might inform the construction of a statute, they credited the allegation that, "during a long series of years previous to the year 1836, it was the practice in New Orleans for tobacco inspectors to furnish samples without any extra charge."[151] Thus, usage actually cut against the legality of the extra fee. In this way, the court construed usage strictly, so that it would not merely include recent practice but the whole history of officer-citizen dealings, which could reveal recent practice to be a usurpation. Applied in this manner, the doctrine of usage would cease to provide cover for ongoing negotiation.

As to the main issue—whether the inspectors' duty should be interpreted expansively to encompass sampling and labeling and thereby prohibit nonstatutory charges for those tasks—the court argued for expansiveness:

> The argument that the [extra] charge is made, not by the inspector in his official capacity for official services, but by the individual in his individual capacity for individual services, is specious [i.e., superficially plausible], but involves an unsafe doctrine. It seems to us very dangerous, when a law prescribes for the public officer certain fees *and no more*, to draw distinctions between the individual and the public officer, except, at any rate, when such a distinction is indispensable to do justice between the parties, by reason of services which it is clearly impossible to class as official, and where his public character has given the claimant no advantage over the citizen in making the bargain.[152]

Essentially, the court was establishing a principle of statutory interpretation under which an officer's fee-paid duty was to be construed expansively, with a strong presumption against charges for "unofficial" services, particularly where the officer enjoyed monopolistic or otherwise coercive power over the service recipients. Officer-citizen negotiation was fundamentally unequal. So judges ought not to trust it.

This relatively expansive view of official duty, driven by the desire to tighten regulation, became conventional. As New Jersey's supreme court explained in 1853, the vagueness and constant evolution of official duty meant judges had to be vigilant against overreaching officers: "The statutes of the legislature and the ordinances of our municipal corporations seldom prescribe with much detail and particularity the duties annexed to public offices; and it requires but little ingenuity to run nice distinctions between what duties may and what may not be considered strictly official; and if these distinctions are much favored by courts of justice, it may lead to great abuse."[153] The sentence was quoted by John F. Dillon in his authoritative treatise on municipal corporations, first published in 1872.[154] A treatise in 1892 indicated that judicial approval of nonstatutory charges for unofficial services was normally confined to tasks performed physically outside the officer's jurisdiction (e.g., the state or county) or substantively far afield from the officer's job, such as a police justice employed to revise the city ordinances.[155] To be sure, there were exceptional cases in which lawmakers and judges countenanced a broader view of unofficial services and thereby allowed an undercurrent of negotiation to continue in limited contexts,[156] but the new regime was predominantly a regulated one.

## A HINT OF THINGS TO COME: ABOLITION OF FACILITATIVE PAYMENTS IN CERTAIN OFFICES OF THE EARLY REPUBLIC

As I have argued throughout this chapter, the main thrust in the development of facilitative payments from the mid-1700s to the mid-1800s was for legislators to permit such payments while regulating them. However, in the case of some offices during this period, peculiar circumstances caused lawmakers to reject not simply unregulated exchange but exchange itself, meaning that facilitative payments had to be stamped out altogether. Here, I note two of these particular cases: the outright abolition of facilitative payments for U.S. diplomats and for federal judges, both in the 1790s. The political concerns of the early republic made reciprocity itself seem unusually and especially hazardous in these two offices. In the case of diplomats, civic republicans had a special aversion to European diplomacy's culture of reciprocity; in the case of federal judges, lawmakers were anxious about the new national judiciary transgressing its limited jurisdiction by entrepreneurially seeking out cases. Later on, starting in the second half of the nineteenth century, a larger change in the nature of American politics—the rise of rival mass interest-group claims to public resources— would lead to a more general reaction against customer-seller reciprocity across all offices. That broader and later reaction is the subject of Chapter 4. The early reforms pertaining to diplomats and federal judges prefigured the later reaction in that they involved anxieties about reciprocity itself, though the reasons for these early anxieties were idiosyncratic to the types of offices at issue.

Consider the first case: diplomats. As noted in Chapter 1, it was lawful and expected for a European diplomat to receive a "gift" from a foreign sovereign upon completing his tenure or concluding a treaty. This gave each diplomat a personal interest in winning the favor of, and reaching agreements with, the government with whom he dealt. It was part of the European diplomatic culture of reciprocity, alliance, and intrigue.[157]

The American revolutionaries had special reasons to be wary of the diplomatic culture of reciprocity. As civic republicans, they accepted the Enlightenment critique of princely diplomacy as corrupt, scheming, devious, and immoral.[158] Further, they knew their own nation was weak—vulnerable to manipulation and domination by stronger and more cunning European "allies." From its very first international dealings, the United States tried to make its alliances as limited as possible, to safeguard the fledgling republic's autonomy.[159]

Americans expressed their apprehension about the diplomatic culture of reciprocity from the moment they broke with Britain, particularly in the area of gift-giving. The draft Articles of Confederation, drawn up in the summer of 1776, barred U.S. officers from receiving gifts from foreign states.[160] When ratified in 1781, the Articles maintained that bar.[161] Yet (as we saw in Chapter 1) this anti-gift provision was so out of step with European custom that it had little effect throughout the 1780s. U.S. diplomats ignored it, and the Continental Congress made exceptions to it.[162] The new U.S. Constitution of 1787–88 largely continued this pattern: by default, no federal officer could accept a gift from a foreign government, but Congress could give permission.[163] This provision might have given rise to a legislatively regulated system of diplomatic gifts, much like the legislatively regulated fees of other offices that were common in the nineteenth century.

But as American politics moved in a more radically republican direction, Congress decided that mere regulation of diplomatic gifts was not enough. In 1798, the House of Representatives, driven by its Jeffersonian members, resolved never to permit U.S. diplomats to accept gifts.[164] One Federalist vainly tried to defend the culture of exchange, pointing out "the good will which was produced by this interchange of civility between nations"—there were "advantages of reciprocal civility in private life, and it was still more necessary in Governments and nations."[165] But to the Jeffersonians, the reciprocal culture of diplomacy was too dangerous for a fragile republic in a world of intriguing monarchies. Diplomatic gifts, warned one Republican congressman, "opened an avenue to foreign influence—an influence, among monarchs—which has always proved the destruction of Republics."[166] Congress ought to exercise its power "to lock up every door . . . to the influence of [royal] Courts and Monarchies."[167] Another member declared himself unwilling "to lay this country under an obligation to a foreign country by our Ministers accepting presents."[168] European monarchs were unlikely to be offended, argued a third member, for it was "well known to the European Courts that our Government is established on principles totally different from theirs."[169] This precedent of 1798 stuck.[170] The United States thus became the first Western power to opt out of money-based reciprocity among diplomats.[171]

Besides diplomacy, a second early instance of Americans rejecting reciprocity altogether came in the case of federal judges. In Chapter 1, we saw that English judges had famously competed with one another to expand remedies in order to attract plaintiffs and fees.[172] At least some colonial judges did the same, particularly the powerful vice-admiralty judges who offered friendly treatment to privateers seeking condemnation of the vessels they captured.[173] The Constitution of 1787–88 authorized a new corps of federal judges, whose main business was inherited from the old admiralty courts. Significantly, the Constitution appeared to mandate salaries for these judges rather than fees.[174] When a federal judge in South Carolina during the 1790s proceeded to take admiralty fees according to the old colonial schedule (based on custom, not statute), Congress reacted not by regulating the fees but by barring their receipt completely, in 1793.[175] No direct evidence survives of the reasons for the new anti-fee rule. But probably it had to do with the fact that the federal courts' jurisdiction was limited (the exact limit being a fraught political question), so congressmen did not want the judges entrepreneurially seeking more plaintiffs and more business. The formidable anti-Federalist "Brutus" had warned in 1788 that "it is highly probable the emolument of the [federal] judges will be increased, with the increase of the business they will have to transact and its importance. From these considerations the judges will be interested to extend the power of the courts, and to construe the Constitution . . . in such a way as to favor it." He pointed to the example of the business-seeking English courts.[176] Congress's prohibition on fees for American federal judges (which preceded the equivalent English reform by several years)[177] may well have been a response to these peculiar concerns about the federal courts.[178] Reciprocity, so long a hallmark of the relations between Anglo-American officers and laypersons, now seemed a danger that had to be controlled or, in this case, smothered altogether.

# 3

## A REGULATORY NIGHTMARE

*Salaries as a Remedy for Corrupt Exchange and Official Lucre*

The legal and ideological transformation chronicled in Chapter 2—whereby lawmakers and judges came to believe that officers and laypersons must never make exchanges except those authorized and regulated by legislative power—led to an administrative nightmare. The fee regulations that legislators wrote proved crude and incomplete, and they became obsolete quite easily and rapidly. Because the fixed payments fell so far out of phase with business needs, officers who took fees according to the regulations had incentives to crazily misallocate their efforts. But many reacted to the regulations' perversity by simply disobeying them, continuing to make bargains with laypersons just as officers had done for centuries. Judged against the new principle that fees required legislative authorization, these bargains were now branded as "corrupt." And it was hard to stamp out corrupt bargains while still permitting officers to take regulated fees. The regulated fee system signaled a general moral approval of officer-recipient exchange, and it served as a convenient cloak for illegal payments. In the period circa 1870–1920, lawmakers concluded that fee-based compensation of officers, even when regulated by statute, led unavoidably to "corrupt" fee-taking outside the statute. To stop officers from taking *unlawful* fees, one had to prohibit them from taking *any* fees and give them salaries instead. The general aspiration to subject officer-layperson exchange to law drove legislators, educated by experience, to block all exchanges between officialdom and laity.

The effort to prevent corrupt exchange was not the only regulatory challenge that pushed lawmakers to give up on facilitative payments and adopt salaries instead. As the final section of this chapter recounts, there was also the regulatory challenge of preventing each individual officer from earning too high an income in the aggregate, which became more pressing in the second half of the 1800s, when rising population and advancing office technology meant that certain officers did far more business, and earned much greater totals of facilitative payments, than ever before. As these incomes came to light, lawmakers came under pressure to regulate them, for they ran afoul of populist and reformist ideologies descended from revolutionary republicanism's hostility to official lucre. Theoretically, lawmakers might have regulated each officer's total income by fiddling with the statutory prices he could charge for individual services, but that proved extremely difficult, for reasons similar to those that hobbled the effort to regulate corrupt individual transactions: unforeseeable changes in business might swell the totals once again, or officers might manipulate the new schedule to achieve the same result. As with the regulation of corrupt individual transactions, the regulation of total incomes ultimately required salarization as a crude but sure solution to the problem.

## MISMATCHES BETWEEN BUSINESS NEEDS AND THE STATUTE'S FIXED PRICES

Throughout the nineteenth century, the fee system's proponents expected it to continue its age-old mission of encouraging officers to meet recipients' needs.[1] But there was a profound tension between the fee system's ancient usefulness for customer service and its new, post-1850 status as a creature of legislation, which outlawed the officer-recipient negotiation that had historically been the system's essence. To be sure, this tension was not irreconcilable in every context. There were many instances, even in the late nineteenth century and early twentieth, in which statutory fees, for better or worse, continued to encourage officers to provide recipients with what they wanted (as I discuss in Chapter 4.) But there were also many instances in which statutory fees did not match the business that needed to be done, either because (1) the legislature from the get-go failed to identify all the services that officers performed, (2) the labor involved in a certain enumerated service varied so much from recipient to recipient that any uniform payment imposed by statute was arbitrarily high or low for many actual cases, or (3) the business evolved after the passage of the statute to require new tasks unanticipated by the schedule.

Close observers of the statute-controlled fee system were keenly aware of these three mismatches between permissible payments and actual business. As to the first of the three mismatches—that the schedule missed services in existence at the time of enactment—the chief justice of Pennsylvania noted in

1815 that it was "impossible for human wisdom to foresee every service which will arise" and that " for many services there may be no compensation at all."[2] The U.S. House Judiciary Committee in 1852, reporting the bill for a uniform fee schedule covering federal court officers, said it was "not pretended" that the new schedule "embraces every item of service which the officers . . . may be called on to perform, but it has been the object and design of your committee to give compensation on a scale so liberal, for the services which are usually and necessarily performed in the courts, that the officers will be well indemnified for such as have not been specified."[3] Wisconsin's high court in 1874 explained that "services required of [officers] by law for which they are not specifically paid, must be considered compensated by the fees allowed for other services."[4]

As to the second of the three mismatches—that an officer's statutory fee for a service did not match the effort he had to expend every time he performed it—the Massachusetts high court in 1822 observed that the statutory fee "is an inadequate compensation in some cases" but "a liberal one in others."[5] New York's chancellor in 1835 thought it an "absurdity" to hope that a statutory fee would be "a full and adequate [compensation] for the performance of the service in each particular case." "If this allowance is more than the service is worth in one class of cases," he continued, "the officer has the benefit of it," but the officer would conversely "sustain the loss in other cases, if it should turn out that this fixed compensation is an inadequate allowance for the service performed."[6] Another New York judge in 1874 conceded that the fees, fixed "upon the judgment and consideration of the legislature," might "in some cases be extravagant for the specific services, while in others they may furnish a remuneration that is wholly inadequate."[7]

As for the last of the three mismatches—novel services arising as business evolved after enactment—consider the comments of a New Jersey judge in 1853: "[T]he incessant changes which the progressive spirit of the times is introducing, effects, almost every year, changes in the character, and additions to the amount, of duty in almost every official station." Such changes were inevitably giving rise to "claims [of compensation] for extra services," which courts ought to resist.[8] Similarly, a New York judge in 1874 explained that "time and occasion may, from change of circumstances, render the services onerous and oppressive, and the Legislature may also increase the duties to any extent it chooses, yet nothing additional to the statutory reward can be claimed by the officer."[9] The state's high court in 1877 expressed the same concern, noting that the statutes defining the duties of the county clerks had been amended repeatedly, whereas the statute defining their fees had not. New legislation would be necessary "to make certain and definite the fees to which county clerks are entitled for their services under the various laws now in force, essentially different as these laws are from those in force at the time of the adoption of the fee bill."[10] The U.S. attorney general in 1883 pointed out the same difficulty in the case of federal court officers: since the enactment of the fee statute, "there has been much new legislation, and a variety of suits have been carried on that were not contemplated at the time of the passage of the original fee [statute]."[11]

Of course, a conscientious and technocratic legislature might monitor the evolution of official services and constantly amend the fee schedule accordingly, but legislatures were not often conscientious or technocratic. Fee levels mattered for the incomes of patronage appointees and the burdens on various constituencies. Adjustments involved political deals, and it was too much of a logistical and political headache for the legislature to make such adjustments whenever it enacted new substantive law that altered officers' duties, much less when officers' duties changed organically. As one economist observed in 1898, fees "when once fixed are not likely to be changed very soon. The inertia of such legislation is very great; all the political forces are against it."[12]

## EFFECTS OF THE MISMATCHES:
## IRRATIONAL EFFORTS AND "CORRUPT" EXCHANGE

When statutory fee schedules were mismatched with the actual business pressures on officers, two alternative dangers might arise. First, the officer might respect the statute, taking only the payments it allowed, but also respond to the irrational incentives that this created, thus allocating his effort disproportionately toward the subset of services to which statutory fees happened to be attached. When New York law granted trial judges fees for some classes of business but not others, one commentator warned in 1839 that this was "a temptation to devote too exclusively [the judge's] attention to this fee-ing business."[13] Henry Bixby Hemenway, a prolific writer on administration and public health, elaborated on the problem in 1914: "[T]he fee compensation [of officers] tends to give the preference to matters paying the larger fees, rather than to the affairs which are essentially the most important, or the most urgent."[14]

The second alternative danger was that the officer and the person seeking the service, in cases in which the statute did not allow the latter to pay the former, would engage in extra-statutory negotiation to ensure the job got done. Perhaps the officer, unenthusiastic about doing the subset of his duties that were inadequately paid, would demand money from the layperson. Or perhaps the layperson, fearing that the officer would refuse work for which the law did not allow enough pay, would make the offer without direct prompting. In either case, the statutory gap resulted in a "corrupt" payment.

Such exchanges were extremely common because they had constituted the often-legal way of doing things for centuries prior to the novel imposition of absolute statutory control. Such control became the ideal of lawmakers, judges, and (apparently) the bien-pensant middle class. But old habits died hard. The eighteenth-century justifications for nonstatutory charges—voluntariness, custom, and just recompense—survived in the folk understandings of many officers and recipients of the nineteenth century. So did the loose reading of statutes to permit charges for "extra" service, plus even the idea that statutes could become obsolete.

This can be illustrated by some events in New York City during the 1870s. When rumors arose in 1878 that Henry Gumbleton, the county clerk and a Tammany mainstay, was taking "illegal and exorbitant fees," he held a public meeting of friendly lawyers who regularly purchased his services. Gumbleton told the meeting that the "extra charges" had "originated about 25 years ago, and had [their] origin in the fact that it was necessary at certain times to expedite the business of the office." Some of the lawyers supported Gumbleton by saying that they "never knew of an unreasonable or unfair charge" under this heading, and that the officer "never exacts the extra fee; it is optional with the lawyer."[15] Similar ideas were articulated that same year by William Quincy, another Tammany man and a top administrator in the county sheriff's office, in charge of taking bail on civil process. According to an anonymous source, Quincy, when confronted with the mismatch between the fee statute and his office's charges for taking bail, replied: "It is the universal practice of the bar of this city to pay $10 extra. If I could only get the legal fees of 37 ½ cents, I never would accept the bail offered by any defendant. . . . If the person under arrest seems inclined to give [my subordinates] $5 or $10 for extra politeness received, I know of no law that hinders the acceptance of the gift. As far as fees go, I am willing to stand before the Governor [in a removal proceeding for misconduct] or any one else."[16] At another point, Quincy was said to have insisted, in demanding a nonstatutory fee, that it was the "usual" payment.[17]

As it turned out, the New York City Bar Association did initiate removal proceedings, before Governor Lucius Robinson, against Gumbleton and against Quincy's boss, Sheriff Bernard Reilly. Gumbleton continued to loudly assert the custom argument, despite its having lost force in elite legal circles, though he apparently dropped voluntariness and reasonable recompense, and hedged by adding a variety of other defenses having nothing to do with the ancient doctrines.[18] To no avail: Robinson removed Gumbleton, vociferously denouncing the custom argument in strong positivist terms. Indeed, the governor thought Gumbleton's willingness to make the custom argument aggravated his crime: "[W]here a public officer stands out as a bold and habitual violator of the statutes of the state, and defiantly justifies his guilt by that of his predecessors, a toleration of his course will naturally and surely lead to the disregard of all law in the community and to a state of anarchy."[19] When Reilly's removal proceeding unfolded a few months later, Quincy did not dare mount any legal defense of nonstatutory payments; he simply denied taking any.[20] The same went for his boss, Reilly, who said he delegated all fee-taking to his subordinates, had no share in what they took, and did not know of their nonstatutory charges.[21]

These stories reveal that extra-statutory exchange between officers and recipients lived on, premised on the inadequacy of the statutes to the business at hand, as well as informal folk justifications descended from the old common-law doctrines. But officers who actually faced elite, formal law dared not assert these folk ideas, or, if they did, they were severely punished. To be sure, officers in less adversarial settings did sometimes mention such justifications without suffering punishment, though they usually donned the fig leaf that the service at issue was "unofficial"—the only excuse still countenanced by formal law. Thus, when the health officer of New York City, who ran the quarantine system for incoming ships, admitted before a legislative committee in 1881 that he took a nonstatutory fee for boarding vessels at night, he was careful to note—in addition to invoking voluntariness and custom—that night work was not encompassed by his statutory duties.[22] Even then, elite observers disparaged the payment as unfortunate and improper. The committee in its report, which the governor quoted approvingly in his annual message of 1884, had "no hesitation in saying that such a state of things ought not to exist with any officer of the State authorized to collect fees."[23] The *New York Times* called the fee an "unauthorized practice," adding that "[i]rregularities like this" were "needless impositions upon the commerce of the port."[24] What the *Times* ignored, in calling the fee an "imposition," was that it arose to facilitate the provision of a service that shipowners strongly desired but for which the statute did not provide.[25] The fee system maintained its capacity to foster mutually beneficial negotiation and flexibility, but within much tighter constraints and under a cloud of suspicion.

## GIVING UP ON PRICE REGULATION AND ABOLISHING FACILITATIVE PAYMENTS ALTOGETHER

The dynamics described above fueled the perception, widespread during the mid- to late nineteenth century, that fee-based compensation of officers, even when formally under absolute statutory control, led unavoidably to nonstatutory fee-taking, which was now defined as "corruption." The period from the late eighteenth to early nineteenth centuries had witnessed a quest by lawmakers and jurists to subject facilitative payments to positive law. But these reforms clashed with the logic of negotiation that had always been the essence of such payments. The conflict between the system's essence and its reformed structure meant it was perpetually falling short of professed ideals.

I think this is the best way to make sense of the widespread assertions of various observers, which might seem puzzling at first glance, that the statutory system of lawful fees was the root cause of officers' tendency to take unlawful fees, meaning that the best way to rid the nation of unlawful fees was to abolish lawful fees and instead compensate officers by salary. The *New York Times* adopted this reasoning when it criticized the health officer's nonstatutory fee for night boarding in 1881: such "[i]rregularities" were "sufficiently numerous to give additional weight to the argument . . . against the present fee system" and in favor of salaries.[26] In 1871, the *Albany Law Journal* suggested that "very much official corruption" could "be prevented by uniformly paying public officers salaries, instead of allowing them fees." Noting the "prevalence" of the practice "of charging illegal fees," the journal posited that converting to salaries would cause "very many of the petty extortions which disgrace our public service" to "disappear."[27] In 1884, a Maine congressman, after a long investigation of the fee system, concluded that it was "a temptation to wrongdoing, and should, as far as practicable, be abolished."[28] Frank Goodnow, in a book on administrative law in 1893, said the fee system's "disadvantage is to be found in the fact that on account of the smallness of the fee usually required [i.e., fixed by statute], extortion is not infrequently practiced by officers and submitted to by the public."[29] Newspaper writers made similar points across the nation.[30] Justice John Dean of the Pennsylvania Supreme Court, looking back in 1895 on his state's replacement of statutory fees with salaries, recalled that fees' abolition was intended to remove "all motive for illegal exactions,"[31] for the old system "held out a constant temptation to extortion upon the public by the officers."[32] A federal court clerk, urging Congress to convert the clerks' offices to salaries in 1918, summed it up: "The fee system is now almost universally regarded as . . . conducive to petty graft."[33]

The problem was not only that every statutory fee schedule's inevitable incompleteness and crudeness led officers and recipients to engage in nonstatutory exchange. It was also that the statutory regulations could be manipulated in various ways by the officers. When recipients or officers felt that a statutory schedule needed a little "adjustment," they could give or receive a nonstatutory sum outright, but it was often easier (and less detectable) for the officer to charge, and the recipient to acquiesce in paying, a sum that fell within the statutory scheme by some stretched interpretation. This dynamic was identified by Montesquieu back in 1748. Urging a blanket prohibition on payments to officers, as opposed to letting them take regulated payments, he warned that regulations opened the way for endless manipulation: "[I]t is easier to convict the one who ought to take nothing but takes something than it is to convict the one who takes more when he ought to take less and who always finds plausible pretexts, excuses, causes and reasons for doing so."[34]

Complaints about officers' manipulative interpretation of statutory fee schedules arose just as soon as American lawmakers and jurists started clamping down on nonstatutory payments. Once officers were legally confined to taking their fees on the basis of the statute, they tended to find that every labor they performed fell within one of the service definitions (allowing a charge), and often that the service could be subdivided so it counted as more than one service and fell within more than one definition (allowing more charges), and often that one service required ancillary services that were also enumerated (yet more charges!).[35] Lawmakers discovered that their regulations never constrained officers as strongly as they hoped.

Complaints of such behavior began in the 1700s in Maryland and North Carolina, which (not coincidentally) were among the first colonies to assert absolute statutory control. The Maryland House of Delegates in 1771 lamented that the current statutory schedule was "so loosely expressed, that not a few of the officers . . . palliate their excessive charges from the doubtfulness of its expressions."[36] The North Carolina rebel leader Herman Husband recounted that, when he confronted court officers about their aggressive charges, they insisted that applying the statutory schedule to their labors was a complicated undertaking: "[The officers] generally tell me that it takes a good lawyer to make out a fee-bill, and that few men in the Province could do it . . . , and intimated it as vain and a crime for any common man to pretend to understand the fee-bill."[37] A committee of the North Carolina assembly believed the statute would be an effective constraint if only the schedule were simpler and therefore understandable by the recipients, who would then have the knowledge to resist improper charges. It therefore recommended in 1771 that an "explanatory act . . . be passed and that the same be ascertained in a plain manner suitable to the understanding of every capacity."[38]

The same courts that consolidated the nineteenth century's new positivist concept of fees also tried to address the problem of officers' manipulative construction of the (now all-important) statutes. John Gibson, the revered chief justice of Pennsylvania, imposed a strict interpretation on the fee statute for justices of the peace in 1827, solemnly pronouncing that "[n]othing is more liable to abuse than the right which the law gives to compensation for official services, and nothing requires to be more strictly guarded."[39] But a judicial principle disfavoring abusive interpretations of a statute was much less precise, and harder to enforce, than a principle disfavoring payments that lacked any statutory basis. Also, as a practical matter, not every fee transaction was going to be litigated, which meant that most interpretations of fee statutes, day to day, would be done not by disinterested courts but by the fee-taking officers themselves. Even in the case of officers (such as court clerks) who took their fees by approval of a judge, the judge typically was not a proactive monitor of his subordinates' charges, instead relying on citizens to come to him with complaints.[40]

The great hope was for service recipients to protect themselves, but for that to happen, the fee schedule had to be comprehensible to them. Another Pennsylvania judge in 1844 concluded that the only "efficient remedy" for "abuses" of the fee statute was "to simplify" it "in such a manner that it may be easily understood by suitors, making the items to consist of as few particulars as possible," since it was "impracticable for men to protect rights which they do not understand."[41] But simplification caused problems of its own: the simpler the list of services, the more it would fail to reflect officers' actual business and labor, potentially aggravating the problems that led officers and recipients to depart from (or stretch) the statute to begin with.

Legislators who tried to simplify the fee schedule and suppress officers' manipulative constructions found themselves playing an endless, exhausting, and darkly comic game of cat and mouse against the fee takers. The New York legislature in 1844 made a laborious investigation of the state's probate judges and found that they were making numerous barely plausible interpretations to increase their charges.[42] The legislature amended the fee statute in a way that (it believed) would cut off all the abuses. Yet, while "there should have been no doubt" about the reformed schedule's meaning, the officers by 1845 were using their "ingenuity and devices" to make yet more questionable charges, prompting a legislative committee to warn that the probate judges "may devise some further innovations unless expressly restrained" and to propose yet another round of amendments "for the purpose of removing all ground for doubt."[43] Similarly, congressmen in 1852 were confident they had devised a fee statute for federal clerks, marshals, and U.S. attorneys that was "explicit and definite, so as to prevent abuses arising from ingenious constructions."[44] And yet, a few

decades later, one federal judge told Congress that the schedule was "so indefi-
nite" and left "so much open to construction as to make bills very confusing and
uncertain,"[45] and another said that only one person in all of Massachusetts was
"perfectly cognizant" of the federal fee statute's meaning: the (fee-taking) clerk
of the U.S. Circuit Court![46] A third federal judge said it best: "[I]t is hard for
human ingenuity to discover language for the purpose [of fee regulation] which
may not be perverted by ingenious misconstructions."[47]

Reformers gradually concluded that legislators could not win the game of cat
and mouse and should therefore stop playing, that is, put officers on salary. A
New York legislative committee in 1839 noted that "the construction of the law
of fees" by the state's court clerks was the object of "[m]uch complaint," but the
committee announced it had "abrogated all temptation to [the abuse's] future
practice, by proposing to change the compensation" of the officers "to a fixed
salary."[48] Similarly, the commissioners of the U.S. General Land Office in the
1870s and 1880s told Congress that field officers were making excessive charges
against land-grant applicants, who were all too willing to pay them, in order
to win friendly treatment from the officers.[49] To prevent overcharges, which
occurred "under the forms of the law," one commissioner thought the best solution was to cut off even the lawful fees and convert the officers to salaries.[50]

To be sure, the substitution of salaries for lawful fees was not a panacea for
the problem of unlawful fee-taking. It was quite possible for a salaried officer to
demand or receive illegal payments from service recipients.[51] Still, lawmakers
had very good reasons to believe that, by transferring officers from statutory fees
to salaries, they were removing a major aggravating factor that promoted unlawful charges. The statutory fee system invited officers and recipients to agree
upon unlawful charges because it created a particularized class of services that
legitimately needed to be performed yet were uncompensated (or inadequately
compensated) by law. It also signaled a generalized moral approval of exchange
between officer and recipient, and it established, as a matter of office practice,
a cash nexus between the two, which could be used as a cover for charges that
pushed the edge of the law or went beyond it. It was much easier for enforcers, recipients, and officers themselves to recognize the illegality of exchanges
where they were not allowed at all, as opposed to being allowed restrictively.

The positivist reformers of the Upper South during the eighteenth century
and of the rest of America during the nineteenth century had sought to banish negotiation from official compensation, and this turned out to require not
merely regulating officer-recipient exchange but abolishing it altogether. Negotiation was too inherent an aspect of exchange to be expunged, unless exchange
itself was suppressed.[52]

## A RELATED REGULATORY CHALLENGE: ABOLISHING
## FACILITATIVE PAYMENTS TO LIMIT OFFICERS' TOTAL INCOME

The quest to prevent corrupt exchange was not the only regulatory challenge that pushed lawmakers to give up on facilitative payments and adopt salaries instead. There was also the regulatory challenge of preventing each individual officer from earning too high an income in the aggregate, which became acute as certain nineteenth-century developments caused officers' total incomes to rise higher than ever before.

Hostility to men making fortunes in public office was a deep-rooted feature of American political culture. As discussed in the Introduction, civic republican leaders of the revolutionary period, such as Franklin, had tried to divorce political power from self-interest and ensure the reign of virtue by prohibiting official income altogether. Although Americans recognized this as a utopian ideal unreachable in a society that lacked enough landed gentlemen to staff its whole government, they did agree that public office should not be too remunerative. The authors of Pennsylvania's revolutionary constitution in 1776 recognized that when "a man is called into public service . . . he has a right to a reasonable compensation," but they feared that lucrative offices would sow "faction, contention, corruption, and disorder among the people." So they mandated that "whenever an office, through increase of fees or otherwise, becomes so profitable as to occasion many to apply for it, the profits ought to be lessened by the legislature."[53] This attitude remained strong in the next century. "It is not according to the genius of our systems," observed a Boston judge in 1827, "to provide a liberal compensation for public servants."[54] The attitude only grew stronger with the rise of Jacksonian egalitarianism, which said that government should never privilege one white man over another. As a Jacksonian newspaper proclaimed in 1831, officers "should not be raised by distinctive marks or unusual incomes, above their fellow-citizens."[55] In 1870, a delegate to the Illinois constitutional convention urged that fees be abolished if their totals grew too high, so they would "not go to establish and maintain these [officers] as aristocrats or nobles."[56]

Though lawmakers by the mid-1800s asserted the power to fix the facilitative payment for each particular service that an officer might perform, they initially did not think to regulate or even monitor the officer's total income, which rose and fell with the aggregate number of services provided.[57] But as population grew and office technology advanced, it became increasingly apparent that the total facilitative payments earned by a single officer could grow to a large sum, especially in a big city. "This fee system was put into existence some sixty odd years ago," editorialized the *Atlanta Constitution* in 1897, "when it was never thought there would be such a big town as Atlanta in the state. Now these fees and perquisites have grown to an enormous amount."[58] A delegate to the Illinois constitutional convention in 1870, recounting the advent of printed forms during his tenure as a county recorder, explained that fee incomes in many offices had increased because of "the facility with which county business is now transacted."[59]

The total incomes of individual officers, particularly in big cities, increasingly became the subject of excited gossip and alarm. A Michigan newspaper in 1897 explained that, "as officials do not report the [total] amount of fees collected, their compensation is frequently far beyond what the most liberal would think a fair salary for the work performed."[60] Rumors spread of burgeoning incomes in big-city offices. Estimates at midcentury for the largest cities ranged from $15,000 to $50,000 per office per year.[61] By the 1890s, certain county officers, particularly in urban areas like New York City and Chicago, were whispered to make $20,000, $50,000, and even $100,000 per year.[62]

As such incomes came to light, lawmakers came under pressure to control them. Theoretically, a legislature might have regulated officers' total incomes by fiddling with the statutory prices that were fixed for each individual service. But that solution was apparently not workable, for reasons similar to those that hobbled the effort to regulate individual exchanges, described earlier in this chapter. The legislature might reduce the prices for certain particular services in an effort to control the officer's total income, but future changes in the demand for services and the technologies for providing them were unknowable and might swell the total once again, or the officer might find new ways to manipulate the schedule that would have the same effect. This is presumably what the economist Thomas K. Urdahl had in mind when he concluded in 1898 that "it is almost impossible to invent a fee bill [i.e., fee schedule] for an office which has been yielding $50,000 a year so as to make it yield only $5,000. The easiest way for legislation to accomplish its purpose [to keep down the officer's total income] is to place the office on a salary."[63] As with the regulatory challenge of corrupt exchange, so with the regulatory challenge of too-high total incomes: salarization was a crude but sure means to solve the problem.

Thus, as the fee totals of officers grew, critics frequently cited their bigness as a sufficient reason for salarization. As one newspaper said in 1849: "The evil of the system of paying public officers by fees instead of salaries, is shown by the fact that the fees of the Health Officer in New York are estimated to amount to over thirty thousand dollars annually—while some persons estimate them even as high as seventy thousand."[64] The fee system in Baltimore, attested a delegate to the Maryland constitutional convention in 1851, "paid to [officers] a sum far beyond what was required to furnish the requisite ability, industry, and integrity for the offices in question. What was the remedy? The only mode would be to let the legislature fix a salary, justly proportioned to the services performed, and make such a disposition of the surplus fees as [lawmakers] might think proper."[65] Looking back on a salarization statute of 1871, the supreme court of Indiana explained that, until its passage, "a demand existed upon the part of the people for a reform in the laws awarding compensation to county officials, as it was manifest that under the fee system these officers, in many of the more populous counties, were too highly rewarded for their services," and the salarization law "was accepted" by the people "as supplying their demand."[66] In New Jersey, where state officers made "little fortunes annually," one newspaper reported in 1879 that "[p]ublic sentiment has demanded, with growing vigor each year, that the officers be given fair salaries, and that the enormous receipts of their offices go into the State Treasury."[67] A commentator on constitutional reform in Tennessee wrote in 1916: "Probably no change is more widely insisted upon than the abolition of the fee system of remunerating county officials. Instances are on record of fees to a single official running above $50,000 a year."[68]

Hostility to high official earnings sprang not only from populist outrage but also from the fear that high income attracted "the wrong kind of person" to public office, especially since incumbents were chosen through elections or patronage—methods susceptible to unscrupulous tactics, which hopefuls were more likely to exploit the more money they could get. The argument was a direct descendent of eighteenth-century aspirations to banish self-interest from the political process. "The effect of such excessive perquisites," warned one commentator on the fee system in 1849, "is to stimulate [hopefuls] to resort to mean and despicable ways to obtain office, and to sacrifice every noble principle of their natures to retain it."[69] The "result" of the fee system's high incomes, pronounced the *New York Times* in 1884, was "that men are nominated for these positions with no regard for their qualifications for the duties to be performed"—"they practically buy their election as well as their nomination. . . . The cure for the evil is obvious. In the first place, the officers themselves should be deprived of direct personal interest in the fees paid for a public service by being themselves remunerated by fixed salaries."[70] "The present [fee] system," lamented a Texan reformer in 1894, "makes public office a matter of speculative value and gambling fever. . . . This fee system fills your counties with candidates for office and leads to a reckless and corrupt expenditure of money to obtain votes."[71] The public administration professor John Fairlie wrote in 1906: "[I]n populous counties many county officers receive very large

[fee] incomes. . . . Such offices are the goal of unscrupulous politicians; and are a constant incentive to corrupt political methods."[72]

The notion that large total incomes corrupted the political process grew even stronger because the fee system came to be associated with political machines. Under the spoils system, a share of every officer's fees went into machine coffers, through the "assessments" which the machine made on the income of all offices in its gift.[73] In itself, though, this was no reason for machines to prefer fees to salaries, since they assessed official salaries, too. However, it was politically easier to preserve a high official income in the opaque form of a fee total than in the transparent form of a salary; the conversion of a lucrative fee-paid office to salary generally meant a reduction in the office's income.[74] Insofar as fee-paid offices tended to be richer than salaried ones, they provided a larger "base" for the machine to assess. Also, lucrative fee-paid offices served as rewards that the machine could hold out to its workers for meritorious service.[75] Accordingly, party machines would sometimes become the protectors of high-earning fee offices against lawmakers' proposals for salarization.[76] As the fee system became increasingly identified as a source of machine funding that machines protected, the sharpening of reform sentiment against those machines made the fee system more of a target.[77]

----●●----

The twin regulatory challenges discussed in this chapter—preventing corrupt individual exchanges and preventing too-high official incomes—proved so difficult to meet by tinkering with statutory fee schedules that lawmakers opted to jettison such schedules altogether and adopt salaries instead. So long as officers could make exchanges for profit with the lay public, those exchanges (and the total incomes they produced) were practically impossible to regulate. But as we shall see in the next chapter, these were not the only reasons that lawmakers abolished facilitative payments. They also soured on the very idea of officer-layperson exchange, irrespective of the problems of regulating it.

# 4

---●●●---

# A GOVERNMENT CAPABLE OF SAYING NO

*Salaries as a Reaction against Customer Service*

The principle that facilitative payments had to be fixed by legislation, which prevailed among lawmakers and judges by 1850, was not enough to kill profit-seeking "customer service" in American government. Customer service lived on. This was partly because officers and service recipients continued to reach individualized bargains over the prices of services (albeit illegally), as recounted in Chapter 3. It was also because, even in cases where officers and service recipients conformed to uniform statutory prices, fees still caused officers to view recipients *as a class* as their "customer base." They continued to cater to the wishes of that base, for they wanted to encourage its members to keep showing up and requesting services. This pattern of reciprocity persisted—and sometimes even intensified—in several areas of government from the mid-1800s through the early 1900s, as this chapter documents.

This chapter also shows how lawmakers by the early 1900s had become disenchanted with the very idea of reciprocity between officials and laypersons. This disenchantment was a further reason that they abolished facilitative payments (on top of the unworkability of price regulation and public hostility to official lucre, discussed in Chapter 3).

Officials who lived by facilitative payments tended to cater to the needs of service recipients, paying relatively little attention to other interests that were less immediate and more diffuse. This comparatively one-dimensional approach to administration came to seem increasingly out of place around the turn of the twentieth century. It was inconsistent with a new pattern that was coming to characterize American politics: mass interest-group rivalry. That is, Americans increasingly mobilized and organized to advocate for interests and values that had previously been diffuse and voiceless—the very kinds of interests and values that customer-focused officers had ignored. Relatedly, an increasing sense of scarcity overtook political discourse. Compared to the nineteenth century, it seemed by the early 1900s that every grant of governmental largesse came at the expense of some other pressing interest or value. To stop officers from catering too exclusively to the desires of service recipients, lawmakers increasingly vested decision-making power in salaried officers. Salarization severed the bond of customer-seller reciprocity between officials and service recipients, vesting the former with the financial independence to say no to the latter. Officers thus acquired the capacity to give more attention to a wider range of interests than under the old customer-focused regime. This is not to say that salaried officials were always careful in how they balanced competing interests. In the worst cases, salarization replaced crude indulgence of recipients with an equally crude indifference to their needs. In general, however, the new salaried regime better accommodated the diversity and rivalry of interests that came to characterize modern political life.[1]

I trace this story through three case studies. The first is the process for deciding immigrants' applications for citizenship, conducted by federal and state judges and court clerks. The second is the process for deciding veterans' applications for disability benefits, conducted by federal examining surgeons. The third is the process for deciding Western settlers' applications for land under the Homestead Act and other settlement laws, conducted by the registers and receivers of federal land offices. Each of the three systems has been the subject of prior secondary work, but no scholar has analyzed the role of facilitative payments in any of the systems in depth.[2]

In each of the three case studies, my analysis progresses through the same four points, as reflected in the four numbered sections of each case study. First, I show that, during the pre-salary era in each system, decision makers possessed wide discretion and generally used it to treat applicants liberally. Second, I argue that a major reason for decision makers' liberality was the profit motive. They wanted to maximize facilitative payments. Many of the adjudicators received fees only when they granted applications. And even the adjudicators who received a fee for every application they processed (whether they granted it or not) had reason to build reputations for generosity, to attract more "customers" in the future. Third, I point out that, in the case of each system during its pre-salary period, congressmen knew that the system was generous and rejected administrative reforms to make it less so. That is, fee-driven liberality was not corrupt or accidental but a deliberate legislative choice to confer benefits freely.[3] Fourth, I show how lawmakers turned against facilitative payments amid the intensified interest-group rivalry and perceived scarcity of the early 1900s. In the case of naturalization, this took the form of the nativist movement, which argued that free admission of immigrants to the polity diluted the value of native-born citizens' votes. In the case of veterans' benefits, it took the form of (1) the fiscal transition from the tariff to income taxes and corporate taxes, which rendered taxation more visible and concentrated, and (2) the fiscal strain of new spending, especially for World War I, which forced lawmakers to be more careful about claims on the Treasury. In the case of land applications, it took the form of the conservation movement, which demanded that land claims be scrutinized more carefully and in some areas halted altogether, for the sake of future users and sustainable use.

I believe that the basic story of each case study—an initial regime of fee-driven liberality and reciprocity, then a reaction arising from interest-group rivalry and perceived scarcity, then a salary reform that alienated officials from their "customers" and rendered them more responsive to other interests—has much wider application. It fits with perhaps the best study of facilitative payments in the literature, Allen Steinberg's book on low-level magistrates in Philadelphia. These officers, known as aldermen, handled the initial stage of the criminal process. Their job was to forward meritorious accusations to the city's grand jury and its superior courts. Accusations often came from laypersons living in the neighborhood, and because aldermen received a modest fee for every case, they treated these lay accusers as customers, forwarding their complaints with little discrimination or scrutiny. This meant that laypersons—most of them poor and many of them female and/or black—had ready access to the protection of the criminal law when they thought themselves victimized. They approached criminal justice as a trusted and familiar institution, responsive to their need for protection and dispute resolution. By the 1870s, however, a coalition formed—consisting of overburdened officials of the superior court, grand jurors, prison reformers, and city business leaders—which argued that the city's criminal justice system was overloaded, that the supposedly petty tribulations of poor Philadelphians were not important enough to deserve the attention of the criminal law, and that the system's resources should be conserved and carefully targeted at "a special 'dangerous' class of citizens," who, in the view of reformers, were its "proper objects." This coalition succeeded in converting the aldermen to salaries, which—combined with a few other reforms—made them far less indulgent toward lay accusers. This limited the access of the city's poor to criminal law's protection.[4] The essential dynamic that Steinberg discerns in Philadelphia criminal justice has much wider application, as

I aim to demonstrate below in the stories of citizenship, veterans' benefits, and Western land.

## DECIDING IMMIGRANTS' APPLICATIONS FOR NATURALIZATION

Facilitative payments did much to foster the liberality of naturalization throughout the nineteenth century. When salaries came in the early twentieth century, they did much to kill that liberality.

To appreciate the stakes of the shift, we must begin with a sense of why naturalization mattered. The period from the early nineteenth century to the early twentieth century saw a titanic influx of immigrants. The foreign-born share of the U.S. population rose rapidly from the 1820s to the 1850s and reached a high plateau, where it generally stayed until the restrictive legislation of the 1920s.[5] For huge numbers of these immigrants, U.S. citizenship was the precondition for valuable rights, mostly determined by state law,[6] the foremost being the right to vote. Though some states permitted aliens to vote, those states mostly shifted to requiring citizenship by the early twentieth century,[7] and the big northeastern states with the nation's largest foreign-born populations—New York, Pennsylvania, and Massachusetts—always required citizenship.[8] The right to vote was particularly precious because one's vote provided access to the local party machine, with its favors and protections, which were necessities in the era before the welfare state.[9] The days before an election always saw long lines of immigrants eager to be naturalized.[10]

### 1. Loose Criteria, Official Discretion, and Liberality

From the founding era through the early twentieth century, Congress vested the power to naturalize immigrants not only in the federal courts but also in state courts, so long as they were courts of record, with "common law jurisdiction, and a seal and clerk."[11] Given the breadth of this category (covering lots of minor local tribunals), a large and motley class of courts had power to naturalize. By about 1900, they numbered more than five thousand.[12]

When immigrants came to court seeking citizenship, what did they have to show? The criteria for naturalization were set by federal statute. Initially, the applicant had to be a "free white person."[13] People of African background became eligible after the Civil War, but restrictions remained in place excluding Asians, and those continued well into the twentieth century.[14] Husbands' and wives' citizenship were independent until 1855, when Congress declared that a man's U.S. citizenship automatically gave the same status to his wife, if she were otherwise eligible. This principle, too, continued well into the 1900s.[15]

European men—the large majority of applicants and the focus of my discussion—became citizens upon meeting three requirements. These requirements remained largely the same from the 1820s to the big reform of 1906.[16] Taken together, they gave courts great discretion to be liberal, if they chose.[17]

The first requirement was residency. The court had to be "satisfied" that the alien had lived in the United States for five years, and in the state where the court was located for one year.[18] But the law did not say how a court was to "satisfy" itself. Some courts required one witness to corroborate the applicant's story, others two.[19] There was little else to go on, for as yet, there were no official records of when people entered the country.[20]

The second requirement was that the applicant have made, at least two years prior to his application, an in-court declaration of his intent to become a citizen.[21] But the law did not require the immigrant to produce any certificate of his prior declaration, nor any particular kind of proof that he had made it.[22] Even when courts asked for a certificate (which they usually did), the applicant could claim that he'd received one from the court but lost it, in which case the court could give him a replacement, often doing little to verify his identity.[23] Moreover, the applicant was excused from the declaration requirement altogether if he demonstrated "to the satisfaction of the court" that he had been living in the United States going back at least three years before his twenty-first birthday and had intended (in his own mind) to become a citizen for at least two years.[24] On this point, a court needed nothing beyond the applicant's say-so.[25] According to critics, this exception invited mass fraud,[26] though it may be that many applicants, coming from peasant societies, did not know their true ages and were not so much lying as guessing in their own favor.[27]

The third requirement was character and loyalty. It had to "appear to [the court's] satisfaction" that the applicant, during his U.S. residency, had "behaved as a man of a good moral character, attached to the principles of the Constitution of the United States, and well disposed to the good order and happiness" of the nation.[28] As with residency, the applicant usually brought one or two witnesses to vouch for him on this point. It was easy and common for the courts to take the witnesses' word for it.[29] (Critics bemoaned this liberal norm, insisting that the law implicitly required the court to scrutinize the witnesses closely or to quiz the applicant to see that he actually understood the "leading principles" of the U.S. Constitution.)[30]

The three criteria left much room for the court to be liberal, and furthermore, there was no opposing party to push back against the applicant's claims, pose tough questions, or dig up counterevidence.[31] Nativist organizations sometimes sent "challengers" to ask questions at naturalization hearings just prior to elections,[32] but courts might halt this practice as an "encroachment on the rights of the alien,"[33] and, in any event, this was not viable as a comprehensive or permanent solution. If inquiries were to be consistently searching, the initiative would have to come from the government itself, and the government's only representative, in this period, was the court.

In general, courts of the nineteenth century used their discretion to give applicants famously (or notoriously) liberal treatment. "Naturalization proceedings in the 19th century," states one historian, "were extremely loose and casually administered," and many immigrants, "particularly in the large eastern cities, voted with fraudulent papers."[34] Judges and clerks freely admitted the absence of scrutiny and the applicants' near-universal success.[35] Nativists denounced the process as outrageously permissive.[36]

The courts' solicitude toward applicants was evident not only in the liberality of their decisions but also in other customer-friendly acts. A New York City court in the 1840s kept interpreters on hand (presumably German) to help applicants just prior to elections.[37] Courts made special efforts to accommodate large numbers of immigrants when they showed up before a fast-approaching election. Describing a New York City court in 1840, one attorney explained that, "during an election," the court found it "necessary," given "the number of applicants," "to make systematic and rigid arrangements for preparing the documents, and for the ingress and egress of persons, so as to expedite business and prevent confusion."[38] Judges, clerks, and observers estimated that the city's courts managed to naturalize one immigrant every two to six minutes during the preelection crush.[39] Courts were permissive in allowing a single witness to vouch for numerous applicants, sometimes "twenty or thirty," or "50, 60, or 100."[40]

## 2. Facilitative Payments as a Cause of Officials' Liberality

Why were the courts so liberal? Previous scholars have focused on officials' loyalty to the local party machine, which wanted aliens naturalized to get more votes.[41] This was certainly important. But another big factor—which could reinforce the officers' party-machine loyalty but also operate independently of it—was the pecuniary stake that officials had in the applications.

Though federal statutes said nothing about fees for naturalization services,[42] state legislatures frequently recognized and regulated fees for those services in state courts. In New York, for example, the legislature in the early 1800s set the "fees in full on granting [a] certificate of naturalization" at $2.50.[43] The fee was paid only when the application was granted,[44] which was presumably justified on the ground that a grant involved more paperwork than a denial. In one of New York City's three big naturalization courts—named the Marine Court because some of its business focused on sailors[45]—all fees went directly to the three judges, who shared them with the clerk.[46] In the city's other two big naturalization courts—the Superior Court and the Court of Common Pleas—the fees went entirely to the clerks, not to the judges.[47]

Thus, the clerks of all three courts, as well as the judges of the Marine Court, stood to make money the more aliens they naturalized. Even in the Superior Court and the Court of Common Pleas, where the pecuniary stake was confined to the clerks, the profit motive very likely influenced the naturalization process. The efficiency and attitude of the clerk determined the speed at which a court naturalized.[48] Further, it seems likely that clerks affected the substance of decisions. In all three courts, it was standard for the clerks to examine the applicants and witnesses before the judge did.[49] The degree to which judges relied on clerks' recommendations is not entirely clear, but they probably relied heavily, given the press of business prior to elections.[50]

Immigrants seeking citizenship were customers of the New York City courts, and the courts competed for them. It was lawful and common for an applicant rejected in one court to go straight to another and succeed.[51] As the newspaper editor Loring D. Chapin wrote to Congress in 1838, naturalization was "a well-known matter of competition among the courts," as the "fees" for granting citizenship yielded "a large revenue." So it was "not . . . a matter of wonder that [the courts] gladly naturalize all who make application, and that, too, without putting such questions to the applicants and to the witnesses as would deprive them of the advantages of the fee; nor is it singular that the clerk . . . should hurry through the few ceremonies, without regard to particulars."[52] An attorney in 1845 agreed that "the officers [of the courts] are interested in the fee, and that a competition for the business is created about the time of the election."[53] Nativists therefore believed that abolishing fees would be to their advantage. A nativist and former inspector of elections in 1845 urged the "abolition of all fees for naturalization, so that no pecuniary motive would operate on any officer applied to for that purpose."[54] Pro-immigrant forces also recognized the importance of fees in facilitating naturalization. After Philadelphia Germans organized a vote drive in 1856, one of them gratefully recalled: "We have here three courts where men can be naturalized; and in each of two of these one judge was employed incessantly for weeks before the election, while the [fee-taking] clerks, *who reaped a golden harvest*, did everything to expedite the business."[55]

Vote-seeking party machines often fostered naturalizations by paying the fees of friendly aliens, who were usually poor.[56] The machine would deposit a pile of cash with the court and give vouchers to prospective applicants. When an applicant showed up with a voucher, the clerk would draw the fee against the machine's cash. All three of New York City's big naturalization courts made such voucher arrangements with party organizations during the 1830s and 1840s.[57] Moreover, all three coupled these arrangements with volume discounts, performing naturalizations for voucher applicants at less than the statutory rate.[58] (It was lawful for courts to sell services for less than the statute said.)[59] The same happened in Philadelphia.[60]

Thus, courts competed for naturalizations not only on the dimensions of liberality and speedy service but also on the dimension of price. Chapin, in an 1838 message to Congress, sardonically recounted the jockeying that occurred in New York City's naturalization market:

> [The Marine Court] does manufacture by far the largest portion of these American freemen; so that a valuable perquisite is secured. . . . In this spirit of competition the court has endeavored to monopolize this profitable kind of business, and, indeed, did so for many years; but when other courts succeeded in obtaining a share of the trade . . . by cutting down the price of fees, the price of the former [i.e., the Marine Court] was regulated [i.e., set by the court], according to the common expression, "as they could light on chaps [i.e., as they could attract customers]." In some instances it was three dollars, in others two, in others one, and in others nothing. Some [presumably professional procurers of applicants], who engaged to bring all they wished to naturalize to that market, were accommodated by the "lump" [i.e., given volume discounts], and "on time" [i.e., given credit]. One of these customers, who dealt very largely in this way, a distinguished partisan and municipal officer, had run up a certain score [i.e., tab] at this court.[61]

Another nativist, Heman Childs, recalled a scene during the 1840 election that vividly reflected the importance of fees: "I saw Henry E. Riell," the president of the New York City Naturalization Society and Tammany Hall's point man for naturalization, "stand near the clerk [of the Marine Court] with quite a number of $5 bills in his hands. . . . As often as two of the papers were passed, he gave the clerk a $5 bill," that is, the statutory fee of $2.50 for each paper. "I should think the time occupied in passing the two [papers] would not exceed seven minutes," added Childs. "There appeared to be very few questions asked."[62] Note that Childs assumed that the clerk *should* be asking questions—that is, clerks were involved in the substance of the decision—and that the clerk's fee-maximizing speed precluded such scrutiny.

We may wonder: Were these fees redundant? Did they merely reinforce the pro-naturalization incentives that big-city judges and clerks had anyway, since they owed their jobs to the machine? Only partly. Fee incentives appear to have operated somewhat independently of the incentives imposed by the machine-as-employer. In New York City, the Democratic machine at Tammany Hall eventually achieved a near monopoly on foreign-born voters, but that had not yet happened during the sharp fee-driven competition of the 1830s. The nascent Whig party initially sought foreign-born votes. As late as 1838 it was playing "a dangerous double game," courting both immigrants and the increasingly assertive nativists.[63] This helps explain why Chapin, writing that year, did not view the naturalization-friendly courts as creatures of the Democratic Party but instead emphasized the "almost equally balanced power of the two contending parties here," which had "impelled rash and over-heated politicians to resort to this . . . most baneful . . . means of adding strength and numbers to their cause," that is, permissive naturalization, whose "spirit" had "infused itself into some of our courts, and evinced itself in a manner in which aliens have purchased, for a bare pittance, the sacred rights of American freemen."[64] Consistent with this, observers in the mid-1840s stated that operatives of both parties—Democrats and Whigs—were (or had been, until recently) escorting aliens to the courts to be naturalized, making voucher arrangements with the courts, paying the fees of applicants, and obtaining volume discounts on those fees.[65] Philadelphia and New Orleans likewise had fee-seeking court officials who each treated both parties as customers.[66]

To be sure, once the fee system helped establish the norm of liberal and speedy naturalization, it was possible for the machines, by filling court offices with their minions, to maintain that norm even when fee compensation disappeared. In the late 1840s and 1850s, the New York state legislature converted the clerks of the Superior Court and the Court of Common Pleas from fees to salaries (for all business, not just naturalization), and it took away the Marine Court's power to naturalize, channeling nearly all applications to the other two courts.[67] Around the same time, the local Democratic machine obtained tighter control over the courts' offices.[68]

Under these conditions, naturalization continued at a steady clip, and Tammany managed to push through the courts an incredible forty thousand applicants for the 1868 elections.[69] This kind of connection between officers and vote-seeking machines continued to promote liberal naturalization across the nation up to the early twentieth century.[70]

### 3. Support for Liberal Administration among Lawmakers and the Public

Fees fueled liberality in naturalization. Such liberality manifested itself in New York City, Philadelphia, and elsewhere at midcentury, and it was known to Congress. Indeed, my principal sources for the foregoing discussion are Congress's investigations of big-city courts. Reformers throughout the 1840s and 1850s importuned Congress to make naturalization harder, both by strengthening the formal criteria and by altering administration so the criteria would be applied more exactly, but their proposals always went down to defeat.[71] There were simply too many pro-immigrant congressmen who liked the easy system, most of them Democrats whose party depended upon foreign-born votes. Apart from the short-lived nativist successes in a few states during the 1840s and 1850s, naturalization restrictionists won little legislation at the state level until the late nineteenth century and almost none at the federal level until the big reform of 1906.

In the debates of the era, reformers seeking tougher naturalization administration often couched their proposals as efforts to prevent "fraud" and promote good government, but pro-immigrant forces refused to accept those assertions at face value. In the view of pro-immigrant types, any "reform" that made it harder for immigrants to become citizens was motivated by hatred of immigrants and should be rejected as such. For instance, when New York state legislators in 1840 proposed various anti-fraud reforms (for example, to stop witnesses from presenting preprinted affidavits and instead make them undergo oral examination), a pro-immigration pamphlet declared that the "object of the bill was to produce delay, and shut out, perchance, on the day of election, some three or four hundred aliens from the privilege of citizens. It would have been still more in keeping with the character of partial legislation . . . to have passed at once a law to close our courts on the day of election."[72] In 1870, when Congress enacted modest reforms pertaining to naturalization fraud, one Democratic congressman proclaimed that "the cry of fraud is a pretext merely. . . . It comes here moved and inspired by [the Republicans'] ancient hate and hostility of the Irish and German voter in particular, and the Catholic population which we have received from foreign countries in general. Its main-spring, its moving motive, is partisan malignity, religious bigotry and intolerance."[73] When the campaign for an overhaul of naturalization administration finally succeeded in 1906, one California congressman found the bill's stringent institutional and procedural framework "entirely too complicated." He predicted that "men who would make entirely satisfactory citizens will be deprived of the blessing of citizenship with no corresponding good in any other direction." And then he revealed his underlying preference: "[S]ubstantially every one who should be permitted to come in [to the United States] should be permitted to enjoy the full blessings, privileges, and burdens of citizenship. . . . [H]aving admitted them to our territory, no good will come from making naturalization complex and difficult."[74]

Liberal administration was a way of approaching universal citizenship for European men, almost as if it were written into substantive law.

Support for liberal naturalization (in both formal criteria and administration) depended upon a widespread sense that immigrant citizens were not using up scarce resources. There was more than enough land and employment for everybody. For example, when the Democratic House Judiciary Committee rejected a petition for tighter naturalization administration in 1846, it declared: "[W]hen our almost boundless wilderness shall be teeming with a dense population; when labor becomes cheap, employment difficult or scarce, and the means of procuring the necessaries of life precarious, then, and not till then, will it be necessary to inquire whether our present policy [of easy naturalization] should be changed."[75]

The same view was expressed by Henry Riell, Tammany's director of naturalization, who (as noted earlier) stood over the clerk of the Marine Court during the 1840 election, handing him $5 for every two naturalizations.[76] During that same election, Riell published a pamphlet defending liberal naturalization. "As a native American," he wrote, "I exult in the triumphant truth that the country which gave me birth, is destined, both politically and physically, to be the free asylum for the oppressed and the distressed of the universal world. As an American, with far more than a million millions of the square acres of my native soil around me, I cannot so far crush my feelings of philanthropy and honest pride as to tell mankind that this wide world affords no asylum for suffering humanity—no refuge for the oppressed. On the contrary I would tell them that it is here without money and without price." "[N]ever had a people so much to give at so slight a sacrifice," concluded Riell, for "the whole commonwealth becomes enriched by the labor, the skill, the industry," which the inflow of foreigners produces.[77]

Riell's use of the fee system arose not from a grubby desire for votes but from a well-articulated ideology of open citizenship. Fee incentives undergirded a coherent vision of governance in which the state should freely dispense the benefit of citizenship, since conferral of the benefit was costless (indeed, positively remunerative) to the polity. Since the grant of citizenship did not harm (indeed, benefited) persons not party to the transaction, it made sense to view it as a simple customer-seller relation.

### 4. The Reaction against Liberality, the Salarization of Officials, and the Alienation of Service Recipients: Nativism Ascendant

Against the liberal view that naturalized immigrants used up no scarce resources and should therefore be encouraged through a generous, transactional, and customer-friendly approach, there arose an opposing view that all this openness and generosity did, in fact, have costs. The new zero-sum thinking was evident as early as the 1830s and 1840s, among the minority of voters and lawmakers who took up nativism at that time. For example, a petition of New Yorkers in 1838, complaining of the substantive generosity of the naturalization laws and the ease of fraud under them, attested that "the great and rapidly increasing influx of foreigners into this country . . . and the indiscriminate freedom with which . . . they are allowed to exercise the elective franchise, are . . . evils which wrongfully deprive *us* of *our* native rights, and fearfully tend to the destruction of *our* Government and *our* liberties."[78] Immigrant votes diluted the value of native citizens' votes and adulterated the governance of native citizens.

Though nativism subsided by the 1860s, it returned, in a more sustained and successful form, in the late nineteenth and early twentieth centuries.[79] One harbinger of this shift was the Chinese Exclusion Act of 1882, which outright banned Chinese immigrants from citizenship. Another was the repeal, by 1900, of alien suffrage in half the states that had once authorized it.[80] Even those who supported open immigration began taking a harder line on the distinct issue of citizenship. For example, the *Nation*, though liberal on immigration, declared in 1893: "The harm [immigrants] do to the country as additions to the voting population is undoubted, notorious, and undeniable"; permissive naturalization "has had an influence on our public men, on our press, and on our legislation of the most deleterious kind. . . . Nearly all the economic absurdities produced on the stump or embodied in legislation are due to a desire to 'capture the foreign vote.'"[81] Whereas "the demand for naturalization reform" through most of the nineteenth century had been driven largely by calculations of partisan advantage, the century's final years witnessed "a new tone of xenophobia and chauvinism," which fed a "growing demand, in Congress and out, for ending our easy naturalization policy."[82]

Furthermore, the surge of nativism received somewhat less pushback from urban political machines than it would have a generation or two earlier. By the late 1800s, machines in several cities, including New York, were so comfortably entrenched that they no longer depended upon the kinds of mass naturalizations that were common at midcentury.[83] In addition, most states by the early twentieth century mandated the secret ballot, thus making it hard for machines to verify that the voters whom they helped become citizens would "deliver the goods" on election day.[84]

*How Restriction Was Initially Thwarted: State Strictures and the Liberality of Fee-Driven Federal Courts, from the Gilded Age to 1906.* Even as nativists began winning laws in state legislatures to tighten naturalization administration in state courts, they saw their plans frustrated by a competing set of institutions: the federal courts, in which fee incentives continued to promote liberality into the early twentieth century. A good illustration can be found in Massachusetts, which ranked fourth among the states in foreign-born population from the mid- to late nineteenth century.

As of the 1880s, the Massachusetts legislature permitted the state's Superior Courts to naturalize immigrants, which they did in large numbers,[85] no doubt partly because their clerks earned fees for naturalizations (along with all other court business).[86] At the same time, the clerks of the U.S. District Court and U.S. Circuit Court at Boston—the only two federal courts in the state—also took fees for grants of naturalization.[87] Consistent with the customer-service mentality that fees fostered, Boston's federal courts by the 1860s were competing hard for naturalization business.[88] By the early 1880s, they may have overtaken the state's Superior Courts. Much like New York's midcentury courts, they were accepting repeat witnesses, garnering a reputation for "loose business," and making "large sums" in fees.[89] Though they appear not to have accepted vouchers or offered discounts, they did go farther than the midcentury New York courts in another respect: the fee-taking clerks—with the knowledge and acquiescence of the judges—took over processing of applications completely, often examining the applicant and witnesses and making the final decision, without the judge playing any role.[90] In this, they also went farther than Massachusetts's Superior Courts, where the judges appear to have been somewhat more involved.[91]

The Massachusetts legislature in 1885 attempted to tighten naturalization through its control of the state courts, only to have its efforts negated by the continuing "customer service" of the fee-taking federal clerks. The new state law struck a compromise between nativists and their opponents: naturalization power would be extended from the state's Superior Courts to its more accessible local courts, but under new procedures that were more searching and burdensome for applicants.[92] Further, the nativists won a provision severing the pecuniary link between applicant and clerk. All the state clerks' naturalization fees—which hitherto had gone into their pockets—now went to the public fisc.[93]

This reform—terminating the state clerks' pecuniary interest in attracting applicants and raising the procedural hurdles to their provision of services— drove applicants further into the arms of the federal clerks, who operated under looser procedures and still had a pecuniary motive to exploit that looseness. As a congressional committee concluded in 1891: "When the [state] law [of 1885] was put into practice, aliens no longer applied to the state courts, with rare exceptions, but went from all parts of the state . . . to Boston, where they found in the United States courts much more convenient methods in accomplishing their purposes."[94] Asked whether the "liberal practice of the United States court defeats the very wholesome law Massachusetts has enacted," the U.S. District Court judge answered that "it does," at least for the eastern part of the state: "The effect of it has been to drive all the naturalization cases in Boston, and all about Boston, Essex, and Middlesex and Norfolk County, to Boston."[95]

The immigrants' attraction to the federal courts was understandable: naturalization in those tribunals was easy. As the district court judge recognized, "substantially all" applications were granted.[96] Though the judge felt there should be some limit on repeat witnesses, the clerks understood this to permit one for "eight or ten" applicants.[97] Whereas the state legislature in the 1885 statute aspired to use local courts and the publishing of applications to expose the frauds of immigrants who claimed to have resided where they really did not, the federal courts' wide geographic jurisdiction meant they dealt with applicants and witnesses who were complete strangers, and they generally took their stories at face value. For example, when asked "[to] what examination, if any, do you subject these [repeat] witnesses in order to ascertain their means of knowledge concerning . . . the residence of the applicants, their moral character and all that," the clerk of the circuit court replied, "We ask them, that is all that we can do."[98] The clerks refrained from making applicants state their street address, which might have allowed for verification of their residency claims. They also refrained from taking down physical descriptions of persons making declarations of intent, which might prevent impersonation by persons claiming to have misplaced their declarations.[99]

The absence of scrutiny permitted the clerks to move like lightning. Just prior to elections, when the judge often took part in the process at least formally, each court could grant citizenship to three hundred or four hundred applicants per day.[100] On days when they operated completely without the judge, the clerks and deputies naturalized up to one hundred per day.[101]

The clerks and judges explicitly recognized the incentive effect of fees. The U.S. Circuit Court judge agreed that "the fees paid for [naturalizing] aliens in the different courts, State and United States courts, have a tendency to create a competition between the clerks and the officers for the business"; that "the abolition of fees . . . would have a tendency to discourage naturalization in the respective courts rather than encourage it"; and that there was "great competition going on between said different courts, the State and United States courts, to accumulate this business."[102]

Indeed, the two federal courts (district and circuit) engaged in some degree of fee-driven competition with each other. For a few years, the district court was ahead, then the circuit court, then they pulled even.[103] A deputy clerk of the district court admitted that, while there was "no open competition" between the two, "[e]ach office used to like to do as much as they could."[104] Another district court deputy said it was "the impression in the building" that there was "an effort made by clerks" of the circuit court "to direct and have procured applicants to go through the Circuit Court for naturalization." He added there was "not really a contest" between the two courts, "although a good deal of grumbling because [the circuit court clerk] got so much."[105]

Profits were considerable. The circuit court clerk testified that his yearly earnings from naturalizations were $5,000, which was more than half the income from his job.[106] It was said he had "accumulated a very large fortune" from naturalization fees.[107]

The federal clerks took advantage of political machines as procurers of immigrant customers, but they were not the mere creatures of any machine. To be sure, federal court naturalizations in Gilded Age Boston continued to be heaviest during election campaigns.[108] A band of applicants might be led by an individual candidate,[109] or by a party "agent."[110] Candidates or parties sometimes paid the applicants' fees (though there were no vouchers or discounts).[111] The immigrant vote tended Democratic nationwide, and Massachusetts was no exception: the most numerous applicants were Irish,[112] and those voters were generally associated with the Democratic machine.[113] But at the same time, Massachusetts had other immigrant groups that tended Republican, such as Englishmen and Scandinavians.[114] One deputy clerk testified that at least some applicants were sent by the Republican organization as well as the Democratic one.[115] And a newspaper reported in 1887 that an unnamed federal clerk "under the guidance of the Republican State committee" was taking declarations of intent from English-born immigrants "in the privacy of the [Republican] party headquarters, and afterward in the convivial presents of a clubhouse." He was doing this, suggested the paper, "for the purpose of getting as large a number of declarations as possible," "for the sake of fees."[116]

That Boston's federal clerks served *all* paying customers, Democrat or Republican, is no surprise, for the officers were not controlled by any machine. Rather, they served at the pleasure of the life-tenured judges of the court,[117] and they did so for long periods, without party-based turnover.[118] To the extent that any party affiliation might be imputed to the clerks, their behavior cut against it: Republican appointees held all the judgeships from 1869 to the 1890s, yet the clerks' take-all-comers mentality helped Democrats more than Republicans.

Although Boston's federal judges—reacting to the adverse publicity of congressional hearings in 1890—imposed several new strictures on their clerks' processing of applications,[119] federal courts elsewhere continued to display fee-driven solicitude for immigrants. In an echo of Massachusetts, the New York legislature in 1895 imposed more stringent procedures on naturalization in the (already-salaried) state courts,[120] but this effort was greatly undermined, at least in Brooklyn, by the fee-taking clerk of the U.S. District Court there, Richard Morle, who (as in Boston) effectively controlled the process.[121] A grand jury presentment in 1900—reported under the headline "A Naturalization Mill"—complained that Morle used less stringent methods than did the state courts; that grants of citizenship "appeared excessive in number"; that many applicants did not know the names of their witnesses; that a professional procurer of aliens had set up shop in the clerk's office; and that in some instances, the ratio of applicants to witnesses was an eye-popping eighty to one. The "fees taken and retained by the clerk," added the grand jury, "may be an explanation" for the looseness of the proceedings, for otherwise it could be explained only by "incompetency or recklessness."[122] (The presentment apparently had no repercussions for Morle, who stayed in office.)[123]

It seems that Morle's fee-driven conduct typified the "customer service" of many federal courts. Soon after Minnesota began requiring citizenship for voting in 1896,[124] a deputy federal clerk "opened a citizenship bargain counter" at Minneapolis, announcing that "for one month" final papers would "be issued at his office . . . for 50 cents each. If the business justifies it, the bargain counter will run from 9 in the morning until 9 in the evening."[125] According to a report by the U.S. Department of Justice in 1905, federal clerks' fee incentives kept them from "a too strict observance of the requirements of the law," which judges indulged out of "a consideration for the revenues of the clerks." Restrictive state statutes, according to the report, had been "almost entirely . . . nullified" not only in Boston and New York but also in "Baltimore, and other cities," while there was a similar lack of "due regard to precautionary measures against fraud" at federal courts in Philadelphia and Pittsburgh.[126] And although the majority of state court clerks by the turn of the twentieth century were on salary, fee-driven solicitude for applicants was evident among the minority who still were not.[127]

*Restriction's Triumph: Congressional Reforms from 1906 to the 1920s.* Nativism ultimately spread from the state houses, like those in Massachusetts and New York, to the U.S. Capitol. The decisive step was Congress's enactment of the Naturalization Act of 1906.[128] This was, as the political scientist Rogers M.

Smith notes, part of the "exclusionary thrust" of federal legislation in the early 1900s.[129] The act made one change in the substantive criteria for naturalization: applicants had to "speak the English language," though they did not have to read it, and Congress said nothing about how to test them. Probably more important than this vague substantive addition was the act's sweeping reform of institutions and procedures. It established the new Bureau of Naturalization in Washington, DC, which kept a national registry of all incoming immigrants and declarations of intent (against which applicants' stories could be checked) and could investigate any application.[130] And while the act continued to vest the naturalization power in federal courts and a large number of state courts, it beefed up the procedures they had to follow.

The 1906 act greatly altered the fee structure for naturalizations, effectively destroying its facilitative character. A major reason that fee-taking clerks had been able to profit by naturalization prior to 1906 was that the process, when administered liberally, was low cost. But the 1906 act imposed new obligations that made the process far more expensive to those who carried it out. Clerks now had to gather far more data about applicants than before (e.g., body weight, ship names), copy and store numerous documents, and correspond with the bureau about every proceeding.[131]

To cover the materials and labor for these tasks, the statute fixed the fees for naturalization and allowed the clerk of every court, federal or state, to retain 50 percent of them, up to $3,000, the rest going to the federal treasury.[132] While the drafters assumed that these fees would generally go to pay the wages of additional clerical assistants,[133] it was also lawful for the clerk, state or federal, to pay himself from these funds, for his own extra labor.[134]

Though the 1906 act might look superficially like a reaffirmation of the old profit-seeking, customer-serving regime, it was actually the opposite. First, it did nothing to roll back the nonprofit status of the numerous state court clerks who had already been converted to salary by state law.[135] Also, the act withdrew naturalization power from the states' small-claims courts.[136] Because such courts were the most likely to have fee-paid clerks (or judges), state-court naturalization was now more dominated by salaried officials than ever before.

And for those clerks (federal and state) who still took fees as their personal compensation, the act restructured the fees so as to reverse the old customer-serving incentives. The sums fixed by the act were very low, given the onerous new procedures. The committee studying the issue had proposed fees totaling $11 per immigrant to cover all the new work, but Congress cut it down to $5 by a floor amendment.[137] Plus, no matter how great the number of applications and the consequent expenses, the statute's ordinary payment mechanism never allowed the clerk more than $3,000 to cover the cost, even though the cost far exceeded that cap in the big cities with large immigrant populations that needed service the most. To be sure, the bureau could give extra funding to courts that exceeded the $3,000 cap,[138] but it needed a special congressional appropriation every year for the purpose,[139] on which Congress was not generous. This left the hardest-pressed courts with inadequate funding.[140]

These factors—tough caps on both individual fees and on total earnings—meant that naturalization was no longer economical for many courts. For state courts, the gap could sometimes be filled by supplemental funding from the state or local government,[141] but that worked only if the state or locality was sympathetic to immigrants and had cash to spare, which they often did not. As naturalization had always been optional for state courts, many now quit doing it.[142] Or, if they stayed in business, they cut their services to the economical level, taking only a set number of applications per day and then shutting their doors.[143] Or, if they refrained from such explicit rationing, they invested less in personnel, which resulted in slow, low-quality service.[144] For example, three years after the 1906 act, a commission on state court naturalization in New York City found that "applicants . . . have been subjected to unnecessary delays, and have often been treated with marked discourtesy." In a survey of successful applicants, 30 percent "complained of delays, of being compelled to reappear many times with their witnesses, of flagrant favoritism, and of contemptuous and insulting treatment."[145] Customer service was in decline.

Federal clerks faced essentially the same funding problem as state clerks. Before 1906, they had been able to draw the (low) expenses of naturalization against the gross receipts of their offices arising from all judicial business.[146] But now, they had to segregate the (much increased) expenses of naturalization and draw them solely against the naturalization fees.[147] If those expenses broke the $3,000 cap, the clerks would personally lose money, barring a special appropriation. In one respect, the federal clerks were in an even tougher position than their state counterparts, since the federal courts, unlike the state courts, could not legally quit doing naturalizations. Worse, federal courts were receiving all the more applications precisely because state courts were shutting their doors or rationing.

As a result, federal courts facing high demand formally remained open but practically had so little capacity to handle the business that applicants were forced to wait in line and often gave up. For example, the personnel of the U.S. Circuit Court in Manhattan, explained the director of the federal Naturalization Bureau in 1908, could only "handle about 25 per cent of the applicants," so the "other 75 per cent waits and comes and goes. Some [applicants] have been there as many as six times, with their witnesses, and it puts the applicants to a heavy expense." The clerk wearily explained that, under the $3,000 cap, he could "not afford to employ more than three [assistant] clerks." As a result, the applicant "loses his day's time and the wages of the two [witnesses] that go down with him."[148] Across the river at the U.S. District Court in Brooklyn, clerk Richard Morle—who had made a fortune on rapid and liberal naturalization in the bygone era of vague statutes, low costs, and uncapped revenue—was caught in the same vise. As he hit the $3,000 cap, the expenses to keep up with demand were eating up his finite revenue. He feared that the expenses would soon have "to come out of [his] own pocket." By 1908, he was begging Congress for special appropriations.[149] In the end, federal courts facing high demand provided such slow service that applicants walked away or did not show up to begin with. According to a Senate committee, many federal clerks, in spite of their obligation to serve all comers, were so little funded that they were trying "to avoid [their] obligation by sending applicants for citizenship to other courts."[150] The problem only got worse in 1912, when Congress abolished the old circuit courts, thus channeling even more naturalizations to the district courts, whose clerks did not get any relief from their respective $3,000 caps.[151] Thus, when Congress officially converted federal clerks to salaries in 1919,[152] the clerks' fee-driven view of immigrants as customers was already long dead.

In addition to this perverse restructuring of clerks' fees, the 1906 act made one other key change that helped kill fee-driven customer service. It authorized the newly established Naturalization Bureau to investigate individual applications. To do that, the agency built a corps of full-time salaried examiners, who effectively seized the substantive decision-making power that, prior to 1906, had been formally exercised by judges and (often) practically by clerks. By the early 1920s, the bureau examiners were vetting the overwhelming majority of applications, interviewing the immigrant and witnesses, and making recommendations at the court hearing. Judges, having no other information on which to rely, generally became rubber stamps for the examiners, while clerks receded to a paper-pushing role.[153]

Exercising the power they had obtained, the salaried examiners were far less indulgent than the fee-seeking clerks of the old regime.[154] In contrast to the observation of a federal judge circa 1890 that "substantially all" aliens were admitted at Boston,[155] the nationwide rate of unsuccessful applications in the decade after the 1906 act hovered between 10 percent and 16 percent.[156] A survey of judges published in 1922 found that they typically viewed "the naturalization examiner as a zealous young man, intent upon straining every technical point to its utmost—against the petitioner [i.e., the applicant]."[157] "In the majority of the courts," concluded a Carnegie Foundation study in 1922, the judge followed the examiner's "recommendations and contentions": "there being no one in court to represent the frightened or embarrassed petitioner, the point of view of the examiner becomes that of the judge, and the law is handed down accordingly."[158]

Free of pecuniary dependence on applicants, examiners employed the discretion supplied by the law's vague criteria to narrow the previous openness of U.S. citizenship. Following the nativist view, they reinterpreted the old requirement that the applicant be attached to the Constitution to require testable knowledge of the Constitution.[159] Looking back on nearly ten years under the new law, the secretary of labor in 1916 emphasized the large number of denials "for educational deficiency and ignorance of American institutions."[160] The Carnegie study of 1922 explained that denials for "ignorance" turned "in the majority of cases" on "the understanding of the petitioner as to the form of government, and sometimes decidedly minute details of the history, of the United States." It quoted one judge, "who has large experience with naturalization," as saying: "Too much stress is laid upon information concerning details of our governmental system," and "too much technical information is demanded by the young men who represent the Bureau of Naturalization."[161] This is consistent with the conclusion of a recent study that the bureau as a whole was "firmly aligned with restrictionists" during this era.[162]

Given the mythology of Progressive Era rationality—and the common social science view of salaried employees as working under top-down control—it is tempting to assume that the stringency of the examiners arose from some national test handed down by Washington headquarters. In this view, the examiners' salaries would give them the independence to apply a uniform standard without fear or favor, guaranteeing fairness. But that is false. The examiners had about as much discretion as their fee-taking predecessors; they just exercised it in a less immigrant-friendly manner. The bureau would not develop a standard citizenship test until the late twentieth century.[163] A 1920 Carnegie study found that, although the bureau "has had during the last decade an increasingly excellent opportunity to develop an educational standard for admission," its standards were instead "as various almost as the temperaments of the 62 examiners, certainly as the temperaments of the 11 chief examiners it employs. There is no uniformity of view among these men."[164] A huge amount depended on the field officers' individual judgment.[165]

The new administration—with its unhelpful clerks and its adversarial examiners—meant that immigrants of the 1910s were less integrated into the American polity than their predecessors from the 1890s. As the Carnegie study of 1922 explained:

Many persons believe now that it is "easy to get naturalized," that upon payment of a few dollars, or in consideration of political subserviency, promised or expected, any alien can go, as it were, straight from the vessel that brings him to the naturalization court and thence to the ballot box! It used to be almost like that, but with the enactment of the law of 1906 a revolution set in, and the condition now, generally speaking, is quite otherwise. The pendulum has swung to the other extreme. It is as difficult now to be naturalized as it used to be easy. And it is quite natural that it should be so, in the reaction of public sentiment from the old happy-go-lucky days, with the law's administration in the hands of a corps of men [the Naturalization Bureau] who, from top to bottom, answer any test of honesty and zeal.[166]

The new salaried regime increased the alienation of immigrants from the polity. The foreign-born in the early twentieth century were substantially less likely to become citizens than their predecessors. The sociologist Irene Bloemraad finds that "the predicted probability of naturalization for a 10-year resident in 1900 is 0.49, whereas in 1920 it is only 0.20, a significant drop."[167] Contemporaries recognized the drop in naturalization and felt alarm at the alienation of foreigners from the polity.[168] To be sure, the drop was partly due to the advent of the English-speaking requirement, combined with rising immigration from non-English-speaking countries.[169] Significantly, however, Bloemraad finds that literacy (which the law did not require for citizenship) proved a better predictor of admission to citizenship than the ability to speak English, thus suggesting that the English-speaking requirement "was not necessarily onerous, but bureaucratization privileged literacy through the need to read and understand forms and/or to negotiate a formal, standardized regulatory process."[170] She says nothing about official compensation, but surely the disappearance of facilitative payments was a major cause of immigrants' increased difficulty in negotiating the process. Furthermore, her findings—combined with the contemporaneous accounts cited earlier—suggest that the new administrative apparatus was not simply a means to faithfully and precisely implement a set of statutory criteria that had previously been corruptly ignored. We can say only that naturalization became harder and less friendly to immigrants, not that it became more accurate.[171]

## DECIDING VETERANS' APPLICATIONS FOR DISABILITY BENEFITS

As with naturalization, so with veterans' benefits. The compensation of decision makers played an important role in shaping the government's treatment of the lay public. Facilitative payments formed part of a relatively generous regime, whereas salary compensation helped make the regime more restrictive.

Just as in the case of naturalization, the stakes were high. Pensions for disabled veterans and widows of the Civil War constituted a major welfare program by any measure and the largest welfare program in U.S. history to that time. By 1900, the federal government was paying pensions to about one million veterans and widows (many of whom had dependents) in a national population of about seventy-six million.[172] Pensions exceeded 10 percent of federal spending in the 1870s, 20 percent in the 1880s, and peaked at more than 45 percent in the 1890s. They continued between 20 percent and 30 percent through the 1910s, when the program began gradually dying out with the Civil War generation. The system thrived on strong support from the Republican Party, identified as it was with the North, the Union cause, and the veterans (especially their lobby, the Grand Army of the Republic). It also won the support of many Northern Democrats, who endorsed it for the sake of their constituents.[173]

This enormous welfare system required millions of decisions about which persons were eligible. For widows, the government wanted to know whether the woman had been married to the soldier and whether she was presently remarried (or cohabiting).[174] For disabled veterans, the government wanted to know whether the man was disabled, how badly, and (in some instances) whether his disability resulted from his military service. It was in the latter case—decisions about disabled men—that facilitative payments played a defining role. Such decisions are the focus of my case study.

### 1. Loose Criteria, Official Discretion, and Liberality

Under the definition devised by Congress, a veteran had a "disability" and was therefore eligible for a pension if he was incapable of doing manual labor (regardless of his actual occupation before or after the disability). Congress granted a certain level of pension for a "total" disability and lesser pensions for lesser levels of disability, graduated to the disability's severity.[175] Initially, Congress allowed pensions only if the disability resulted from military service, but in 1890 it established an alternative schedule of pensions for disabilities arising from any cause (though it left standing the old service-connected schedule, side by side with the new, which some eligible veterans preferred for its higher awards).[176]

How did the government decide whether a veteran was eligible, and for what sum? In the usual scenario, a veteran with a new claim for a pension—or for an increase in his existing pension by reason of worsened disability—sent an application to the Pension Bureau's all-salaried headquarters in Washington.[177] If the claim was plausible, the Washington office ordered the applicant to undergo a medical exam to determine whether he was disabled and how badly. Exams were conducted by "examining surgeons" appointed by the Pension Bureau in various localities across the nation. These surgeons—the "main characters" of our story—were paid a fee for every examination. At first, the surgeons made their exams individually, but starting in the early 1880s, they usually acted in boards of three, making decisions by majority vote.[178] At the system's height in the 1890s, there were about 1,400 boards nationwide.[179] After finishing the exam, the surgeon(s) sent a report to the Washington headquarters. Officers there made the final decision, based on the surgeons' report and on the records at their disposal (of the veteran's enlistment, of his wartime medical treatment, and so forth).

While the determination of whether a disability resulted from military service was firmly under the control of the Washington headquarters (given its access to war records),[180] the determination of whether the veteran was disabled to begin with, and how badly, rested mainly with the examining surgeons. They sent the Washington office a description ("pen picture") of the veteran's condition, plus a recommended finding as to whether he was disabled and how badly (the "rating"), expressed as the monthly dollar amount they thought he should receive.[181] While the Washington office drew up intricate rules for what maladies warranted what ratings, these rules did little to constrain the examining surgeons. Quite often they ignored them.[182] Even if they paid attention, ratings called for many subjective judgments that rules could not control. While the Washington headquarters could depart from the surgeons' rating,[183] this was not easy, for Washington had no knowledge of the applicant's condition except what the surgeons chose to pass along.[184] Thus, the surgeons' report was normally decisive.[185]

Decisive as the surgeons' decision was, it involved a great deal of discretion. Though we might casually assume that veterans' maladies were objective and obvious, like missing limbs or bullet wounds, such stereotypical battlefield claims proved far less common than those for diseases (such as chronic diarrhea, rheumatism, and heart trouble), which were often harder to verify and evaluate.[186] As Jerry Mashaw puts it, disability decisions of this kind, then as now, were inherently subjective—"analogous to fact-based determinations by one-person juries" and "influenced by the subjective understandings of the adjudicators."[187] Theda Skocpol agrees that "[m]uch room for initiative and interpretation was introduced into the system," given the vagueness of the criteria.[188] This subjectivity was recognized by people at the time. As one examining surgeon told Congress in 1881: "In certain cases it is a nice point to determine accurately the precise disability which is present, and there is frequently room for doubt." The decision depended "upon our impressions as to the candor and reliability of the applicant himself. . . . If he appears like an honest man and not disposed to exaggerate, we are very likely to give him the benefit of the doubt." In "doubtful cases," concluded the surgeon, "it is a matter of judgment[;] our judgment may sometimes be different. Doctors do not always agree, you know; that is proverbial."[189] Two decades later, a commentator discerned the same difficulty, noting that the results of one board, compared to the next, "are at startling variance."[190]

It was easy for examining surgeons to use their discretion to be generous toward applicants, for the proceeding was one sided. There was nobody to oppose or question the veteran's claim. "No one representing the government," explained a commentator in 1884, "is brought face to face with the applicant except the examining surgeon. In a word, the system is based upon the hypothesis that the applicant is an honest ex-soldier."[191]

According to the conventional wisdom of lawmakers, high officials, and opinion leaders, this discretionary system was indulgent toward applicants. Senator J. J. Ingalls—a Kansas Republican, former chairman of the Committee on Pensions, and leading advocate of the pension system—acknowledged in 1876 that "the pensions always go up and never down" and estimated that "at least one-sixth part of the entire amount that is paid to pensioners is fraudulently and wrongfully paid."[192] In 1893, a longtime official at the bureau's Washington office and one of its top claim-reviewers said that he "heard the statement made by a supervising examiner in 1888, that thirty percent of the claims which were then being admitted were entirely without merit. This statement was probably an exaggeration; but it expressed an opinion which I think was not uncommon among the employees of the bureau."[193] Writing in the *North American Review* that year, the chair of the House Pensions Committee acknowledged that "the undeserving class . . . unfortunately . . . constitutes a considerable portion of the [pension] list."[194] Skocpol documents the "apparently overwhelming opposition of educated public opinion toward the legacies of Civil War pensions," a system the educated class considered extravagant and easily abused.[195] A recent study of newspaper coverage of the pension system finds that, while Republican and Democratic papers portrayed the system according to their partisan predilections (Republicans positive, Democrats negative), independent, Mugwump, and "liberal" papers were about as accusatory as the Democratic ones, or more so, portraying the system as too generous to the undeserving.[196]

Today's scholars find it hard to verify or refute the system's indulgent image. Hugh Rockoff offers this measured assessment: the system "was often perceived, with some justice, as a system rampant with abuses."[197] In Skocpol's view, "nothing exact can be said about the proportions of illegitimate pensioners or expenditures. We can only speculate that some (undetermined) thousands, or conceivably tens of thousands, of the nearly one million pensioners in 1910 were bogus."[198]

But it is a mistake to frame the question in terms of abuses and bogus claims. Although some claims can be categorized as undeniably fraudulent (like false impersonation), disability adjudication is inherently subjective and contestable. Rather than try to judge the system from an Archimedean point, we might say that it was far more generous than most contemporaries who publicly reflected about the issue wanted it to be. That in itself suggests the system, judged by contemporaneous cultural standards, had institutional features causing it to resolve doubt in favor of claimants.

What were the institutional features that did this? For one thing, the Washington office appears to have been particularly indulgent toward applicants in electorally important areas, seeking to garner votes for the incumbent party.[199] But the examining surgeons—the actors of interest to us—were also frequently pegged as key contributors to the system's liberality and looseness. Officials critical of the system's indulgence placed much responsibility on the surgeons, as did critics in the press.[200] Skocpol agrees.[201]

## 2. Facilitative Payments as a Cause of Officials' Liberality

Why were examining surgeons so inclined to give veterans the benefit of the doubt? The reason most often posited by contemporaries for surgeons' generosity was that surgeons did government work only part-time and spent the rest of their time practicing medicine in the very communities where they did government examinations. Thus, said many observers, the surgeons viewed applicants as neighbors, friends, and potential patients to whom they wanted to ingratiate themselves, and they feared that being stringent would harm their reputation in the neighborhood.[202] In Skocpol's acclaimed study of the system, these social and business ties are the sole reasons given for the surgeons' laxity.[203]

But this is not the whole story: in addition to their concerns about attracting and keeping patients in their private practice, the examining surgeons' fee-based compensation for the examinations themselves was a major factor inclining them to be liberal. Surgeons wanted to maintain a reputation for generosity so that veterans would keep coming to them with fee-producing claims.

Since the inception of the pension system, surgeons had been paid a fee for every examination they performed, regardless of the outcome. Under the codification of the pension statutes in 1873, the fee was $2 per exam.[204] When

Congress in 1882 mandated that exams be conducted by three-member boards whenever practicable, it set the fee at $2 for each board member ($6 total).[205] From 1885 onward, Congress provided that, when multiple veterans were examined in a single day, the fee for each surgeon was $2 for each of the first five exams and then $1 for every one after that. By 1908, the fee for each of the first five was $3, then still $1 for each thereafter.[206]

Fees for the examinations themselves were potentially good business for the surgeons. Medicine in the late nineteenth century had not yet achieved high status, and its profitability was even lower than its status. Estimates of the income of a typical private doctor at the turn of the century varied but generally fell between $750 and $1,500 per year.[207] The average examining surgeon during the 1890s made about $265 per year from his part-time governmental business,[208] roughly one-quarter of a midrange private income. And of course the pension business was bigger in more populated areas. In a large city, the position of examining surgeon was "a very desirable billet," still leaving time for private practice,[209] with the pension fees amounting to a "considerable" sum.[210] In an especially heavy year, the fee income per surgeon on the multiple boards in Boston and Philadelphia exceeded $2,500 and in Washington exceeded $2,000.[211]

For examining surgeons to make examination fees, veterans had to make claims. Those claims might be initial applications for new pensions or follow-up applications for increased pensions by reason of worsened disability. Both required exams, and surgeons received the same fees for both.[212] Both types of claims—initial and increase—were important parts of the pension business: in the early 1880s, the two types of applications were about equal in number, and by the late 1880s, increase applications were more numerous.[213] A longtime staff member at the Washington office wrote in 1893: "[N]o sooner is a pension granted, usually, than the pensioner files another claim for increase. In many admitted claims, an application for increase has been filed as often as once a year, on an average, for many years."[214] In the period up to 1900, each individual veteran filed twelve claims on average.[215]

Thus, examining surgeons had a pecuniary motive to encourage veterans to enter the system and, once there, to keep asking for more benefits. Furthermore, the three-member boards were in competition with one another to attract veteran claims. Pretty much every Northern county had at least one board, and some had several.[216] Thus, for the typical applicant, a second board was only a train ride away. In a large city, there were often two or three boards, even as many as six.[217] If rejected by one board, a veteran (or his attorney) had the option to ask the Washington office to send him to another, and the office generally obliged.[218]

Examining surgeons had reason to maintain reputations for generosity not only among veterans themselves but also among the private intermediaries—known as "pension agents" or "pension attorneys"—who drummed up applications and channeled veterans to boards. There were thousands of these attorneys, some in Washington, but most in various cities and towns across the nation.[219] Veterans had attorneys in 85 percent of applications.[220] Notoriously aggressive,[221] and required by statute to work on a contingent-fee basis,[222] the pension attorneys were "repeat players" who could monitor the generosity of each board and influence the assignment of examinations accordingly. They were proactive in the medical examination process, sometimes accompanying their clients on visits to the board.[223]

It seems the attorneys were making judgments about the relative "customer-friendliness" of various boards and trying to allocate their business accordingly, thus encouraging the examining surgeons to be generous so as to attract more applicants. We catch a glimpse of this phenomenon in the reports of the reformist bureau commissioner H. Clay Evans and his top medical officer Jacob F. Raub. Evans and Raub took over the Washington office in 1897 and stayed until 1902, when the veterans' lobby had them ousted.[224] Until 1897, the Washington office had been in the practice of mailing orders for medical exams to a veteran's attorney rather than to the veteran himself. It had become common—what Raub called a "prominent abuse"—for attorneys to mail the orders right back to Washington, "with a request that claimants be ordered before different boards." The practice had grown to "such magnitude" that Evans directed that orders be mailed to the veterans themselves (with notices to the attorneys). Nevertheless, both veterans and attorneys were still sending letters to Washington on a "daily" basis "requesting that orders for medical examination be changed to some other board of examining surgeons."[225] And it was "not an infrequent incident" for an attorney to visit his client, physically take the order, and mail it back to Washington with a request for a different board, "this when the local medical examining board *does not meet the demands of the attorney.*"[226]

Raub, in an 1899 report, keenly discerned how the desire for examination fees drove the examining surgeons' effort to serve the wishes of claimants and attorneys. Though Raub found fault with many aspects of the system—especially the too-frequent selection of an incompetent country doctor "on the ground that he stands well in his community as a general practitioner"—he judged fees to be a key factor in themselves. The surgeons cared too much about money: "It is too much a question with them of the number of examinations they make and the amount of fees that may be coming to them at the end of a quarter." "It were far better," he attested, "if the Bureau could employ two experienced physicians in each Congressional district and pay them a reasonable annual salary to make these examinations," for "[i]n paying an annual salary *all temptation to cater to the wishes of claimants and attorneys would be removed*, and there would be no inducement to hurry examinations so as to swell the pay account for each day." The "ratings of many boards" were "unreasonably extravagant," as "an assurance to the claimant . . . that the members of the board of surgeons are his friends."[227] (Raub's analysis deserves particular weight, given his deep experience: as an army surgeon during the war, as an examining surgeon in Pennsylvania for two decades, and as a Washington-office reviewer of surgeons' reports from around the nation for seven years.)[228]

   The importance of fee incentives was also recognized by E. M. Brown, an examining surgeon from Vermont, in a paper he gave at a meeting of examining surgeons in 1905. "It would seem to me better," stated Brown, that examining surgeons "be paid by the day, for each day they meet, and the same pay whether they examine one or ten applicants." He went on:

> If this were done the feeling of a money consideration to encourage a soldier to apply for an examination would not exist. Neither would be there be the same desire that the Board preserve a standing before the pensioned as one likely to recommend an increase of pension.
>
> The Bureau [i.e., the Washington office] in its leniency allows the applicant to appear before any Board he may select. This makes each sagacious Board very careful not to lisp to those appearing before them a possibility that they might not receive an increase, as their disability did not warrant it. In other words, each U.S. Pension Examining Board under the present system, must look out for the maintenance of its own standing and existence.[229]

Raub and Brown's unease about fee incentives resonated with a fear expressed decades earlier (in a less precise way) by J. A. Bentley, the most earnest reformer to hold the commissioner's job prior to Evans. In 1877, Bentley reported that "some of these [examining] surgeons used their commissions more to serve their private interests than to serve the public, by seeking to draw to themselves, through advertisement and other means, for examination, as many pensioners as possible." Though this passage did not expressly mention fees, they seem the only explanation. On the next page of his report, Bentley recommended placing all surgeons on salary.[230]

   The press also picked up on the issue, as when the *Minneapolis Journal* in 1898 recounted the story of a board that examined five applicants in a single day, finding they all "had exactly the same ailment and symptoms." It "was found that this board took one case as a sample and drew fees for examining five cases, reporting all five alike." This, said the *Journal*, was but one illustration of "the way the treasury is mulcted by pension examining boards," and "hundreds, per- haps thousands, are annually certified as entitled to pensions who have not the slightest claim on the government." If the boards were "abolished and a certain number of physicians employed on salaries to do the work of examining for the whole state[,] it would save millions of dollars to the government every year."[231] Note how the story draws a link between adjudication's speed and its generos- ity: surgeons who decided cases quickly would have more time for their private practice, and while speed meant lower-quality decisions, this was unlikely to occasion complaint if the decisions favored the claimants, since nobody was hurt except the taxpayer.

### 3. Support for Liberal Administration among Lawmakers and the Public

Congress knew well the generosity of the adjudicatory system, and it repeat- edly rejected efforts to rein it in, whether by salarization or other means. Admin- istrators throughout the 1870s proposed replacing the local, part-time, fee-paid surgeons with traveling, full-time, salaried surgeons.[232] A Senate committee in 1880 favorably reported a bill to do just that, but it never came up on the floor.[233] As one journalist pointed out in 1884, the examining surgeons' strong presump- tion in favor of the veteran was "backed up by a sentiment in Congress which demands that the laws be construed liberally, and the benefit of a doubt always given to a soldier."[234] In 1893, some House members proposed a reform package to tighten the pension system, providing for (among other things) a corps of salaried field doctors that would rival and perhaps supplant the fee-paid exam- ining surgeons.[235] Notably, the opponents of the package refused to credit its professed status as a mere anti-fraud measure, aimed at the unobjectionable end of guaranteeing the faithful execution of the pension statutes. In the words of George Ray, a New York Republican, Union veteran, and future chair of the (famously pro-veteran) Pension Committee, "the object of the proposed legislation is not to weed out fraudulent cases, if any there be, but to under- mine the system, to destroy the law, to deprive the old soldier of the pittance to which he is now entitled, to send the crippled veteran . . . 'over the hills to the poorhouse.'"[236] Ultimately, one part of the reform package (including the salary proposal) failed on a parliamentary technicality, and the remainder was then rejected by the House on the merits.[237]

It was not only congressmen but also presidents who defended the status quo of loose administration. When Commissioner Bentley in the late 1870s proposed reforms to tighten administration (including the salarization of the

examining surgeons), the pension attorneys "succeeded in making him unpopular among the former soldiers." President Garfield fired him shortly after taking office in 1881, even though he was of Garfield's party.[238] Two decades later,
when Evans adopted a similar stance (reviving Bentley's salarization proposal),
he incurred the displeasure of the veterans' lobby, which persuaded Theodore
Roosevelt to push him out.[239]

In defending the status quo of lax administration, the veterans' lobby pushed
policy outcomes in the direction of its true goal, which from the 1880s onward
was to abolish the requirement of disability altogether, conferring benefits on
all veterans simply by reason of their service.[240] The looseness of the adjudicatory system was a means for the Grand Army of the Republic to get nearer that
goal, even if it could not achieve it formally. Public opinion would not accept
the formal enactment of a purely service-based pension, yet public opinion, in
the view of many observers, *was* willing to accept a system so lax that it achieved
most of the same outcomes as a service-based system, under another name.
Said one commentator in 1893: "It is easier to recognize the fact that abuses
have been practiced than to suggest a proper remedy. Public sentiment does
not demand and would not sanction radical measures, conceived in any spirit of
unfriendliness to the veterans as a class."[241] The economist William Glasson, for
all his criticism of the system's liberality, conceded in 1918 that it was supported
by a popular political judgment about the relative importance of false negatives
and false positives: "It has been felt that the veterans served the country when
it was in need and that many of them may be worse off physically or otherwise
because of their military service, without being able to furnish legal proof. In
this state of the public feeling, the people have endured a great deal of obvious
extravagance and fraud in order that meritorious claimants for places on the
pension roll should not suffer by restrictions and safeguards framed to keep out
the undeserving and corrupt."[242]

The willingness of lawmakers and the public to bear the cost of the pension
system depended on their perception that public money was not scarce. From
the 1860s to the 1910s, there was a strong political coalition for high tariffs as a
protectionist measure, and as trade grew, the federal treasury often had money
to spare. Indeed, the frequent surpluses were something of an embarrassment
to protectionists, who liked pensions in part because they provided a way to get
rid of the money, thus making the tariff look more necessary for revenue.[243] Free
traders recognized this link and therefore disliked the pension system, but they
could not muster the votes to change things.[244] Overall, the federal government
saw itself as living through an age of plenty that made the pension system seem
affordable. The burden of the tariff was borne by consumers at large, to whom

it was invisible. Glasson, looking back on the system's history, wrote in 1918: "If federal taxation for [Civil War] pensions had been direct and personal, if the average head of a family had been required to pay out eight or ten dollars annually as a tax for this specific purpose, it is very doubtful whether the pension system could have reached its present proportions," but the tariff was a "system of taxation comparatively invisible and painless."[245]

Politicians seeking to expand pensions directly invoked the absence of scarcity. Ingalls asked in 1884, "What better use can be made of our surplus than to pay to the utmost farthing these most sacred of all our national obligations?" Justifying pensions in 1907, the chairman of the Senate Pension Committee proclaimed that the "country now . . . is wealthy. The Treasury is bursting with its load of coin."[246]

#### 4. The Reaction against Liberality, the Salarization of Officials, and the Alienation of Service Recipients: World War I and Fiscal Scarcity

War with Germany in 1917 confronted politicians with the question of whether the existing benefits regime should be extended to the huge crop of new veterans who were about to come into being. A few years prior to 1917, the waste and looseness of the Civil War system had been the object of embarrassment and hand-wringing, but all of it seemed academic, since the system was both (1) too deeply entrenched to be rolled back for the persons already covered and (2) certain to fade away naturally in a decade or two, as the Civil War generation died.[247] The second point reinforced the first: there was no reason to be *that* upset about the Civil War system circa 1910, since its specificity to a certain generation meant that its days were numbered. But all that changed when the United States in 1917 entered the World War (as Americans at the time called it). Suddenly, there was a stark choice: the nation had to either double down on the old veterans' benefit system or make a radical change.

Politicians opted for radical change. The system for World War veterans would seek to conserve money in a way the Civil War system had not. Whereas the politicians who abetted the expansion of the Civil War system in the course of the Gilded Age had faced a highly organized veterans' lobby and relied on a tariff-centered tax regime that was "comparatively invisible and painless,"[248] the politicians of 1917 faced a quite different landscape. There were no veterans as yet, so they could not form a lobby. And national finance, given the looming conflict with Germany, looked forbidding. Federal spending and debt were sure to explode, and veterans' benefits were sure to be a significant part of that explosion.[249] Also, beginning in 1916, President Wilson and congressional Democrats used the preparedness campaign and the war itself as opportunities to transform federal taxation so that it concentrated far more on wealthy individuals and corporate profits—sources unwilling to be plucked quietly, like consumers under the tariff. The struggle over federal taxation and budgeting entered a new, more intense era.[250]

As the United States entered the war, Congress declared that the Civil War pension laws would continue to apply to the Civil War veterans and their widows, but that a completely new statutory regime would govern World War veterans, indeed all new veterans going forward.[251] The new scheme—proposed by Treasury secretary and former railroad executive William Gibbs McAdoo—was enacted unanimously in autumn 1917.[252] Rather than frame the system as an amendment to the Civil War pension laws, McAdoo had it tacked on to the War Risk Insurance Act of 1914, which until then had mainly concerned government-sponsored insurance for commercial shipping and seamen. This allowed for the bill to go through the committees on interstate commerce rather than the (notoriously pro-veteran) committees on pensions. At every turn, McAdoo and his top congressional allies distanced themselves from Civil War precedent. "The authors of the new law," writes one historian, "wanted to protect themselves and the new measure from the charges of partisanship and corruption levied against the Civil War pension system by progressive reformers in the North."[253] The new generation of soldiers, said McAdoo to Congress, must not "be left . . . to the scandals of our old pension system."[254]

The amended War Risk Insurance Act differed from the old system in several ways. First, it gave benefits only for genuine disabilities resulting from military service, in contrast to the Civil War system, which in 1890 had dropped the requirement of service connection and was generally viewed as giving benefits for conditions that were barely disabling, if at all. To this end, the new regime conferred many of its benefits not in cash but in forms that only a truly disabled person would want: hospital care and rehabilitation.[255]

Still, the reformers reluctantly acknowledged the need for some degree of cash assistance. Each veteran disabled in service was to receive such assistance in proportion to the loss of earning power normally associated with his injury or disease.[256] But, in contrast to the Civil War system, he was to receive nothing if the loss were less than 10 percent.[257] In addition, Congress changed the name of the assistance from *pension* (the Civil War term) to *compensation*. As the House Commerce Committee explained, it was "of the utmost importance both for the practical results and for the psychological effect upon the men, their families, and the people of the country, that a new point of view be established," which was to be "accomplished" in part by "designating the payments to them as compensation and not as pensions."[258] The term *compensation*—a deliberate invocation of then-burgeoning laws on workers' compensation—embodied the requirements of actual disability and service connection that had been dropped or weakened in the prior era.[259]

Perhaps most important, the supporters of the new bill implicitly repudiated the old system of local, part-time, fee-paid examining surgeons. They insisted that World War compensation be administered by expanding the War Risk Insurance Bureau (WRIB), which had previously handled only commercial shipping and seamen, rather than having it administered by the Pension Bureau, which was the more obvious choice. In fiscal 1916–17, the number of Civil War pensioners (including widows) was only one-third less than its turn-of-the-century peak.[260] The Pension Bureau's Washington office was among the largest in the capital, employing more than one thousand people. Across the nation, there were more than 1,200 boards of examining surgeons open for business.[261] Yet the reformers, while never questioning that the Pension Bureau and its surgeons should continue to handle all Civil War benefits, demanded that World War cash assistance be vested in a completely separate agency that would have to be frenetically expanded to do the job. The oddity of this approach, from an organizational perspective, was pointed out by several congressmen, some of whom had no particular love for veterans' pensions and simply considered the duplication of effort wasteful.[262] But the reformers were adamant in bypassing the old apparatus.[263]

In truth, the reformers wanted to exclude the Pension Bureau because they viewed it as irredeemably linked to the excessive, corrupt, and irrational Civil War system. Back in 1905, a paper given at a meeting of examining surgeons had acknowledged that "no department of the government is so much calumniated as is the Pension Commissioner and his subordinates."[264] The House Commerce Committee in 1917 did not even consult the Pension Bureau about how to design the new system.[265] It announced that "the bill strikes a new keynote as against the former pension legislation. *For that reason alone*, its administration should be separated from that of the present pensions."[266] The quest to establish a "new point of view" about benefits required "separating the administration of this law absolutely and completely from the administration of the [Civil War] pension laws."[267] The chairman of the Senate Finance Committee, in hearings on the new scheme in 1917, was especially clear in linking this point to the old system's excessive generosity: "What is hoped is that [this bill] will do away with the pension system at the Pension Bureau, *where the leak is*."[268]

Congress's pension committees (identified with the old system) campaigned to bring World War benefits under the existing apparatus and to make them more generous, but to no avail.[269] In 1919, the House Committee on Pensions reported a bill to transfer World War compensation to the Pension Bureau, noting the bureau's "force of medical examiners which is available and readily accessible to claimants in every part of the United States. . . . These boards are maintained at a minimum cost, for the reason that each member is paid only for the examinations made by him." The committee cited the waste of having two separate agencies perform such similar missions. Further, it proposed that the World War scheme, which provided "a much less liberal allowance" than the old pensions, be substantively altered to match those pensions.[270] It was quite logical to couple a return to the fee-paid examining surgeons with a proposal for increased generosity. But the tide was against the committee. Its bill never came up on the floor.[271]

The central aim of the reformist plan was long-term fiscal discipline. As McAdoo told Congress, "the cost" of covering World War veterans under the old pensions laws "would likely exceed that of the proposed plan."[272] The bill's floor manager in the House, Sam Rayburn, said it aimed to avoid "'another saturnalia of pension frauds' such as that which followed the Civil War."[273] The House Commerce Committee reasoned that, if Congress started the war effort with a reasonable and measured promise of benefits, carefully confined to disabilities that were service-connected and substantial, it would gain public acceptance and thereby hopefully "erect a certain moral barrier" to the future expansion of the system.[274]

Consistent with this transformed view of veterans' benefits, the WRIB quickly embraced salaries for its field service. So that we appreciate the importance of this field service, let me first note that the steps for determining World War compensation were much like those of the Civil War system: the veteran initially applied to the Washington office; a physician in the field performed an exam and reported a recommended disability rating to the Washington office; and that office, drawing upon the report, decided what benefits the veteran would receive.[275] As in the Civil War system, the physician's report was of paramount importance in deciding the claim.[276] The 1917 statute let the WRIB decide how to carry out the exams, so long as they were done by "a duly qualified physician designated or approved" by the agency.[277] By the time veterans returned en masse in 1919, the WRIB had enlisted the U.S. Public Health Service (PHS) to perform all exams for World War compensation.[278] The PHS, in turn, established a nationwide corps of salaried doctors (some full-time, others part-time), numbering more than 1,500 by mid-1920.[279] The PHS, explained a top official, strongly preferred salaried doctors, finding that on the "fee basis," exams were "not satisfactory," because they were not sufficiently thorough.[280]

When the Veterans' Bureau formed in spring 1921, it absorbed several preexisting agencies, including the WRIB and the (largely salaried) force of doctors at the PHS who performed veteran exams.[281] In the first half of 1922, 92 percent of Veterans' Bureau exams were performed by salaried doctors and only 8 percent by fee-paid ones.[282] The salaried proportion reached 97 percent by fiscal 1924–25, when the bureau referred to its "policy of performing as much work as possible through salaried personnel of the bureau, with the elimination so far as practicable of fee-basis personnel."[283] The policy was motivated, at least in part, by a desire to suppress generosity. The bureau director in 1921 observed that outside physicians on contract "have been, to say the least, most lenient in the reporting of cases of claimants who are simply exaggerating the most trivial complaints into major disabilities."[284]

In addition to placing adjudicators on salary, the new regime prevented the development of a customer-seller ethos in another way: by banning private intermediaries. Recall that Civil War examining surgeons could expect their generosity to produce fees in part because private pension attorneys channeled business toward liberal boards. In early 1918, attorneys began contacting families of men killed in the World War, offering to help them claim death benefits (also promised by the 1917 statute) for a contingent fee. When McAdoo learned of this, he sent a furious message to Congress, calling the attorneys "sharks" and decrying their "heartlessness" and "rapacity."[285] Congress, acting with the precision of a meat-axe, ordered the WRIB *never* to recognize *any* attorney in the adjudication of *any* claim for benefits under the 1917 statute, not only death benefits but also disability compensation.[286] The conceit was that attorneys were unnecessary because adjudication would be fast and straightforward (a belief soon proved utterly false).[287] In any event, the prohibition of attorneys further evidenced the ardent congressional desire to exclude any middlemen who might promote a customer-seller ethos.

World War benefits adjudicators, unlike their Civil War predecessors, had no monetary incentive to give veterans the benefit of the doubt, and to a significant degree, they were less inclined to do so.[288] Let me preface this by emphasizing that "the benefit of the doubt" was still crucial to disability adjudication. To be sure, promoters of the 1917 act aspired to decide "every just claim impersonally and as a matter of right."[289] But despite advances in medical science, disability adjudication remained a highly subjective enterprise (as it is today). "[O]f all the work which the Veterans' Bureau is called upon to perform," wrote an agency lawyer in 1924, disability ratings were "perhaps the most important," yet "at the same time, the most unsatisfactory," because they rested, "in their adoption and application, largely upon matters of judgment and opinion."[290] Indeed, disability adjudication after the World War was perhaps more subjective than ever, since newly recognized neurological disorders accounted for a quarter of Veterans' Bureau clients and "severely tested and often eluded the diagnostic . . . techniques of psychiatry and neurology."[291]

The discretion inherent in disability adjudication allowed for adjudicators' solicitude toward veterans to weaken as their customer-serving incentives disappeared. To be sure, it was not the stated policy of the WRIB, the PHS, or the Veterans' Bureau to be less accommodating of veterans. The Veterans' Bureau director in 1921 drew up a memo saying the agency was always to presume in favor of the claimant.[292] But adjudicators' tendencies are the product not merely of official policy announcements but also of the whole institutional environment, particularly amid crushing caseloads like those faced by the veterans' agencies just after the World War.[293]

Consistent with the idea that salarization severed the bond of reciprocity between adjudicators and claimants, many World War veterans found the government doctors who performed examinations and ratings to be horribly callous. This contrasted with the Civil War regime, in which veterans generally found the examining surgeons congenial.[294] On this point, a key source is an in-depth 1923 report that the Rehabilitation Committee of the American Legion (the biggest veterans' group) drafted on one of the bureau's medical districts, the one covering California, Nevada, and Arizona. Nevada Senator Tasker Oddie, one of three members of a select committee conducting a major investigation of the bureau, had the report printed, calling it a "masterly piece of work" that would be "to the interest of ex–service men throughout the country," and adding that "many of the suggestions made will apply to other districts."[295]

The report explained that bureau doctors, who (among other things) "examine men to determine whether or not they are entitled to compensation" and "pass upon disability ratings," fell into "one or more" of ten classifications. Two of these were positive: the "few" who took pride in their work and the "limited number" who worked in the bureau temporarily for "clinical opportunities" before going into private practice. The remaining classifications, covering most bureau doctors, were all negative, including the "time server," with "no other ambition than to draw his salary"; the "weakling," who "fears to even make a diagnosis"; the "red-tape slave," who "gives little time or thought to patients"; and the doctor "so lacking sympathy as to antagonize everyone to whom he renders service." After citing two examples of bad examiners, including one who cut a veteran's compensation despite obvious disability, the committee attested that these were "but two of many examples of the type of medical men that are in the Veterans' Bureau pretending to render service to disabled veterans. On doctors like these [veterans] are dependent for disability ratings, diagnosis, and medical treatment. Is it any wonder that the ex–service people damn the Veterans' Bureau and the Government?" The committee went on to "cite examples of the so-called 'hard-boiled' examiner," telling of one doctor who refused to reopen a claim to consider additional evidence, accused the claimant of fraud, and rudely and unreasonably denied another claim. "This type of doctor is all too numerous, and the results of his service are complaints and dissatisfaction that cannot be excused." The report added further examples, including one of a doctor responding angrily when a claimant complained about waiting in line. "Numberless other cases might be cited," concluded the committee, "[b]ut these are sufficient to show the callous attitude of the present medical staff toward patients." In general, the veterans had a "critical, complaining, and resentful feeling" toward the staff.[296] The committee attributed the poor quality of bureau doctors to (1) the low level of salary offered and (2) the civil service selection process, which weighed years of experience, an objective factor, above all others.[297]

Alienation between veterans and the salaried agency staff was not confined to the West. An investigator for the Senate committee, having observed the New York office, worried about "the mental attitude of a large proportion of the employees of the office. There is too much cynicism and too little sympathy. Undoubtedly a great many of the applicants have unfounded claims, but there seems to be a tendency on the part of some of the employees to assume that this applies to all claimants." He further noted that veterans really had nobody on their side and often lacked the initiative necessary to push their claims. Without an advocate, "the average applicant's case falls by the wayside. He has either to collect the necessary proof or else he falls into despair at the delay and quits."[298] Civil War veterans, by contrast, had enjoyed the services of attorneys who assiduously sought their business.

The American Legion, despite its bitter criticism of the WRIB and Veterans' Bureau,[299] refused to endorse the idea of transferring World War veterans' compensation to the old Civil War Pension Bureau and its examining surgeons. The Legion committed itself to reform the new agency, not bypass it.[300] In that respect, the Legion recognized, accommodated, and even internalized the reaction against the old system's laxity. The Legion was influential because it was moderate and sensitive to nationwide and elite opinion beyond the ranks of veterans. Throughout the 1920s, the Legion emphasized that genuine service-connected disabilities were its top priority, holding up that morally unassailable claim as a shield against charges of greedily raiding the Treasury.[301] Working with the Veterans' Bureau to improve service, the Legion in 1924 succeeded in persuading Congress to carve out an exception to the prohibition of attorneys:

the Veterans' Bureau was now permitted to recognize designated members of the Legion and other veterans' organizations as lay representatives of claimants.[302] The alienation of veterans from the officialdom was thereby mitigated, but the lay representatives did not have the benefit-maximizing incentives of the old pension attorneys. The old distributive style of administration was no more.

Admittedly, Congress's initial stringency loosened as veterans became more organized in the course of the 1920s. This was particularly evident in the determination of whether disabilities were service connected (which was not mainly the bailiwick of the examining physicians). For certain widespread diseases, Congress imposed a rebuttable or conclusive presumption in favor of finding the disease to be connected with military service.[303] The pressure on Congress to make these legislative changes can be seen as a testament to the independence of the administrative system from the veterans. Those seeking benefits could no longer rely upon indulgent administration of the existing statute, so their only hope was to change the statute, which required concentrating their efforts to demand new law from Congress—that is, doing battle openly and collectively in the mass interest-group struggle over public resources.[304]

When the government's fiscal situation worsened amid the Great Depression, the Veterans' Bureau demonstrated a formidable capacity to defy veterans' wishes. It set up review boards that cut the disability rolls in half during the early 1930s, mainly by applying the criteria for service connection more stringently, often getting into caustic exchanges with lay representatives from the Legion.[305] The officialdom had learned to say no.

## DECIDING SETTLERS' APPLICATIONS FOR LAND

A third key area in which official compensation shaped the government's treatment of the lay public was in land distribution. For many years, the fees by which adjudicatory officers made their living helped render the process loose and liberal. Only with salarization did distribution become less indulgent to claimants and more sensitive to broader interests.

Seldom in world history has a government acquired and distributed such a huge amount of real estate as the U.S. government did in the nineteenth and early twentieth centuries. U.S. land acquisition and distribution were vast, complex, and multistage projects. Facilitative payments were important at a key juncture, but we first need a sense of the larger processes in which that juncture was located.

In its first eighty years of independence, the United States acquired sovereignty over its present continental territory, sometimes by war and sometimes by purchase. For most of this land, the federal government acquired not only sovereignty but also ownership. On tracts that were uninhabited and unclaimed, federal ownership came automatically with sovereignty. On Indian-occupied tracts, the federal government had to extinguish Indian title. It sometimes did this by war, but also commonly by formally consensual cessions, which it acquired by various forms of coercive pressure and often-underhanded means. Advancing white settlement on nearby federal land was one factor that pressured Indians to cede, for such settlement led to white trespass on Indian land, sparked white-Indian violence, and thinned the game populations on which some Indians relied, thus rendering their land less attractive to them.[306] The work of fighting the Indians, negotiating with them, removing them, and containing them on reservations was mainly carried out by the U.S. military and the Bureau of Indian Affairs, whose officers took no facilitative payments and had no reason to treat Indians as customers.[307]

Once the federal government acquired land, there was the question of how to distribute it among the numerous state governments, railroad corporations, absentee investors, white settlers, and others who were clamoring for it. Of the hundreds of millions of federal acres distributed over the 1800s and early 1900s, about one-third consisted of grants to entities like state governments and railroad corporations. The other two-thirds went to individuals, either through auction sales or through "settlement laws" such as the Homestead Act, by which individuals could acquire land for a low price, or even for free, if they worked it themselves. Of these two methods, auction sales were prevalent at first, but the settlement laws came to predominate in the middle of the nineteenth century and remained dominant through the early 1900s.[308] Both the auction sales and the settlement laws were administered by the federal district land offices.

My case study here analyzes how these district land offices decided individuals' claims under the settlement laws — in particular, how they decided whether frontiersmen seeking land had worked the land enough to earn the right to keep it. It was for these decisions that the officers received facilitative payments in the pre-salary era.

## 1. Loose Criteria, Official Discretion, and Liberality

This section lays out the federal system for distributing land and explains how the settlement laws came to be the dominant mode of distribution by the mid-1800s. As we shall see, those laws reflected a paradox. On the one hand, they arose from a Jeffersonian belief that the government should grant land in strictly limited amounts and only to people who cultivated it themselves; nobody should be allowed to accumulate large amounts of land or to speculate on land. On the other hand, a truly effective ban on all accumulation and speculation would have rendered the Western agricultural economy practically unworkable, not least for poor migrants who wanted to start farms there. Thus, Westerners, including poor aspiring farmers, wanted to engage in some degree of accumulation and speculation. And the settlement laws were so vaguely drafted as to let them do that, so long as the officers administered them in a loose and liberal manner—which in fact they did.[309]

The workaday process of distributing federal land—whether it was the implementation of land grants, the conduct of auctions for cash, or the adjudication of claims under the settlement laws—occurred largely on the frontier itself. The portion of the United States containing substantial amounts of federal land was divided into districts, and the land in each district was administered by a district land office. When the district land offices were first established in 1800, there were four, but the number grew to about one hundred by the late nineteenth century and stayed there into the early twentieth. At each office, the principal personnel (sometimes the only personnel) were the register and the receiver. Though the register was formally responsible for decision-making and the receiver for handling money, it appears that the two officers frequently acted jointly. The district land offices were officially under the U.S. General Land Office, a branch of the Interior Department, with its headquarters in Washington.[310]

In the early years of the U.S. government, Congress aspired to auction off the federal lands for cash and use them as a revenue source. The main job of the registers and receivers was to administer these cash sales. But squatters soon undermined this approach. The prevention of squatting would have required a significant military or police force, which Congress was not inclined to provide, especially since several Western states contained large numbers of squatters, who pressed their representatives to block or weaken enforcement.[311] And because the law required each auction to physically take place in the district where the land was located, squatters were able to assemble at the auction, to intimidate any nonresident purchaser from bidding on "their" land, and to collude among themselves to ensure that each of them paid only the statutory minimum (which, for most land, was $1.25 per acre).[312]

As the years passed, it became increasingly common for squatters in this or that geographic area to petition Congress for an act giving them a preferential right to purchase the land that they had cultivated and improved, at the minimum price. Pushed by Western representatives, Congress frequently obliged, granting such "preemption" rights to squatters in selected geographic areas, act by act, through the early 1800s.[313] During the 1830s, Congress passed a series of more general statutes, each of which granted preemption rights nationwide to persons squatting at the time of enactment, so long as they made their purchase by some deadline, often one or two years hence.[314] The registers and receivers now had an additional job: deciding which applicants for preemption rights under each statute had actually met the act's requirements for residency, cultivation, and so on.[315]

Squatters and their congressional backers did not, of course, couch their demands as simple grasping. They argued that settlers' residency and labor on the land were precisely what gave it value, which meant that settlers had a moral claim to capture all the money that could be wrung from it, in contrast to Eastern absentee speculators who purchased the land simply to let it rise in value and then sell, thus capturing a portion of the surplus while supposedly adding no value.[316] Furthermore, attested the squatters and their allies, a nation of numerous small settler-owners was morally better—and more suited to republican government—than one in which financiers hoarded the land. The squatters held a Jeffersonian vision of land policy, premised on the mythical dichotomy between wholesome settlers and evil speculators.

Jeffersonian policy scored its biggest win to date in the Preemption Act of 1841, which granted a preemption right to every American household prospectively.[317] Any head of household could, by living on a plot of land and improving it, obtain a right to purchase it at the minimum price (for most land, $1.25 per acre). The plot was to be a quarter section (160 acres), meaning the usual total price was $200—less than a year's wages for a common laborer.[318] The statute aimed to distribute land widely in small amounts: a person could buy land via preemption only once, and a person who already owned 320 acres or more anywhere in the United States was barred.[319]

No more than one month after settling on the land (or three months, depending on the category of land), the applicant was to file a "written statement" with the register, declaring "the intention . . . to claim the [land] under the provisions of this act." The applicant then had up to one year to return to the register and make the purchase at the minimum price.[320] To make the purchase, the applicant had to make "proof," to "the satisfaction of the register and receiver," of "the settlement and improvement" required by the statute,[321] which were vague: the applicant was to "inhabit and improve the [land]" and "erect a dwelling thereon."[322] Further, the applicant had to swear compliance with the statute, including that he or she had not settled on the land "to sell the same on speculation, but in good faith to appropriate it to his or her own exclusive use or benefit" and that he or she had not made an agreement to sell or give the land to anybody else.[323]

The culmination of Jeffersonian policy arrived in the Homestead Act of 1862, which followed the model of the Preemption Act, but with even more emphasis on settlement and less on paying cash.[324] Any head of household could acquire a 160-acre plot, but instead of paying the modest price of $200 plus fees, he or she could acquire the land for the fees alone (which normally totaled only $18) plus five years of living on the land and cultivating it. The applicant began the process by making a sworn statement "that such application is made for his or her exclusive use and benefit" and "for the purpose of actual settlement and cultivation," and not for any other person. After five years (or, at most, seven), the applicant could obtain title by returning to the land office and proving that he or she had "resided upon or cultivated the [land] for the term of five years immediately succeeding" the initial application.[325] Applicants lost their rights if during the five-year period they "actually changed" their "residence" or "abandoned the said land for more than six months at any time."[326] In keeping with Jeffersonian distributive concerns, a person could acquire land by the act only once.[327]

Notably, the Homestead Act did not repeal the Preemption Act: the two statutes operated simultaneously, and a settler could obtain land by both (though not at the same time, since both required residency).[328] Indeed, applicants for homesteads could convert their applications to preemption; they just needed to come up with $200.[329]

By the last three decades of the nineteenth century, the nature of land policy—and the workaday business of the registers and receivers—had shifted significantly away from auction sales and toward settlement-based claims. Congress passed additional statutes that were variations on the Preemption and Homestead Acts, promising title to land, at a low price or free, in exchange for various kinds of cultivation.[330] These statutes were known collectively as the settlement laws. Though the government as of 1862 had designated substantial amounts of land as available for eventual auction sale (and did in fact auction such land in subsequent years), it moved relatively few new acres into that category.[331] Thus, the settlement laws became the only method for individuals to acquire federal land in "[a]pproximately two-thirds of Kansas, a larger fraction of Nebraska, all of Oklahoma and the Dakotas, and all of the public land farther west except for California and small areas in Colorado, New Mexico, and Washington."[332] Congress completely abolished auction sales in 1888–91, leaving only the settlement laws standing.[333]

Under the strongest Jeffersonian reading, the settlement laws mandated that the West be settled exclusively by yeomen obtaining small plots from the government and intending to stay on them indefinitely. But numerous Americans seeking land in the West had reason to prefer a different outcome. First, although the federal government was giving away *land*, starting a farm also required *capital*, and speculation was a ready way to obtain that, even (or especially) for poor people trying to make a start in a rapidly developing locality.[334] Second, a Jeffersonian distribution of land might fit republican political theory, but it would not permit profit-maximizing farms, or even (in many cases) economically viable ones.[335] Western lands were agriculturally diverse, and in many areas, 160 acres was smaller than the economical plot size, especially because the West was relatively arid, meaning that parts of farms needed to lie fallow each year to accumulate the necessary moisture.[336] Those who wanted to use the land profitably, or to gain from trade with those who did, sought ways of assembling units exceeding Jeffersonian limits. "No matter by whom they are held," wrote one commentator in 1881, "the public lands will be used for the purposes they are best adapted to, and the people who occupy them will ever be a law unto themselves as to acquirement and disposition of them."[337]

Thus, many Westerners stood to gain from a flexible administration of the settlement laws, one that allowed for a degree of speculation and accumulation. And while the settlement laws might seem to mandate a static economy of self-sufficient yeomen, their actual language did not clearly impose on settlers the kind of exacting requirements that would have been necessary to force settlers into that mold. In both the Preemption Act and the Homestead Act, the key requirements were that the applicant settle the land and intend to hold the land. But in neither statute were those requirements carefully drafted. As to the first requirement, there were many unanswered questions.[338] How much of a crop did the homesteader have to plant? How soon? How big a dwelling did the homesteader need to build? How soon? How long must the settler remain between six-month absences? How much leeway for bad weather? For sickness? As for the second requirement, the statutes only required applicants to swear that, at the time of the initial and final applications, they had no intent or agreement to sell the land.[339] There was nothing to prevent settlers, once they took title, from changing their minds and selling.[340] Even if settlers sold soon after taking title, they could simply say, "I changed my mind," and without additional evidence of their intent prior to taking title, there was nothing to stop them.

Even if the statutes had been clearer, they did not provide much of an enforcement mechanism. The law regarded the assertions of the settlers themselves as sufficient. The onus was on the government to disprove these, and it was under no requirement to investigate. As one official explained, "The laws are such that a man's title to land is determined by his own ex parte showing, and if he makes an ex parte showing which is good upon its face . . . , in the absence of somebody to go to the field to ascertain whether the showing itself is true, of necessity he gets title to the land."[341]

Thus, the registers and receivers confronted (1) statutes that, if read a certain way, practically allowed a good deal of speculation and accumulation; (2) applicants eager to speculate and accumulate; and (3) nobody to push back against the applicants. Registers and receivers reacted by indulging the applicants. "The idea prevails to an almost universal extent," wrote one commissioner of the General Land Office, "that, because the government in its generosity has provided for the donation of the public domain to its citizens, a strict compliance with the conditions imposed is not essential. . . . Our [district] land offices partake of this feeling in many instances, and if they do not corruptly connive at fraudulent [applications], [they at least] modify their instructions and exceed their discretionary powers in examination of final proof."[342]

Let me explain some of the most common techniques by which Westerners were able to speculate and accumulate, given the loose drafting of the laws, the absence of enforcement, and the indulgence of officials. Here are three.

*Pro Forma Compliance Followed by Sale.*   The simplest trick was for someone in a rapidly developing area to apply for land under a settlement law, make minimal improvements (thereby leaving time for other business), assert that the requirements were fulfilled, acquire the land, and sell, profiting not by the improvements but by rising values in the area. This route was available to all persons who found themselves in the right location at the right time, even those of little means. That is significant, because in the conventional telling, the exploiters of the land system were all fat cats and large "interests."[343] But, as we learn from the historian Paul W. Gates, it was not only the magnates but also the small fry who took advantage of the system. Though critics focused on "speculators who had considerable capital," says Gates, "the fact was that many people on the frontier were ready to evade the laws to gain additional land and they came to feel little repugnance about shading the truth in so doing." Against the monopolists "were arrayed 'honest' farmers who . . . might be taking advantage of loopholes in the land laws," for example, "to swear that they had made improvements—including a house 12 by 14 that might be nothing but a portable doll house 12 by 14 inches."[344] Speculators came in all sizes.[345] The settlement laws did not abolish speculation so much as confine it to persons physically present in the West (or to persons who could hire somebody physically present in the West), and many of those physically present were not rich. Small-time speculation in low-cost government land could sometimes open the way for a poor man to "finally establish himself as a stable farm maker. . . . [A] very considerable portion of the misuse of the public land laws resulted, it appears, from the credit needs of actual settlers."[346] To actually achieve Jeffersonian ends, settlers needed a flexible and indulgent system.

*Selling Relinquishments.* This was a way to capture some of a plot's speculative value without waiting to make final proof, even pro forma. Say that A initiated a homestead claim and wanted to take advantage of rising values before the five-year mark. B wanted the land. B paid A to find out exactly when A would go to the land office to relinquish the application. Then, right after A relinquished, B filed an application for the same land. In this way, A extracted some of the value of the property, without giving up the once-in-a-lifetime homestead right. In itself, this kind of agreement was lawful. Still, critics thought it dangerous, since it encouraged people to make applications in contemplation of selling the relinquishment, with no intent ever to make final proof. *That* was clearly illegal.[347] But again, the statutory looseness that permitted this trick may have served Jeffersonian ends in the long run: the sale of relinquishments "permitted persons who lacked the means with which to begin farming to acquire some cash, farm machinery, and stock and after two or three false starts and sale of relinquishments to succeed finally in establishing ownership of a going farm."[348]

*Dummy Applicants.* Now say that A needed land but found it inconvenient to make applications under the settlement laws or had maxed out his entitlement. He therefore hired B to make an application. B might make a few improvements on the land to comply formally with the law, then acquire the land and quickly sell to A. This violated the rule that applicants awaiting title could not make agreements to sell. But proving the violation would require proving B's intent prior to taking title, which was difficult. It was especially common for an employer to ask his employees to act in this way as dummy applicants, paying each for doing so. The payoffs could go as high as $1,000.[349] That was enough to buy a farm in a lower-cost area without the aid of the settlement laws. Serving as a dummy applicant meant helping somebody else acquire big tracts in violation of Jeffersonian principle, but the payoff could serve as a nest egg for a poor frontiersman—yet another ironic way to further Jeffersonian ends.

## 2. Facilitative Payments as a Cause of Officials' Liberality

In order to work, all of the settlers' techniques for speculation and accumulation required registers and receivers to take applications and final proofs at face value—to refrain from scrutinizing the applicants' actual physical improvements of their respective lands and their potential agreements with other persons to sell their rights. Why did the registers and receivers refrain from scrutiny?

A major reason was their stake in fees for accepting and granting applications. To be sure, this was not the only reason. Prior to 1903, registers and receivers also lacked the power to compel the attendance of witnesses, which diminished the chance of proving alleged violations.[350] And they did not have much time or staff to conduct investigations.[351] Still, fees appear to have been important.

In the early 1800s, registers and receivers were entitled to a commission on all cash raised from auctions,[352] which surely gave them reason to see that land was sold and perhaps to seek higher prices for it. But as auction sales went into eclipse during the second half of the century, the field officers came to depend mainly on flat fees for transactions under the settlement laws, meaning that they benefited not from higher prices but simply from the amount of land distributed. Within a single office, the register and receiver each received identical fees for every transaction, regardless of which of them did the work. In preemption cases, each received fifty cents (raised in 1864 to $1) for the initial application, apparently without regard to whether it went forward or not,[353] plus $2 if the applicant successfully made final purchase.[354] In homestead cases, each officer received $2 for an initial application and $2 for a successful final application.[355] The fee structure was similar for other settlement laws.[356] In the late nineteenth and early twentieth centuries, the registers' and receivers' fees under the settlement laws were their greatest source of official income.[357]

Given that registers and receivers made money from settlement-law applications and particularly from successful ones, they had a pecuniary reason to be liberal, so that people would feel encouraged to apply and so that applications would go through. Leading scholars have made this point, though not in any depth. Leonard D. White notes that "[r]egisters and receivers . . . depended on fees for their income; they were naturally disposed to accept claims fair on their face rather than to reject them."[358] Paul W. Gates suggests that the land officers tolerated bad-faith relinquishments because they "benefited from the number of entries [i.e., applications] that went over their desks."[359] In addition, Gates observes that the institutional culture of the General Land Office favored disposing of land, as opposed to managing it. On that point, he mentions that the agency's "principal local officials in the West [registers and receivers] were largely dependent on the fees they received and had shown in the past favor for legislation that would facilitate and increase the flow of land into private ownership."[360]

Sources from the period also suggest the influence of fees. William Sparks, a rare reformist General Land Office commissioner, urged in 1885 that registers and receivers be converted to salaries. He said he "found land offices conducted apparently with an eye single to their emoluments." "While a common complaint against local officers is the exaction of illegal fees," he continued, "there is reason to believe that a still more serious evil lies in connection with cases uncomplained of, because the parties paying the excess fees do so will-ingly in order to avoid scrutiny of their proofs."[361] Though Sparks was referring to illegal fees, he believed that the system of lawful fees provided cover for such illegal payments, and he was connecting officer-citizen exchange with unwarranted official indulgence. A newspaper in 1906 reported that an Idaho register and receiver had "induced settlers to take up land" in a certain area by telling them falsely that the land was to benefit from a public irrigation project. "It was natural," said the reporter, "that [the officers] should desire to increase the business before their office, since increased business means increased compensation."[362]

Because Westerners frequently sought to stretch the settlement laws, reg-isters and receivers who scrutinized applications closely would have to reject applicants, losing fees in those particular cases and potentially discouraging future applicants. Sparks, from his position at the (all-salaried) Washington headquarters, made a short-lived crackdown in 1885, ordering the suspension of all pending initial applications, plus closer scrutiny for new applications going forward. This caused political trouble for the Cleveland administration, which soon fired Sparks. Prior to turning against Sparks, the interior secretary in 1887 observed that "the new methods adopted by the Land Office to insure a more strict compliance with law" had apparently caused a "falling off" in settlement-law applications. "This decrease," he concluded, was "proof that the new meth-ods are bearing legitimate fruit, and that speculators and other evaders of the law have found out that . . . it is not safe for them to attempt to patent land without honest compliance with the necessary legal prerequisites. It also shows that many patents hitherto issued 'without the investigation necessary to deter-mine their bona fide or fraudulent character' went to those who did not desire them for homes."[363] Low scrutiny attracted fee-paying applicants, while high scrutiny repelled them. Once Sparks was fired, applications shot back up.[364] Presumably, any registers or receivers who contemplated crackdowns in their own districts would fear a similar blow to their business.

The pushback felt by an overly stringent register or receiver would come not merely from the diffuse decisions of potential applicants to refrain from applying but also in more concentrated form, from the private intermediaries who drummed up applications at each of the district land offices throughout the country. These intermediaries, known as land agents or land attorneys, had a large interest in the kind of laxity that attracted applicants. Indeed, applicants who stretched or violated the law were often abetted by a land agent who told them that their behavior was lawful, or that everybody did it.[365] Every such agent would presumably monitor the nearby register and receiver for any departure from the easy administration that fostered business.

On top of all this, there was yet another way that facilitative payments entered settlement-law procedure: the person doing the face-to-face adjudication often was not the federal register or receiver but rather a state or territorial officer (also paid by fees). For the convenience of settlers, Congress in 1864 had authorized settlement-law hopefuls to make their initial application before the clerk of a local county court (state or territorial). The clerk would mail the application and the register's and receiver's fees to the district land office, where the register and receiver would process the claim without ever seeing the applicant.[366] Since most rural court clerks in this era were paid by fees, the applicant would need to pay a sum to that officer on top of the others, but in doing so would save a long trip to the federal office. Congress in 1877 extended this local process to cover final applications.[367] Theoretically, the involvement of local officers might have allowed for stricter application of the settlement laws, since these officers lived nearer to the applicants and could more easily investigate them. Yet these officers were also more susceptible to local influence, and they typically lived by fees and therefore had the same interest as the federal officers in attracting applications. Sparks in 1887 believed that "the majority of proofs" were made before local officers and that only a "small proportion" of them were presented directly to the registers and receivers. The "only interest" of these local officers, he lamented, "is to get attestation fees. Accordingly, . . . there is not scrutiny of the statements of applicants. The widest possible opportunity is thus given for imposing false affidavits and proofs."[368]

As a qualification to the foregoing discussion of registers' and receivers' fee incentives, let me note that there was a long-standing statutory cap on the total fees that a register or receiver could take home each year. To be exact, each officer had an automatic salary of $500, on top of which he could earn fees, but no more than $2,500, for a maximum annual income of $3,000.[369] A sampling of fee data at five-year intervals from 1885 through 1915 reveals that the percentage of district offices reaching the cap varied between 30 percent and 63 percent. The average was 47 percent.[370] Thus, in busy offices, fee incentives were presumably softened to the extent that officers felt assured that they could reach the cap by relying simply on high exogenous demand. Of course, the fee incomes of local officers taking applicants' papers face-to-face were matters of state or territorial law, and they might well be subject to no cap.[371]

## 3. Support for Liberal Administration among Lawmakers and the Public

The settlement laws originated from the wishes of frontier congressmen who represented squatters. That class of congressmen continued to dominate public-land debates throughout the nineteenth century. In the administration of the laws for which they had pushed, Western congressmen wanted "flexibility," as Gates calls it. That is, they wanted administrative indulgence for a degree of speculation and accumulation by their own constituents. To be sure, they often invoked the dichotomy between the virtuous yeoman and the evil speculator. But in fact, they sought to protect the chance for their constituents to engage in some degree of speculation and accumulation—something that could be helpful not only to their rich constituents but also to their poor ones.

Speculation and accumulation depended on registers and receivers maintaining a liberal attitude. The absence of the power to compel witnesses, the relative paucity of staff, and the fee system all encouraged such an attitude. Western lawmakers knew all this, and they fought to keep administration as it was. "[A]s long as Interior and Land Office administrators were interpreting and administering [the land laws] in a way satisfactory to the West, allowing always for flexibility," explains Gates, "there was little conflict between the Washington authorities and Western people. But if the administration became inflexible and threatened to interpret laws in a way the West did not like, it could, and on a number of occasions did, incur the wrath of the West."[372] The most famous case was of Commissioner Sparks, discussed earlier, whose campaign of administrative reform led to his defenestration.[373] His successors got the message: none of them disrupted business as usual for the following sixteen years.[374] In this climate, we can appreciate why proposals to abolish fees went nowhere, given that such fees encouraged the free distribution that Westerners preferred.

As with citizenship and pensions, the permissive attitude toward accumulation and speculation in Western land depended on a perceived absence of scarcity. Millions of acres passed into private hands, lamented Sparks, "upon the single proposition that nobody but the government had any *adverse* interest."[375] As the U.S. military and Bureau of Indian Affairs removed the Indians ever farther west and ultimately confined them to reservations, there seemed (in the eyes of Congress) to be more than enough land for the advancing white population. The nineteenth-century United States, writes one historian, was "too much of a land of plenty to be worried over alleged or impending scarcities."[376]

#### 4. The Reaction against Liberality, the Salarization of Officials, and the Alienation of Service Recipients: Conservation Ascendant, 1891–1934

The facilitative payments that encouraged registers, receivers, and local officers to give away land fit nicely with the freely distributive Western vision. It was a vision premised on the absence of scarcity: there was enough land for everybody, so everybody could have what they wanted. But there gradually arose an opposing political movement for conservation. By the 1890s, as William

Cronon explains, there was a "general concern that American abundance was giving way to scarcity." Many Americans began to fear "that good farmland would no longer be so easily available for would-be homesteaders" and "that other resources might also disappear from the American landscape."[377]

Creepingly in the 1890s and then forcefully in the early 1900s, four changes occurred in policy and administration that promoted the preservation and careful management of the federal domain. The overarching idea was to distribute resources in a more targeted fashion that respected their finitude or to halt distribution altogether. This meant a departure from the old pattern of following the preferences of private land-seekers. As the new approach took hold, fee-taking officers lost power and salaried officers gained it, thus severing the transactional connection between officer and layman that had fueled the old regime of free and easy distribution. Let us consider the four changes in turn.

*The Transfer of Lands to the Salaried Forest Service.* Up to 1891, there had been no stable mechanism for the acquisition of land for timber. When offers for cash sale declined after 1862, timber firms had no way to acquire land except through manipulation of the settlement laws.[378] Congress in 1891 authorized the president to set aside timber lands as forest reservations, to which the government would retain title while allowing commercial use under the administration of salaried superintendents.[379] Acreage set aside by the first presidents after 1891 was modest,[380] and the early superintendents did not carve out much of an identity for themselves, for they were patronage appointees, working under the distribution-oriented General Land Office.[381]

Entering the White House in 1901, Theodore Roosevelt changed course. He reserved three times as much forest land as his predecessors, constituting most of the national forests to this day.[382] After winning a tenfold increase in appropriations for the superintendents, Roosevelt and his allies persuaded Congress in 1905 to transfer those officers to the Department of Agriculture, where they ultimately became the Forest Service.[383]

By reason of sloppy classifications and Roosevelt's aggressiveness, a large portion of "forest" reservations actually were not forests.[384] In truth, these reservations, encompassing diverse landscapes, constituted a complete rival system of public-land administration—an alternative to the old land officers' distributive attitude.[385] The Forest Service's aim was "to prevent [the lands'] destruction so that they could be managed and harvested in perpetuity as a resource for future generations of Americans."[386] That kind of program—sensitive to the needs of future generations—was a major departure from the registers' and receivers' solicitude for the immediate wishes of paying customers. Western congressmen, who represented those paying customers, greatly resented the new system, but they could not stop it.[387]

*The Use of Salaried Special Agents to Investigate Settlement-Law Claims.*    Rising anxiety over scarcity not only originated the new forest laws; it also reshaped the administration of the preexisting settlement laws. "As long as there was an overabundance of public land available for agriculture, timber, water, and fuel," explained Roosevelt's interior secretary, "few, if any, complaints were made regarding either the misappropriation or misuse of the public domain, but the rapidly increasing population in the public-land States has changed this condition," for now Westerners were, he believed, finally recognizing that resources were "not inexhaustible."[388] According to Roosevelt himself, people who complied with the settlement laws were in a zero-sum game against people who did not: "In so many cases the success of the fraudulent claimants means the prevention of the establishment of a home by some honest home seeker."[389] "The essential fact about public land frauds is not merely that public property is stolen," he later attested, "but that every claim fraudulently acquired stands in the way of the making of a home or a livelihood by an honest man."[390]

Roosevelt accordingly expanded the role of the General Land Office's special agents, salaried investigators whose job was to scrutinize applications.[391] The employment of such agents had been authorized by Congress since the 1870s, ad hoc each year through the appropriations statutes, but their numbers were small.[392] Amid a series of events that put settlement-law compliance in the spotlight,[393] Roosevelt in late 1906 issued an executive order barring any applicant from taking title under the settlement laws "until by an examination on the ground actual compliance with that law has been found to exist." "For this purpose," the president told Congress, "an increase of special agents in the General Land Office is urgently required."[394] This was a radical departure. It effectively divested the registers and receivers of their unilateral power to grant final applications, requiring a salaried officer to investigate the application first. To pay for the additional special agents, Roosevelt demanded a bigger appropriation, complaining that those to date "have been utterly insufficient."[395]

After a brief delay, Congress gave Roosevelt the increase he wanted. To measure it, we can take as a baseline the average of real appropriated dollars per final homestead application for the years 1885, 1890, 1895, and 1900. Fiscal 1905 already exceeded that baseline by 105 percent, and while there was no increase (and even some decrease) over the following few years, fiscal 1908–09 surpassed the baseline by 284 percent; fiscal 1909–10, by 706 percent; fiscal 1910–11, by 443 percent; and fiscal 1911–12, by 388 percent.[396] It diminished thereafter, but

Roosevelt himself had promised that the appropriation could be "continually diminishing" once the initial backlog was cleared.[397] As to the number of special agents, it is hard to find perfectly comparable figures from year to year, but they appear to have grown by a factor of three or four.[398] The number of applications investigated rose rapidly, from 3,903 in fiscal 1906–07 to 8,700 in fiscal 1907–08 to 22,077 in fiscal 1909–10, in which range it stayed.[399] By 1912, 17 percent of final applications underwent on-site investigations, which were targeted on the basis of high-risk categories, tip-offs, and information acquired incidentally in the investigation of separate cases.[400]

The watchful eye of the special agents made it much harder for Western-ers to acquire land by pro forma compliance with the settlement laws. The agents inspected the land to verify the value and extent of improvements and cultivation, asked neighbors whether the applicant had been living there con-tinuously, and sought to discover contacts between the applicant and hidden parties in interest.[401] The investigations were serious: the rate of adverse reports was between 30 percent and 40 percent from 1911 to 1914.[402] To be sure, an ap-plicant receiving an adverse report could demand a hearing before the (histori-cally pro-claimant) register and receiver, but the special agent would represent the government at that hearing.[403] This made the application a far more costly undertaking than in the old days. Furthermore, the special agent was a "repeat player," having no stake in the success of applicants. He could report registers and receivers to the Washington headquarters if they were overly pro-claimant. In addition, the incentives of registers and receivers to seek application fees may have been partly neutralized, since they were also entitled to fees for hearings, and the special agents were big initiators of hearings.[404] After 1909, it became even harder for applicants to contest their failure to comply with cultivation requirements, for in that year Congress passed the Enlarged Homestead Act, authorizing applicants in dry regions to take up 320-acre units (often still too small to be economical),[405] but with the proviso that they meet cultivation re-quirements far more exact than in the 1862 law: "cultivation of one-sixteenth of the acreage entered beginning with the second year, and one-eighth to be continuously cultivated from the beginning of the third year following the tak-ing up of the claim."[406]

The special agents severed the bond of reciprocity between officials and Westerners, who felt quite alienated. The new "critical examination" of applica-tions "was not well received in the West."[407] On-site inspections were "slow" and "bound to work hardship on the settler." They made it "increasingly difficult for a homesteader to get his patent."[408] Jeffersonian principles of land acquisition, when implemented without the liberality of the prior era, turned out to be onerous and unreasonable. Farming was full of uncertainty, particularly in the arid regions being settled circa 1910, and cultivation requirements could be cruel if strictly enforced. Senator William Borah—a "progressive" on many fronts, but not when he witnessed the pain that rationalization inflicted on his own constituents—lamented in 1912 that "these land laws have come to be in their operation extremely harsh, forbidding to go upon the public domain those who have not the means to remain there for a long period of time and continue to develop and reclaim their land at a comparatively heavy expense."[409] That year, Congress reduced the residency requirement for homesteads from five years to three, acknowledging that "on the remaining [dry] land the average family could not hold out for five years. The point of starvation was reached short of that, and consequently it would be humane to shorten the required time of residence to three years."[410] Now that administrators were no longer liberal, Congress had to loosen the requirements of formally enacted law.

Special agents became hated men in the places where they worked. Western congressmen condemned their "spying" and accused them of harassing home-steaders.[411] "At best the work of a special agent is most difficult," observed the in-terior secretary in 1909, for "[n]o matter how honestly, how effectively, he works, he is constantly subjected to the criticism of every [applicant] upon whose claim an adverse report is made." The secretary acknowledged charges (which he con-sidered "wholly unwarranted") that special agents, "as a class, are dishonest, ty-rannical, or ignorant of their work and the conditions on the public domain."[412] Concerned about excessive adversarialism, administrators in Washington made sure agents were "definitely instructed that they are not to presume any man guilty of violating the law" and that they were to give "the settler a favorable re-port whenever good faith was shown and a real intent to make a home could be drawn from all the circumstances of the case."[413] Plainly, the special agents and the settlers had different ideas about what constituted "good faith."

*The Drop in Applications to Registers and Receivers.* In addition to the changes in forest policy and settlement-law enforcement, a third factor leading to the mar-ginalization of the fee-taking officers was the organic diminution in the amount of attractive land and, therefore, of settlement-law applications. The number of initial applications fell by more than half between 1916–20 and 1925–30. It never recovered.[414] The number of district land offices accordingly fell. There were about one hundred such offices in the 1910s but only twenty-three by 1934.[415] This is significant, for it was only with the decline of applications and offices that the last of the Westerners' techniques for speculation and accumulation (especially the sale of relinquishments) finally faded away.[416]

*The Transfer of Lands to the Salaried Grazing Division.* Already in decline, the old fee-taking officers were driven to the brink of extinction in 1934 by our fourth factor, the reform of grazing law, which was again premised on scarcity concerns. By the 1930s, the attractive land that remained under the district land officers' jurisdiction was generally suitable for grazing and nothing else.[417] Grazing had much bigger economies of scale than farming and often required one thousand acres or more, thus making it an especially bad fit for the settlement-law model of small plots.[418] Historically, owners of cattle and sheep had not acquired federal land at all but instead used it as a commons, though they did hire dummy applicants to acquire plots with special resources, like water.[419] Some of the "forest" lands under control of the Forest Service were actually range lands, where the service tackled the problem of overutilization through its usual method of regulating for sustainable use. Conservationists wanted a similar regulatory model for all grazing land, as did wealthy stockmen concerned about overgrazing of the commons.[420] But instead Congress (over stockmen's objections) made a quixotic attempt to extend the settlement-law model to grazing, passing a settlement law for owners of cattle and sheep in 1916.[421] The law allowed units of only 640 acres, larger than under the farming laws but still insufficient for cattle or sheep, not to mention the fact that breaking up the range into small units could harm its capacity.[422] Finally, in the Taylor Grazing Act of 1934, Congress gave up on distributing grazing lands and embraced the regulatory model: it placed the range under control of a new (salaried) Grazing Division within the Interior Department, which would permit exploitation on a regulated basis without giving the land away.[423] As a result, "practically all" that remained of "desirable land" was withdrawn from eligibility under the settlement laws.[424]

In all three of the personnel transformations discussed here—the rise of the Forest Service, of the special agents, and of the Grazing Division—a regime of facilitative payments, with a direct transactional bond between the officer and the layperson, gave way to a salaried regime with no such bond. In the first two cases (Forest Service and special agents), power became vested in officers who had secure tenure and stable careers within a top-down command structure. Hence, these two cases fit the common assumption in social science that salaries are part of a "package" with these other indicia of bureaucratization. But this view of salaries does not fit the story of the Taylor Grazing Act of 1934. In that case, power was vested in the Grazing Division, but only nominally. It was actually exercised, within each locality, by an advisory board of the locally powerful stockmen, who worked out the distribution of resources among themselves through a local political process, while shutting out "nomadic" stockmen unestablished in the area. The Grazing Division, thinly staffed and not professionalized, rubber-stamped the boards' decisions.[425] This model departed from the attitude of the old fee-taking officers, who impersonally gave land to anybody who paid, and it succeeded in mitigating the overutilization that had been the great disadvantage of the old distributive paradigm. Yet it did not fit the social science heuristic mentioned earlier: the members of an advisory board, sharing power in their parochial oligarchy, were the opposite of career bureaucrats operating within a top-down command structure. This story indicates how facilitative payments can be suppressed independently of the other indicia of bureaucratization.

After 1934, the district land officers, though still on the fee system, were completely marginalized. So was the distributive vision, oriented to the wishes of individual customers, which those officers embodied. A few fee-making registers survived up to the General Land Office's replacement by the Bureau of Land Management in 1946.[426] In their last years, they were like museum exhibits recalling a bygone era when it made sense to think of the relationship between official and layperson as one between seller and customer.

*Part Two*

———●●———

# BOUNTIES TO SALARIES

# STATE AND LOCAL TAXATION

## *The Tax Ferrets*

Part Two of this book traces the transition from bounties to salaries. As discussed in the Introduction, governance in the early modern period consisted mostly of familiar imposition, in which officers were members of the community and enforced norms that were in keeping with the community's social expectations. Under alien imposition, by contrast, an external sovereign sought to impose demands that violated community norms, often relying on outsiders to the community as enforcers. Although alien imposition had always existed in isolated pockets, lawmakers in the nineteenth century grew more ambitious, and alien imposition spread dramatically. The bounty—a reward that an officer received for doing something the affected person did not want—held great promise as an instrument to make alien imposition work, for it gave officers an extrinsic motivation to enforce sovereign directives faithfully and aggressively even when faced with the scorn and resistance of the communities and individuals whose expectations were being violated. Accordingly, lawmakers from the mid-1800s through the early 1900s experimented with bounties more intensely than ever before. But the very intensity of the experiment proved to be the bounty's undoing. Lawmakers were so disappointed, disillusioned, and disturbed by the results that they rejected bounties altogether. Though such rewards encouraged the aggressive exercise of coercive power, lawmakers concluded from experience that coercion alone could not achieve mass compliance with alien demands, for the state would never have enough enforcers to produce the requisite deterrence. Mass compliance required the population to trust the state and voluntarily cooperate with it, but bounties placed the officialdom and the citizenry in an adversarial relation that vitiated trust and cooperation. Official selflessness was necessary to vest the state's novel and alien demands with legitimacy.

In the nineteenth-century surge of alien imposition, no area was more important than taxation. Compared to the past, American lawmakers in the second half of the 1800s imposed taxes that were higher, fell on more kinds of wealth and activity, and entailed more intrusive surveillance into citizens' affairs. This chapter focuses on the dramatic growth of tax demands at the state and local level; Chapter 6 does the same for the federal level.

In the early 1800s, state and local taxation—consisting mainly of property taxes—was familiar imposition. The burdens on property owners were decided, in each locality, by an assessor who was elected by the locality and did the job part-time for a per diem allowance. This officer was deeply enmeshed in the local community's social and political life. Assessment was a face-to-face, participatory process of small-time political negotiation between the assessor and his neighbor-constituents. This consensual style of administration was sufficient to meet the government's financial needs. That was because (1) those needs were small and (2) most people's property took the form of farmland and livestock, which the assessor and everybody else in the community could see, so there was a focal point to foster agreement about the allocation of the tax burden. Personal property—and especially intangible assets like bank accounts and securities—was much harder for the assessor to find, and a social expectation developed that such assets, even if formally subject to taxation, would not be assessed, as a practical matter. This was not much of a fiscal worry, for such assets were still rare in comparison to land and animals.

But in the mid- to late 1800s, taxation went from familiar to alien. Legislators became far more ambitious and intrusive in their tax demands, knocking taxation out of equilibrium with social expectations. They began seeking much larger amounts of revenue, to cover new projects in sanitation, public health, policing, schooling, and highways. Meanwhile, industrialization and urbanization meant that intangible property replaced farmland as the primary form of wealth. Given intangible property's new prevalence, lawmakers decided they had to tax it. Doing so seemed all the more imperative in light of the rise of the liberal ideal of formal equality, which required that government tax all wealth at an equal rate, no exceptions. But these new demands collided with the expectation of the owners of intangibles, built up over the preceding years, that their wealth fell within a tax-free zone of privacy. Thus, by about the 1860s, lawmakers were demanding more taxes than ever before, and mainly from owners who expected that their property was practically tax-free. Taxation had become alien imposition.

Or, at least, legislators were *trying* to make taxation into alien imposition. But they were hobbled in that attempt by their continuing reliance on the local assessors, whose offices had been structured to engage in familiar imposition, not the intrusive and feather-ruffling investigations that lawmakers now wanted. Local assessors were beholden to the communities that elected them, through a neighborly kind of "hand-shaking politics." They were loath to upset any of their constituents, so they dared not violate the settled expectation of intangibles owners that their property was not to be taxed. With local assessors afraid to enforce, evasion remained the norm for taxes on intangibles, even as those assets became the bulk of national wealth. Tax evasion became an incredibly common and therefore unserious offense, like jaywalking today: "everybody does it."

Desperate to make their alien demands stick, state legislators—as well as the local lawmakers of big cities—adopted bounty-seeking as the seeming solution to their problem. From the 1870s through the early 1900s, they increasingly hired "tax ferrets": investigators who would discover tax liabilities (especially intangibles) that the ordinary assessors had missed, in exchange for a percentage of the proceeds. The people who became tax ferrets were usually outsiders to the counties and towns where they did their work. Their profit motive and their disconnect from the local community meant that they worked coldheartedly to maximize collections, in stark contrast to the neighborly accommodation of the old assessors. In particular, the tax ferrets invented and aggressively carried out new and intrusive methods of surveillance against the owners of intangibles, systematically searching county mortgage records, corporate stock books, and other sources of personal financial data.

But lawmakers' intense experiment with bounty-seeking ultimately caused them to lose faith in the practice. They found that tax-ferreting, which sought to achieve compliance through coercion and deterrence, in fact produced at most an incremental improvement in compliance and might actually worsen it. Lawmakers became convinced that a sound tax system depended on a high degree of voluntary taxpayer compliance—legitimacy—which the ferrets did not foster and might well undermine. This was in part because intangible assets were so easy for taxpayers to conceal and move. The payment of tax on such property required taxpayer goodwill toward the government. Starting circa 1900–10, reformers proposed a method for winning that goodwill: lawmakers should "classify" intangibles as a special category of property enjoying a lower rate. In the view of those who advocated this proposal, the mass of laypersons were not narrowly self-interested tax-minimizers but instead had some intrinsic desire to be law-abiding, so long as the law, in terms of its demands and administration, seemed reasonable and worthy of cooperation. By this thinking, bounty-seeking enforcement was counterproductive. It meant that state agents benefited when citizens violated the law en masse and were then forced to comply. This placed state and citizen in an adversarial relation and alienated them from each other, thus undermining the intrinsic desire of citizens to comply with law for its own sake and poisoning their trust in the state. Bounties aggravated the preexisting legitimacy deficit of lawmakers' alien demands. By rejecting the tax ferrets and classifying intangibles at a lower rate, lawmakers sought to reduce adversarialism, foster mass lay cooperation, and achieve legitimacy.

This chapter is the first historical treatment of the tax ferrets. Scholars in the time of the ferrets sometimes wrote about them, up till about 1930.[1] But since them, nobody has given them serious attention. The most notable mention is by C. K. Yearley, in his 1970 history of state government finance, and it totals little more than one page, during which Yearley unfairly repeats the depiction of the tax ferrets drawn by their most hysterical critics: that they were crooks and rascals. Further, Yearley refers to tax ferrets in only two states.[2] In fact, they were active in twenty. It is time we heard their story.

## THE EARLY PART OF THE 1800s: STATE AND LOCAL TAXATION AS FAMILIAR IMPOSITION

In about the first half of the 1800s, state and local taxation was a matter of familiar imposition. Paying taxes was something that people experienced as a local community event, not as the intrusive demand of some outside power. For the most part, state and local taxes fell on property, and they were assessed, in each locality, by a single assessor. This officer was socially enmeshed in the community he assessed: he did the job part-time and was normally elected by the locality—in some states by the county, though in other states by the (even smaller) town. The assessor worked out the allocation of the tax burden with his constituents by deciding valuations for their taxable property, which he did through a localized, face-to-face, participatory process of small-time political negotiation and accommodation.[3]

This kind of consensual, neighborly administration worked fine, for two reasons. First, the assessors were not asking for much, in terms of dollars. In the early part of the 1800s, revenue demands per capita were low compared to the levels they would reach by midcentury (to say nothing of later), even accounting for inflation and per capita income growth.[4] And the proportion of revenue dependent on taxes was also low: government land sales, government investments in infrastructure and banks, and other nontax sources of money provided a bigger fraction of state and local revenue than was ever to be the case again.[5]

Second, the assessors were not asking for much in terms of information. The economy was agricultural, so people's wealth largely took the form of land and livestock, which were easily visible, not just to the assessor but to the whole community.[6] The obviousness of townspeople's wealth provided a focal point that made it easier for the assessor to reach agreement with them about the allocation of the burden across the community. Tax-paying did not entail the invasion of privacy.

To be sure, there also existed less visible forms of wealth: personal property, especially intangibles like bank accounts, stocks and bonds, and "credits" (i.e., mortgage loans to individuals, a common form of real-estate investment). Intangible assets were "practically impossible" for the assessor to discover, "except through the declaration of the owner."[7] Admittedly, there might be evidence of such ownership in institutional records (of banks, corporations, or county recording offices). But for the taxpayers of any given locality, the relevant institutions might be scattered across the country. And there was no systematic index of such institutional information, much of which was private and confidential—something that did not change for the remainder of the nineteenth century.[8]

But the invisibility of intangible wealth did not cause much concern. It was not very prevalent compared with land and livestock, so governments did not feel much need to find it. The fact that officials could not easily discover intangibles—combined with the fact that politicians did not see much reason to try—gave rise to a social expectation that such assets, even if formally subject to taxation, would not actually be assessed, as a practical matter.

## THE LATTER PART OF THE 1800s: LAWMAKERS' HOPES FOR ALIEN IMPOSITION AND THEIR PRACTICAL FAILURE TO ACHIEVE IT

Up to the mid-1800s, state and local taxation had been a relatively placid affair. Government reached the bulk of wealth, since it was visible. Owners of such wealth paid light taxes through a localized process of neighborly political negotiation. And government was content to leave untouched the invisible remainder. But from midcentury onward, several developments caused lawmakers to become far more ambitious and intrusive in their tax demands.

First, the mass of wealth taking the form of personal property (and especially intangible property) grew too big to ignore. This trend had several causes. The industrial sector expanded. People left farms and moved to cities. More business was done through corporations. This meant that people with wealth increasingly held it in bank accounts, stocks and bonds, and credits.[9]

Lawmakers at the state and local level became more and more desperate to reach this less visible property. This was not only because of the assets' rising importance in the economy but also because of three other factors. First, the depression of 1837–42 wiped out many of the infrastructure and banking enterprises in which governments had invested, discrediting those sources of revenue and forcing lawmakers to rely more on taxes.[10] Second, public spending per capita grew dramatically. This upward trend was already evident in the antebellum period.[11] Outlays then spiked in the 1860s and remained high thereafter, driven by new initiatives in sanitation, public health, policing, schooling, and highways.[12] Third, lawmakers became enthralled with an abstract liberal ideal of formal equality, which required that all wealth equally bear the burden of supporting government, with no privileges or exemptions.[13] The liberal ideal was embodied in a standard scheme called the general property tax, under which every single item of property within a jurisdiction, whether a state or locality, was taxed according to its actual value at a uniform rate. Between the 1820s and 1860s, more than half the states committed themselves to the general property tax or something like it, either by statewide legislation or by constitutional provision.[14] All other kinds of taxes became suspect and were repealed or cut back. The general property tax became "virtually the sole source of revenues" for states and localities by the late nineteenth century.[15] This made it imperative for intangible property to pay its equal share.

Thus, by the 1870s, lawmakers were demanding more tax money than ever before, particularly from owners who had previously come to expect that their property was practically tax-free. Insofar as lawmakers succeeded in making people pay these newly ambitious demands, people would experience such payments as alien imposition.

But lawmakers did not succeed in making people pay, for they did not have the kind of officialdom necessary to do the job. They were still relying on the office of the local assessor, which had been structured to engage in familiar imposition, not to make the intrusive investigations and unprecedented demands that lawmakers now wanted. As a rule, the assessor was low paid (usually on a per diem basis), had no professional qualifications; had little to no funding for assistants, and had a mandate to complete his yearly work in a few months, thus leaving little time to conduct investigations.[16] Most important, he was part-time and typically elected by his locality (the county or even the town), such that he was deeply enmeshed in the local political community. He was accountable to the local electorate and subject to little or no supervision from farther away.[17] This meant he was "controlled politically by the very persons" whom he was "expected to assess."[18] The assessor wanted, above all, to avoid upsetting his constituents, and constituents who owned intangibles were likely to be extremely upset if he searched them out. The gradual historical process by which intangibles had become prevalent, combined with the incapacity of prior assessors to put such property on the rolls, had created settled expectations that such property was practically tax-free. Plus, owners of intangibles had a ready moral justification for their evasion: that taxing intangibles amounted to "double taxation." Mortgages were taxable to both borrower and lender; bank deposits, to both bank and depositor; corporate property, to both the corporation and the shareholders (taxed on their shares).[19] Since the moral theory of the general property tax was to allocate the burden equally and uniformly according to true wealth, owners of intangibles had an arguable claim that taxation of their property was unjust.[20]

And there was a further problem. The burden of the *state* property tax was determined for each locality by dividing that locality's total dollar assessment by the sum of all the total dollar assessments of all the localities in the state. Because of this, each assessor tried to make his locality's total dollar assessment as low as possible, to minimize the share of the state burden that his constituents would collectively have to pay.[21] In doing this, the path of least resistance was to ignore intangibles and undervalue real estate. Decades of realty undervaluation, in turn, caused state legislators and local lawmakers to push tax rates sky-high, on the assumption that a high rate on realty would be softened by a low assessment. But these sky-high rates could have disastrous consequences when intangibles came into the picture. Most intangibles were incapable of under-assessment, since they had dollar denominations or were traded on public markets. Thus, *if discovered*, intangibles would suffer an extremely high effective rate—much higher than on realty, indeed so high as to consume one-third or one-half of the asset's annual income, which was beyond almost anybody's notion of a reasonable tax rate.[22] This gave owners of intangibles yet more reason to feel unjustly violated if the assessor listed their assets.[23]

Pushback against such taxpayer expectations was dangerous to the assessor, whose continued employment and advancement depended on a neighborly kind of "'hand-shaking politics'" within the county or town.[24] Assessors were "afraid to be over-diligent in the discharge of their duty," wrote Richard Ely in a discussion of Ohio personalty in 1888, "knowing that in such a case they would not be re-elected."[25] Another commentator in 1904 explained the ineffective assessment of intangibles by noting that the officers were "dependent on public favor" and did "not wish to make enemies."[26]

By the strict terms of the general property tax, intangibles in the late nineteenth century should have been shouldering most of the state and local tax burden, but, given the timidity of the assessors, evasion was the norm—an unserious offense that everybody committed, like jaywalking. "Before the enactment of Prohibition," writes Yearley, "probably nothing in American life entailed more calculated or premeditated lying than the general property tax."[27] A longtime Ohio tax official told Ely in the 1880s that "there is not a wealthy man in the state of Ohio who is not a perjurer."[28] Statistics bore this out. Between 1860 and 1880, the nationwide total of nominal assessments for realty grew 87 percent, whereas for personalty it fell 24 percent.[29] This was crazily at odds with reality: nominal gross domestic product nearly tripled in that time period, and wealth was undoubtedly shifting *toward* personalty, given industrialization.[30] Intangibles accounted for much of the gap. In Ohio, all banks in 1900 reported their total deposits, the sum of which more than doubled the statewide assessment of all intangible property.[31] Observers believed the escape of intangibles was particularly widespread in cities, where most intangible property owners lived. This made sense: the local electorate's domination of the assessor meant that, in the localities where owners of intangibles were most numerous, the assessor was least inclined to burden them.[32]

Against this background, the few evaders who were caught and forced to pay experienced the enforcement action as an arbitrary injustice—and an antisocial, illegitimate act on the part of the officer. They "feel, if compulsory steps are taken against them," said the jurist Thomas Cooley in 1881, "something like a sense of personal wrong."[33] In the candid words of one state supreme court: "[S]o general has been the evasion of the law that the citizen has been compelled to choose between following the custom [that is, evading] and suffering a wrong [that is, paying]."[34] One commentator, in an essay published widely in 1903–04, said: "The citizen against whom [the tax] is enforced feels that it is spite work on the part of the taxing officers, because his neighbors escape, and he is soured for life. He determines that he will never be caught a second time and he never is. He becomes a student of the subject, 'How to Escape Taxation,' and as the lesson is readily and easily learned, he becomes a master in it."[35] Ely counseled that tax systems ought to be designed to "appeal to the intuitive feelings of justice in the community"—which the general property tax did not.[36]

## BOUNTIES AS A PROMISING MEANS OF ALIEN IMPOSITION: THE TURN TO TAX FERRETS, CIRCA 1880–1915

The general property tax, as applied to personalty and especially intangibles, was in flagrant violation of the expectations and norms of the owners of that property. The traditional assessment machinery of American counties and townships, premised on neighborly negotiation backed up by the visibility of property, could not do the kind of intrusive and anti-social work that the general property tax required, least of all at the sky-high rates that lawmakers had imposed.

And yet state and local lawmakers could not simply give up on their alien demands. Their need for tax revenue was desperate and growing, so they could hardly ignore such an important category of wealth. Plus, the tax reformers of the mid-1800s had often used constitutional provisions to eliminate or curtail taxes besides the general property tax, thereby leaving lawmakers of the late 1800s with no choice. And politically, the general property tax enjoyed strong and continuing support among rural voters, who maintained control of state legislatures even as cities grew, thanks to malapportionment.[37] This rural support may seem odd, given that the tax was far easier to enforce against (and therefore fell more heavily upon) farms and livestock.[38] Nevertheless, rural voters remained devoted to the tax, exhibiting a "superstitious reverence" for its formal equality. They wanted the authorities to find some way—any way—to force the city dwellers to pay what they owed by the letter of the law.[39]

Driven by these factors, state legislators and local lawmakers turned to a classic instrument of alien imposition—the bounty—to enforce their demands on the population. They designated agents with the specific mission to discover tax liabilities that taxpayers had not admitted and that the ordinary assessors had missed, in exchange for a percentage of the collections arising therefrom. The official names for these agents varied, but they were generally known by the informal name of *tax ferret* or *tax inquisitor*.

### Where the Tax Ferrets Were

The use of tax ferrets spread across the nation from the late 1870s to the 1910s. One of the first states to try the idea was Ohio, a leading jurisdiction. It was the third-largest state by population from 1840 to 1880 and the fourth largest from 1890 to 1930. In the late 1870s, Hamilton County (containing Cincinnati, then the eighth-largest U.S. city) contracted with two men to "hunt up property omitted from the tax duplicate."[40] The state legislature in 1880 approved the county's actions, though only for property omitted up till that time. In 1885, it prospectively authorized the state's four biggest urban counties (containing Cincinnati, Cleveland, Columbus, and Toledo) to contract for the discovery of any omitted taxable property, in exchange for a commission. It then extended that authorization to the remaining counties in 1888, this time with a cap of 20 percent on the commission.[41] The contractors in Ohio were called tax inquisitors — initially by their critics, but eventually by everybody,[42] including their staunchest defenders,[43] as well as the courts.[44] In the mid-1890s, more than half of Ohio's counties had contracts with tax inquisitors, including all the major urban ones.[45]

Similarly Indiana, in 1880 the eighth-largest state, would move to the forefront of tax-ferreting. Marion County (containing Indianapolis) contracted in 1878 for the discovery of omitted property for a percentage,[46] and the legislature in 1879 authorized such contracts whenever the county authorities found a "public necessity."[47] It reversed course and banned such contracts in 1881,[48] but then authorized them again in 1891.[49] After the state supreme court clarified this reauthorization,[50] the press reported that "the business of the 'ferret' has increased wonderfully . . . , and there is hardly a county in the State in which contracts have not been made."[51] A state commission in 1916 declared that "[t]he 'tax-ferret' has been with us for years."[52]

Southern states also embraced tax ferrets, styling them as officers rather than contractors. The Kentucky legislature in 1880 created a corps of "revenue agents" whose job was similar to the Ohio and Indiana contractors: discover omitted property for a 20 percent commission.[53] Observers recognized these Kentucky officers as "tax ferrets" and referred to them as such, sometimes analogizing them to the Ohio contractors.[54] Later, in the 1890s, three other Southern states created similar officers: Mississippi, a "state revenue agent" with a corps of hired deputies;[55] Tennessee, a set of "revenue agents";[56] and Alabama, a corps of "county tax commissioners."[57] All were paid by commission, and at least in Mississippi and Alabama, people called them "tax ferrets."[58]

Meanwhile, there were attempts to unleash tax ferrets in Illinois, the third-largest state. In 1884, Cook County (containing Chicago, then the third-largest U.S. city) hired tax ferrets to discover omitted property, though its power to do so was questioned.[59] It soon began lobbying the legislature for a grant of such power,[60] renewing the effort repeatedly over the following quarter century.[61] Other Illinois counties hired ferrets as well, though the state supreme court in 1905 held such contracts illegal, reasoning that local governments could not assign duties to agents other than those designated by law.[62] Nonetheless, Chicago politicians planned and publicized ferret schemes (and perhaps carried them out) into the 1910s.[63]

Intrepid county governments contracted with tax ferrets in other states, as well. They were doing so by the late 1890s in Iowa, then the tenth-largest state. In 1900 the Iowa legislature authorized the practice, limiting commissions to 15 percent.[64] Over the following decade, well more than two-thirds of Iowa counties, including all the urban ones, engaged tax ferrets, many of them repeatedly.[65] The contractors organized themselves into the "Association of Iowa Tax Ferrets," which gathered data, published pro-ferret pamphlets, and lobbied the legislature.[66]

Farther north and west, tax-ferreting made some inroads, if limited ones. Counties contracted with tax ferrets in the 1890s in Minnesota, but the state supreme court in 1900 held that they lacked the power to do so.[67] Hennepin County (containing Minneapolis) made an attempt in 1903, only to have a court block it.[68] Something similar happened in Kansas, where counties took up ferret contracts in the 1890s—one newspaper predicted in 1904 that ferrets would "no doubt spread to every county in the state"—but the supreme court in 1908 held that counties lacked the requisite power.[69] Tax ferrets next appeared in South Dakota, winning a contract with Minnehaha County (containing Sioux Falls, the state's biggest city) in 1909, only to have it invalidated by the supreme court in 1912 for the usual reasons.[70] In Colorado, ferrets were hired in multiple counties, including El Paso County (Colorado Springs), in the 1890s, but the supreme court held in 1906 that the county commissioners lacked power to hire them.[71] Still, this ruling arguably left open the door for the county *treasurer* to do so, which the treasurer of El Paso County did as late as 1913.[72]

Meanwhile, tax ferrets had better luck in the Southwest. The Oklahoma legislature authorized counties to contract with them in 1907,[73] and counties "commonly" exercised the power over the following few decades.[74] In Texas, ferrets contracted with several counties in the 1910s (including those containing Fort Worth and Austin),[75] and the state courts upheld such contracts as impliedly within the power of local governments.[76] The Texas legislature recognized and regulated the practice in 1930–31, requiring the approval of the state comptroller and attorney general and capping the commission at 15 percent.[77]

The attraction of tax ferrets was evident again in the attempt of two big Midwestern cities to adopt the practice in 1911. Kansas City, Missouri, made such a contract, only to be shut down by a court.[78] Meanwhile, Milwaukee—then under Socialist Party control—did the same. Socialists and tax ferrets may seem like strange bedfellows, but remember that ferreting was a ready method to mulct the owners of capital. Ultimately, the Milwaukee socialists' scheme was blocked in the courts, though socialist lawmakers attempted to get the practice approved by the Wisconsin legislature, both for the city and the whole state—a battle they lost.[79]

The tax ferrets' final inroads came in the South. The Georgia legislature, in what may have been ratification of an existing practice, authorized counties to engage tax ferrets in 1913.[80] Atlanta garnered attention in the 1930s when the city and county governments there contracted with a tax ferret who discovered several million dollars' worth of taxable property over about five years.[81] And in 1935, tax-ferreting took an absurdist turn as Huey Long, U.S. senator from Louisiana and effectively dictator of the state, had the state tax commission award a tax-ferret contract to a firm consisting of himself and one of his associates, with one-third of the proceeds as their reward.[82] Long was felled by an assassin's bullet four months later, so he never collected. (There was a trickle of late ferret activity in a couple of sparsely populated states: North Dakota, where it was attempted in Burleigh County, containing Bismarck, but shut down by the courts in 1924;[83] and Montana, where the courts approved it in 1930.[84])

Altogether, tax ferrets received the approval of the legislature in ten states and were employed by at least some localities (often the biggest cities) in ten others. The ten states giving legislative approval included 30 percent of the national population as of 1900, while the other ten included 21 percent.[85] Ferreting was of such great interest that the *American Law Reports* in 1921 compiled an entire commentary titled "Authority of County to Employ Tax Ferret."[86]

As noted earlier, it was in the taxation of personalty (especially intangibles) that people's expectations and norms were most averse to assessment and the need for official fearlessness greatest. Accordingly, the tax ferrets, almost everywhere they operated, focused on that area. For example, the Ohio legislature made clear it had intangibles foremost in mind,[87] and Ohio inquisitors did in fact overwhelmingly focus on intangibles.[88] In Indiana, the statutes permitted contracts for the discovery of omitted property, which implied a focus on personalty, since realty normally was not omitted (it was undervalued instead).[89] And in their operations, Indiana ferrets were mainly associated with intangibles.[90] The same pattern—statutes focused on omitted property and operations focused on intangibles—held in Iowa, Georgia, and Oklahoma.[91] In Texas, tax ferrets similarly focused on intangibles, both in the early years when they operated under judicial authorization and after they were regulated by the legislature.[92] Intangibles were likewise prevalent in the shorter-lived ferreting schemes of Colorado,[93] Illinois,[94] Kansas,[95] Missouri,[96] South Dakota,[97] and Wisconsin.[98] In the four Southern states that established tax ferrets as public officers (Kentucky, Mississippi, Tennessee, and Alabama), those officers had a somewhat more mixed portfolio: they certainly went after omitted personalty (particularly intangibles), but they also went after undervaluations of realty and evasions of license and privilege taxes.[99]

## The Promise of the Tax Ferrets: From Local Community Accommodation to Adversarial Bounty-Seeking

For lawmakers seeking revenue in the face of resistant social expectations, tax ferrets promised to make alien imposition work. Unlike elected assessors—enmeshed as they were in the "hand-shaking" politics of their localities and skittish about making constituents angry—tax ferrets worked single-mindedly to maximize their profits (and, with them, public revenue). They did so not only because of their right to a percentage of the taxes but also because their jobs were generally structured so as to cut them off from local political account-ability. Below, I discuss both aspects of the tax ferrets: their profit motive and their social insulation from the local community where they enforced the law. These were the twin guarantees of the tax ferrets' faithfulness as enforcers of alien policy.

First, some specifics about the tax ferrets' profit motive. All of the contractors and officers discussed in the preceding section were paid a substantial percent-age of the taxes arising from the property they uncovered. In many states, a statute set or capped the percentage, anywhere from 10 percent to 25 percent.[100] In unregulated states, percentages tended toward the higher end of this range, occasionally ranging well above it, to 50 percent.[101]

This made for a stark contrast with the local assessors, who in most states were paid a flat sum, usually $2, for each day on the job.[102] Some jurisdictions had begun paying their assessors annual salaries, which were often low to re-flect the part-year nature of the work.[103] Such pay schemes did nothing to spur aggressive assessment and may well have discouraged it, insofar as the low pay encouraged the officers to finish their part-time assessment work as fast as pos-sible, to free up more of the year for better-paid employment.[104] A newspaper noted that in Ohio "[a]ssessors are paid by the day, and as a rule, do their work with the least possible trouble to themselves, sometimes missing large amounts of property entirely."[105]

The tax ferrets' drive for bounty rewards was their crucial feature, as both their supporters and critics recognized. C. L. Poorman, the Ohio legislator who successfully proposed expanding the tax-ferret system to the whole state in 1888, explained the importance of the profit motive. Ohio's locally elected tax offi-cers were "required to look after omitted taxes," but "all of them have failed to do so, because there is no incentive, no inducement to assume responsibility or incur the expense necessary to produce results."[106] The auditor of Hamilton

County (Cincinnati), speaking in favor of tax ferrets after having worked with them, declared that "a clerk working on a specified salary" would not achieve nearly the results the ferrets did, since the clerk "would be sure to be paid his salary whether he succeeded in furnishing any information or not."[107] Similarly, the governor of Mississippi in 1924 opposed putting the state revenue agent on a fixed salary: those who supported the change, he warned, did so "because they knew that a man working on a salary would not prosecute them as vigorously and relentlessly as if he were getting a percentage of the tax."[108]

In addition to profit-seeking, the second key feature of the tax ferrets was their social insulation from the local communities where they did their dirty work. In most states where tax ferrets operated, they did so by contract with the county, as we have seen. The prevailing custom was for the county to hire contractors who were outsiders to the community. In Ohio, noted one observer, the tax inquisitor was "usually someone living outside the county, away from local political influences."[109] A survey in the mid-1890s found that, of the Ohio counties employing ferrets, 73 percent had one from outside the county.[110] The logical corollary of the ferrets' nonlocal status was that each ferret could service multiple counties, for a single county usually was not a full-time undertaking. In Ohio, it was "quite common for the same individual or firm to have a contract in several counties at once."[111] Contracting with multiple localities allowed an individual to make ferreting into a full-time job and even a career, thus acquiring experience and expertise unimaginable for the ordinary assessor. As one Ohio newspaper explained in 1906, "[t]he Inquisitors to be efficient have to be expert and of long experience."[112] The same pattern—of a single ferret holding contracts in many localities ranging beyond his home—definitely obtained in Iowa,[113] and there is also evidence of it in Georgia,[114] Indiana,[115] Oklahoma,[116] and Texas.[117] Nonlocal ferrets were likewise central to the shorter-lived tax-ferret schemes of Colorado Springs,[118] Milwaukee,[119] and Kansas City.[120] Critics of tax ferrets invoked the contractors' "foreign" status as part of their indictment, condemning them as "rank outsiders,"[121] or as "foreigners—persons who do not reside here and never expect to—who, it would seem, have no reputation to make or lose here."[122] It was far better, argued the anti-ferret Wisconsin Manufacturers' Association in 1911, for local government to follow the "judgment" of the locally elected assessors "in the administration of laws consonant with public opinion than to accept the services of non-residents."[123]

To the ferrets' defenders, of course, this was precisely the advantage of the tax ferrets: their insulation from the local social and political network and their consequent coldhearted devotion to the maximization of bounties (and public revenue). Accordingly, anti-ferret legislators in Iowa sought in 1902 to require that tax ferrets be residents of the counties where they operated, but pro-ferret forces defeated the proposal.[124]

Why would a locality contract for the services of an agent who would violate the social expectations of many of its constituents? The reason is simple: revenue. In nearly all the states where counties contracted with tax ferrets, the entity that contracted on behalf of the county was its elective legislative body, the board of county commissioners.[125] The commissioners, unlike local assessors, were responsible for—and elected on the basis of—the county's general well-being, including the amount and quality of public services. This gave the commissioners a much bigger political stake in raising county revenue than the local assessors had. Hiring a tax ferret was potentially a "win-win" proposition for the commissioners: they reaped the political benefit of higher revenue, and they acquired that revenue without having to do the "dirty work" in person, as the assessor would have had to. Indeed, once the tax ferrets had mulcted enough taxpayers, they could be sent on their way, like outside consultants hired by a present-day company to decide which employees should be laid off. (Note also that in several states the assessors were elected not at the county level but at the town level, where the electorate was even smaller and more neighborly; in such states, the difference between the county board and the assessors in terms of social distance from taxpayers would have been even greater.)[126]

In the four Southern states where tax ferrets held the legal status of officers rather than contractors, the incumbents generally enjoyed a similar insulation from local politics. None of the Southern ferret officers was locally elected. In Alabama, Kentucky, and Tennessee, they were appointed by a statewide officer.[127] In Mississippi, selection was by statewide election,[128] which presumably allowed the officer to maintain a more impersonal attitude toward his targets than if the election had been local. Like the Mississippi ferret, the Tennessee ferrets and several of the Kentucky ferrets were assigned to the state "at large" and not to a particular county.[129] Only Alabama confined every ferret to a single county, and it is probably no coincidence that the state at times had especially great trouble finding people to take the job and that the Alabama ferrets—despite their monetary incentives—sometimes exhibited the same softness as did the ordinary assessors.[130]

Defenders of the tax ferrets viewed the substitution of profit-seeking for "hand-shaking politics" as their great advantage. These enforcers would focus on money-making instead of constituent favor. To justify the ferrets' high commission, Poorman attested that "something is due to services employed in an unpopular business."[131] The auditor of Hamilton County, Ohio, insisted that a tax ferret was far superior to a salaried public employee, since the latter "would of course be selected from the city in which he is employed and would have a great many friends and would be inclined to favor such friends rather than make them enemies."[132] Opponents of the tax ferrets basically agreed with this description but thought it an evil rather than a good. "No elective officers," stated an anti-ferret Ohio lawyer, "would dare to perform the functions of a tax inquisitor."[133] A Kansas City newspaper, commenting on that city's ferret contract of 1911, summed up the matter perfectly: "Most of the aldermen contend that the 'tax ferrets' could discover nothing that an efficient and zealous city official cannot find. This is true; the only difference being that the 'ferret' would receive 20 per cent of the taxes recovered, whereas the city officials would have nothing but a sense of duty well performed and a fine lot of active enemies."[134]

### Tax Ferrets as Pioneers of State Surveillance

A big obstacle that prevents a government from truly penetrating the communities under its jurisdiction is a lack of accurate information about those communities—about the resources and activities of the people who inhabit them. To govern effectively, an external sovereign must find ways of making the population *legible*, to use James C. Scott's term.[135] The success of alien imposition requires the state to build up capacities of surveillance.

Tax ferrets had the incentive and the will to engage in surveillance in a way the local assessors never had. Further, the ferrets' nonlocal status allowed them to take up jobs in many localities—enough jobs that they could devote themselves full-time to this surveillance and perform it more systematically than assessors ever could. Said one county official: "[I]t requires a man of considerable business qualifications to be a successful tax inquisitor."[136] Several were accountants by trade.[137] At least one was a former U.S. internal revenue agent.[138]

In several ways, the tax ferrets pioneered techniques of seeking "information-at-source" that would later be used by state tax agencies. As mentioned earlier, it was common during this period for individuals to invest their wealth by making mortgage loans. Such mortgages were typically set down in the records of the county where the land was located.[139] Thus, in some cases, a tax ferret would systematically search the records of the county that hired him, looking for taxpayers who had invested locally.[140] An apparently more common technique was to search for mortgages in records of other counties, including out-of-state ones.[141]

The ferrets' investigations ranged further to include other public proceedings and records that might disclose personalty, such as those of probate courts.[142] Another source was divorce proceedings, where tax ferrets were known to sit in the audience, waiting for disclosure of the couple's personalty.[143] Yet another was receivership proceedings. For example, when a bank went under, the depositors had to file claims publicly, which could then be observed by a watchful tax ferret, looking for the names of anyone who lived in his jurisdiction(s).[144] (Solvent banks fiercely resisted disclosure of their depositors' names to tax authorities, for the high rate on intangibles might cause everybody to withdraw their money on assessment day, causing a run on the bank.[145] Such disclosure generally was not required,[146] or if it were, tax officers let it go unenforced.[147])

Tax ferrets also sought information about corporations, seeking the names of persons who owned their securities. Under this heading, out-of-state corporations were the most important, since their securities were less likely to be tax-exempt. Discovering such securities was a challenge: it required investigators with "state or nation-wide scope on stocks and bonds."[148] Tax ferrets tried everything they could. They sent spies to shareholders' meetings to take down names of those present.[149] Ideally, they wanted a glimpse of the corporate stock books, since these included the dates of purchase, which might allow for collections going back several years.[150] Such books might be accessed by several means, like purchasing shares in the corporation and making demand on the directors,[151] or paying off a New York broker.[152] By the 1910s and 1920s, it was rumored that the tax ferrets had constructed an interstate network to exchange and compile information among themselves regarding the ownership of securities across the country.[153] Whatever the exact means, it was clear that tax ferrets frequently had to pay for information.[154]

## THE CRITIQUE OF TAX-FERRETING: THE FAILURE TO FOSTER VOLUNTARY COOPERATION AND LEGITIMACY

The tax ferrets had plentiful enemies and inspired numerous critiques, but the debates arising from many of these critiques appear to have been inconclusive, in part because the ferrets and their defenders often had quite reasonable rebuttals. For example, critics complained that ferrets pressured their targets into settling for more than they owed,[155] but the ferrets' defenders insisted that taxpayers were well protected by procedural safeguards, which always included judicial review of the ferrets' claims, and often a precourt hearing before a tax administrator.[156] Another critique was that tax ferrets mainly pursued "poor widows and orphans," whose property was exposed in probate proceedings and who were (supposedly) too unsophisticated to hide their intangibles.[157] But ferrets and their defenders countered that the profit motive pushed their enforcement efforts away from targets who were truly poor—widows, orphans, or anybody else—for it simply did "not pay a tax ferret to go after the 'small fry.'"[158] Yet another critique was that tax ferrets too often drew their claims from evidence that was easy for ordinary assessors to discover—and which those assessors perhaps *had* discovered but refrained from using. The fear was that ordinary assessors, knowing that ferrets provided a backstop, might be even more lax in their assessments, or worse, that the ferrets might bribe the assessors to be lax, to manufacture more cases of evasion on which to profit.[159] But to some degree, this critique was beside the point: the state and county authorities were not paying merely for the labor and expertise of the tax ferrets in listing intangibles, but also for their political and social willingness to make those listings— something elected assessors could never be counted on to do.

What ultimately convinced lawmakers to abandon the bounty-seeking strategy was a deeper objection: that a sound tax system depended on a high degree of voluntary taxpayer compliance—legitimacy—which the ferrets did not foster and might well undermine.

The proponents of tax ferrets generally viewed the tax-evading mass public as overwhelmingly and incorrigibly committed to narrow monetary self-seeking. In this view, the citizenry would comply with law only to the extent they were coerced by direct enforcement or the fear of it. A leader of the Ohio Grange, the state's main farmer organization and a strong defender of the tax ferrets, wrote in 1896 that owners of intangibles were returning millions of dollars out of "a wholesome fear that some [tax inquisitor] would unearth their hidings."[160] The Kentucky revenue agents, said one observer, aimed "to patch up the assessment by putting fear into the hearts of the people so that they would be afraid not to list their property with the assessor."[161] To abolish the tax ferrets, warned their defenders, was effectively to abolish the taxation of intangibles, for enforcement was the only thing that made people pay. The *Ohio Farmer*, organ of the state's Grange, declared that "[o]wners of these investments [stocks and bonds]—many of them—would never pay a cent of tax on them if not compelled to do so. The [tax-inquisitor] law is the only thing that will ferret out this and other hidden property."[162] "Eighty-five per cent of the taxpayers are dishonest," proclaimed one Iowa official, and "[w]ith the present tax ferret law shelved there would not be over fifteen per cent of the taxpayers who would list their money and credits correctly."[163]

But *were* the tax ferrets, through coercion and fear, *actually* fostering compliance with the general property tax? Some asserted that the ferrets had achieved results, but others asserted the opposite.[164] On this point, we must especially consider the two serious academic studies that attempted to gauge the effect of the tax ferrets. The first, published on Ohio in 1897, was by the economist Thomas Nixon Carver, then teaching at Oberlin (before moving to Harvard). The second, published on Iowa in 1911, was by the economist John E. Brindley of Iowa State College. While neither took a clear political stand for or against the ferrets—a testament to the two authors' intellectual honesty—they converged on one key point: whatever the effect of tax ferreting might be, it was certainly no more than an incremental improvement of an institution—the general property tax—which was, in the broader scheme of things, hopeless. The tax ferrets had not made compliance a norm. There had been no quantum leap. Tax-ferreting was "not capable of reforming the general property tax," concluded Carver. The listings secured by the inquisitors were "small . . . as compared with the taxable property in the state." Tax-ferreting "seems . . . like a last attempt to buttress up the decaying general property tax."[165] Similarly, Brindley, after condemning the general property tax as "antiquated," stated that the "few" Iowa tax ferrets whom he considered "thorough and careful" had "temporarily resurrected this worn out system and made it at least the shadow of a success in some of the counties of Iowa."[166]

Amid the apparent failure of the tax ferrets to shift the norm from evading to paying, commentators and lawmakers around 1900–10 began formulating an alternative way of thinking about property taxation. According to this new approach, the return of personalty and especially intangibles was, to a large degree, a voluntary act by the taxpayer, and government could not make it otherwise. One major reason for this inherent voluntariness was that such property was very easily concealed. And even if the owner were discovered and forced to pay taxes going back for a few years—say by a tax ferret searching mortgage records or corporate stock books—the owner could then sell the asset (not even suffering a tax discount, so long as the buyer did not live in a tax-ferret jurisdiction) and invest the proceeds in some new investment that the tax ferret had not yet discovered and probably never would.[167] Given that tax ferrets assigned to a jurisdiction tended to search for records of investments that were most convenient for residents of the jurisdiction (say, mortgage records of the county itself or nearby counties), taxpayers seeking to dodge the ferret would transfer their wealth to investments farther from the locality. Or if taxpayers still had trouble escaping the ferret, they could move to a different jurisdiction that did not employ one. (As the general property tax could take one-third to one-half an asset's income, it was plausible that people dependent on such income would move.) As a result, the government employing the ferret gained little in tax revenue over the long run and hurt itself by driving investment and perhaps population out of its bounds and environs. The mobility of persons and capital limited the practical effectiveness of coercion and fear.

This thinking was key to the argument against tax-ferreting as it evolved in the early 1900s. The idea that the tax ferrets would drive intangibles farther into hiding and cause them or their owners to flee the jurisdiction or avoid it to begin with—undermining the fisc and harming the local economy—came up in virtually every jurisdiction that employed tax ferrets.[168]

As taxpayers could move their intangible property or themselves beyond the sight and reach of the jurisdiction, some observers concluded that governments ought to give up trying to tax intangibles at all. Crucially, however, others argued that governments could succeed in drawing revenue from intangible property, so long as they did so in a way that recognized the largely voluntary nature of such taxation. Governments ought not to force taxpayers to comply so much as induce them to. The most common method proposed for doing this— not just in tax-ferret jurisdictions but everywhere—was to abolish the general property tax's uniform rate on all property and instead "classify" intangibles as a special category enjoying a lower rate. The purpose of the low rate was partly to redress the injustice of intangibles' having to pay sky-high rates that lawmakers had set in reliance upon the undervaluation of realty, but it was also a concession to the brute fact that owners of intangibles could easily conceal and move their wealth.[169] The Harvard economist Charles Bullock, a leading advocate of this "classification" proposal, explained it at a conference with state tax administrators from across the nation in 1909: "Intangible property is the easiest of all [kinds of property] to conceal or remove from one jurisdiction to another. It can be taxed successfully only by making the rate moderate and uniform throughout the widest possible area." "[A]ny rate exceeding what the property will bear," he warned, "must result in loss of revenue, injury to industries and such general demoralization as accompanies widespread evasion of law." Using the voluntaristic vocabulary of the market, Bullock noted that his proposal was consistent with "the ordinary business principle of adjusting charges and prices to 'what the traffic will bear.'"[170]

The promise of classification received empirical confirmation from some early experiments. When the city of Baltimore adopted one of the nation's first low-rate taxes on intangibles in 1896, the returns for that category increased more than ninefold in a single year.[171] When Minnesota did the same in 1910, its one-year increase was eightfold.[172] Admittedly, the reduction in the rate could limit or even eliminate revenue increases, but even then, the tax would be extracted in reasonable amounts from a large number of people,[173] as opposed to confiscatory amounts from a small number of people, who might then remove themselves or their wealth from the jurisdiction. In any case, the voluntaristic approach in Baltimore and Minnesota was achieving quantum leaps in compliance, far greater than what Carver and Brindley had concluded the tax ferrets were capable of doing.

Importantly, many proponents of classification posited that the mass public was not purely and narrowly self-interested but instead had some intrinsic desire to be law-abiding, so long as the law, in terms of its demands and administration, seemed reasonable, fair, and worthy of cooperation. An Iowa newspaper in 1910 attested that there were "many" citizens "who might cheerfully pay a fair tax on their moneys and credits" but who objected "to a confiscatory tax" and therefore were fleeing the state.[174] Minnesota, explained the state's tax commission in 1913, had recently tried classification, on the assumption "that the average man desired to be honest and that a low rate would permit him to make a truthful return" of his intangible property, "without the fear of having most of its income confiscated for taxes."[175] The Kentucky tax commission in 1914, discussing Baltimore's successful experiment in classification, emphasized that "practically the whole assessment is based upon returns of taxpayers," not on any kind of coercive enforcement; indeed, "the force at the disposal of the assessing department is so small that a complete annual assessment could not be had." That Baltimore had attained good results "under such circumstances" showed "that people will voluntarily return for taxation at a reasonable rate far more property than the most arbitrary dooming law can place upon the assessment list." A top Maryland tax official, in words cited by the Kentucky commission, explained that it was "generally admitted and recognized" that the rate was "reasonable," and so "public opinion fully supports the law and frowns upon any attempted violation of it."[176]

With this thinking in mind, we can now appreciate the deep objection to the tax ferrets—indeed to the very notion that enforcers should have a monetary self-interest in the act of enforcement. Bounty-seeking meant that the enforcer gained insofar as the citizen violated the law and the enforcer coerced the citizen to comply. The bounty reward publicized a state interest in noncompliance and coerced compliance, as opposed to voluntary compliance. It prevented the citizen from attributing good motives and good faith to the state—a prerequisite for trust. This placed state and citizen in an adversarial and mistrustful relation and alienated them from each other, undermining whatever intrinsic desire citizens might have to comply with law for its own sake. This was especially problematic where the government's demand did not arise organically from the local community but was instead a novel program of a sovereign separate from the community (like intangibles taxation). In this context, bounty-seeking aggravated the preexisting legitimacy deficit.

Some observers were quite explicit about the toxicity of the tax ferrets for cooperation and trust between the state and the lay public. Nelson W. Evans, an Ohio lawyer who wrote extensively on his state's tax system, offered this assessment of bounty-seeking in 1904 (when bounties consisted of 20 percent to the tax inquisitor, plus 4 percent to the county auditor and 5 percent to the county treasurer):

> The tax inquisitor law is necessarily demoralizing. It demoralizes the tax in-
> quisitor, the auditor, the treasurer and the tax victim. No victim of a tax in-
> quisitor can ever feel towards his state as he did before his treatment by the
> tax inquisitor. No man could ever feel justly patriotic to a state which sold
> him out to the tax inquisitor, the auditor, the treasurer for 29 per cent [i.e., the
> sum of these enforcers' commissions] of what they could wring out of him.
> A citizen thus feels that he ought to change his domicile and does it when he
> can. . . . [T]he tax inquisitor law cannot sustain the general property tax in
> Ohio, but only make it more odious.[177]

Relatedly, Evans concluded that the tax-inquisitor system had "increased the withholdings of moneys and credits from taxation."[178] Similarly, the Brookings Institution in 1932 urged the government of Mississippi to abolish the state tax ferret's office, arguing that the "very existence" of that office "rests on the assumption that taxpayers and officials are intentionally dishonest. The purpose back of [the office] is to make citizens . . . honest by fear. The existence of the office is subversive of that public spiritedness and morale which is indispensable for sound taxation and public service." The office had to be discontinued "to create that morale in the citizens of the state which is so necessary for good government."[179]

These explicit discussions of citizen psychology by Evans and the Brookings Institution suggest the kind of thinking that presumably underlay the common point, made by many informed observers, that tax-ferreting had a negative effect on mass compliance that might offset whatever increases in compliance resulted from the ferrets' coercive acts and the fear they inspired. E. R. A. Seligman, the nation's foremost tax professor, articulated the idea in 1913: "When an effort is made to introduce still more drastic methods [to enforce the general property tax] by the employment of so-called 'tax-inquisitors' or 'tax-ferrets,' . . . the situation becomes still worse. The only result of more rigid execution of the law is a more systematic and widespread system of deception" by the taxpayers.[180]

Many observers who lived under the tax ferrets made similar points. Consider the testimony of M. E. Ingalls, the prominent railroad executive and future president of the National Civic Federation, before the Ohio legislature in 1896. The personalty assessment of Cincinnati had fallen during the reign of the inquisitors. To explain this, Ingalls argued that the tax inquisitors increased the salience of the general property tax's injustice and thereby reduced the inclination of more conscientious people to comply voluntarily. The decline "has been the result of an attempt to enforce an unjust law or one that the people believe to be such. When you attempt that, you draw attention to it, and people will evade the law in every way in the world. . . . Men who are paying tax for any thing, when the law is passed, enforcing it which they think unjust, their attention being thus especially called to its injustice, the returns thereupon always decrease." "Chicago," continued Ingalls, "has very nearly the same law as in Ohio for taxing unseen things, but they have never allowed the appointing of an inquisitor. They leave it to the auditor to get what he can, and to the conscience of the people; and as a result, more personal property is put on the duplicate than you have."[181] Five years later, the Ohio legislator James R. Garfield echoed the point before a National Civic Federation conference, contending that the tax-inquisitor system "has proved not only useless but demoralizing"— "[d]emoralizing because it has produced contempt for the law."[182] An Ohio tax commission estimated in 1908 that, "after more than fifty years of experience, with all conceivable methods in the way of inquisitor laws, severe penalties and criminal statutes, designed to force the owners of moneys and credits, stocks and bonds, to put their holdings upon the tax duplicate," the "percentage of such property returned" was "less than ever before." Worse, "public sentiment seems to be more and more openly approving an evasion of the law."[183] In Wisconsin, the Manufacturers' Association warned that the employment of tax ferrets, judging by the experience of other states, would result in "obliterating from the tax rolls much of the personal property that is now found thereon."[184] In Georgia, declared the Princeton economist Harley Lutz, "the practice of employing tax ferrets" caused "transfers of residence, transfers of trusts and estates to banks and trust companies outside of the state, and other methods of escape," leading to "the disappearance of intangibles" from the tax rolls.[185]

The notion that tax ferrets placed the state in an adversarial stance toward the citizen, one that was counterproductive in a context where cooperation and trust were essential, resonated with a major study of state tax administration conducted by Walter Heller, the great economist, at the start of his career in 1941, in which he argued:

In most government activities, the official is offering substantive services to the public. The tax gatherer has nothing to offer but his claims. To sell such wares requires a gifted salesman. . . . [A] chip on the auditor's shoulder can create [in the taxpayer] a "come and get me" attitude which will be costly to

the state in added auditing outlays and reduced revenues. Technical competence must be tempered with personality traits that elicit taxpayer cooperation. Those traits . . . should be encouraged in the . . . promotional system
of the tax department. By overemphasizing tax productivity as a promotional
basis, the federal government and many states inculcate in their field audit
personnel an attitude which damages an otherwise valuable asset, viz., taxpayer good will.[186]

Heller was writing about the salaried employees of a public agency, not about
tax ferrets. But if an emphasis on "productivity" could be counterproductive in
an agency's promotional system, how much more counterproductive might it
be to have enforcers depend for their living on the maximization of collections,
as did the tax ferrets?

Consistent with this, the tax ferrets themselves tended to lobby in favor of
retaining the general property tax as opposed to classifying intangibles.[187] This
was understandable in raw business terms. A lower rate would reduce the tax
for each dollar discovered, whereas the cost of discovering that dollar would
remain the same, thus reducing tax ferrets' profits. But the tax ferrets' opposition to classification likely had a deeper reason: their business thrived on the
norm of noncompliance. To the extent that classification threatened to reverse
that norm and foster voluntary cooperative taxpaying, it struck at the tax ferrets'
reason for being.

## THE REPUDIATION OF THE TAX FERRETS AND
## THE QUEST FOR VOLUNTARY COOPERATION

To see how lawmakers addressed the problems of legitimacy, trust, and cooperation described in the preceding section, I offer case studies of the repudiation of the tax ferrets in three states: Iowa in 1910–11, Ohio in 1906–10, and
Wisconsin in 1911. I select these three because, among the bigger states that
experimented with tax ferrets, their rejections of that method occurred in relatively concentrated statewide legislative reforms on which there is a reasonable
amount of source material (no small thing, since state legislatures in this era
kept almost no substantive records of their deliberations).

My main finding is that, in all three states, the repudiation of the tax ferrets
was closely associated with the low-rate classification of intangibles (or something like it), which reflected a program to reduce adversarialism, foster voluntary cooperation, and achieve legitimacy. I begin with Iowa, because the
process there was straightforward. Knowing the story of Iowa helps us discern

the underlying meaning of the more complicated events that occurred in the other two states. We then move to Ohio, which is of particular interest because it was a very big state whose experience was closely observed by people across the nation. We close with Wisconsin, which is of interest because, at the same time that it rejected the ferrets and lowered the burden on intangibles, its lawmakers replaced the intangible property tax with a close substitute—an income tax focused mainly on income from intangible property—and this proved to be the first permanent income tax ever to be successfully implemented in the United States, providing an important model in the long-term development of American taxation.[188]

To ensure that we appreciate what great faith American tax reformers of the early 1900s placed in low-rate classification and voluntary cooperation as substitutes for the tax ferrets' adversarial methods, I shall point out below that the legislatures of Iowa and Ohio, when they committed themselves to nonprofit tax administration, did very little else to strengthen their tax systems apart from low-rate classification (or something like it). In particular, the new nonprofit regimes in Iowa and Ohio did nothing to vest tax administrators with secure tenure and career stability, and they did relatively little to subject them to top-down control. As I said in this book's Introduction, it is a common view in social science that salaried jobs tend to be associated with secure tenure, career stability, and top-down control. But in these states, that association did not hold. In Iowa and Ohio, the lawmakers who rejected the tax ferrets believed the voluntarist potential of the low rate would by itself meet the challenge of compliance. These lawmakers may have been inspired by some of the early experiments in classification, which greatly increased compliance without a centralized career bureaucracy.[189]

On this point, the story of Wisconsin was somewhat different. There, the lawmakers who rejected the ferrets did not rely solely upon the lowering of the burden on intangibles. Instead, they coupled that lowering with major reforms of the assessment apparatus, providing secure tenure and career stability to the assessing officers and placing them under top-down control. Compared with the pre-reform assessors (who had been elected annually by the town),[190] officials under this reform enjoyed greater independence and insulation from the assessable population, and they were therefore more fearless in enforcing the law, but without the extreme alienation associated with profit-seeking tax ferrets. Wisconsin reformers viewed *both* reform measures—the lowering of the burden to promote voluntary compliance *and* the insulation of administrators through career stability and top-down control—as essential to the tax's success. Thus, the not-for-profit, voluntarist vision was a freestanding reform in Iowa and Ohio and a key element of a larger reform package in Wisconsin.

As I discuss below, the reforms in Iowa and Ohio increased compliance, but they were less successful in doing so than those of Wisconsin. The reason for Wisconsin's greater success may well be that it coupled bounty abolition and the lowering of the burden on intangibles with career stability and top-down control for officials. But my aim here is not to identify the measures that optimize administrative performance. Rather, it is to identify the considerations that in fact convinced lawmakers to swear off bounty-seeking. Lawmakers of Iowa and Ohio may not have achieved as great success as Wisconsin, and the approach they adopted—lessening the burden on intangibles to foster citizen cooperation but not providing officials with career stability or putting them under top-down control—was sometimes criticized as incomplete. But what matters is that they found it superior to bounty-seeking, so much so that they never took up bounties again. This confirms that the vision of voluntary cooperation—the only factor present in all three of the states at the time they repudiated the ferrets—was the actual and proximate cause of the nonprofit regime that has been handed down to us. Furthermore, it appears that, even in Wisconsin, reformers considered the lessened burden and the cooperative vision to be a necessary (if not sufficient) basis for the nonprofit regime.

## Iowa, 1910–11

Though Iowa had seen various unsuccessful efforts to abolish the tax ferrets prior to 1910,[191] the voluntarist critique of the ferrets got a major boost that year from the release of the decennial U.S. census, which showed that Iowa had lost population in the preceding decade. Numerous Iowans attributed this unwelcome fact, at least in part, to the application of the general property tax to intangibles and its enforcement by tax ferrets. These factors, it was said, had driven people to move out of the state (or to refrain from moving in) and had caused a flight of capital that hampered economic development, further constraining population.[192] At its session in early 1911, the legislature banned the hiring of tax ferrets and then, later in the same session, classified intangibles as a special category to be taxed at a low uniform rate throughout the state; both bills passed both houses by margins of three to one or better.[193] Newspaper accounts leading up to the session and commenting on it afterward viewed tax-ferret abolition and intangibles classification as two parts of a single reform, with the new low rate effectively substituting for the tax ferret as the means to foster compliance.[194] As one article stated: "Coupled with the new law abolishing tax ferrets[,] the exemption of moneys and credits [from the high general property tax rate] is regarded as an invitation to capital to remain in and come to the state, whereas the former subjection of moneys and credits to the ordinary rate of taxation and the employment of agents to ferret out this class of personal property . . . has been cha[r]ged to [be] one of the influences responsible for the loss of population of the state."[195] Another newspaper put it more color-fully: "Iowa has wiped out the tax ferret law and replaced the old money tax with a small uniform rate. Iowa says to those who have gone elsewhere for in-vestments: 'Bring back your money.'"[196] Stories abounded about how attracting persons and capital to the state required the repeal of the tax ferret,[197] or the classification of intangibles,[198] or both.[199]

Low-rate classification and its potential to foster voluntary cooperation made up the entirety of Iowa's program to meet the compliance challenge after giving up bounty rewards. Indeed, the state senate at the same session considered and rejected a bill to establish an appointed statewide tax commission that would impose top-down control on the town assessors.[200] The bill, reported one news-paper, "was regarded as entirely too drastic and expensive," and the senate de-feated it 22–18 (with ten senators not voting).[201] Within the senate, the balance of power was held by a bloc that embraced the new voluntarist vision of tax administration while rejecting top-down control of the assessors: fourteen sena-tors voted to abolish the tax ferrets and to place a low rate on intangibles but against the tax commission, and another five voted the same way, except they abstained from voting on the tax commission when it was narrowly defeated.[202]

The results of Iowa's reform were mixed and, to some, disappointing. The immediate effect on the intangibles assessment was more muted than in Balti-more or Minnesota; it grew by only one-half as of 1915. Still, it doubled by 1918 and tripled by 1920. The Brookings Institution posited that "[p]robably most of the increase" that had occurred "may reasonably be credited to the leniency of the tax," though some was due to economic growth.[203] Revenue declined some-what, but a much larger number of people shouldered the burden, making its distribution far more equitable,[204] which could reduce the flight of population and capital.

Observers gave multiple explanations for why the reform had not achieved a bigger instant leap in compliance. Several of these explanations were logically consistent with the voluntarist concept: (1) the reforms granted no amnesty for property unassessed in the pre-reform years; (2) they allowed tax ferret contracts that had been signed prior to February 1911 to run their course, which might be a couple of years; and (3) taxpayers feared that the reform might soon be repealed (though it never was).[205] Some observers, though, attributed the prob-lem to the legislature's refusal to provide for top-down control of the assessors.[206]

From its 1920 peak, the intangibles assessment receded over the following decade, though this may have been due to the deteriorating Iowa economy and a small increase in the tax.[207] In any case, the rejection of the tax ferrets remained final. The legislature refused to revive them, retaining a salaried regime backed up simply by the voluntarist vision.[208] Only in 1929 did the assembly begin to move in the direction of top-down control, establishing a statewide tax commission.[209] And it never provided its tax administrators with secure tenure or career stability: as late as 1958, the commission hired by patronage, resulting in one-third turnover when a new party came to power, concentrated among field auditors.[210]

## Ohio, 1906–10

Events in Ohio were more complicated than in Iowa, but they embodied a very similar dynamic: the repudiation of bounty-seeking enforcement in favor of a less adversarial strategy, aimed at fostering trust, voluntary cooperation, and legitimacy.

The Ohio legislative session that ran from January to May 1906 saw an attempt to abolish the tax inquisitors, which would have succeeded but for a "hasty adjournment," according to the *Ohio Farmer*.[211] Then, a few weeks after the session ended, Ohio's supreme court struck down the tax-inquisitor system in its entirety, but in a way that left the door open for the legislature to reenact virtually the same system if it chose. The court's decision rested on a minor technicality. The legislature had authorized the inquisitors under two statutes, one for the urban counties without a cap on the commission, and the other for the rest of the state, with a cap of 20 percent.[212] Because one statute had a cap and the other did not, the two were not quite uniform. The Ohio constitution required that all statutes must "have a uniform operation throughout the state" if they were "of a general nature."[213] In recent years, the court had been expanding the definition of "general nature" to include ever more kinds of statutes.[214] In the 1906 decision (*State v. Lewis*), it expanded the category to cover the tax-inquisitor laws and, since they were not perfectly uniform, struck them down.[215]

*Lewis* elicited a few different kinds of reactions. The *Ohio State Journal*, a leading Republican newspaper in Columbus, stretched to claim the decision as a victory for its own local crusade against inquisitor "graft." (The paper had supported a separate lawsuit against a different inquisitor from the ones in *Lewis*, for pocketing commissions for "discovering" property that was known to the ordinary tax officers, or should have been.)[216] The *Cleveland Plain Dealer*, a leading Democratic paper, did not present *Lewis* as having anything to do with graft. It just stated dispassionately that the decision might save public money in the short run by knocking out inquisitor commissions but hurt the fisc in the long run by weakening the deterrent to evasion.[217] For its part, the *Ohio Farmer* condemned *Lewis* as the work of high-priced attorneys in hock to tax-dodging "moneyed interests."[218]

In any event, *Lewis* left the door open for the legislature to reenact a virtually identical tax-inquisitor system if it chose. Between the decision's announcement in summer 1906 and the reassembly of the legislature in January 1908, observers anticipated a fight over reenactment.[219]

At the legislative session of 1908, one lawmaker initially managed to sneak a bill through the house that would have revived the inquisitors through an indirect arrangement that most of his colleagues did not recognize for what it was. The bill's true purpose came to light when it reached the senate. Both the senate and house then took multiple votes on various versions of the bill, ultimately killing it. The debates were unrecorded, but the votes made clear that substantial majorities in both chambers opposed reviving the tax inquisitors. In the last of these votes, reported one newspaper, a "chorus of 'noes'" in the house made sure "the tax inquisitor system is still dead."[220]

Importantly, the very same session of the Ohio assembly that repudiated the tax inquisitors also endorsed a low-rate tax on intangibles, just as in Iowa. Specifically, the Ohio legislators submitted for referendum a constitutional amendment to rescind the state constitution's stricture that all property be taxed at the same rate, thus empowering the legislature to classify property.[221] (Iowa's constitution never had any such stricture.) Ohio legislators planned to use this proposed new power to classify intangibles.[222] However, at the referendum in autumn 1908, the amendment failed to pass. This may have been partly because of rural voters' devotion to the general property tax, but it was mainly because of Ohio's notoriously high hurdle for constitutional referenda, in which blank ballots counted as no votes.[223]

Thus, the Ohio legislature in 1908 attempted the same "one-two punch" as in Iowa, only to be thwarted by its more restrictive constitution. With their hands tied, Ohio lawmakers at the 1909 short session did not touch personalty tax administration. But they did reform realty taxation, reducing the lag between reassessments from ten years to four.[224] This precipitated a crisis in personalty taxation. Anticipating realty reassessment, the state auditor held a conference in December 1909 of all county auditors and town assessors, hoping to redress the lamentably deep, unequal, and illegal undervaluation of realty. Remarkably, the local officials, backed by popular sentiment among landowners, told the state auditor and governor that they would continue to undervalue realty (i.e., violate the law) unless they received a guarantee against the possibility that an honest valuation of realty would cause the tax burden to fall even more disproportionately on realty than personalty. To satisfy the assessors,

Governor Judson Harmon, a Democrat known for good-government and pro-business views, promised "that he would see that intangible personal property was listed at its real value."[225]

In the new legislative session that opened in January 1910, the lawmakers, encouraged by Harmon, adopted a next-best substitute for the (constitutionally barred) reduced rate on intangibles: a reduced rate on *all* property, including realty, known as a "rate limitation." The legislature essentially "promised" the public that it would never raise the state tax above a certain percentage, and it capped the rates that localities could impose.[226] The measure commanded broad support, passing the house unanimously and winning the continued endorsement of both major parties in their platforms that summer.[227] This rate limitation was expressly understood, by Governor Harmon and others, as a way of imitating the low-rate classification of intangibles, within the limits of the state constitution.[228]

Importantly, numerous supporters of rate limitation embraced the voluntarist idea that the measure could, by itself, build up a culture of citizen-state cooperation and trust. Such was the recollection of Ohio tax scholars as they looked back on the events of 1910 over the following decade. Oliver Lockhart, an economist at Ohio State, noted that "many advocates of a classified property tax" believed "that a low rate of taxation will of itself bring intangible property out of hiding. To many, this belief in the coaxing power of a low rate became the principal reason for advocacy of rate limitation."[229] In the view of the original "advocates of the tax [rate] limit law and its present defenders," wrote the economist Harley Lutz, then teaching at Oberlin, "[e]very owner of intangibles should be glad to return them for taxation under tax rates so beneficently limited in his favor."[230] Similarly, the economist Clair Wilcox, teaching at Ohio Wesleyan, observed that the "hopes of some of the proponents of the tax limit legislation had been that a promise of a lower rate would be sufficient greatly to increase the [personalty] return"—to "coax onto the tax list much personal property which had hitherto escaped taxation." Furthermore, "[t]he law was regarded by its advocates as a contractual obligation assumed by the state giving a guarantee to property owners that the return of their property at its full value would not increase the burden."[231] Relatedly, the rate limitation act of 1910 was amended in 1911 to grant amnesty from back-tax collections to all taxpayers who began complying under the new, low rates. Harmon endorsed this amnesty by condemning the state's harsh back-tax statute as a relic of the tax-inquisitor system, for which the inquisitors themselves had lobbied. It was so harsh as now to stand in the way of mass compliance under the new law.[232] The old, adversarial system of tax enforcement was to be swept away.

A vivid articulation of the cooperative vision came from Allen Ripley Foote, president of Ohio's Board of Commerce, who helped stage the 1909 assessor conference that sparked rate limitation and who made numerous speeches urging passage of the 1910 reforms.[233] (Foote had also founded the National Taxation Association in 1907, which became the nation's leading tax-reform organization.)[234] In a lecture in summer 1910, Foote condemned the now-dead tax-inquisitor system as "demoralizing," exalted in the recent enactment of rate limitation, and finally proclaimed:

> Intelligent public sentiment cannot be created and maintained on this subject without the creation of *voluntary organizations* through which all taxpayers can *cooperate*. For this reason I have recommended that the taxpayers in each taxing district in the State [of Ohio] organize an efficient committee through which they can cooperate with the taxing officials of their district, and with each other, to secure an intelligent enforcement of the tax laws of the State. This is the only way in which the vicious system of tax evasion . . . can be broken up. Every one knows this system is vicious, but no one can break it up single-handed. This cannot be accomplished by the officials and taxpayers in a single district or county. It can be accomplished only by a statewide *movement* that will reach and organize the taxpayers in every taxing district in the State.[235]

As to personalty assessment specifically, Foote insisted that "public sentiment and the voluntary action of taxpayers, cooperating with public officials of all classes, must make it certain that all personal property that can be discovered is entered on the tax list at its true value."[236]

Ohioans' strong faith in rate limitation and its power to promote cooperation and trust in the post-ferret era is evident from the 1910 reform's lack of any other serious measures to strengthen the personalty tax system. In particular, the reform left the assessing officials quite decentralized, without top-down control, and it did not provide them with secure tenure or career stability. The leaders of Ohio's rate limitation movement had also been leaders of the state's thwarted classification movement, and this movement, noted Lockhart, had "seldom gone so far as to suggest the administrative measures by which the taxation of intangible property could be made effective; for the most part, they seem to have assumed that" a low rate "would result in a satisfactory voluntary return of such property."[237] Admittedly, the legislature in 1910 did establish a new statewide tax commission, with formal power to give orders to the local assessors, but those assessors continued to be elected by their respective towns,

and although they could be punished by fines and forfeiture of office if convicted in court of disobeying a commission order, the commission could not
simply fire them.[238] In truth, the main intent behind establishing the commission was to improve the assessment of realty and of public utilities: the statute
focused overwhelmingly on those issues, and the commission's efforts and ac-
complishments in 1910–13 were concentrated in those areas, not in the area of
personalty.[239] The evidence seems doubtful that the commission did anything
during those years with respect to personalty assessment beyond moral exhortation of the local officials.[240]

The rate limitation of 1910 achieved results, though it fell short of the hopes
of many. The personalty assessment did instantly increase by 133 percent, with
some categories of intangibles increasing less than that.[241] This was better than
the tax inquisitors had ever done, and it was better than Iowa would do in 1911.
But it fell short of expectations.[242] It did not match the eight- and ninefold increases of Minnesota and Baltimore, and it meant that probably only one-fifth
of intangibles were returned. Ohio had succeeded in "vastly improving" the
assessment, yet it still was not "reasonably complete."[243] As in Iowa, there were
plausible explanations for the shortfall that were consistent with the voluntarist concept of taxation, particularly that the rate, though limited, was still too
high—three times higher than Iowa would adopt for intangibles in 1911.[244]

To some observers, the reason for the disappointing result was that assessors
were still too decentralized, accountable only to their respective town elector-
ates. The seeming solution was top-down control, and in 1913 this was tried
(though it would not last). The legislature abolished the ancient practice of
electing assessors by township and empowered the state tax commission to appoint an assessor for each county, who then appointed a crew of deputies. Assessors were removable by the state tax commission with the governor's consent.
The deputies reported to the county assessor on a daily basis, who then reported
to the state commission on a weekly basis. This integrated hierarchy allowed for
the systematic sharing of information about mortgage and securities ownership
across the state.[245] (This was something the tax ferrets had done by different
means, like selling their information to each other.) The progressive Democratic governor James M. Cox presented the new system as the means to reach
personalty. Appointing the officers, rather than electing them, was key: "Courageous performance of duty by the listing officers" was "a thing unknown under
the elective system," for the "assessor who did his duty was never re-elected."[246]
The insulation from society that the tax ferrets had achieved through bounty
incentives was now being achieved through top-down bureaucratic control—
officers' loyalty to the central agency to which they owed their salaried jobs.[247]

But like rate limitation in 1910, top-down control in 1913 fell short of expectations. The reform increased the intangibles assessment by only 65 percent in the first year. This was not a quantum leap in compliance, and it meant that two-thirds of the state's intangible property, by a conservative estimate, was still escaping.[248] As with rate limitation, the disappointing results may well have been caused by the too-high rate.[249] This suggests that lowering the burden and fostering cooperation were very much necessary to a workable system. Centralizing the officers was no panacea.

In any event, the legislature repealed the top-down centralization scheme in 1915, after fewer than two years of operation, and restored the town-elected assessors.[250] Centralized assessment had proved "to be politically unpopular."[251] There was "general opposition to its replacement of *locally elected* assessment officials by the *political appointees* of the state government."[252] Significantly, the appointed county assessors in 1913 were not selected under civil service rules, so the state-level Democratic machine exploited them for its own gain. Because of this, the system elicited hostility not only from advocates of local autonomy and from partisan Republicans, but also from many progressives.[253]

The 1915 statute was itself struck down by the courts in 1917 as violative of the state constitution, since it did not restore the locally elected assessors quite as completely as the constitution required. (The centralizing statute of 1913 would have been struck down on similar grounds, had it not been repealed first.) The legislature in 1917 then established another scheme, still retaining the town-elected assessors and largely relying, as before 1913, on taxpayer self-assessment. The county auditor now had somewhat greater power over the local assessors than he had possessed prior to 1913 (including the power to remove them), but no central state authority appointed anybody, and the county auditor himself remained elected.[254] Though counties were bigger than townships, county officers in Ohio and elsewhere were still notorious for their accommodating attitude toward taxpayers, who were also their constituents.[255]

Later years would see refinements of the system and a moderate increase in top-down control, but all this came well after the nonprofit status of tax administration was established. In 1929, the Ohio electorate approved a constitutional amendment authorizing classification, and the legislature in 1930 took the opportunity to enact a low-rate tax on intangibles, finally adopting "for real" a measure that it had imitated for the previous two decades.[256] The lowness of the rate made it possible for the government to win, for the first time, the cooperation of banks in reporting the wealth of their depositors.[257] In 1931 the legislature gave the state tax commission power over the assessment of intangibles for all individuals owning $5,000 of such property or reaping $500 in annual income from it, although it stopped short of a completely centralized approach, leaving the assessment of lesser owners to the (still-elected) county auditors.[258]

## Wisconsin, 1911

As we have seen, the socialist government of Milwaukee in 1911 hired tax ferrets to search for intangibles, but the campaign to have the Wisconsin legislature legalize this contract—and to extend authorization for tax ferrets to the entire state—failed.[259] The arguments that defeated tax ferreting in Wisconsin included voluntarist appeals that would have sounded familiar in Iowa and Ohio. The tax ferrets would succeed only in "driving capital into hiding and obliterating from the tax rolls much of the intangible personal property that is now found thereon."[260] Intangibles owners "would withdraw their money from the banks" and transfer them to other investments, causing a "depression."[261]

When the Wisconsin legislature of 1911 rejected the tax ferrets, the alternative it adopted was not universal rate limitation (as in Ohio) or low-rate classification of intangibles (as in Iowa), but instead an income tax.[262] This turned out to be the first permanent income tax ever to be successfully implemented in U.S. history, making it a model for many American jurisdictions thereafter.[263]

But despite its seeming uniqueness, Wisconsin's new income tax was actually quite similar to the rate limit and the classified property tax. It was really just another way of doing what those other schemes sought to do: elicit greater cooperation from owners of intangibles by moderating the state's demands on them. Although we today think of the income tax mainly as a tax on labor, people in the 1910s viewed it mainly as a tax on income from intangible property. (Early income taxes had high exemptions and fell only on high-income people, who tended to live on investments.) In the words of T. S. Adams—an economist at the University of Wisconsin, state tax commissioner, and leading proponent of the income tax—the new tax, in "its most important aspect," was "a substitute for the personal property tax." When the income tax came into effect, the old property tax was accordingly rolled back so as to exempt "practically all personal property," except for certain tangible items.[264] In several other states over the following few decades, the income tax would likewise serve as a replacement, in whole or in part, for personalty taxation.[265]

Just like classification and rate limitation, the Wisconsin income tax aimed to lower the effective burden on what it covered, and in this respect, Wisconsin went even farther than Iowa or Ohio. In the first year of its operation, the Wisconsin income tax imposed an average rate of about 2 percent on an asset's income,[266] whereas the Wisconsin general property tax had averaged about 1.8 percent of an asset's *value*,[267] which was equivalent to an income-tax rate of 30 *percent*, assuming a rate of return of 6 percent, which was typical for that era.[268] So the reform cut the actual economic burden on intangibles—so far as they were discovered—by about nine-tenths. This burden was much lower than even the post-reform intangible tax in Iowa, to say nothing of the post-reform Ohio rate.[269]

Offering an even lower economic burden than post-reform Iowa or post-reform Ohio, Wisconsin aimed, like those states, to encourage voluntary co-operation. Wisconsin governor Francis McGovern, fervently defending the income tax during his 1912 reelection campaign, explained this rationale. Under the old general property tax, he said, "the easiest way to hide securities and dodge taxes" had been "to invest in other states," but under the new income tax, the rate was "low and just," and the "low rate" would "take away the incentive to dodge taxes by investing in other states," thus bringing investment back to Wisconsin.[270]

Though Wisconsin policy makers in 1911 had *some* faith that the low rate of their new tax would help raise compliance above the miserable levels associated with the general property tax, they did not have as complete faith as the lawmakers of Ohio in 1910 or Iowa in 1911, who believed that the low rate could spark a revolution in compliance by itself, with little to no reform of assessment administration, save for the banishment of the bounty-seeking ferrets. To the Wisconsin reformers, effective assessment also required officials to take some initiative, and if officials were going to do that, they had to be socially insulated from the communities they assessed. Many states and localities had, of course, achieved this kind of social insulation through tax-ferreting, but at the cost of citizen-state trust and voluntary cooperation. Wisconsin aimed to achieve social insulation in 1911 through the alternative means of bureaucratic restructuring: officials were to have secure tenure and be under top-down control. The 1911 statute replaced the old locally elected assessors with officers appointed by the state tax commission under civil service rules.[271] "The greatest need of the [new] tax system," attested Adams, looking back in 1913, "was a set of officers not dependent for the retention of their offices upon the favor of the people whom they assess."[272]

Hired and supervised by a revenue-seeking central authority, rather than beholden to local taxpayer-constituents, the Wisconsin administrators brought to realization a new approach to information-gathering, originally pioneered by the tax ferrets: they sought out the sources from which taxpayer incomes were paid and worked backward from those to check the returns. But whereas the tax ferrets had been forced to purchase such "information at source" from private sellers or to find chance disclosure of it in public records, the Wisconsin authorities were able to require its disclosure by all income sources in the state. The tax commission ordered all Wisconsin residents and corporations to report the interest, dividends, and wages they paid to other Wisconsinites.[273] (One imagines that the lowness of the rate helped make this reporting requirement politically possible, as with the Ohio banks.) The Wisconsin bureaucracy's power to demand information from all sources statewide—rendered feasible by the lowness of the burden—went beyond what the tax ferrets had been able to do. Information at source was and remained a key instrument of the Wisconsin tax bureaucracy, as it would be for income-tax agencies in other states in the future.[274]

That said, the role of information at source should not obscure the substantial degree to which Wisconsin's tax authorities still had to rely upon individual citizens' voluntary self-assessment. The state's power to require disclosure did not extend to out-of-state sources. For those sources, the bureaucracy had to do basically what the tax ferrets had done: acquire information unaided by sovereign authority. In discussing this matter, Adams made only the vague comment that information about out-of-state sources was "constantly being received from various quarters."[275] Hence, taxpayers' opportunity to transfer their investments out of state—what the governor himself called "the easiest way to . . . dodge taxes"[276]—was probably no less available under the new bureaucracy than under the tax ferrets. The state tax agency's lack of jurisdiction over out-of-state sources would continue to be a factor as the income tax spread to other states in future years.[277] (Though the federal Internal Revenue Bureau began collecting information at source in the 1910s,[278] Congress did not officially open federal tax records to the states until 1926, and then only to states with income taxes.[279] Even then, the federal bureau was extremely restrictive about allowing nonfederal officers to see information, at least through the 1930s.[280] And the states were very slow to exchange information with one another.[281])

Altogether, the Wisconsin tax system of 1911 had an extraordinarily low rate (to foster voluntary cooperation) and an extraordinary degree of career stability and top-down control (to step up official pressure and information-gathering), and it achieved extraordinary results. During the income tax's first year, the state commission collected data on the value of the intangibles whose income was assessed, to make a direct comparison with the assessment for the last year of the general property tax. The increase was sevenfold. Revenue approximately doubled.[282]

Though scholars have emphasized that Wisconsin's success had much to do with its bureaucratic restructuring and information at source,[283] the architects of the Wisconsin tax attributed its success not merely to those factors but also to a nonadversarial, cooperative, and good-faith relationship between taxpayer and officer that is difficult to imagine between taxpayer and tax ferret. Although Wisconsin reformers did not treat voluntarism as sufficient to achieve tax compliance (as did Iowa and Ohio), they did treat it as necessary. This is no surprise, given that tax shelters in the form of out-of-state investments remained largely out of the government's sight. The fraction of Wisconsin taxpayers' income that came from out-of-state sources, wrote Adams in 1913, "is adequately known through the common honesty of the average citizen." Consistent with this, Adams believed taxpayer cooperation to be of great practical utility to successful administration: "The taxpayer usually knows better than does any one else the amount of his income and the value of his property. . . . In the past, far too little use has been made of the taxpayer and the facts which he can contribute." Judging by the "Wisconsin experience," continued Adams, there was no truth in "the catch-phrases 'self-assessment is poor assessment' and 'don't tax anybody for anything that can move because it will move.'" Although "a tax which is left completely to the taxpayer for assessment" would go unpaid, this did not mean that "the taxpayer cannot be made and ought not to be made to cooperate in the fixing of his own assessment. It is equally untrue that taxes should be levied only on those tangible things which the assessor can see and appraise without the help of the owner or taxpayer."[284]

This kind of good-faith communication in the first instance between taxpayer and officer would have been much harder between taxpayer and tax ferret. The Wisconsin legislature itself recognized the importance of taxpayer cooperation when it drastically lowered the high intangibles rate on which the ferrets had thrived. The commissioners who headed the Wisconsin bureaucracy, explaining their successful 1911 assessment, paired official initiative with the low rate as the twin reasons for the leap in compliance: "A year's experience with the income tax serves to establish the refreshing fact that the average taxpayer is honest and will tell the truth provided assessors will take the trouble to ask him direct questions and provided the rate is reasonable."[285] Several economists agreed that the voluntary element of mass tax compliance could not be eradicated: the strictest and most centralized bureaucracy then imaginable would nevertheless be unable to achieve mass compliance without a reasonable rate.[286]

The importance of taxpayer cooperation—and the need for administrators to cultivate it—entered the conventional wisdom about the income tax. Lutz in 1920 spoke of how the "necessarily inquisitorial character of income tax administration must and can be tempered by the establishment of a relationship of goodwill and mutual respect between assessor and taxpayer."[287] Mark Graves, the longtime New York tax commissioner, argued in 1936 that it was "highly desirable" that "the administrator consider himself the arbiter, umpire or third man in the ring, whose duty it is to see that the state on the one hand and the taxpayer on the other, receive just and equitable treatment," for if taxpayers "believe they are being unfairly treated, they will view the subject as a game and devise ingenious methods of trying to beat the department."[288] Heller in 1941 attested that "a self-assessed tax based on a concealable subject like income is peculiarly dependent on taxpayer education and cooperation for its success. In view of this dependence, every effort should be bent to make the taxpayer the best possible source of information."[289] "By overemphasizing tax productivity," agencies risked "inculcat[ing] in their field audit personnel an attitude which damages an otherwise valuable asset, viz., taxpayer good will."[290]

It seems tax ferrets had disappeared in nearly all the jurisdictions where they once operated by about 1940. At the same time, state and local intangibles taxation generally moved in the direction of classification. Close analysis of these events and their possible links in individual states besides Iowa, Ohio, and Wisconsin is beyond the scope of this book. As the story of Ohio suggests, the ferrets' demise and related events could get very complicated, so a comprehensive survey is not feasible.[291] Still, the experience of these three states suggests that, in the realm of taxation, the abandonment of bounty-seeking rested in large part on the aspiration to establish the state and its officialdom, in the eyes of the populace, as reasonable and nonadversarial—worthy of trust and cooperation. In a word, *legitimate*.

# 6

## FEDERAL TAXATION

### *The Moiety Men*

Having examined how lawmakers relied upon and then rejected bounties in the realm of state and local taxation, we now tackle those same issues in federal taxation. In the history of American public finance, the federal level is just as worthy of study as the state and local levels. Contrary to the myth that federal power began in the twentieth century, historians' estimates for the period before 1900 indicate that federal revenue was comparable to the nationwide total of state and local revenue. The state-and-local total usually exceeded the federal total, but never by more than 50 percent, often far less.[1]

Federal revenue in the nineteenth century overwhelmingly came from taxes,[2] and the most important federal tax of the century was the customs duty. From 1801 to 1860, with a brief exception during the War of 1812, the customs was the sole federal tax. The Civil War drove Congress to impose a variety of internal duties, which, at their 1865 peak, made up 71 percent of the federal tax total. But after the war, Congress rapidly phased out most of the internal taxes, keeping only the excises on liquor and tobacco. The customs pulled ahead of internal revenue in 1869 and remained there, with the exception of only six years, until 1910.[3]

Up to the second half of the nineteenth century, bounties were available to officers in both the customhouses and internal revenue. In both areas, the bounties consisted of percentage shares, set by statute, of the forfeitures that federal law imposed for intentional evasion. Each share was known as a "moiety," and the officers who sought them, in the customs particularly, were nicknamed "moiety men."[4]

Bounties (moieties) were abolished for internal revenue officers in 1872,[5] and for customs officers in 1874. This chapter focuses on bounties for customs officers, since the customs duty was the more important of the two forms of taxation by dollar value, and because the published debate on bounties was far more extensive for customs.

At first glance, the history of bounties in the customhouses presents us with a puzzle. Customs officers had been eligible for bounties since the inception of the federal government in 1789 and, before that, through much of the colonial period. Yet it was only in the 1860s and 1870s that merchants, lawmakers, and opinion leaders concluded that such bounties were bad and had to be abolished (as they were in 1874). The specific complaint of the merchants, which Congress found to be true, was that (1) merchants' business records were so voluminous and complex that they inevitably contained occasional mistakes that led to accidental underpayment of taxes and (2) moieties were driving the officers to interpret every mistake as an intentional evasion that subjected the merchant to forfeiture. Hence the puzzle: why did moieties, which had been available for generations without raising significant objections, suddenly start having perverse effects in the 1860s and 1870s?

The reason, I argue, is that moieties' effect depended upon the larger governance structure of which they were a part, and that structure changed over time. Through the early 1800s, the customhouses were sites of familiar imposition. Offices were filled by "local notables" — men socially enmeshed in the port community, who had cozy relations with the merchants and were not about to sacrifice their ties to make a quick buck. Tax rates were relatively low, so there was not much incentive to evade or suspicion of evasion. The rules for imposing and calculating forfeitures were relatively mild, which meant that officers could not threaten merchants very effectively. And merchants' business records were off-limits to official surveillance, so the officers had little information on which to base accusations. Under these conditions, officers administered the customs laws in an accommodating and indulgent manner, and merchants, thinking the government's demands were generally reasonable, complied willingly, if somewhat loosely.

But in the mid-1800s, familiar imposition gave way to alien imposition. For one thing, the national political parties took over federal administration and began filling the customhouses not with local notables but with party functionaries, usually from outside the port community, who did not have social ties to the merchants who might be targeted. Further, Congress became far more aggressive and intrusive in its demands on the merchants, driven especially by its desperation to finance the Civil War and its postwar ambition to impose a permanent protective tariff. Legislators enacted higher tax rates and harsher forfeiture rules, and they armed the officers with unprecedented power to search merchants' books and papers, giving them far more evidence to use in prosecutions.

While the moiety had been a feeble counterweight to the coziness of the old familiar regime, it held great promise as a fitting motivational engine for the new alien regime (at least at first). The new regime gave officers much greater reason and opportunity to seek profits. They no longer had social ties to their targets; higher taxes made violations (and reward opportunities) more plentiful; more severe forfeitures meant bigger moieties; and more access to information made it easier to make accusations. And just as the new regime encouraged bounty-seeking, so bounty-seeking seemed (on the surface) to strengthen the new regime. Congress had decided to "get tough" on the merchants: it was demanding more money, threatening worse punishments, and authorizing more intrusive surveillance of their affairs. Moieties seemed the perfect motivational fuel to ensure that government exercised its new powers and made its demands stick. Indeed, Congress in 1867 reaffirmed and expanded the moiety rewards.

Moieties proved effective—terrifyingly effective!—in promoting adversarial enforcement. Accusations skyrocketed in the 1860s and early 1870s. Officers put the screws to the merchants, successfully pressuring them to agree to harsh settlements, quite often in cases in which the underpayments appeared to be innocent mistakes.

Faced with these results, congressmen in 1874 recoiled. They concluded that bounties were dangerous, not just to the merchants but to the workability of modern government. Congressmen very much wanted to maintain the protective tariff, and they knew that high rates, serious punishments, and intrusive surveillance would be necessary to do that. Yet Congress feared that, if officers continued to operate the ambitious new revenue system in such an adversarial and narrowly self-interested manner, they would radically alienate the merchants from the officialdom and make it impossible to build and maintain mutual trust and confidence between the two. Trust and confidence, as congressmen came to conclude, were necessary for the system to be workable. There were too many imports and not enough officers for government to rely on coercion alone. Mass compliance required the merchants' voluntary cooperation and goodwill. To foster that, congressmen in 1874 abolished moieties, believing that nonprofit officers would be more likely to exercise forbearance and discretion in making the fundamentally subjective judgment of whether an underpayment was an innocent mistake or a punishable fraud. If officers could make that judgment credibly, they would be more likely to win the trust of the merchants under their jurisdiction, and the government would have the benefit of a more compliant and cooperative taxpayer culture—that is, of legitimacy.

The role of customhouse moieties and their demise in the process of American state-building has been almost entirely ignored by scholars, several of whom have narrated the story of the 1874 abolition law, but not in much depth. They hardly cite the rich congressional hearings and the profound congressional debate that occurred on the subject.[6] These works mostly treat bounty-driven enforcement as mere Gilded Age corruption and its abolition as a minor episode of good-government cleanup. Such treatment is woefully incomplete.[7] Examination of the hearings and debates reveals that, although many lawmakers and other observers became disillusioned with moieties, they mostly characterized the moiety men's actions as lawful.[8] In truth, the main story was not the venality of individual rascals but a challenge of institutional design, which this chapter seeks to recover.

A final point before we embark: the story below focuses largely on the customhouse at New York City, due to its overwhelming importance in customs administration. Near the time of the founding, New York surpassed its rivals to become the nation's busiest port, and its position only grew more dominant in the course of the nineteenth century. By the 1840s, its customhouse was taking in more than half of all customs receipts.[9] By the 1850s, the figure was two-thirds,[10] where it remained in the 1870s, with Boston a far-distant second, at about one-tenth.[11] When bounty-seeking reached its crisis, in the 1860s and 1870s, New York officers were earning the largest reward incomes, by far.[12] Congressmen legislating on customs officers and their incentives had the New York customhouse foremost in mind, and rightly so.

## BACKGROUND: WHAT CUSTOMS OFFICERS DID

To understand this story, we need some background on what customs officers did. Their job was to see that everybody bringing goods into the United States passed through a customhouse and paid duties according to law. The most obvious way for an importer to foil the officers was smuggling, that is, introducing goods into the country without having them processed at the customhouse at all, say, by sailing to shore under cover of darkness, or sneaking across an unwatched stretch of the Canadian border. Smuggling was punishable by forfeiture of the goods, in which the customs officers were entitled to shares (moieties). Another way to evade duties was by false documentation; that is, the perpetrator processed his goods at the customhouse but gave the authorities inaccurate data as to their quantity, nature, or value. This kind of evasion, too, was punishable by forfeiture, in which the customs officers likewise had moieties.

By the mid-1800s, false documentation was the more important of the two forms of evasion.[13] And the controversy leading to the abolition of officers' moieties in 1874 centered on the question of how to enforce the law against false documentation, especially as to the goods' value. To appreciate why this became a problem, we need a basic understanding of how duties were defined and calculated.

Customs duties could be set in one of two ways. The first was by quantity (say, four cents per pound of sugar); this was known as a specific duty. The second was by value (say, 15 percent on the value of each shipment of sugar); this was known as an ad valorem duty. Congress employed both kinds of duties, imposing specific duties on some goods and ad valorem duties on many others.[14]

Ad valorem duties presented a big administrative challenge. How did one discern the value of a good? On this point, the relevant legislation gradually took shape in the federal government's early decades and was fairly settled by the 1840s. Under it, Congress adopted two alternative definitions of value, one for each of two common scenarios: (1) for goods that had been purchased, the importer was to submit an invoice stating the price actually paid; and (2) for goods that had never been purchased but were instead arriving on consignment from a foreign manufacturer, the importer was to submit an invoice stating the "market value" of the goods in the country of export. In both scenarios, there were complex and oft-changing statutory rules about what additional charges the invoice should include, such as packaging, insurance, commissions, and so on. To make things yet more complicated, Congress decided that those who purchased below market value should not receive a tax benefit from the favorable bargains they had struck. Hence, taxable value for purchased goods (at least from the 1810s onward) was defined as the purchase price or the market price, whichever was higher. To ensure that purchased goods did not get the benefit of submarket bargains—and to ensure that invoices for nonpurchased goods were accurate in their statement of "market value"—Congress established a system for appraising all taxable imports, initially relying on private merchants who served ad hoc, but increasingly moving toward full-time governmental appraisers. Bottom line: the invoice price served as taxable value, unless it fell short of the appraisal, which would then be substituted.[15]

Theoretically, the invoice price should have controlled only in cases where it happened to give a price exceeding appraised market value.[16] On the basis of that, we might assume that invoices did not matter much. But in fact, they mattered enormously. The reason was that the appraisers failed to challenge the assertions that importers made through their invoices. In the federal government's first few decades, appraisers were private merchants serving ad hoc. Essentially, the merchants were deciding one another's liability, and they had a common interest in keeping taxable values low. Though the government eventually hired more full-time appraisers, they tended to be unqualified: salaries were low,[17] and the "spoils system" ensured that turnover was frequent and that selection depended mainly on patronage considerations.[18] Appraisement was a difficult task calling for expertise on foreign markets and international commerce,[19] but the people filling the offices were typically ignorant, sometimes unable to read the foreign languages in which invoices were written.[20] Because appraisal was so inadequate, the invoice became, by default, the decisive evidence of taxable value.[21] This remained the case for the whole period that concerns us. Only in 1890 was appraisement overhauled to establish a board of career experts.[22] Even after that, appraisement was difficult enough that invoices still exerted major influence.[23]

It was essential for merchants to submit accurate invoices, and so Congress imposed punishments for inaccuracies. There were two tiers of punishments.[24] The first applied to all inaccuracies, regardless of whether the merchant intended to evade. If an invoice price fell short of an appraisal by more than a specified percentage, the importer was strictly liable for a penalty equal to the duty on a specified percentage of the appraisal. After repeatedly fiddling with the percentages, Congress in 1842 settled on a stable rule: any shortfall greater than 10 percent would trigger the penalty, and the penalty would be the duty on 20 percent of the appraisal.[25] The second tier of punishments—tremendously harsher than the first—applied to importers who submitted inaccurate invoices with intent to evade. The most important of these punishments was the forfeiture of the goods fraudulently invoiced[26] or, if the goods had passed out of the importer's hands, of their appraised value.[27]

Crucially, customs officers had a moiety only of the money that arose from intentional fraud, not from the automatic penalty for every undervaluation that exceeded 10 percent.[28] In other words, the official aim of the bounty system was to discover intentional (fraudulent) undervaluations, not accidental ones.

## THE EXPLOSION OF COMPLAINTS ABOUT ENFORCEMENT IN THE 1860s AND 1870s

As the preceding section indicates, the question of intent was crucial in customs enforcement. And it was precisely on this point that congressmen in the 1860s and 1870s concluded that the moiety system was operating perversely and had to be abolished. The congressional investigations and debates on customs enforcement of the period contain several patterned horror stories. The most prevalent one went as follows. A clerk at an importing firm gave a tip to the customs officers that the firm was committing fraud, usually through its invoices. The officers seized the firm's books. Examining those books, they discovered irregularities, which suggested that the invoices were false and had resulted in underpayment of duties. The firm responded (truthfully!) that the irregularities were innocent mistakes. But the officers, driven by the profit motive, charged the firm with intentional fraud, invoking the law's draconian forfeiture provisions in terrorem. The firm, though innocent, was loath to take the risk of such a large forfeiture and was, in any event, reluctant to prolong the proceedings, since governmental custody of its books disrupted its operations. Therefore, the firm settled the case for a large sum, when it justly owed nothing.

The most commonly invoked example of the above pattern was the case of Phelps, Dodge and Company, one of the nation's most venerable importing firms, which settled a fraud charge with the New York customhouse for a large sum in early 1873. When the details of the case became public later that year, they sparked newspaper editors across the country to denounce the government's conduct.[29] The firm's lead partner, William E. Dodge, became the star witness for the complaining merchants at congressional hearings early in 1874, and his case was the main exhibit presented by the congressmen who pushed through the abolition measure that June.[30]

The irregularity in Phelps Dodge's books—which the firm insisted was a mistake—deserves our attention as a telling example of the problem of how to distinguish mistake from intentional fraud. The firm was in the habit of purchasing tinplate in England on long-term contracts, setting the price far in advance of delivery. The market for this product was generally rising, meaning that the contract price was usually (but not always) less than the market price at the time of shipment. Clerks in the firm's Liverpool house drew up the invoices using market values at the time of shipment, apparently not understanding that U.S. customs law required them to use the contract prices. Crucially, these clerks also sent memoranda to the New York house that *did* state the contract prices. On searching the firm's books, the customs officers discovered these memoranda. For most shipments, the market value was greater than the contract price; by paying on that basis, Phelps Dodge had simply paid what it lawfully owed (but practically might not have had to pay if it had simply listed the contract price, since the incompetent U.S. appraisers might well have failed to notice that the contract price fell short of market value). But for a few of the shipments, the market value was less than the contract price—

technically a false valuation in favor of the importer, which, if intentional, triggered a forfeiture.[31]

But was it intentional? The transactions at issue—in which the market value was less than the contract price—were few, and the differences were small: lost duties amounted to only $1,658.78 over a five-year period, during which Phelps Dodge *had* paid about $8 million in U.S. duties on its firmwide business. Further, as the firm repeatedly emphasized in the press and before Congress, its undervaluations (where the market value it listed was less than the contract price) were more than offset by the transactions in which its mistake had the opposite effect (that is, where the market value it listed was greater than the contract price). In this way, Phelps Dodge implied—and allowed its congressional allies to believe and repeat—that the firm had paid more tax than it owed, overall.[32] This was somewhat misleading: the offsetting transactions did not constitute overpayments of tax in a legal sense; they were merely instances of the firm giving up the practical benefit that it ordinarily would have reaped from the government's incompetence at appraisement. Nevertheless, it does seem that the firm practically paid more than it would have if there had been no irregularity. This fact—combined with the smallness of the duties lost—made it hard to believe that the irregularity constituted intentional fraud. Yet if a court could be convinced otherwise, the forfeiture would be terrifyingly large. Under traditional doctrines dating to the eighteenth century, forfeiture would have covered all the goods undervalued (amounting to $271,000). That was scary enough, but under more recent laws and judges' interpretations of them, the forfeiture could be even larger, covering all the goods in the invoices that included the undervalued items (amounting to $1,750,000). Faced with such a staggering potential loss and fearful about the costs of the proceedings themselves, Phelps Dodge settled for the amount of the goods undervalued—$271,000.[33] Of this, the three principal officers who ran the customhouse each received a moiety of about $22,000. A top customhouse detective (Special Agent Benaiah G. Jayne) got about $66,000, of which he kept one-third, having promised the rest to the clerk who gave him the tip. And the U.S. attorney received about $5,400.[34]

Learning the details of the case after the settlement, outraged critics said that the customs officers should never have imposed such a high penalty. They should have recognized Phelps Dodge's innocence, but they failed to do so, since they wanted the money. To be fair to the officers, the existence of a double (and mismatched) set of prices for a single set of transactions *usually was* a red flag indicating fraud.[35] Further, the officers apparently had no knowledge, during the settlement negotiations, of the offsetting overpayments.[36] Still, one could certainly argue that, despite this ignorance, the smallness of the lost duties ought to have been enough to convince the officers that the case did not warrant such harsh punishment. Furthermore, the officers' ignorance of the overpayments was itself a product of their excessively adversarial approach to the whole case: throughout the negotiations, they were quite selective in what they revealed about the case they were building (letting the firm know the value of the goods and invoices covered by the undervaluations but not the duties lost), apparently thinking that this kind of selective disclosure would win them a richer settlement. Dodge testified that he did not know the amount of the lost duties until after he had agreed to settlement and never would have settled had he known how small it was.[37] Better communication would have afforded him a chance to better explain the irregularity.[38]

In the view of many congressmen and other observers, the Phelps Dodge case, though extreme, typified a widespread problem: the system was punishing merchants who, at least in a moral sense, were guilty of nothing except a mistake. Legal doctrines helped open the way for this kind of harshness. For one thing, fraudulent intent could be inferred from the mere fact of undervaluation.[39] In addition, a mistake of law was no defense to intentional fraud—only a mistake of fact was. Thus, if an importer claimed that he miscalculated in adding up a column of figures, that could in principle be a defense, assuming the jury believed him. But if he claimed that he misunderstood some complicated clause in the tariff schedule, that was not a defense at all, even if he was telling the truth.[40] For merchants who made innocent mistakes of law, the escape hatch was supposed to be the Treasury secretary's discretionary power to remit or mitigate punishments.[41] But merchants viewed this as ineffective, since the secretary (and his clerks) had little time or capacity to review proceedings at faraway ports, especially since officers seeking their moieties were likely to retain counsel and use their (sometimes great) connections to Republican political bosses to press the secretary to let the forfeiture stand.[42]

Only a few critics of customs enforcement had an exact understanding of the complex doctrine on intent, but very many of them expressed the more general view that, whatever the particulars of the law, officers too frequently extracted harsh forfeitures from merchants who were blameless as a matter of morals and did not deserve punishment as a matter of policy. On this point, merchants and their congressional allies argued that every firm was inevitably going to have at least a few irregularities—as to both fact and law—in drawing up invoices and calculating duties. The inevitability of irregularities meant officers should be understanding and accommodating in drawing the line between mistake and fraud. A firm's processing of information about prices, market values, and additional charges (like packaging) was inherently complex. What is more, the tariff laws themselves were complex, frequently amended, and confusingly drafted.[43] Given all this, irregularities were simply a fact of life. In the words of a merchant lawyer: "[T]here is not a large importing merchant in any large city of this Union whose books and papers, if taken and examined, would not show mistakes, and where, if the law was rigidly enforced to the letter, he would not be liable to forfeiture, especially if an accidental mistake is to be construed by the Government into an intentional fraud." "Of course," he added, "it would be a pleasant thing if we never made mistakes, but I do not suppose that is possible."[44] Numerous others made the same point.[45]

Nowhere was the problem of distinguishing mistake from fraud more acute than in the Phelps Dodge case, in which the irregularity appears to have been a mistake of law.[46] Dodge himself said, "We admit that we undervalued our goods by mistake," later adding, "we have never refused to admit . . . that we had committed irregularities, and had unintentionally made ourselves liable to the law."[47] Dodge, in the words of a congressional ally, was "[u]nwilling to go into court where upon the technical letter of the law without any dishonest intention his firm might be subjected to a penalty of over $1,000,000."[48]

One might think the task of distinguishing between mistake and intentional fraud would be made easier by considering the amount of the duties unpaid: the higher that amount, the more likely the irregularity was fraudulent.[49] But the smallness of the duties lost was not an infallible guide to the merchant's intent. A tiny irregularity might be detected on a single invoice, but that same irregularity — if repeated over numerous invoices — might add up to a large sum of duties lost, making fraud seem more likely.[50] What is more, a firm that evaded customs duties might be motivated not by the wish to retain the amount owed but rather by the opportunity to undersell its taxpaying competitors and thereby gain market advantage. Obviously, it was imperative that the government prevent fraud in such situations, for otherwise the honest merchants would be forced to choose between evading tax or losing business. The amount of tax evasion necessary to gain competitive advantage in a commodities market might be very small.[51] One senator even suggested that the amount of duties lost in the Phelps Dodge case — though small — might have allowed the firm to undersell its rivals.[52]

In the end, there was no automatic, objective way to tell mistaken irregularities from intentional ones. The officers had to make a subjective, holistic judgment about the merchant's inner thoughts.

## THE PUZZLE OF WHY UNWARRANTED ENFORCEMENT
## AROSE WHEN IT DID

In the view of contemporaries, the excessive tendency of officers to construe irregularities as fraudulent arose mainly from their pecuniary interest in finding fraud. "We believe," declared one merchant spokesman, "that this moiety system is at the bottom of the trouble."[53]

This presents a puzzle. The moiety system had been in place in the federal customhouses since 1789, and even earlier than that in the colonial customhouses. Why did it come to have perverse results and spark outrage only in the 1860s and 1870s? "Moieties," as the U.S. attorney for New York City quizzically observed in 1874, "certainly have always existed since the creation of this Government down to the present time." And "if the result of the moiety system . . . is to ruin the merchants, as we have heard dinned into our ears for several months [by the newspapers and the merchants themselves], then it is very extraordinary that there are any merchants [left] in this country, and that they have not been ruined in the seventy or eighty years that the moiety system has prevailed."[54] Similarly, John W. Candler, a leader in the Boston merchants' campaign to abolish moieties, acknowledged that "the moiety and spy system" went back to the 1700s, while adding that it "has never been brought before the people in the objectionable form in which it has come until within a short time past."[55]

Secondary scholarship presents the same puzzling timeline. The historian Gautham Rao, in a deeply documented study of the customhouses in the late 1700s and early 1800s, characterizes their administrative culture as one of "accommodation": merchants complied willingly but loosely with the law, insofar as its demands were reasonable, and officers in return administered it in an indulgent manner, giving merchants the benefit of the doubt and allowing them to exploit loopholes.[56] Rao's research goes up to the 1820s and 1830s, in which decades he finds that officials became somewhat less deferential toward merchants, though his analysis on that point does not focus on anti-evasion enforcement.[57] A broadly consistent narrative appears in an 1897 history by John Dean Goss, who says that the customhouses began in 1789 "with slight preventives against fraud, and apparently [were] administered for the first quarter of a century [to circa 1815] upon the basis of confidence in the importer." The penalties established in the late 1700s "were rarely resorted to" at first. But enforcement "increased gradually as time went on" and finally became "rigorous" after 1861.[58]

Consistent with this, congressional reports, the testimony of merchants, and statistical data indicate that customs enforcement suddenly became much more intense in the 1860s. (I examine these sources later in this chapter.)[59] Again: why then?

## THE ANSWER TO THE PUZZLE: MOIETIES AND THE SHIFT FROM FAMILIAR TO ALIEN IMPOSITION, 1820s TO 1860s

The reason it took until the 1860s for moieties to spark consistently severe enforcement is that the rewards' effect depended upon the larger governance structure of which they were a part, and that structure changed over time. Up till about the 1820s, the customhouses operated under a regime of familiar governance, to which moieties were a feeble counterweight. It was a world in which social relations between officers and merchants were cozy, tax rates were relatively low, forfeiture rules were relatively mild, and officers had almost no power to intrude on merchants' privacy to gather incriminating evidence. From the 1820s to the 1860s, all these things changed. Familiar governance gave way to a new alien regime in which governmental demands were far more impersonal, ambitious, and intrusive. To be specific, (1) the new national political parties took over the customhouses, throwing out the "local notables" who had been socially connected to the merchants and installing "spoilsmen" with no such ties; (2) Congress, driven by protectionism and ultimately by war, greatly increased tax rates, raising the temptation to evade and the suspicion of evasion; (3) Congress and the courts, bent on enforcing the high rates, altered the definition of forfeiture to be more severe toward the merchant; and (4) Congress armed officers with greater power to seize merchants' books and papers, which gave them more information on which to base accusations and more leverage in settlement talks. To be sure, not all these changes were neat or linear. Some occurred episodically, or in zigzagging fashion, finally falling into place in the 1860s. But the overall trend was unmistakable.

Bounty offers, though old, seemed like they might fit perfectly with this tough new approach to taxing imports. The new regime allowed officers to take advantage of profit-seeking in a way they never had before: the substitution of spoilsmen for local notables removed the social brake on enforcement, higher taxes made violations (and therefore paydays) more plentiful, more severe forfeitures meant bigger moieties, and more access to information made violations easier to find.

And just as the new regime encouraged bounty-seeking, so bounty-seeking seemed (on the surface) to strengthen the new regime. The old accommodationist attitude was out. A new positivist attitude was in: less trusting and deferential toward the merchants, more exacting in its demands for compliance with the letter of the law. What better way to get officers to force compliance with the law than give them a percentage of the penalties imposed? Thus, Congress not only maintained the moiety system throughout the period of transformation but also reaffirmed it in 1867, making clear that moieties were widely available to all customs officers. It was only after witnessing the results of this experiment that lawmakers (as we shall see later) determined in 1874 that profit-seeking was perverse when mixed with this new mode of governance.

### The Shift to Alien Imposition at the Customhouses

As noted above, there were four changes in customs administration between the 1820s and 1860s that shifted governance from familiar to alien: new personnel, higher tax rates, more severe rules of punishment, and greater official access to information. We begin with new personnel. As Rao documents, the customs officers of the late 1700s and early 1800s were generally appointed from the ranks of local notables. They were men known, respected, and socially enmeshed in the merchant communities of their respective ports, often by ties of commerce, family, and social life.[60] Such men made it their first priority to accommodate the merchants within their jurisdiction, who were also their neighbors, friends, former or future business associates, and even relatives. "[I]t is hardly too much to say," writes Jerry Mashaw in a gloss on Rao, "that in the early years of the republic, the major custom houses were run by the local merchants."[61] These men were not about to sacrifice their ties to make a quick buck.

The personnel arrangement of Rao's story met its death by the 1830s, when the new political parties—organized as mass nationwide bodies with systematic patronage networks—began allocating federal offices to effective party workers rather than to local notables.[62] To trace this transformation, I have collected data on the incumbents of the collectorship of the port of New York. Consistent with Rao's view, the first four collectors, whose tenures covered the period from 1789 to 1830, were all merchants. But of the next seventeen collectors, whose tenures covered the period from 1830 to 1878, only three were merchants (and those three served a total of only five years).[63] As the chairman of the New York board of trade put it in 1874, the merchants of the city "do not dictate whom the President shall appoint as collector of the port of New York. The merchants have had very little to do of late years even in nominating anybody. . . . The merchants have but very little to do with selecting subordinates."[64] The spoils system made officers into creatures of the national party and not of the local mercantile community. This increased the social distance between them and the merchants with whom they dealt.[65]

Back in the days of familiar governance, moieties had pushed against the strong social tendency of the officer to give his merchant friends the benefit of the doubt. But once local notables were replaced by spoilsmen, moiety incentives were no longer subject to that social brake. It is no accident, I think, that the first major moiety-related scandal occurred not long after the New York collectorship switched from notables to spoilsmen. Jesse Hoyt, the second nonmerchant and spoilsman to occupy that office (1838–41), engaged in a campaign of zealous and abusive enforcement against supposed undervaluations. His purposes, concluded an investigating committee, were to make money for himself via moieties,[66] and to ingratiate himself politically to the merchants' sworn enemies—protectionist New England manufacturing interests.[67] Indeed, Hoyt expressly condemned the former accommodationist tendencies of the customhouse in an 1840 letter: "The laxity with which the revenue laws have heretofore been executed in this district . . . produced a general repugnance to all ideas of considering the laws as having any binding force."[68]

Hoyt's campaign was crude. He pressured appraisers to find that merchants were undervaluing goods, he seized those goods, and he delayed trial until merchants submitted to settlements.[69] Perhaps because the blunt instruments at his disposal made the abusiveness of his actions so obvious, he apparently inspired no immediate copycats. The advent of the spoils system was necessary but not sufficient to produce the kind of sustained overenforcement that led to the abolition of moieties in 1874. Additional components of the new regime of alien imposition still had to fall into place.

The second component of the transition from familiar to alien governance was Congress's increase in tax rates. The idea of permanently high tariffs for the protection of domestic industry entered American political discourse in the 1810s. From that time up to the Civil War, the average rate on dutiable goods fluctuated between 20 percent and 33 percent,[70] except for the extraordinary "tariff of abominations" (1828–32), which reached 49 percent,[71] though it proved difficult or impossible to enforce in New York and elsewhere (not to mention that it caused the near rebellion of South Carolina).[72] With the coming of the Civil War, Congress inaugurated a new epoch of persistently high duties— higher than any prior duties except for the tariff of abominations—that would last for generations. Initially enacted to pay for the war, high duties remained in place because Republicans stayed in control and pushed an ambitious protectionist agenda. Thus, Congress in 1862 put the average rate on dutiable goods at 35 percent and in 1864 at 49 percent. Congress briefly cut the rate in 1872, but only to 39 percent. Congress raised it in 1875, so that it averaged 43 percent for the next several years, then raised it again in 1883, to 45 percent.[73] The height of the tariff gave merchants a strong incentive for evasion, which in turn increased the suspicion that they were evading.[74]

Only in the 1860s and 1870s do we observe the coincidence of moieties, spoils-based office-holding, and persistently high tariff rates. Back when the spoils system came into its own during the 1840s and 1850s, rates were generally falling: Congress cut them from 32 percent to 26 percent in 1846 and then to 20 percent in 1857.[75] These comparatively low rates help explain why Hoyt inspired no imitators prior to the Civil War.[76] Lower rates lessened the temptation to undervaluation and the suspicion that it was occurring—a trend that suddenly reversed in the 1860s.

The third component of the transition was that Congress and the courts increased the harshness of punishment for undervaluations. Under the original statutory regime of the late 1700s, forfeiture for a fraudulent invoice applied only to those goods about which the invoice gave false information.[77] In 1830, things got somewhat harsher. Congress set forth examination procedures for all goods passing through the customhouse. If a fraudulent invoice were caught during that examination (as opposed to being caught after the goods had passed into consumption), the jury had the option to impose forfeiture (1) only on the goods actually undervalued, (2) on all goods in the same package as those undervalued, or (3) on all goods in the same invoice as those undervalued.[78] Then in 1863, Congress—clamping down on the increased evasion that arose from heightened wartime duties—passed an act to tighten enforcement. Though its provision on forfeiture was not perfectly clear,[79] Chief Justice Chase, riding circuit in 1869, construed it to mandate the forfeiture of all goods in the invoice, without exception.[80] That same year, the U.S. District Court in New York City, which handled all the port's customhouse business, followed the same interpretation.[81] Though forfeitures had always been deliberately greater than the amount of duties evaded, they were now greater by an even higher ratio. In New York City from 1869 to 1873, the ratio of total fines, penalties, and forfeitures to unpaid duties recovered was about fourteen to one.[82] Some cases involved extreme disproportions, which merchants and their congressional allies cited to argue that the rule was excessively harsh and irrational. The primary exhibit was Phelps Dodge.[83]

The fourth and final component of the transformation was that Congress armed the officers with new powers to surveil merchants' business. Surveillance powers grew modestly up to the 1860s and underwent a quantum leap in 1863. To use James C. Scott's term, the merchants' private activities became more *legible* to the officialdom than ever before.[84]

From the founding of the U.S. customhouses in 1789, officers had possessed the authority, dating back to England, to search for and seize, in virtually any location (including a private building), *goods* on which duties had not been paid.[85] Books and papers were a different story. Officers had little access to them prior to the 1860s. Though Congress in 1832 authorized customhouse appraisers to order the production of documents, the penalty for defying such orders was so light that firms likely preferred to incur it rather than reveal evidence of fraud.[86] The government gained a bit of additional leverage in 1846, when the U.S. Supreme Court held that, if officers seized goods with probable cause, the jury was "at liberty to presume" that any books a merchant refused to produce "would have operated unfavorably to his case."[87]

The big change came in 1863. That year, Congress—aiming to make new wartime duties stick—went far beyond all prior measures. It provided that, whenever any person (an officer or private informer) made it "appear, by affidavit," to the satisfaction of any U.S. District Court judge that an importer had committed revenue fraud with respect to any merchandise, that judge was to issue a warrant authorizing the customhouse officers "to enter any place or premises where any invoices, books, or papers relating to such merchandise or fraud are deposited, and to take and carry the same away to be inspected."[88] An amendment in 1867 required that the person seeking the warrant submit a written complaint setting forth "the character of the fraud alleged, the nature of the same, and the importations in respect to which it was committed, and the papers to be seized."[89]

Congress's empowerment of the officers was without precedent. The solicitor of the Treasury, asking lawmakers to pass the new measure in 1863, said as much,[90] as did judges and other legal observers in later years.[91] So did the U.S. Supreme Court, looking back from the 1880s, when it characterized the 1863 enactment as "the first legislation of the kind that ever appeared on the statute book of the United States." It was "the first act . . . either in this country or in England . . . which authorized the search and seizure of a man's private papers, or the compulsory production of them, for the purpose of using them in evidence against him in a criminal case, or in a proceeding to enforce the forfeiture of his property." Even the British statutes of the revolutionary period had not gone so far, for they had only authorized searches for goods, not records.[92]

Officers wielding warrants under the statutes of 1863 and 1867 could access a very wide range of books and papers. One of the merchant lawyers, S. B. Eaton, testified in 1874 as to the usual process in New York City, which was "to issue a warrant authorizing the seizure of all books of account and papers relating to certain specified importations. . . . When the marshal executes the warrant, he is in utter ignorance what books and papers relate to the specified invoice, and, not knowing which to take, he naturally errs in favor of the Government, and takes all." Thus, most or all of the merchant's books might end up in the government's possession.[93] The statutory provision calling for particularity in the complaint was not much of a practical constraint.[94] It seems that officers who came across compromising information unrelated to the transactions specified in the warrant may have used that data against the merchant nonetheless.[95]

The seizure of merchants' books was not only a source of accusatory evidence but also a means to annoy and pressure the merchants into settling. The investigatory process had always imposed costs on merchants, as when officers as far back as the 1700s seized a suspected firm's goods or store, thereby disrupting its business.[96] The power to seize books and papers, established in 1863, allowed for yet more disruption.[97] Generally, the books remained in governmental custody throughout the examination.[98] This could take weeks or even months.[99] A firm without books found it hard to carry on business.[100] Merchants might settle simply to return to normal operations.

A final change that intensified surveillance was the Treasury Department's assignment of specialized government detectives to customs evasion—the first men ever to do such investigations as a full-time job. The officers who took up this detective role were known as "special agents" of the department. Originally, they had the job of rooting out corruption within customhouse ranks.[101] But they were increasingly assigned to anti-evasion duty, first to gather price data in European markets in 1863,[102] and then to investigate merchants in domestic ports (especially New York) by 1869.[103]

Equipped with the new draconian forfeiture rules and surveillance powers, the customhouse officers—and especially the full-time detectives—devised sharp techniques for interrogating merchants and extracting settlements from them. They told the merchants of the gravity of their offenses in vague and menacing terms and held meetings in a windowless room lit by gaslight.[104] During the 1874 hearings, no fewer than five merchants used the word *terrorism* to describe the process.[105]

### Moieties as an Instrument of the New Alien Regime: How Congress Embraced Them

By the 1860s, customhouse officers were more socially distant from merchants, demanded higher taxes from them, had power to impose harsher punishments on them, and enjoyed greater access to their private information. Under these conditions, officers were more inclined to seek moieties and more capable of winning the forfeitures that produced moieties.

The moiety incentive, thus unleashed, promised to further intensify the adversary posture of the officers—faithful to the positive demands of the sovereign against a recalcitrant population. As the *New York Tribune* argued in 1871, moieties were guarantees against any social accommodation that might still exist between the officers and the merchants: "Your Collector, Surveyor, &c., like to stand well with the importers—to enjoy the popularity secured by their favor. Are they likely to be keen on the scent of suspected undervaluers of known wealth and high mercantile and social standing when it makes no penny's difference to them whether goods are undervalued or not? We perceive and admit the faults of the 'moiety' system: we do not yet see how the requisite vigilance and fearlessness are to be secured without it."[106]

Congressmen were the prime movers behind the transformation of the 1860s: they were the ones seeking war revenue and protective tariffs, which led them to raise rates, step up punishments, and authorize more surveillance. And congressmen understood quite well that moieties could play a key role in this new, harsher, more adversarial mode of governance. Indeed, Congress in the 1860s would explicitly reaffirm and strengthen those rewards.

To appreciate how Congress did this, we need a bit of background on the different kinds of customhouse officers and their moiety rights. Each customhouse was run by three principal officers: the collector, the naval officer (who had no connection to the navy), and the surveyor. At the New York customhouse, subordinate staff had grown by the 1860s to more than one thousand (far more than any other port), and New York's three principal officers acted as the chiefs of that large force. In particular, the three made all final decisions regarding enforcement actions. They had the power to direct their subordinates' enforcement activities and often did so proactively.[107]

Under the moiety statute adopted by Congress in 1789 (which remained the same till the 1860s), the three principal officers of a port were each entitled to a one-sixth moiety of any forfeiture occurring at the port, with the U.S. Treasury taking the remaining one-half. Where the forfeiture occurred pursuant to a tip from an "informer," that informer could take one-fourth, with the three principal officers each taking one-twelfth and the Treasury its usual half.[108] Thus, the principal officers always had a substantial share. Their shares, combined with their expansive powers, positioned them to intensify enforcement amid the changes discussed above (social distancing, higher taxes, worse penalties, more information).

But the three principal officers were not the only ones doing enforcement; many lesser officers also played a role.[109] Were these nonprincipal officers also eligible for moieties? Up to the 1860s, it was uncertain. One might interpret the 1789 statute to mean that a nonprincipal officer who uncovered fraud could enjoy a one-fourth moiety by presenting himself as an "informer," but one could alternatively interpret the word *informer* to benefit only private tipsters, outside government service. The sources contradict each other on whether nonprincipal officers could share under the pre-1860s regime. It may be that the Treasury Department did not have a uniform and consistent policy on the matter.[110]

In any event, Congress in the 1860s confirmed its faith in bounty-seeking by amending the law to make certain that nonprincipal officers were eligible to share. A modest step in this direction came in 1863, when Congress granted a 2 percent commission on all forfeitures to the U.S. attorney, who played an important role in enforcement decisions.[111] The big step came in 1867. In that year, the Senate Commerce Committee reported a bill mandating (among other things) that in cases where there was no informer, the Treasury should receive not only its usual one-half of the forfeiture but also another one-fourth, with the three principals receiving only one-twelfth each, just as they would in a case with an informer.[112] The bill thus lessened moiety incentives. However, on the floor, an amendment was offered by George Edmunds, a leading Senate Republican from Vermont, eminent lawyer, chairman of the Judiciary Committee, and protectionist. Edmunds was under the impression that nonprincipal officers presently had no right to moieties.[113] But he strongly believed they ought to have such a right. His amendment altered the text of the moiety statute to say that, in every case, one-half of the forfeiture went to the U.S. Treasury; one-twelfth to each of the three principal officers; and one-fourth to the informer or—here was the innovation—if there were no informer, to "the officer making the seizure."[114] The purpose, declared Edmunds, was "to provide a stimulus" to the officers, "to reward the zeal and fidelity of the seizing officer," and to counteract the temptation to receive bribes—all of which he thought "would greatly improve the public service."[115] With no senator questioning Edmunds, the Senate adopted his amendment and passed the bill by unrecorded votes, and the House then passed the amended bill by a voice vote.[116]

With these revisions, the congressional commitment to bounty-seeking was as strong as it ever had been, perhaps stronger. During the early 1870s, moieties regularly went to nonprincipal officers (who, in turn, might give a cut to a private tipster).[117] Especially prominent among these profit-making officers were the new "special agents." Dodge described the special agents as the most dangerous men at the customhouse—"very anxious to secure their large moieties."[118]

## The Result: An Explosion of Unwarranted Enforcement in the 1860s

Most factors contributing to alien governance emerged, or came to their culmination, in the 1860s: the persistently high tariff in 1862; the power to search merchants' books in 1863; the U.S. attorney's commission in 1863; the universal "whole invoice" rule in 1863 (or, if we focus on judicial interpretation, in 1869); the confirmation of nonprincipal officers' moiety rights in 1867; and the assignment of special agents to anti-evasion duty by 1869.

Consistent with this, people who complained about unwarranted enforcement in the early 1870s generally said the problem was of recent origin, which they often dated to the Civil War or thereabouts. As one congressman said in 1874, "[T]his system of revenue service . . . has existed now for the last ten or fifteen years, growing every year in the enormities of the amounts [i.e., moieties] gathered in by these men, . . . until it becomes the great and overshadowing complaint that is now presented."[119] "In olden times, or previous to the rebellion," declared an advocate for New York merchants in 1874, "an omission found on an invoice, or any error of any kind whatever, was, on its discovery, communicated to the importer in order to have the correction made," in contrast to the present practice of using the irregularity as justification to search the firm's books and engage in aggressive enforcement.[120] Another merchant advocate observed that same year: "[D]uring the [Civil] war, there grew up a very large force of detectives and special agents, and there grew up in the Government a system of informers, which had never practically existed in the Government before the war."[121] A Boston merchant and former congressman attested that "[t]here was no such injustice under the law of 1799, and there were very few complaints." It was only under the legislation of 1863–67 that "this gigantic system of prosecution and robbery of honest men has grown up in this country."[122] Dodge himself in 1874 recalled that "[a]s the custom-house was managed a quarter of a century ago," the "course pursued" in the case of error or suspected fraud would have been to bring the irregularity "to the notice of the firm, that they might have an opportunity for explanation," rather than instantly resort to prosecution, as the officers now did.[123]

Consistent with these comments from the early 1870s, observers in the mid-1860s had noticed increases in enforcement and its abusiveness that prefigured later and more spectacular cases. Three New York merchants testified that during 1863 they had been subjected to official treatment quite similar to that later meted out to Phelps Dodge: officers seized their books, discovered mistakes, and pressured them into settling for sums far exceeding the duties lost.[124] A. T. Stewart, a leading importer in business since the 1820s, observed in April 1864 that "[d]uring the past year" the customhouse officers at New York "made more strict and rigid investigations respecting the values of goods imported than I have ever before known, resulting in great changes."[125] A congressional committee noted in March 1867 that, back in 1864–65, the troubling enforcement pattern had been "comparatively in its infancy" and that the cases of "hardship and great oppression," though in existence, had been "scarce sufficiently numerous and general in their character" to "authorize the asking" of legislative reform. Since then, however, "[a]buses" had "greatly multiplied; revenue officers have from habit become more fearless. . . . Certainly something, somewhere and somehow, is wrong, to beget an apprehension, at home and abroad, that our seizing revenue laws are worked more in the interests of informers and seizing officers than to protect the honest merchant and the revenues of the government."[126]

Statistics confirm that enforcement became far more intense in the 1860s. We can measure the intensity of enforcement by calculating the ratio, for each fiscal year, between (1) the total customs fines, penalties, and forfeitures paid into the Treasury in a given year and (2) the total customs duties collected during that same year. This measure controls for inflation, the volume of trade, and the height of the tariff. Figure 6.1 graphs the ratio from fiscal 1854–55 through fiscal 1879–80. The ratio spikes in fiscal 1863–64 and 1864–65, reaching a level more than double that of any previous year in the period. It then dips briefly (but not back to the prewar level). The ratio then spikes again in fiscal 1867–68, and from there on it remains at least double (or triple or even quintuple) the highest figure in the pre-1863 period. (This continues until fiscal 1874–75, when the ratio crashes and stays low. The crash is obviously connected to Congress's abolition of moieties in June 1874, shortly before fiscal 1874–75 began on July 1, as I shall discuss later.)

While there are no statistics on the moiety incomes of individual officers prior to 1862, it seems fair to assume that the incomes of the 1860s and early 1870s were larger than ever before. Certainly, they were tremendous in an absolute sense. During the period 1862–73, each of New York's three principal officers received an average of more than $35,000 in moieties per year.[127] The most feared special agent at New York, Jayne, served from 1869 to 1874 and officially received about $328,000. Less the side deals he made with private tipsters, his personal share was "about $140,000 to $160,000," for annual earnings of about $30,000.[128] This income, like that of each principal officer, was triple the salary of the Treasury secretary ($10,000).[129]

## THE ABOLITION OF MOIETIES IN 1874:
## LEGITIMATING POWER BY TEMPERING ITS EXERCISE

The aggressiveness and perversity of customs enforcement in the 1860s and 1870s—particularly the inclination of the officers to construe mistaken

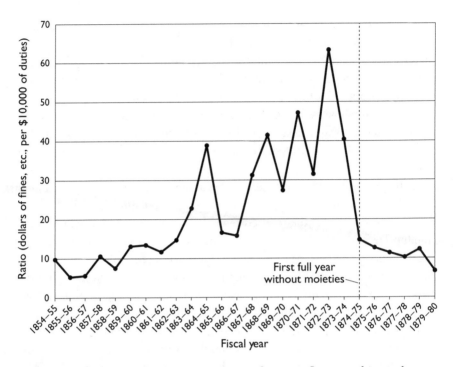

*Figure 6.1.* Ratio between U.S. Treasury receipts of customs fines, penalties, and forfeitures, and of customs duties, 1855–1880.

*Sources*: The Treasury's receipts from customs duties are from *HSUS* series Ee428. The Treasury's receipts of fines, penalties, and forfeitures are from the following sources. For fiscal 1854–55 through 1866–67, see H.R. Exec. Doc. No. 34–40, at 673 (1856); H.R. Exec. Doc. No. 34–86, at 615 (1857); H.R. Exec. Doc. No. 35–13, at 687 (1857); H.R. Exec. Doc. No. 35–20, at 629 (1859); H.R. Exec. Doc. No. 36–7, at 605 (1860); H.R. Exec. Doc. No. 36–12, at 567 (1860); H.R. Exec. Doc. No. 37–36, at 543 (1862); H.R. Exec. Doc. No. 38–8, at 409 (1863); H.R. Exec. Doc. No. 38–84, at 341 (1864); H.R. Exec. Doc. No. 38–73, at 359 (1865); H.R. Exec. Doc. No. 39–12, at 391 (1866); H.R. Exec. Doc. No. 40–315, at 449 (1868); H.R. Exec. Doc. No. 42–29, at 443 (1871). For fiscal 1867–68 through 1869–70, see Treasury Report, 1868, p. 44; Treasury Report, 1869, p. 67; Treasury Report, 1870, p. 59. For fiscal 1870–71 through 1876–77, see Treasury Report, 1877, p. xxix. For fiscal 1877–78 through 1878–80, see Treasury Report 1878, p. 321; Treasury Report 1879, p. 265; Treasury Report 1880, p. 249.

irregularities as frauds—arose from the explosive combination of the moiety system with novel forms of alien imposition: stranger officers, higher taxes, worse penalties, and more intrusive surveillance. Congress in 1874 reacted to these perversities by enacting a statute, popularly known as the "Anti-Moiety Act,"[130] which (1) moderated some of the novel forms of alien governance, but refused to give them up, and (2) abolished moieties to ensure that officers would temper the future exercise of their still-substantial powers, so as to build a less adversarial and more cooperative and trusting relationship between the merchants and the unavoidably alien state.

### Congress Moderates Alien Imposition but Refuses to Give It Up

Alien imposition did not disappear in 1874. In many ways, it remained just as strong as it had been. First, officers would continue to be strangers to the merchant community. There was no going back to the regime of "local notables." Congress in 1874 favored maintaining the spoils system in the customhouses, and even when limited numbers of customs officials moved toward civil service beginning in 1879,[131] that was itself just another form of alien governance. Second, the tariff would remain very high for the foreseeable future: the average ad valorem rates from the mid-1870s to 1890 were 43 percent to 45 percent.[132] This would remain an ever-present temptation to fraud and reason for suspicion. Third, special agents continued in their capacity as full-time detectives.[133]

In the areas of punishment and information-gathering, the Anti-Moiety Act moderated the novel forms of alien governance, but it surely did not eliminate them.[134] As noted earlier, the courts had construed the enforcement act of 1863 in draconian fashion to forfeit the entire invoice in every case of fraud. Congress in 1874 moderated the forfeiture so that it was confined to the package that contained the undervalued goods. This was still a harsher sanction than had prevailed in the early republic, when only the items undervalued were forfeit. And it could be harsh in an absolute sense: the $271,000 for which Phelps Dodge settled was the value of items undervalued; a package-based sanction would have been greater. What is more, Congress in 1874 additionally provided for a fine up to $5,000 and imprisonment up to two years for each offense,[135] that is, for each false invoice.[136] Since the typical invoice was less than $5,000,[137] this fine was potentially more severe than the draconian rule of 1863.[138] To be sure, the fine, though potentially severe, was not automatic like forfeiture: its amount was in the judge's discretion, up to $5,000. But the 1874 act vested the officers with a new power to seize, even in advance of trial, *any* goods belonging to the merchant equal in value to *double* the maximum of all fines *claimed*.[139] As one merchant fearfully pointed out, the officers, "[w]henever fines are incurred, can aggregate them, on a basis of a penalty for each offense of $5,000" and then seize any goods "equal in value to the aggregate of all such penalties."[140] In fact, it was worse: they could seize double the aggregate!

As with punishment, so with investigatory power. The Anti-Moiety Act moderated that power, but not very much. Congress took away the power of customs officers to seize books from a merchant's building. But it empowered the U.S. attorney, when litigating a fraud case, to describe any document that would "tend to prove" a government allegation and to demand that the merchant produce it. If the merchant refused and failed to explain why "to the satisfaction of the court," the allegation was "taken as confessed."[141] If a firm claimed that an asked-for paper did not exist, the burden was on the firm to prove it.[142]

Such information-seeking power was significant, though it had more safeguards than before 1874. First, it was routed through the U.S. attorney, whereas the law previously had allowed any customhouse officer to obtain a warrant.[143] But this made little difference: New York officers had already been checking all warrant requests with the U.S. attorney.[144] Second, the new process became available only after the government brought a lawsuit, as opposed to the ex parte process of obtaining a warrant.[145] Some feared the lawsuit could provide the fraudster with advance warning, allowing him to destroy incriminating papers.[146] But, as one congressman argued, merchants might well be afraid to destroy papers, since their doing so would indicate the truth of the fraud charges.[147] Third, there were new protections against fishing expeditions. The U.S. attorney had to "particularly describ[e]" the documents he sought, and he could only look at the entries related to his allegations, and then only in the presence of the merchant's lawyer. But a court could be generous to the government in applying the vague particularity requirement.[148] Fourth, the court had to approve the U.S. attorney's demand and could block the demand "at its discretion," whereas previously the judge had been required to issue a warrant upon the "appear[ance]" of fraud.[149] Finally, the sanction for the merchant's unjustified refusal was not contempt of court but instead confession of the allegation. This was still a formidable threat. As one Supreme Court justice later put it, the U.S. attorney would "always be sure to state the evidence expected to be derived from [the asked-for document] as strongly as the case will admit of."[150] So the sanction could "be made more severe" than "fine and imprisonment."[151]

There was one other limit on information-gathering, though probably not a very great one. The Anti-Moiety Act declared that compulsory production was available in all proceedings under the revenue laws except "criminal" ones. As the bill was initially reported by both the House committee and Senate committee, it provided for no jail term but contemplated that both the forfeiture and the $5,000 fine would occur in civil proceedings, so the government could force production of documents when seeking those sanctions.[152] However, a last-minute amendment on the Senate floor added the prison term and altered the wording of the punishment clause so that not only prison but also the $5,000 fine were apparently confined to criminal proceedings.[153] Though nobody mentioned it (or perhaps even realized it), this apparently meant that the production order was available only in prosecutions to win forfeitures, not fines.[154] Still, this may not have been a great limitation. Under federal law at the time, if a merchant were forced to divulge information in any judicial proceeding, the government would be unable to use that same evidence against him in a criminal prosecution, but it could still criminally prosecute him for the offense to which the evidence pertained. It just needed to gather other evidence on which to prove the charge.[155] Thus, the government could sue a merchant for civil forfeiture, force him to produce documents, learn the particulars of the fraud from them, gather other evidence on the basis of those particulars (the testimony of clerks, perhaps), and then prosecute the merchant criminally on the basis of that evidence.[156]

Because it preserved these still-formidable elements of alien governance, Congress felt obligated to try to ensure that officers would no longer use their powers to press fraud cases against merchants who had merely made mistakes. In pursuit of that end, lawmakers began by reaffirming the intent requirement and addressing two of the oddities that had sometimes undermined it prior to 1874: (1) that a merchant who underpaid because he honestly mistook the law was treated as an intentional fraudster and (2) that a merchant who underpaid because of a mistake of fact might have difficulty asserting his innocence, since the jury could infer evil intent from failure to pay. The new statute stated that, if a fraud accusation went to trial, the jury had to make a "special finding" as to whether the merchant had the "actual intention" to evade taxes.[157] The phrase "actual intention" meant that a merchant who mistook the law was no longer guilty of fraud.[158] And the need for a "special finding" drew the jury's attention to the intent issue and perhaps made the jurors less likely to infer intent from the act of underpayment.[159]

## Congress Abolishes Moieties to Legitimate Alien Imposition

The reforms discussed above, aiming to moderate alien imposition, were well and good. But if the intent requirement were truly to protect merchants against the traps and hard edges of modern customs law and its enforcement machinery—if it were to succeed in rendering alien imposition bearable and legitimate—there remained the problem that intent (even in its revised formulation) rested on an irreducibly subjective judgment: what had the merchant been thinking? This subjectivity gave enforcers wide latitude to prosecute. In making the subjective judgment, officers could stretch or hang back.

The aim of abolishing officers' moieties, which the act did in its very first substantive section,[160] was to take away the officers' reason to stretch, so that they would be more understanding toward merchants' assertions of mistake, thus mitigating the risk of prosecution for mere technicalities. In pursuing this aim, lawmakers were heeding Dodge's warning that officers were "very anxious to secure their large moieties," creating "great danger of their assuming that there has been fraud where there never had been."[161] Lawmakers were also seeking to breathe life into the Treasury Department's existing instructions to the special agents, which cautioned that the "severity" of official powers granted by Congress was "such that extreme caution, discretion and forbearance are requisite in their enforcement and exercise. They are not to be put in operation upon hasty or trivial charges, nor ever used in full force, except when absolutely necessary in extreme cases."[162] Rising official power called for "caution, discretion, and forbearance," but such things were practically impossible when officers operated on the profit motive. "Under the stimulus of the moieties," explained Representative Ellis Roberts, an upstate New York Republican and floor manager for the House bill, "the large interests of the officers has led [them] . . . to extreme constructions classifying[,] as criminal[,] acts without intent of wrong, . . . and to the enforcement of penalties disproportionate to the offense and ruinous to men who had no crime in their hearts."[163] Representative Niblack, an Indiana Democrat on the House Ways and Means Committee, which reported the bill, praised "especially that provision which repeals all moieties, which takes away from the officer the incentive to seize upon, to pounce upon, the importing merchants for slight and trivial offenses."[164]

It was the distinctly subjective character of judgments about intent that drove Congress to abolish moieties for the officers who scrutinized underpayments. Congress implicitly acknowledged this by maintaining a system of bounties (albeit an anemic one, consisting of discretionary bonuses from a measly appropriation) for officers detecting outright smugglers who tried to avoid the customhouse completely, as by sneaking goods across a desolate stretch of the Canadian border.[165] In that context, fraudulent intent was plain in the act itself, in contrast to underpayments arising from the reporting or processing of data, where mistake was a very real possibility.

The banishment of the profit motive reconciled lawmakers to maintaining a large degree of official power, even though such power had been so terrifyingly exercised up to 1874. After so many complaints of unwarranted enforcement, both the House and Senate were skittish about preserving *any* official power to gather merchant data by coercion. In debate on the act, each chamber initially voted to strike the bill's production-order provision—that is, to return the customs officers to their pre-1863 blindness—before finally being persuaded to accept this moderate degree of investigatory power.[166] In a careful argument favoring the production-order provision, Representative John Kasson, an Iowa Republican and member of the Ways and Means Committee, prefaced his defense of this official surveillance power by emphasizing that it would be divorced from bounty-seeking: "I condemn, as heartily as any man on this floor, laws which allow extraordinary powers, in the name of the Government, to interested men, tempted by the acquisition in a single day of an enormous fortune."[167] Nor was the compulsory production of documents the only power whose exercise Congress sought to temper by decoupling it from profit-seeking. Recall that the bill authorized the officers, prior to trial, to seize a merchant's goods in an amount double the total fines claimed.[168] The New York merchants' top lobbyist warned Congress that the officers, "[w]henever fines are incurred, can aggregate them, on a basis of a penalty for each offense of $5,000" and then seize any goods "equal in value to the aggregate of all such penalties."[169] Defending his committee's decision to grant this power, Representative Roberts cited the abolition of moieties as a guarantee that officers could be trusted to forbear when appropriate: "If the district attorney or collector had a direct personal interest in multiplying and magnifying suits, some grounds might exist for this sort of complaint. But all that has been removed by the bill. The customs officers have no moiety; the district attorney has not even a commission to impel him to exaggeration of this kind."[170]

Congress's ultimate purpose, in tempering the exercise of official power through the banishment of the profit motive, was to win legitimacy for the ambitious revenue system it had constructed over the preceding years—to cultivate a less adversarial and more cooperative and trusting relationship between officers and merchants and, with it, a culture of voluntary compliance among the merchants.

As one leading merchant emphasized in his testimony before the House committee, the voluntary cooperation of the merchants was crucial, for there was little to stop them from evading duties if they really wanted to. The government simply did not have enough competent officers to detect and punish violations if they occurred en masse. Enforcement and punishment would always have less impact than the communal norms and values of the merchants.[171] Representative Fernando Wood, the former political boss of New York City and now a top House Democrat seeking to woo merchants and reformist voters,[172] explained that the merchants were essential "intermediaries" between the federal Treasury and the mass of American consumers who ultimately bore the economic burden of the tariff. "This force"—the intermediary merchant class—"is one as yet entirely unrecognized by the Government, too little respected by our laws," whose members "have been the objects of oppression." "Is it not . . . our duty as a Government," asked Wood, "to nourish, protect, and encourage the source upon which we mainly depend for revenue?"[173]

Roberts, the House floor manager, warned that immoderate, profit-driven enforcement was undermining the taxpayer goodwill that was necessary to compliance: "Our institutions," he said, "depend on the good-will of the citizen. For the collection of the revenue, one of the primary essentials is the moral support of those who pay." But this had "been to an alarming degree lost. Sympathy has been aroused for those charged with offenses against the customs. Penalties enforced in accordance with the letter of the law have excited odium." As a result, "[v]iolation of the laws has ceased to affix opprobrium. Their enforcement carries a taint as in the case of the old fugitive-slave law." Roberts concluded, "[Y]ou must guard against such cruel measures as will render frauds respectable and will raise false importations into a short of chivalry."[174]

Abolishing bounties seemed necessary to rescue the mutual trust between government and merchants. Profit-seeking enforcement, attested the New York merchants' chief lobbyist, had lost the government the "affection and the loyalty" of importers.[175] The Treasury Department's commissioner of customs agreed, observing that merchants had come to view their government "as alien in interest and hostile in feeling to themselves."[176] Wood said the pattern of enforcement had "alienated the affections of a large class of liberal and patriotic citizens."[177] The Treasury secretary warned that the moiety system "impairs the efficiency of customs officers by subjecting them constantly to the imputation of interested motives in the discharge of their official duties, and hence lowering them in the public estimation."[178]

At times, contemporaries explicitly discussed the mechanisms by which moiety-seeking caused enforcement to become excessive and merchants to become alienated and uncooperative. Analyzing the "moiety and spy system," the Boston merchant John Candler explained that unwarranted adversarialism by the government would elicit a reciprocal response from the taxpayer, which the government lacked the resources to counteract through sheer deterrence: "There is something in a man's heart that, if you take from him that which you have no right to take, if an opportunity comes he retaliates. This is something which we cannot prevent. If you wrong a man to-day, he tries to-morrow to circumvent the Government so as to get his own again. And no regulations, and no penalties, in my opinion, can meet and effectually change that fact."[179] The notion that citizens reciprocate the attitude of regulators resonates powerfully with present-day social science on law enforcement, as does the fear, also expressed in the 1870s, that officials could undermine citizens' intrinsic willingness to comply if they approached enforcement with the presumption that citizens were generally noncompliant.[180] "Can it be considered sound public policy," asked Wood, "to frame and execute laws based upon the theory that such a people [merchants] are naturally dishonest?"[181] Indeed, moiety-driven enforcers do appear to have approached their jobs assuming that evasion was the norm (which is no surprise, since their income depended on evasion). One merchant lawyer recalled a conversation with a special agent who told him: "The truth is, all these importers are scoundrels and frauds, every one of them; they are all engaged in cheating the revenue. That's their business; that's the way they make their money. There isn't one of them honest."[182]

Another mechanism by which moiety-seeking led to excessive enforcement and undermined trust and cooperation, in the eyes of contemporaries, was that profit-maximizing officers failed to exercise the subjective judgment and forbearance that complex and imperfect laws necessitated, resulting in too much enforcement for "technical" violations. Said the New York merchants' top lobbyist: "[E]ven bad and imperfect laws, when administered by good men with good motives, are very often run on for a long time harmoniously and pleasantly. But when you get technical men, selfish men, who are interested in their enforcement, then you begin to see the hardships of the laws."[183] Writing to Congress in support of moiety abolition, Treasury Secretary Richardson made the same point and linked it with Candler's point about how regulatees tended to mirror the adversarialism of regulators: there were "powerful inducements for [the merchant] to take any possible technical advantage in his own favor. When this is met by a corresponding technical enforcement of the law on the part of its executive officers, a feeling of antagonism between the merchant and the Government is insensibly developed, the results of which cannot but be demoralizing and injurious."[184] "[D]isregard petty irregularities," promised one merchant advocate, "and then, sir, you make every honest importer and merchant a watchman for the Government."[185]

To those holding these views, the abolition of moieties promised to foster a relationship of trust, confidence, and mutual cooperation between taxpayers and officialdom. Nonprofit status, contended Richardson, would exempt officers from "any suspicion of bias," and they would "be elevated in public estimation," and "[c]onfidence will take the place of distrust" and "antagonism."[186] According to the commissioner of customs, ending moieties would remove from the "customs-officer" the "reproach under which all spies and informers, for contingent rewards, labor in popular estimation."[187] He hoped that "both officials and importers, by being on a better footing toward each other, may act together for the prevention of such frauds and abuses."[188] The abolition of an analogous system of bounties for internal revenue officers back in 1872, in the view of many, had been salutary for officer-taxpayer relations and for compliance—a result that the opponents of moieties hoped to replicate in the customhouses. During his testimony, Candler answered affirmatively to the question: "Since the abolition of moieties to informers [in internal revenue], is not the class of men who were affected by it [i.e., makers of taxable items like liquor and tobacco], getting along with the Government more harmoniously, and is not the Government getting its revenues more fairly?"[189] Similarly, Representative James B. Beck, a Kentucky Democrat on the Ways and Means Committee, attested that, after the abolition of moieties in internal revenue, the "revenues of the Government are better secured and more cheerfully paid. Instead of increased distrust, confidence and good-will between the distiller, tobacco manufacturer, and others who pay revenue and the Government is the rule and not the exception. It will be so with the customs revenue when this bill becomes a law."[190]

Representative Roberts, convinced that coercion and deterrence were of limited effectiveness, summed up his vision of legitimacy for the revenue system, to which he believed nonprofit enforcement was necessary:

> Their [the merchants'] aid is better than police. Their support is better than armed men. Against their sense of wrong, against their aroused moral sentiment, laws and officers can do little. Just laws, reasonable penalties, humane enforcement, enlist the conscience, the interest, the active support of those who are affected. If we retain the processes, the spirit, the harsh severity of barbaric ages in laws and administration, we must expect the restiveness, the attempts at fraud, the moral resistance which extreme measures always invite. Every step of amelioration in general legislation, every removal of unreasonable penalties and punishment, has tended to diminish crime and to develop better citizenship. The like result may be anticipated from a mitigation of the harshness of proceedings, and of the extortionate forfeitures under our customs laws.[191]

Strikingly, the defenders of moieties largely admitted that the rewards and the pattern of enforcement they promoted rendered odious the officials and the law they enforced. For moieties' defenders, this kind of alienation, distrust, and resentment were inevitable aspects of alien imposition, even of positive law itself. Legitimacy was simply unachievable, and coercion was the only solution. In a speech critical of the anti-moiety bill, Senator Aaron Sargent, a California Republican, insisted that "[r]evenue laws are from their very nature unpopular," which meant that bounties for informers were necessary. "[T]o compete with dishonor," he said, "dishonor must be used."[192] According to George Bliss, the U.S. attorney for New York City, the use of spies and private informers—methods characteristic of the bounty-seeking special agents—was "a necessary result . . . of any attempt to enforce a law, certainly unless that law has some basis of moral principle away down in the bottom of the hearts of men to which you can appeal. Now . . . with reference to any question of evading the tax or evading the duties, there is not any basis of moral principle in the ordinary human being to which you can appeal which will keep him from doing what is really wrong, as it is a violation of the statute law, because he does not feel that it is morally wrong."[193] Bliss believed "you have got to fight self-interest with self-interest."[194] For many other contemporaries, too, bounty-seeking was unfortunate and distasteful yet necessary. Pennsylvania Republican Senator Simon Cameron, who supported the preservation of moieties for officers, admitted that "the whole system of employing spies and all the bad people in their train is one of the worst features of our later history. . . . But you cannot collect your revenue unless you have informers of some kind."[195]

In this debate, it seems congressmen were truly interested in what kind of enforcement regime would be most workable. It does not appear that lawmakers' underlying preferences about the substance of tariff policy controlled their views on moieties. Most obviously, Congress maintained considerable tariffs throughout the 1870s, yet the Anti-Moiety Act passed the House by a voice vote and cleared the Senate with only three dissenting votes.[196] Furthermore, the members of the House Ways and Means Committee who spoke at length in favor of moiety abolition included committed protectionist Republicans (Henry Dawes of Massachusetts, as well as Roberts), a moderate protectionist Republican (Kasson), a moderate anti-protectionist Democrat (Wood), and a strong anti-protectionist Democrat (Beck).[197] It is noteworthy that Roberts and Wood, despite their partisan and policy differences, were the most articulate of all congressmen regarding the link between nonadversarial enforcement and voluntary compliance.[198] As Roberts declared, "This is not a question of free trade or protection." If anything, moiety abolition was necessary to legitimate and bolster the protective regime: "It becomes especially the advocates of protection," explained Roberts, "to show that their policy can be maintained without gross wrongs to individuals." Protectionists "must prove by action that annoying litigation, onerous fines, and ruinous forfeitures are no part of a protective system."[199] To be sure, some of the few senators who expressed sympathy for moieties were protectionist Republicans, but so was the main architect of the Senate anti-moiety bill, John Sherman.[200]

Despite the connection that social science often draws between salaried jobs and career stability, it would be wrong to view moiety abolition as part of a package by which lawmakers moved the customhouse officialdom toward secure tenure or, relatedly, civil service reform. The quest for nonadversarial administration to foster cooperation and trust was an end in itself, independent of roughly contemporaneous civil service trends. To be sure, friends of civil service reform generally (though not universally) supported the campaign to abolish moieties.[201] Yet the Forty-Third Congress, while passing the Anti-Moiety Act with almost no dissenting votes,[202] simultaneously killed the first U.S. Civil Service Commission by cutting its appropriations to zero.[203] For many lawmakers, moiety abolition clearly had attractions independent of civil service reform.[204] Even when the leading customhouses began to undergo civil service reform, first by executive order in 1879 and then by statute in 1883,[205] the officers who had been (and would remain)[206] the most active in anti-fraud enforcement—the collector and special agents—remained conspicuously outside the system. Indeed, collectors would remain political appointees at least through the 1910s.[207] The special agents, too, were excepted from civil service regulations until 1889,[208] and even then, they were subjected only to noncompetitive examinations that left room for patronage, in which status they remained for the next couple of decades.[209] Between 1885 and 1894, turnover among the special agents was 86 percent.[210] Political considerations remained a factor in personnel decisions for special agents till about 1910 at the earliest.[211]


## AFTERMATH: ALIEN IMPOSITION IN THE LONG RUN

Fostering voluntary compliance is a tricky endeavor, since the rate of compliance is often difficult or impossible to measure, in contrast to the amount of enforcement, which is easier to gauge. Lawmakers aiming at voluntarism must guess. On this point, the Anti-Moiety Act was no exception.

In the single fiscal year following the act's passage (which began July 1, 1874, after the president signed the act on June 22), our gauge of the intensity of enforcement—the ratio between the Treasury's receipts of fines, penalties, and forfeitures and its receipts of customs duties—fell by an astonishing 63 percent. And it stayed in that low range, close to its pre-1863 level (see figure 6.1). Another metric of enforcement, the number of forfeiture suits filed in New York

City, also fell precipitously in 1874 and stayed at its new low level.[212] This crash clearly resulted from the Anti-Moiety Act, though we cannot be certain about the relative importance of the act's various provisions—abolition of moieties, strengthening of the intent requirement, and moderation of punishments and investigatory power. In any case, the numbers surely suggest that enforcement had become less adversarial.

Whether the decline of adversarialism had the intended effect of fostering mass compliance is hard to tell. Customs revenue fell in the year after abolition, and continually until 1877, but it then recovered to its previous level by 1882.[213] Most and perhaps all of these fluctuations are attributable to the business cycle, as the nation entered a depression in 1873 and recovered in 1877. John Sherman, the Senate floor manager for the Anti-Moiety Act and later Treasury secretary, worried in 1877 that the drop in forfeitures resulted not from increased compliance but from more lax enforcement. Still, he did not advocate the reinstatement of moieties for officers, instead issuing a vague call for increased incentives to private tipsters.[214] Ultimately, compliance levels were unknowable, and opinion on the level of compliance was divided. In 1885, Treasury Secretary Daniel Manning asserted that the law against undervaluation was effectively a "dead letter," though he attributed the situation only partly to the Anti-Moiety Act and mainly to the inherent difficulty of enforcing a high tariff (he was an ardent free trader).[215] Yet Joseph Solomon Moore, a leading writer on international commerce and also a free trader, insisted that same year that undervaluation was marginal.[216]

Whatever the actual results of their actions, the lawmakers who repudiated the profit motive in federal tax enforcement intended to temper the exercise of a growing and permanent arsenal of alien official powers. To be sure, one of the most important of these powers—to compel the disclosure of documents—ran into some obstacles. In 1886, the U.S. Supreme Court held in *Boyd v. United States* that the production-order provision of the Anti-Moiety Act, limited though it was by comparison with the regime of 1863–74, violated the Fourth and Fifth Amendments of the Bill of Rights.[217] Yet *Boyd* only hindered, and did not stop, the long-run growth of state surveillance. For one thing, the decision itself made a huge exception for the "supervision . . . exercised by officers . . . over the manufacture or custody" of goods subject to excise taxes, as well as the "entries" of such activities "in books required by law to be kept for [the officers'] inspection."[218] This meant that *Boyd* had limited application to the realm of federal internal revenue (consisting mainly of excise taxes on liquor and tobacco), where Congress required all distillers and tobacco-product manufacturers to keep minute records of their sales, purchases, and other activities. These records were not "private" under *Boyd*, so the government had power to inspect them. By the 1890s and early 1900s, courts recognized this exception as covering required records not merely of excisable goods but of any "transactions which are the appropriate subjects of governmental regulation."[219] Also, the Supreme Court in 1906 made an exception to *Boyd* for the records of a corporation, which was then becoming the standard business form.[220] Over the twentieth century, what remained of *Boyd* would also disappear.[221]

Even within the realm of customs enforcement, it is not clear that *Boyd* made much of a difference. Congress apparently ignored the holding. In 1890, it imposed a fine per day for a merchant's failure to produce papers demanded by a customs collector, which it reenacted in 1909 and apparently strengthened in 1913.[222] The statute provided for no immunity, yet no reported case held it unconstitutional or even discussed its constitutionality.[223]

Further, it appears that customs officers, if determined, could access merchants' books in spite of *Boyd*. When the exceptionally aggressive William Loeb (formerly a close aid to Theodore Roosevelt and afterward an executive in the Guggenheim steel empire) became collector at New York in 1909,[224] he enlisted the special agents in a campaign against undervaluation, and they proved capable of obtaining merchants' books in large numbers.[225] An agent's success in obtaining books, in the words of one congressman, was "dependent upon his ability as a diplomat or a bluffer."[226] Some agents apparently threatened importers with bad publicity if they failed to comply.[227] In some cases, it seems, physical force was used. In 1910, Loeb and his men, acting on the basis of an anonymous letter and nothing else, raided the offices of New York's top art-dealing partnership and seized numerous invoices on which to base undervaluation charges. Although the dealers were advised by counsel who apparently understood the constitutional issues and raised them with the U.S. attorney, they pled guilty, were each assessed fines of $10,000 or more, and made a civil settlement of more than $1 million.[228]

Thus, despite the efforts of the Supreme Court, it seems that Congress in 1874 correctly anticipated that alien official power would be a persistent and growing element of American government, one that needed to be tempered by reforms (like the banishment of profit-seeking) that were more hardwired into the officialdom's internal structure than was judicial review. Notably, Loeb in 1911 told Congress that, in addition to using the special agents for enforcement, he was relying upon their excellent ideas for how to revise customhouse regulations and procedures to make fraud more difficult, and less likely, to begin with.[229] It is hard to imagine the "moiety men" being so enthusiastic about fostering mass compliance.

# 7

## CRIMINAL PROSECUTION

### *Cash for Convictions*

We now turn to criminal justice, another realm in which lawmakers experimented intensely with bounties as instruments of state-building before ultimately rejecting them. Our focus will be the public prosecutor (known by such diverse titles as district attorney, state's attorney, or, at the federal level, U.S. attorney). Interestingly, this officer did not exist in England, where criminal prosecutions were ordinarily carried out by private individuals. North American colonists invented the office, for reasons that historians today do not fully understand.[1] Once the office was created, the public prosecutor became the single most powerful actor in the American criminal justice system. The nature and timing of the process by which the officer acquired such power is the subject of research by many scholars, to which this chapter seeks to contribute.

Through much of the nineteenth century and sometimes into the twentieth, American public prosecutors made their income from fees, usually based on the number of cases they brought or the number of convictions they won, depending on the jurisdiction. For a crime that had a particular victim, such a fee was simultaneously a facilitative payment, in that it motivated the officer to serve the desire of the individual victim to have the suspect prosecuted, and a bounty, in that it motivated the officer to go after the suspect, who would rather be left alone. Depending on the conditions for collecting the fee, its facilitative aspect might predominate over its bounty aspect, or vice versa.

When the fee was simply for bringing the case (regardless of whether it resulted in conviction), its facilitative aspect predominated. Private citizens came forward claiming to be the victims of crime, and the public prosecutor—

entitled to fees on the basis of the number of cases he brought—maximized his income by sending all their accusations to trial without much scrutiny or discrimination, thus allowing accusers free access to court to tell their stories to the jurors. In this way, private accusers had effective control over the machinery of criminal prosecution, and the public prosecutor played a facilitative role by holding the courthouse door open for them. This arrangement motivated the public prosecutor to impose *some* hardship on defendants, in that he forced them to go through the annoyance of a trial, but he had no interest in seeing them actually convicted or punished. Further, it was common for private accusers to treat the matter as a neighborly dispute and drop the case upon reaching some private resolution with the accused. Thus, defendants experienced the system as coercive, but the coercion was relatively mild, it came from one's own neighbors, and one had equal right to exercise the same accusatory power oneself. In this way, the lay members of the community effectively shared, and collectively exercised, control over criminal prosecution. Insofar as there was imposition, it was of the familiar variety.

When the public prosecutor's fee was not merely for bringing a case but instead for winning a conviction, its facilitative aspect faded and its bounty aspect became stronger. Instead of taking all comers, the officer had an incentive to scrutinize private accusations, concentrate his efforts on cases that he judged to be winners, and shut the door to the accusers whose cases looked like losers. And once the officer picked a case as a winner, he had the incentive to win it— to see that the defendant was not merely tried but also found guilty. Under these conditions, the public prosecutor had reason to take a less customer-serving attitude toward complainants and a more adversarial attitude toward defendants. Thus, the conviction fee was predominantly a bounty. It implied a new and different concept of the public prosecutor. He was not simply a conduit for the aggregate complaints of the community; he was instead a proactive gatekeeper. Defendants experienced prosecution not as a neighbor-to-neighbor dispute but as an intervention by a more independent and external force. In that respect, imposition was more alien than under the regime of case-based fees.

Things went even farther in this direction when the crime at issue had no particular victim. In prosecutions of such crimes (say, for violating laws about gambling, liquor, or taxes), the victim-customer disappeared altogether. Gone was any glimmer of service to a private individual. The prosecution was a purely official state attack on the defendant, and the fee for making the attack was simply a bounty, with no trace of a facilitative payment. Further, it was common for a legislature to offer especially high fees for convictions of victimless crimes, to encourage the official initiative that was necessary in the absence of a victim-accuser. Since statutes criminalizing victimless acts often clashed with the norms of whole neighborhoods or communities, such bounties were clear instruments of alien imposition.

Until now, scholars have said very little about public prosecutors' fees, with the exception of Allen Steinberg's justly acclaimed study of the criminal courts in nineteenth-century Philadelphia, where the fees were by the case, not the conviction.[2] I rely upon Steinberg to understand the institutional and social implications of case-based fees. I rely mainly on new primary research (1) to show which American jurisdictions had case-based fees and which had conviction-based fees, and (2) to explain the implications, promise, and ultimate demise of the conviction-based type.

I begin this chapter by examining case-based fees (basically facilitative payments), which were the type of fee that prevailed in most early American jurisdictions. I then show that legislatures between about 1800 and the 1860s shifted toward conviction-based fees (basically bounties), adopting them in about two dozen states and territories and at the federal level—more jurisdictions than ever had case-based fees. As part of this shift, lawmakers frequently offered special fees (i.e., high ones) for convictions under statutes that criminalized victimless acts, especially when those statutes were unpopular in certain neighborhoods or localities. The adoption of conviction fees was a major experiment in alien imposition, setting up the public prosecutor as a proactive gatekeeper to the criminal justice system and as a proactive enforcer of locally unpopular laws against victimless acts. It was an enterprise in state-building.

Then, in the latter part of the chapter, I consider why lawmakers abandoned bounties in favor of salaries. I offer a case study of Congress's decision to convert the U.S. attorneys from conviction fees to salaries in 1896.

In federal law enforcement, as in many other contexts, bounties for a time held great promise as tools of alien imposition. Though Congress never singled out particular crimes for special high fees (as the states did), I think that U.S. attorneys' conviction fees *generally* were special fees for the enforcement of alien law, since nearly all of federal criminal law was alien. A very large proportion of federal criminal statutes prohibited victimless acts and clashed with the norms of many local communities. The prime example was the excise tax on liquor and tobacco, which Congress initially imposed to help finance the Civil War and then retained into the twentieth century. Congress devised a highly technical regulatory framework to ensure payment of the tax, which included criminal penalties for anybody who produced or sold even the slightest amount of liquor or tobacco without conformity to the regulations. This was alien imposition in the extreme, for the production and sale of liquor and tobacco were common folk practices in numerous rural communities of the South and West. True to their promise, bounties for convictions motivated U.S. attorneys to enforce these locally unpopular laws to the letter.

Yet, as in Chapters 5 and 6, lawmakers concluded from experience that bounty-driven enforcement made it impossible to build the legitimacy that was necessary for a workable state. Conviction fees motivated U.S. attorneys to convict as many people as possible, and because the regulations of liquor and tobacco were so minute and technical, this meant they convicted countless people who were guilty of small-time violations. Such prosecutions, as congressmen increasingly realized, radically alienated the population from the federal government and made it impossible to build the kind of community sentiment that would promote voluntary cooperation with the law. For federal law to win the trust and goodwill of the laity, concluded lawmakers, public prosecutors would have to ease up, letting go a substantial portion of the people who were guilty and convictable, particularly those guilty of small-time offenses. Congressmen in 1896 placed federal prosecutors on salaries so that they would have the financial independence to exercise prosecutorial discretion. This would "sand off" the hard edges of modern positivist legislation (which was inevitably broad and rigid) and thereby vest it with legitimacy.

A final note: Throughout the chapter, I refer without specific citation to the dates at which American states and territories converted their public prosecutors from fees to salaries. These dates are all listed and documented in the book's Appendix.

## CASE-BASED FEES: CUSTOMER SERVICE FOR THE VICTIM, FAMILIAR IMPOSITION FOR THE ACCUSED

As of the early nineteenth century, the most common fee arrangement for American public prosecutors was to receive a fee whenever a case went to trial, regardless of whether it resulted in conviction. Let me begin with a word about the establishment of this norm, which needs to be understood in conjunction with the availability of sources to pay the fees.

In the seventeenth century, English practice "ordinarily required the payment of [officers'] fees by defendants even when they were acquitted."[3] This rule made its way to several North American colonies,[4] where the fees included those of the public prosecutor. Forcing the defendant to pay fees regardless of the verdict had the effect of ensuring that the public prosecutor received the same sum regardless of whether he won or lost. Though this might help guarantee the officer's impartiality, many colonists thought it "contrary to natural

justice."[5] Around the time of the Revolution, American lawmakers freed acquitted defendants from liability for fees. But this raised the question of how
officers—and especially the public prosecutor—were to be paid in cases of acquittal. A common solution was to pay them out of the public treasury, and to
do the same with fees in cases of insolvent convicts. Several states adopted this
solution, or something similar, by the period circa 1780–1810: Massachusetts,[6]
Connecticut,[7] Rhode Island,[8] New York,[9] Vermont,[10] Pennsylvania,[11] Delaware,[12] Maryland,[13] South Carolina,[14] and Louisiana.[15] The approach remained
in place in all these states (except South Carolina and Louisiana[16]) until salarization. And it would spread to a few of the new governments that were established in later years: Maine in 1820,[17] Texas in 1836,[18] Iowa by 1847,[19] Nebraska
territory in 1855,[20] and the Dakota Territory as of the 1870s.[21]

Our best information about the impact of such case-based fees comes from
Steinberg's work on Philadelphia. His book, *The Transformation of Criminal
Justice: Philadelphia 1800–1880*, focuses on that city's minor judiciary and police force, but it also includes discussion of the city's public prosecutor,[22] which
Steinberg further details in an article.[23] In these works, Steinberg shows that
compensation schemes profoundly shaped the office of the Philadelphia district attorney.

We first need some background on Philadelphia criminal justice and the
district attorney's role in it. Although the American public prosecutor today
actively exercises vast discretion over the initiation and termination of criminal
cases, the Philadelphia district attorney through most of the nineteenth century
did no such thing. Typically, a case began when a private citizen made an accusation, most commonly of assault and battery or theft,[24] before a neighborhood magistrate, known as an alderman.[25] Because the alderman earned fees
from private accusers, he had reason to give his customers what they wanted,
that is, to let their accusation go forward.[26] The city's grand jury, possessing
little initiatory role of its own,[27] had the job of screening the private accusations
as they poured in.[28] If the grand jury approved, the case went for trial before
the petit jury. Within this system, the district attorney "was essentially a clerk,
organizing the court calendar and presenting cases to grand and petit juries."[29]
He processed the cases like widgets on an assembly line, automatically and
indiscriminately moving each one to the next phase of the process, unless some
other actor plucked the case from the system: the private accuser, who might
drop the accusation; the grand jury, which might reject it; or the petit jury,
which might acquit the defendant.[30]

A major reason for the district attorney's indiscriminate approach was the
case-based fee structure, which took no account of cases' outcomes. The district

attorney was guaranteed, from the treasury, (1) a fee of $3 for every case that he submitted to the grand jury that was rejected and (2) a fee of $5 for every case submitted to the grand jury that was returned a true bill, thus sending it to trial.[31] The extra $2 for a true bill probably had little or no net incentive effect, since it was coupled with the extra labor of processing a case for trial. And once a case was at trial, the district attorney had no pecuniary reason to care how it came out. Thus, in cases where the private accuser did not retain trial counsel of his or her own, "the public prosecutor did not often assume that role. Rather, he simply placed the private [accuser] on the stand and let him state his case, then instructed the defense to do the same."[32] The public prosecutor's role was basically to process all private accusations through the system as quickly as possible, regardless of their merits. That was how he made money. The fee structure gave him "a built-in incentive to channel all cases to the grand jury and beyond, leaving others with the responsibility of dismissing them."[33]

Formally, the district attorney's case-based fee was simultaneously a facilitative payment (vis-à-vis the private accuser, who wanted the case to go forward) and a bounty (vis-à-vis the accused, who wanted the case to stop). But the facilitative aspect predominated. Case-based fees encouraged the district attorney to treat private accusers as his customers, moving their complaints forward without question or delay, thereby giving the citizens of Philadelphia easy access to the machinery of criminal prosecution whenever they believed they had been wronged. Notably, this "customer service" regime was not skewed in favor of the wealthy. Since aldermen's fees were low and the district attorney's fees were publicly financed, the system's solicitude extended to poor accusers (often battered wives), who used the criminal courts extensively.[34]

To be sure, the fees encouraged the district attorney to impose hardship on accused persons, in forcing them through the annoyance of a trial.[35] But the officer had no interest in actual conviction, which helps explain his passive attitude in the courtroom. Most likely, defendants felt themselves to be targets not of the officer but of their respective private accusers, usually other people from the neighborhood, for whom the officer was merely holding the courtroom door open. As Steinberg emphasizes, private accusers had great control over whether to keep the prosecution going, and they typically dropped it prior to the verdict (by failing to show up for the inquest or trial), often because they had reached a private resolution with the accused.[36] The conviction rate was accordingly very low.[37] And even when convictions occurred, private accusers often requested that punishment be nominal, to which the court usually assented.[38] Thus, the hardship for defendants usually was not terribly great, and they probably experienced it as emanating from the private accuser, not the public prosecutor. Further, the defendant's vulnerability "was, in part, off-set" by his or her own ability "to adopt the role of private prosecutor [i.e., accuser]."[39]

Insofar as this regime involved coercion, its openness (indeed deference) to citizen accusations and citizen discretion meant the imposition was familiar. Because the community's lay members effectively controlled the system's machinery, that system served as a conduit for community values in criminal law. "Very low conviction rates and high rates of cases being ignored by grand jurors or abandoned by [private accusers]," explains Steinberg, "reflected a criminal justice process easily negotiated by the public and dependent upon community-based definitions of crime." The system "gave citizens the power, in practice, to define crime. . . . The determination of what acts would provide grounds for a criminal charge was made among the participants in the communities where the acts took place." The "people" enjoyed "the freedom to police themselves, to determine when the law should be invoked and, often, how far the criminal justice process should continue, even though in an imperfect and sometimes exploitative way." The system's accessibility to private accusations produced "a vibrant and effective means of neighborhood-based self-government."[40]

Conversely, this regime was ineffective when it came to alien imposition, that is, the enforcement of laws criminalizing victimless behavior that the community accepted. Occasional spasms of political or judicial pressure to enforce regulations of consensual acts like gambling, drinking, and prostitution had little effect, for the system—dependent as it was on victim-accusers—could not do this kind of thing. As Steinberg says, this "was not a form of law enforcement well suited to the suppression of popular activities."[41]

The Philadelphia district attorney's fee structure remained the same until he was converted to salary in 1874. That conversion helped work a revolution in the office. Facilitation faded. Liberated from the pecuniary imperative to push all cases through the system, the officer was now able—and expected—"to carefully sift through cases, evaluate them and the people involved, and treat them differently, allowing only some access to the judiciary."[42] This reform—coupled with another that salarized the aldermen and cut their electoral ties to local neighborhoods—meant that private accusers could no longer set the criminal justice system in motion according to their own needs.[43] They now had to submit to the judgments of newly independent public officers.[44]

Salarization severed the customer-seller relationship between the public prosecutor and private accusers. The transformation was similar to the changes (recounted in Chapter 4) that accompanied the abolition of facilitative payments for naturalization, veterans' benefits, and homestead rights, including a distancing of officers from laypersons. It entailed "the reduction of the place in criminal justice of proactive citizen participation."[45] Summarizing the transition, Steinberg says that the "era of widespread citizen manipulation of criminal law has given way to an era of widespread citizen distrust of the criminal law, especially among those most likely to need it."[46]

No longer in direct control of the machinery of criminal prosecution, the members of lay communities lost the capacity to influence charges and punishment according to their personal dispute-resolution needs. Laymen became more passive and the system more punitive.[47] The ratio of serious charges to minor ones rose, as did the proportion that ended in conviction.[48] The proportion of prosecutions for victimless crimes rose, too.[49]

## THE RISE OF CONVICTION FEES:
## BOUNTY-SEEKING AND THE QUEST FOR ALIEN IMPOSITION

### Conviction Fees Generally:
### The Public Prosecutor as Gatekeeper and Adversary

Steinberg's assessment of the institutional and social effects of prosecutorial fees in Philadelphia is compelling. But does it apply to the rest of the United States? I suspect it does, insofar as other jurisdictions allowed fees to public prosecutors according to the number of cases, as Pennsylvania did. As noted earlier, there were several other states that had case-based fees. These were concentrated on the East Coast and had mostly adopted public financing to guarantee the arrangement by about 1810.

Yet the period from about 1800 to the 1860s saw the spread of an alternative fee structure, especially in the newer states and at the federal level: fees based largely or entirely on the number of convictions won. By the 1860s, this scheme prevailed in more jurisdictions than did case-based fees. It implied a new concept of the public prosecutor. It incentivized the officer to sift accusations and pick out the ones that seemed likely to result in conviction, instead of taking all comers. And once accusations were selected for prosecution, it incentivized the officer to actually win the case. Thus, the fee structure encouraged the public prosecutor to be less customer-friendly toward accusers and more adversarial toward defendants. Defendants would not experience the prosecution as a more or less private dispute, as did defendants in Philadelphia, where prosecution reflected merely the ire of some neighbor, with little official effort to convict. Rather, defendants would experience prosecution as the act of the state, distinct from some neighbor with whom they had a quarrel. This type of imposition was less familiar, and more alien, than the Philadelphia model. The conviction fee was a harbinger of modernity.

Let us begin this discussion by tracing the spread of conviction fees. Lawmakers established such fees in a couple of East Coast jurisdictions during the eighteenth century: New Jersey in 1748,[50] then South Carolina in 1791.[51] Their rise to prominence began in earnest after the turn of the nineteenth century, starting in the Old Northwest and Old Southwest. Lawmakers adopted conviction fees in Indiana during the territorial period in 1807,[52] keeping them long past statehood. Illinois adopted them right after statehood, in 1819.[53] Mississippi Territory initially had its public prosecutors on pure salaries, and when in 1817 it split into the new state of Mississippi and the territory of Alabama, both jurisdictions stuck with this approach.[54] But when Alabama became a state in 1819, it switched to conviction fees.[55] And Mississippi in 1848 began supplementing its public prosecutors' salaries with conviction fees.[56] Meanwhile, Tennessee established conviction fees in 1832.[57] Shortly after Florida entered the Union in 1845, its legislature adopted conviction fees, in 1851.[58]

Beyond the Mississippi River, conviction fees likewise became the norm. Louisiana Territory in 1807 initially used public financing to equalize fees in cases of conviction and acquittal.[59] But, after splitting off from the territory, the new state of Louisiana in 1820 placed public prosecutors on conviction fees,[60] as did Missouri in 1825,[61] and Arkansas by 1837.[62] Meanwhile, Texas converted from case-based fees to conviction fees in 1848.[63] Such fees also took hold in New Mexico Territory in 1846,[64] Oregon Territory in 1853,[65] Washington Territory in 1854,[66] the state of California in 1856,[67] Colorado Territory in 1861,[68] and Arizona Territory in 1864.[69] (New Mexico, Oregon, and Colorado would keep these arrangements till after statehood.) Back east, when West Virginia split off to become its own state during the Civil War, it adopted the same scheme.[70] And North Carolina, after several years of an odd fee structure (which I discuss later in this chapter), adopted a straightforward conviction-fee scheme in 1874.[71]

Some additional states adopted arrangements that operated in a similar way. Kentucky from the 1850s onward paid each public prosecutor a percentage of the fines imposed in the court where he practiced.[72] Georgia did something quite similar.[73]

The federal government followed the trend by granting conviction fees to U.S. attorneys. Back in the 1790s, Congress had said that U.S. attorneys should receive the same fees as their counterparts in the state courts of their respective districts.[74] Thus, as states increasingly adopted conviction fees, U.S. attorneys practicing in those states began receiving such fees.[75] Then, in 1853, Congress enacted a uniform fee schedule for all U.S. attorneys. Some of the fees did not depend upon outcomes (e.g., $20 for a jury trial, $5 per diem for examining a defendant), but the statute also empowered the court, for every jury conviction, to give the U.S. attorney an additional fee, on top of all the others, of up to $30, "in proportion to the importance and difficulty of the cause."[76] According to several sources, it became common and perhaps routine for judges to give the $30 maximum, even in minor cases.[77] Observers in the late 1800s described U.S. attorneys' fees as "bounties or premiums on prosecutions and convictions."[78]

To nineteenth-century lawmakers, the attraction of the conviction fee was that it incentivized the officer to prosecute vigorously. Admittedly, the primary record on this point is sparse, since the nineteenth-century state legislatures that adopted conviction fees kept almost no substantive records of their deliberations. But other sources suffice to confirm that policy makers were thinking in terms of incentives. In 1837, the governor of Tennessee, discussing a statute criminalizing certain weapons, noted that the legislature had offered a $20 conviction fee to the public prosecutor (plus fees to other officers) "to stimulate the detection, apprehension, and conviction of such culprits."[79] In 1869, after New York changed to salaries, a reform group urged that the state give public prosecutors "a fee for each conviction, instead of fixed salaries," since "[u]nder the present system, the district attorneys get as much for doing nothing as for doing something; and this fact, human nature being as it is, has a paralyzing influence."[80] In 1884, U.S. Attorney General Benjamin H. Brewster, after reversing his earlier support for U.S. attorneys' fees,[81] continued to acknowledge the fear that federal prosecutors "would be less attentive to their duties if paid by salary."[82] The *Chicago Tribune* in 1897 explained that Illinois lawmakers had maintained the conviction-fee system in part because they believed it "would encourage vigorous prosecutions."[83] The governor of Kansas in 1911 vetoed a bill abolishing certain conviction fees, because it took away from the officer "one great incentive to prosecute."[84]

But wouldn't conviction fees dangerously incentivize public prosecutors to convict the innocent? Did the dozens of American legislatures that established such fees not care about that risk? It appears that legal observers of the first half of the nineteenth century, when most conviction fees were adopted, thought the risk very small. To their minds, the American Revolution had guaranteed the triumph of Whig principles in criminal procedure, which were considered extremely protective of the defendant. For example, nineteenth-century judges and lawyers were quite comfortable with the near absence of appellate review in criminal cases, for they believed the trial process made wrongful conviction extremely unlikely: "Criminal proceedings have thrown around the innocent so many guards," wrote a New York judge in 1827, that appellate review would be "almost useless."[85] "[D]efendants, if innocent," attested the Alabama Supreme Court in 1831, "have never much to apprehend from the laws, as administered in this country, even with the aid of the ablest counsel for the State."[86] Further, public prosecutors of the era were not a formidable class. They were typically young, inexperienced, and overburdened.[87] They did not have the apparatus of governmental police and detective services that they would later acquire. As for defense attorneys, representation in serious criminal cases had high prestige value for the nineteenth-century bar, creating the impression (if not the reality) that criminal defendants tended to get good lawyers.[88] In a system apparently so favorable to the defendant, it probably seemed that conviction fees would not increase the likelihood of wrongful conviction above a negligible level.

Indeed, I would go farther and contend that contemporaries viewed conviction fees as affirmatively protecting the innocent. If a jury was vanishingly unlikely to convict an innocent person, then the criminal justice system's greatest threat to the innocent was not the possibility of wrongful conviction, but the injustice of putting an innocent person through the hardship of a trial, albeit one ending in acquittal. Conviction fees encouraged public prosecutors to allocate their resources toward cases that would "pay," which gave them reason to avoid initiating prosecutions likely to end in acquittal and to shut down such prosecutions when started by some other actor, like a private accuser. In other words, the public prosecutor's monetary stake in convicting the guilty incentivized him to prevent the harassment of the innocent. To get paid, he had to sift accusations to find the "convictable" suspects.[89]

Despite the absence of records of state legislative deliberations, there are some other sources that articulate this innocence-protecting rationale for conviction fees. One is an 1897 case from the Tennessee Supreme Court, which concerned a recent statute providing for the compensation of sheriffs and witnesses by conviction fees. (The statute did not address public prosecutors.) The court concluded that the conviction-fee statute was a boon to the innocent, comparing it favorably with a previous statute that gave sheriffs and witnesses the same fees regardless of conviction or acquittal:

> If the new law says, in effect, "Convict, and you shall be paid," the old law says, "Prosecute, and you shall be paid whether you convict or not." If the new law offers an inducement to convict, the old law offers a still more potent and ready inducement to prosecute whether there is or is not a ground for it. . . . Whether it is a greater evil to incur the remote probability that some innocent man may be convicted from mercenary motives, or to encourage the . . . wholesale bringing of trivial and baseless charges and prosecutions

in order to obtain fees, can hardly admit of question, and the legislature has passed this act to remedy [the problem]. . . .

The voice of this act is . . . one of caution and warning. To officers and witnesses it utters salutary words. In effect it says: "Beware that you do not set on foot frivolous, vexatious, or malicious prosecutions, that . . . oppress and annoy the citizen. . . .["][90]

Similar thinking apparently underlay a brief 1867 commentary on conviction fees for New Jersey public prosecutors by Cortlandt Parker, then the public prosecutor of Essex County, who went on to become one of that state's leading attorneys.[91] Parker wrote: "This system of payment [by conviction fees] seems theoretically wrong. Practically, it works well. . . . [T]he character of the bar of New Jersey is such, and the fees themselves so small, that it is not believed that the necessity of success to emolument leads any men to improper exertion. Indeed, the possibility of such a thing protects the innocent from undue prosecution. Too great zeal defeats itself."[92] In the same vein, the North Carolina congressman Thomas Settle, after eight years as a state-level public prosecutor, remarked in 1896 that, under North Carolina statutes, in cases of acquittal "the witnesses and officers receive half fees only; and that provision operates to keep out of our courts frivolous and insignificant prosecutions."[93] Settle's reference to "half fees" refers to North Carolina's law-enforcement officers generally. Public prosecutors in that state received *no* fees in cases of acquittal, so his reasoning applied to them even more strongly.[94]

To be sure, the innocence-protecting rationale for public prosecutors' conviction fees made sense only if public prosecutors actually had the legal power to select which persons would be prosecuted. On this point, Steinberg's work might give us pause, since he finds that Pennsylvania statutes, through the time of salarization in 1874, greatly restricted the formal power of the Philadelphia district attorney to halt cases that private accusers had introduced into the system. But it seems Pennsylvania was an outlier: cases in the courts of numerous other states and at the federal level during the early to mid-1800s recognized the broad power of public prosecutors to drop prosecutions. And though many states continued to vest the formal power to initiate prosecutions in the grand jury through the end of the nineteenth century, it is quite possible—and confirmed by evidence in some states—that public prosecutors in the first half of the nineteenth century were already dominating the grand jury and turning it into their puppet—a status that it would eventually assume in every jurisdiction where it survived. The federal government never formally gave up the grand jury, yet the U.S. attorneys came to dominate it quite early in the nineteenth century.[95]

Not only may the public prosecutor have enjoyed practical power to initiate cases in jurisdictions that formally vested that power in the grand jury, but also there were several states that simultaneously maintained conviction fees for the public prosecutor and deprived the grand jury of even the formal power to initiate cases, vesting that power in the public prosecutor alone. These states—Illinois, Kansas, Louisiana, and Texas—are clear examples of lawmakers basing the public prosecutor's fees on conviction with certain knowledge that he selected which persons to prosecute.[96] They furnish strong evidence that lawmakers understood conviction fees as instruments to guide public prosecutors' selection of defendants—an understanding that makes much more sense if they viewed such fees as protecting the innocent.

Admittedly, incentivizing public prosecutors to target convictable defendants and prosecute them vigorously was not the only conceivable rationale for conviction fees. Lawmakers may have liked such fees for an additional reason: it was possible to offer them without burdening the acquitted defendant or the public treasury. Recall that many legislatures in the early republic were considering how best to abolish the unjust English rule that defendants pay officers' fees even when acquitted. The states discussed in the preceding section opened their treasuries to cover the fees in cases of acquittal, but an alternative solution was to abolish fees altogether in cases of acquittal, leaving the public prosecutor to collect fees only from defendants he convicted. That is, the law would allow the public prosecutor to make money in those cases—and only those cases—in which he could justly mulct a non-treasury source (the convicted defendant). In fact, several of the conviction-fee states had just such a financing scheme: the public prosecutor got his conviction fees only when he could collect them from the defendant (sometimes by forcing the convict to labor while incarcerated).[97]

Though this treasury-protecting rationale may have motivated some of the lawmakers who adopted conviction fees, I still think that incentivization of the public prosecutor was the primary rationale. The best evidence is that numerous legislatures—often for extended periods of time—paid or guaranteed their public prosecutors' compensation out of the public treasury yet continued to structure that compensation so the officers received fees only for winning convictions, or a much higher fee for convictions than acquittals (at least double). The lawmakers of these states must have viewed the conviction basis of the fee as a good in itself, not merely as a response to a financing challenge.

To wit, New Jersey adopted public financing in 1813,[98] yet it maintained its conviction-fee structure until salarization in the late nineteenth century. Tennessee was already paying all costs in criminal cases from the treasury when it established conviction fees in 1832,[99] and public financing of conviction fees

continued there until salarization in the 1890s. Missouri began paying all public prosecutors' fees from the treasury starting in 1845,[100] yet maintained their
conviction-based structure until salarization (which occurred in St. Louis in
1866–69, Kansas City in 1893, and the rest of the state in the twentieth century). A few years after converting to conviction fees, Texas by 1858 opened
the treasury to pay all such fees for felonies (though not for misdemeanors);[101]
this continued into the twentieth century. Florida, amid shifts between many
different schemes, had two stints of publicly financed conviction fees (1851–55
and 1883–95).[102] Conviction fees were also publicly financed in Oregon from
1853 until salarization in 1898;[103] in Washington from 1854 until salarization
in 1881;[104] in California from 1856 until salarization county-by-county over the
following several decades;[105] and in Colorado from 1861 until salarization in
1891.[106] Louisiana opened the treasury to finance the conviction fees of the New
Orleans district attorney in 1884[107]—an arrangement that prevailed until the
office's salarization in 1916. Other examples include North Carolina[108] and Arizona Territory.[109]

The most striking example of public financing for conviction fees was the
federal government. Congress in 1792 provided for all U.S. attorneys' fees in
criminal cases to be paid from the Treasury.[110] Thus, when it made conviction
fees available to U.S. attorneys nationwide in 1853, those fees were publicly
financed,[111] all the way up to the salarization of the U.S. attorneys in 1896.

On top of all this, there is one further item of evidence that lawmakers who
adopted conviction fees cared about public prosecutors' incentives, not merely
about finding non-treasury sources of fee financing. In cases of acquittal, it was
possible to mulct the private accuser, and there were some private accusers
whose charges were so frivolous that they arguably deserved to suffer some kind
of penalty, for wasting the time of the defendant and the court. If lawmakers had
cared simply about scrounging up non-treasury sources of pay for the public
prosecutor and not about that officer's incentives, they would have allowed the
officer to mulct the private accuser for trying cases where the charge turned
out to be frivolous. (The incentive here would be perverse because the officer
would have reason to bring the very flimsiest cases.) But in fact, state legislatures generally did not do this. There are a few exceptions that prove the rule.
North Carolina in 1818 provided for the public prosecutor to extract a fee from
the defendant in cases of conviction or a fee from the private accuser in cases
of acquittal *when the court found the accusation to be frivolous,* but he received
no fee at all in other cases of acquittal.[112] That said, the North Carolina public
prosecutor's entitlement to fees from frivolous accusers was confined to "inferior offenses" with relatively low fees,[113] and in 1874 the legislature dropped its

provision for the payment of fees in frivolous cases, fully aligning itself with the conviction-fee norm.[114] Also, in 1868, Kansas adopted a scheme similar to North Carolina's 1818 scheme,[115] though Kansas's particular doctrines on malicious prosecution may have counteracted the fee scheme's apparently perverse incentives.[116] A couple of other states had certain limited arrangements that bore some similarity to this odd scheme,[117] but legislatures generally steered clear of it. This indicates that they were using conviction fees to perfect official incentives, not simply to scrounge up non-treasury sources of financing.

## Special Conviction Fees under Locally Unpopular Laws against Victimless Acts

As argued in the preceding section, the conviction fee insulated the public prosecutor from the wishes of lay accusers and placed him in a more adversarial posture toward those defendants he selected for prosecution, whom he had to convict in order to profit. In both ways, conviction fees rendered criminal prosecution more of an alien imposition.

Conviction fees also furthered alien imposition in another way: lawmakers placed special reliance upon such fees—offering unusually high amounts—for convictions under statutes that clashed with the norms of local communities. These statutes usually criminalized victimless acts that were popular in the community, like gambling and drinking. The victimless nature of these crimes meant there was nobody to enforce the statutes except officers, and the statutes' unpopularity meant that officers needed some extrinsic motivation to do the job. Case-based fees, which allowed officers to make money simply by relying on private accusations, were quite ineffective for the enforcement of such laws, as Steinberg's work on Philadelphia confirms. Conviction-based rewards, the bigger the better, seemed a promising solution.

Special conviction fees were most prevalent in the enforcement of statutes on gambling, where they originated in the Old Southwest and spread to the New Southwest. First, a bit of background: in most states, as a default, conviction fees rose with the severity of the crime's authorized punishment. There was often one fee for misdemeanors, a higher one for felonies, and perhaps an even higher one for capital offenses.[118] But in setting fees for gambling convictions (which were misdemeanors or minor felonies, often punishable only by fine), lawmakers often deviated from this pattern. The pioneering state was Alabama, which in 1819 offered its public prosecutors $50 for each conviction of exhibiting or housing a gaming table (which equaled the fee for the most heinous felonies) and $20 for all other gaming offenses (double the general fee for penitentiary offenses).[119] In 1841, the legislature raised the gaming-conviction fees to $40 and $100 (depending on the offense), while pricing general felony convictions at a mere $20.[120] When California banned gambling in 1855, it offered its district attorneys 25 percent of all fines collected under the ban, then in 1857 switched to a conviction fee of $100, which it reduced in 1860 to $50, though that was still equal to the fee for capital offenses and double the fee for other felonies.[121] We observe similarly disproportionate fees in New Mexico and Nevada.[122] Other states—Texas, Mississippi, and Arkansas—adopted less spectacular fees for gambling convictions that nonetheless departed upward from the ordinary punishment-based schedule.[123] Tennessee did the same on the subject of illegal lotteries.[124]

In Alabama, especially, the statutes make clear that high incentive fees were to operate in conjunction with public prosecutors' initiative. When the legislature doubled the gaming conviction fees of public prosecutors in 1841, it also vested those prosecutors with extraordinary power, well beyond that available under the common law, to summon witnesses before the grand jury and force them to answer open-ended questions about gaming violations.[125] The state supreme court called the process "inquisitorial."[126]

Besides gambling, another set of laws yielding high conviction fees were those restricting the sale of liquor—something the states regulated ever more aggressively over the nineteenth century.[127] Mississippi instituted such fees in 1839,[128] at a time when its public prosecutors were otherwise almost purely salaried. Kentucky's system of paying its public prosecutors by a percentage of all fines began in embryo with a statute granting them a share of the fines under a few particular laws, including those on liquor.[129] After Massachusetts in 1852 adopted a revolutionary prohibition on the manufacture and sale of liquor,[130] the legislature soon turned to conviction fees, offering them specifically for liquor convictions (the public prosecutors being otherwise salaried).[131] But the best example of all is Kansas. Recall that this state since the 1860s had maintained an odd system in which the public prosecutor received a fee only if it could be collected from a convicted defendant or—if the court determined the prosecution to be malicious—from the complaining witness.[132] After enacting the nation's most restrictive liquor law in 1881,[133] the legislature in 1885 instituted a $25 fee for each count in a prohibition case, but this time the legislature made it collectible only upon conviction,[134] departing from the odd provision about malicious complainants and opting for a more rational incentive structure. The $25 fee equaled that for murder convictions and nearly doubled the $15 for ordinary felony convictions.[135] Most significant, the statute vested the public prosecutor with "extraordinary powers . . . for eliciting testimony by inquisitorial process."[136] The grand jury's role in Kansas had already been much narrowed back in the 1860s,[137] empowering the public prosecutor to operate unilaterally. Here, as in Alabama, lawmakers deliberately combined increases in prosecutorial power with pecuniary incentives to channel that power. When Kansas replaced prosecutors' fees with salaries in 1898, it made an exception for the liquor fee, retaining it into the twentieth century.[138] Later, during the era of national prohibition, the Indiana legislature in 1927 offered an extraordinary $25 fee for each drunk-driving conviction. As one district attorney wrote, "I seem to hear the state saying to me, 'All right, young man, you may not like to do this. It may be an unpopular thing for you to do, so we will make it worth your while.'"[139]

Though gambling and liquor were the most common subjects for special conviction fees, they also appeared in other areas where regulation was in tension with community norms. One was gun control (and its predecessor, the regulation of bowie knives).[140] Another, more dramatic instance arose when lawmakers in the Reconstruction South, seeking to establish racial equality in the face of fierce resistance from the white population, offered special conviction fees under statutes criminalizing the Ku Klux Klan. Obviously, the Klan committed numerous acts that had particular victims, such as murder and arson. But the statutes under which lawmakers offered special fees criminalized the organization itself and association with it, as a prophylactic measure, so the state could prosecute without having to wait for direct acts of bloodshed. Tennessee in 1868 outlawed "any secret organization . . . that shall prowl through the country . . . for the purpose of disturbing the peace, or alarming" the citizenry, and it further made it criminal for any person to "unite with, associate with, promote or encourage" such an organization, or to possess "any uniform or regalia . . . for any unlawful purpose." Much as in the Alabama gambling statute or the Kansas liquor statute, Tennessee public prosecutors were granted both extraordinary powers (to summon any person who, according to the officer's "well-grounded belief," had "any knowledge" of the Klan) and extraordinary incentives (a fee of $100 for each conviction under the statute, five times the fee for capital crimes).[141] Republicans in Arkansas adopted a similar statute and copied the $100 fee provision.[142]

The advent of antitrust law at the state level in the 1880s occasioned one last surge in legislative adoption of special conviction fees. To be sure, antitrust does not perfectly fit the pattern, since restraint of trade and monopolization were not victimless. They drove other firms out of business and raised prices for consumers. But depending on the circumstances, and especially if the victims were mainly consumers, their harms might be so diffuse that no victim would have enough incentive to come forward. And surely antitrust law was alien, for it threatened to shut down businesses that had large numbers of employees in the locality where they operated. As one governor put it, the "fear and favor which the wrongdoers inspire and exert in the community" created "local conditions" under which a public prosecutor "naturally shrinks" from enforcing the law.[143] To make officials overcome their fear, legislatures offered potentially huge bounties in Missouri, Tennessee, Texas, and North Carolina, as an "inducement" to "stimulate" the officers, in the words of one state supreme court.[144]

## FROM CONVICTION FEES TO SALARIES: THE TRIUMPH OF PROSECUTORIAL DISCRETION AND THE LEGITIMATION OF ALIEN IMPOSITION

The purpose of replacing *case-based* fees with salaries was to take prosecutorial decisions out of the hands of lay community members and vest those decisions in a public officer. As Steinberg found in Philadelphia, two of the major effects of this transfer—which reformers anticipated and intended—were to raise the proportion of prosecutions that ended in conviction and increase prosecutions for victimless crimes.

But conviction-based fees had the potential to serve quite similar purposes. They incentivized the public prosecutor to allocate the system's resources toward convictable defendants, especially toward defendants convictable of victimless crimes that would go unenforced if lay accusers were in control. In that sense, conviction fees and salaries might be partial substitutes for each other. Both compensation schemes reflected a legislative desire—growing stronger throughout the nineteenth century—to liberate prosecutorial decisions from the individual wishes of lay community members and make those decisions more responsive to collective, legislatively expressed desires to regulate consensual behavior like drinking and gambling, to enforce taxes, and so on. Consistent with the idea that salaries and conviction fees were two alternative means of modern positivist state-building, states with case-based fees generally switched to salaries sooner, while those with conviction-based fees generally switched to salaries later (see this book's Appendix).

But the promise of conviction fees as instruments of alien imposition proved only temporary. Every conviction-fee jurisdiction eventually switched to salaries. Why? What fatal defect prevented conviction fees from fulfilling their promise? As I argue below, modern positivist legislation created broad and rigid liability, criminalizing much conduct that lay communities thought normal and harmless, and conviction fees pushed public prosecutors to exploit the law's breadth and rigidity, piling up convictions for small-time or technical offenses.

Lawmakers concluded that this pattern of enforcement aggravated the law's pre-existing legitimacy deficit, and they converted public prosecutors to salaries so they would have the financial independence to forbear in prosecuting small-time offenses, thereby "sanding off" the hard edges of modern positivist law. Lawmakers hoped this would open the way for a more trusting relationship between citizens and an increasingly ambitious state.

### A Case Study: The Salarization of U.S. Attorneys, 1880s to 1896

In tackling the question of why lawmakers rejected conviction fees in favor of salaries, I offer a case study of Congress's salarization of the U.S. attorneys in 1896. The federal government is the obvious place to begin, for it has the best sources, by far. Congress recorded its deliberations far more extensively than any state, and it considered the issue for several years. The House of Representatives held hearings in 1884, passed a salarization measure that same year (which Senate conferees rejected for procedural reasons), debated another bill in 1886–87, and held more hearings in 1890. The Senate then considered a bill in 1892 and the House another in 1894. Finally, the two chambers extensively debated and enacted a salarization measure in 1896. These deliberations furnish us with rich discussions of the fee compensation of U.S. attorneys, sometimes as a topic in itself, or sometimes in conjunction with fee compensation of other federal law enforcement officers, such as U.S. marshals and their deputies. Even when the conduct of marshals or deputies was under discussion, the incentives of U.S. attorneys were always implicitly at issue, since the U.S. attorneys' decisions did much to shape the behavior of field personnel who brought suspects to them.[145] (The statute of 1896 that salarized the U.S. attorneys did the same for the U.S. marshals, making them the first two classes of federal law enforcement officers to go on salary.)[146]

In federal law enforcement, as in many other contexts, bounties for a time held great promise as tools of alien imposition. Though Congress never singled out particular crimes for special high fees (as the states did), I think that U.S. attorneys' conviction fees *generally* were special fees for the enforcement of alien law, since nearly all of federal criminal law was alien. A very large proportion of federal crimes were victimless and clashed with the norms of numerous local communities.

To appreciate this point, we must begin with some background. In the early republic, federal criminal law had been marginal, covering obscure areas like piracy or robbing the mail. It did not attempt to penetrate most of the nation's communities.[147] This changed in the second half of the nineteenth century. Having levied no internal taxes since the War of 1812, Congress during the

Civil War suddenly imposed such taxes on a wide range of goods, then rolled them back just as quickly once the war ended. Crucially, however, it retained the excise on liquor and tobacco, establishing that tax as a permanent feature of federal finance. The United States would depend upon the excise for at least one-third of its revenue every year for the rest of the century.[148]

Because liquor and tobacco were so much a part of everyday life, the criminal statutes for enforcing the excise were the first permanent, peacetime federal criminal laws to practically intrude on the conduct of millions of ordinary people. The statutes were broad and rigid. Take liquor. It was now a crime to produce any quantity of distilled spirits (no matter how small) without registering with the federal government and giving bond.[149] Every distillery had to post a sign announcing its registration, and it was a crime for anybody to work in a distillery without a registration sign (even briefly), to bring any supplies to such a distillery, or to carry any liquor from it.[150] Plus, it was a crime to sell any quantity of spirits (no matter how small) without registering and paying an annual tax.[151] Though the big-time distillers developed a norm of compliance early on, that was not true of the countless farm communities in which small-time, casual distilling was an old folk practice and a convenient (sometimes important) source of income. The inhabitants of these communities did not take kindly to a distant government's sudden effort to regulate and tax an activity that they had undertaken for generations.[152] Furthermore, it was a common practice in many neighborhoods for people to sell one another small amounts of liquor on a casual basis—"the petty neighborhood retailing of whisky," as one judge called it.[153] Jarringly, the law now required everybody in this casual economy to register and pay tax, as "retail sellers" of liquor. From one perspective, the new laws seemed unreasonable and extreme, in that they touched any amount of production or sale, even if tiny. Yet from another perspective, they seemed necessary: though small-time production and traffic were not big sources of revenue, they could (if completely ignored) grow quietly and steal customers from law-abiding distillers and saloons.[154]

The excise on tobacco was similar: it imposed novel and minute requirements on seemingly harmless everyday conduct. It was now a crime to sell or even purchase any quantity of tobacco (no matter how small) except in a package stamped with proof of compliance with the tax.[155] As with liquor, it was common for people to make small-time casual sales and exchanges of tobacco, which this law now covered.[156] Criminal liability also extended to trivial acts like emptying a cigar box or snuff box without first destroying the container's proof-of-payment stamp—regardless of whether one intended to defraud the revenue.[157]

In light of all this, one U.S. Supreme Court justice declared in 1875 that the excise on liquor and tobacco had conjured up "a system of legislation for its enforcement harsh beyond everything known to our history."[158] It led, said President Cleveland in 1885, to the "multiplication of small and technical offenses" in criminal dockets.[159] Indeed, it appears that annual federal indictments per capita in the 1870s were about *ten times* higher than in the 1820s, and they kept rising into the 1890s.[160] (Unfortunately, there is no collected data for the period 1830–70.) In each year from 1870 to 1896, internal revenue crimes accounted for between 49 percent and 75 percent of all federal indictments, dwarfing any other type of offense.[161] Perhaps the next-most common offense was taking timber from (usually vacant) federal land, which, like small-time dealing in liquor and tobacco, was an act that local communities usually found harmless: "many farmers or settlers saw nothing wrong with cutting down a few trees for heat and shelter."[162]

The intrusiveness of federal law and the proliferation of federal prosecutions were nationwide issues. To be sure, the issue burned hottest in the "moonshine" districts in the mountains and hills of the South, where folk distilling was most prevalent.[163] Yet the issue was also important in the West, especially because of timber violations.[164] By the 1890s, even congressmen from Massachusetts, Minnesota, and Iowa cited the expansion of federal prosecution as a salient issue in their home states.[165]

As so often with alien imposition, federal criminal statutes depended heavily on officials to take the initiative in the face of popular opposition. In moonshine districts, violators could hide behind the "wall of solidarity" maintained by their neighbors.[166] "These [internal revenue] laws," commented one federal judge, "have but few defenders except the courts and the officers of the Government."[167]

Under these conditions, bounties struck many federal lawmakers as a crucial instrument for making alien imposition work. In 1887, Thomas Brackett Reed, the Republican leader of the House of Representatives and former chair of its Judiciary Committee, defended the fee incentives of U.S. attorneys and other federal officers:

[I]n order to prevent [crimes] the United States must make it for the interests of its officials to look them up and to destroy them.
. . . [T]he crimes against the State and crimes against the United States are entirely different in their character. Crimes against the State are crimes which are under the common law, and every lawyer knows that crimes which are punished by the common law have in their punishment and in their

detection the support of every individual in the community. The officers of the law are there sustained by a vigorous and healthy sentiment, whereas the crimes against the United States are not those which are universally recognized as moral criminalities.

The whole community is awake to detect murder and to punish theft. But what community ever bestirred itself against frauds on the internal revenue, against moonshine distilleries, against smuggling, against a hundred things which are crimes against the United States? What, then, do you need in order to bring your criminals against the United States laws to detection? You need to have the officials stimulated by a similar self-interest to that which excites and supports and sustains the criminal.[168]

To be sure, Reed was wrong to identify alien imposition exclusively with federal law. The numerous special conviction fees offered by state legislatures show that the states also faced the challenge of enforcing laws unbacked by a "vigorous and healthy sentiment." Yet Reed was absolutely right that federal law presented an especially strong case of alien imposition, which caused many federal lawmakers to put their faith in bounties.

Yet lawmakers' faith in bounties died of experience. In the 1880s, federal lawmakers and other observers began to argue that U.S. attorneys' fees were perverse and counterproductive—a conclusion that Congress accepted with virtually no dissent when it put those officers on salary in 1896. The core complaint about U.S. attorneys' fees, repeated over and over in the 1896 debate, was that they resulted in an excess of prosecutions, which congressmen denounced as "frivolous," "petty," "technical," "vexatious," "trivial," "unnecessary," "useless," and the like.[169]

In using these epithets, congressmen do *not* appear to have been expressing fear that U.S. attorneys were convicting the innocent. The extensive debates of 1896 contain almost no explicit references to the idea of convicting innocent people—something we would expect anti-fee politicians to trumpet had they believed it was happening.[170] Though congressmen did complain frequently that prosecutions were legally meritless, these complaints seemed to focus generally on subjecting the innocent to the hardship of the preverdict criminal process: arrest, transportation to faraway courts, trial, or simply the process in general.[171] A few congressmen talked about incarceration of the innocent, but without referring to conviction or sentencing, so they probably meant pretrial detention (which could last for months).[172]

Theoretically, of course, a conviction-fee policy was supposed to spare the innocent from the hardship of the preverdict process, by incentivizing the public prosecutor to target persons who could be convicted. Congressmen's complaints suggest they believed that U.S. attorneys' fee compensation was not living up to this theory. But one could easily explain this failure without losing faith in conviction fees per se, for U.S. attorneys' fees were not based solely on convictions. Besides a fee up to $30 for each trial conviction (which was routinely granted),[173] federal law offered certain noncontingent fees, such as $20 simply for a trial.[174] If preverdict hardship for the innocent had been Congress's sole concern, it could have responded by abolishing the noncontingent fees and keeping the conviction fees. Yet instead it abolished all fees—including conviction fees—and put the officers on salary. Why?

Crucially, there was another consideration at play, one that gave congressmen a decisive reason to reject conviction fees specifically: such fees incentivized the officers to convict as many people as possible, but congressmen increasingly felt that not everybody who was guilty and lawfully convictable ought to be punished as a matter of policy. Some of the guilty—especially those guilty of only small-time liquor sales and other casual offenses—should be left alone, at least most of the time. Essentially, congressmen acknowledged that (1) federal criminal legislation was ever more alien, intrusive, and rigid, and (2) the way to render it bearable and acceptable to the population was to "sand off" its hard edges with discretionary nonenforcement and forbearance. Thus, conviction fees fell out of favor not because of the risk of convicting the innocent, but because such fees ran afoul of congressmen's emergent view that law's legitimacy required many of the guilty to be spared. In converting U.S. attorneys to salaries, congressmen were establishing prosecutorial discretion as a softener of modern positivist legislation.

Forbearance garnered prominent advocates beginning in the 1880s. The argument came from congressmen, social reformers, field investigators for the Department of Justice, and officers of the Internal Revenue Bureau.[175] Consider the remarks of John White, a Democratic representative from Kentucky, in 1884. At a committee hearing, he complained that federal prosecutions were "for the most part for trifling, petty offenses, like selling half a pound of tobacco, or a pint of whisky."[176] Then, on the floor of the House, he reminded his colleagues of a rather delicate fact—the small-time sale of liquor occurred in the Capitol building, with congressmen themselves as buyers, even though it was illegal under the resolution Congress had enacted:

> The men who keep the restaurants in this Capitol building, in either wing of it, by a joint resolution, have no right to sell intoxicating liquor. But does any gentleman who hears me doubt if he wanted to get a glass of wine, or a glass

of beer, or a milk-punch, or a whisky-straight in a tea-cup he can get it in this Capitol? Yet you know that a joint resolution of the two Houses of Congress prohibit the sale of intoxicating liquors on the Capitol grounds, and no one has a Government license or city license to do so. Why, sir, what would you think if the United States marshals should raid on them?

Now apply that to North Carolina, Virginia, Tennessee, or Kentucky, and imagine a man, not a member of Congress but a poor man, living fifty or a hundred miles from a railroad, who had gone to one of the saloons or little distilleries operated according to law there and bought a gallon of whisky or apple brandy. If he should turn around and give a pint of it to a man passing on the road and that man the next day should give him a little tobacco, . . . that act would be construed by the beneficiaries of the miserable fee system into a violation of the law. . . . The records are full of such cases.[177]

In White's telling, congressmen themselves conducted their personal affairs in reliance upon a certain amount of breathing space when it came to broad and rigid regulations. They should allow that same breathing space to the American public.

Federal lawmakers, when they finally enacted salarization in 1896, accepted this argument with virtually no dissent. Proponents of salarization in the 1896 debate made clear that many of the cases they felt should go unprosecuted—the ones they labeled "frivolous," "petty," "technical," and so forth—were cases in which the defendant was in fact guilty but should get a pass. Of the four members of the House committee reporting the bill who spoke most extensively on it,[178] two made this point with particular clarity. Foster Brown, a Tennessee Republican and former state-level prosecutor, recounted the outrageous prosecution of a "good old lady" for using leaf tobacco to pay her cook—probably an ordinary transaction in the casual neighborhood economy of tobacco. For this, the lady "was doubtless guilty of a technical violation of the internal-revenue laws, but no right-thinking man would insist that the ends of justice were promoted by her prosecution."[179] The second committee member, Republican Charles Burton of Missouri, quoted a federal judge saying that "[o]ne-half of the offenses alleged against [internal revenue defendants], while technically within the statute, could well be ignored without injury to the public welfare."[180] Many other congressmen similarly urged that a large subset of legally guilty people should be spared, not only for liquor and tobacco violations but also for public-land trespasses and even hypertechnical postal violations.[181]

Congressmen got what they sought. Salarization in 1896 apparently caused a dramatic and permanent shift toward forbearance—that is, sparing the guilty.

Figure 7.1 is a graph of the annual number of federal prosecutions terminated nationwide after indictment, per one hundred thousand population, for the fiscal years 1886–87 through 1905–06. The word *terminated* includes all ways in which a prosecution could end (e.g., conviction, acquittal, dropping the charge, quashing the indictment), making this figure a good proxy for the number of cases officers were sending through the pipeline to begin with. The graph shows a sudden drop of 42 percent between fiscal 1895–96 and fiscal 1896–97. This is by far the largest single fluctuation, up or down, in the whole period. It coincides perfectly with salarization.[182] Burton predicted that salarization would cause a drop of this magnitude, and the attorney general, upon observing the drop, attributed it to "the new salary system."[183] (A simultaneous change in the hiring of marshals' deputies may also have contributed to the drop, though it likely would have been large even without that.[184] There were no other likely contributing factors.[185])

Significantly, it seems that the numerous cases that went unprosecuted by reason of salarization were mostly cases in which convictions would have been won had they gone forward. We can infer this because, while the number of cases fell by nearly half and stayed low, the conviction rate remained pretty stable, in the 50–60 percent range (see figure 7.2).[186] Thousands of convictable persons were now getting a pass.

Having established that congressmen in 1896 sought and obtained a massive reduction in the prosecution of guilty (but presumably small-time) offenders, we must now consider what impact congressmen hoped this change would have on the effectiveness of law enforcement and the whole enterprise of state-building. For one thing, it would let prosecutorial resources go toward different and presumably better uses. For years prior to 1896, attorneys general and other observers had complained that the fee system's imperative to maximize convictions pushed U.S. attorneys to round up the bit players in criminal operations rather than pursue the leading men—too many convictions of the workers at a moonshine distillery (rather than the owner) or the axmen on a timber raid (rather than the ringleader).[187] In fact, the House hearings in 1890 turned up insinuations that, in at least some districts, federal officers were deliberately focusing on the bit players because they wanted the criminal operations to keep going, so they could continue making small-time prosecutions for fees.[188] In some instances, this might lead to a vicious cycle: (1) U.S. attorneys prosecuted small-time offenders; (2) judges, recognizing the offenses as minor, imposed light sentences or suspended sentences; (3) future defendants, knowing the judges were lenient, happily pled guilty; and (4) U.S. attorneys felt all the more inclined to pursue small-time offenders, since they got easy guilty pleas and easy fees

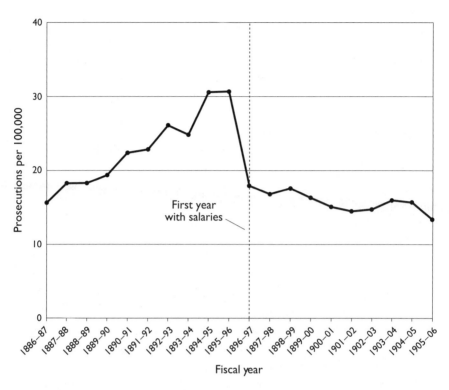

*Figure* 7.1. Annual federal prosecutions terminated nationwide, per 100,000 population, 1886–1906.

*Sources:* National population data are from *HSUS* series Aa7. All remaining data are from AG Report 1886, pp. 24–27; AG Report 1887, Exhibits, pp. 4–7; AG Report 1888, Exhibits, pp. 4–7; AG Report 1889, Exhibits, pp. 4–7; AG Report 1890, Exhibits, pp. 4–7; AG Report 1891, pp. 18–21; AG Report 1892, pp. 22–25; AG Report 1893, pp. 18–21; AG Report 1894, pp. 28–31; AG Report 1895, pp. 60–63; AG Report 1896, pp. 30–33; AG Report 1897, pp. 18–21; AG Report 1898, pp. 22–25; AG Report 1899, pp. 72–75; AG Report 1900, pp. 68–71; AG Report 1901, pp. 66–69; AG Report 1902, pp. 20–23; AG Report 1903, pp. 144–49; AG Report 1904, pp. 176–83; AG Report 1905, pp. 114–21; AG Report 1906, pp. 92–97. I exclude data for two districts. The first is the Southern District of New York, since Congress had already replaced that officer's prosecutorial fees with a fixed salary back in 1861. 12 Stat. 317 (1861). The second is the District of Columbia, since the U.S. attorney there always vastly exceeded the $6,000 cap on fees, to a much greater degree than did any other U.S. attorney, meaning that he could earn the maximum without effort and was really salaried de facto. H.R. Exec. Doc. No. 48–92, at 3 (1884). On the cap, see note 78 to this chapter.

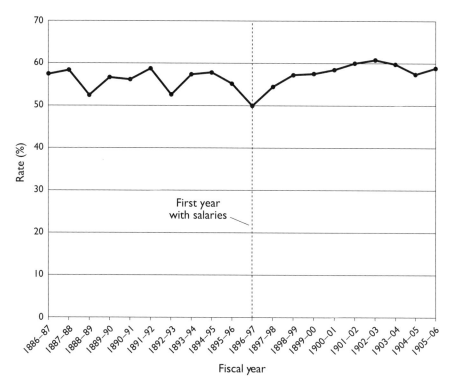

*Figure* 7.2. Rate at which terminated federal prosecutions ended in conviction, nationwide, 1886–1906.

*Sources:* Data are from the same pages of the AG Reports cited in figure 7.1. I exclude the Southern District of New York and District of Columbia, for reasons stated in figure 7.1. Convictions consist of an unknown mix of trial convictions and guilty pleas; the reports give no data on the breakdown between the two prior to 1905.

without having to hurt anybody very much.[189] (Though a U.S. attorney winning a guilty plea made only $10—less than the $20 trial fee and the common $30 conviction fee—he saved the effort of trial and got more than the $5 he would receive if he simply dropped the charge.)[190] This pattern of prosecution, where it occurred, perverted bounty-seeking into a crime-nurturing enterprise, and it caused the public to view law enforcement as a racket.[191] But the phenomenon may not have been very prevalent: congressmen debating salarization in 1896 hardly raised the issue.[192] Nor did they give any serious attention to the idea that ignoring small-time offenders would free up resources for bigger offenders.

A point that congressmen emphasized a great deal—and one that resonates with Chapters 5 and 6—was that salarization would bolster the population's trust in the federal government as a legitimate institution, soothe popular hostility to federal power, and foster voluntary cooperation with federal law. In congressmen's view, bounty-seeking might motivate aggressive enforcement of unpopular laws, but its incentive to enforce broad and rigid laws to the letter— combined with how it cast the officialdom as self-seekers in a zero-sum game against the population—had the effect of aggravating the lay public's resentment, distrust, and resistance.

Legitimation was a key issue at this stage of federal state-building. As Wilbur Miller argues in his history of the liquor tax, the federal government in the late nineteenth century more or less succeeded in building an effective internal revenue regime (in contrast to its recent failure to reform the South's racial caste system).[193] The process, says Miller, saw two periods of high friction: (1) during the late 1870s and early 1880s, when federal officials first sought to penetrate the moonshine districts, and (2) in the economic depression of the mid-1890s, "when farmers became desperate for cash that could be earned from mountain dew and Congress raised the liquor tax to compensate for a growing federal deficit."[194] As I argue below, the first of these two periods of crisis saw an initial burst of discourse about bounty-seeking, forbearance, and legitimacy, and the second saw the intensification of that discourse, culminating in bounty-seeking's abolition in 1896. As Miller shows, internal revenue's success rested upon balancing enforcement with leniency.[195] I believe salarization was key to finding that balance. Though Miller documents certain abuses of the fee system and their effect on the government's reputation, he refers only briefly to the reform of 1896 and fails to identify it as the self-conscious project of legitimation that it was.[196]

Let us first consider the initial burst of discourse on bounty-seeking, forbearance, and legitimacy that occurred in the 1880s. We must take care in analyzing this discourse, since it sometimes registered not only people's views on the best way to achieve legitimacy but also their underlying disagreements on whether it *should* be achieved—that is, on the good or evil of federal authority. Historically, internal revenue and federal power were associated with the Republican Party, while Democrats tended to be critics of both, especially in the South. It is therefore significant that those warning of the fee system's dangers to legitimacy during this period were often northern Republicans with a stake in federal law's success. In 1882, Internal Revenue commissioner Green Raum, an Illinois Republican deeply dedicated to enforcement,[197] urged salaries for U.S. attorneys and other federal officers, warning that "institution of criminal prosecutions under the internal-revenue laws for trivial and technical offenses . . . is a constant cause of complaint in various parts of the United States, and is continually productive of irritation in the enforcement of the laws."[198]

Around the same time, Attorney General Brewster, a Philadelphia Republican, initiated a brave and politically costly investigation of his own department's field personnel, touching on several matters, including fees.[199] It found that bounty-seeking was enormously aggravating popular distrust of federal law in the moonshine regions. Brewster's chief investigator (and nephew), also a Pennsylvania Republican, reported in 1884 that "the abuses of the fee system" were "so prevalent and so odious that it is not to be wondered at that deputy marshals and deputy collectors of internal revenue have been shot down as if they were the enemies of the people." He added that "poor men" arrested in "remote county districts" of Alabama were saying, "'Now, we ought to love our Government, but what is there to love? These deputy marshals come to our homes and they arrest us for some little trivial or technical offense.'"[200]

With the support of Brewster and the Republican administration, a Democratic House committee in 1884 reported a proposal to salarize the U.S. attorneys and marshals.[201] On the House floor, the committee chairman, Illinois Democrat William Springer, cited Brewster's statement that "[c]itizens have been repeatedly arrested on frivolous and trumped-up charges, and similar outrages have been practiced in some districts to such an extent as to render the Government odious to the people, making them hostile to the courts of the United States." Springer added that "these oppressions on frivolous prosecutions have become so great in some localities that . . . the officers of the Government are regarded as public enemies. . . . The laws should be administered in a spirit of fairness and justice, so that even the citizen who has done wrong shall respect and revere the arm which punishes him."[202]

Though this initial effort to legitimize federal law through salaries was serious and bipartisan, salarization had certain obstacles to surmount before it could become law. One such obstacle was the substantive counterargument in favor of bounties. Reed, ignoring the views of fellow Republicans like Raum who had actually been in the trenches of enforcement, argued powerfully for the necessity of bounties in the debate on Springer's proposal in 1884 and again on a similar bill in 1887. But the substantive counterargument was only one of multiple obstacles, and apparently a diminishing one: Reed had only a few allies to echo him in 1884 and none in 1887.[203] When Congress finally enacted salarization in 1896, sentiment for it was universal. Nobody questioned the principle of the measure through all the lengthy, open-ended discussions,[204] and several lawmakers said that the rightness of the reform had been obvious for years.[205] (Reed himself, by then Speaker, silently reversed his opposition in allowing the bill to reach the floor.[206]) Yet there were other, nonsubstantive obstacles to overcome, which help explain why reform did not occur earlier. One was the controversy over whether to enact salarization through a regular bill or an appropriations bill. Though the House initially passed Springer's proposal as part of an appropriations bill in 1884, the Senate conferees questioned it on this procedural ground, and with the session's clock running out, the proposal failed.[207] An even more important obstacle, which came to the fore in the late 1880s, was the extreme difficulty of reaching agreement on the amounts of the salaries that the various U.S. attorneys and marshals should each receive. Each lawmaker fought for high salaries in his own district, since the U.S. attorneys and marshals were patronage appointments.[208] And each salary level was hard to determine (and therefore highly contestable) because the jobs were part-time,[209] meaning the amount should depend on the volume of business, yet one could not rely upon existing volumes, as they were driven by the very evil (fee incentives) that salarization sought to remedy.[210] One bill reached the House floor in 1886–87, only to disappear after congressmen complained mightily about its salary levels.[211] Another reached the Senate floor in 1892, only to have senators nitpick the salary levels one by one, so the bill "lost all shape and form" and had to be withdrawn, even though nobody questioned salarization in principle.[212]

Congress finally acted on the emergent consensus in favor of salaries because the existing problems of federal criminal justice — including the legitimation issue — became more intense and salient during the depression of 1893–97. Let me first note, as background, that while many Democrats had initially opposed the excise, their party generally accepted the tax by the 1880s, realizing it was necessary to achieve their more-cherished goal of tariff reduction.[213] After the crash of 1893 plunged the federal budget into deficit, the Democrats — in control of both chambers and the White House — sought to balance the books even as they reduced the tariff, and so in 1894 they enacted a package that *raised* the liquor tax and established a new income tax (though the Supreme Court struck down the latter in 1895).[214] The excise was now more entrenched in federal finance than ever, and both parties had a big stake in making it work. But the depression and the tax hike made evasion more attractive to the population,[215] increasing resistance and violations, big-time and small-time.

Under these conditions, the drive for alien imposition was more intense than ever. Prosecutions hit unprecedented levels in fiscal 1894–95.[216] This produced two crises. The first was moral and social: with evasion and enforcement at a peak, the fee-driven pattern of enforcement was more prevalent and problematic than ever. The second crisis was fiscal: the federal treasury was liable for the costs of every prosecution — not only the fees of the U.S. attorneys, marshals, and deputies but also the transportation of prisoners and the payment of witnesses and jurors—so that excessive and ever-increasing prosecutions worsened the depression's budget crunch. Salarization, which everybody knew would reduce prosecutions, could therefore help the deficit.[217] This fiscal attraction gave lawmakers an immediate reason to overcome their differences about salary levels.[218] Furthermore, the congressional session of 1895–96 proved an opportune moment: the depression had given Republicans a big new House majority, but with Cleveland still in the White House, the only viable bills were those with bipartisan support, and support for salarization was universal.[219] It was during a floor debate on law enforcement appropriations early in the 1895–96 session that House members began moaning that something finally had to be done about excessive prosecutions. At that point, Virginia Democrat Claude Swanson and North Carolina Republican Thomas Settle seized the opportunity to remind their colleagues that the issue involved far more than money, and they demanded a salarization bill, which the Judiciary Committee soon reported.[220]

While a few members spoke of salarization as simply a money-saving measure,[221] we must remember that the law enforcement crisis of the mid-1890s involved not only the budget but also moral and social factors, especially the buildup of trust and legitimacy for the federal government. Most congressmen speaking on the matter expressly stated that they considered the moral and social factors just as important as, or more important than, fiscal ones: the "frivolous and unnecessary" nature of the prosecutions, their "oppressions" of the people, their "demoralizing" effect on the population, the "harass[ment]" of "poor men" for "trivial offenses," and danger to "the good name of the government."[222]

Foster Brown, one of the four members of the House committee reporting the bill who spoke most extensively on it, dwelled at length on the matters of legitimacy, trust, and the buildup of community sentiment for voluntary cooperation. He was in a good position to appreciate these issues. On the one hand, his district was in East Tennessee, a moonshine region.[223] On the other hand, there are reasons to think he earnestly wanted to establish the authority of federal law on a stable, cooperative, and peaceful basis. First, he was a member of the Republican Party, which was historically most committed to the excise. Second, he recognized that the excise was "now structurally fixed in our governmental economies" and that neither "this [n]or the next generation" would consent to the "radical change" in federal taxation that would be necessary to abolish it.[224] Third, his district included Chattanooga,[225] where he lived, and this at a time when middle-class inhabitants of Southern cities had been turning against the illicit moonshining of the lower-class highlands.[226] Finally, he had until recently been the law partner of Charles Dickens Clark,[227] who in 1895 had become the U.S. District Court judge for East Tennessee and fast garnered a reputation for seriousness in upholding the excise.[228]

Noting that the bill had "been submitted to a number of United States judges and they have all approved it," Brown explained that the "present [fee] system brings on the courts discredit which they want to see removed by taking away temptation from the officers to bring frivolous and unnecessary prosecutions." Brown submitted a statement from his friend Judge Clark, who had "given the subject much study," and who declared: "The [salary] legislation not only will not weaken, but will greatly add to a clean, reputable, and proper administration of the law." After bemoaning the prevalence of prosecutions for slight, casual violations—against "some old white woman without money" who "gave a colored woman a twist of tobacco to do a day's washing"—Clark argued that the "spectacle" of such prosecutions "in any community is thoroughly demoralizing. . . . The oppression that is practiced every day is a reproach in the eyes of any civilized community and creates much of that ignorant prejudice against Federal authority which you know to exist in communities where this [fee] system is in force." Brown also quoted an anonymous federal officer who wished "to see taken away from the courts the odium which necessarily attaches to the present pernicious fee system." Perhaps most interesting, Brown spoke of reaching an equilibrium between the level of enforcement and local public opinion. Consistent with Miller's account of rising middle-class sentiment in favor of cooperation, Brown attested that in "all Southern States there is without question now (although it has not always been so) a strong and healthy public sentiment which will sustain the officials in the proper enforcement of the revenue laws." By "proper," Brown presumably meant an enforcement pattern that would ease up on small-time violators of such broad and rigid statutes. "This bill is by no means intended to cripple the *proper* administration of the law," he continued, "but on the contrary, the friends of the bill hope and believe to accomplish a cleaner and more efficient administration of that system of laws. That strong sentiment in the South in favor of the *proper* administration of the law will encourage the prosecution of all *real* violations of the law."[229]

Charles Burton, another of the four most engaged members of the committee and (like Brown) a Republican from a border-state highland district,[230] echoed Brown's view. After narrating the prosecution of a technical liquor offense, he asked whether it tended "to uphold the majesty of our flag and the glory of our Government" and "to create in [the defendant's] mind or in the minds of his neighbors respect for law and love of country? I say no." Burton also submitted a statement from a federal judge noting that, while salarization would save money, that was a "secondary consideration. The good name of the

Government and the integrity of public officials, especially in connection with the courts of justice, are of supreme concern."[231]

Brown and Burton were not the only congressmen to emphasize legitimation and trust. Another was Claude Swanson, the later-famous Virginia Democrat who helped bring attention to the issue early in the session. His district contained some moonshine areas,[232] and in 1894 he had expressed hostility to the whole idea of the excise.[233] Later that year, however, he had accepted its entrenchment, voting in favor of his party's tax package, which raised the liquor tax to allow for reduction of the tariff (another of his favorite causes).[234] If the excise was to stay, its administration should be reformed to build a trusting and cooperative relationship between population and officialdom. Attuned to the dangers of adversarialism, Swanson predicated that, with salarization, the "intense friction and harshness witnessed in the past in the administration of the law would disappear. . . . The people would no longer feel that they were made by law subjects to be preyed upon by officials who received fees and riches in proportion to the people's ills and misfortunes." "Quiet, peace, and satisfaction will again reign in places where there are now only fear, discord, and bitterness." Perceived motives were key. "If there is any place where the fee system ought not to exist it is in the judiciary department," that is, law enforcement. The reason was that "the judiciary department is one that should have the complete confidence of every citizen. A citizen, when he is arrested and brought before a commissioner [i.e., magistrate] and incarcerated in jail, should feel that the officers of the law have no interest in inciting the prosecution against him or conducting it to a successful termination, except the desire to perform their sworn duties as officers of justice. With the fee system you make every man who is arrested think that he is the victim of the greed of some official who is trying to enrich himself at the expense of the man he has arrested and prosecuted."[235]

Further insight on legitimacy and especially on voluntary cooperation came from Representative Thomas Settle, who also represented a Southern highland district (in North Carolina) but was a Republican. Settle submitted a statement by his local U.S. District Court judge, Robert P. Dick, an old Republican scalawag and intimate of Settle's father.[236] Though Dick (as Miller notes) was genuinely committed to making the liquor tax work,[237] he thought the fee-paid officers' focus on small-time offenses was undermining the favorable public sentiment necessary to mass cooperation:

> The strict and rigid enforcement of this law does not and never will stop the petty neighborhood retailing of whisky, and I can see no public good that can

result from the prosecution of every person who sells or offers for sale without payment of the special tax. . . .

From long experience I find that criminal and penal laws are difficult in enforcement unless the policy of such laws is approved and sustained by the public sentiment of the good citizens of the country. I think this public sentiment is now very decidedly against illicit distilling and the illicit traffic in whisky *as a regular business*; but a very large number of good citizens do not approve of the rigid prosecution of petty transactions of sale in remote country sections, in small neighborhood dealings where whisky can not be conveniently obtained from regular saloons and grogshops. The revenue officers are very active in hunting up such cases. The evidence generally makes out a clear case of violation of law, and honest juries convict, while they do not approve of such prosecutions and regard the law as too stringent and "iron clad."

If such prosecutions could be stopped, Dick felt confident that the change "would be approved and appreciated by the best public sentiment, and the internal-revenue laws would cease to be such a prominent and disturbing factor in politics in this State."[238] Dick, like Brown, thought law enforcement would be more effective once it reached a reasonable accommodation with (increasingly pro-compliance) community opinion.

Congress's solution to this problem of legitimacy was to give U.S. attorneys the financial independence to exercise prosecutorial discretion. Indeed, the salary reform of 1896 was a profoundly important step in the triumph of prosecutorial discretion as a dominant factor in federal criminal justice. Congress gave its approval to the selective, subjective, case-by-case, and (in the view of critics) capricious approach to criminal prosecution that prevails in America to this day. Fee-driven enforcement had been excessively, perversely rule bound: it had incentivized officers to push the letter of the law to the edge in order to maximize convictions. Salaries, by contrast, were meant to win public allegiance by "sanding off" the hard edges of modern positivist legislation. They aimed to stop officers from standing on the letter of the law and instead focus on its more amorphous "spirit." There was no exact rule for distinguishing the violations that were "technical," "slight," "trifling," or "petty" from the violations whose prosecution would promote the "ends of justice," secure the "public welfare," and give "benefit to society." Lawmakers allowed the scope of statutory criminal liability to remain broad while trusting in street-level discretion to remedy its overbreadth, case by case. One can imagine an alternative history in which lawmakers tried to delineate the bounds of liability more narrowly instead of relying so heavily on official forbearance, and we can speculate on why they did not: maybe they thought it too hard to define an objective boundary between technical and genuine offenses,[239] or maybe they feared that any exact definition would be gamed by criminals.[240] In any event, they chose the path they did. And so public prosecutors became, for better or worse, the "real lawmakers" in American criminal justice.[241]

Theoretically, the Washington headquarters of the Department of Justice might have made up for the lack of clear statutory rules by imposing its own guidelines on the U.S. attorneys' decision-making. This would have fit with the connection, often drawn by social scientists, between salaried jobs and top-down control. But in fact, congressmen did not contemplate that the headquarters would impose guidelines, and indeed it did not. Lawmakers in 1896 seem to have believed that individual U.S. attorneys, once vested with the financial independence of salaries, would each recognize and spare "technical" and "trifling" violations in their own way and that such adjustments would be satisfactory, making salarization by itself a remedy for excess prosecutions. Settle predicted that "the desired adjustment will be largely reached if we place these officers on salaries."[242] Consistent with this thinking, the Department's Washington headquarters did not react to salarization by imposing any guidelines on the U.S. attorneys' prosecutorial decisions.[243]

Nor does the salarization of U.S. attorneys bear out the common social-science view of salary as part of a package with secure tenure and career stability. Most U.S. attorneys were still part-time in 1896,[244] and it remained permissible for them to engage in part-time private practice for nearly sixty years afterward.[245] Further, they were major patronage appointees prior to the 1896 reform and remained so afterward. Indeed, they remain so to this day, coming and going with changes in politics, not spending their lives climbing a bureaucratic career ladder.[246]

## Converting State Prosecutors from Conviction Fees to Salaries: A Brief Look

Having examined the salarization of U.S. attorneys, let us briefly consider the analogous reforms that occurred in all of the conviction-fee states. The sources for these jurisdictions are far less plentiful and detailed, but we can at least explore some apparent similarities with the federal story.

First, as with the U.S. attorneys, the salarization of state district attorneys was not part of any package to place them under top-down control or give them secure tenure and career stability. Whereas the U.S. attorneys were theoretically subject to the Department of Justice but in fact enjoyed great autonomy, centralization at the state level hardly existed even in theory, to say nothing of

reality. Though some states vested their respective attorneys general with supervisory powers over district attorneys to varying degrees, a comprehensive study of
these reforms in 1934—after salarization had nearly swept the states—found this
centralization practically "negligible."[247] It remains so today. Nor did the job of
state-level district attorney become a career position. Lawmakers in nearly all
the states during the nineteenth century converted it to locally elected status,
which it retains today.[248] And most state prosecutors remained part-time far into
the twentieth century, well after fees had virtually disappeared.[249]

It is possible that anxiety about convicting the innocent contributed to the
rejection of conviction fees, though I suspect it was not the main factor. Critical comments about conviction fees sometimes invoked an ideal of the public
prosecutor as an impartial and quasi-judicial officer.[250] But the embrace of the
quasi-judicial ideal was not universal. Some jurists, and especially the popular
press, viewed the public prosecutor as a rightly adversarial figure.[251] Also, the
quasi-judicial view and the importance of protecting the innocent were hardly
novel ideas in the late 1800s. Defendants' rights had been a core value of American political culture since colonial times, and there were many articulations of
the quasi-judicial ideal of the public prosecutor in the early nineteenth century,
when conviction fees were being adopted.[252] Remember that such fees could
be rationalized as *protecting innocents*: because the jury was supposedly unlikely to convict an innocent person, prosecutors seeking conviction fees would
spare the innocent the trouble of trial. A more plausible argument for the quasi-
judicial ideal's contribution to the abolition of conviction fees is that Americans
in the late nineteenth century were losing faith in the *jury* as a protector of the
innocent (though the evidence on this is not very clear).[253] In the end, I am
skeptical that concerns about innocence were decisive, since they received so
little attention in the lengthy deliberations on U.S. attorneys' conviction fees.
Had innocence been a major issue at the state level, one would expect it to be
more prevalent in the federal debates.

A more promising explanation at the state level, I think, is one analogous
to the federal level. Lawmakers increasingly concluded that many of the guilty
should be left alone, so public prosecutors needed the financial independence
to ignore technical and trivial offenses. An anonymous but well-informed commentator made this point about the conviction fees of the New Orleans district
attorney in the 1870s. After suggesting that the fees were "intended to increase
the zeal of the District Attorney to obtain convictions," he argued that their
effect was perverse, for they caused "the prosecuting officer to fritter away the
time of the Court in prosecuting petty offenders, where convictions are easily
obtained, while heinous offenders go untried, unpunished."[254] In the 1880s, a

newspaper editor praised the Alabama legislature's decision to abolish the conviction fees of its public prosecutors, for such fees encouraged the officer to "bring into the courts trivial offences that should not be noticed."[255]

Why would it have seemed increasingly important for public prosecutors to ignore technical and small-time offenses? One reason was the trend toward alien imposition, in particular the increasing breadth and rigidity of state criminal legislation throughout the nineteenth and early twentieth centuries, in areas like alcohol, gambling, business regulation, and so on.[256] An especially interesting example is the rise of Jim Crow statutes in the late 1800s, which sought to impose rigid order on an interracial social life that was inevitably fluid—and made stringent demands on businesses to maintain that order.[257] A Texas newspaper in 1909 lambasted a county prosecutor for his fee-driven excesses in prosecuting railroads that failed to comply perfectly with regulations of race-mixing in train cars: "There had perhaps been unintentional technical violations of the separate coach law—a railroad company can hardly prevent such things at times—but not defiance of law or flagrant disregard for the statutes. . . . Railroads, like plain citizens, should be punished when they intentionally disregard the law, but neither the roads nor the citizens should be persecuted on trivial and unsubstantial grounds."[258]

A related reason that lawmakers might increasingly want public prosecutors to ignore minor offenses was the growth of cities. Urbanization meant the geographic concentration and higher salience of behavior (often victimless) that the law criminalized. Such criminalization might be recent, as with certain business regulations, or long-standing, as with public drunkenness or profanity. In either case, city life increased the volume of potential offenses through which public prosecutors had to sort. Also, urbanization meant greater social distance between officers and the population, thus weakening social brakes on officers' power to exploit the letter of the law in seeking fees. Cities thus made law enforcement more alien. A committee of the Tennessee Bar Association reported in 1896 that the fee system's excesses could be attributed to the growth of an urban underclass that frequently engaged in conduct that the law criminalized but that should not always be prosecuted. The authors viewed the matter through the lens of their racist ideology: white virtue versus black debauchery. Despite this, they did provide some insight into the connection between excessive criminal prosecution and urbanization. The fee system, they said, had not caused trouble back when the state had been "sparsely settled" by whites. But now, amid African American migration to cities, things were different: "when population has been congested in our towns and cities; when our citizenship has been swelled by an ignorant and irresponsible race, prone to such crimes as delight the hearts of the fee hunters, the system has indeed become unbearable." Taking the fee system as an unfortunate given, the committee proposed certain procedural reforms that might ameliorate its bad effects, assuming it was even "necessary to so vigorously prosecute profanity, assault and battery, crapshooting, lewdness and other almost inalienable rights of certain of the negro race"—something the committee clearly believed was *not* necessary.[259] When Tennessee abolished public prosecutors' fees the next year, discourse centered on the state's cities.[260] Also, in four other conviction-fee states, the legislature salarized one or more big cities before the state at large.[261]

Whether they arose from new legislation or urbanization, excessive petty convictions were especially disturbing when they promoted a dynamic of mutual accommodation between the public prosecutor and the underworld. In this scenario, the public prosecutor would pursue large numbers of small-time offenders and get them punished lightly, effectively allowing the criminal operations in which they participated to survive and flourish, providing a continuous flow of convictions and fees. The governor of Tennessee, making a successful call for salarization in 1897, identified this dynamic in the state's cities, particularly as to "lewdness, gambling, and the illegal selling of intoxicating liquors."[262] The *Tulsa World* in 1911 declared that salarization of the city's public prosecutor had stopped such a pattern, particularly with respect to public drunkenness.[263] The Kansas Supreme Court in 1925 ousted the fee-paid prosecutor of Kansas City for engaging in such behavior.[264] Though the federal debates of 1896 ignored the issue of prosecutor-criminal accommodation, it may have been more common at the state level, where public prosecutors were usually elected and therefore had reason to reach a modus vivendi with lawbreakers, at least when the criminalized conduct was a popular pastime among enfranchised persons.[265]

Whether conviction-maximizing prosecution was adversarial or accommodative, it could be a drain on government funds, since the state often paid certain costs of running the system, such as juror fees, transportation of prisoners, and so on. Such expense was a spur to salarization at the state level, just like the federal level. Friends of successful salarization measures invoked the issue in Mississippi in 1888, in Tennessee in 1897, and in Georgia in 1916.[266]

There is reason to think the conversion of state prosecutors from conviction fees to salaries was part of a legitimation project, as it was at the federal level. On this point, a striking example is alcohol prohibition in Kansas. Here we discover John S. Dawson, a public prosecutor deeply committed to enforcing alien law, who successfully persuaded his legislature to abolish the conviction fees of his own office, in an effort to bolster the legitimacy of his mission and trust in his motives.

Recall that Kansas in 1881 had enacted the nation's most restrictive liquor prohibition statute. Prohibition had a majority in the legislature, but it was unpopular—a decidedly alien imposition—in the state's urban counties and mining counties. In 1885, the legislature offered the county attorneys a $25 reward for every liquor conviction.[267] But this bounty was not enough to overcome the (locally elected) county attorneys' reluctance to enforce the law in the "wet" counties. In response, the legislature authorized the state's attorney general (who was elected statewide and therefore more sympathetic to prohibition) to appoint assistants in localities where the county attorney was lax, and in 1887 it made the attorney general and assistants eligible for the $25 rewards.[268] The attorneys general initially showed some enthusiasm for enforcement, then eased up in the 1890s, then returned to the fray amid resurgent statewide prohibition sentiment in about 1905.[269] Republican Fred Jackson held the office from 1907 to 1911 and continued to step up enforcement. As convictions increased, so did his income,[270] and the conviction-fee system became the subject of "considerable criticism," as he himself put it.[271]

In 1911 the office was filled by Dawson, a Republican known for being an ardent and principled dry. Dawson foresaw, in his own words, "that this [conviction-fee] system of compensation was fraught with danger to the attorney-general," and he persuaded the legislature in 1911 to pass a bill abolishing it. Even Jay House, a cynical muckraker and wet, had to admit that Dawson's bill "seemed to be an honest attempt to prevent a repetition of the 'talk' that had followed Jackson's administration of the office."[272] Yet the bill was vetoed by Governor W. R. Stubbs, also a vehemently dry Republican, but committed to a more adversarial and combative style of enforcement than the cerebral Dawson.[273]

The dangers that Dawson foresaw in the fee system were to his own legitimacy, and they soon came to fruition when he embarked on a campaign that summer to enforce prohibition in Kansas's mining counties. In those parts of the state, the population was so hostile to prohibition that angry mobs were gathering, and county commissioners were conspiring to undermine the law. Dawson had to carry a gun to protect himself.[274] Most telling, he encountered the (locally elected) Judge E. E. Sapp, of wet sympathies, who publicly undermined the campaign by questioning the enforcers' motivations. Traveling to the state capital and meeting personally with Dawson and his associates, apparently in front of reporters, Sapp announced that, historically, "the whole enforcement of the liquor cases" in the mining region "had been a scandal, the people of the county believed that the farcical attempts at liquor enforcement was a fee-grabbing proposition." "I believed then and I believe now," said Sapp to Dawson's face, "that the underlying scheme of it all was to make fees. And I believe that the highest ideal of your liquor prosecutions in our county is for the fees."[275] Sapp may even have implied that Dawson and his men were prosecuting in such a way as to let liquor violations continue, so they could keep prosecuting and making fees.[276] Painfully aware of how the fee system caused the population to distrust his motives, Dawson responded that none of his assistants were directly pocketing the bounties awarded, which he was collectivizing in a contingent fund out of which to pay them.[277] At the following session of the legislature, after the governorship had passed to a dry with a less combative approach, Dawson succeeded in getting a bill enacted to explicitly transfer all his liquor conviction fees as attorney general to the public treasury.[278] At its next session, the legislature went further, enacting an appropriations provision (which became standard from then on) that all liquor conviction fees won by the attorney general's assistants were to go into the office's contingent fund.[279]

Dawson's experience in Kansas reflects the legitimation problem with conviction fees that was central in the federal story and likely to the stories of other states, as well.[280] These rewards initially held promise for imposing positivist legislative demands on the population, but state builders ultimately found out that a display of disinterestedness might be more valuable.

8

# INCARCERATION

*Jailors' Fees and Penitentiary Profits*

The experiment with bounty-seeking as an instrument of modern governance was particularly intense in the context of incarceration, to which we now turn. Though the other chapters in Part Two rely mainly on primary research, here I rely mainly on Rebecca McLennan's *The Crisis of Imprisonment*, a justly acclaimed recent history of incarceration in the Northern states, particularly its profit-seeking aspect.[1] While McLennan obviously does not use my concepts of alien imposition, bounties, and so on, I think those ideas map well onto the narrative she constructs. (Though there are valuable studies of profit-seeking incarceration in the South, including the rise and demise of convict leasing, the role of the profit motive in Southern imprisonment has not received the degree of synthesis that McLennan provides for the North.[2] Therefore, I focus here on the territory McLennan has covered.)

Throughout Anglo-American history, incarceration has been a significant public function, and for about the past two hundred years, it has been the principal punishment for crime. The tasks of incarcerators—jailors, keepers, turnkeys, wardens, guards, and so forth—have been several. One has been simply to keep the inmates inside. Another has been to provide the inmates with some degree of care and sustenance: food, shelter, and other goods and services. A third—prevalent only for the past couple of centuries, and then only inconsistently—has been to see that the inmates engage in productive labor, which can be for many different purposes, such as defraying the cost of imprisonment, rehabilitating the inmates, or warding off the mental and social pathologies of idleness. Taken together, these tasks have created many opportunities for the incarcerators both to coerce the inmates and to make mutually beneficial exchanges with them. Accordingly, the history of incarcerators' compensation—and the broader history of social relations between them and their charges—has involved a complex and changing mixture of facilitative payments, bounties, and salaries.

Our story begins with the eighteenth-century jail, which was a site of familiar imposition. The eighteenth-century jailor typically allowed the inmate community to govern itself according to its own norms, and he acted as a kind of innkeeper to the inmates, accepting facilitative payments in exchange for giving them various privileges and services. But then, starting in the 1780s, lawmakers came up with the idea for a different kind of carceral institution—the penitentiary—in which the warden would proactively control inmates' lives (in particular, forcing them to labor), in order to reform their morals. To ensure that the warden would govern the inmates rather than treat them as customers, lawmakers banned this official from taking facilitative payments and placed him on salary. Also, starting around the 1810s, the new penitentiaries invited small businesses (contractors) to set up shop inside their walls and use the inmates as laborers, selling what they produced. These contractors (backed by salaried prison staff) sometimes used coercion to make inmates work but also offered them many positive rewards for doing so. This give-and-take produced a stable work environment.

However, in the 1870s, legislators became worried that small-time contractors were prone to work interruptions that threatened prison order and productivity. These lawmakers considered the profit motive such a promising means to keep the convict population disciplined and productive that they "doubled down" on the contractor system. Specifically, they had each prison place all its inmates at the disposal of a single big contractor, and that contractor then acquired extraordinary control over inmate discipline, especially corporal punishment. Vested simultaneously with power and profit motive, the new big contractors relied intensely and overwhelmingly on the naked threat of physical pain to force inmates to labor harder than ever before. Prison labor became a purely coerced act, and the contractors' profit became a bounty for extracting it. This forced labor was alien imposition taken to a frightening extreme. In reaction, inmates rioted in unprecedented numbers, forcing lawmakers to realize that it was impossible to maintain prison order by adversarial coercion alone. Acting on this realization, governments starting in the 1880s abandoned the contractor system. They ultimately replaced it with a nonprofit regime that would seek the inmates' voluntary cooperation through less adversarial means, including the provision of recreational activities and the offer of "good time" credits. Even (perhaps especially) in the most intensely state-controlled environment, order required the legitimation of power and the cooperation of the governed.

## THE EIGHTEENTH-CENTURY JAIL:
### INCARCERATION AS FAMILIAR IMPOSITION

In the 1700s, incarceration was generally a form of familiar imposition. Officials indulged the inmates' preferences and accommodated the expectations of the inmates' "community" to a degree that seems remarkable today. To understand how this could be, we must first observe that, in England, incarceration was not primarily a punishment. Persons were commonly held in jail for nonpunitive purposes. For one, private citizens had one another jailed for debt. Also, the state used jail as a waiting area for persons scheduled to go on trial, or for persons awaiting sanguinary punishments like whipping or hanging. (Though jail itself was also sometimes a punishment for misdemeanors.) Similarly, in the American colonies, the main function of carceral institutions was not "as instruments of criminal punishment."[3] For the large number of inmates jailed for nonpunitive purposes, the Anglo-American jailor's responsibility was not to punish them but to keep them from escaping, and he had various incentives to see to that (for example, that he might become personally liable for the obligations of a debtor who ran off).[4] But so long as confinement was maintained, the jailor and the inmates had much latitude to negotiate over its terms. Notably, many inmates had money: since jails were generally open to outsiders, the people confined could obtain cash from relatives and friends or by begging.[5] The jailor would then accept facilitative payments from inmates in exchange for providing them with nicer rooms or apartments; a nicer bed; tastier food, alcoholic beverages, or coffee; copies of court papers; and various privileges, such as going outside the prison during daytime or going outside their cells after dark.[6] In England during the 1700s, local justices of the peace would often approve fee schedules for their respective jails, though sometimes they let the fees go unregulated.[7] The jail was not typically a place for inmates to labor.[8] It was rather a place where they had to stay, trying to get the best living conditions they could.

In keeping with this customer-serving attitude, jailors allowed inmates remarkable freedom to act as they pleased, so long as nobody absconded. Jailors "did not enforce a 'discipline' in the nineteenth century sense of the term. Internal order, such as it was, was enforced chiefly by the inmate subcultures themselves," and it reflected the expectations of those subcultures, rather than a sovereign program.[9] Inmates in England and early America even established their own "courts" to maintain their customary rights and norms.[10] Largely free of official efforts at internal control, the jail was a site of familiar imposition.

### A TRANSITIONAL PHASE: THE ADVENT OF THE PENITENTIARY AND OF CONTRACTING, 1780s–1860s

In a departure from the old regime, English and American lawmakers of the late 1700s and early 1800s adopted a revolutionary program under which (1) traditional criminal punishments like whipping and hanging were abolished or greatly curtailed; (2) imprisonment per se became the main criminal punishment; and (3) imprisonment was to involve a strict regimen of labor, aimed at morally reforming the convict. The main carceral institution was no longer the jail, in which confinement was merely an incident of some later sanguinary punishment or civil process, but a new establishment—the penitentiary—in which the state used confinement itself (combined with labor) to punish criminals and make them see the error of their ways. In contrast to the jail's organic internal order and its openness to the surrounding society, the penitentiary was to be a closed, officer-controlled environment, structured to perform a sort of surgery on inmates' personalities.[11] In contrast to the jailor, who was essentially an innkeeper to his forced guests, the penitentiary warden was to be a patriarchal figure and work boss, administering a reformative program.[12] The penitentiary was among the earliest and most ambitious endeavors in modern positivist state-building. Some divines considered the idea hubristic and sacrilegious, for it presumed a God-like capacity "to operate upon the souls of mortals."[13]

Pennsylvania was the first state to move in the direction of the penitentiary model, when it reorganized the Walnut Street Jail in the 1780s. New York followed, ordering the construction of what became Newgate Prison in lower Manhattan in 1796. By 1810, eight Northern states had penitentiaries, and imprisonment had become the North's standard criminal punishment.[14]

These reforms necessitated changes in how carceral officers made money. Conditions in the traditional jail reflected the inmates' wishes and their ability to pay, which was supported by the flow of resources from outsiders. But the new program required incarcerators to fill a very different role. They were not only to keep the inmates inside but also to control their behavior while inside, forcing them into a labor regimen they might not like. It therefore seemed necessary, at the very least, to sever the customer-seller bond between the institution's inmates and its officers. This required a ban on facilitative payments. As one historian writes of Pennsylvania's legislation on Walnut Street Jail in 1789: "To end the keeper's dependence on jail fees and the provision of (sometimes illegal) services to inmates, the Assembly made the keeper a salaried officer. . . . [N]o longer (so the Assembly hoped) would the keeper be able to profit from the traditional social economy of the prison."[15] Similarly, the New York statute establishing Newgate in 1796 provided that the keeper was to be salaried.[16]

The separation of carceral institutions from society—and of their personnel from exchange relations with inmates—was a tall order, and it got off to a rough start. In the early decades of the new program, inmates at places like Walnut Street and Newgate did not accept the novel labor regime, and they frequently rioted and engaged in slowdowns and sabotage. Further, "many of the families and friends of America's first penitentiary inmates were ill-disposed toward the strange new laws that provided for the sequestration of their loved ones," and they "asserted a right of access to the prisoners, which ran directly contrary to the penitentiary's foundational principle of segregating convicted offenders away from the community. Their efforts made the [early] penitentiary a notoriously porous institution," not unlike the traditional jail. "A voluminous traffic in goods, people, money, and news flowed through the penitentiary's gates on a daily basis." This flow of resources presumably gave inmates the means to pay officers for what they wanted, and customer-seller exchange lived on. In the early nineteenth century, "the inspectors of Walnut Street still complained of keepers who brazenly traded all manner of contraband with the prisoners. In 1820, Walnut Street's Board of Inspectors criticized guards for 'laxity of discipline' and their 'considerable collusion' with convicts." Inmates' influence over their internal governance continued: they still had "courts" to maintain their own group norms.[17]

Recognizing the failure of the original vision of the penitentiary, lawmakers and administrators—beginning in New York in the 1810s and 1820s—modified the program in the hope of making it more workable. Departing from the humanitarianism of the late eighteenth century, they expanded the power of officers to use corporal punishment to maintain discipline. Wardens accordingly ratcheted up the level of coercion, and they also cracked down on, and curtailed, the collusion between their subordinate officers and the inmates. They also shut down the inmates' "courts." The wardens then used the increasingly disciplined atmosphere of the prison to induce private manufacturers (contractors) to set up shop inside the prison walls and pay the state for use of the inmates' labor.[18] At New York's Sing Sing prison, for example, nine contractors had set up shop by 1841 and were using the "great majority" of the inmates.[19] Effectively, salaried government personnel kept the inmates disciplined while the manufacturers kept them occupied. Inmates rioted far less after the 1810s than they had before.[20] And the contractors' payments proved a valuable source of state income. The apparent success of New York's system—heightened corporal punishments and on-site contractors—caused its spread to nearly every Northern state by 1850.[21]

The contractor-based approach that swept the North in the 1830s and 1840s was not simply a matter of coercing the inmates. Though a baseline of coercive order was necessary to induce manufacturers to set up shop to begin with, contractors often used carrots, not sticks, to get the best work out of their inmate-laborers. They would often smuggle in items that inmates wanted, such as tobacco, and give it out in exchange for better work. Whereas the archetypal form of intraprison exchange had once been the inmate giving money to the jailor to facilitate better service, it now became increasingly common for the contractor to give goods to the inmate to facilitate better labor.[22] Contracting thus softened the penitentiary's official harshness.[23] New York even banned flogging in 1847.[24] Altogether, the contracting regime that became standard by 1850 was a workable and stable accommodation between the institution and the inmates.

## VESTING CONTRACTORS WITH ABSOLUTE POWER: ALIEN IMPOSITION AND BOUNTY-SEEKING IN THE 1870s AND 1880s

In the 1870s, lawmakers confronted a sudden and unexpected crisis in prison order, and they reacted by shifting toward a more intense and coercive regime of prison labor management, turning incarceration into alien imposition of an especially pure and radical kind. Up to the 1870s, the typical Northern prison had contained the workshops of many contractors, each a small business. But the depression of 1873–77 caused many of those firms to abandon their contracts or fail altogether. This cost the states dearly, and it left the inmates in a sudden and dangerous idleness, sparking internal disorder. Responding to this crisis, state legislatures decided that contractors ought to be big firms strong enough to weather a downturn: each prison was now to contract with one big firm (or at most a few big firms) that would use the labor of all its inmates. New York once again set the tone by adopting this approach in 1876. For example, the oven molder John Sherwood Perry undertook an enormous contract with Sing Sing that made his business the largest oven-making enterprise in the world. Nearly all Northern states rapidly followed.[25]

By subjecting a whole institution's population to the use of a single firm, lawmakers fused the profit-seeking extraction of labor with the coercive power of prison management in a way that had never happened before. Previously, the contractors at an institution had been so small and numerous that none rivaled the salaried governmental staff for practical control over the means of coercion. But now that the institution had only one big firm to deal with, that firm acquired tremendous power, for the institution was dependent on the firm to keep the mass of inmates occupied and productive.[26] With the big firm in such a commanding position, its personnel rapidly acquired de facto control over the prison's disciplinary practices. As McLennan shows:

> Overseers and foremen employed by the contractor exercised considerable authority over prisoners by reporting, and threatening to report, prison labor- ers to the state's keepers for real or alleged incidents of slacking, disobedience, or poor workmanship. The states' guards still executed corporal punishment, but its imposition became tightly tethered to the contractor's setting of targets and standards, the prisoner's performance as a laborer, and the overseer's as- sessment of the quality and quantity of the prisoner's labor.
>
> At the same time, the state's prison keepers effectively became auxiliaries of the contractor—a relationship that many contractors affirmed and but- tressed by putting the state's guards on the company payroll. In the 1870s and 1880s contractors commonly supplemented the wages of guards and other state officials. . . . In return, prison officers coordinated punishments with overseers and surveilled and recorded prisoners' work performances. Civilian foremen commonly referred prisoners to the state keepers for punishment, and pressured state officers to drive prisoners to higher levels of productivity through more liberal infliction of punishments.[27]

"With the advent of large-scale, rationalized contracting in the mid-1870s," McLennan continues, "the observance of industrial discipline eclipsed all other disciplinary objectives and became the foundation of prison order in general. . . . Unsatisfactory work, accidents involving damage to machinery or materials, acts of insubordination, failure to meet task (that is, produce a set amount of goods on any one day), refusal to work, and sabotage became the most commonly punished offenses." Indeed, it seems the big contractors' ea- gerness to punish inmates was a major reason the 1870s saw the "proliferation and refinement" of more terrifying punishments: paddling, stringing-up by the thumbs, ice-baths, and solitary confinement.[28] Newly vested with control over the "stick," contractors were now far less inclined than in the previous era to use the "carrot." They "increasingly substituted nakedly punitive forms of coercion for reward-and-incentive-centered techniques of motivation."[29]

The fusion of profit-seeking labor extraction with disciplinary control that McLennan documents in the 1870s should, I believe, be understood as a kind of bounty-seeking. As defined throughout this book, a bounty is money that a state agent receives for doing something the affected person does not want. Contractors now put inmates to a stark choice between labor or physical punishment and profited by doing so, while inmates did not want to be put to that choice. (In the era before the 1870s, by contrast, inmates were far less likely to be averse to the choice presented to them by a contractor, which would often include the prospect of substantial positive rewards in exchange for good work.)

The bounty-seeking penitentiary contractor of the 1870s was engaged in alien imposition of the most radical kind. "Both in practice and in the administrative imaginary," writes McLennan, "the prison became an amoral domain, dominated almost entirely by instrumental rationality."[30] Typically, alien imposition means that the sovereign makes demands that violate the norms of a community and the expectations of the mass of its inhabitants. Places like Sing Sing in the 1870s saw this taken to an extreme: the profit-maximizing goals of the sovereign agent (the contractor) threatened to exclude organic communal norms altogether, and the contractor refused to recognize the expectations (or even personalities) of its wards beyond their animal fear of physical pain. Reflecting the views of many prison administrators, the head of the New York system, Louis Pilsbury, "now openly and publicly condemned reformatory and other 'moral' approaches to incarceration, dismissing them as misguided 'sentimentalism': Felons, Pilsbury declared [in 1880], 'have passed beyond moral influence,' and 'can only be governed by fear of bodily punishment.'"[31]

The profit-seeking penitentiary contractors of the 1870s were the polar opposite of the profit-seeking jailors of the 1700s. Eighteenth-century jailors had been profit seekers, but the money they sought took the form of facilitative payments. Because of this, the carceral institution had possessed no independent internal order, for it simply reflected the aggregate preferences of the inmate-customers and the norms they developed as a community. Now, in the 1870s, the incarcerator was profit-seeking once again, but this time for bounties. Accordingly, the prison's internal order was radically independent of inmates' preferences, threatening to reduce inmates to things that existed merely to have their labor extracted. This was alien imposition of an acute, even dystopian, variety.

## THE EXPULSION OF THE CONTRACTORS: FOSTERING INMATE COOPERATION AND LEGITIMACY

As in Chapters 5, 6, and 7, bounty-seeking reached the peak of its intensity only to cause a backlash, which led lawmakers to banish the profit motive. The new regime of super-powerful contractors sparked a huge increase in riots and strikes by the inmates. These "mutinies" flared up all across the nation, and they were much bigger and more frequent than before the 1870s.[32] They nearly always resulted from "the efforts of contractors to raise production levels, cut costs, inflict punishments, or a combination of these things."[33]

The whole point of the post-1876 regime of big-firm contracting had been to make "the prison a secure and profitable institution,"[34] yet the very intensity of contractor control rendered the system unbearable for the inmates and motivated them to assert collectively the irrepressible autonomy that they still possessed, in spite of the seeming absoluteness of the contractor's power. "Rebellions exposed a vital link between the conditions of prison life, on one hand, and the convicts' *ability and willingness* to work hard and well for their contractors, on the other. . . . Even with the prison guard[s] . . . at their disposal," contractors needed "a significant degree of cooperation from the convicts." Indeed, the very nature of modern manufacturing rendered inmate cooperation especially important, for the division of labor was so minute and integrated that if workers at one stage of the process struck, they could disrupt the whole enterprise.[35]

Inmate mutinies and disruptions demonstrated that even (perhaps especially) in the most intense state-controlled environments, some degree of voluntary cooperation was still necessary for governance to be workable. Coercion had its limits. Walls, guard towers, and guns might suffice to keep inmates inside prison walls, but maintaining and shaping social order within those walls required the officialdom to elicit inmates' cooperation and build legitimacy, as with so many other state-building endeavors.

Lawmakers and voters were soon confronted with this reality, for the riots and strikes were catalysts in the political process. They received lots of press.[36] They "helped reopen public debate over both the efficacy and the ethical value of the prevailing system of penal servitude." In particular, they "palpably refuted the claim of contractors and the authorities that their system imposed order in the prisons,"[37] which had been a primary argument in its favor. Further, the disruptions galvanized the key interest group that would spearhead the drive to banish profit-seeking from the prisons: the labor movement. For unions, the abolition of prison contracting was both a pocketbook issue (to protect their members from low-cost competition) and a broader moral issue (to prevent the dehumanization of labor).[38]

The union-led reaction against the contract system would ultimately succeed across the North.[39] McLennan takes New York as her case study. Just as big-firm contracting had originated in New York, the backlash began there as well, in the early 1880s. The state was closely divided between Democrats (who tended to oppose the contractors) and Republicans (who tended to favor them).[40] Yet this was not simply a story of anti-contractor Democrats defeating pro-contractor Republicans. The disorder and abuse were so obvious that Republicans were on the defensive, and public misgivings about the system extended well beyond Democratic ranks. There were mutinies at Sing Sing soon after Perry's contract began in 1877, then more at another New York prison in 1882, then more at Sing Sing in 1883 while a legislative committee was investigating the place.[41] When the committee reported, the Democratic minority demanded that the contract system be "wiped out," and even the Republican majority set forth a "damning critique" of vesting profit seekers with disciplinary power, though it held out hope that "a new, less injurious" contract labor regime could be devised.[42] The legislature submitted the issue to a popular referendum in the November 1883 elections. The electorate voted to abolish contract penal labor by a margin of nearly two to one.[43] In the late 1880s and early 1890s, the New York Republican party would officially join the Democrats in opposition to the contract system.[44]

New York voters rejected the contract system in 1883 because they judged it unstable and morally unacceptable in an absolute sense; there was no obvious arrangement to replace it.[45] Still, in accordance with the referendum, prison contracting wound down, and its last vestiges disappeared in the mid-1890s.[46]

Finally, in 1895–1900, the new State Prison Commission drew up an affirmative plan for a less adversarial mode of management. Inmates were still to labor, but only under salaried state supervision and only to make goods for the government.[47] In truth, this "state-use" solution would never produce enough demand, or be efficient enough, to occupy the inmates in the way that private manufacturing had.[48] Anticipating this, the commission and other administrators began planning supplementary activities for the inmates, such as classes, libraries, and prison newspapers.[49] Perhaps most important, the new plan curtailed corporal punishment, replacing it with "softer (though potentially no less powerful) techniques of persuasion,"[50] which mixed positive incentives with comparatively subtle negative incentives. Inmates would be divided into grades within each prison, through which they could be promoted or demoted depending on their behavior, which would affect their prospects of early release. They could also be transferred between the state's multiple prisons (which differed greatly in conditions), again on the basis of behavior.[51]

In the commission's original vision of the late 1890s, all these arrangements — manufacturing for state use; the administration of promotions, demotions, and transfers; and the control of corporal punishment — were to be carried out through top-down control, and prison employees were to enjoy secure tenure and career stability. The statewide commission and superintendent would control the whole system, the wardens of the individual prisons would act as their agents, and the guards would become civil servants.[52] In some ways, the vision became a reality. Guards did gain civil-service protection.[53] Each prison did develop grades.[54] And transfer became a common disciplinary tool.[55]

In these respects, the conversion of penitentiaries to nonprofit status fits with the common social-science view of salary compensation that associates it with top-down control and career stability. Yet it would be wrong to say that lawmakers initially opted against the profit motive as part of a self-conscious program to rely instead on centralization and civil service reform, since (as noted above) the voters in 1883 rejected the profit-seeking system as unacceptable in an absolute sense, without a clear idea of any alternative. Still, the vacuum left by the referendum did open the way for reformers to go in the direction of top-down control and career stability, although these ideals fell short of full realization, sometimes very short. Communications between statewide authorities and wardens, and between wardens and guards, remained predominantly oral and unsystematic for many years.[56] Guards did not necessarily obey official directives: corporal punishment lost the terrifying pervasiveness and rationalized intensity of the contractor era, but it continued as an underground practice, shielded by the guards' conspiracy of silence.[57] The wardens remained within the spoils system, and their turnover was quite high through the 1910s. Further, wardens asserted complete control of prisoner grades within their respective institutions, foiling the attempts of the statewide authorities to develop a more centralized and rationalized scheme of promotions and demotions.[58] During the 1910s, the reformist politician Thomas Mott Osborne—as warden of New York's Auburn penitentiary and then Sing Sing—pushed prison management even farther away from top-down control. He established a remarkable degree of inmate self-government (for example, inmate-staffed disciplinary boards), obtained loads of unauthorized nonstate funding for the enrichment and entertainment of inmates from sources like philanthropic groups and universities, and generally ran each prison as his personal creative endeavor, defying the statewide authorities on issues like transfers, hiding information from them, and breaking personnel rules.[59]

Prison management finally reached a stable equilibrium in the 1920s, when Lewis Lawes, in charge of Sing Sing, curtailed and co-opted the inmates' self-government arrangements, maintained the incentives associated with grades and other privileges, and expanded entertainment and enrichment (athletics, movies, radio, classes). The profit motive was long gone. Labor itself was increasingly marginal. Gone, too, was the aspiration to reform the convicts' morals that had given birth to the original penitentiary and had cropped up periodically during the intervening years. The idea was simply to keep the convicts cooperative and docile, through a relatively soft touch. When Sing Sing avoided the wave of riots that hit other New York prisons in 1929, Governor Franklin D. Roosevelt made Lawes's approach the model for the whole state, and it soon became the standard for most other states, too.[60]

The equilibrium that ultimately prevailed under the post-contractor, non-profit system was quite unlike the old regime of the 1700s. In the traditional jail, officers had given inmates free rein to develop an intraprison society and even to shape official action through their buying power. By contrast, mid-twentieth-century wardens like Lawes affirmatively and proactively managed the inmate population. And yet they did so with an eye toward nurturing the cooperation of the inmates. In this respect, their approach was also quite different from the bounty-seeking regime of the big contractors in the 1870s. Wardens like Lawes took a far less adversarial tack, seeking to manage the inmates rather than break or exploit them. The absence of any profit motive, whether of the facilitative or bounty-seeking variety, meant that the officialdom stood in a middle distance from the population it governed.

# 9

NAVAL WARFARE

*Prize Money and Blood Money*

From its earliest years, the U.S. government, copying Britain, made its naval officers and seamen eligible for two kinds of bounties. The first consisted of shares in the proceeds from enemy merchant vessels and cargo they captured, known as prize money. The second consisted of rewards from the public treasury for sinking enemy warships, pegged to the number of enemy sailors on board, officially known as head money, though the seamen nicknamed it "blood money." Because the early U.S. government was willing to build only a small permanent navy, it supplemented the force, when facing a superior naval foe, with privately owned ships (privateers) that were licensed to capture enemy merchant vessels and cargo. Privateers could win prize money for their captures, just as navy ships could. (Head money was irrelevant to privateers, since, as amateurs, they were not expected to fight enemy warships.)

Prize money and head money were uncontroversial throughout the U.S. maritime wars of the nineteenth century—until 1899, right after the Spanish-American War, when Congress suddenly abolished them for all U.S. naval personnel. Why this abrupt change? That is the question of this chapter.[1]

As recounted in Chapters 5–8, lawmakers generally abolished bounties to confer legitimacy upon alien imposition—that is, upon novel assertions of governmental power, especially those that were unprecedented in their ambition and intrusiveness. For these assertions of power, a display of disinterested motives seemed necessary to win the trust and goodwill of an alarmed population. The same dynamic underlay Congress's decision to abolish bounty-seeking in the U.S. Navy.

To see the commonality, we must first appreciate a peculiar aspect of military power, particularly in the American context. We begin with the obvious: a military force, when fighting an ordinary war, engages in alien imposition against foreigners (say, when it attacks them or seizes their property). It was for such impositions against foreigners (captures and sinkings) that naval personnel received prize money and head money. Such rewards provided straightforward incentives to fight and win. But—and here is the key point—a military force can also engage in alien imposition against the domestic population of its home country.

To Americans during the late eighteenth and nineteenth centuries, this point was especially salient. In their view, the buildup of a big permanent military establishment by the U.S. government would inexorably lead to fearful alien impositions on the American population. First, such an establishment would require high taxes by the federal government, the level remotest from America's self-governing local communities. Second, an establishment would entail the formation of a socially distinct, nationally oriented, and quasi-aristocratic class of military officers, which might come to dominate national politics. Third, an establishment would draw the United States into the rivalries, intrigues, and alliances of the great European powers, thus robbing Americans of their capacity to make decisions for themselves, free of foreign interference. Fourth, an establishment would draw the United States into wars against the European powers, thus subjecting Americans to attack by foreign forces.

Because of these factors, Americans felt themselves at risk of alien imposition arising from *their own* military, should it ever become too big, professionalized, or ambitious. Indeed, a common American view was that the military establishments of all the world's powerful nations mutually reinforced one another—through alliances, intrigues, rivalries, and arms races—so as to impose alien demands on their own populations (through taxes, conscription, officerclass power, and foreign obligations) and on one another's populations (through invasions, battles, and the like). In this view, the military establishments of all Europe were collectively engaged in a conspiracy of alien imposition against all the peoples of Europe.[2]

For the first 120 years after independence, Americans avoided such terrors of alien imposition by simply refusing to build up a big permanent military establishment, escaping the cruel game of great-power rivalry. They kept their regular army and navy small, relying mainly on temporary amateur personnel to fight the War of 1812, the Mexican War, the Indian Wars, and the Civil War. Such forces quickly melted back into civil society when each conflict ended.

Also, Americans worked to avoid alien imposition through an additional mechanism: they repeatedly sought international humanitarian agreements to reduce the harm that warring states imposed on civilians and their property, especially at sea. From its founding, the U.S. government sought protective guarantees for the nationals of neutral countries and their ocean-borne property during wartime. By the early nineteenth century, Americans went even farther, pushing for treaties to protect all ships and cargo belonging to noncombatants (even nationals of countries currently at war with each other). This would confine maritime war to a chivalric duel between navies, leaving untouched the economic life of noncombatants on both sides. This narrowing of violence (it was thought) would foster international commercial ties and international peace. Wars would become less likely and, when they did occur, less extensive in their destructiveness.

Against the background of the anti-establishment tradition and the humanitarian diplomatic program, prize money and head money for U.S. naval personnel seemed acceptable. Such rewards were useful motivators to fight and win. And they seemed otherwise harmless, for two reasons. First, the U.S. Navy was so tiny that its monetary stake in war inspired little fear of warmongering. (American ships that obtained privateering licenses were more numerous, but they had no stake in war, for they could make larger risk-adjusted profits by engaging in peacetime commerce.) Second, though the stake of all navies (including the U.S. Navy) in capturing merchant ships and cargo formed part of a fearsome regime of belligerent state imposition on noncombatants, the U.S. agenda for treaties protecting noncombatants allowed Americans to tell themselves that the progress of world civilization—which they were proud to lead—would inevitably bring an end to all maritime war against commerce, including prize money. On that, Americans were content to look to the long run.

But in 1899, Congress suddenly abolished prize money and head money in the U.S. Navy. It did so by an overwhelming consensus: the House acted unanimously, and the Senate without a roll call.[3] So far as U.S. lawmakers knew, their country was the first in the world to do anything like this. (The British—the world's experts at naval war—would reaffirm naval bounty-seeking in 1900 and abolish it only in an incremental and cautious manner between the 1910s and 1940s.) Congressmen in 1899 were responding to a wave of near-universal popular American revulsion against naval profit-seeking that hit during the brief Spanish-American War of the summer of 1898. Why did this wave arise then? Why not at some earlier point in U.S. history?

It was because the United States, as a result of the war with Spain, suddenly acquired an overseas empire—the possessions Hawaii, Puerto Rico, Guam, and the Philippines, and the satellite Cuba—which everybody knew would require a huge permanent navy to maintain (rendering amateur privateers obsolete). Thus, the anti-establishment tradition suddenly collapsed. This was a wrenching and alarming change. It portended the various alien impositions—high taxes, officer aggrandizement, entangling alliances, and frequent overseas wars—that Americans had always feared. The proponents of this novel military establishment sought to legitimate the institution—for the public and for themselves—by focusing on the purity of its *motives*. They endlessly repeated the original humanitarian justification for fighting Spain (to save the Cubans from Spanish concentration camps) and expanded that justification to encompass a "civilizing" mission in the new overseas possessions. In response to anti-imperialists who told scary stories about the self-interestedly aggressive European establishments, the defenders of the new U.S. Navy cast it as an instrument of selfless humanitarianism, civilization, and enlightenment.

In this debate, U.S. naval profit-seeking was an embarrassment for the hawks. It clashed with the notions of selflessness and progressive civilization that they invoked to justify the new empire. Further, it gave the navy a motive to start wars, and that motive now presented an obvious hazard, since the navy was slated to expand greatly, with numerous points of foreign contact around the globe. Thus, with the full support of U.S. naval officers and their allies, Congress terminated naval profit-seeking as soon as it convened after the victory against Spain.

Also, in a further effort to soothe fears about the nation's new imperial role and to confirm its humanitarian aims, the McKinley administration loudly reasserted the traditional American program to win protection for noncombatants' ocean-borne property against the depredations of warring states, initiating another drive for international agreement on that point. Thus, Americans told themselves that, even if wars were now more likely, their destructiveness would be more narrowly confined. The abolition of prize money served as a guarantee of the U.S. commitment to ameliorate war, despite the nation's entry onto the imperial stage.

Thus, in the case of maritime war as in so many others, lawmakers abolished bounties to confer legitimacy on alien imposition. Americans consented to the buildup of a naval establishment that had the physical and organizational potential to involve the nation in more destructive conflicts than ever before. Yet the new selflessness of the navy, so Americans hoped, would keep it from fulfilling that dreadful new potential.

I should note that there are some differences between my analytic narrative in this chapter and in Chapters 5–8. In the previous chapters, lawmakers were seeking to win the trust of the very population against whom officers had been engaged in bounty-seeking imposition. Here, congressmen were seeking to win the trust of the American population, who were not the same people as those against whom the U.S. Navy had been fighting to win bounties. Also, in the previous chapters, the goal of winning people's trust was to achieve their direct compliance with alien demands—to induce them to obey personally the statutes and official actions that lawfully applied to them. Here, congressmen were seeking the *political support* of the American population, in their capacity as voters, not as law abiders or law violators.

Despite these discrepancies, I think the similarities are deeper and more profound than the differences. Although Americans were not subject to attack by the U.S. Navy, they (or their property) would be subject to attack by foreign navies in conflicts that a warmongering U.S. Navy might start, as part of a transnational system of bounty-seeking in which U.S. naval personnel (until 1899) took part. And although congressmen were seeking Americans' political support rather than their personal obedience, the former was quite essential to the new navy's success. Altogether, the abolition of bounties, in the case of the U.S. Navy, as in this book's other case studies, was about the legitimation of power. Lawmakers used selflessness to elicit the population's trust in an otherwise threatening officialdom.

The new U.S. Navy, ushered in by rhetoric of humanity and civilization, did in fact win broad support from the American public. But legitimacy is a double-edged sword, giving the navy's story an ironic conclusion, which I recount toward the end of this chapter. Because they no longer had a sordid pecuniary stake in war against civilian commerce, U.S. naval officers after 1899 enjoyed greater credibility in arguing for the effectiveness of that kind of war, purely as a strategic matter. Under pressure from top naval officers—whose anti-humanitarian strategic views were no longer tainted by monetary self-interest—the U.S. government gradually abandoned its traditional sympathy for the protection of noncombatants' commerce in maritime war. In World War I, the nation cooperated (first implicitly, then openly) with Britain's "starvation blockade" of Germany, which killed a half million German civilians and drove the Germans to engage in unrestricted submarine warfare. This was exactly the kind of reciprocal escalation of war against civilians that nineteenth-century Americans had feared. Hence a great irony of the modern state: selflessness helps legitimate modern state power, and once a state is legitimate, it has more capacity than ever to carry out all kinds of acts, including terrible ones.

(An aside: This chapter's focus on water does not mean that American land forces received no bounties. On the contrary, during the colonial period and early republic, Americans fighting in the militia and even the U.S. Army were sometimes eligible for various bounties, such as captured enemy property or cash rewards for enemy scalps.[4] But the decline of those bounties is difficult to trace, since much of American land warfare during the nineteenth century was decentralized and informal, and the public official sanction for certain kinds of profit-seeking was murky.[5] Bounties in American land wars must await future research.)

## BACKGROUND: BOUNTIES FOR COMBAT IN EUROPE

In medieval and early modern Europe, soldiers on land could lawfully take for themselves the personal property of a defeated population, known as booty.[6] This was a key motivator for soldiers to enlist, fight, and win. But between the late 1600s and early 1800s, the governments of Europe increasingly outlawed and curtailed booty-seeking by their respective armies. At the same time, however, they maintained and expanded the more systematic practice of contributions, whereby the invading army, acting as a corporate body at the direction of its top officers, extorted resources from the subject population. The idea of contributions was to supply the invading army and (sometimes) strike at the foe's economy, not to let the invading soldiers enrich themselves personally.

European governments had a couple of reasons for outlawing booty. For one thing, they wanted to solve the problems of army discipline that arose when each individual soldier could seize booty for himself. Also, the centralization of resource extraction made it possible to control and moderate such extraction, so that an invading army would not invite the mass civilian resistance that excessive plundering might spark.[7]

The profit motive also thrived in European sea war, where it would prove more persistent than on land. Throughout history, belligerent nations have sought to obstruct one another's maritime trade. In England during the Middle Ages, kings made agreements with private shipowners whereby the latter were authorized to capture enemy merchant ships and cargo, the proceeds of which they would then share with the king.[8] The king also might own some ships himself, for which he would directly employ the crews, but those ships were not assembled into a permanent or distinct body. Medieval England's maritime fighting force was "less an institution than an event"—the ad hoc sending of ships, some owned by the king and others by private parties, to prey on foreigners when the need arose.[9] In this context, it is not surprising that compensation for those who manned the king's ships and the privately owned ships was similar: both received shares of what they took.[10] When Henry VIII assembled the king's ships into a permanent and institutionalized public force—a *navy*—during the 1500s, the right of naval personnel to a share of captures continued, as did the practice of licensing private ships (privateers) to raid for profit in addition to the navy. The experience of other European powers was similar: they all granted prize shares to their naval personnel and all licensed privateers.

Taking ships and cargo at sea was different from taking property on land. At sea, only a narrow slice of the enemy population directly felt the pain of the taking. Violence fell only on merchant seamen, and immediate economic loss fell only on the owners of ships and cargo. Thus maritime takings did not excite as much social disruption or moral outrage as booty-seeking. Further, it was easier for the top officers of a maritime force to monitor and control the depredations of their subordinates, since maritime takings occurred in a confined space, unlike takings on land.

In light of these conditions, early modern governments did not find it necessary to abolish combatant profit-seeking at sea. They were able to regulate it in a way that mitigated disciplinary problems. Traditionally, the personnel of a successful raiding ship had been entitled to pillage: each man could take for himself whatever he personally found above the gun deck of the captured ship, much like soldiers grabbing booty after battle. But in the early modern era, European governments abolished the right to maritime pillage, effectively protecting the personal property of enemy sailors. England, for example, did so circa 1700.[11]

While abolishing pillage, governments preserved the raiding personnel's right to the prize money (i.e., the proceeds from the captured ship itself and its commercial cargo), which the sovereign, by law, divided among the naval crew, according to rank. For example, by regulations of 1708, the British crown granted three-eighths to the ship's captain, one-eighth to its next-highest class of officers (which included lieutenants and masters), and so forth down the ladder.[12] (On privateers, division was by contract.) In this way, prize-taking, unlike pillage, was integrated into the rationalized, hierarchical disciplinary structure of the warship. The men could profit only to the extent that they worked successfully as a unit to find and take the prize. Even then, they shared it according to their places in the hierarchy.

In this comparatively rationalized phase, prize-taking remained quite important. In the British navy during the 1700s, it "was the chief attraction of the naval service."[13] As James Stephen, a prize lawyer and key government adviser, wrote in 1806: "The wise, liberal, and efficacious policy of this country, has been, to vest the property of maritime prizes wholly in the captors; and hence, much of the vigilance, activity, and enterprise, that have so long characterized the British navy."[14]

Though prize-seeking was generally more orderly and less fraught than booty-seeking, it did present one thorny problem: collateral damage to neutrals.[15]

It was common for enemy merchant ships to carry neutral cargo, or for neutral merchant ships to carry enemy cargo. The latter case was especially vexing, for belligerents (including Britain) asserted the power of their armed ships to stop every neutral vessel and search it for enemy goods. To be sure, belligerent sovereigns—in another example of the comparative orderliness of prize-seeking—provided some protection for neutrals against a wrongful taking: the men of the captor ship (whether naval or privateer) could not pocket the proceeds of the enemy ship and cargo until a court of the captor's home country found that they did indeed belong to nationals of the enemy country and condemned them. But this judicial safeguard did not completely solve the problem, for if a neutral ship held cargo that was even arguably of enemy status, it could be forced into a port of the captor's country to await a judicial decision on the question—a costly waste of time. Neutral shipowners hated this. They also complained that prize-seeking subjected them to much harassment that was wholly unauthorized, especially by privateers, whose crews were less disciplined than those of naval ships. What the neutrals really wanted was carte blanche to carry any and all goods for both sides—what they called the principle of "free ships, free goods."

Driven by these grievances, the traditionally neutral nations of the eighteenth century (e.g., Sweden, Russia, Holland) repeatedly formed alliances to retaliate against chronic belligerents like Britain and France. Much as warring sovereigns on land worried that excessive bounty-seeking would spark resistance among an occupied population, warring sovereigns at sea worried that excessive bounty-seeking would spark resistance among neutrals. This issue came to a head in 1854, when Britain and France fought the Crimean War against Russia. Britain and France sought the goodwill of strategically located neutrals like Sweden by promising, for the duration of the war, to give up privateers and to honor the principle of "free ships, free goods." The Declaration of Paris, which ended the war in 1856, adopted these two principles as permanent rules of war as between Britain, France, and most other European powers. But despite the end of privateering, the distribution of prize money to *naval* personnel lived on. Indeed, nearly all the powers continued it into the twentieth century, as I discuss later.

Like every incentive scheme, naval prize money had its imperfections. It encouraged the interdiction of enemy trade, but sovereigns also needed their navies to perform other tasks—like attacking enemy warships—from which prize money might be a distraction. Moreover, naval ships could be assigned to different kinds of duty, and some of these offered much better chances of prize-taking than others, causing feelings of unfairness and resentment in the service, particularly since the least lucrative assignments might be very dangerous, like serving on slow, gun-heavy ships that were key for big battles.[16]

The British responded to the imperfections of prize money by devising an additional form of bounty to counterbalance it. Parliament in 1708 established something called head money, which became known among the sailors as "blood money." This was a cash reward, paid from public revenue, to every armed British ship that sank an armed ship of the enemy. The award consisted of £5 for each enemy sailor on board the sunken ship at the start of the fight, which sum the British officers and seamen shared according to rank, just like prize money.[17] Plus, if British ships won a major victory, Parliament would often vote the crews head money ad hoc at a special rate higher than £5 per enemy sailor. After the Royal Navy triumphed at Trafalgar in 1805, Parliament voted £300,000 for those who fought in the battle. Of this, each captain got more than £3,000,[18] compared with annual captain's salaries of about £200 to £400.[19]

## U.S. NAVAL POLICY, 1776–1861: AVOIDING ALIEN IMPOSITION

Military power entails alien imposition in two senses. The first is obvious: the fighting force of one nation inflicts an alien imposition on the people of the opposing nation, whom it physically assaults or whose resources it seizes or destroys. We may call this *imposition from without*. The second sense is less obvious but still important: a fighting force may impose alien demands upon its own population. It may do so in a variety of ways: by directly threatening them with violence, by more subtly infiltrating their previously nonmilitarist politics, by making novel demands on their resources in the form of taxes or conscription, by drawing them into alliances with foreign powers, or by drawing them into actual wars, which (in turn) lead to more militarized politics, more taxes and conscription, and more alliance obligations. We may call this *imposition from within*.

To understand the history of American military bounty-seeking, we must understand the larger history of American attitudes toward military power. For the first 120 years of U.S. independence, this was a story of (1) avoiding alien imposition from within, by refusing to build a big, permanent military establishment, and (2) avoiding alien imposition from without, by avoiding war with the great powers and by seeking liberal humanitarian treaties to limit the destructive scope of war should it come—a limit Americans sought for their own benefit and (so they told themselves) for the benefit of all the world.

## The Anti-Establishment Tradition:
## Avoiding Alien Imposition from Within

Americans from the founding of the republic through the 1890s over-whelmingly opposed building a substantial military establishment. They were willing to fight, but only in a way that preserved the localist autonomy and self-government they held dear. Accordingly, their preferred military unit was one organized within a local community, composed of amateurs serving for a lim-ited term and electing their officers, who were usually neighborhood notables and local politicians, perhaps with military experience but very often not. This was the structure of the old militia units, which formed the bulk of U.S. land forces in the War of 1812, and of the later volunteer units, which played the same role in the Mexican War and Civil War.[20] The republic had a regular army, but it was quite small: in each of the wars just listed, the amateur units swelled the ranks sixfold or more, then rapidly shrank back.[21] For the numerous small wars against Indians, local amateur units were extremely prevalent.[22]

Maritime warfare was similar. Americans relied on privateers, "our marine militia."[23] Just as the men of standing in a rural community might raise a com-pany of locals to fight on land, so the leading merchants of a seaport would fit out their fastest ships with a few guns and gather a crew from the port's sailors to make a raiding voyage. These privateersmen and their ships would melt back into civil society when the conflict ended, just as the militia and volunteer com-panies did. To be sure, there was a regular U.S. Navy, but it was tiny compared to the privateers. The U.S. government in the War of 1812 sent only twenty-two naval cruisers to sea, but it commissioned more than five hundred privateers, more than two hundred of whom took at least one prize.[24]

The early United States' heavy reliance on militiamen, volunteers, and priva-teers ensured that military violence was firmly under local, popular, amateur con-trol. The nation's war-fighting capacity was undifferentiated from civil society and practically nonfunctional without a large amount of favorable popular sentiment.

The exact opposite war-fighting model was the large, permanent, profes-sional military establishment, such as existed in Britain, France, Prussia, or Russia. Such an organization was differentiated and alienated from civil so-ciety. Americans therefore considered it poisonous to localist republican self-government. Whereas the militia was incapable of attacking the people be-cause it *was* the people, a big standing army was distinct from the people and therefore could turn against them.[25]

Although a navy (unlike an army) could not venture inland to conquer the domestic populace, Americans still found a naval establishment to be dangerously anti-republican.[26] There were a couple of reasons for this. First, a naval establishment required enormous fixed investment and a crushing tax burden. Americans feared the example of the mother country, where the Royal Navy's budget had made the British the most taxed people in Europe.[27] Second, Americans feared the idea of a career military officer corps, whether of the army or navy. It was a distinctly European, aristocratic, and anti-republican institution. Americans vividly remembered the abuses of British redcoats and naval officers in the 1760s and 1770s, not to mention the unnerving attempt of American revolutionary veterans—including naval ones—to establish a hereditary Society of the Cincinnati during the 1780s, which looked like an effort "to create a European-style hereditary aristocracy in America."[28] In the 1830s and 1840s, Jacksonians maintained this suspicion of career military officers and put their own spin on it, viewing the officers as privileged elites and therefore illegitimate.[29]

Given these perceived evils, Americans were loath to build a big permanent navy unless it had some large offsetting benefit. But what benefit did such a navy provide? A small navy—coupled with a swarm of privateers when necessary—was enough to make other nations respect American commerce. The only reason for a nation to have a big permanent navy was if it wanted to participate, on a continuing and systematic basis, in the global rivalry of the European powers, particularly for overseas colonies. To Americans of the early republic, such participation was not a "benefit" at all, but a horror. Participation in the global rivalry of European empires would require the United States to ally itself with at least some of them. That kind of entanglement threatened American self-determination.[30] The nation risked becoming a dependent or pawn. If foreign obligations dictated America's policy, then Americans were not really free to govern themselves. As George Washington warned in his Farewell Address of 1796, the "attachment of a small or weak, towards a great and powerful nation, dooms the former to be the satellite of the latter."[31]

Even if the United States were to build up a navy for some reason besides participation in great-power rivalry, the mere possession and operation of such a navy would inevitably draw the nation into the European vortex. Because a navy interacted frequently with foreign nations during peacetime (as an army did not), it was at risk of getting into altercations that would drag the United States into war.[32] In that respect, a navy was actually more dangerous than an army. It could be a *"war-creating"* institution, as one critic said.[33] On this point, American concern about foreign intrigue merged with American fear of the officer class, for career military officers were distinct not only in their aristocratic status but also because of their professional self-interest in war. "[M]ilitary

aristocrats welcomed war as an adventure, an opportunity for fame and glory."
And they were to be feared "because of the influence [they] could wield over
civil government." Americans wished to avoid the situation in Britain, where a
"large numbers of militia, army, and navy officers served as members of Parliament, giving the legislature a distinctly military character and military aristocrats a great deal of power in government."[34] Government by military professionals was alien, not popular.

Americans' myriad fears of a military establishment (including a naval establishment) shared a unifying theme: the aversion of local democratic communities to alien imposition. Such imposition might take the form of a faraway
federal Congress levying higher taxes. It might take the form of foreign "allies"
dictating terms to the United States. It might take the form of career naval
officers—with an outlook oriented toward nation and empire rather than state
or town—starting wars in foreign ports or insinuating themselves into American
politics. Adherence to the anti-establishment tradition avoided all these threats
to local civilian communities' self-determination.

To be sure, the anti-establishment tradition did not imply pacifism. Nineteenth-century Americans violently seized much of the North American continent from the Indians and Mexicans. But they did so through wars that were
geographically confined, brief, or both. This made it possible to rely largely on
nonestablishment forces and remain aloof from great-power rivalries.

### Anti-Establishment's Implications for U.S. Strategy and Force Structure

The anti-establishment principle necessitated a very particular approach to
maritime war. To understand this, we need some general background on strategy and ships. This is merely a sketch, but it will suffice for our purposes.[35]

The most basic way for a belligerent government to catch enemy merchant
vessels (or neutral vessels carrying enemy cargo) was to scatter its own ships
far and wide across the high seas, allowing each one to search for and capture
merchant vessels individually. This decentralized approach was known as commerce raiding. The type of ship suited to commerce raiding was the cruiser: a
relatively small, fast, lightly armed ship, capable of catching and overpowering
merchant vessels, which were themselves fast but had little to no firepower.

A more advanced way of interdicting enemy trade was to assemble a cluster
of cruisers off an enemy port and have them chase and capture any merchant
vessel that tried to get in or out. This was a blockade. It was a relatively novel
weapon of war. The British in the 1790s had been the first to make it workable, once they figured out effective techniques to keep ship bottoms from
rotting and sailors from getting scurvy.[36] In terms of efficiency, blockade was

an improvement on commerce raiding, for it focused on the narrowest bottle-neck in enemy shipping. Yet blockade had an Achilles' heel: the enemy navy could assemble a fleet of capital ships—big, slow, heavily armed vessels—and advance on the port, giving the blockading cruisers a choice between being pulverized or running away. Either way, the blockade would be broken. Thus, if the blockading force was to remain in place, it required not only cruisers but also a fleet of capital ships, sufficient to defeat the enemy's capital ships.

If two warring nations each had fleets of capital ships, one might concentrate its own fleet to prevent the opposing fleet from concentrating, or, failing that, attempt to destroy the enemy fleet once it had concentrated. This led to climactic fleet battles (the classic being Trafalgar). When one nation destroyed its enemy's fleet, or when it possessed a fleet so powerful that its enemy dared not engage in fleet-based operations like blockade, the nation was said to have "command of the sea."

All the foregoing activities—commerce raiding, blockade, and battle—involved profit-seeking. A cruiser engaged in commerce raiding on the high seas received the value of the enemy ships and cargo it captured. Similarly, cruisers blockading a port received the value of the blockade-runners they captured (by the usual rule, every ship within signal distance at the time of capture got an equal share). Capital ships and cruisers that destroyed enemy warships in battle got head money.

We can now appreciate the distinct roles of naval ships and privateers. Naval ships engaged in every type of maritime combat. There were naval cruisers, which might be assigned to commerce raiding or blockade duty. And there were naval capital ships, which guarded blockades and fought fleet battles. By contrast, privateers had a more confined role. Recall that a privateer was simply a fast merchant ship, fitted temporarily with a few guns. It was by definition a cruiser. (Capital ships were too slow and specialized for peacetime commercial use, so only governments built and owned them.) Like naval cruisers, privateers engaged in commerce raiding. But that was all they did. They never took part in blockades. Because privateers were private enterprises (albeit licensed ones), their government could not affirmatively order them to do anything, which meant that it was impossible for them to undertake the kind of elaborate coordination that a blockade required.

A nation devised a maritime war strategy by choosing from the menu of ships and activities described above. Different nations made different choices. By the early 1800s, Britain had developed the *guerre d'escadre* (fleet war), a strategy aimed at using a fleet centered on capital ships to win command of the sea and blockade the enemy coast. At the other end of the spectrum was the United

States, which clung to the *guerre de course* (war of chase), a strategy consisting of commerce raiding and little else. This was the nation's approach in the War of 1812, and it remained the U.S. war plan for any conflict against a superior naval power up to the 1890s.

Britain's and America's choices followed from their respective priorities. Britain was willing to bear the huge cost of capital ships and to maintain a huge officer corps to operate them. The United States was willing to do neither. Instead, it relied mainly on privateers, which meant commerce raiding. The small U.S. Navy, consisting of a handful of cruisers, did largely the same thing as the privateers: its ships sailed the high seas on solo voyages, chasing enemy commerce. Because the U.S. naval cruisers had more firepower and more professional crews than the privateers, they captured merchant ships at a much higher rate. But the United States had so many more privateers than naval ships that the former were more important in the aggregate. But in another respect, the U.S. naval cruisers did more work than the privateers: upon encountering enemy naval cruisers on the high seas, they stood and fought, whereas privateers normally ran away. The reason was that privateer crews had to protect their shipowners' investment and were therefore unwilling to risk fighting a warship, whereas U.S. naval officers, though motivated partly by prize money, were also motivated by the prospect of promotion, by honor, and by head money.

## U.S. Naval Profit-Seeking

To Americans of the period 1776–1861, the profit-seeking status of the tiny U.S. Navy seemed perfectly ordinary. It was a status shared by the swarm of privateers that accompanied the navy to war. It was also a status shared by all foreign navies.[37] And though Americans considered foreign navies to be menacing institutions, they simultaneously believed that, insofar as the United States was going to have a navy, it was fine for it to follow conventional worldwide naval practices, so long as the force itself remained within its confined political and institutional space.

Following conventional practices usually meant following British practices.[38] From the time Congress established the U.S. Navy at the turn of the nineteenth century, it granted its personnel shares of prize money on the model of corresponding British statutes. Congress also offered head money, though it was not as generous as Parliament. It granted a reward (of $20 per enemy sailor) only when the enemy ship was of equal or superior force to the U.S. naval ship.[39] Congress also followed Parliament's custom of voting ad hoc rewards, on top of the ordinary head money, for especially significant victories.

For the tiny U.S. Navy, these various profit opportunities were a "major motivator."[40] During the War of 1812, the commanding officer of a cruiser averaged total annual rewards from prize money and head money that were about equal to his annual salary.[41] Some hit the jackpot: at least eight navy captains won prizes greater than five times salary, sometimes much greater.[42] Further, there were eight ad hoc rewards granted by Congress (usually for one-on-one engagements, since U.S. Navy ships operated solo and did not seek multiship battles).[43] As a result of one such reward, Commodore Stephen Decatur became the war's top earner, pocketing more than $30,000, compared with an annual salary of less than $2,000.[44]

### Liberal Humanitarianism: Avoiding Alien Imposition from Without

In refusing to build a big, permanent military establishment, Americans avoided alien imposition from within. But they also feared alien imposition from without—that is, victimization by the formidable military establishments of the European powers. In particular, Americans, as neutrals, feared harassment of their commerce by belligerent European navies.

Neutral grievances about belligerent harassment had already become widespread before the United States came into existence. Owners of neutral ships greatly resented being stopped and searched, to say nothing of being dragged to belligerent ports for adjudication, or worse. This was more of a problem for commerce raiding, which occurred on the high seas and therefore affected the ships of all nations, than for blockade, which was confined to designated ports that neutrals could opt to avoid. By the eighteenth century, traditional neutrals like Sweden and Holland had formulated an ideology of "neutral rights," most importantly the principle of "free ships, free goods"—a purported right of neutral ships to carry belligerent-owned goods without interference on the high seas.[45] Obviously, this served the neutrals' self-interest. But it also reflected a larger moral aspiration: to limit the harms of war.

The logical implication of America's aversion to European great-power rivalry was neutrality. "Bred in the doctrines of the enlightenment," writes one historian, "America saw herself as a perpetual neutral in European conflicts, with a neutral's antipathy to wars against commerce."[46] This stance made the United States "the harbinger of a new liberal era: with a large merchant marine and no effective navy, the United States intended that her wealth proceed by commerce not war."[47]

The United States began putting this ideology into practice in 1776, when the Continental Congress drew up a template for treaties. This model agreement provided that, whenever one signatory was belligerent and the other neutral, the former would recognize the principle of "free ships, free goods" as protecting the latter. By 1785, the United States concluded such pacts with France, Holland, Sweden, and Prussia. And when the French Revolutionary and Napoleonic Wars of 1793–1815 shifted British and French shipping to American merchant vessels, the new nation's interest in neutral rights grew even stronger.[48] One of the United States' principal aims in the War of 1812—the only overseas war it declared in the 120 years after independence—was to vindicate neutral rights.

By the 1820s, the American commitment to the protection of neutral commerce expanded into an even wider humanitarian ambition to protect all private property on the high seas in wartime. The United States sought international agreements by which belligerents would refrain from capturing any merchant ship or cargo on the high seas, even if it belonged to nationals of the enemy. There would be an exception for direct military supplies (contraband), but ordinary trade would go untouched. It was not enough to protect the people of noncombatant *countries* from the destructive power of warring states; Americans now wanted to protect all noncombatant *individuals*, even nationals of the warring states. Individuals should enjoy absolute protection for their property, even from a government with whom their own government was at war. This was the ultimate bar against alien imposition from without. It meant that, should the United States go to war in the future, its civilian population would be insulated from economic attack, as would the civilian population of its opponent.

In seeking such agreements, Americans thought of themselves as humanizing and civilizing international relations, ending barbarism. They sought to guarantee a private sphere of individual rights inviolable by any government.[49] As Secretary of State John Quincy Adams wrote in 1823, it was "unjust . . . that any private property of individuals should ever be destroyed or impaired by national authority for national quarrels."[50]

In addition to guaranteeing individual rights, the American plan for international law would open as wide a field as possible for commerce, which by the early 1800s seemed the key to more pacific, cosmopolitan, and mutually beneficial relations among Western peoples.[51] Such thinking was in keeping with the fading of mercantilism and the rise of market-based utilitarianism.[52] In the words of an 1820 petition against commerce raiding signed by New England luminaries, "Commerce is in the interest of the world; it connects distant regions, multiplies and distributes the fruits of every climate, and makes every country a sharer in the natural, intellectual, and moral wealth, of all the others."[53]

The idea of shielding all commerce from war might seem quixotic, but it fit with the postmillennial Protestantism that was common in bourgeois circles during the nineteenth century, according to which society was progressing inexorably toward more humane, civilized, and less barbarous ways.[54] Many examples could be cited, including the abolition of the slave trade and of sanguinary punishments. Even more relevant was the abolition (at least formally) of booty-seeking in land warfare: Americans and their European sympathizers frequently noted that international law now recognized private property as sacred in land warfare and should do the same in maritime warfare.[55] (This was false, for armies were still permitted to be quite aggressive in forcing contributions, but many people wanted to believe the falsehood and did.) In light of all this, commerce raiding, which was literally state-sanctioned piracy, seemed to be on the wrong side of history. "History," attested Adams, showed "that the influence of Christianity has been marked in a signal manner by the gradual establishment of rules in the hostile conflicts of nations tending to assuage the evils of war." The enslavement of prisoners of war, for example, had been abolished, indicating a "progressive amelioration in the condition of man," which, he hoped, would result in the protection not only of persons caught in the midst of war but also of their possessions.[56]

But the world was not quite as "civilized" as the United States would have liked. The efforts of the Monroe administration in the 1820s to win international agreements prohibiting the capture of property on the high seas failed.[57] Though its dream of ending all commerce raiding faded temporarily around 1830,[58] the U.S. government continued to advocate for neutral rights, which was a second-best solution. "[J]udging from the slow progress of civilization," explained Secretary of State Henry Clay in 1826, "it would be too much to indulge any very sanguine hope of a speedy, universal concurrence in a total exemption of all private property from capture," yet "[s]ome nations may be prepared to admit the limited . . . principle" of "free ships, free goods."[59]

## Tension between the Anti-Establishment Tradition and Liberal Humanitarianism

America's anti-establishment tradition aimed to prevent alien imposition from within, while its liberal humanitarian tradition aimed to prevent alien imposition from without. In that respect, the two traditions were in harmony. They protected Americans from the threat of professional military power, domestic or foreign. Further, the traditions were in harmony in that both (it was thought) tended toward peace. By rejecting a military establishment, the United States removed itself from the destructive game of European rivalry. And by seeking treaties to make the world safe for commerce, the United States promoted pacific and mutually beneficial relations among peoples that would reduce their inclination to fight each other.[60]

Yet, at another level, America's anti-establishment tradition and its liberal humanitarian project were in tension. Because of the anti-establishment principle, the United States had to rely on the *guerre de course*, and not only that, but a *guerre de course* carried out largely by privateers. While privateersmen lacked military discipline and were driven solely by profit, naval officers and crews had stronger discipline and, though driven partly by prize money, were also motivated by the promotion system and honor. For these reasons, privateers were notoriously less respectful of neutral rights than were naval cruisers.[61] America's anti-establishment tradition deprived it of the elements of military professionalism (discipline, hierarchy, honor) that were necessary to civilize fighting men in their dealings with noncombatants.

This tension came to a head in 1856, when (as noted earlier) the European powers in the Declaration of Paris proposed adopting the principle of "free ships, free goods" and prohibiting privateers. Both of these were neutral-friendly measures, and the United States had always cast itself as the champion of neutrals. Yet the ban on privateers was a deal breaker for the United States. The nation's aversion to a naval establishment meant it had little maritime defense without privateers. In rejecting the 1856 proposal, Secretary of State William L. Marcy made this explicit. He considered "powerful navies," like "large standing armies," to be "detrimental to national prosperity and dangerous to civil liberty." When faced with a conflict, the American people were "content . . . to rely, in military operations on land, mainly upon volunteer troops [i.e., amateur units], and for the protection of their commerce . . . upon their mercantile marine," in the form of privateers. The United States was no more willing to give up its privateers at sea than its volunteers on land.[62] Privateers, as one congressman declared that same year, were "the only legitimate marine defense that can to any very considerable extent be recognized by a republican Government." They were "our marine militia."[63]

Rejecting the Declaration of Paris in order to preserve privateering was potentially embarrassing for the United States. Having long posed as the Galahad of international relations, the nation was now defending a particularly retrograde practice. Marcy tried to argue that privateers were no more abusive of neutral rights than were naval ships, but everybody knew that was wrong. Britain and France had offered to ban privateering as consideration for neutral goodwill in 1854, and neutrals besides the United States were eager to make the ban permanent in 1856.[64] The *New York Times* candidly acknowledged that the declaration presented the United States with "the difficulty of reconciling a decent deference to the apparent demands of civilization with a proper regard to our own interests."[65]

To save face and maintain America's sense of moral superiority, Marcy reintroduced his government's thirty-year-old proposal to immunize private property from capture on the high seas, regardless of whether it belonged to an enemy or a neutral, and regardless of whether the captor was a naval ship or privateer. This bid to maintain his country's humanitarian prestige worked, at least to some degree. There were many European liberals who embraced America's rhetoric about pacific international relations. Marcy's proposal won much favorable press coverage in Europe.[66]

When the European governments rejected the U.S. plan for universal immunity, Americans were able to tell the world (and themselves) that the United States therefore had to reject the Declaration of Paris because it was *not humanitarian enough*. It immunized private property from capture only when the captor happened to be a privateer, whereas the true principle of civilization was to grant immunity universally, whether the captor was a privateer or naval ship. Americans told themselves that the Declaration's ban on commerce raiding *for privateers only* was not truly humanitarian, for it fell short of American principle and was really a cynical European effort to ban commerce raiding selectively in a way that would disadvantage the United States.[67] Dismissing the declaration as a ploy, Americans preserved their cherished self-image as the champions of individual rights and of commerce-based human brotherhood against the abuses of warring states.

## U.S. NAVAL PROFIT-SEEKING IN THE CIVIL WAR: AS ACCEPTED AS EVER

The Civil War was a turning point in many aspects of American life, but not on the issues of naval policy and naval profit-seeking. Though the United States took extraordinary temporary measures to put down secession, it did not adopt a permanent, European-style naval establishment. With no alteration of their fundamental role in the American polity, U.S. naval personnel earned their requisite shares of prize money and head money for the duration of the Civil War emergency. In general, lawmakers and the public viewed those rewards as ordinary and appropriate, as much as they ever had. The Civil War experience confirms that U.S. naval profit-seeking remained a very stable practice through-out the nineteenth century (not changing until the shock of 1898–99, which I discuss in the next section).

The Union naval war effort, if temporary, was impressive while it lasted. Up to 1861, the United States had been a relatively weak naval power, confined to commerce raiding. But the rebellious South had almost no navy whatever, plac-ing the United States in an unaccustomed position of relative strength. Accord-ingly, the U.S. government, for the first time in its history, took up the weapon of the superior power: blockade. As noted earlier, privateers' independent legal status made them useless for blockade. The Union would have to rely on its navy to carry out the task, but in 1861, that navy was not remotely big enough to cover the three-thousand-mile Confederate coastline. Therefore, the U.S. Navy, in the course of the war, purchased about 500 vessels and built about 150 more.[68] Its personnel increased sixfold.[69] As the navy swelled, the blockade grew tighter, and it ultimately played a major role in the economic destruction of the South.[70]

Still, for all its success, the U.S. naval effort in the Civil War reflected no last-ing shift in U.S. naval policy. The anti-establishment principle allowed for the massive expansion of the public armed forces, so long as they contracted just as rapidly at war's end and left behind no permanent apparatus. The Civil War fit that pattern. Once the Confederacy fell in 1865, it took only until 1867 for the U.S. Navy to shed enough personnel as to be only slightly larger than in 1861.[71] And it took only until 1870 for it to sell off or scrap more than two-thirds of its vessels.[72] By the 1870s, the U.S. Navy was fully recommitted to the traditional weak-navy strategy of the *guerre de course*.[73] Indeed, it became so weak as to be outmatched in a spat with Chile in the early 1880s.[74]

While the Civil War emergency lasted, its sheer scale meant that naval per-sonnel made a good deal of money—something that just about everybody ex-pected and accepted. As one newspaper said in looking back, "The Civil War saw the [prize money] system well established and more popular than ever."[75] Prize payouts totaled about $12 million, of which about half went to officers.[76] Dividing $6 million by the approximate number of man-years that officers spent in the four years of war,[77] we get a rough average of more than $300 per officer per year. Of course, actual prize incomes diverged greatly from this average: some ships took big prizes while others took none, and an officer's proportion increased greatly with rank. Still, the $300 average confirms that prizes were a noticeable income source. At this time, the most numerous officers were mid-shipmen, whose annual salary was $500. A lieutenant's was $1,875, and a cap-tain's $3,500.[78]

Rewards for a few officers were huge, particularly squadron commanders, who received 2.5 percent of every prize captured by the ships under them.[79] That made sense: it was the squadron commander who decided the formation and movement of the ships, which largely determined the blockade's effectiveness (and profitability). Acting Rear Admiral Samuel Phillips Lee, who commanded the North Atlantic squadron for two years in the middle of the war, implemented elaborate plans for the movement of his ships, and he adjusted the plans repeatedly to tighten the net. For these efforts, he earned at least $110,000 in prize money over two years, more than twenty times an admiral's annual salary of $5,000.[80] Lee was the record holder for prize money, but at least three other admirals and commodores broke $20,000. Captains and lesser officers could also make fortunes if they captured one or more especially rich prizes. At least ten officers of captain's rank or below broke $20,000.[81]

The widespread acceptance of naval profit-seeking was evident in Congress. The nation's legislature made frequent adjustments to the prize-money system, of the incremental kind that one expects for an institution that was largely uncontroversial. For example, lawmakers tinkered with the shares for different ranks and made improvements in procedures for adjudicating prizes and distributing proceeds.[82]

Prize money seemed to make sense. As one Civil War historian writes, it was "[t]he one big attraction that assured enough officers and men for blockade duty."[83] "Nothing gave the seamen more pleasure at sea," writes another, "than the chase of a blockade runner and the thoughts of prize money."[84] As one senator said shortly after the war, "I suppose experience has shown that [prize money] is a wise system. It stimulates the officers and crews of our vessels to make prizes."[85]

As to head money, the Civil War Congress not only preserved it but expanded it. While the existing statute granted $20 per enemy sailor, and then only if the enemy were of equal or superior force, Congress in 1864 increased the reward tenfold to $200 per enemy sailor, and it added a reward of $100 per enemy sailor for warships of inferior force.[86]

Congress further confirmed its approval of naval profit-seeking when, following the British Parliament's custom and its own practice in the War of 1812, it voted ad hoc rewards, beyond ordinary head money, for especially significant sinkings of enemy warships. Of course, there were not many of these, since the Confederacy had such a small navy. Still, the rewards that were made could be handsome. After the USS *Kearsarge* destroyed the much-feared CSS *Alabama* in 1864, Congress granted $190,000 to the officers and men (equivalent to the sunk vessel's value),[87] far exceeding the $30,000 they had initially pocketed under the head-money statute.[88] Captain John Winslow's share was $19,000, compared with a $3,500 salary.[89] Because of the crush of congressional business and some procedural mishaps, the bill had to go through Congress multiple times, but the votes confirm the broad acceptance of cash rewards for naval victories. The bill passed the House initially by a voice vote, then by a vote of 85–25, then by another voice vote, and (when finally enacted) by a vote of 90–58. It won an unrecorded vote in the Senate.[90] As the Senate committee explained, shortly before the bill was finally enacted in 1872: "[R]esponding to what we believe to be the sentiment of the country toward these gallant men, we think their services should be handsomely recognized."[91]

Naval profit-seeking in the Civil War had critics, but they were few. Leading up to the second divided House vote on the *Kearsarge* award, New York Democrat Samuel Cox declared the whole system of prize money and head money to be "a relic of past ages. There is no reason for applying it to the seas, unless you apply it to the land." Beyond this, he offered no argument against naval profit-seeking per se. Instead, he mainly argued that it was unwise to extend the system ad hoc in selected cases.[92] Cox lost this fight when the House voted to grant the *Kearsarge* award, 90–58. And the fifty-seven members who voted with Cox may well have objected to the selective and extraordinary nature of the award, not to naval profit-seeking itself.

The only other objection to naval profit-seeking per se that I can find in congressional debates of the 1860s or 1870s came in a brief and indirect comment by Senator Charles Sumner, the Massachusetts Republican and humanitarian reformer. In debate on a technical prize-law provision affecting a narrow category of captured vessels, Sumner passingly stated that, "in proportion as nations have become more civilized and more refined, [prize money] is a policy that has been drawn into doubt." But he did not press the point.[93]

Beyond Congress, a few Civil War–era newspaper editorials and letters to the editor voiced criticisms of naval profit-seeking, though it is hard to say how widely felt these were, since they received so little public attention in the legislature. One criticism—to which Cox and Sumner both adverted—was that prize money resembled piracy or plunder and was at odds with the humanitarian ideals of a progressive civilization.[94] Another criticism—which Cox also mentioned—was to point out the anomaly of giving naval personnel a percentage of seizures while denying the same to army personnel. Sometimes this was a genuine invocation of interservice equity, though it could also be simply a restatement of the civilization argument: the navy should catch up with the army's progress toward civilization.[95] A third criticism of prize money was to emphasize the randomness and inequity of the rewards within the naval service—a very old complaint dating to the mid-1700s at the latest.[96]

The nearest that critics of prize money came to changing policy, either during the Civil War or in the postwar years up to 1898, was in 1882. In that year, an anonymous naval officer drew up a bill to collectivize all future prize money and allocate it toward naval pensions, which the officer lamented were "ridiculously small."[97] Navy Secretary William H. Hunt, without endorsing the proposal, forwarded it to Congress, saying it was "entitled to consideration, as containing the views of an eminent and experienced officer in our naval service."[98] Representative Leopold Morse, a Massachusetts Democrat on the Naval Affairs Committee, introduced the bill,[99] and his committee issued a favorable report, which he wrote. Morse's argument for the change focused largely on the need to increase pensions. As for prize money itself, he said only briefly: "The progress in modern warfare, with its tendency to remove all individual and personal motive from the parties engaged therein, and to conduct it upon a plane above the baser passions, induces your committee to believe that this is a wise reform, and that it is better to rely upon the attachment of the sailor to the cause and the flag of his country than to motives which spring from the mere hope of booty."[100] Morse appended a memo from the anonymous officer, which was largely cribbed from an anonymous letter to the editor published near the end of the Civil War.[101] It made the Sumner-like argument about progressive civilization and linked it with the aspiration, articulated by Adams and Marcy, for immunity of wartime commerce. In addition, the author lamented the randomness and inequity of prize money within the navy. Also, he made the interesting argument—which did not appear in the later debates that actually led to abolition—that a blockading squadron had a perverse incentive not to capture the port it was guarding, since doing so would "kill the goose that laid their golden eggs."[102]

These arguments fell on deaf ears. The 1882 bill to collectivize prize money never came up on the House floor.[103] Apart from this bill, Congress gave no serious consideration to abolishing or curtailing naval profit-seeking until after the Spanish-American War.[104] The navy's status as a profit-seeking institution remained firmly established in the United States, as it was around the world.

## THE ABOLITION OF NAVAL PROFIT-SEEKING, 1898–99: LEGITIMATING THE NEW IMPERIAL NAVY

In the 1860s and 1870s, naval profit-seeking had frequently received the attention of the full Congress, and lawmakers' reaction was to preserve and expand the system. When such profit-seeking next received the full Congress's attention, in the winter session of 1898–99, lawmakers voted to abolish it, apparently by total consensus: the House acted unanimously, and the Senate without a roll call.[105] They acted amid applause, and with almost no debate. They took a root-and-branch approach, repealing every provision of law granting either prize money or head money (though preserving claims pending from the recent Spanish-American War).[106] They did not even permit future naval personnel to share on a collectivized basis, as the ignored plan of 1882 had proposed.

Why the big change? What happened between the early 1870s, when Congress was still voting by large majorities to grant extra rewards for successful naval operations, and 1899, when it voted—with no dissent—to obliterate even the ordinary rewards forever?

The transformation is all the more dramatic because the United States was, as far as congressmen knew, the first nation in the world to repudiate naval profit-seeking. Such profit-seeking was still the policy of the world's four largest navies: those of Britain, France, Russia, and Italy. It had been abolished in the then-small Japanese navy in 1894 (and possibly in the then-small German navy sometime after 1871).[107] But it does not appear that Americans in 1899 were aware that any nation had stopped the practice.[108]

### The Context of Abolition: Becoming a Great Power

The United States' pioneering decision to establish a non-profit navy must be understood in light of the peculiar shock that occurred in American naval policy in 1898–99 as a result of the Spanish-American War. Having shifted modestly in the direction of becoming a global naval power in the course of the 1890s, the nation in 1898–99 seized that role suddenly and permanently.

First, some background on the years leading up to the conflict with Spain. After the navy's decline in the late 1860s and 1870s, Congress started a new program of ship construction in the 1880s. But this was not much of a departure. The idea was merely to acquire a state-of-the-art version of the usual small force of commerce raiders. No capital ships. No fleet coordination.[109] Officials agreed the force would need to expand rapidly in case of a major war, and privateering remained a real possibility.[110]

In the 1890s, the nation began to move in a fundamentally new direction, though quite slowly at first. A growing movement of politicians and naval officers became convinced that the United States should more actively engage in global affairs and therefore must acquire a navy nearer the British model, that is, a fleet of capital ships capable of fighting big battles, winning command of the sea, and blockading a serious naval power. The key figure in this movement was Alfred Thayer Mahan, a U.S. naval officer at the War College, who published best-selling books on British naval history during the 1890s and was soon renowned as the world's leading naval theorist. According to Mahan, Britain owed its status as the world's richest and most powerful state to its naval strategy (the *guerre d'escadre*), which he presented as vastly superior to the *guerre de course*. To his American audience, Mahan portrayed a Darwinian world in which nations following the British model could get ahead in the struggle for global markets while others fell behind.[111]

Consulting with Mahan, Navy Secretary Benjamin Tracy in 1889 made a path-marking request to Congress for money to build capital ships. Congress granted the money for four such ships, though it gave them the contradictory and misleading label "sea-going *coast-line* battleships," allowing congressmen to tell their constituents (and even themselves) that the vessels were defensive, not instruments of global ambition. Tracy's successor in 1893–97, after Mahan's books converted him to the *guerre d'escadre*, sought and won funding for five more ships of the same type (and label).[112] In a related development, U.S. Navy ships in 1894 began seriously practicing fleet coordination for the first time.[113] Altogether, average real annual naval spending was 62 percent greater from fiscal 1889–90 through 1896–97 than it had been during the pre-capital-ship building program (fiscal 1882–83 through 1888–89).[114] This was a large increase, but no quantum leap. The United States in 1898 was still behind Britain, France, Russia, Italy, and Germany.[115]

Then came war with Spain. Though neither Congress nor the public could have been sold on a transparent program of overseas expansion, events in the nearby Spanish colony of Cuba led the United States to war under a more selfless rationale. Cubans in 1895 began a fight for independence against their Spanish rulers. In response, the Spanish army in 1896 forced Cuban civilians into concentration camps, where they suffered starvation and disease, resulting in deaths that historians today estimate at one hundred thousand.[116] This atrocity caused outrage in the United States, including demands for intervention. Then, in February 1898, the USS *Maine*, on a customary visit to Havana, exploded. A U.S. naval court of inquiry found (probably wrongly) that a submarine mine had been the cause. U.S. newspapers screamed for war as soon as the *Maine* exploded, and the court's finding only strengthened their demand. Meanwhile, Senator Redfield Proctor, a Vermont Republican of "impeccable conservative credentials," returned from a fact-finding mission to Cuba and gave the Senate a horrifying account of the camps. Many moderates, who had previously been the key group resisting war, changed their minds, swayed by Proctor's highbrow credibility.[117] "In place of a dubious vengeance" for the

*Maine,* says one historian, Proctor "offered war founded on an undiluted humanitarianism."[118]

Under congressional and public pressure to intervene in Cuba, President McKinley in April 1898 asked Congress for authority to do so, emphasizing the humanitarian issue. Congress passed a resolution granting McKinley's request, though it added a disclaimer of imperial ambitions, dubbed the Teller Amendment, forswearing "any disposition or intention to exercise sovereignty, jurisdiction, or control" over Cuba." The Teller Amendment "lent substance to the claim that the United States intended to intervene in Cuba solely on disinterested moral and humanitarian grounds."[119]

Though the United States had finished building only four capital ships, the Spanish navy was so small and decrepit that the Americans were in a position of superiority. The U.S. Navy therefore prosecuted the *guerre d'escadre,* with Mahan dominating the War Board that directed strategy from Washington.[120] The Americans established a blockade of Cuba (to deny supplies to Spanish forces) and sought command of the sea. The U.S. government announced it would commission no privateers. The new strategy made them unnecessary. When Spain's small fleet arrived in the Caribbean, the U.S. fleet bottled it up in Santiago Bay, achieving command of the sea, thus making the blockade invulnerable and allowing the U.S. Army to travel safely to the island. When the Spanish ships ventured from the bay weeks later, the U.S ships destroyed them in battle. The U.S. Army's victory in Cuba came soon after. In addition, the Americans sought to force Spain's surrender by taking its other colonies. With command of the Caribbean, U.S. forces occupied Puerto Rico. Meanwhile in the Pacific, a squadron of U.S. ships, under Admiral George Dewey, had attacked the Philippine Islands, easily destroying the weak Spanish force defending them, and a single U.S. ship had taken the strategically located island of Guam. Spain surrendered in mid-August 1898.[121]

The war, initiated as a humanitarian project, ended up destroying the American anti-establishment tradition—suddenly, decisively, and permanently. It precipitated the acquisition of several overseas possessions, thus committing the United States to a continuous role in the global rivalry of European empires, which required a quantum leap in U.S. naval power.

Start by considering the acquisitions overseas. First came the Hawaiian Islands. Their white-dominated government had been asking for U.S. annexation since the early 1890s, which the Americans had refused. But the war with Spain—especially Dewey's seizure of the Philippines and the consequent need to hold them at least for the duration of the conflict—suddenly made the absorption of Hawaii strategically necessary. Congress passed the annexation measure a month before Spain surrendered.[122] Second, Puerto Rico and Guam had gone unmentioned in the run-up to war, but they seemed too valuable strategically for the United States to relinquish. As peace negotiations began in the summer, McKinley immediately demanded both islands.[123] Third, there was Cuba. It was of great importance strategically, though the Teller Amendment disclaimed annexation. Still, the U.S. war resolution had not recognized the Cubans' rebel government. This allowed the U.S. Army to occupy the island indefinitely, and even when independence was formalized in 1902, the Americans made Cuba into a U.S. satellite.[124] Fourth, there were the Philippines. Their remoteness from North America and their large, independence-seeking population made them costly to hold. Yet abandoning them, in the view of many, would simply allow some ambitious power—Germany, Britain, or Japan—to conquer them, leaving the United States with a worse situation in the Pacific than before the war.[125] And though businessmen had been reluctant about going to war in the first place,[126] many changed their minds once the Philippines were in American hands, for the archipelago was a gateway to Asia.[127] McKinley deliberated on the question for several months, finally deciding by November 1898 that his country must take the islands.[128]

Meanwhile, debate erupted throughout the United States over the nation's sudden overseas expansion.[129] As Congress convened in December, McKinley presented it with the treaty annexing Puerto Rico, Guam, and the Philippines. After bitter debate, focusing on the Philippines, the Senate in early February 1899 barely ratified the treaty by the required two-thirds majority.[130] Even after ratification, popular dissent continued and grew.[131]

America's overseas expansion of 1898–99 was unlike the nation's prior acquisitions on the North American mainland. The new territories were not to be settled by migrants from the preexisting states and absorbed into the U.S. polity. Instead, they were subject possessions, usable mainly in global imperial rivalry. They made the United States a central player in the control of a future Central American canal and of Pacific Ocean commerce.[132]

This meant a transformative naval buildup, and this time it was permanent, unlike in the Civil War. Holding the new territories required a much bigger navy. The territories, in turn, provided the bases that made a global navy possible. And victory in the war with Spain had strengthened politicians' faith in the *guerre d'escadre*. Congress responded dramatically. In its first postwar session (winter 1898–99, the same session in which it abolished naval profit-seeking), it provided funding for "a [naval] building program larger than that of any previous single year." The next year, it dropped the word *coast-line* from the labels of the capital ships, underscoring their global purpose.[133] Naval building skyrocketed. Take as a baseline the total real naval appropriations for the eight fiscal years when the United States built capital ships prior to the war's start (1889–90 through 1896–97). For the eight fiscal years after the war's end (1899–1900 through 1906–07), the comparable total was three times higher.[134] In 1898, the United States had possessed only four capital ships, and its navy ranked sixth in the world. By 1907, it had twenty-two capital ships, and its navy was second only to the British.[135] Privateering was now a thing of the past. Acquiring overseas possessions massively increased the importance and power of the U.S. Navy; unsurprisingly, U.S. naval officers generally supported such acquisitions.[136]

### The Abolition Measure Itself: A Sparse Official Record

It was at this crucial turning point—amid the advent of a huge permanent naval establishment that naval officers supported and from which they benefited—that Congress abolished naval profit-seeking. It did so with no dissent and little discussion. Let us briefly consider this sparse official record.

The abolition measure was incorporated into a more general naval personnel bill that originally said nothing about prize money or head money. Back in November 1897, months before war seemed likely, the Navy Department had convened a board of officers to draft a bill making personnel reforms (1) to integrate the separate corps of line officers and engineering officers, (2) to equalize salaries and wages between the navy and army, and (3) to introduce merit into the promotion system by retiring the "least fit" officers when necessary to ensure that others could reach the high ranks before growing too old.[137] (Note that this last measure would make a difference mainly in peacetime: historically, the executive already possessed authority to promote officers for success in combat.)[138] The House Naval Affairs Committee held hearings on the bill in April 1898, as war neared. It reported the bill, largely in its original form, about a month after the war started. The bill, the hearings, and the report all ignored prize money and head money.[139] Congress went home in July, shortly after the victory at Santiago.

Congress returned in the winter of 1898–99. By then, the Navy Department had issued an extensive postwar report that covered personnel issues, but it did not address prize money or head money.[140] Meanwhile, the full House took up the naval personnel bill in January 1899. Its floor manager was George Edmund Foss, a Chicago Republican and ardent supporter of a big navy, particularly as an instrument to open foreign markets.[141] (In the very next session, he would begin a twelve-year run as chair of the Naval Affairs Committee.) In going over the bill, Foss made the lengthiest comment on the abolition of naval profit-seeking that appears in the official public record: "[W]hen we reach this section in the bill I propose to offer a substitute abolishing the distribution of prize money in the Navy. [Applause.] I may say for the naval officers that they consider prize money a mere bagatelle. It amounts to but little. In the press it is exaggerated one hundred times more than it is worth, but we propose to abolish it in this bill, and I may say that we have the support of all the naval officers to that proposition."[142]

Foss did indeed offer his amendment, and the House adopted it by a voice vote, which the *Washington Post* reported as "unanimous."[143] The House ultimately passed the whole bill by voice vote.[144] In the Senate, nobody even commented on the bill's abolition of naval profit-seeking, and the bill passed, without a roll call, on February 17.[145]

Foss's comment—our biggest nugget of legislative history—is not very helpful. The most significant thing is the "[a]pplause" for abolition, which indicates that congressmen and observers were paying attention to naval profit-seeking and cared about ending it. Yet Foss left unstated the affirmative reason to terminate prize money. He said merely that naval officers did not oppose abolition, without saying why abolition was desirable to begin with. His claim that prize money was a "bagatelle" was not really an affirmative reason to terminate it. Payouts to naval personnel for the Spanish-American War were indeed much lower than in the Civil War (about $300,000),[146] but that was largely because the war was short (less than four months) and the scope of trade interdiction narrow (mainly to Cuba, since the Philippines fell so early). Future wars might be longer and geographically broader (as in fact they were). As to head money, the rewards under the general statute did turn out to be rather low in 1898. (Dewey won the biggest sum, equal to four times his salary for his one battle, but nobody else came close.)[147] But Congress had the power to vote extra sums of head money, beyond the general formula, as it had done in prior wars. Congress in 1899 was clearly in no mood to continue that practice, thus rendering head money a "bagatelle," but that begs the question: why did lawmakers no longer approve of naval profit-seeking?

### The Popular Discourse against Naval Profit-Seeking: The Need for a Selfless Navy

Though the legislative record is nearly silent, the popular discourse of 1898–99 tells us far more. Popular media like newspapers, magazines, and speeches expressed overwhelming opposition to naval profit-seeking. Congressmen's herdlike support of the abolition measure presumably means that, as elected officials, they were following this popular view.

Demands for the end of naval profit-seeking are best understood as part of a larger project to legitimate the revolutionary imperial expansion (and requisite naval buildup) that was occurring simultaneously. Throughout the nineteenth century, Americans had generally viewed their anti-establishment tradition and their liberal humanitarian tradition as twin bulwarks of a distinctly republican foreign policy, embracing peace and rejecting the destructive rivalry of the European powers. The years 1898–99 marked the sudden collapse of the anti-establishment tradition. This conjured the old specters of alien imposition, which now materialized into reality: a big permanent naval establishment, a higher tax burden, an empowered officer class, and entanglements with global imperial rivalries threatening to draw America into big wars.

Proponents of the new military establishment sought to legitimate it by reasserting the other, still-living American tradition of foreign policy—liberal humanitarianism. In particular, they sought to build trust in the new militarized state by declaring that its *motives* were consistent with the liberal humanitarian dreams of old. They insisted that America went to war and governed subject peoples only to further humanity and civilization, to put down barbarism, and for other such selfless reasons. The idea was to present the new empire and its military establishment, not as a self-seeking aggressor inviting the aggression of others, but as a disinterested regime worthy of trust, that would, in its own way, maintain the pacific and progressive vision of international relations that republicanism had always counseled.

Abolishing naval profit-seeking was essential to this project. It removed a glaring inconsistency in the image of the U.S. military as selfless and civilizing. It terminated the direct monetary interest that naval officers had in fomenting war. And it fit closely with a revival of U.S. interest (which occurred simultaneously) in immunizing property from capture on the high seas, raising hope that war, even if it became more likely, would be ever more confined in its destructive scope.

*The Collapse of the Anti-Establishment Tradition and Anxiety about Alien Imposition.* Let me begin this analysis by documenting fears in 1898–99 of the ways in which the new military establishment might intrude on the lives of Americans and take away their autonomy. I shall rely particularly on the statements of the minority of politicians and opinion leaders who opposed overseas acquisition and naval buildup, for I believe that (1) the majority who accepted the new establishment felt the need to present it in such a way as to answer this critical minority, and (2) the fears articulated by the critics were probably felt inwardly by many pro-establishment types, who needed to overcome these fears to justify the new regime to themselves.

First, critics correctly noted that the acquisitions of 1898–99 would drive the nation to build a much bigger navy. The United States, warned the former U.S. House Speaker and Treasury secretary John Carlisle, would now require "such a permanent increase of our naval establishment as will keep it constantly upon a war footing."[148] This meant the federal government would have to squeeze the public harder for taxes. "As has been said of the army-and-navy ridden countries of Europe," predicted Carl Schurz, the former U.S. senator, "every American worker, when at his toil, will have to carry a soldier or sailor on his back."[149]

Most dangerous was the likelihood that the United States' new status as an expansive naval power would draw it into European imperial rivalry, effectively relinquishing the people's right of self-determination. "Here on our own continent," explained Carlisle, "we are not only free from molestation by other powers, but free also from any obligation or interest to participate in their quarrels or wars abroad; but the adoption of the imperial policy of conquest and annexation . . . will at once precipitate us, wholly unprepared, into the vortex of European and Asiatic complications." "The great questions of peace and war," he concluded, "will no longer be determined exclusively by a consideration of our own interests or the judgment of our own people, but by the controlling influences of European intrigues and coalitions."[150] Critics predicted the United States would be forced into a treacherous alliance with Britain.[151] (Indeed, navalists like Mahan did want a British alliance.)[152] America's "entrance upon the stage in the Far East," cautioned Andrew Carnegie, "will not be welcome to any but Britain, and that . . . for British purposes only."[153] "British statesmanship," observed Schurz, "has sometimes shown great skill in making other nations fight its battles. . . . I should be loath to see . . . the American Navy in the situation of a mere squadron to the British fleet."[154]

Whether it had allies or not, the United States would surely invite new enemies. American adventures beyond the Western Hemisphere, argued William Jennings Bryan, would upset the equilibrium of the Monroe Doctrine: when the United States intruded on Europe-dominated regions, the Europeans would intrude on America's backyard.[155] Charles Towne, the former congressman and national leader of the Silver Republicans, summed up the whole problem: "To set up a colonial system is to be ready to trade peace for war, to surrender serenity and security for a state of armed anxiety and weakening incertitude. It is to mix up in alien quarrels, . . . at precisely the time when by all indications they are about to culminate in the most colossal and destructive war of modern times."[156] Taking the Philippines, said Senator Augustus Bacon of Georgia, would put the United States "in danger at any time of being involved in a world's war."[157]

To critics, the imperial navy was not to be trusted. Despite the formalities of democracy, such an institution was not really amenable to democratic control. Because of arms races, governments were forced by their competitors to build up their navies. As Schurz lamented, referring to warships, "[W]e shall . . . be in the situation of those European powers, the extent of whose armaments are determined, not by their own wishes, but by the armaments of their rivals."[158]

As to the personnel of this expanding navy, the civic republican suspicion of professional military officers, though most prominent in the eighteenth century, was still very much alive at the end of the nineteenth century. In 1894, the assistant secretary of the navy attributed congressional neglect of the navy to "that natural prejudice against professional military organizations which always exists, more or less, in republics."[159] In 1898, Carlisle warned of how imperialism could aggrandize the military in American domestic politics: "[I]f we are to adopt and successfully maintain an imperial policy, the glory of the achievement will belong principally to the army and navy. . . . [T]he almost inevitable result will be that their social and political influence will grow until they overshadow all other callings and professions. Military Senators and Representatives in Congress will enact laws for a military President to execute."[160]

Critics warned of the officers' personal interest in imposing war on the United States. Democratic Representative Henry Johnson, in a speech given shortly after both chambers had passed the abolition measure, noted reports that McKinley had agreed to Philippine annexation at the urging of Admiral Dewey. Johnson insisted that Dewey's advice was no justification for McKinley's decision, for the "predilections" of the "officers of our Regular Army and Navy" were "naturally for arms." Military officers, attested Johnson, "have imbibed . . . the prejudices and the preferences of their calling. We can not blame them for desiring to magnify the size and importance of the Army and Navy; for advocating the expansion of our territorial limits and the taking on of a colonial policy. Such a departure will open up to them opportunities for promotion and for honorable service and distinction which they could not otherwise enjoy. For this very reason, their advice as to our national policy should be received with caution."[161] As the president of Stanford University wrote, "A large army and navy must justify itself by doing something. An army and navy we must maintain for our own defense, but beyond that they can do little that does not hurt, and they must be used if they would be kept alive."[162]

*Using Liberal Humanitarian Motives to Legitimate Military Establishment and Empire.*   Those who supported overseas war, acquisition, and naval buildup sought to persuade the public to accept these things on the ground that the motives of the government and the military were selfless, in keeping with the long-standing American discourse of humanity and civilization against savagery. Concerns about new forms of state power were met with assurances of the good motives for which that power would be used.

This was evident in the initial decision to go to war with Spain. Politicians and opinion leaders fervently professed America's selfless mission to vindicate civilization over barbarism. The centrality of such rhetoric is undeniable, and many historians judge that a huge amount of it was sincere.[163] In his war message of April 1898, McKinley proclaimed that, in confronting the Cuban crisis, "I speak not of forcible annexation, for that can not be thought of. That, by our code of morality, would be criminal aggression." Yet Spain's treatment of Cuba had, "by the exercise of cruel, barbarous, and uncivilized practices of warfare, shocked the sensibilities and offended the humane sympathies of our people."[164] The "primary reason why the United States initiated the war," says Warren Zimmermann in a recent account, "was human rights."[165] Responding to McKinley's message, congressmen espoused the same thinking. According to Senator John Spooner, "We intervene to put an end to savagery."[166] Senator George F. Hoar proudly foresaw "a war in which there does not enter the slightest thought or desire of foreign conquest or of national gain or advantage.... I want to enter upon it with the sanction of international law, with the sympathy of all humane and liberty-loving nations, with the approval of our own consciences, and with a certainty of the applauding judgment of history."[167]

Such rhetoric was necessary to reconcile the war with the nation's historic aversion to European-style overseas aggression. Said Schurz: "[I]f the war had been announced as a war of conquest the American people would most certainly not have consented to it."[168] The conflict, he explained, "was to be simply a war of liberation, of humanity, undertaken without any selfish motive.... If a republican nation can undertake any war without injury to the prestige of democracy as an agency of peace, it is such a war of disinterested benevolence."[169]

When the United States concluded its "selfless" war with large overseas acquisitions, proponents of the move loudly reasserted the progressive motive that had begun the war and sought to extend it to a new "civilizing" mission among the Filipinos. McKinley insistently, even defensively, rehashed the war's high motive. The "humanity of our purposes and the magnanimity of our conduct have given to war, always horrible, touches of noble generosity, Christian sympathy and charity," he proclaimed in October 1898. "Passion and bitterness formed no part of our impelling motive."[170] Some historians view Philippine annexation as a devious plot hatched before the war started, while others consider Dewey's sudden victory an unforeseen event, which the U.S. government awkwardly accommodated by annexation.[171] In either case, annexationists had reason to make their professions of moral purpose as convincing as possible. McKinley, as "the main promoter of annexation of the Philippines," emphasized "humanitarian themes."[172] In February 1899, he insisted that the Filipinos were not in a position to govern themselves effectively, making it inhumane for U.S. forces to abandon the islands: "Our concern was not for territory or trade or empire, but for the people whose interests and destiny, without our willing it, had been put in our hands." In fighting Spain and thereby taking control of the islands, "We were doing our duty by them [the Filipinos], as God gave us the light to see our duty, with the consent of our own consciences and with the approval of civilization," performing "a great act of humanity." Annexation notwithstanding, "[n]o imperial designs lurk in the American mind. They are alien to American sentiment, thought, and purpose. Our priceless principles undergo no change under a tropical sun."[173]

But could liberal humanitarian motives really legitimate the United States' embrace of military establishment and empire? Numerous Americans cried no: the motives for this shift were not humanitarian, but selfish and aggressive. They were the exact same sordid motives that actuated the European powers. In this view, the postwar acquisitions perverted the original humanitarian justification of the war or revealed it to have been a fraud from the start.

While McKinley and his allies tried to present the new empire as continuous with Americans' ideal of progress in international relations, critics insisted that empire reversed the progressive American tradition and forced the nation back to a less civilized, more barbarous, and more European stage of development. Towne, after praising the original intent of the war, bemoaned the subsequent acquisitions:

> Ah! what a fall is here, my countrymen. Within the circuit of a single year to have declined from the moral leadership of mankind into the common brigandage of the robber nations of the world.
>
> The contest out of which it is claimed there comes to us this Christian duty of slaughter and subjugation [in the Philippines] began nobly. Not since the devoted manhood of Europe in holy enthusiasm vowed to redeem the tomb of the Saviour from the pollution of the infidel has history witnessed so chivalrous and unselfish a war as that which was commenced by the people

of the United States to free the island of Cuba from the tyranny of Spain. It was not to be a war of conquest. Orators in and out of Congress pictured in glowing colors the disinterestedness of our action.[174]

Yet this selfless war had ended in self-interested conquest, which was anathema to the republic's tradition: "[W]hat can empire offer us? A rivalship with swaggering kingdoms seeking loot and license of their weaker neighbors, snatching our share of plunder that we do not need, marching back three centuries over the fallen and shattered idols of our storied progress, earning the fear of every victim and the jealous hatred of every rival . . . ?" Should the United States become an empire, "[i]t will be ours eternally to bear the odium of having stopped the car of progress and turned it backward."[175]

The question of governmental motive was at the center of this controversy. Though annexationists insisted that their motives were selfless, critics condemned those motives as material and rapacious, drawing comparisons with theft and plunder. "The wrongs of the poor Cuban are forgotten," observed former Vice President Adlai E. Stevenson, "and the dream of the imperialist is now of untold commercial gain."[176] America's enemies and detractors, according to Schurz, were crowing: "'We told you so!'"—"'That is what the unctuous rectitude of the Anglo-Saxon always ends in. He always begins by calling heaven to witness his unselfish desire to help his neighbor, but he always ends up stealing his spoons!'"[177] Hearing the argument that the United States could not abandon the Philippines, since some other empire would simply conquer them, Representative Johnson restated the point sarcastically: "[W]e were obliged to commit grand larceny of the Philippines in order to prevent the great European nations from committing the crime."[178] Senator Hoar proclaimed: "I deny this alleged right of conquest. Human beings—men, women, children, peoples—are not to be won as spoils of war or prizes in battle. It may be that such a doctrine finds a place in the ancient and barbarous laws of war. But it has no place under the American constitution."[179]

To the critics of overseas expansion, the departure from initial war aims was destroying trust in the U.S. government, both among the American people and among foreign nations. While Bryan strongly supported the initial humanitarian intervention, he warned that Americans would "find it difficult to meet the charge of having added hypocrisy to greed" if "a contest undertaken for the sake of humanity degenerates into a war of conquest."[180] "What could our answer be," asked Schurz, "if the world should say of the American people that they are wolves in sheep's clothing, rapacious land-grabbers posing as unselfish champions of freedom and humanity . . . ?"[181]

*Abolishing Naval Profit-Seeking to Build Up the Credibility of Selfless, Humanitarian, and Pacific Motives.*   Against this background, naval profit-seeking was a great embarrassment to the proponents of the imperial navy. It undermined the notion of selflessness. It gave the navy a sinister ulterior motive for aggressive war. And its historical association with older practices of booty-seeking and privateering clashed with any attempt to associate empire with progressive humanitarianism.

When the United States set out to rescue Cuba in April 1898, its first military actions to appear in the press were U.S. naval captures of Spanish merchant ships in the Caribbean. The Philadelphia journal *City and State*, edited by the civic reformer and eventual anti-imperialist Herbert Walsh, argued that such prize-taking tainted the war's professed purpose:

> We hear many justifications of this war from the Christian pulpit. We are told that it is a war of righteousness and liberation. . . . But if it is a holy war, and in accordance with the Christian spirit, why do we not keep it so far as possible in line with that idea? Why permit our seamen to receive "prize money," which is nothing but a survival of the idea of piratical plunder, which on land is justly obsolete? Soldiers who rob the houses of private persons, even in the enemy's country, are subject to severe punishment. Such conduct was permitted in former times, but it is contrary to military ethics now. The spoils of which our sailors cruising off the Cuban coast propose to divide are the property not of the Spanish Government, but of private persons who are the unhappy victims of this war, and not the authors of it. If the bravery of our sailors is due to love of their country and desire to free the Cubans, why mix these high motives with those which inspire the activity of Kurds in Asia Minor or Apaches in the Sierra Madre?[182]

According to the *New York Times*, "the moral sense of the great mass of the [American] people who feel that in setting out to make Cuba free we have undertaken a noble duty is shocked by this eager chase after private property [i.e., Spanish merchant ships], the capture of which appears . . . to be of advantage only in so far as it fills the pockets of the captors with prize money."[183] The *Springfield Republican*, an influential paper, echoed the point: "Overhauling harmless merchant craft" was "inglorious for a nation going to war for an idea"—"our able seamen ought to be actuated in the war to free Cuba by higher motives than greed for prize money."[184]

As the war unfolded, newspapers continued to point out the tension between profit-seeking and the war's ostensibly selfless aim. When one admiral self-interestedly argued that certain ships had been captured by his own force and not by the U.S. Army, the *Washington Post* opined that it was "not such an incident as would furnish nice material for elegant literary embroidery in a history of this war for humanity."[185] "In no war of the past," added the *Post*, "has this ugly inheritance from darker ages appeared so incongruous as it does in this war for humanity."[186] The "prize system in the navy," echoed the *Detroit Free Press*, is "utterly inconsistent with the high grounds of justice and equity on which this government claims to stand."[187]

It was not only the self-interested seizure of others' property that seemed incongruous with humanitarian war motives, but military profit-seeking in general, including the quest for head money. The "head money law," said the *New Haven Register*, "grates upon the nerves of a nation that is claiming to wage a war in the name of humanity."[188] An article in the *National Magazine*— after quoting the line from Byron's *Don Juan*, "Revenge is sweet, especially to women, / Pillage to soldiers, prize money to seamen"—observed that the "avowed policy of the United States in entering upon this war was that it should be for humanity, not for revenge; for the cause of civilization and liberty," but then noted that prize money and head money lived on, despite the disappearance of similar practices on land.[189]

For the majority of politicians and opinion leaders who supported not only the war but also the subsequent imperial program, it was important to resolve this tension between naval profit-seeking and their professed belief in the progressive purpose of war and empire. They resolved the tension by urging abolition of the naval rewards. I believe that such efforts at self-justification, whether fully conscious or not, underlay the outpouring of rhetoric against prize money and head money that occurred in popular media in 1898–99. From everywhere, one heard that naval profit-seeking was barbarous, piratical, savage, and medieval, and that it was anathema to civilization, enlightenment, humanity, progress, and the "spirit of the age." This thinking preserved the postmillennial concept of progress in international relations that went back to the early nineteenth century. (That the pro-imperial majority supported abolition as a measure to legitimate its own program did not mean that anti-imperialists opposed abolition. They, too, would have reason to support abolition, since it would make America's dreaded imperial future somewhat less awful. This helps explain why published opinion on naval profit-seeking in 1898–99 was virtually all negative.[190])

The annexationist *Washington Post* was a leader in developing the civilization-based critique of naval profit-seeking.[191] Such profit-seeking, said the *Post* in one of many editorials on the issue, was "a survival of the middle ages, when

all Christendom was in a state of war; when battle, foray, pillage, and spoliation was the rule on land and sea. . . . Long ago the spread of civilization and
humanity abolished it in the armies of the world, but it still holds a place in our
naval scheme, to its unutterable reproach and shame. . . . It puts us back a century in the march of humanity and enlightenment."[192] It was "out of harmony
with the age."[193]

Many other newspapers took up the same theme. The *Springfield Republican*
condemned the "navy prize rules" as "relics of more savage days," "hostile to the
spirit of the age."[194] The *Syracuse Post* counseled that the system be "relegated
to the past. It smacks too much of piracy to be tolerated by the civilization of today."[195] The *Philadelphia North American* called it "a relic of barbarism which
should have no recognition in the articles of war of an enlightened state."[196]
Prize money and head money, attested the *Omaha World Herald*, were "hardly
proper in this advanced and enlightened age."[197] The *Dallas Morning News*
dubbed the system a "scandal to civilization."[198] The *New Haven Register* found
the system "half savage in its spirit of encouragement and almost brutal in its
instinct."[199] To the *Hartford Courant*, prize money was "a late-lingering survival
of the times in which captured cities were immediately given over to sack and
pillage, and the victorious soldiers cut the throats of their prisoners, held them
for ransom, or sold them as slaves."[200] Perhaps the favorite epithet of newspaper
editors was to say that naval profit-seeking was a "relic of barbarism,"[201] a "relic
of the days of piracy,"[202] or the like.[203]

Giving a commencement address a few months after the abolition measure,
McKinley's attorney general listed the measure as one of the "Advances in
Jurisprudence in the Nineteenth Century," along with such achievements as
the amelioration of England's bloody code and Lincoln's emancipation of the
slaves. He considered naval profit-seeking "[a]nother relic of a ruder system and
more ancient time."[204]

Significantly, Philadelphia's leading Republican newspaper, the *Press*,[205]
seized upon the House's passage of the abolition measure as a refutation of anti-
imperialist critics who asserted that the United States had betrayed its liberal
humanitarian tradition. The measure, declared the *Press*, "is as important an
act in the history of civilization as any for a generation. It begins a great reform. It places the United States again in the van of progress and improvement
in international law. Once more, as in the past, just as a host of loud-voiced
critics are asserting that this country is smitten with a brutal and rapacious appetite for territorial plunder, the House takes one of those disinterested steps
which ameliorate war, advance humanity, and promote human progress."[206]
The *Washington Post* understood the House's action in the same way: "This

republic has always occupied an advanced position in efforts to not only prevent war, but to mitigate its evils. Our recent victories have not changed our national character in this respect."[207] The *Philadelphia North American* announced that the measure "marks a distinct advance in our methods, and it will undoubtedly serve to increase the high opinion of our progress and enlightenment among the nations of the world."[208]

Foss, the navalist congressmen who (as noted above) was most directly responsible for the abolition measure, partook of this popular line of thought. He had published an article on the naval personnel bill in December 1898, in which he telegraphed his plan to abolish naval profit-seeking and gave more of an affirmative reason for it: "[T]he provision of our laws permitting the allowance of prize money to our naval officers in time of war should be repealed, as it is entirely inconsistent with the spirit of the age and of modern naval warfare, and remains simply and purely a relic of barbarism."[209] "Spirit of the age" and "relic of barbarism" were key phrases in the postmillennial rhetoric of the newspapers. And nonprofit status, as a guarantee of disinterestedness and civilization, fit closely with Foss's vision of the imperial U.S. Navy. Consider a speech he gave in April 1900, little more than a year after the abolition measure, defending naval spending:

> [W]e are building our Navy for civilization. This country embarked in the war with Spain for purposes of freeing the suffering Cubans from the tyranny of Spanish rule. . . . What their [the Philippines'] future may be I do not know. Perchance we may annex them permanently to ourselves, or we may civilize them until they arrive at that stage of civilization and of progress where they can erect a government of their own. . . .
>
> This I know, that our duty is now clear; our duty is to civilize those people [the Filipinos], and toward that end there will be ten thousand ministering angels, [including American missionaries, teachers etc.]. . . . I say that the American battle ship, that never bore a commission of duty but what it carried a message of hope, will do more to civilize these people than the ten thousand sweeter and gentler influences which mold the minds of more civilized people. [Applause.][210]

A few years after the abolition measure, people looking back remembered it as resulting from a popular groundswell of humanitarian sentiment. The peace activist Benjamin F. Trueblood, at an international conference in 1907, recalled that the "outcry against the capture of Spanish merchant vessels was so great in the early stages of the Spanish War that our Parliament [i.e., Congress] was compelled by the force of public sentiment to abolish all prize money."[211] The retired U.S. Supreme Court Justice Henry Billings Brown (a onetime admiralty lawyer), who was among the tiny number of public figures to express opposition to the abolition measure, recalled in 1909 that "a wave of humanity suddenly" had taken "possession of Congress" and caused it to pass the reform, on the basis of "sentimental principles."[212]

It seems that naval officers themselves, amid the sudden increase in their power and importance in 1898–99, felt relieved that the public would have less reason to mistrust their motives. As we have seen, Foss attested to the officers' universal support of the abolition measure. So did former Assistant Navy Secretary Theodore Roosevelt, Naval War College President Charles Stockton, and Massachusetts Representative Samuel Barrows.[213] Consistent with this, there is evidence that naval officers before 1899 worried that the public might distrust them as being warmongers. Addressing the Social Science Association in 1895, Commander Caspar F. Goodrich — soon to be president of the War College — felt quite defensive about the issue: "You may, and doubtless will, be surprised to hear that I express the serious opinion of the navy, as a whole, in deprecating war. The service is . . . full of energetic officers who would quickly profit by any offered chance to distinguish themselves through valorous acts of seamanship and tactics; but of officers who would welcome war *because* of such opportunities there are extremely few. . . . [B]elieve me, we are not blood-thirsty Jingoes."[214] Shortly after the war in 1898, when Senator Henry Cabot Lodge was researching his book on the conflict, he found that, during the tense months preceding the war, Captain A. S. Crowninshield, one of the top war planners in Washington, had been instrumental in devising the scheme by which Dewey was ordered to assemble his ships in the Pacific, setting up the fateful battle that placed the Philippines in U.S. hands. When the imperialist Lodge sought to credit Crowninshield and his fellow planners for this highly successful move, the captain asked him not to, fearing it might make naval officers seem too eager for war — "put us in a light of being almost over-prepared — in other words it might seem that the [Navy] Department had as early as February 25 . . . made up its mind and that there was to be a war anyway," even though McKinley was, at the time, still trying to reach a peaceful settlement of the Cuban crisis.[215]

Former Representative Barrows, a Boston Republican and peace activist who had voted proudly for the abolition measure, declared that it would render the navy less war hungry: "To render war less probable, it is important to remove the motives and excuses which lead to it. The abolition of prize money is an important step in this direction."[216]

*Abolishing Prize Money to Reassert the American Commitment to Immunity for Property on the High Seas.* The abolition measure was a broad one that covered both prize money and head money, thus severing all direct links between monetary self-seeking and military combat. Its breadth was necessary to address the whole range of anxieties about national motives and naval warmongering. However, the abolition measure also had a more particular implication as applied specifically to prize money (as distinct from head money): it was, in the view of many, a step toward realizing the long-standing American hope, originated by Monroe and Adams, of immunizing property from capture on the high seas.[217] In all the world's great navies, the incentive of prize money encouraged such captures. The United States' elimination of that incentive, it was thought, would reduce and ameliorate captures. Consistent with this, McKinley in December 1898 asked Congress for authority to negotiate an international agreement for immunity. He did so "to please the peace movement."[218] (As in 1856, the other powers would demur, but nobody knew that until after Congress abolished U.S. naval profit-seeking.)[219]

Proposals for high-seas immunity had always been key to the broader vision of sparing noncombatants from the harms of war. In the late nineteenth century, this vision was the object of great interest. As armed forces became more professionalized and technologically expert, observers predicted and hoped that future wars would be confined to confrontations between those forces, leaving civilians alone. Obviously, World War I and World War II would make a mockery of this prediction, but prior to 1914 it had much credence. Its believability in the naval sphere rested in part on laymen's misunderstanding of the *guerre d'escadre*. Whereas Mahan in fact considered blockade (which could starve a civilian population) essential to this strategy, ignorant lay observers focused on the strategy's emphasis on the fleet battle, which they misinterpreted as a chivalric duel that would by itself settle the dispute between belligerent governments, without either side ever imposing harm on civilians. Representative Frank Gillett, a Massachusetts Republican, articulated this view when arguing in favor of high-seas immunity in summer 1898: "[W]hile [war is] growing ever more terrible and more destructive within its sphere, that sphere ought ever to be growing narrower and wars growing shorter; more destructive momentarily to the actual combatants, but less exhausting to the nation and the world. This has been the history of the development of war, and it is along these lines only that we can aid in future development."[220] Such predictions about the progressive limitation of war—rendered more credible by McKinley's immunity proposal and Congress's abolition of prize money—encouraged Americans to believe that, even as their nation built up its military and became more active abroad, future wars were unlikely to harm *them* personally.

The aspiration to spare noncombatants fit nicely with American pretensions of humanitarian purpose in 1898–99. Urging his government to grant high-seas immunity unilaterally for the duration of the war with Spain, Gillett said the "United States has always aspired to lead the van of [international humanitarian] enterprises such as this, and what more fitting occasion to take a step in the interest of civilization and humanity than a war of which civilization and humanity were the cause?"[221] The Washington lawyer Charles Henry Butler, a leading advocate of immunity, presented the immunity proposal as part of the inexorable amelioration of war, in which America's selfless rescue of Cuba was a milestone: though "[w]ar for humanity's sake sounds ridiculously inconsistent," the United States had been "compelled to take up the sword in the cause of humanity" and "for no other purpose whatsoever."[222]

Americans trumpeted the abolition of prize money—which they believed no other country had undertaken—as a symbol of American leadership on immunity that would lead the world toward a more pacific and humane order. Gillett made the point strongly: "The whole system"—the right of capture and the related right to prize money—"should be ended. And, in ending it, we are the nation which should take the lead. . . . We must do so to be consistent with what is our constant endeavor as well as our boast—to lead the world in progress and civilization." The nation had to "show that in adopting the barbarity of war we do not forget our mission of progress and civilization."[223] The International Law Committee of the American Bar Association predicted that "[d]oubtless the time will come when the principle for which Mr. Marcy contended in 1856 [i.e., immunity], will be adopted by all nations," and in the meantime, the United States ought not to give its naval personnel "a subvention of what is really the legalized plunder of the individual property of citizens of the country with which it is at war."[224] In a 1903 discussion of immunity, the incoming U.S. solicitor general, Henry M. Hoyt, cited Congress's abolition of prize money as "illustrating . . . the advanced attitude at all times of the United States."[225] Many friends of immunity welcomed prize money's abolition as "a great step in the right direction," in Butler's words.[226] The lawyer and scholar Charles Chauncey Binney cast abolition as "one of many steps" in "the advance of civilization," and one that would "probably lead in time to the immunity of all private property from capture on the high seas."[227]

*The Ironic Conclusion: How the Naval Establishment Used Selflessness to Legitimate Total War.* Casting prize-money abolition as a stepping-stone to the immunity of property on the high seas was comforting. It allowed Americans to believe they were progressing toward a world of more limited wars, which, in turn, made the rise of their own military establishment seem less threatening. But this argument was believable mainly to lawyers and newspaper editors, not to naval officers. Such officers may not have cared much about prize money, but they did care about winning wars, and they were in a better position than laymen to understand that victory required destroying not just the enemy's military but its civilian economy, now more than ever. Yet such officers were still inclined to support the abolition of prize money, because they knew that, if they remained financially interested in economic warfare, it would be hard for anybody to trust the arguments they were making for a new level of state imposition—approaching total war—that many Americans found terrifying.

In 1898–99 and the following years, there may not have been complete consensus among U.S. naval officers as to whether immunity was a good or bad idea,[228] but surely many of the most influential officers were against it.[229] At the vanguard of these anti-immunity officers was Mahan himself, the master U.S. naval strategist.[230]

At first glance, it might seem odd that naval officers after 1898 would cling to the right of capture on the high seas. After all, the *guerre d'escadre*—which the U.S. Navy embraced in the 1890s—focused on the blockade of enemy ports, which would be excepted from high-seas immunity. Yet even devotees of the *guerre d'escadre* had good reasons to fear the high-seas immunity proposal. First, high-seas immunity rested on a moral argument that private property deserved protection from warring governments. That argument, taken to its logical culmination, would proscribe blockade, too. Mahan repeatedly warned about this possibility, and other observers were aware of it.[231] Second, the feasibility of a traditional blockade—of the kind prosecuted by Britain in the War of 1812 and Crimean War and by the Union in the Civil War—was increasingly uncertain, given new technologies like submarine mines. Around 1900, strategists began gravitating toward a modified approach known as "distant blockade," in which the interdicting ships would patrol bottlenecks on the sea-lanes leading to the enemy coast, rather than planting themselves immediately off its ports. (This is exactly what Britain did to Germany in World War I.) This approach was still consistent with the *guerre d'escadre*, for it required command of the sea and tight coordination among ships. Legally, however, it was incompatible with high-seas immunity, since the distant patrols were on the high seas.[232]

Fearful that the long-standing American dream of immunity (if actually implemented) would hobble U.S. strategy, Mahan and several of his fellow officers campaigned against it, articulating a strategic vision that approached modern total war. As early as 1894, Mahan published an article rejecting the liberal humanitarian notion of a "private" sphere of individual rights beyond the reach of imposition by a war-making government. "[P]rivate property borne upon the seas," he insisted, "is engaged in promoting, in the most vital manner, the strength and resources of the nation by which it is handled." "[I]s it not clear," he asked, "that maritime commerce occupies, to the power of a maritime state, the precise nourishing function that the communications of an army supply to the army? Blows at commerce are blows at the communications of the state; they intercept its nourishment, they starve its life, they cut the roots of its power, the sinews of its war. While war remains a factor . . . of our history, it is a fond [i.e., vain] hope that commerce can be exempt from its operations, because in very truth blows against it are the most deadly that can be struck."[233] When liberal humanitarians mounted a campaign for high-seas immunity after Spain's surrender in 1898, Mahan publicly opposed them, writing to the *New York Times* with essentially the same total-war argument in November of that year.[234]

As Mahan's dispute with the humanitarians unfolded, he enlisted the help of his War College associate, Commander Charles H. Stockton, a specialist in international law.[235] At Mahan's urging, Stockton published a rebuttal of the immunity advocates, which appeared in February 1899, just as the prize-money abolition measure was nearing passage.[236]

In writing this piece, Stockton explained what he (and Mahan) considered the critical U.S. strategic interest in destroying the enemy's economy.[237] Further, he pointed out that the nation's acquisition of overseas possessions—which he and Mahan endorsed[238]—counseled in favor of maintaining the widest possible bounds for the exercise of its war-making capacity: "To-day, when we are gradually assuming, by the extension of our insular territories, . . . the role of a great possible belligerent, it behooves us to examine closely all such questions [of belligerent rights], and to study them in their relation to ourselves, and to our future complications in the arena of the world. We should not hastily restrict our war powers."[239]

Stockton's piece was risky. His argument for economic warfare went against American humanitarian ideals. And the connection he drew between that argument and the nation's new possessions made it seem that the nightmare version of the imperial navy had become real: the navy acquired new territory, thereby making the nation more warlike, in a never-ending cycle.

Such unfamiliar and dangerous-sounding arguments for the most disturbing kinds of alien imposition would be nonstarters unless U.S. naval officers could build up some degree of trust in their audience. That is where the abolition of prize money came in. At the very opening of his article, Stockton emphasized his support for ending such profit-seeking: "To prevent any misapprehension, I would add that I favor the repeal of any laws that give to naval officers any prize money from the capture of enemy merchant vessels at sea." At the article's conclusion, he said it again, this time adding, "I have endeavored to show that the practice [i.e., capture] should be continued upon its merits as a military measure"—that is, as a thing good for the United States, not for naval officers personally.[240] In a political culture wary of naval aggrandizement, naval officers had to display their disinterestedness, if they were to establish the authority and trust necessary to win public acceptance of the powers they considered necessary to winning wars, particularly the right of capture. As the *Nation* said in response to Stockton, the commander "obviously" disclaimed support of prize money "because he perceives that until the prize-money laws are repealed, there will always be a sinister pecuniary interest affecting the settlement of the controversy" over the right of capture.[241]

In the long run, U.S. naval officers favoring total war prevailed. The U.S. proposal for immunity at the 1899 Hague Peace Conference was peripheral to the agenda, and one of the U.S. delegates was Mahan, who worked to ensure it would not go far.[242] In 1905, a conference of naval officers drew up proposed regulations on maritime war that largely (if subtly) rejected the idea of immunity.[243] To be sure, the U.S. government remained nominally supportive of immunity at the 1907 Hague Conference. But by that time, a top board of naval officers had officially recommended against the reform. The secretary of state and possibly President Roosevelt privately agreed with them. One of the U.S. delegates to the conference was Admiral Charles Sperry, who opposed immunity. Mahan himself, still in the U.S. Navy and acting with Roosevelt's permission, publicly argued against immunity in the British press. Ultimately, the immunity proposal failed to garner the necessary support from other countries, just as many top U.S. Navy men predicted and hoped.[244] As the American public became acclimated to great-power status, its ardor for liberal pacifist doctrines subsided at least somewhat[245]—a testament to the rising legitimacy of the (nonprofit) navy.

When total war finally arrived, in World War I, the United States was a full participant. In 1914, Britain imposed a distant blockade on Germany. It was the tightest campaign of trade interdiction in history—a "starvation blockade" that caused the deaths of an estimated half million German civilians. During the United States' years of "neutrality" (1914–17), President Wilson essentially supported Britain and therefore acquiesced and even cooperated in Britain's starvation strategy. This provoked Germany to initiate unrestricted submarine warfare, sinking neutral merchant ships on sight—exactly the kind of reciprocal escalation of war against civilians that American critics of military establishments had always feared.[246] Submarine attacks, in turn, brought the United States into the war, making the nation a full partner in the starvation blockade. To be sure, Wilson told himself he was engaging in a great-power war only to force a peace settlement that would forever replace such wars with a new liberal internationalist order, including "freedom of the seas." But the United States' prosecution of total war did not, in fact, produce that result. The 1918 elections gave the chairmanship of the Senate Foreign Relations Committee to the militarist yet anti-internationalist Henry Cabot Lodge, who thought it insane to sign away the belligerent rights that had crippled Germany. At Versailles in 1919, Wilson did not even try to win "freedom of the seas."[247]

The abolition of naval profit-seeking was important, in the context of an American political culture wary of military establishments, for winning mass acceptance of this kind of naval power. Mahan himself acutely understood how monetary self-seeking could delegitimate the formidable governmental powers he considered strategically necessary. In 1906, he wrote that the "opprobrium" attached to war against trade was "probably due largely to the practice of prize money."[248] The following year, he published an essay urging Britain (which he considered the most important U.S. ally) not to relinquish the right of capture, and this at a time when the British navy still had prize money. In his essay, Mahan elaborated on the issue of self-seeking, noting that the naval captors' individual gain—historically associated with piracy—had made it difficult for people to understand that capture was really the act of the interdicting *state*, to degrade the practical war-making capacity of the enemy state. "Prize money," said Mahan, had thus unfortunately become "to popular apprehension the exponent, as it were, of maritime capture in war. It summed up the ethics, and the practical aspect, of the system from which it derived. . . . Prize money was the robber's gain, maritime capture the robber's trade, the sufferer the robber's victim." As Mahan saw it, people had begun with an aversion to individualized piratical self-seeking and transferred that aversion to state-level seizure. He believed that such transference was illogical, calling it an "inconsequence" (non sequitur). Still, he thought it "extremely human."[249]

Indeed it was. It exemplified the human tendency to distrust those who exercise power when they are known to have a narrow self-interest in its exercise. Congressional abolition of that self-interest in 1899 was an important step in building public trust in a navy that, ultimately, did more to prosecute the total wars of the twentieth century than vindicate the humanitarian dreams of the nineteenth.

## Managerial Explanations and Why They Are Inadequate

The cluster of reasons for abolishing naval profit-seeking that I have discussed so far—all involving the buildup of legitimacy and trust in a newly empowered but humanitarian navy—were the most prominent ones that appeared in public discourse in 1898–99. Here I consider another possible cluster of reasons for abolition: managerial ones. By *managerial*, I mean having to do with the technical "fit" between bounty-seeking and the navy's internal organizational structures, as opposed to the navy's place in the American polity.

As discussed in previous chapters, there is a common view in social science that associates purely salaried jobs with incumbents' career stability and their subjection to top-down control. Career stability was indeed the norm for naval officers in 1899. But it had been the norm since the early nineteenth century, in stark contrast to the quick turnover in America's spoils-ridden civilian administration.[250] This makes it hard to see the reform of 1899 as part of an effort to provide naval officers with more stable careers. I have seen no affirmative evidence for such an interpretation.

Top-down control merits more attention as a potential explanation, not so much in itself as part of a larger set of concerns about whether prize money had become irrationally misaligned with the kind of official behavior the navy wanted to encourage and reward. Newspapers in 1898–99 occasionally raised the argument that prize money had become irrational and should therefore be terminated. For example, the *Washington Post*, in addition to the legitimation arguments discussed above, called prize money "a demoralizing lottery, in which a few may happen to draw great prizes, while others, equally meritorious, may serve all their lives and not draw a cent."[251]

Despite these occasional newspaper comments, I do not think we can explain the events of 1898–99 as a reaction to some perceived irrationality. Admittedly, the irrationality problem may explain similar reforms that occurred later in other countries, and it may mean that the United States inevitably would have banished the profit motive from its navy sometime in the first half of the twentieth century, even though the actual and proximate cause in 1898–99 was the navy's crisis of legitimacy.[252]

The distribution of prize money and head money was surely uneven, but that was the whole point: an incentive reward system normally produces uneven results. Of course, such a system may be irrational if its payouts misalign with the effort and skill of the payees in meeting the organization's objectives. Yet the degree of alignment or misalignment can be difficult to measure. James Stephen in 1806 thought prize money an "efficacious policy" that motivated "much of the vigilance, activity, and enterprise, that have so long characterized the British navy."[253] Yet by Stephen's time, there had long been complaints that each ship's reward depended largely on whether the Admiralty assigned it to a more or less favorable cruising ground.[254] Some viewed prize money as efficacious and others thought it arbitrary, but on balance, the British government maintained it.

Had anything changed shortly before 1898 to aggravate the misalignment between payouts and achievement of organization objectives? One might argue that the U.S. Navy's concerted shift toward the *guerre d'escadre* rendered the arbitrariness of prize money more extreme or more salient, since ships on blockade duty had less autonomy than under the old regime of solo commerce-raiding missions. (This would fit the oft-posited connection between salaried jobs and top-down control.) Yet blockade duty still required officers and seamen to be constantly vigilant, to react quickly, and to chase successfully. Offering incentives for success arguably made sense. Crucially, the nineteenth century had witnessed three tightly coordinated and highly effective blockades without the blockading power abolishing prize money: the British blockade of the American coast in the War of 1812; the British blockade of Russia in the Crimean War of 1854–56; and the Union blockade of the South in the Civil War. The brief and small-scale blockade of Cuba in 1898 was not particularly new or different. (The Crimean War and Civil War had already seen steamships, and the U.S. Navy did not even begin to take wireless communication seriously until 1912.)[255] In light of this, it is hard to believe that prize money was inherently incompatible with blockade as it existed in 1899.[256]

If some change in naval strategy, tactics, or technology had rendered prize money less rational than before, one would expect the reform to originate among naval experts and pass through official channels. But that did not happen. An expert board of U.S. naval officers had spent the winter of 1897–98 drafting and submitting a bill to overhaul the navy's personnel system, yet that bill ignored prize money. Officers testifying on the bill in April 1898 said nothing about the matter.[257] Nor did the Navy Department's official report of December 1898.[258] The reform occurred through an amendment on the House floor, offered amid "[a]pplause" and adopted without debate or dissent. The discourse surrounding it, as we have seen, was moral, not managerial.

Further, if the abolition measure had been part of a rationalization process that was overtaking the U.S. Navy in 1898–99, one would expect other countries with more advanced navies to have undertaken the reform earlier. Yet each of the world's four largest navies in 1899 still awarded prize money.[259]

Of these foreign countries, the most striking case is Britain, whose navy departed from profit-seeking through an expert-controlled, incremental, and cautious process extending from the 1910s to the 1940s. If we take Britain as the gold standard of rationality in the naval sphere (as we should), it becomes clear that the American reform of 1899 is better understood as a popular and moralistic measure, not a rationalizing one.

The British navy was by far the largest and most advanced on earth. In 1900, it had more than twice as many capital ships as its nearest rival,[260] and it was master of the *guerre d'escadre*. The British were the world's experts in naval warfare. Moreover, the incentives of their officers and seamen were firmly under expert control. In contrast to the United States, where prize money and head money were established (and abolished) by legislative act, Parliament had long since delegated complete control over naval rewards to the cabinet,[261] effectively to the Admiralty.

In the years shortly after 1899, the experts who controlled British naval incentives showed no inclination to abolish profit-seeking. The government issued a new set of regulations in 1900 that reaffirmed prize money.[262] When the French delegate to the Hague Conference in 1907 proposed a nonbinding resolution disapproving prize money, the British delegate opposed the measure, noting that prize money had "certain advantages in the eyes of the British authorities, which they deem it wise to retain." (The resolution failed.)[263]

However, at that time, the British navy was undergoing rapid changes that would render it even more centralized and internally specialized than before. The Admiralty in London was beginning to direct all ships at sea with unprecedented precision, through wireless telegraphy. The British navy had mastered the wireless by about 1907 (well before the U.S. Navy even began to take it seriously in 1912).[264] Further, the Admiralty at this time was seriously considering the "distant blockade" that it would ultimately prosecute in World War I,[265] in which the bulk of the navy focused on bottling up the enemy fleet in port, while a small number of cruisers caught all prizes at the narrow points on the sea lanes. Under these conditions, the division of labor within the British navy would be more minute, and the ships would be under tighter control, than in any nineteenth-century blockade by Britain or the United States.

Against this background, the parliamentary secretary of the Admiralty in 1911 told the House of Commons that awarding prize money to individual ships had come to seem problematic. He suggested that the Admiralty in a future war would use its discretion to "pool" the proceeds of prizes and distribute them to the whole fleet, though it would reserve the power to make awards ad hoc for particularly meritorious captures to individual cruisers.[266]

When Britain declared war on Germany in 1914, the cabinet adopted the pooling arrangement.[267] The Admiralty's parliamentary secretary said it would be "more equitable."[268] According to one peer, the scheme made sense because "all prizes" were now "equally due to the vigilance of the whole Navy."[269] A naval officer wrote in a commentary that pooling was the only "just" alternative now that ships' duties were so specialized and "by far the larger part of the fleet was debarred by the nature of its duties from taking part in the safe, easy work of capturing prizes, and the consequent sharing of profits."[270] Another officer emphasized not only specialization but also the coordinated activity of ships across wide expanses: under "modern conditions," the "taking of a ship in prize might well be dependent on operations which were taking place hundreds of miles away."[271]

The British pooling of prize money in 1914–18 differed from the U.S. measure of 1899, which had abolished the navy's right to prize money altogether, even on a collective basis. The U.S. approach, I would argue, reflected congressmen's moral and political aversion to prize money, beyond the more technical concern of the British about inequitable distribution. On this point, consider the words of Lord Beresford, formerly a top admiral, in defense of naval personnel's (collectivized) right to prize money in 1918: "There have been some remarks made in the press that the wish for prize money [even if pooled] is a sordid wish; that the men ought not to demand it. I do not see why the men should not have this benefit [i.e., their pro rata shares from the pool] the same as those of any other profession."[272] That some of the British press thought it "sordid" to distribute prize money even on a pooled basis reveals that, by completely obliterating naval prize money (rather than pooling it), the U.S. Congress in 1899 had taken a moral stand against the practice, not simply made a technocratic adjustment. (Note that British shares from the pool were not peanuts: about £4,000 for an admiral, £800 for a captain, and £25 for a seaman, at a time when seamen's wages were £40 per year.[273] Pooled or not, these were the profits of starving the Germans.)

The British in World War I also differed from the U.S. approach in another respect: the British preserved head money, without even pooling it.[274] "Human nature being what it is," said one commentator in a British military journal, "some such inducement to active pressure on the enemy is decidedly politic."[275] Shortly before the war, one member of Parliament, while praising the U.S. measure of 1899 for abolishing prize money, specifically criticized the Americans for going too far in abolishing head money.[276] In total, the head money arising from World War I would amount to £176,850.[277] To be sure, the crews of modern British ships had grown so large that individual payouts were mostly small. But the officers and seamen of British submarines—which had small crews and attacked big enemy ships—won large sums.[278] The British government would abolish head money only in 1948, and even then, the debate witnessed a former admiral and former captain opposing the reform. Unlike in America in 1899, there was no consensus against profit-seeking among British naval professionals.[279]

That Britain in 1914 preserved individual head-money awards even while pooling prize money confirms that the U.S. measure of 1899 — which abolished all forms of naval profit-seeking in one fell swoop — was not simply a response to the imperatives of rational military organization. At least one American newspaper in 1899 had endorsed head money while disapproving prize money,[280] but the moral and political imperative to obliterate all naval profit-seeking swept away both, without distinction. The United States, unlike Britain, was going through a wrenching political transition toward great-power status, creating a legitimation crisis that led to a more sweeping reform than the surgical British approach.

# EPILOGUE

## The Salary Revolution and American State-Building

The salary revolution in American government consisted of two distinct though simultaneous transformations, one involving facilitative payments, and the other bounties. Lawmakers replaced facilitative payments with salaries for two main reasons. First, they found officer-layperson bargaining to be fatally inconsistent with republican and liberal principles, and when their attempt to preserve exchange on a regulated basis failed to stamp out bargaining, they abolished exchange altogether. Second, democratic politics saw the rise of mass interest-group rivalry, which made it untenable to have officers cater to a particular "customer class." Meanwhile, lawmakers replaced bounties with salaries for one main reason: they were making unprecedented assertions of legislative power, and after experimenting intensely with bounties as instruments to effectuate those assertions, they concluded that such rewards were so poisonous to the officialdom's legitimacy and to the public's trust as to undermine the mass voluntary cooperation necessary to the modern state.

Social science often casts the salary as one element in a package of intra-organizational features fitting the ideal type of bureaucracy, the other two being that the official enjoys career stability and is subject to top-down control. As I have noted throughout the preceding chapters, this is not an adequate way to understand the triumph of salaries in American government. Though some instances of salarization coincided with the advent of career stability and top-down control, this was very far from universal. Quite often, career stability and top-down control never came at all, or came by a gradual and halting process that only began after the causes I emphasize—the aversion to bargaining, mass interest-group rivalry, legitimation—had already put salaries in place.

That American lawmakers banished the profit motive for reasons independent of bureaucratization resonates with a larger theme in American political development: that the American state differs profoundly from the ideal type of modern bureaucratic government, constructed by Max Weber, to which most other big, rich democracies conform more nearly. Weber's ideal type is a centralized, hierarchical body whose members, hired according to technical qualifications, spend their careers at the institution, climbing the rungs of the promotion ladder. In American government, by contrast, we observe frequent departures from centralization, hierarchy, instrumentally rational hiring, and lifelong civil service careers. In America, power is often fragmented and dispersed to autonomous state governments (even in many "federal" programs) or to autonomous localities (even in many "state" laws). The jurisdictions of agencies are overlapping and crosscutting. A huge number of administrative officials are elected, which makes it hard to keep them under hierarchical control and prevents them from viewing their jobs as permanent careers. Even when appointed, officials often owe their jobs to politics and patronage, and they frequently enter and leave public service through a "revolving door" that leads to the private sector or to the hustings. Even when an agency is internally structured along the lines of Weber's type, America's separation of powers means the agency must answer to multiple masters (legislature and chief executive), so it cannot achieve the role (envisioned by Weber) of simply implementing the value choice made by an external actor. As a recent essay puts it, America has "a different kind of state."[1]

As noted by the sociologist Elisabeth Clemens, scholars typically treat the nonbureaucratic aspects of American government "as the residue of the past, the sticky, less-than-rational predecessor of the modern bureaucratic state."[2] In this view, the bureaucratic ideal has always been the goal of right-thinking, reform-minded people—a goal that every rich democratic nation should reach.

If we tend to view the features of American government that depart from the bureaucratic blueprint as residue and failure, the flip side is that we tend to view the features that *do* conform to the blueprint as the unfinished product of an aborted undertaking, like the foundation or frame of a house whose builder never added the walls or the roof. But to understand the American officialdom's salaried status in this way would be a terribly impoverished view. That status is not the product of some clumsy and incomplete effort to imitate Prussia. Rather, it was (and is) a direct and perhaps necessary response to some of the deepest factors in American political life: republican values like anti-monopolism; liberal values like legislative supremacy, plural interest-group rivalry, and the effort to build a voluntarist and cooperative relation between state and civil society. These factors are at least as characteristic of America as of any other country. Conversely, one suspects that the factors driving salarization in other countries were not, in fact, all reducible to the project of bureaucratization but instead resonated with some of the values prevalent in the American story.

The history suggests that you can recognize the value of nonprofit government even if you are indifferent or hostile to bureaucracy-building more generally. This is significant, for "bureaucracy" has long had negative connotations in American public discourse, especially amid the aversion to "big government" that has been prevalent for about the past four decades. In the 1992 best seller *Reinventing Government*, which typifies the past generation's critical rhetoric on public administration, David Osborne and Ted Gaebler announce "The Bankruptcy of Bureaucracy." They condemn all the principal features of the Weberian ideal type—not only top-down control and lifelong bureaucratic careers but also the absence of the profit-seeking spirit.[3] The wholesale banishment of bureaucracy, in their view, points toward a new era of flexibility, responsiveness, innovation, energy, and entrepreneurship in public service.

A difficulty with this view—apart from the authors' ignorance of how far American government already departs from the bureaucratic model—is that it lumps together American government's nonprofit status with a variety of other (supposedly bad) institutional features that actually have no ironclad connection with it, logical or historical. To the extent that our government is insulated from the profit motive, it is wrong to view that insulation as an import of European statism, suppressing some inherent entrepreneurial spirit just waiting to be unleashed. Americans are an entrepreneurial people, but they are also a people whose other values—such as anti-monopolism, interest-group pluralism, and voluntarism—counsel the separation of the profit motive from the state under modern conditions.

A related point: the recent decline in bureaucracy's cachet encompasses not only public agencies but also private businesses. The rhetoric of private management for several years has favored smaller, flatter, less centralized firms; greater flexibility; and sharper incentives. Skepticism of bureaucracy in the provision of public services is part of a larger disillusionment with bureaucracy that transcends the public-private divide.[4] (When Weber constructed the ideal type of bureaucracy, he thought it "applicable with equal facility to a wide variety of different fields," public and private.)[5] If our belief in a nonprofit officialdom rises and falls with our faith in bureaucracy, then there is nothing to stop us from importing to the public sector the latest thinking on the private sector. Indeed, leading scholars urge us to think about privatization as if the government were a private firm faced with the choice of whether to "make or buy" a service.[6]

There is something to this, but we must be cautious. The imperatives that historically drove salarization in America were especially and sometimes exclusively directed at *public* offices—at their peculiarly monopolistic status, at their unique control of scarce public resources subject to rival democratic claims, or at their distinctive mission to foster the population's cooperation and support for legislative mandates. Our forebears' experience counsels us against automatically applying private-sector thinking to the public sector, and it highlights some of the most important factors that distinguish the two—and that can help us in developing a distinct way to think about *public* organizations.

Insofar as public organizations provide services to individuals who want them, there is a natural tendency to analogize such individuals to the customers of a private firm. But the historical experience shows how generations of lawmakers came to reject that analogy, viewing it as unworkable in light of liberal-republican imperatives to prevent monopoly exploitation and ensure equality of treatment—and to acknowledge and honor the rival interest-group claims to public resources that characterize a modern democracy.

Insofar as public organizations seek to ensure the population's compliance with legal mandates, there is a tendency to model such compliance as a function of public agents' enforcement activities: if you incentivize officers to engage in a certain amount of enforcement activity, that will produce a certain level of deterrence and (therefore) a certain level of public obedience. But the history shows that the very lawmakers who first imposed modern legislative mandates en masse found such a model inadequate, for it ignored the fact that deterrence is rarely sufficient and that laypersons accept law in part because they come to view the officialdom as a legitimate and reasonable body deserving at least a modicum of trust, not as an opponent to be outsmarted. In building that trust, the incentives furnished to government enforcers have an expressive or symbolic effect distinct from their effect on the enforcers' behavior and its effect (in turn) on laypersons' fear of being caught and punished.

Altogether, the salary is not merely an intra-organizational feature that government should adopt or reject for the same reasons that a private firm would consider. Rather, the salary has, through a long process of trial and error, become integral to the vindication of liberal-republican values, the honoring of plural interest-group claims, and the popular acceptance of legislatively enacted programs in a democratic society. To be sure, history never stops: the value we place on these things may change, and so may their connection to the salary. But if we are to evaluate the absence of the profit motive in American government, we must take account of the historical freight that the salary has acquired through its role in the development of American democracy.

# APPENDIX: PUBLIC PROSECUTORS' DATES OF TRANSITION FROM FEES TO SALARIES, BY JURISDICTION

Below are the dates of transition to salary for public prosecutors in every state and territorial jurisdiction in the continental United States (omitting Virginia, because its statutes on this point are impenetrably confusing). I list jurisdictions in three categories, according to their pre-salary compensation schemes: (1) conviction fee jurisdictions, which I define as those with fees only for conviction, or with fees for conviction that were at least double the fees for acquittal; (2) case-based fee jurisdictions, which I define as those with fees in no way contingent on conviction; and (3) leftover jurisdictions, that is, those not fitting either of the two preceding categories. For documentation supporting my assignment of jurisdictions to the conviction fee category and to the case-based fee category, see Chapter 7, text at notes 6–21 and 50–73. In the leftover category, I give a brief description of each jurisdiction's pre-salary compensation mechanism in the entry for that jurisdiction; the endnote for each such entry documents not only the salarization date but also my description of the pre-salary compensation scheme.

## 1. CONVICTION FEE JURISDICTIONS

- *Alabama*: statewide 1887[1]
- *Arizona*: several counties 1885; rest of territory 1893[2]
- *Arkansas*: statewide 1937[3]
- *California*: San Francisco 1856; rest of state, county by county, up to 1907[4]
- *Colorado*: capped statewide 1891; fully converted to salary statewide 1919[5]
- *Florida*: statewide 1895[6]
- *Georgia*: most judicial circuits 1916–33; rest of circuits circa 1930s to 1950s[7]
- *Illinois*: statewide 1913[8]
- *Indiana*: Allen County (Fort Wayne) and Vanderburg County (Evansville) 1907; St. Joseph County (South Bend) and Vigo County (Terre Haute) 1911; Marion County (Indianapolis) 1921; rest of state 1931[9]

- *Kentucky*: commissions on fines capped 1892; all public prosecutors met cap "without effort" by 1960 at the latest; formal salarization 1976[10]

- *Louisiana*: Orleans Parish 1916; rest of state, parish by parish, 1924–50[11]

- *Mississippi*: statewide 1890[12]

- *Missouri*: St. Louis County (misdemeanors) 1866; St. Louis County (felonies) 1869; Jackson County (Kansas City) 1893; a few more counties 1907–13; in the remaining counties, the legislature reduced the importance of fees by greatly increasing salaries in 1919 and formally instituted pure salaries in the late 1940s[13]

- *New Jersey*: the legislature converted all public prosecutors to salaries through local acts in 1874–80, but in 1884 the state supreme court invalidated all the acts for violating procedures on special legislation; the legislature then converted all the public prosecutors again, through a series of local acts; all were on salary by 1919[14]

- *New Mexico*: statewide 1913[15]

- *North Carolina*: statewide 1923[16]

- *Oregon*: Multnomah District (containing Portland) 1898; rest of state 1899[17]

- *South Carolina*: statewide 1877[18]

- *Tennessee*: statewide 1897[19]

- *Texas*: fees capped in 1897, though in the 1910s the legislature loosened the caps for some large counties; it then transferred public prosecutors to salaries by a byzantine series of local acts; all were on salary by 1949[20]

- *Washington*: territory-wide 1881[21]

- *West Virginia*: fee payments capped and made discretionary with county boards 1908; abolished altogether statewide 1915[22]

## 2. CASE-BASED FEE JURISDICTIONS

- *Connecticut*: statewide 1879[23]

- *Dakota Territory*: territory-wide for most prosecutions 1883 (statutes somewhat unclear)[24]

- *Delaware*: statewide 1871[25]

- *Iowa*: statewide 1886[26]

- *Maine*: statewide 1839[27]

- *Maryland*: Baltimore County converted to salary de facto circa 1870s; Cecil County 1892; rest of state, county by county, circa 1902–20[28]

- *Massachusetts*: Suffolk County (Boston) 1822; rest of state 1832[29]

- *Nebraska*: statewide 1867[30]

- *New York*: New York City 1821; rest of state, county by county, 1838 to circa 1880s[31]

- *Pennsylvania*: Philadelphia County, Allegheny County (Pittsburgh), and Luzerne County 1874; rest of state 1905[32]
- *Rhode Island*: statewide 1852[33]
- *Vermont*: statewide 1859[34]

### 3. LEFTOVER JURISDICTIONS (NOT FITTING EITHER CATEGORY)

- *Idaho*: Legislature initially offered conviction fees, then switched to case-based fees in 1881, then converted to salaries in 1887[35]
- *Kansas*: Fees were payable (1) by defendant if convicted or (2) by complainant if prosecution unwarranted. In liquor prosecutions, fees payable only by convicted defendant. Legislature converted all public prosecutors to salaries in 1899,[36] but preserved conviction fees for liquor well into 1900s
- *Michigan*: Legislature authorized board of each county to decide compensation of its public prosecutor, which boards "generally" structured as an "annual salary"[37]
- *Minnesota*: Pure salaries from creation of the territory in 1849[38]
- *Montana*: Initially, legislature authorized case-based fees with small conviction bonuses (no more than half the case-based fee); legislature deleted conviction bonuses in 1889 and converted to salaries in 1891[39]
- *Nevada*: Substantial salaries from the outset, but also conviction fees for selected offenses like gambling and vagrancy; legislature converted individual counties to salaries by local acts from 1880s into 1900s[40]
- *New Hampshire*: A statute of 1789 clearly contemplated payment of some kind of fees but did not specify them; a statute of 1824 provided for compensation to be set by the judge but did not specify whether it was fee or salary; by 1843, pure salaries were in place[41]
- *Ohio*: not entirely clear, but it seems public prosecutors were paid by salaries by 1815 and never had any fees[42]
- *Oklahoma*: Pure salaries from creation of the territory in 1890[43]
- *Utah*: Fees were payable (1) by defendant if convicted; (2) by complainant if no probable cause for the prosecution; or (3) if neither of the above, by county, but this was optional, and only up to half the fee; legislature adopted salaries territory-wide in 1874[44]
- *Wisconsin*: The territory was created in 1838, but I have been unable to locate any relevant statutes prior to statehood in 1848, by which time public prosecutors were already on pure salaries[45]
- *Wyoming*: Initially, legislature authorized case-based fees with small conviction bonuses (no more than half the case-based fee); legislature salarized several counties in 1877 and rest of state in 1879[46]

# ABBREVIATIONS

**AG Report [year].**   Annual Report of the Attorney General of the United States for [year].

**ANB.**   *American National Biography Online*, ed. Susan Ware et al. (New York: Oxford University Press, 2000–, updated semi-annually), http://www.anb.org.

**ATRCF.**   America: Two Returns of Customs Fees, 1751–1771, Treasury Records T 64/45, National Archives of the United Kingdom, Kew. Note: This item is two series of papers. The second starts over at page 1. In each citation to this item, I first list whether it is the first or second series, then a colon, then the page number.

**Gates, *History*.**   Paul W. Gates, *History of Public Land Law Development* (Washington, DC: Government Printing Office, 1968).

**Gates, "Homestead Act."**   Paul W. Gates, "The Homestead Act: Free Land Policy in Operation, 1862–1935," in *Land Use Policy and Problems in the United States*, ed. Howard W. Ottoson (Lincoln: University of Nebraska Press, 1963), 28–46.

**Gates, "Homesteading."**   Paul W. Gates, "Homesteading in the High Plains," *Agricultural History* 51 (1977): 109–33.

**Glasson, *FMP*.**   William H. Glasson, *Federal Military Pensions in the United States* (New York: Oxford University Press, 1918).

**GLO Report [year].**   Annual Report of the Commissioner of the [U.S.] General Land Office for [year].

**GPO.**   [U.S.] Government Printing Office.

**Hearings (1845).**   *Reports of the Committee on the Judiciary of the Senate of the United States . . . with Testimony Relating to the Violation of the Naturalization Laws*, S. Doc. No. 28–173 (1845). Note: Some copies of this source were printed with no title page, but all have the same publication number and pagination.

**Hearings (1864).**   *New York Custom-House*, H.R. Rep. No. 38–111 (1864).

**Hearings (1865).**   *New York Custom-House*, H.R. Rep. No. 38–25 (1865).

**Hearings (1867).** *New York Custom-House*, H.R. Rep. No. 39–30 (1867).

**Hearings (1874).** *Moieties and Customs-Revenue Laws: Evidence before the Committee on Ways and Means Relative to Moieties and Customs-Revenue Laws*, H.R. Misc. Doc. No. 43–264 (1874).

**Hearings (1884).** *Testimony Taken by the Committee on Expenditures in the Department of Justice*, H.R. Misc. Doc. No. 48–38, pt. 1 (1884).

**Hearings (1891).** *Investigation of Certain Alleged Illegal Practices of the United States Courts*, H.R. Rep. No. 51–3823 (1891).

**Hearings (1892).** *Alleged Illegal Practices Connected with the United States Courts, and Abuse of Judicial Process*, H.R. Rep. No. 52–1966 (1892).

**Hearings (1911).** *Hearings before Subcommittee of House Committee on Appropriations Consisting of Messrs. J. A. Tawney, W. I. Smith, George R. Malby, J. J. Fitzgerald, and Swagar Sherley in Charge of Sundry Civil Appropriation Bill for 1912* (Washington, DC: Government Printing Office, 1911).

**Hearings (1923).** *Investigation of Veterans' Bureau: Hearings before the Select Committee on Investigation of Veterans' Bureau, United States Senate, Sixty-Seventh Congress, Fourth Session, Pursuant to S. Res. 466*, 2 vols. (Washington, DC: Government Printing Office, 1923).

**HSUS.** *Historical Statistics of the United States, Earliest Times to the Present: Millennial Edition*, ed. Susan B. Carter et al. (New York: Cambridge University Press, 2006), online edition at http://hsus.cambridge.org.

**Md. Arch.** *Archives of Maryland*, ed. W. H. Browne and others, varying in subsequent years, 72 vols. (Baltimore: Maryland Historical Society, 1883–1972).

**NC Recs.** *The Colonial Records of North Carolina*, ed. William L. Saunders and others, varying in subsequent years, 30 vols. (various locations, beginning with Raleigh, NC, and various state printers, beginning with P. M. Hale, 1886–1907). Note: The later volumes in this series have the title *The State Records of North Carolina*.

**Parrillo diss.** Nicholas Richard Parrillo, "Against the Profit Motive: The Salary Revolution in American Government, 1780–1940" (Ph.D. diss., Yale University, 2012).

**Pension Bureau Report [year].** Annual Report of the Commissioner of [the U.S. Bureau of] Pensions for [year].

**PHS Report [year].** Annual Report of the Surgeon General of the [U.S.] Public Health Service for [year].

**Purdy Report.** *Report to the President of the Commission on Naturalization Appointed by Executive Order March 1, 1905*, H.R. Doc. No. 59–46 (1905).

**RC-Fees.** "Reports of the Commissioners Appointed by Act 25 Geo. III cap. 19. to Enquire into the Fees, Gratuities, Perquisites, and Emoluments, Which Are or Have Been Lately Received in the Several Public Offices Therein Mentioned" (1786–88), in House of Commons Parliamentary Papers, vol. 7 (report and its appendices take up whole volume), 1806 (309).

**RC-PA.** *The Reports of the Commissioners Appointed to Examine, Take, and State the Public Accounts of the Kingdom*, 3 vols. (London: H. M. Printers, 1783–87).

**RFCC.** Returns of Fees Charged in the Colonies, 1764, Colonial Office Records CO 325/5, National Archives of the United Kingdom, Kew.

**ROE.** *Republic or Empire? The Philippine Question* (Chicago: Independence Co., 1899).

**Schurz Papers.** Carl Schurz, *Speeches, Correspondence, and Political Papers of Carl Schurz*, ed. Frederic Bancroft, 6 vols. (New York: G. P. Putnam's Sons, 1913).

**Stat. of Penn. (1682–1801).** *The Statutes at Large of Pennsylvania from 1682 to 1801*, ed. James T. Mitchell and others, varying in subsequent years, 17 vols. (Harrisburg: Various state printers, beginning with Clarence M. Busch, 1896–1915).

**Steinberg, "FPP."** Allen Steinberg, "From Private Prosecution to Plea Bargaining: Criminal Prosecution, the District Attorney, and American Legal History," *Crime & Delinquency* 30 (1984): 568–92.

**Steinberg, TCJ.** Allen Steinberg, *The Transformation of Criminal Justice: Philadelphia, 1800–1880* (Chapel Hill: University of North Carolina Press, 1989).

**Treasury Report [year].** Annual Report of the [U.S.] Secretary of the Treasury for [year].

**Trial of Prescott.** *Report of the Trial by Impeachment of James Prescott, Esquire . . . before the Senate of Massachusetts* (Boston: Daily Advertiser, 1821).

**USRS.** *Revised Statutes of the United States*, 2nd ed. (Washington, DC: Government Printing Office, 1878).

**Veterans' Bureau Report [year].** Annual Report of the Director, United States Veterans' Bureau for [year].

**Weber, ES.** Max Weber, *Economy and Society: An Outline of Interpretive Sociology*, ed. Guenther Roth and Claus Wittich, 2 vols. (Berkeley: University of California Press, 1978).

# NOTES

## INTRODUCTION

1. Throughout this book, I use terms like *profit motive* and *profit-seeking* to denote income that has a relatively immediate and objective relation to the recipient's conduct. A leading economist refers to this kind of income as a high-powered incentive, as opposed to the low-powered incentives that employers supply for workers on fixed salaries. Oliver E. Williamson, *The Economic Institutions of Capitalism* (New York: Free Press, 1985), 132, 140. For the use of a similar distinction, see Bengt Holmstrom and Paul Milgrom, "The Firm as an Incentive System," *American Economic Review* 84 (1994): 972 (contrasting the payment of a "fixed wage" with payment "only for quantities supplied"). Present-day writing on government commonly assumes, explicitly or implicitly, that the profit motive traditionally is, or ought to be, absent in government agencies. E.g., John D. Donahue, *The Privatization Decision: Public Ends, Private Means* (New York: Basic Books, 1989), 11, 39; David Osborne and Ted Gaebler, *Reinventing Government: How the Entrepreneurial Spirit Is Transforming the Public Sector* (New York: Plume, 1992), 198; Oliver Williamson, "Public and Private Bureaucracies: A Transaction Cost Economics Perspective," *Journal of Law, Economics, and Organization* 15 (1999): 336; James Q. Wilson, *Bureaucracy: What Public Agencies Do and Why They Do It* (New York: Basic Books, 1989), 115–16.

2. Let me add a word about the exact boundaries of this category, especially as it pertains to officers whose job was to decide whether an applicant should receive some kind of advantage or not (e.g., a permit). In some instances, the officer would receive a payment only if he granted the advantage that the applicant sought. Such a payment, by my definition, would certainly be facilitative. In other instances, the officer would receive a payment simply for the act of deciding whether to grant the advantage or not, regardless of whether the decision was favorable to the applicant. That kind of payment, by my definition, would still be facilitative, since the applicant, at the time of requesting the decision, preferred that the decision be made rather than that it not be made. In that sense, the decision was a service the applicant wanted.

3. This distinction—between a service that the affected person wanted done and a task that the affected person did not want done—is an intuitive one. Broadly similar distinctions appear in the literature on governance. E.g., Susan Rose-Ackerman, *Corruption and Government: Causes, Consequences, and Reform* (Cambridge: Cambridge University Press, 1999), 51; James C. Scott, *Comparative Political Corruption* (Englewood Cliffs, NJ: Prentice Hall, 1972), 67; Tom R. Tyler and Yuen J. Huo, *Trust in the Law: Encouraging Public Cooperation with the Police and Courts* (New York: Russell Sage Foundation, 2002), 32, 42–43. To be sure, it would be possible to set the parameters of a facilitative payment and of a bounty so as to make them equivalent to each other from a strict economic perspective, much as a fine, given certain parameters, can be economically equivalent to a price, even if the two still differ in terms of formalities and framing. But what matters for my argument—as I summarize in the following few paragraphs of the text and elaborate throughout the book—is that facilitative payments predominantly gave rise to mutually beneficial exchanges that were socially much like customer-seller relations, whereas bounties predominantly gave rise to adversarial interactions, socially alienating laypersons from the officialdom and from government more broadly. Because of their different social dynamics, each of the two kinds of payment inspired a distinct rationale for why it was evil and should be replaced by salary. For a profound and wide-ranging argument that monetary payments can be differentiated on the basis of their social meaning, see Viviana A. Zelizer, *The Social Meaning of Money: Pin Money, Paychecks, Poor Relief, and Other Currencies* (Princeton, NJ: Princeton University Press, 1997), esp. 21–30. To be sure, there were crosscutting scenarios, in which facilitative payments led to adversarialism and bounties to cooperation. In the course of this book, I also explore those scenarios and consider the particular reasons why they, too, inspired arguments leading to salarization:

- As for facilitative payments leading to adversarialism, this occurred when service recipients wanted the service but griped about the price they were paying. That is, exchange was still mutually beneficial, but recipients were unhappy with the distribution of the surplus. This issue underlay the campaign to regulate the prices of official services in order to control officers' monopoly power (see Chapter 2).

- As for bounties leading to cooperation, this occurred in certain enforcement schemes where the punishment was slight, such that the enforcer and the targets built up a mutually beneficial relationship in which the enforcers allowed the targets to continue their violations, so long as they submitted to a limited degree of enforcement and punishment (which produced bounties to enrich the enforcers). See the text in this Introduction at notes 135–36, and Chapter 7, text at notes 187–92 and 262–65. A bounty scheme that morphed into a cooperative relationship in this way would be vulnerable, politically, to the charge of corruption.

4. The story is so little a part of the conventional American narrative that a leading sociologist of the modern Western state says of the United States: "*All* federal officials have been salaried, from the late 1780s to the present day" (emphasis in original). Michael Mann, *The Sources of Social Power*, vol. 2, *The Rise of Classes and Nation-States, 1760–*

1914 (Cambridge: Cambridge University Press, 1993), 457. This is completely wrong. See the fee and commission totals for hundreds of federal internal revenue officers, customs officers, postmasters, and others in "Roll of the Officers, Civil, Military, and Naval, of the United States" (1802), in *American State Papers, Miscellaneous* (Washington, DC: Gales and Seaton, 1834), 1:260–319.

5. Weber, *ES*, 1:220, 235–36; 2:958–69, 1028–38.

6. Most comprehensive are the works of G. E. Aylmer on the seventeenth century, when the profit-seeking regime was well established: *The King's Servants: The Civil Service of Charles I, 1625–1642*, rev. ed. (London: Routledge & Kegan Paul, 1974), 160–252; *The State's Servants: The Civil Service of the English Republic, 1649–1660* (London: Routledge & Kegan Paul, 1974), 106–21; *The Crown's Servants: Government and Civil Service under Charles II* (Oxford: Oxford University Press, 2002), 101–13. There have also been briefer synthetic discussions of the English transition to salaries during the late 1700s and early 1800s. See John R. Breihan, "William Pitt and the Commission on Fees, 1785–1801," *Historical Journal* 27 (1984): 59–81; Norman Chester, *The English Administrative System, 1780–1870* (Oxford: Clarendon Press, 1981), 14–16, 61–64, 134–41, 142–55; John Torrance, "Social Class and Bureaucratic Innovation: The Commissioners for Examining the Public Accounts, 1780–1787," *Past and Present* 78 (1978): 56–81, esp. 62, 64, 67–68.

7. There was a published dissertation on the subject in the 1890s, Thomas K. Urdahl, *The Fee-System in the United States* (Madison, WI: Democrat Printing Co., 1898), but it does not meet modern standards of evidence and was written while the transformation was still very much in progress. Leonard D. White's four-volume history of federal administration up to 1901 discusses official compensation only in a few brief passages. *The Federalists: A Study in Administrative History* (New York: Macmillan, 1948), 298–300; *The Jeffersonians: A Study in Administrative History, 1801–1829* (New York: Macmillan, 1951), 403–04; *The Jacksonians: A Study in Administrative History, 1829–1861* (New York: Macmillan, 1954), 388–91; *The Republican Era, 1869–1901: A Study in Administrative History* (New York: Macmillan, 1958), 123–26, 205. More recently, Karen Orren has discussed the matter, but only as one point in her much broader theory of officers' rights. See Karen Orren, "The Work of Government: Recovering the Discourse of Office in *Marbury v. Madison*," *Studies in American Political Development* 8 (1994): 60, 64, 67; Karen Orren, "'A War between Officers': The Enforcement of Slavery in the Northern United States, and of the Republic for Which It Stands, before the Civil War," *Studies in American Political Development* 12 (1998): 343, 352–53; Karen Orren, "Officers' Rights: Toward a Unified Field Theory of American Constitutional Development," *Law and Society Review* 34 (2000): 873, 883–84. There is also a brief synthetic discussion of profit-seeking in Jerry L. Mashaw, *Creating the Administrative Constitution: The Lost One Hundred Years of American Administrative Law* (New Haven, CT: Yale University Press, 2012), 60–62, but not on its decline.

8. Only four function-specific works take compensation as a principal subject. Beverly McAnear, *The Income of the Colonial Governors of British North America* (New York: Pageant, 1967); Robert Ralph Davis Jr., "Diplomatic Gifts and Emoluments: The Early National Experience," *Historian* 32 (1970): 376–91; Harold D. Langley, "Dewey,

Sampson, and the Courts: The Rise and Fall of Prize and Bounty Money," in *New Inter-pretations in Naval History: Selected Papers from the Thirteenth Annual Symposium Held at Annapolis, Maryland, 2–4 October 1997*, ed. William M. McBride (Annapolis, MD: Naval Institute Press, 1998), 93–107; Donald A. Petrie, *The Prize Game: Lawful Looting on the High Seas in the Days of Fighting Sail* (New York: Berkley Books, 1999). McAnear and Petrie say almost nothing about the transition to salaries. Langley's treatment of the abolition of naval prize money is brief and inadequate, as it largely ignores the issues that were key to the transition (see my discussion in Chapter 9). Several other function-specific works touch on official profit-seeking; the following is a list of those that go into relatively greater depth, although most of their treatments are still fairly brief:

- On judges, justices of the peace, and court administration: Julius Goebel Jr. and T. Raymond Naughton, *Law Enforcement in Colonial New York (1664–1776)* (New York: Commonwealth Fund, 1944), 731–48; I. Scott Messinger, *Order in the Courts: A History of the Federal Court Clerk's Office* (Washington, DC: Federal Judicial Center, 2002), 9–12, 20–45; Robert C. Post, "Federalism, Positive Law, and the Emergence of the American Administrative State: Prohibition in the Taft Court Era," *William and Mary Law Review* 48 (2006): 113–16; Steinberg, *TCJ*, 28, 38, 101–02, 172–75, 190–94, 222–29; Michael Willrich, *City of Courts: Socializing Justice in Progressive Era Chicago* (Cambridge: Cambridge University Press, 2003), 12–22.

- On public prosecutors: Dirk G. Christensen, "Incentives vs. Nonpartisanship: The Prosecutorial Dilemma in an Adversary System," *Duke Law Journal* 1981 (1981): 323n94, 325–28; Goebel and Naughton, *Law Enforcement in Colonial New York*, 731–48; Tracey L. Meares, "Rewards for Good Behavior: Influencing Prosecutorial Discretion and Conduct with Financial Incentives," *Fordham Law Review* 64 (1995): 880–82; Steinberg, "FPP," esp. 577–78, 580–83.

- On sheriffs, constables, and police officers: Carl V. Harris, *Political Power in Birmingham, 1871–1921* (Knoxville: University of Tennessee Press, 1977), 207–15; David R. Johnson, *Policing the Urban Underworld: The Impact of Crime on the Development of the American Police, 1800–1887* (Philadelphia: Temple University Press, 1979), 45–51, 64–67; James F. Richardson, *The New York Police: Colonial Times to 1901* (New York: Oxford University Press, 1970), 17, 19, 30–31, 38–39, 46, 61–63, 119, 212; David A. Sklansky, "The Private Police," *UCLA Law Review* 46 (1999): 1193–1229.

- On federal law enforcement officers: Stephen Cresswell, *Mormons & Cowboys, Moonshiners & Klansmen: Federal Law Enforcement in the South and West, 1870–1893* (Tuscaloosa: University of Alabama Press, 1991), 118, 166–71, 223–24, 248, 252–54; Wilbur Miller, *Revenuers and Moonshiners: Enforcing Federal Liquor Law in the Mountain South, 1865–1900* (Chapel Hill: University of North Carolina Press, 1991), 117–25, 183–85.

- On the federal tariff: Andrew Wender Cohen, "Smuggling, Globalization, and America's Outward State, 1870–1909," *Journal of American History* 97 (2010):

380–82, 393–94; R. Elberton Smith, *Customs Valuation in the United States: A Study in Tariff Administration* (Chicago: University of Chicago Press, 1948), 104–17.

- On naval prize money: in addition to the works by Langley and Petrie cited at the beginning of this note, see Christopher McKee, *A Gentlemanly and Honorable Profession: The Creation of the U.S. Naval Officer Corps, 1794–1815* (Annapolis, MD: Naval Institute Press, 1991), 341–47.

- On bounties in Indian conflicts: James Grenier, *The First Way of War: American War Making on the Frontier, 1607–1814* (New York: Cambridge University Press, 2005), 39–42, 50–51, 61–65, 68, 125, 167; Peter Silver, *Our Savage Neighbors: How Indian War Transformed Early America* (New York: Norton, 2008), 161–72.

- On the Post Office: Richard R. John, *Spreading the News: The American Postal System from Franklin to Morse* (Cambridge, MA: Harvard University Press, 1995), 103–05, 121–23.

- On imprisonment: For Northern penitentiaries, see, most importantly, Rebecca M. McLennan, *The Crisis of Imprisonment: Protest, Politics, and the Making of the American Penal State, 1776–1941* (Cambridge: Cambridge University Press, 2008). On Southern convict leasing, there is a substantial literature, in which perhaps the most comprehensive works are Matthew J. Mancini, *One Dies, Get Another: Convict Leasing in the American South, 1866–1928* (Columbia: University of South Carolina Press, 1996); Robert Perkinson, *Texas Tough: The Rise of America's Prison Empire* (New York: Metropolitan Books, 2010).

9. Steinberg, *TCJ*; Steinberg, "FPP," esp. 577–78, 580–83.
10. McLennan, *Crisis of Imprisonment.*
11. See especially James Lindgren's doctrinal history of extortion, which, though not concerned with lawful official compensation per se, helps us understand the legal boundaries of the facilitative payment—a picture that I flesh out with further primary research in Chapters 1 and 2. Lindgren, "The Elusive Distinction between Bribery and Extortion: From the Common Law to the Hobbs Act," *UCLA Law Review* 35 (1988): 815–909. See also Jack P. Greene, *The Quest for Power: The Lower Houses of Assembly in the Southern Royal Colonies, 1689–1776* (Chapel Hill: University of North Carolina Press, 1963), 148–68. Greene's discussion of colonial fee regulation is excellent, though his finding that Southern colonial assemblies controlled fee-taking does not apply to the North and is, I believe, mistaken as to South Carolina (see my discussion in Chapter 1, note 134). An important intellectual and cultural history of bribery is John T. Noonan Jr., *Bribes* (Berkeley: University of California Press, 1987), though it is superseded by Lindgren so far as the legal history of England and America goes.
12. The distinction between facilitative payments and bounties has received no serious attention in modern scholarship on state development. Indeed, it has not even been fully recognized. Weber gives it only glancing recognition in his discussion of premodern official income. In several instances, he refers to fees for official services but without mentioning the alternative of the bounty. Weber, *ES*, 1:230–31, 239–40; 2:1029,

1032. He also sometimes says that premodern officers made money through "fees or taxes" (or some similar phrase). Ibid., 1:235, 236; 2:1100. We might read these comments as recognizing a distinction between fees-for-service and tax farming (the latter being a bounty scheme), but even then, these comments all cast fees and taxes as similar items in a series. Because Weber attaches no analytic importance to the distinction and almost elides it, he has no trouble describing premodern official compensation as a single type—a uniform regime characterized by the incumbent's appropriation of the office. E.g., ibid., 2:959, 966, 967. More recent scholars of the modern state similarly speak in terms of a relatively unitary premodern type, defined by appropriation. Mann, *Sources of Social Power*, 2:444, 446; Edward L. Rubin, *Beyond Camelot: Rethinking Politics and Law for the Modern State* (Princeton, NJ: Princeton University Press, 2005), 25–26, 29–31, 34–35.

13. Jeremy Bentham, "The Rationale of Reward" (written circa 1780, first published 1825), in *The Works of Jeremy Bentham*, ed. John Bowring (Edinburgh: William Tait, 1843), 2:191, 239, 241, 250–51. For an American newspaper implicitly making the distinction, with the same normative views as Bentham, see "A Note of Warning to Farmers," *Ohio Farmer* 88 (Nov. 14, 1895): 386; "Influencing Legislation," *Ohio Farmer* 89 (Feb. 13, 1896): 130 (simultaneously advocating abolition of the fee system for county officers, which consisted mainly of facilitative payments, and maintenance of the "Morgenthaler law" establishing tax inquisitors, which provided for bounties).

14. E.g., Lawrence M. Friedman, *A History of American Law*, 3rd ed. (London: Touchstone, 2005), 128; Gordon S. Wood, *The Radicalism of the American Revolution* (New York: Vintage, 1992), 83–84.

15. On how the weakness of Tudor-Stuart state finance led the crown to rely upon officers raising their fees for services, see Joel Hurstfield, *Freedom, Corruption and Government in Elizabethan England* (Cambridge, MA: Harvard University Press, 1973), 161. On the importance of fees relative to other sources of Stuart royal finance, see Aylmer, *King's Servants*, 240–52.

16. That it was even a necessary condition is unclear. It was possible for the fees of several officers to be pooled and for fixed annual salaries to be paid out of the pool. In this way, officers could be placed on salary even though the financing of their work continued to depend entirely on fees rather than on general public revenue. Several British government departments adopted this arrangement in the late 1700s and depended on it until Parliament began providing appropriations in the early 1800s. Chester, *English Administrative System*, 138–40. Admittedly, this kind of arrangement—particularly if the officers in the pool were geographically dispersed—would require a mechanism to ensure that they faithfully paid all their receipts into the pool, plus another mechanism to disburse salaries from the pool. See Scott, *Comparative Political Corruption*, 49 (on the absence of such mechanisms in Stuart England); White, *Federalists*, 298 (on their absence in the early U.S. government).

17. Here are some examples:

- The fees of federal court clerks, U.S. marshals, and U.S. attorneys in criminal cases were paid out of the Treasury beginning in 1792. § 4, 1 Stat. 275, 277 (1792).

This remained the rule more than eighty years later. "Fees of District Attorneys, Marshals, and Clerks" (1877), in *Official Opinions of the Attorneys-General of the United States*, ed. A. J. Bentley (Washington, DC: W. H. and O. H. Morrison, 1880), 15:386–88. The marshals and attorneys were not converted to salary until 1896 (see Chapter 7). And clerks were not converted until 1919. 40 Stat. 1182 (1919).

- In the federal veterans' benefit system, the fees of the numerous examining surgeons were paid from the Treasury throughout the late 1800s and early 1900s, as indicated by the appropriations for those fees. E.g., 19 Stat. 8 (1876) ($100,000); 31 Stat. 787, 788 (1901) ($700,000). Appropriations lessened as the Civil War generation died out. 39 Stat. 1132 (1917) ($60,000).

- In the French and Indian War (1754–63) and Revolutionary War, several colonies and states offered bounties to their soldiers from their treasuries for the scalps of enemies (see Chapter 9, note 4).

- In the U.S. Navy, officers and seamen were eligible for "head money," paid from the Treasury for sinking enemy warships. The award was established by 1800, was increased in 1864, and remained in place till 1899 (see Chapter 9, text at notes 39, 86, 105–06).

- State-level prosecutors often had their fees (by the case or the conviction) paid by the government, and this arrangement often went on for decades before they were converted to salary. In Connecticut and Pennsylvania, for example, publicly financed fees lasted about seventy years or more. Compare the discussion of the states' financing mechanisms (see Chapter 7, notes 6–21, 98–109) with the states' dates of salarization (see the Appendix).

- In New York, the fees of justices of the peace, constables, court clerks, district attorneys, and sheriffs in criminal cases were ordered paid by the counties in the 1820s. *The Revised Statutes of the State of New-York* (Albany, NY: Packard and Van Benthuysen, 1829), 2:753. Many of these officers did not go on salary until scattered special acts in the late 1800s and early 1900s. For documentation of this point as to district attorneys, see my entry for New York in the Appendix.

- In Texas, public funds covered the fees of all law enforcement officers in felony prosecutions, starting in the 1850s. A *Digest of the General Statute Laws of the State of Texas*, ed. Williamson S. Oldham and George W. White (Austin, TX: John Marshall and Co., 1859), 675 (statute of 1856). This was still the case in 1932. S. B. McAlister, "The Fee System as a Method of Compensation for the Texas County Officials," *Southwestern Social Science Quarterly* 12 (1932): 27.

The examples cited here all involved officers receiving payments from general governmental revenues (normally from taxes) that did not arise from their own activities. In addition, there were also many officers who received shares of tax revenues, or tax-related revenues, that they themselves collected. See Chapter 5 (on tax ferrets, who took a share of tax collections) and Chapter 6 (on customs officers, who took a share of tax forfeitures).

It should also be noted that the federal government kept the compensation of many officers—such as court clerks, examining surgeons, and land-office registers and receivers (Chapter 4) and U.S. attorneys and marshals (Chapter 7)—largely in a profit-seeking format until the 1890s or later, even though it had been evident since the 1830s that general federal revenue was sufficient to pay salaries to all federal officers. See Secretary of State Edward Livingston's argument in S. Doc. No. 22–83, at 3–4 (1831).

When critics in the late 1800s and early 1900s urged salarization, they often argued that facilitative payments or bounties were creating perverse incentives for officers to run up costs to the treasury, meaning that salarization would *save* money overall. See, e.g., Pension Bureau Report 1877, p. 732 (regarding examining surgeons); "The Resolutions," *Colorado Springs Weekly Gazette*, Sept. 13, 1890, p. 4 (regarding county officials). See also Introduction, text at note 128.

18. Weber, *ES*, 2:968, 959; see also ibid., 1:220–21; 2:962–63. For more recent scholars making similar associations, see Mann, *Sources of Social Power*, 2:444; Daniel P. Carpenter, *The Forging of Bureaucratic Autonomy: Reputations, Networks, and Policy Innovation in Executive Agencies, 1862–1928* (Princeton, NJ: Princeton University Press, 2001), 377n31 (referring to a steady upward increase in "income" along the career ladder).

19. At the federal level, see, e.g., Ari Hoogenboom, *Outlawing the Spoils: A History of the Civil Service Reform Movement, 1865–1883* (Urbana: University of Illinois Press, 1961); Ronald N. Johnson and Gary D. Libecap, *The Federal Civil Service System and the Problem of Bureaucracy: The Economics and Politics of Institutional Change* (Chicago: University of Chicago Press, 1994); Stephen Skowronek, *Building a New American State: The Expansion of National Administrative Capacities* (Cambridge: Cambridge University Press, 1982); Paul P. Van Riper, *History of the United States Civil Service* (Evanston, IL: Row, Peterson, 1958); White, *Republican Era*. State systems have received less attention. Anirudh V. S. Ruhil and Pedro J. Camões, "What Lies Beneath: The Political Roots of State Merit Systems," *Journal of Public Administration Research and Theory* 13 (2003): 27–42.

20. Weber, *ES*, 1:220–21; 2:963, 967–68, 988. For a more recent analysis in this vein, see Rubin, *Beyond Camelot*, 25–26, 29–31.

21. Donahue, *Privatization Decision*, 39–48; Holmstrom and Milgrom, "Firm as an Incentive System," 972–74; Herbert A. Simon, *Administrative Behavior: A Study of Decision-Making Processes in Administrative Organizations*, 4th ed. (New York: Free Press, 1997), 144–45; Williamson, "Public and Private Bureaucracies," 322–24, 331–33.

22. Weber himself noted the failure (or slowness) of England and America to conform to his ideal type of rational bureaucracy. *ES*, 2:970–71, 976, 987. For more on the American departure from the ideal-typical path of career stability and top-down control, see Bruce Ackerman, "The New Separation of Powers," *Harvard Law Review* 113 (2000): 702–12; Brian Balogh, *A Government Out of Sight: The Mystery of National Authority in Nineteenth-Century America* (Cambridge: Cambridge University Press, 2009); Christopher R. Berry and Jacob E. Gersen, "The Unbundled Executive," *University of Chicago Law Review* 75 (2008): 1399–1401; Elisabeth S. Clemens, "Lineages of the Rube Goldberg State: Building and Blurring Public Programs, 1900–1940,"

in *Rethinking Political Institutions: The Art of the State*, ed. Ian Shapiro, Stephen Skowronek, and Daniel Galvin (New York: New York University Press, 2006); Mirjan R. Damaška, *The Faces of Justice and State Authority: A Comparative Approach to the Legal Process* (New Haven, CT: Yale University Press, 1986); Mirjan Damaška, "Structures of Authority and Comparative Criminal Procedure," *Yale Law Journal* 84 (1975): 480–544; Samuel P. Huntington, *Political Order in Changing Societies* (New Haven, CT: Yale University Press, 1968), 93–139; Lloyd I. Rudolph and Susanne Hoeber Rudolph, "Authority and Power in Bureaucratic and Patrimonial Administration: A Revisionist Interpretation of Weber on Bureaucracy," *World Politics* 31 (1979): 218; Bernard S. Silberman, *Cages of Reason: The Rise of the Rational State in France, Japan, the United States, and Great Britain* (Chicago: University of Chicago Press, 1993), 1–2, 10–15, 227–31, 259–61, 264–65, 277, 281; Skowronek, *Building a New American State*, 204–11, 285–92; Wilson, *Bureaucracy*, 297–301. I wholeheartedly agree with recent works emphasizing that America's departure from the Weberian path should not be construed to mean that the American state is "weak"; in fact, it is merely *different* from the continental state. Desmond King and Robert C. Lieberman, "Ironies of State Building: A Comparative Perspective on the American State," *World Politics* 61 (2009): 555, 561–62, 569–71; William J. Novak, "The Myth of the 'Weak' American State," *American Historical Review* 113 (2008): 761–62.

23. This was often true of the transition from bounties to salaries. See my discussion in Chapter 5, text at notes 188–290; Chapter 6, text at notes 201–11; Chapter 7, text at notes 242–49; and Chapter 8, text at notes 47–59. In the case studies of facilitative payments in Chapter 4, the correlation of salarization with career stability and top-down control is somewhat stronger, but there are still many exceptions. For example, salaried naturalization examiners engaged in quite decentralized decision-making (text at notes 163–65); Public Health Service doctors responsible for deciding disability claims were salarized even while many were part-time, such that they could not have viewed their government work as a career (text at note 279); and salaried grazing-land administrators had their decisions effectively controlled by local private interests across the nation, not by a central agency headquarters (text at note 425). Also, the abolition of diplomatic gifts in the 1790s (see below, Chapter 2, text at notes 157–71) occurred at a time when diplomats were still quite decentralized and autonomous. George C. Herring, *From Colony to Superpower: U.S. Foreign Relations since 1776* (Oxford: Oxford University Press, 2008), 76.

24. The civil service reform movement came into being in the 1860s. The federal government began experimenting with the idea in the 1870s but did not convert officers to civil service by a statutory mechanism until the Pendleton Act of 1883. Hoogenboom, *Outlawing the Spoils*. Even then, it took until the 1910s for 80 percent of federal employees to be converted. Johnson and Libecap, *Federal Civil Service System*, 61. A few states began converting in the 1880s, but the large majority did not do so until after 1900. Ruhil and Camões, "What Lies Beneath." By contrast, the salary revolution was under way earlier, in some ways much earlier. Its first stage was the movement for complete legislative regulation of facilitative payments, which began by the mid-1700s. See Chapter 2. Several offices underwent salarization between the late 1700s and the

1860s, such as federal judges and diplomats (see Chapter 2, text at notes 157–78) and public prosecutors in several states (see the Appendix). Even after the advent of the civil service movement, it was possible for a leading federal administrator like Green Raum to vocally support salarization and reject civil service. Miller, *Revenuers and Moonshiners*, 98–99, 119. More broadly, many of the offices that I analyze in my case studies of bounty abolition were not converted to civil service until well after salarization, if ever. See Chapter 5, text at notes 210, 250–58; Chapter 6, text at notes 201–11; Chapter 7, text at notes 244–46, 248–49; Chapter 8, text at note 58. Also, Steinberg's study of the reform of Philadelphia's minor judiciary in the 1870s (which replaced facilitative payments with salaries) finds that, even fifty years afterward, the offices retained their patronage status (and seedy reputation). *TCJ*, 228. Conversely, naval officers acquired career stability generations before their bounties were terminated. See Chapter 9, text at note 250. That said, civil service reform was significantly linked with salarization in at least one important respect: big-city political machines often reaped more handsome "assessments" from fee-paid offices than from salaried ones, which helped make fee-based offices a target for anti-spoils reformers. See Chapter 3, text at notes 73–77.

25. One was Senator George F. Edmunds. On his successful effort to strengthen customhouse bounties in 1867 and his skepticism of abolishing those bounties in 1874, see Chapter 6, text at notes 112–16, and note 201. On his affinity to civil service reform in 1869–71, see Hoogenboom, *Outlawing the Spoils*, 59, 101. A second was Senator George F. Hoar. On his support of bounties for federal law-enforcement officers at least through the late 1880s, see 28 Cong. Rec. 3183, 3229 (1896) (noting that he "very reluctantly" came to support salarization sometime in the previous six years). On his strong support of the Civil Service Reform Act in 1883, see Hoogenboom, *Outlawing the Spoils*, 240. A third was House Republican leader Thomas Brackett Reed. On his support of bounties for federal law-enforcement officers and customhouse officers, see 18 Cong. Rec. 1502 (1887). Though Reed was not himself a "reformer," he also was not "particularly successful" with patronage either, and he voted for the Civil Service Reform Act in 1883. William A. Robinson, *Thomas B. Reed: Parliamentarian* (New York: Dodd, Mead, 1930), 97, 100.

26. For a good synthesis of Weber's thinking on this point, see Joseph Bensman, "Max Weber's Concept of Legitimacy: An Evaluation," in *Conflict and Control: Challenges to Legitimacy of Modern Governments*, ed. Arthur J. Vidich and Ronald M. Glassman (Beverly Hills, CA: Sage, 1979), 17–48. For a sense of more recent scholarship on the state and legitimacy, see *Trust and Governance*, ed. Valerie Braithwaite and Margaret Levi (New York: Russell Sage Foundation, 1998).

27. In the literature on the historical development of taxation, for example, there is very little attention to the relation of official monetary incentives to legitimacy. For a discussion of ancient Roman tax farming that somewhat addresses the issue, see Margaret Levi, *Of Rule and Revenue* (Berkeley: University of California Press, 1988), 85, 88–94, 182. The leading social-scientific account of European tax-farming treats citizens as profit maximizers and ignores issues of legitimacy. Edgar Kiser, "Markets

and Hierarchies in Early Modern Tax Systems: A Principal-Agent Analysis," *Politics &*
*Society* 22 (1994): 284–315. On the general need for more historical investigation of the
processes by which modern states acquire legitimacy and elicit compliance, see Assaf
Likhovski, "'Training in Citizenship': Tax Compliance and Modernity," *Law & Social*
*Inquiry* 32 (2007): 669.

28. Wood, *Radicalism of the American Revolution*, 104–08.

29. Montesquieu, *The Spirit of the Laws* (1748), ed. Anne M. Cohler, Basia C. Miller, and
    Harold S. Stone (Cambridge: Cambridge University Press, 1989), 68.

30. On the tendency of justices of the peace to remit their fees, as an attestation of their
    financial independence and disinterestedness, see Norma Landau, *The Justices of the*
    *Peace, 1679–1760* (Berkeley: University of California Press, 1984), 184–85, 204–05; We-
    ber, *ES*, 2:1060.

31. William E. Nelson, "Officeholding and Powerwielding: An Analysis of the Relation-
    ship between Structure and Style in American Administrative History," *Law and So-*
    *ciety Review* 10 (1976): 191–92, 198; Wood, *Radicalism of the American Revolution*,
    83–84; Michael Zuckerman, *Peaceable Kingdoms: New England Towns in the Eigh-*
    *teenth Century* (New York: Knopf, 1970), 85–86.

32. Wood, *Radicalism of the American Revolution*, 288.

33. *Debates on the Adoption of the Federal Constitution, in the Convention Held at Phila-*
    *delphia, in 1787*, ed. Jonathan Elliot (Philadelphia: J. B. Lippincott, 1891), 5:144–47.

34. On urban justices of the peace who lived on the fees of office, see Landau, *Justices of*
    *the Peace*, 184–90; Norma Landau, "The Trading Justice's Trade," in *Law, Crime, and*
    *English Society 1660–1830*, ed. Norma Landau (Cambridge: Cambridge University
    Press, 2002), 46–70.

35. Aylmer, *King's Servants*, 241–46 (on the royal courts and Exchequer); Daniel A.
    Baugh, *British Naval Administration in the Age of Walpole* (Princeton, NJ: Princeton
    University Press, 1965), 108–18; John Brewer, *The Sinews of Power: War, Money and the*
    *English State* (Cambridge, MA: Harvard University Press, 1988), 108 (on the excise);
    Chester, *English Administrative System*, 138–40 (on the Treasury and other central
    departments); Alan James Guy, *Oeconomy and Discipline: Officership and Adminis-*
    *tration in the British Army, 1714–63* (Manchester, UK: Manchester University Press,
    1985), 88–115; Elizabeth Evelynola Hoon, *The Organization of the English Customs*
    *System, 1696–1786* (New York: D. Appleton-Century, 1938), 211–21.

36. Wood, *Radicalism of the American Revolution*, 287, 293.

37. *Debates on the Adoption of the Federal Constitution*, 5:147; Wood, *Radicalism of the*
    *American Revolution*, 290–92.

38. *RC-PA*, 3:187.

39. For discussion of such arguments, see Huntington, *Political Order in Changing Soci-*
    *eties*, 68–69; Rose-Ackerman, *Corruption and Government*, 16.

40. On how the illegality of payments promotes secrecy and related bad consequences,
    see Rose-Ackerman, *Corruption and Government*, 12.

41. Rose-Ackerman raises the possibility of such legalization but is cautious about it. *Cor-*
    *ruption and Government*, 17, 26, 79.

42. What appears to be "corruption" is often a combination of the continuation of old patterns of conduct and the advent of new, more stringent norms. See Huntington, *Political Order in Changing Societies*, 60; Scott, *Comparative Political Corruption*, 7.

43. For a discussion of the relative merits of defining corruption by public opinion, public interest, and applicable law, see Scott, *Comparative Political Corruption*, 3–5. See also Huntington, *Political Order in Changing Societies*, 59 (defining corruption by "accepted norms"); Susan Rose-Ackerman, *Corruption: A Study in Political Economy* (New York: Academic Press, 1978), 7 (focusing analysis on illegal payments, but noting that her analysis can "often be easily extended to legal activities with similar public policy consequences").

44. Scott, *Comparative Political Corruption*, 26; James C. Scott, "Corruption, Machine Politics, and Political Change," *American Political Science Review* 63 (1969): 1142–44. Scott's analysis is nuanced, and he acknowledges that corruption may open the way for some kinds of broader group influences, as well as particular ones. James C. Scott, "The Analysis of Corruption in Developing Nations," *Comparative Studies in Society and History* 11 (1969): 326; Scott, *Comparative Political Corruption*, 23, 27.

45. Terry M. Moe, "The Politics of Structural Choice: Toward a Theory of Public Bureaucracy," in *Organization Theory: From Chester Barnard to the Present and Beyond*, expanded ed., ed. Oliver E. Williamson (New York: Oxford University Press, 1995), 116–53.

46. Theodore J. Lowi, "American Business, Public Policy, Case-Studies, and Political Theory," *World Politics* 16 (1964): 690.

47. Richard L. McCormick, *The Party Period and Public Policy: American Politics from the Age of Jackson to the Progressive Era* (New York: Oxford University Press, 1986), 203–14. For more recent scholarship drawing on McCormick's argument for the importance of distributive policy in this era, see Carpenter, *Forging of Bureaucratic Autonomy*, 60; Theda Skocpol, *Protecting Soldiers and Mothers: The Political Origins of Social Policy in the United States* (Cambridge, MA: Harvard University Press, 1992), 81–83. For a valuable critique of McCormick, introducing a volume of case studies of significant policy areas that did not fit the distributive definition, see Richard R. John, "Ruling Passions: Political Economy in Nineteenth-Century America," *Journal of Policy History* 18 (2006): 1–20.

48. On the work of the military and especially the Bureau of Indian Affairs in removing Indians from their lands and containing and isolating them on reservations, see Stephen J. Rockwell, *Indian Affairs and the Administrative State in the Nineteenth Century* (Cambridge: Cambridge University Press, 2010). It should be noted that easy acquisition of federally owned land by white settlers did indirectly further the expropriation of nearby Indian lands, for the advance of white agricultural settlement tended to cause violence between white settlers and Indians and to thin the game populations on which some Indians relied, thus making the land less attractive to the Indians and pressuring them to cede it to the U.S. government. Eric Kades, "The Dark Side of Efficiency: *Johnson v. M'Intosh* and the Expropriation of American Indian Lands," *University of Pennsylvania Law Review* 148 (2000): 1065–1190.

49. McCormick, *Party Period and Public Policy*, 223–27.

50. As to naturalization, Congress added an English-speaking requirement, but it was very vague. As to veterans' benefits, Congress began offering part of the benefit package in the form of goods that only a truly disabled person would want (such as medical care and job training), as opposed to cash, but it also continued to offer substantial cash benefits. As to the settlement laws, Congress specified the cultivation requirements more closely for a certain class of larger plot sizes.

51. Weber, *ES*, 2:990.

52. On how the difficulty of balancing multiple goals complicates the provision of incentive compensation in government, see Avinash Dixit, "Incentives and Organizations in the Public Sector: An Interpretive Review," *Journal of Human Resources* 37 (2002): 696–727; Jean Tirole, "The Internal Organization of Government," *Oxford Economic Papers* 46 (1994): 1–29. On the distinction between the direct beneficiaries of a government program and those in whose name it is enacted, see Mark H. Moore, "Privatizing Public Management," in *Market-Based Governance: Supply Side, Demand Side, Upside, and Downside*, ed. John D. Donahue and Joseph S. Nye Jr. (Washington, DC: Brookings Institution Press, 2002), 297–305.

53. For case studies of governance that fit the "familiar" type in early modern England, see Colin Brooks, "Public Finance and Political Stability: The Administration of the Land Tax, 1688–1720," *Historical Journal* 17 (1974): 281–300; Margaret Gay Davies, *The Enforcement of English Apprenticeship: A Study in Applied Mercantilism, 1563–1642* (Cambridge, MA: Harvard University Press, 1956), 161–62, 249, 252, 255–56; Henrik Langelüddecke, "Law and Order in Seventeenth-Century England: The Organization of Local Administration during the Personal Rule of Charles I," *Law and History Review* 15 (1997): 76; Weber, *ES*, 2:1059–64 (on justices of the peace). For discussion of similar modes of governance in colonial and early republican America, see Balogh, *Government Out of Sight*, 31–37; Laura F. Edwards, *The People and Their Peace: Legal Culture and the Transformation of Inequality in the Post-Revolutionary South* (Chapel Hill: University of North Carolina Press, 2009), esp. 4–8, 44, 65, 67–68, 71, 73, 79; David H. Flaherty, *Privacy in Colonial New England* (Charlottesville: University of Virginia Press, 1972), 189–205, 211–18; Jack P. Greene, "Law and the Origins of the American Revolution," in *Cambridge History of Law in America*, ed. Michael Grossberg and Christopher Tomlins (Cambridge: Cambridge University Press, 2008), 1:447–81, esp. 1:470; Hendrik Hartog, "The Public Law of a County Court: Judicial Government in Eighteenth Century Massachusetts," *American Journal of Legal History* 20 (1976): 314; James A. Henretta, "Magistrates, Common Law Lawyers, Legislators: The Three Legal Systems of British America," in *Cambridge History of Law in America*, 1:556–82; Nelson, "Officeholding and Powerwielding," 191–99; Wood, *Radicalism of the American Revolution*, 77–92; Zuckerman, *Peaceable Kingdoms*, 85–89. William J. Novak, who argues convincingly that early America was highly regulated rather than laissez-faire, recognizes that this early regulation tended to be more local, more oriented toward community consensus, and more based on common law and custom (as opposed to positive enactment) than the later regulatory paradigm that arose

over the course of the 1800s. *The People's Welfare: Law and Regulation in Nineteenth-Century America* (Chapel Hill: University of North Carolina Press, 1996), esp. 235–48.

54. The distinction I draw between the ideal types of familiar and alien imposition resonates with the work of others scholars on the development of law and society. Paul Bohannan distinguishes between primary societal customs, which evolve organically, and law, which he defines as the restatement of a norm through a special institution. Law, argues Bohannan, "is always out of phase with society"; "it is the very nature of law, and its capacity to 'do something about' the primary social institutions, that creates the lack of phase. Moreover, even if one could assume perfect legal institutionalization [of primary societal customs], change within the primary institutions would soon jar the system out of phase again." To this, Bohannan adds a historical claim: "the more highly developed the legal institutions, the greater the lack of phase." That is, imposition becomes less familiar and more alien as we reach modernity. Paul Bohannan, "The Differing Realms of the Law," *American Anthropologist*, n.s., 67 (1965): 37. My distinction between the familiar and the alien also resonates with the contrast that Robert C. Post draws when he notes that a legal system can establish one form of social order (community) when it "seeks authoritatively to interpret and enforce shared mores and norms," or a different form (management) when "it organizes social life instrumentally to achieve specific objectives." Robert C. Post, *Constitutional Domains: Democracy, Community, Management* (Cambridge, MA: Harvard University Press, 1995), 2. "Managerial legislation," adds Post, "typically strives to sweep with scythe-like precision and indifference through the entangled fields of . . . contextualized community norms." Ibid., 11. Like Bohannan, Post observes a broad historical shift: "In general the twentieth century has witnessed a significant shift from [community] to [management]." Ibid., 4–5. (This is equally true, I think, of the nineteenth century.) In a similar vein, Charles Tilly claims that, over the long run, Western states have shifted from "indirect rule," in which the sovereign allows local elites to govern their respective localities in exchange for some kind of collective tribute and allegiance, toward "direct rule," in which the sovereign regulates and taxes individuals without the intermediation of the local community or local elite. Charles Tilly, *Coercion, Capital, and European States, AD 990–1992* (Malden, MA: Blackwell, 1990), 99–107. This, too, is consistent with my framework. Familiar imposition is the experience of individuals under indirect rule, for whom the sovereign's wishes are highly mediated by local social hierarchies, arrangements, and norms, whereas alien imposition is the experience of individuals once the sovereign regulates directly. For more scholarship resonating with the familiar-alien distinction, see Robert L. Kidder, "Toward an Integrated Theory of Imposed Law," in *The Imposition of Law*, ed. Sandra B. Burman and Barbara E. Harrell-Bond (New York: Academic Press, 1979), 289, 297; Marc Galanter, "The Modernization of Law," in *Modernization*, ed. Myron Weiner (New York: Basic Books, 1966), 153–65.

55. E.g., Gautham Rao, "The Creation of the American State: Customhouses, Law, and Commerce in the Age of Revolution" (Ph.D. diss., University of Chicago, 2008) (on U.S. customhouses in the early republic); Brooks, "Public Finance and Political Stability" (on British land tax of the 1700s).

56. In the examples of familiar governance that appear in the sources cited in note 53 above, officers were generally unpaid or very low paid. In the English studies, see Brooks, "Public Finance and Political Stability," 287, 299 (commissioners received only their expenses; their subordinates the assessors were unpaid, though they sometimes doubled as collectors, who received a commission); Davies, *Enforcement of English Apprenticeship*, 161–62 (contrasting community-based enforcement by unpaid justices of the peace and constables with profit-seeking *qui tam* informers); Langelüddecke, "Law and Order in Seventeenth-Century England," 76 (noting that justices of the peace and parish officers, who mediated or undermined royal directives, were unpaid). In the American studies, see Edwards, *People and Their Peace*, 67–68 (noting that magistrates administering local justice, though they received fees, "did not take the position solely for the money" but considered it "a duty that they performed in addition to farming or other business pursuits"); Nelson, "Officeholding and Power-wielding," 191–92, 198 (colonial offices received little to no pay); Zuckerman, *Peaceable Kingdoms*, 85–86 (persons initially elected constable in Massachusetts towns normally refused to serve and paid fine instead).

57. On the resilience of prelegislative community norms in the face of top-down "reform-ist" legislation, see Hendrik Hartog, "Pigs and Positivism," *Wisconsin Law Review* 1985 (1985): 899–935; Sally Falk Moore, "Law and Social Change: The Semi-Autonomous Social Field as an Appropriate Object of Study," *Law and Society Review* 7 (1973): 723, 742.

58. Peter J. Bowden, *The Wool Trade in Tudor and Stuart England* (London: Macmillan, 1962), xv–xviii, 107–54.

59. Ibid., 144, 152.

60. M. W. Beresford, "The Common Informer, the Penal Statutes and Economic Regula-tion," *Economic History Review*, n.s., 10 (1957): 223–24, 231 (giving data).

61. Bowden, *Wool Trade*, 135–36, 140.

62. Davies, *Enforcement of English Apprenticeship*, 1–5, 10–11.

63. Ibid., 17–19.

64. G. R. Elton, "Informing for Profit: A Sidelight on Tudor Methods of Law-Enforce-ment," *Cambridge Historical Journal* 11 (1954): 149–50, 154, 166–67; G. D. Ramsay, "The Smugglers' Trade: A Neglected Aspect of English Commercial Development," *Transactions of the Royal Historical Society*, 5th ser., 2 (1952): 138–47. For data on informers in this area, see Beresford, "Common Informer," 223–24, 228–29. On cus-toms officers' shares of forfeitures in the 1700s, see Hoon, *Organization of the English Customs System*, 219, 270–89; Leon Radzinowicz, *A History of English Criminal Law and Its Administration from 1750* (London: Stevens and Sons, 1956), 2:64–67.

65. On the rise of tax-farming in the English customs, see Ramsay, "Smugglers' Trade," 147–48. On its demise, see Brewer, *Sinews of Power*, 92–94. On tax-farming as an anti-corruption measure, see Kiser, "Markets and Hierarchies in Early Modern Tax Systems," 294.

66. On the nature of offenses covered by *qui tam*, see J. Randy Beck, "The False Claims Act and the English Eradication of *Qui Tam* Legislation," *North Carolina Law Re-view* 78 (2000): 567–73, 590–601; Beresford, "Common Informer," 221–22, 226, 228; Radzinowicz, *History of English Criminal Law*, 2:142–47.

67. Beck, "False Claims Act," 597–601; Radzinowicz, *History of English Criminal Law*, 2:11–13, 147. Note also that the reward system for apprehending vagrants defined such vagrants as outsiders to the locality where they were found, as opposed to the "known poor," who were entitled to remain in the locality and seek relief from the community. Deborah Valenze, *The Social Life of Money in the English Past* (Cambridge: Cambridge University Press, 2006), 199–222.

68. On the federal government, see Beck, "False Claims Act," 553n54. On Virginia, see the University of Virginia's 1969 reprint of *The Statutes at Large; Being a Collection of All the Laws of Virginia, from the First Session of the Legislature in the Year 1619*, edited and first published in the early 1800s by William Waller Hening. This collection has been transcribed by the genealogical organization VaGenWeb on its website, at vagenweb.org/hening (last accessed Aug. 3, 2012). A search for "inform" in 1741–50 (volumes 5–6) yields several dozen informer provisions, overwhelmingly targeting offenses in areas like taxation; commerce in tobacco, meat, flour, liquor, and other goods; movement of persons (including emigration, concealment of sailors, forging of indentured-servant passes); regulation of rivers, other public ways, and innkeepers; fees and oaths of lawyers; usury; and abuses of governmental subsidies. There are also numerous informer provisions targeting neglect or irregular conduct by public officers. Beyond that, there are also occasional provisions on vagrancy, military desertion, stealing hogs, and unlawful interactions by free persons with slaves (e.g., allowing another's slaves to gather on one's property).

69. "Article V," *Christian Examiner and General Review* 8, n.s. 3 (no. 34, n.s. no. 9, July 1830): 356–59 (review of William Oldnall Russell's A *Treatise on Criminal and Indictable Misdemeanors*). For Austin's authorship of this unsigned article, see *Index to the Christian Examiner: vols. I–LXXXVII, 1824–1869* (Boston: J. S. Cushing, 1879), 127. On Austin, see *Cyclopaedia of American Literature*, ed. Evert A. Duyckinck and George L. Duyckinck (New York: Charles Scribner, 1856), 2:61.

70. On the history and scope of rewards, see J. M. Beattie, *Crime and the Courts in England 1660–1800* (Princeton, NJ: Princeton University Press, 1986), 50–59, 148–67; J. M. Beattie, *Policing and Punishment in London, 1660–1750: Urban Crime and the Limits of Terror* (Oxford: Oxford University Press, 2001), 376–417; Radzinowicz, *History of English Criminal Law*, 2:57–64, 74–82, 84–88, 97–98.

71. On the special anxiety about property crime in and near London and the city's particular importance in new criminal legislation, see John Beattie, "London Crime and the Making of the 'Bloody Code,' 1689–1718," in *Stilling the Grumbling Hive: The Response to Social and Economic Problems in England, 1689–1750*, ed. Lee Davison et al. (New York: St. Martin's Press, 1992), 53–54, 70. For more on the uniqueness of property crime in London, see Beattie, *Crime and the Courts*, 149, 159–60, 163–64.

72. E. A. Wrigley, *People, Cities, and Wealth: The Transformation of Traditional Society* (Oxford: Basil Blackwell, 1987), 133–35, 163–64.

73. Robert B. Shoemaker, "Reforming the City: The Reformation of Manners Campaign in London, 1690–1738," in *Stilling the Grumbling Hive*, 100–01.

74. Beattie, "London Crime," 70–71 (referring generally to the criminal legislation circa 1700, including harsher punishment and rewards).

75. Davies, *Enforcement of English Apprenticeship*, 47–50; Radzinowicz, *History of English Criminal Law*, 2:147. For a study of one such professional, active in diverse localities, see Elton, "Informing for Profit," esp. 153.

76. Beattie, *Policing and Punishment*, 228–47, 379, 404, 410–17. Though the thief takers were sometimes in a collusive relationship with the criminals with whom they dealt. Compare my discussion in this Introduction, text at notes 135–36.

77. Edward Coke, *The Third Part of the Institutes of the Laws of England* (London, 1797), 194 ("viperous vermin"); Davies, *Enforcement of English Apprenticeship*, 63 ("lewd"), 156–57 ("base"). On the despised status of *qui tam* informers and reward seekers, sometimes giving rise to popular violence against them, see Beck, "False Claims Act," 548n30, 577–79, 597–601; Davies, *Enforcement of English Apprenticeship*, 47, 64, 65, 70, 72, 156; Radzinowicz, *History of English Criminal Law*, 2:97, 147, 151, 154, 332. Beattie notes that thief-takers would be publicly hated insofar as they enforced economic or liquor regulation; he says it is "unclear" how the public would regard their activity in catching those guilty of crimes like robbery. *Policing and Punishment*, 234. But he adds, in discussing a robbery case, that thief takers were "hated by a large part of the population." Ibid., 416–17.

78. Flaherty, *Privacy in Colonial New England*, 208.

79. Ibid., 195–201. For more on tythingmen, including their great reluctance to enforce the law and people's refusal to serve in the office, see David W. Conroy, *In Public Houses: Drink and the Revolution of Authority in Colonial Massachusetts* (Chapel Hill: University of North Carolina Press, 1995), 38, 53, 59, 62, 64–81.

80. Flaherty, *Privacy in Colonial New England*, 210.

81. Hartog, "Pigs and Positivism," 926. For the bounty offers, see ibid., 904 (in 1817, repealed 1818), 922 (1847), 928–30 (1832).

82. [Austin], "Article V," 358. For the full citation to this article, see note 69 above.

83. Edward Livingston, *A System of Penal Law for the State of Louisiana* (Philadelphia: James Kay Jr. and Co., 1833), 206. The reward provision was article 20 of the Code of Procedure. Ibid., 478.

84. Richard Hill, *The Prizes of War: The Naval Prize System in the Napoleonic Wars, 1789–1815* (Portsmouth, UK: Royal Naval Museum, 1991); Petrie, *Prize Game*; Nicholas Parrillo, "The De-Privatization of American Warfare: How the U.S. Government Used, Regulated, and Ultimately Abandoned Privateering in the Nineteenth Century," *Yale Journal of Law and the Humanities* 19 (2007): 1–96.

85. Grenier, *First Way of War*, 39–42, 50–51, 61–65, 68, 125, 167.

86. Ibid., 68, 125, 167.

87. The grants of shares to public and private captors were technically offered under distinct statutes. But the rules of capture and the adjudicatory process were uniform across the two. On British captors, see Baugh, *British Naval Administration*, 112–15. On U.S. captors, see Parrillo, "De-Privatization of American Warfare," 23–25.

88. Beattie, *Policing and Punishment*, 120–34, 150–58, 244–47, 404, 411–12 (quote at 153).

89. Richardson, *New York Police*, 19; *Laws of the State of New-York, Revised and Passed at the Thirty-Sixth Session of the Legislature* (Albany, NY: H. C. Southwick and Co., 1813), 2:27.

90. Hoon, *Organization of the English Customs System*, 271, 287–88. The statute is 14 Car. II, c. 11, § 16 (1662).

91. Thomas C. Barrow, *Trade and Empire: The British Customs Service in Colonial America, 1660–1775* (Cambridge, MA: Harvard University Press, 1967), 54 (act of 1662), 184 (act of 1764).

92. § 38, 1 Stat. 29, 48 (1789), superseded by the very similar § 91, 1 Stat. 627, 697 (1799).

93. On local community pushback against customs enforcement in the colonial period, see Barrow, *Trade and Empire*, 35 (late 1600s), 178 (1760s). On the early national period, see my discussion in Chapter 6, text at notes 56–61.

94. See, e.g., Edwards, *People and Their Peace*, esp. 8–9, 13, 29–31, 44, 46, 47, 210 (on the decline of a relatively flexible and participatory "localized law" and the rise of a more exacting and uniform "state law," imposed from above by officials who, though they might be elected, were at a greater social remove from affected laypersons); William J. Novak, "The Legal Origins of the Modern American State," in *Looking Back at Law's Century*, ed. Austin Sarat et al. (Ithaca, NY: Cornell University Press, 2002), 270–71 (referring to "a separation of ownership from control of the American polity"). The beginnings of this acceleration may go back farther. Henretta, "Magistrates, Common Lawyers, Legislators," 582–92 (on how legislatures in the late colonial and revolutionary periods increasingly enacted substantive legislation and overrode local justice-of-the-peace government).

95. On the transition from notables to spoilsmen, see Martin Shefter, "Party, Bureaucracy, and Political Change in the United States," in *Political Parties and the State: The American Historical Experience* (Princeton, NJ: Princeton University Press, 1994), 63–72.

96. The "legibility" of a population is essential to the imposition of law upon it by an external state. James C. Scott, *Seeing Like a State: How Certain Schemes to Improve the Human Condition Have Failed* (New Haven, CT: Yale University Press, 1998).

97. Hooper v. Fifty-One Casks of Brandy, 12 F. Cas. 465, 466 (D. Maine 1848).

98. 18 Cong. Rec. 1502 (1887).

99. Tom R. Tyler and Yuen J. Huo, *Trust in the Law: Encouraging Public Cooperation with the Police and Courts* (New York: Russell Sage Foundation, 2002), 102. See also Bensman, "Max Weber's Concept of Legitimacy."

100. This is true even when we account for withholding and third-party reporting. James Andreoni, Brian Erard, and Jonathan Feinstein, "Tax Compliance," *Journal of Economic Literature* 36 (1998): 821–22, 850–52, 855. For a study indicating that tax compliance depends partly on one's trust in government and fellow citizens, see John T. Scholz and Mark Lubell, "Trust and Taxpaying: Testing the Heuristic Approach to Collective Action," *American Journal of Political Science* 42 (1998): 398–417. This is not to deny that detection and punishment are major factors, indeed the primary factors, in explaining differences in the level of compliance across taxpayers. On the large variations in compliance depending on the ease with which the IRS can detect taxpayers' liabilities through withholding and third-party reporting, see Joel Slemrod, "Cheating Ourselves: The Economics of Tax Evasion," *Journal of Economic Perspectives* 21 (2007): 29–30, 35–41. For an interview-based study of evasion among taxpayers

with relatively invisible liabilities, see Susan Cleary Morse, Stewart Karlinsky, and Joseph Bankman, "Cash Businesses and Tax Evasion," *Stanford Law and Policy Review* 20 (2009): 37–67.

101. For examples of modern state legitimacy beyond taxation, consider military conscription. There has been variation in compliance between nations across modern history that is not explicable in terms of variation in their respective governments' enforcement capacities. Margaret Levi, *Consent, Dissent, and Patriotism* (Cambridge: Cambridge University Press, 1997), 77. See also ibid., 160–63. In the realm of illegal drugs, Robert J. MacCoun and Peter Reuter find that people's use of such drugs does not much depend on changes in the degree of enforcement and punishment, but they suggest that outright legalization may greatly increase use, in part because of the interaction between a drug's legal status and informal norms about it. *Drug War Heresies: Learning from Other Vices, Times, and Places* (Cambridge: Cambridge University Press, 2001), 78–100. On how the breakdown of legitimacy can result in a perverse equilibrium in which high enforcement coexists with high noncompliance, see William J. Stuntz, *The Collapse of American Criminal Justice* (Cambridge, MA: Harvard University Press, 2011), 28–32, 50–56, 244–46.

102. Tyler and Huo, *Trust in the Law*, 12, 96.

103. See, e.g., Lars P. Feld and Bruno S. Frey, "Tax Compliance as the Result of a Psychological Contract: The Role of Incentives and Responsive Regulation," *Law & Policy* 29 (2007): 102–20; Margaret Levi, "A State of Trust," in *Trust and Governance*, 90–96.

104. Tyler and Huo, *Trust in the Law*, 8.

105. Ibid., 15.

106. Ibid., 59, 62–64.

107. Tyler and Huo's only mention of the issue is a brief reference to bribery. Ibid., 64.

108. Tyler and Huo focus mainly on the formation and effect of trust that is based on a person's personal contact with the authorities, but the authors note that it is also possible for people to form trust in authorities with whom they have no personal contact and that such trust likewise makes those people more likely to accept the authorities' actions. See ibid., 67–68, 206. See also Tom R. Tyler, *Why People Cooperate: The Role of Social Motivations* (Princeton, NJ: Princeton University Press, 2011), 133. Seeing as how the bounty compensation of an enforcer was usually notorious in the community of potential enforcees, it is fair to assume that such compensation would influence the process by which individuals developed (or failed to develop) trust in the state, even if they did not personally experience enforcement themselves.

109. Relatedly, another study finds that an officer's use of fair procedures and treatment ("procedural justice") has a greater positive effect on a layperson's compliance when the layperson disagrees with the law the officer is enforcing. Kristina Murphy, Tom R. Tyler, and Amy Curtis, "Nurturing Regulatory Compliance: Is Procedural Justice Effective When People Question the Legitimacy of the Law?" *Regulation and Governance* 3 (2009): 1–26. This study focuses on procedural justice, not motive-based trust, which Tyler and Huo treat as a distinct phenomenon. Tyler and Huo, *Trust in the Law*, 16–17, 76–77, 84. Still, motive-based trust and procedural justice are very much "intertwined," as noted in Tyler, *Why People Cooperate*, 105–07.

110. Ian Ayres and John Braithwaite, *Responsive Regulation: Transcending the Deregulation Debate* (New York: Oxford University Press, 1992), 19, 22.

111. Ibid., 24–26, 47–48.

112. Ibid., 26–27, 50. For another major study in this vein, see Eugene Bardach and Robert A. Kagan, *Going by the Book: The Problem of Regulatory Unreasonableness* (1982; New Brunswick, NJ: Transaction, 2002), 58–119.

113. For example, to individual tax compliance and enforcement. See *Taxing Democracy: Understanding Tax Avoidance and Evasion*, ed. Valerie Braithwaite (Aldershot, UK: Ashgate, 2003).

114. *The Lord Coke His Speech and Charge. With a Discoverie of the Abuses and Corruption of Officers* (London, 1607). The volume has no page numbers; this quotation appears on the sixth-to-last page.

115. Coke, *Third Part of the Institutes*, 194.

116. Bentham, "Rationale of Reward," 223. Although the quoted words reflect the thrust of the passage from which they come, other passages in Bentham's essay recognize nuances in the interrelations between profit-seeking enforcement, positive law, and popular legitimacy. It may be that the essay as a whole does not yield a consistent view of the problem. See ibid., 214, 216–18, 250–51.

117. Davies, *Enforcement of English Apprenticeship*, 156–57. See also Radzinowicz, *History of English Criminal Law*, 2:152.

118. [Austin], "Article V," 358. For the full citation to this article, see note 69 above.

119. Scott J. Basinger, "Regulating Slavery: Deck-Stacking and Credible Commitment in the Fugitive Slave Act of 1850," *Journal of Law, Economics, and Organization* 19 (2003): 307–42; Stephen Lubet, *Fugitive Justice: Runaways, Rescuers, and Slavery on Trial* (Cambridge, MA: Harvard University Press, 2010), esp. 42–45; Thomas D. Morris, *Free Men All: The Personal Liberty Laws of the North, 1780–1861* (Baltimore: Johns Hopkins University Press, 1974).

120. Basinger, "Regulating Slavery," 324; Lubet, *Fugitive Justice*, 43.

121. One fugitive-slave commissioner, facing a hostile anti-slavery community, publicly forswore taking the extra fee. Lubet, *Fugitive Justice*, 154.

122. Gautham Rao, "The Federal *Posse Comitatus* Doctrine: Slavery, Compulsion, and Statecraft in Mid-Nineteenth-Century America," *Law and History Review* 26 (2008): 22–26, 32–37.

123. E.g., Lubet, *Fugitive Justice*, 133–35.

124. For Weber's characterization of modern official action as rule bound and nondiscretionary, see Weber, *ES*, 1:218, 221; 2:958, 988.

125. Davies, *Enforcement of English Apprenticeship*, 156 (quoting Sir Edwin Sandys). See also ibid., 257.

126. William M. Landes and Richard A. Posner, "The Private Enforcement of Law," *Journal of Legal Studies* 4 (1975): 38. On the inadequacy of written rules to fully delineate the behavior needed to make any human institution function properly—and the consequent necessity of less formal and more flexible processes—see Scott, *Seeing Like a State*, 6, 255–56, 310–11.

127. Galanter, "Modernization of Law," 163–64.

128. An example is the concern about the budgetary cost of enforcement that helped convince Congress to put U.S. attorneys and U.S. marshals on salary in 1896, in the hope of scaling back enforcement activity. See Chapter 7, text at notes 213–22. See also H.R. Doc. No. 56–566, at 59 (1900) (discussing law enforcement in Baltimore); Emmett O'Neal [governor of Alabama], "Reorganization of the Judicial Administration of Justice," *Central Law Journal* 86 (1918): 407.

129. On the increasing number and minuteness of statutory prohibitions during the nineteenth century (particularly economic regulation and vice), including the increased number of prohibitions lacking intent requirements, see Lawrence M. Friedman, "On Legalistic Reasoning—A Footnote to Weber," *Wisconsin Law Review* 1966 (1966): 167; Friedman, *A History of American Law*, 216–19, 442–49, 452–53; Livingston Hall, "The Substantive Law of Crimes—1887–1936," *Harvard Law Review* 50 (1937): 622–63.

130. For discussion of the tension between profit-seeking and prosecutorial discretion, both as a theoretical matter and with attention to English history, see Landes and Posner, "Private Enforcement of Law," 39–40; Beck, "False Claims Act," 583–85, 610–11, 627–33. Both these articles focus on bounty schemes in which any person can seek the bounty. My focus, by contrast, is on designated state agents (i.e., persons enjoying a monopoly on enforcement) entitled to bounties. As Chapters 6 and 7 make clear, the offer of bounties to state agents caused many of the same pathologies identified by Landes and Posner and Beck. This suggests that, where the profit motive is present, a monopoly of enforcement does not eliminate the problem.

131. Discretion does not play a major role in Chapter 5. The tax ferrets simply forced taxpayers to pay the tax itself (for which they were strictly liable), not any penalties on top of it. So there was not much of a rationale for treating evaders differently from one another.

132. On the excess of fee-driven enforcement for "trivial," "technical," or "minor" matters, and the like, see Charles Richmond Henderson, *An Introduction to the Study of the Dependent, Defective and Delinquent Classes* (Boston: D. C. Heath and Co., 1893), 193; "The State Press," *Dallas Morning News*, Jan. 20, 1894, p. 6; "West Haven Police Force," *New Haven Register*, May 9, 1895, p. 1; "The Fee System," *Fort Worth Star-Telegram*, Sept. 18, 1907, p. 4; Emmett O'Neal [governor of Alabama], "Reorganization of the Judicial Administration of Justice," *Central Law Journal* 86 (1918): 407.

133. Carl V. Harris, *Political Power in Birmingham, 1871–1921* (Knoxville: University of Tennessee Press, 1977), 207–15.

134. On the various supports for a "system of domination" apart from legitimacy, including appeals to expediency and to fear, see Bensman, "Max Weber's Concept of Legitimacy," 31, 47n3.

135. For instances of perverse cooperation in English bounty-seeking, see Davies, *Enforcement of English Apprenticeship*, 20–21, 154–55; Radzinowicz, *History of English Criminal Law*, 2:281, 310; Torrance, "Social Class and Bureaucratic Innovation," 62 (on the excise). On American law-enforcement officers periodically raiding a

red-light district "for revenue only," thus acting as parasites on the prostitution business, see Willrich, *City of Courts*, 21.

136. "The Fee System," *Fort Worth Star-Telegram*, Sept. 18, 1907, p. 4 (noting that, in Alabama, "the sheriff or some other official receives a fee for every arrest made whether the charge is proven or not. The result is that Italians and other foreigners who have no vote in Alabama are often subject to frequent arrest for mere technical offenses.").

CHAPTER 1: THE OLD REGIME

1.  James Lindgren, "The Elusive Distinction between Bribery and Extortion: From the Common Law to the Hobbs Act," *UCLA Law Review* 35 (1988): 864–65, 883–84; James Lindgren, "The Theory, History, and Practice of the Bribery-Extortion Distinction," *University of Pennsylvania Law Review* 141 (1993): 1696–97.

2.  Lindgren, "Elusive Distinction," 839.

3.  Edward Coke, *The First Part of the Institutes of the Laws of England* (London, 1794), vol. 2, sec. 701, bracketed page marker [368.b] ("wresting or unlawfully taking by any officer, by color of his office, any money or valuable thing of or from any man, either that is not due, or more than is due, or before it be due").

4.  William Blackstone, *Commentaries on the Laws of England* (Oxford, 1769), 4:141.

5.  Fleetwood v. Finch, 126 Eng. Rep. 517, 518 (C.P. 1793) (Eyre, C.J.).

6.  William Sheppard, *An Epitome of All the Common & Statute Laws of This Nation Now in Force* (London, 1656), 781; Mathew Bacon, *A New Abridgment of the Law* (London, 1736), 2:463. At this point, Bacon is apparently describing officers "who have to do with the administration of justice." But he means the point to apply to all officers. See ibid., 2:464 ("allowed by act of Parliament, or is the known and settled fee," referring simply to "any officer").

7.  Michael Dalton, *The Countrey Justice: Containing the Practices of the Justices of the Peace Out of Their Sessions* (London, 1677), 71, 77; Michael Dalton, *The Country Justice: Containing the Practice, Duty, and Power of the Justices of the Peace as Well in as Out of Their Sessions* (London, 1746), 82, 89; Richard Burn, *The Justice of the Peace, and Parish Officer* (London, 1755), 1:401.

8.  Lindgren, "Elusive Distinction," 849 (referring to the troika of "coercion," "bribery," and "false pretenses").

9.  The cases in this category are discussed in Lindgren, "Elusive Distinction," 839–40, 842, 850–51, 855n226, 880–81. See also ibid., 885, 885n443 (citing case in which denial of space to use a public market would support an extortion charge).

10. The cases in this category are discussed in Lindgren, "Elusive Distinction," 840, 842–43, 850, 878, 879, 880n413, 894–95. For confirmation that *People v. Whaley*, 6 Cow. 661 (N.Y. Sup. 1827), cited in Lindgren, "Elusive Distinction," 894, is a false-pretenses case, see the case itself.

11. The cases in this category are discussed in Lindgren, "Elusive Distinction," 839–41, 843–44, 853–59, 860n258, 877–81, 883, 884–85. See also ibid., 869–70 (noting statutes defining a crime of "extortion" based on briberylike conduct).

12. In writing his history, Lindgren's principal aim is to show that the Hobbs Act of 1946—a U.S. statute making a federal crime of common-law extortion affecting

interstate commerce—encompasses behavior that we today think of as bribery. On this point, Lindgren is convincing, and the U.S. Supreme Court has rightly relied upon his research in holding that the Hobbs Act extends to briberylike behavior. Evans v. United States, 504 U.S. 255, 260 (1992).

13. Lindgren, "Elusive Distinction," 859 (on statutes covering East India Company enacted in 1773, 1784, and 1793), 866–70 (on statutes covering England), 870–72 (on certain colonial statutes), 896–900 (on postrevolutionary New York statutes).

Lindgren also provides an analysis of the famous Statute of Westminster I, enacted in 1275 and on the books until the twentieth century. Ibid., 844–48. This statute mandated "that no sheriff, nor other the king's officer, take any reward to do his office, but shall be paid of that which they take of the king." Westm. I, 3 Edw. I, c. 26 (1275). If read literally, this appears to prohibit (except as allowed by subsequent statute) the receipt of any reward for official action, from anybody except the king, by any "king's officer," which might cover most or all of English government. But the statute should not be taken literally. In general, medieval statutory construction was not literal. J. H. Baker, *An Introduction to English Legal History*, 4th ed. (London: Butterworths Lexis-Nexis, 2002), 206. This provision of Westminster I was enacted as part of Edward I's effort to quell discontent in the countryside by halting oppressions by local officers at the county level or below. See Helen M. Cam, *The Hundred and the Hundred Rolls: An Outline of Local Government in Medieval England* (London: Methuen and Co., 1930); J. R. Maddicott, "Edward I and the Lessons of Baronial Reform: Local Government, 1258–1280," in *Thirteenth Century England I: Proceedings of the Newcastle upon Tyne Conference* (Woodbridge, UK: Boydell Press, 1985), 1–30. I think it is best understood as applying to the local officers existing at the time: sheriffs, their subordinates (e.g., bailiffs), coroners, and the like. This is consistent with subsequent texts on those officers, which say they are prohibited from all receipts not authorized by statute. E.g., Michael Dalton, *Officium Vicecomitum: The Office and Authoritie of Sherifs* (London: For the Company of Stationers, 1623), 182v.–183r.; *The Compleat Sheriff, Wherein Is Set Forth, His Office and Authority* (London, 1696), 415, 420. It is also consistent with the many sources that clearly assume it was lawful for other officials— those who were nonlocal (e.g., in London) or whose offices postdated 1275 (e.g., justices of the peace)—to take nonstatutory, customary payments, making no mention of Westminster I. E.g., Margery Bassett, "The Fleet Prison in the Middle Ages," *University of Toronto Law Journal* 5 (1944): 394–95 (royal investigation in 1561 to discern true customary fee levels); Francis Bacon, "Sir Fran. Bacon's Arguments against the Bill of Sheets," in *The Works of Francis Bacon*, ed. James Spedding et al. (London: Longmans, 1868), 10:286 (memo of 1606 referring to "ancient fees" of many offices); King James I, *The Copie of His Maiesties Commission, Touching the Fees of Officers and Ministers Belonging to the Courts of Justice* (London, 1623), 5 (royal investigation so that "ancient and due fees" can be "made known and settled"); Dalton, *Countrey Justice* (1677), 78–79 (justice-of-the-peace fees "vary according to the custom of the country"); William Oldnall Russell, *A Treatise on Crimes and Misdemeanors* (London: Joseph Butterworth and Son, 1819), 1:221–22 (discussing common law of extortion by analyzing Westminster I and then adding: "Justices of the peace, whose office was instituted after the act [i.e., after Westminster I], are bound by their oath of office to taking nothing for their office of justice of the peace to be done, but of the king, and fees accustomed, and costs limited by statute. And generally no public officer may take any other fees or rewards for doing any thing relating to his office than some statute in force gives him, or else as have been anciently and accustomably taken"). Consistent with this, Julius Goebel Jr. and T. Raymond Naughton, in a discussion of England in the seventeenth and eighteenth centuries, state: "A pious maxim [cited to Coke's *Institutes* and tracking Westminster I] that no officer would take reward for doing his duty had yielded to the practical argument that fees were perquisites allowed for labor and trouble and, where established by usage, were not assailable. . . . For the most part the English fees were regulated by ancient usage." *Law Enforcement in Colonial New York (1664–1776)* (New York: Commonwealth Fund, 1944), 732.

14. Some of this commentary concerns Westminster I. Lindgren, "Theory, History, and Practice," 1729n144. I believe Westminster I applied only to ancient local offices. See my discussion above, in note 13 to this chapter. Other commentary by Lindgren concerns later statutes. Lindgren, "Elusive Distinction," 865, 868, 872.

15. Lindgren invokes this troika ten times across two articles. "Elusive Distinction," 829, 847, 849, 863, 882, 908; "Theory, History, and Practice," 1697, 1703, 1717, 1739. He uses the term *false pretenses* for deception.

16. Two of these cases, *Stotesbury v. Smith*, 97 Eng. Rep. 635 (K.B. 1760) (cited in Lindgren, "Elusive Distinction," 850), and *Badow v. Salter*, 82 Eng. Rep. 34 (K.B. 1625) (cited in Lindgren, "Elusive Distinction," 885), concerned bailiffs, who, as sheriffs' officers, fell under the anti-receipt mandate of Westminster I. See my discussion in note 13 above. The third case, *Miller v. Aris*, 170 Eng. Rep. 598 (K.B. 1800) (cited in Lindgren, "Elusive Distinction," 850–51), concerned a jailor, whose receipts were in violation of regulations set by the county magistrates, 170 Eng. Rep. at 598, which were presumably promulgated under the scheme established by Parliament in 2 Geo. 2, c.22, § 4 (1729).

17. G. E. Aylmer, *The King's Servants: The Civil Service of Charles I, 1625–1642*, rev. ed. (London: Routledge & Kegan Paul, 1974), 176 (emphasis in original).

18. Aylmer, *King's Servants*, 179. See also Robert Latham and William Matthews, "Introduction," in *The Diary of Samuel Pepys*, ed. Robert Latham and William Matthews (Berkeley: University of California Press, 1970), 1:cxxiii.

19. For examples of commissioners discussing gratuities without intimation of illegality, see *RC-PA*, 1:79 (Navy Pay Office), 82–85 (Army Pay Office), 87 (Exchequer Auditor of Receipt), 102 (Exchequer Usher), 111 (general discussion of gratuities and the possibility of abuse); *RC-PA*, 2:104 (controller of army accounts, received until recently), 182 (Exchequer auditors of imprest); *RC-Fees*, 5 (secretary of state's subordinates), 96–99, 101 (Admiralty), 176–80 (Navy Office), 281–86 (Deptford Dockyard), 566–67 (Navy Victualling Office). On the possibility of abuse in general, see *RC-PA*, 1:111; *RC-PA*, 2:185–86; *RC-Fees*, 14, 100. For particularized examples of gratuities being abused, see *RC-Fees*, 574.

20. *RC-PA*, 2:184–85. The gratuities are first introduced in ibid., 2:180. See also *RC-Fees*, 16.

21. The passage was the same in Matthew Bacon, *A New Abridgment of the Law*, 6th ed., ed. Henry Gwillim (London: A. Strahan, 1807), 3:108. On the intervening English editions, see Morris L. Cohen, *Bibliography of Early American Law* (Buffalo, NY: William S. Hein and Co., 1998), 2:216.

22. William Oldnall Russell, *A Treatise on Crimes and Misdemeanors* (London: J. Butterworth, 1819), 1:222. It was also reproduced in John Lord Viscount Dudley and Ward and T. Cunningham, *The Law of a Justice of Peace and Parish Officer* (London, 1769), 2:164.

23. Matthew Bacon, *A New Abridgment of the Law* (London, 1740), 3:744. Note that the first and second volumes were dated 1736.

24. Boyter v. Dodsworth, 101 Eng. Rep. 770, 771 (K.B. 1796). Though the case concerned an Anglican Church office rather than a civil one, the Anglican Church was established and therefore a public institution. The case was cited by a later authority as pertaining to "offices" generally. Matthew Bacon, *A New Abridgment of the Law*, 6th ed., ed. Henry Gwillim (London: A. Strahan, 1807), 5:199.

25. Davies was the chief clerk to the comptroller for bills and accounts. *RC-Fees*, 205. On the importance of the chief clerks in Navy Office administration, see ibid., 182.

26. *RC-Fees*, 207. On his total income from fees and gratuities (more than £1,737), see ibid., 175.

27. Two clerks in the Navy Office testified in 1787 that, "when an account [to be processed] occasions more than usual trouble, the fee is increased," though payment of the increase was "optional." *RC-Fees*, 225–26. Similarly, one of the top administrators in the Navy Office in 1787 testified that he would often receive "a gratuity . . . for dispatch in examining and checking [certain] victualling accounts . . . , which gratuity is optional, and not paid after any fixed rate, but is from two shillings and sixpence to three guineas, according to the size of the account." Ibid., 217. The chief clerk for examining and stating imprest accounts in the navy's Victualling Office testified that there were "no established fees" in his section but that gratuities were "in general expected to be" paid at a certain rate, though they were "sometimes more and sometimes less." Ibid., 602.

28. The naval administrator Samuel Pepys, notes a scholarly introduction to his famous diary, "could not see anything wrong in a gift made merely to expedite business or to establish good personal relations." Latham and Matthews, "Introduction," in *The Diary of Samuel Pepys*, 1:cxxiii.

29. Jeremy Bentham, "The Rationale of Reward" (written circa 1780, first published 1825), in *The Works of Jeremy Bentham*, ed. John Bowring (Edinburgh: William Tait, 1843), 2:241.

30. Sparrow v. Cooper, 96 Eng. Rep. 769, 769 (C.P. 1778). See also Bentham, "Rationale of Reward," 241 (under the fee system, "[t]he regulated hours of business are employed in doing nothing, or in doing the least possible, that extraordinary pay may be received for what is done out of office-hours.").

31. Aylmer, *King's Servants*, 176. See also G. E. Aylmer, "Charles I's Commission on Fees, 1627–40," *Historical Research* 31 (1958): 58 (noting "a chronic tendency . . . for unofficial perquisites and gratuities to be formalized into recognized fees, and for additional 'tips' to take their place.").

32. *RC-PA*, 1:111.
33. *RC-Fees*, 207. For a similar story, see ibid., 602.
34. *RC-Fees*, 243, 245, 247. See also clerks of dockyards, ibid., 332, 333.
35. Richard J. Ross, "The Memorial Culture of Early Modern English Lawyers: Memory as Keyword, Shelter, and Identity," *Yale Journal of Law and the Humanities* 10 (1998): 259–61.
36. E.g., *RC-Fees*, 10 (Secretary of State's Office, at least a century old).
37. Bentham, "Rationale of Reward," 241.
38. King James I, *Copie of His Maiesties Commission*, 7 (emphasis omitted).
39. Jean S. Wilson, "Sir Henry Spelman and the Royal Commission on Fees," in *Studies Presented to Sir Hilary Jenkinson*, ed. J. Conway Davies (London: Oxford University Press, 1957), 464. See also Aylmer, *King's Servants*, 195.
40. 3 W. & M., c. 5, § 54 (1691).
41. *RC-PA*, 1:355, 359–60.
42. When the Lords of the Treasury collectivized all their subordinates' fees into a single fund from which salaries would be paid (see *RC-Fees*, 55–56), they also ordered one clerk to research the fees and reduce them into a single accessible schedule. This clerk testified that he had compiled the schedule "from the returns of clerks who executed the different branches of business, and formerly received [i.e., pocketed] the fees thereon." *RC-Fees*, 74. Had the fees rested on any higher or more formal authority than the lists kept by the clerks, we can assume that the commission would have cited it, as it did in the case of ordinances and departmental schedules for other agencies. E.g., ibid., 10 (ancient table in Secretary of State's Office), 111 (Privy Council order for Admiralty clerks).
43. This is based on testimony of Navy Office clerks before a parliamentary commission in 1787. In at least thirty-three cases, a Navy Office clerk stated the annual total of his fees and/or gratuities and submitted his own personal, individualized schedule of the rates of payment that he received for each transaction. *RC-Fees*, 208, 208–09, 209, 210, 211, 213 (two clerks), 223, 224, 225, 227–28, 228, 229 (two clerks), 230 (two clerks), 231 (two clerks), 232, 235, 236, 239, 240, 241, 243, 244, 245 (two clerks), 245–46, 246, 246–47, 247 (two clerks). In at least twenty other cases, the clerk stated the annual total of his fees and/or gratuities but submitted no schedule of rates, though in some of these cases he stated the rates directly in his testimony or stated the range into which the rates usually fell. *RC-Fees*, 207, 212, 217, 217–18, 218, 225, 226, 237 (two clerks), 238 (two clerks), 241, 242, 244, 248, 254, 256 (three clerks), 257 (two clerks). In no case did any member of the Navy Office cite any more official authority for the rates of the fees he was taking, such as a departmental ordinance, or even a departmental schedule. Had one existed, the commissioners would have cited it, as they did in the case of other agencies. See note 42 above.
44. *RC-PA*, 1:80.
45. William Holdsworth, *A History of English Law*, 7th ed., ed. A. L. Goodhart et al. (London: Methuen and Co., 1956), 1:256 (quoting parliamentary commission of 1818).
46. Aylmer, *King's Servants*, 189, 194; Aylmer, "Charles I's Commission on Fees," 60, 65–66.

47. *Commons Debates*, 1621, ed. Wallace Notestein et al. (New Haven, CT: Yale University Press, 1935), 3:150.
48. Aylmer, *King's Servants*, 190–91.
49. A *Discourse on Fees of Office in Courts of Justice* (London, 1736), 28, 30.
50. Fleetwood v. Finch, 126 Eng. Rep. 517, 518 (C.P. 1793) (Heath, J.).
51. Queen v. Coles, 115 Eng. Rep. 802, 807 (Q.B. 1845).
52. Veale v. Priour, 145 Eng. Rep. 492 (Ex. 1666).
53. 43 Eliz., c. 12 (1601).
54. *Veale*, 145 Eng. Rep. at 494–95.
55. Ballard v. Gerard, 88 Eng. Rep. 1553, 1553 (K.B. 1702) (Holt, C.J.) (citing "Beal and Prior," in "Hard.," which means *Veale v. Priour*, in Hardress's reports).
56. *Discourse on Fees*, 31, 33.
57. Herbert A. Johnson, *Imported Eighteenth-Century Treatises in American Libraries, 1700–1799* (Knoxville: University of Tennessee Press, 1978), 3–4, 59. This ranking excludes law dictionaries and formularies. On imported treatises' importance in America, see ibid., xvi.
58. Cohen, *Bibliography of Early American Law*, 2:216–18.
59. A *New Conductor Generalis: Being a Summary of the Law Relative to the Duty and Office of Justice of the Peace* (Albany, NY: D. & S. Whiting, 1803), 163; Nathan Dane, A *General Abridgment and Digest of American Law, with Occasional Notes and Comments* (Boston: Cummings, Hilliard and Co., 1824), 7:21; William Oldnall Russell, A *Treatise on Crimes and Misdemeanors*, 1st American ed., ed. Daniel Davis (Boston: Wells and Lilly, 1824), 1:222.
60. Thomas C. Barrow, *Trade and Empire: The British Customs Service in Colonial America* (Cambridge, MA: Harvard University Press, 1967), 189.
61. Alfred S. Martin, "The King's Customs: Philadelphia, 1763–1774," *William and Mary Quarterly*, 3rd ser., 5 (1948): 210.
62. RFCC, 73. He also cited usage.
63. ATRCF, 2:9 (Salem).
64. A Rhode Island customs officer claimed payment for filling out certain forms, on the ground that it was "optional in the merchant," since he could fill out the forms himself if he chose. Ibid., 1:11. A New Hampshire customs officer listed fees "paid with the consent of the merchants trading people." RFCC, 73; see also ATRCF, 1:7 (copy of same).
65. RFCC, 37.
66. RFCC. This quoted language appears on a page between the numbered pages 45 and 52, with the words "Province of New Hamp." in large letters at the left.
67. RFCC, 31.
68. Kilty v. Hammond, 3 H. & McH. 149, 149–51 (Md. Gen. Ct. 1793).
69. *Trial of Prescott*, 170. Note that Webster went on to say: "Most of the services [for which Prescott is accused of taking illegal fees] were not, strictly speaking, official services. As before observed, the petition, bond, etc., might have been prepared elsewhere, if the party had so chosen." Ibid. This perhaps supports Lindgren's idea that the payments referred to by Bacon were not "under color of office." Lindgren, "Elusive

Distinction," 888. Webster's opposing counsel, Shaw, seemed to concede Webster's point, but only as to ministerial, nonjudicial officers. *Trial of Prescott*, 183.

70. *The Colonial Records of South Carolina: The Journal of the Commons House of Assembly, November 10, 1736–June 7, 1739*, ed. J. H. Easterby (Columbia: Historical Commission of South Carolina, 1951), 345.

71. *Stat. of Penn. (1682–1801)*, 10:39–40 (emphasis added).

72. Irwin v. Commissioners of Northumberland County, 1 Serg. & Rawle 505, 508 (Pa. 1815) (Yeates, J.). Judge Yeates said he could not give the statute's exact citation or year, since he did not have the books in front of him, but this is clearly the statute to which he was referring. See also Judge Tilghman's opinion, ibid., 506 (stating that customary fees had been "indirectly recognized by acts of assembly").

73. 10 Geo. 3, c. 37, § 2 (1770). An earlier provision to the same effect, though not quite as explicit about the usage basis of pre-1764 fees, was 5 Geo. 3, c. 45, § 27 (1765).

74. RFCC, 2:71.

75. ATRCF, 2:28 (Bermuda customs officer).

76. *Journals of the House of Representatives of Massachusetts 1729–1731* (Boston: Massachusetts Historical Society, 1928), 335 (message from governor, referring to his own fees).

77. ATRCF, 1:30 (James River Lower Part); ibid., 1:32 (Currituck, Virginia).

78. RFCC, 72 (Salem).

79. ATRCF, 1:16 (Perth Amboy); ibid., 1:38 (Charlestown, referring to the searchers). The collector at New Haven, Connecticut, listed customary fees dating "from the establishment of the port." ATRCF, 1:14. But that probably refers to New Haven's assuming the status of a legal port of entry, which did not occur till 1757 or later. Barrow, *Trade and Empire*, 124. A customs officer at "Wynyaw" (i.e., Winyah Bay), South Carolina, dated his fees from the establishment of the office there. ATRCF, 1:37 But it was established only in about 1738–50. Barrow, *Trade and Empire*, 138.

80. RFCC, 49 (collector at Piscataqua, New Hampshire), 114 (New York chancery clerk, referring to "an old accustomed fee before I came to the office"). For a somewhat stronger assertion of antiquity, see RFCC, 70 (Massachusetts customs officers, referring to fees that "had been [received] for several years before we came into" the office).

81. RFCC, 175 (Virginia governor, referring to a fee "by prescription," received "as I am informed by the late Lt. Governor Robert Dinwiddie Esq.," his immediate predecessor); ATRCF, 1:28 (customs officer at Rappahannock, referring to several customary fees that "his predecessor Mr. Reid we believe" also received).

82. RFCC, 121–22 (New York clerk of the circuits, referring to "usual and customary fees," "having been always taken by my predecessors allowed and taxed by the judges"), 126 (New York clerk of Kings County, referring to a customary fee that "has been allowed to former clerks" by the judges), 128–30 (New York clerk of Queens County, referring to customary fees taken by "predecessors"), 205 (South Carolina vice admiralty judge, referring to fees "established by long usage and custom" that "have been constantly allowed to be taken by all the judges of this court for a great number of years past"), 206 (South Carolina register in chancery, referring to customary fees that have "always

been taken by the present master and his predecessors to me and my predecessors in office").

83. RFCC, 47 (New Hampshire naval officer: "custom"), 124 (New York high sheriff of Richmond County: "custom"), 204 (South Carolina surveyor general: "long usage"), 222 (South Carolina Secretary's Office: "custom"); ATRCF, 1:31 (customs officers at James River Upper Part: "custom only"); ibid., 1:34 (customs officers at Bath, North Carolina: "by custom"); 1:48 (Bahamas customs officers: "customary"); ibid., 2:16 (New York customs officers: "by custom only"); ibid., 2:22 (York River customs officers: "custom only"). See also ATRCF, 1:19 (Philadelphia collector and comptroller: "usually taken"). For confirmation that *usually* means "customary," see the contemporaneous statutory schedule of customs fees (enacted in 1751–52), in *Stat. of Penn.* (1682–1801), 5:174, in which most of the claimed fees do not appear. See also *NC Recs* 4:1126 (1750) (colony secretary, referring to governor's fee, founded on "some foregoing law or proscription I cannot say").

84. ATRCF, 2:9–10.

85. "Opinion on the Power of the General Court to Establish Fees" (1774), in *The Letters and Papers of Edmund Pendleton, 1734–1803*, ed. David John Mays (Charlottesville: University Press of Virginia, 1967), 1:84.

86. Colden to Board of Trade (Aug. 9, 1764), in *Collections of the New York Historical Society for the Year 1876: The Colden Letter Books*, vol. 1, 1760–1765 (New York: For the Society, 1877), 340 (emphasis added). On the forty-year usage, see Colden's subsequent letter to the Board (Oct. 13, 1764) in ibid., 387.

87. RFCC, 66–67 (emphasis added).

88. Compare *The Acts and Resolves, Public and Private, of the Province of Massachusetts Bay* (Boston: Wright and Potter, 1874), 2:44–45 (statute of 1716), with RFCC, 67. The amounts are the same for entering and clearing a foreign vessel and for entering and clearing a provincial vessel. The 1764 report claims 3*s*. 4*d*. for entering and clearing a New England vessel, whereas the statute only allows 2*s*. And the 1764 report omits the fee for entering and clearing other North American vessels, which in the statute is 5*s*. and 6*s*. for inward and outward passage, respectively.

89. Compare the tenth to twelfth items in RFCC, 67, with *Acts and Resolves*, 2:44–45 (statute of 1716).

90. *Journals of the House of Representatives of Massachusetts 1735–1736* (Boston: Massachusetts Historical Society, 1932), 205.

91. Compare *Journals of the House of Representatives of Massachusetts 1735–1736*, 205 (claiming, for "cancelling bonds," 3*s*., though he actually takes only 2*s*., currency unspecified), with RFCC, 67 (claiming, for "recording the certificate of bond being given in Great Britain for vessels that design to load enumerated commodities, or for taking bond for vessels loading those commodities, when no such bond has been given, in either case the fee is," 1*s*. 6*d*. sterling or 2*s*. proclamation money; and claiming, for "cancelling such bond taken upon a certificate being returned," 6*d*. sterling, or 8*d*. proclamation money).

92. Compare *Journals of the House of Representatives of Massachusetts 1735–1736*, 205 (claiming, for "going on board ships or vessels, viewing and examining them if

qualified for a Mediterranean pass, certifying thereon and taking bond for said pass," 15s., though he actually takes only 12s., currency unspecified), with RFCC, 67 (claiming, for "surveying vessels, passing a certificate and taking bond for those bound to the Mediterranean or those parts which requiring the taking out an Algerine pass, in the whole," 4s. 6d. sterling, or 6s. proclamation money).

93. Barrow, *Trade and Empire*, 189–90.
94. *Md. Arch.* 31:65 (1755). However, they added that remoteness of some localities and the hostility of local juries might make it practically difficult for an officer to collect such payments, so it helped to have a special statutory collection process.
95. See my discussion in this chapter, text at notes 120–23.
96. RFCC, 202. See also ATRCF, 2:9–10 (Salem collector, justifying one fee simply "as a reasonable fee for the services" without mention of usage).
97. The chief justice of New York reported in 1767 that this was the norm in his colony. Goebel and Naughton, *Law Enforcement in Colonial New York*, 742. A justice of the supreme court of Pennsylvania said the same in recalling the eighteenth-century practice of his colony-state. Irwin v. Commissioners of Northumberland County, 1 Serg. & Rawle 505, 508 (Pa. 1815) (Yeates, J.). See also my discussion in note 116 below.
98. See my discussion in this chapter, text at notes 162–69. See also *Waldron v. Tuttle*, 4 N.H. 149, 152–53 (1827) (stating that officer can "demand and receive" extrastatutory fees, apparently without mediation of a fee-taxing judge).
99. *Trial of Prescott*, 162 (citing "1. *Salkeld*. 333," which is *Ballard*), 163 (citing "*Hard.* 355," which is *Veale*).
100. *Trial of Prescott*, 185 (Shaw). See also my discussion in this chapter, text at notes 135–39.
101. ATRCF, 2:10.
102. RFCC, 202. See also ibid., 95 (New York vice admiralty judge: "example of my predecessors with a view to a *quantum meruit*"), 120 (New York customs officers: "cheerfully paid by the merchants . . . for many years past"), 209 (South Carolina clerk of the Court of Common Pleas: "by custom taken . . . as a *quantum meruit*").
103. E.g., RFCC, 103 (New York attorney general, analogizing to English attorney general), 202 (South Carolina master in chancery, claiming fees received "by other public officers for the like business"), 213 (South Carolina chief justice of Court of General Sessions, analogizing to chief justice of the Court of Common Pleas). One of the attorneys prosecuting Prescott admitted that "perhaps, by rules of analogy, [Prescott] might [lawfully] have taken the same sum as is established by law" in an analogous type of case. *Trial of Prescott*, 83.
104. *Md. Arch.* 35:219. See also *Md. Arch.* 32:495 (referencing the 1719 statute).
105. *Md. Arch.* 35:179–80. On office-holding in the upper house, see Newton D. Mereness, *Maryland as a Proprietary Province* (London: Macmillan, 1901), 182, 470 (referring to such office-holding in 1730s and 1750s).
106. *Md. Arch.* 36:125, 495–96. On the upper house's request for veto, see Mereness, *Maryland as a Proprietary Province*, 178.
107. See Wynne's opinion in *Md. Arch.* 32:495–96 (1730).
108. *Md. Arch.* 35:442.

109. Paraphrase in Mereness, *Maryland as a Proprietary Province*, 381.
110. *Md. Arch.* 36:165.
111. *Md. Arch.* 37:502–03. See also *Md. Arch.* 62:426 (message of judges of Land Office to governor during a subsequent controversy in 1770, looking back on events occurring shortly after expiration of 1719 statute).
112. *Md. Arch.* 37:502.
113. *Md. Arch.* 28:31–44. On the return of at least temporary stability, see Mereness, *Maryland as a Proprietary Province*, 381–82. For background, see *Md. Arch.* 36:328–29 (1729); *Md. Arch.* 32:497–98 (1731); *Md. Arch.* 39:183 (1735).
114. *Md. Arch.* 35:442–43 (1726) (assembly proposal); *Md. Arch.* 36:159 (council proposal).
115. Nothing relevant appears in the indexes of *Md. Arch.* vol. 33 (Council Proceedings 1732–53) or *Md. Arch.* vol. 39 (General Assembly 1732–36).
116. A final word should be said about the several officers, in both England and America, who were attached to courts and had to have bills for some or all of their fees approved by the judge before they could collect. These included clerks, registers, sheriffs, constables, and the like. One might think that judicial supervision would restrain negotiation between these fee-taking officers and the public. But that was not necessarily the case. Frequently, a judge knew little about the customary fee-charging practices of his own court and did not immerse himself in such matters, leaving them to a (fee-seeking) clerk. E.g., *Journals of the House of Commons* (London: House of Commons, 1803), 1:606 (statement of Mr. Downes in Parliament of 1621); RFCC, 308–09 (South Carolina vice admiralty judge); also, see my discussion in this chapter, text at note 127 (on Pennsylvania admiralty judge and his register). And even if the judge were aware of negotiation between court officers and the public, he might let it go on. Several Anglo-American judges in this period had a share in the fees of their subordinates. Bentham, "Rationale of Reward," 241 ("heads of departments" will "connive" at improper fee-taking by subordinates, for their "share of the benefit"); NC Recs 6:173 (assembly's statement that chief justice is "exacting from the clerks a considerable part of the legal fees" they charge). And even when they did not, they often acted permissively "out of kindness to their inferiors, or for fear of rendering them discontented." Bentham, "Rationale of Reward," 241 (referring to "heads of department" generally as supervisors of fee-taking by their subordinates).
117. *Trial of Prescott*, 161–62.
118. *Walker v. Ham*, 2 N.H. 238, 239 (1820).
119. *Discourse on Fees*, 26, 32. For similar points, see ibid., 12, 42.
120. *Laws of New Hampshire*, ed. Albert Stillman Batchellor (Concord, NH: Rumford Printing Co., 1913), 2:335–36 (statute of 1719). For the schedule itself, see ibid., 275–81 (statute of 1718).
121. RFCC, 43–44. The judge and register divided the court's fees between themselves "by agreement." Ibid. A New Hampshire customs official made a similar report. Ibid., 47.
122. The ordinance is *An Ordinance for Regulating & Establishing Fees. By His Excellency Robert Hunter, Esq* (New York, 1710?), Evans Early American Imprints No. 1482. Compare ibid., 2 (no officers shall take an unlisted fee "for any service or services . . . to be done and performed in their respective offices"), with ibid., 19 (no officer shall

take "any greater or other fee for or in respect of any the services herein before mentioned").

123. RFCC, 128–31 (emphasis added). Also, see my discussion in this chapter, text at note 158.

124. *Stat. of Penn. (1682–1801)*, 5:177 (statute of 1752) (emphasis added).

125. *Stat. of Penn. (1682–1801)*, 10:40 (statute of 1779) (emphasis added).

126. George Everett Hastings, *The Life and Works of Francis Hopkinson* (Chicago: University of Chicago Press, 1926), 257–64; Dixon Wecter, "Francis Hopkinson and Benjamin Franklin," *American Literature* 12 (1940): 208. See also the memorial of Hopkinson's enemy Sergeant, in *The Pennsylvania State Trials, Containing the Impeachment, Trial, and Acquittal of Francis Hopkinson, and John Nicholson, Esquires* (Philadelphia, 1794), 27. (This book says "Vol. I" on its title page, but no subsequent volume was ever published.) On extortion being the most serious charge, see ibid., 59.

127. *Pennsylvania State Trials*, 38–39. Robeson corroborated his boss's story. Ibid., 50. On Robeson's age and tenure, see J. Thomas Scharf and Thompson Westcott, *History of Philadelphia, 1609–1884* (Philadelphia: L. H. Everts and Co., 1884), 2:1577, 1577n6.

128. *Pennsylvania State Trials*, 50–51. For the statute, see *Stat. of Penn. (1682–1801)*, 10:39–40.

129. *Pennsylvania State Trials*, 60. Reed's characterization of Pennsylvania law was confirmed a few decades later by the justices of the state supreme court, who recalled that, during the eighteenth century, "compensatory fees for services rendered by public officers, not enumerated in any fee bill [i.e., fee statute], were uniformly received, under the sanction of this court, and of all the courts of justice in Pennsylvania," "under a supposed *quantum meruit*." Irwin v. Commissioners of Northumberland County, 1 Serg. & Rawle 505, 508 (Pa. 1815) (Yeates, J.). See also ibid., 506 (Tilghman, J.) (referring to "long standing" practice). This case concerned a claim by a sheriff for fees from a county, but clearly the justices were referring to customary fees that could also be charged to individuals.

130. *Pennsylvania State Trials*, 61–62.

131. Ibid., 52.

132. Ibid., 62.

133. *The Statutes at Large of South Carolina*, ed. Thomas Cooper (Columbia, SC: A. S. Johnston, 1839), 5:153 (statute of 1791) (emphasis added).

134. The issue was "not decided in so many words, but it [was] in substance; because the Court did in that case sanction many items of charge, for services alleged to be performed, which are not comprised in the act." Butler v. Ryan, 3 Des. Eq. 178, 182 (S.C. Cir. Eq. 1810), discussing an apparently unreported aspect of *Shubrick v. Fisher*, 2 Des. Eq. 148 (S.C. App. 1802). But note the judge in *Butler* qualified this point by concluding that such nonstatutory fees could not be by the officer's "own arbitrary charge" but had to be sued for, or taxed by the master in chancery. *Butler*, 3 Des. Eq. at 183.

Jack P. Greene argues that the colonial assembly of South Carolina held effective control over fee-taking despite the fact that its acts on the subject were not officially in force. *The Quest for Power: The Lower Houses of Assembly in the Southern*

*Royal Colonies, 1689–1776* (Chapel Hill: University of North Carolina Press, 1963), 155–58. I disagree. Nine South Carolina officers answered the Board of Trade survey in 1764 by claiming one or more fees on nonstatutory grounds. RFCC, 202 (master in chancery), 204 (surveyor general), 205 (vice admiralty judge), 206 (register in chancery), 207 (provost marshal), 208 (clerk of crown and peace), 209 (clerk of common pleas), 213 (chief justice of general sessions), 222 (secretary's office). The governor in 1767 sent the secretary of state a list of fees taken in the province, which (he said) "he found difficult to obtain, as few of the fees, are ascertained by Act of Parl[iament], but are regulated, either by custom, or by an act of assembly, that . . . never received the royal assent." Abstract of Dispatch from Governor Charles Montagu to the Earl of Shelburne (Aug. 14, 1767), 56:103, Papers of William Petty, 1st Marquis of Lansdowne, 2nd Earl of Shelburne, Clements Library, University of Michigan.

135. 1796 Mass. Acts 523, 535 (emphasis added). This volume contains statutes passed at a session beginning in 1795 and ending in 1796. Lawyers, apparently using different sets of volumes of the Massachusetts session laws, varied in whether they cited this statute to a volume labeled 1795 or 1796.

136. The discussions that come nearest to textual analysis on this point are in *Trial of Prescott*, 90 (defense counsel Hoar: "The statute in making provision for certain services does not say that the judge shall have no compensation for other services"), 141 (defense counsel Blake: "I must beseech the learned Managers, . . . that they would be pleased to put their finger upon any prohibitory clause of the statute, . . . inhibiting a judge of probate, at the peril of impeachment, from receiving a reasonable compensation, a mere *quantum meruit*").

137. Ibid., 71. See also Leland's argument on Prescott's departure from his own usage. Ibid., 83–84.

138. Ibid., 162–63.

139. Ibid., 185.

140. Walker v. Ham, 2 N.H. 238, 240 (1820). New Hampshire officers were permitted to make these charges directly against the citizen, even without the mediation of a judge who was taxing the fees. Waldron v. Tuttle, 4 N.H. 149, 152–53 (1827).

141. Commonwealth v. Shed, 1 Mass. 227, 228–29 (1804).

142. *Trial of Prescott*, 83 (emphasis added).

143. Commonwealth v. Shed, 1 Mass. 227, 229 (1804). The court added that the payor might be able to recover the extra charge in a civil action. Ibid. Attorneys prosecuting Prescott seemed to recognize a similar doctrine. *Trial of Prescott*, 199.

144. Regulation XXIV, appended to 12 Car. 2, c. 4 (1660). The regulation is printed in *The Statutes of the Realm . . . from Original Records and Authentic Manuscripts* (Buffalo: W. S. Hein, 1993), 5:205.

145. For the London table, promulgated in 1662, see *RC-PA*, 3:386–92. For tables of the eight head ports (each governing the head's respective member ports), promulgated in 1662 and 1670, see *RC-PA*, 3:392–93, 395–96, 397, 398, 722, 741, 770, 779, 787, 795, 809. On how the tables at all the non-London ports covered only the patent officers, see *RC-PA*, 3:157.

146. *RC-PA*, 3:157.

147. John Brewer, *The Sinews of Power: War, Money, and the English State, 1688–1783* (Cambridge, MA: Harvard University Press, 1988), 66.

148. The commissioners warned that "[s]ome of the officers have no salaries: Many have salaries so small as not to afford common support"; if they did not take fees, they would "endure an official situation whence the means of livelihood cannot be derived." *RC-PA*, 3:185.

149. *RC-PA*, 3:185.

150. *RC-PA*, 3:79–80.

151. The comparison is introduced in *RC-PA*, 3:80. For the 1662 parliamentary table, see *RC-PA*, 3:386–92. For the fee lists of the 1780s, see *RC-PA*, vol. 3, appendix to the 14th report, item numbers 27, 42, 47, 50, 53, 61, 73, 82, 88, 98, 109, 115, 118, 123, 129, 132, 140.

152. *RC-PA*, 3:80.

153. *RC-PA*, 3:157.

154. Quite frequently, the table of fees actually charged at a head port or member port dwarfed the parliamentary table for the head port. For all the tables beyond London, see *RC-PA*, 3:722–819.

155. *RC-PA*, 3:157.

156. At least fifteen witnesses referenced fees "grounded on usage" or some similar phrase. *RC-PA*, 3:365, 367, 403, 438, 449, 458, 461–62, 463, 482, 484, 499, 506, 526, 661, 721. John Dalley, one of the highest customs officers nationwide, referred to "law or usage" as the two "authorities" on which fees were taken. *RC-PA*, 3:579. On Dalley's status, see *RC-PA*, 3:4.

157. *RC-PA*, 3:823–25. Also, in three cases, they cited agreement and arbitration between officers and merchants.

158. *RFCC*, 90–91.

159. *RFCC*, 88–89.

160. *Documents Relative to the Colonial History of the State of New-York*, ed. F. B. O'Callaghan (Albany, NY: Weed, Parsons and Co., 1856), 7:924–25. Kempe reported on the same subject in *RFCC*, 102. See also the report of the New York chancery clerk on the obsolescence of this and some other gubernatorial ordinances regulating fees. *RFCC*, 114 (front and back of page).

161. *Journal of the Votes and Proceedings of the General Assembly of the Colony of New-York* (New York, 1766), 2:672.

162. *Ordinance for Regulating & Establishing Fees*, 2, 15. For the full cite to this source, see note 122 above.

163. The instruction is in *Royal Instructions to British Colonial Governors, 1670–1776*, ed. Leonard Woods Labaree (New York: D. Appleton-Century Co., 1935), 2:579 (no. 820). Though the wording seems to impose the limit only on grants of "resumed lands" to "late patentees" (and, after 1753, on "resumed lands" to any patentees), it was apparently understood to apply generally. See Ronald W. Howard, "The English Province (1664–1776)," in *The Empire State: A History of New York*, ed. Milton M. Klein (Ithaca, NY: Cornell University Press, 2001), 152 ("After Cornbury [i.e., in 1710], the Board of Trade instructed New York governors to limit grants to two thousand acres (reduced to one thousand acres in 1753) per patentee").

164. Patricia U. Bonomi, *A Fractious People: Politics and Society in Colonial New York* (New York: Columbia University Press, 1971), 204–05; Catherine Snell Crary, "The American Dream: John Tabor Kempe's Rise from Poverty to Riches," *William and Mary Quarterly*, 3rd ser., 13 (1957): 189; Howard, "English Province," 152.

165. See Kempe's report on his fees in 1767, in *Documents Relative to the Colonial History of the State of New-York*, 7:925.

166. RFCC. This is on the back of page 96, facing page 97.

167. See Colden's report to the board in 1764, in *Collections of the New York Historical Society for the Year 1876*, 387.

168. RFCC, 103–04. Kempe repeated these justifications in a 1767 report. *Documents Relative to the Colonial History of the State of New York*, 7:924–25.

169. RFCC, 96–97. See also Bonomi, *A Fractious People*, 205n47.

170. J. H. Parry, "The Patent Offices in the British West Indies," *English Historical Review* 69 (1954): 211.

171. Committee report of 1766, printed in *An Appeal to the Public on Behalf of Samuel Vaughan* (London, 1770), 126.

172. Order in Council of 1765, printed in *Appeal to the Public on Behalf of Samuel Vaughan*, 122–23. The assembly was free to pass a new statute, but the crown would approve it only if it were "adequate to the present state of [the officers'] business, and the circumstances of the times." Ibid., 123. Shocked by this rebuke, the assembly did not regulate the fees of any officers for the rest of the century (with minor exceptions). Parry, "Patent Offices," 211.

173. Committee report of 1766, printed in *Appeal to the Public on Behalf of Samuel Vaughan*, 126. For similar events in Barbados, see Parry, "Patent Offices," 211–12.

174. When institutions for administering the empire first emerged in the 1670s, the crown began issuing a boilerplate instruction telling every royal governor, "with the advice and consent" of his council, "to take especial care to regulate all . . . fees belonging to places [i.e., offices]," so they would "be within the bounds of moderation" and "no exaction" be made. *Royal Instructions to British Colonial Governors*, 1:371–72 (no. 521). Though the instruction did not reference the assembly, it became common for assemblies to participate in fee regulation, jointly with the governor and council, through the enactment of statutes. The Board of Trade considered such participation acceptable, indeed laudable. See the board's messages to North Carolina's Governor Dobbs. *NC Recs* 5:750 (1757); ibid., 6:726–27 (1762). See also Greene, *Quest for Power*, 153–55. That said, the Privy Council made clear in 1754 that the governor and colonial council could enact new fees without the assembly, via statutelike ordinance, if need be. Jack P. Greene, "The Case of the Pistole Fee: The Report of a Hearing on the Pistole Fee Dispute before the Privy Council, June 18, 1754," *Virginia Magazine of History and Biography* 66 (1958): 404–05.

175. "Their occasional efforts" at reform in several areas (including fee regulation), observes one historian, "produced only limited and temporary results." Parry, "Patent Offices," 207.

176. *Acts of the Privy Council of England: Colonial Series*, ed. W. L. Grant and James Munro (Hereford, UK: Hereford Times Co., 1910), 2:142–43 (order in 1689 upholding

fee "as being an ancient and customary fee, and paid only by such who receive a considerable benefit thereby"); Parry, "Patent Offices," 205–06, 211–12 (on treatment of Barbados in 1710s to 1730s).

177. *RC-PA*, 3:187.

178. William Hawkins, *A Treatise of the Pleas of the Crown* (London, 1716), 1:171. But note Hawkins was a proponent of regulating the level of facilitative payments.

179. Bacon, *New Abridgment*, 3:744. This is the first edition, dated 1740.

180. Paraphrase by Mereness, *Maryland as a Proprietary Province*, 387.

181. *Pennsylvania State Trials*, 60.

182. Anonymous [Richard Champion], *Considerations on the Present Situation of Great Britain and the United States of North America, with a View to Their Future Commercial Connections*, 1st ed. (London, 1784), 110–11. Champion was making this statement in reaction to a recent crackdown against such reciprocity and a recent proposal in Parliament to abolish customs officers' fees altogether. Ibid., 106–14. For background on fee-based negotiation and accommodation between English customs officers and merchants (with a more negative take than Champion gives), see *RC-PA*, 1:111; *RC-PA*, 3:166, 183–84. Note Champion published a second edition of this tract, much expanded, that same year, with the same title and publisher, and revealing his name, but that edition omits the quoted passage.

183. RFCC, 103–04.

184. RFCC, 96–97.

185. Mary Lou Lustig, *Privilege and Prerogative: New York's Provincial Elite, 1710–1776* (Madison, NJ: Fairleigh Dickinson University Press, 1995), 160–64, 169. In his arguments to the crown, he may have been referring not only to the royal acreage cap but also to a 1767 royal proclamation against grants of land in what is now Vermont.

186. Commonwealth v. Shed, 1 Mass. 227 (1804).

187. *Discourse on Fees*, 26.

188. Adam Smith, *An Inquiry into the Nature and Causes of the Wealth of Nations* (Dublin, 1776), 3:86–87. Smith also stated that fees could be "precisely regulated and ascertained" so as to prevent "corruption." Ibid., 3:84–85. For a recent analysis of English judicial fee-taking, see Daniel Klerman, "Jurisdictional Competition and the Evolution of the Common Law," *University of Chicago Law Review* 74 (2007): 1179–1226.

189. *NC Recs* 3:367 (1732).

190. D. B. Horn, *The British Diplomatic Service 1689–1789* (Oxford: Clarendon Press, 1961), 57–60.

191. William Temple Franklin to Thomas Jefferson (Apr. 27, 1790), in *The Papers of Thomas Jefferson*, ed. Julian P. Boyd (Princeton, NJ: Princeton University Press, 1961), 16:364. I located this source through Robert Ralph Davis Jr., "Diplomatic Gifts and Emoluments: The Early National Experience," *Historian* 32 (1970): 377–80.

192. Davis, "Diplomatic Gifts and Emoluments," 377.

193. Charles Ronald Middleton, *The Administration of British Foreign Policy, 1782–1846* (Durham, NC: Duke University Press, 1977), 223.

194. Horn, *British Diplomatic Service*, 57 (thirty-five thousand livres). For the exchange rate between British and French currency in 1763, see John J. McCusker, *Money and Exchange in Europe and America, 1600–1775: A Handbook* (Chapel Hill: University of North Carolina Press, 1978), 97.

195. Horn, *British Diplomatic Service*, 57.

196. François de Callières, *The Practice of Diplomacy* (1716), trans. A. F. Whyte (London: Constable and Co., 1919), 25.

197. Thomas Jefferson, "Notes of Presents Given to American Diplomats by Foreign Governments" (circa 1791), in *Papers of Thomas Jefferson*, 16:366. Jefferson's denominations are in Louis d'Ors. To convert to pounds, see Shepard Pond, "The Louis d'Or," *Bulletin of the Business Historical Society* 14 (1940): 79 (in period before 1789, Louis d'Or stabilized at twenty-four livres); David R. Weir, "Tontines, Public Finance, and the Revolution in France and England, 1688–1789," *Journal of Economic History* 49 (1989): 99n13 (exchange rate of twenty-four livres to the pound in 1780s).

198. *Journals of the Continental Congress, 1774–1789*, ed. Gaillard Hunt (Washington, DC: GPO, 1910), 18:1114–15.

199. Louis W. Potts, *Arthur Lee: A Virtuous Revolutionary* (Baton Rouge: Louisiana State University Press, 1981), 241.

200. *Journals of the Continental Congress, 1774–1789*, ed. John C. Fitzpatrick (Washington, DC: GPO, 1934), 30:95.

201. Articles of Confederation (1781), art. 6, cl. 1.

202. Jefferson, "Notes of Presents," 366. For conversion to pounds, see note 197 above. See also Richard B. Morris, *The Peacemakers: The Great Powers and American Independence* (New York: Harper and Row, 1965), 434–35.

203. Jefferson, "Notes of Presents," 366.

204. 8 Annals of Congress 1583 (1798) (Rep. Bayard).

205. 8 Annals of Congress 1585 (1798) (Rep. Otis).

## CHAPTER 2: BARGAINING OUTLAWED

1. Linda Levy Peck, *Court Patronage and Corruption in Early Stuart England* (Boston: Unwin Hyman, 1990), 166–67, 184.

2. G. E. Aylmer, *The King's Servants: The Civil Service of Charles I, 1625–1642*, rev. ed. (London: Routledge & Kegan Paul, 1974), 188–91; Peck, *Court Patronage and Corruption*, 185, 188; Statute of Monopolies, 1624, 21 Jac. I, c. 3.

3. William Petty, "A Treatise of Taxes and Contributions" (1662), in *The Economic Writings of Sir William Petty*, ed. Charles Henry Hull (Cambridge: Cambridge University Press, 1899), 1:75–76. See also Aylmer, *King's Servants*, 247–48.

4. William Hawkins, *A Treatise of the Pleas of the Crown* (London, 1716), 1:171.

5. Bentham, "Rationale of Reward," 241.

6. Ibid., 241; *The Colonial Records of South Carolina: The Journal of the Commons House of Assembly, September 12, 1739–March 26, 1741*, ed. J. H. Easterby (Columbia: Historical Commission of South Carolina, 1951), 216 (message of the House seeking posted tables).

7.  Patrick K. O'Brien and Philip A. Hunt, "England 1485–1815," in *The Rise of the Fiscal State in Europe, c. 1200–1815*, ed. Richard Bonney (Oxford: Oxford University Press, 1999), 58–61.

8.  "Unable to tax the subject to pay for the ever-growing government service, the Crown left the civil servants to raise their own fees—in every sense of the word!" Joel Hurstfield, *Freedom, Corruption and Government in Elizabethan England* (Cambridge, MA: Harvard University Press, 1973), 161.

9.  Edward Coke, *The Second Part of the Institutes of the Laws of England* (London, 1797), 533. This is repeated in William Blackstone, *Commentaries on the Laws of England* (Oxford, 1765), 1:262.

10. *Journal of the Votes and Proceedings of the General Assembly of the Colony of New-York* (New York, 1764), 1:224. See also ibid., 1:238.

11. *The Colonial Laws of New York from the Year 1664 to the Revolution*, ed. Charles Z. Lincoln et al. (reprint; Clark, NJ: Lawbook Exchange, 2006), 1:623.

12. *Journal of the Votes and Proceedings*, 1:274. For the governor's 1709 recommendation that the statute be disallowed by reason of unreasonably low charges, see *Documents Relative to the Colonial History of the State of New-York*, ed. F. B. O'Callaghan (Albany, NY: Weed, Parsons and Co., 1855), 5:82.

13. E.g., *Journal of the Votes and Proceedings*, 1:637, 660, 722.

14. Gordon S. Wood, *The Radicalism of the American Revolution* (New York: Vintage, 1992), 98.

15. Montesquieu, *The Spirit of the Laws*, ed. Anne M. Cohler et al. (Cambridge: Cambridge University Press, 1989), 67.

16. Andrew Kippis, *Considerations on the Provisional Treaty with America and the Preliminary Articles of Peace with France and Spain* (London, 1783), 147–48. On Kippis's associations, see Caroline Robbins, *The Eighteenth-Century Commonwealthman* (1959; Indianapolis: Amagi, 2004), 249–50, 322, 324, 328. On the early modern concept of official services as favors rather than rights, see James C. Scott, *Comparative Political Corruption* (Englewood Cliffs, NJ: Prentice Hall, 1972), 44–45.

17. G. E. Aylmer, *The State's Servants: The Civil Service of the English Republic, 1649–1660* (London: Routledge & Kegan Paul, 1974), 115, 120. Radical pamphleteers wanted fees abolished and replaced with salaries. Ibid., 120.

18. *Severall Proposals for the Generall Good of the Common-wealth with the Grounds and Reasons Thereof* (London, 1651), 3–4. I located this pamphlet through Aylmer, *State's Servants*, 287.

19. G. E. Aylmer, *The Crown's Servants: Government and Civil Service under Charles II, 1660–1685* (Oxford: Oxford University Press, 2002), 101.

20. Robbins, *Eighteenth-Century Commonwealthman*; Bernard Bailyn, *The Ideological Origins of the American Revolution* (Cambridge, MA: Harvard University Press, 1967).

21. Jack P. Greene, *The Quest for Power: The Lower Houses of Assembly in the Southern Royal Colonies, 1689–1776* (Chapel Hill: University of North Carolina Press, 1963), 148–49.

22. *NC Recs* 3:262 (1731). See also Greene, *Quest for Power*, 149.

23. *NC Recs* 23:284 (1748).

24. *NC Recs* 6:599 (1761).
25. *NC Recs* 7:485 (1767). Greene interprets this, mistakenly I think, as an admission of "unchallenged" assembly power. *Quest for Power*, 155.
26. *NC Recs* 9:255 (1772). See also *NC Recs* 9:165 (1771) (Martin's message to assembly asking for revised statute); *NC Recs* 8:271–72 (Tryon's schedule of his own fees).
27. *Debates on the Adoption of the Federal Constitution, in the Convention Held at Philadelphia, in 1787*, ed. Jonathan Elliot (Philadelphia: J. B. Lippincott, 1891), 4:243 (emphasis added).
28. Greene, *Quest for Power*, 158–59. See *The Statutes at Large; Being a Collection of All the Laws of Virginia, from the First Session of the Legislature in the Year 1619*, ed. William Waller Hening (reprint; Charlottesville: University of Virginia Press, 1969) [hereafter *Hening's Statutes*], 4:340–41, 350–51 (1732 act presaging general language of the 1745 act but covering only a named subset of the colony's officers).
29. *Hening's Statutes*, 5:326, 342 (1745) (emphasis added).
30. Quoted in Glenn Curtis Smith, "The Affair of the Pistole Fee, Virginia, 1752–55," *Virginia Magazine of History and Biography* 48 (1940): 214.
31. Quoted in Smith, "Affair of the Pistole Fee," 217. On this controversy, see also Jack P. Greene, ed., "The Case of the Pistole Fee: The Report of the Hearing on the Pistole Fee Dispute before the Privy Council, June 18, 1754," *Virginia Magazine of History and Biography* 66 (1958): 399–422; Greene, *Quest for Power*, 159–66. The Privy Council ultimately confirmed the technical power of the governor-in-council to settle fees, though practically the enacted fees were overwhelmingly by act of assembly up to the Revolution.
32. For the Virginia returns generally, see RFCC, 171–97. For the one gratuity, see RFCC, 175.
33. On the royal inquiry, see RFCC, 29–52 (New Hampshire), 53–78 (Massachusetts), 79–153 (New York), 198–225 (South Carolina). Interestingly the inquiry on New Jersey, as in Virginia, indicated virtually complete statutory control. RFCC, 154–70. On Pennsylvania, see my discussion in Chapter 1, text at notes 129–32.
34. ATRCF, 1:28, 31; ATRCF, 2:22. On confusion about these fees in the 1760s, see Thomas C. Barrow, *Trade and Empire: The British Customs Service in Colonial America, 1660–1775* (Cambridge, MA: Harvard University Press, 1967), 189.
35. Frank L. Dewey, *Thomas Jefferson, Lawyer* (Charlottesville: University of Virginia Press, 1986), 96–101.
36. *The Letters and Papers of Edmund Pendleton, 1734–1803*, ed. David John Mays (Charlottesville: University of Virginia Press, 1967), 1:82–85.
37. Dewey, *Thomas Jefferson*, 101–04; David John Mays, *Edmund Pendleton 1721–1803: A Biography* (Cambridge, MA: Harvard University Press, 1952), 1:247.
38. Dewey, *Thomas Jefferson*, 104.
39. Ibid., 104–05. For the memo itself, see ibid., 127–29. The memo mentions but does not really confront the issue of *quantum meruit*.
40. Virginia Constitution of 1776 (no numbered subdivisions).
41. *The Papers of Thomas Jefferson*, ed. Julian P. Boyd (Princeton, NJ: Princeton University Press, 1950), 2:320 (arguing that Jefferson probably "drew" several of the bills in the revisal of 1779, including No. 75, on extortion).

42. *Papers of Thomas Jefferson*, 2:521 (emphasis added).

43. *Hening's Statutes*, 12:335–36 (1786).

44. *Md. Arch.* 44:630 (1747).

45. Newton D. Mereness, *Maryland as a Proprietary Province* (London: Macmillan, 1901), 386.

46. *Md. Arch.* 62:426 (1770).

47. *Md. Arch.* 62:425 (1770).

48. *Md. Arch.* 62:xxvii–xxviii.

49. The lower house viewed the officers' unilateral takings as a kind of proclamation and therefore a tallage. It declared that the land-grant officers "have thus daringly insulted the whole legislature at that time assembled for the very purpose of regulating officers' fees, by attempting to introduce a regulation of fees by proclamation"—*proclamation* being the term for a unilateral ordinance of the king (or proprietor). *Md. Arch.* 62:380 (1770).

50. *Md. Arch.* 62:301 (1770).

51. This is explained in *Md. Arch.* 63:225 (1771) (governor's message).

52. *Md. Arch.* 62:xxix. For the ordinance's text, see *Md. Arch.* 63:227.

53. *Md. Arch.* 62:xxix.

54. *Md. Arch.* 63:196–97 (1771). Compare Coke, *Second Part of the Institutes*, 533.

55. *Md. Arch.* 63:199 (1771).

56. *Md. Arch.* 63:229–30 (1771).

57. *Md. Arch.* 63:198 (1771).

58. *Md. Arch.* 63:226, 230 (1771).

59. Perhaps notably, Coke's discussion of fees downplayed custom, and it said nothing of *quantum meruit*, since *Veale* and *Ballard* were not decided until long after Coke died. Edward Coke, *The First Part of the Institutes of the Laws of England* (London, 1794), vol. 2, sec. 701, bracketed page marker [368.b]; Coke *Second Part of the Institutes*, 176, 209–10. See also my discussion of the Statute of Westminster I, in note 13 to Chapter 1.

60. Maryland Constitution of 1776, Declaration of Rights, § 12 (emphasis added).

61. The statute said that no officers, "by reason or color of their office or offices, shall have, receive, or take of any person or persons, directly or indirectly, any other or greater fees . . . than are hereafter limited and allowed to the several officers herein mentioned." See Maryland Session Laws, November 1779 session, ch. 25, § 2. The volume has no page numbers.

62. State v. Martin, 1 H. & J. 721, 721 (Md. 1805).

63. *Md. Arch.* 30:251 (1715).

64. *Martin*, 1 H. & J. at 728–36.

65. Ibid., 736.

66. Ibid., 737–39 (citing 2 Hardress 355, which is the nominate citation to *Veale*, and 1 Salkeld 333, which is *Ballard*). Interestingly, Martin—perhaps sensing that custom and *quantum meruit* went against the political climate—mixed the two arguments with an invitation to the court to suppose that there was some lost statute, enacted in the seventeenth century, that authorized the fee.

67. *Martin,* 1 H. & J. at 740.
68. Ibid., 743.
69. Consider these examples from various cases in Chapters 1 and 2:

    - *Federalists and Whigs for regulation:* Pennsylvania Chief Justice Tilghman (see Chapter 2, text at note 83); Massachusetts Chief Justice Parker (see Chapter 2, text and accompanying note 87); New York State Senator Tracy (see Chapter 2, text at note 102).

    - *Jacksonians for regulation:* New York Chancellor Walworth (see Chapter 2, text at note 102); Justices Eustis and Slidell of the Louisiana high court in *Kernion v. Hills* in 1846 (see Chapter 2, note 132).

    - *Federalists and Whigs against regulation:* Daniel Webster (see Chapter 1, text at note 138); several justices of the Louisiana high court in *Hills v. Kernion* in 1844 (see Chapter 2, note 132).

    - *Jacksonians against regulation:* New York Vice Chancellor McCoun (see Chapter 2, text at note 99).

70. William E. Nelson, "Officeholding and Powerwielding: An Analysis of the Relationship between Structure and Style in American Administrative History," *Law and Society Review* 10 (1976): 191–99.
71. Matthew A. Crenson, *The Federal Machine: Beginnings of Bureaucracy in Jacksonian America* (Baltimore: Johns Hopkins University Press, 1975); Lynn L. Marshall, "The Strange Stillbirth of the Whig Party," *American Historical Review* 72 (1967): 445–68; Wood, *Radicalism of the American Revolution,* 302–05.
72. Jack P. Greene, "Law and the Origins of the American Revolution," in *Cambridge History of Law in America,* ed. Michael Grossberg and Christopher Tomlins (Cambridge: Cambridge University Press, 2008), 1:447–81; Larry D. Kramer, *The People Themselves: Popular Constitutionalism and Judicial Review* (New York: Oxford University Press, 2004), 24–34; William E. Nelson, *Americanization of the Common Law: The Impact of Legal Change on Massachusetts Society, 1760–1830* (Cambridge, MA: Harvard University Press, 1975), 13–14.
73. Laura F. Edwards, *The People and Their Peace: Legal Culture and the Transformation of Inequality in the Post-Revolutionary South* (Chapel Hill: University of North Carolina Press, 2009); Nelson, *Americanization of the Common Law,* 173–74.
74. On the constitutional ideal of uniformity, see Howard Gillman, *The Constitution Besieged: The Rise and Demise of Lochner Era Police Powers Jurisprudence* (Durham, NC: Duke University Press, 1993). On general incorporation, see Oscar Handlin and Mary Flug Handlin, *Commonwealth: A Study of the Role of Government in the American Economy: Massachusetts, 1774–1861,* rev. ed. (Cambridge, MA: Harvard University Press, 1968), 161–228. On the general property tax, see Sumner Benson, "A History of the General Property Tax," in *The American Property Tax: Its History, Administration, and Economic Impact,* ed. George C. S. Benson et al. (Claremont, CA: Institute for Studies in Federalism, 1965).

75. Louis Hartz, *Economic Policy and Democratic Thought: Pennsylvania, 1776–1860* (Cambridge, MA: Harvard University Press, 1948), esp. 309–20; Helen Tangires, *Public Markets and Civic Culture in Nineteenth-Century America* (Baltimore: Johns Hopkins University Press, 2003).

76. *Stat. of Penn. (1682–1801)*, 5:177.

77. *The Pennsylvania State Trials, Containing the Impeachment, Trial, and Acquittal of Francis Hopkinson, and John Nicholson, Esquires* (Philadelphia: Francis Bailey, 1794), 60.

78. *Stat. of Penn. (1682–1801)*, 15:372 (emphasis added).

79. Two high-court judges, Tilghman and Yeates, appeared to assume that compensatory fees were lawful right up to 1814. Irwin v. Commissioners of Northumberland County, 1 Serg. & Rawle 505, 506, 507–08 (Pa. 1815). There is perhaps some counterevidence in the briefly reported *Milne v. Davis*, 2 Binn. 137 (Pa. 1809).

80. 1813 Pa. Laws 352, 364 (session went into 1814).

81. *Irwin*, 1 Serg. & Rawle at 506 (Tilghman, J., paraphrasing plaintiff's argument) (emphasis added). Though the sheriff in this case was seeking a fee from a county, the theory would surely apply to fees from individuals.

82. ATRCF, 1:19 (Philadelphia collector and comptroller: "A List of Fees that have been generally and usually taken by the Collector & Comptroller"). Most of these fees do not appear in the contemporaneous statutory fee schedule for those officers (enacted in 1751–52), in *Stat. of Penn. (1682–1801)*, 5:174.

83. Richard E. Ellis, *The Jeffersonian Crisis: Courts and Politics in the Young Republic* (Oxford: Oxford University Press, 1971), 183.

84. *Irwin*, 1 Serg. & Rawle at 506–07 (emphasis added).

85. Brown v. Commonwealth, 2 Rawle 40, 43–44 (Pa. 1829).

86. 1796 Mass. Acts 523, 535. This volume contains statutes passed at a session beginning in 1795 and ending in 1796. Lawyers, apparently using different sets of volumes of the Massachusetts session laws, varied in whether they cited this statute to a volume labeled 1795 or 1796.

87. Shattuck v. Woods, 18 Mass. 171, 177 (1822). Contrast *Commonwealth v. Shed*, 1 Mass. 227, 229 (1804) (allowing extra payment for "extra trouble and expense"). *Shattuck* was written by Chief Justice Isaac Parker, whose background was Federalist. ANB.

88. *The Revised Statutes of the Commonwealth of Massachusetts* (Boston: Dutton and Wentworth, 1836), 713. But see ibid., 736 ("for performing any service or any official duty, for which the fee or compensation is established by law"). In the 1860 revision, only the latter provision survived. *The General Statutes of the Commonwealth of Massachusetts* (Boston: William White, 1860), 814 (ch. 163, § 22). But it appears the courts understood it to prohibit all fees for services not enumerated by statute. Brophy v. Marble, 118 Mass. 548, 551 (1875) (allowing no fees for service to an officer where none were provided for according to the terms of the statute, and citing *General Statutes*, ch. 163, § 22, for this proposition: "Being a public officer for whose compensation provision is made by law, the plaintiff cannot recover anything for official services except as so provided, even if he performed such services at [the recipients'] requests").

89. *Acts and Laws of the State of Connecticut in America* (Hartford, CT: Hudson and Goodwin, 1796), 177–81 (saying simply that "the establishment of salaries and fees of the several officers of this state[] shall be as follows").

90. *The Public Statute Laws of the State of Connecticut: Book II. Commencing October Session, 1808.* (Hartford, CT: Hudson and Co., 1818?), 268, 269 (ch. 3, § 6). The statute is listed as from the October session of 1816.

91. Preston v. Bacon, 4 Conn. 471, 477 (1823).

92. Butler v. Ryan, 3 Des. Eq. 178, 182 (S.C. Cir. Eq. 1810), discussing an apparently unreported aspect of *Shubrick v. Fisher*, 2 Des. Eq. 148 (S.C.App. 1802).

93. *The Statutes at Large of South Carolina*, ed. David J. McCord (Columbia, SC: A. S. Johnston, 1839), 6:2–3 (statute of 1827).

94. See my discussion in Chapter 1, text at note 140.

95. *The Revised Statutes of the State of New Hampshire* (Concord, NH: Carroll and Baker, 1843), 474 ("If any person shall demand and take any greater fee for any service than is allowed by law, or any fee to which he is not by law entitled, he shall forfeit [etc.]"). See also *Fox v. Whitney*, 33 N.H. 516, 518 (1856) (noting the provision penalizes "demanding and taking a fee for a service . . . , greater than is allowed by law for that service, or for which no fee is allowed"). Compare the wording of an earlier statute of 1796 printed in *The Laws of the State of New-Hampshire* (Exeter, NH: C. Norris and Co., 1815), 132 ("any greater fee or fees for any of the services mentioned in this act").

96. The 1789 statute contained an opening clause that appeared to preclude pay for unenumerated services and a penalty clause that appeared to permit it. *Laws of the State of New York Passed at the Sessions of the Legislature Held in the Years [1789–1796]* (Albany, NY: Weed, Parsons and Co., 1887), 3:39, 58–59. The 1801 statute had the same problem. *Laws of the State of New York Passed at the Session of the Legislature Held in the Year 1801* (Albany, NY: Weed, Parsons and Co., 1887), 5:553, 571. There is a similar tension between two provisions of *The Revised Statutes of the State of New-York* (Albany, NY: Packard and Van Benthuysen, 1829). Compare ibid., 2:650 (no officer "or other person to whom any fees or compensation shall be allowed by law for any service, shall take or receive any other or greater fee or reward for such service, but such as is or shall be allowed by the laws of this state"), with ibid., 2:753 ("provisions of law prohibiting the taking of fees for services in civil cases, other than such as are allowed by statute, shall apply to the taking of fees for services in criminal cases beyond the amount allowed by law for such services").

97. Smith v. Birdsall, 9 Johns. 328 (N.Y. Supreme Court 1812) ("Where the law is silent as to charges for particular services, the court, if they allow any thing, must allow what is reasonable.").

98. Hatch v. Mann, 9 Wend. 262, 262–63 (N.Y. Supreme Court 1832).

99. That McCoun decided the case is evident from the title of the reporter, *Reports of Chancery Cases, Decided in the First Circuit of the State of New-York, by the Hon. William T. McCoun, Vice-Chancellor*, ed. Charles Edwards (New York: Gould, Banks and Co., 1837), vol. 2. McCoun was appointed in 1831. Edgar A. Werner, *Civil List and Constitutional History of the State of New York* (Albany, NY: Weed, Parsons and

Co., 1889), 330. The governor appointing him was Enos Throop, an associate of the great Jacksonian Martin Van Buren.

100. City Bank v. Bangs, 2 Edw. Ch. 95, 97–98 (N.Y. Ch. 1833). In the end, McCoun decided that the policemen, though eligible in principle, were not actually the moving force behind the discovery as the terms of the reward mandated, though he added that they still might recover in *quantum meruit* for the more limited extra service they had provided. Ibid., 107.

101. Hatch v. Mann, 15 Wend. 44 (N.Y. 1835).

102. Tracy served in Congress as a Whig. On Walworth's affiliation, see *ANB*.

103. *Hatch*, 15 Wend. at 46 (Walworth: noting he thinks best to rule broadly), 49–50 (Tracy: constable's theory would apply to "any other officer").

104. *Hatch*, 15 Wend. at 46 (Walworth: discussing extortion statute), 49 (Tracey: same). See also *Parker v. Newland*, 1 Hill 87 (N.Y. Supreme Court 1841) (citing *Hatch* as pertaining to extortion).

105. *Hatch*, 15 Wend. at 48 (referring to "the obvious distinction between the performance of extra services by a public officer, and the performance of the services specified in the fee bill in a more vigilant and faithful manner than usual").

106. Ibid., 48.

107. Ibid., 46–47.

108. Ibid., 49.

109. For a similar view expressed by the high court of Pennsylvania, see *Smith v. Whildin*, 10 Pa. 39, 40 (1848).

110. *Hatch*, 15 Wend. at 49–50.

111. Crofut v. Brandt, 13 Sickels 106, 112–15 (N.Y. 1874). See also the strong statement in *People v. Green*, quoted in Chapter 2, text at note 116.

112. *Laws of the State of New York Passed at the One Hundred and Fourth Session of the Legislature* (Albany, NY: Weed, Parsons and Co., 1881), 3:140 (Penal Code § 557).

113. Strong statutory regulation of official pay came to prevail at the federal level, as well. The story was a bit different there, for federal officers were more frequently paid from the Treasury than by service recipients, and their nonstatutory compensation came in the form of pay for extra services allowed by heads of departments and by fee-taxing federal judges. But Congress cracked down on such discretionary allowances in a series of statutes in 1839–53, seeking to confine officers to explicit statutory fee schedules. Parrillo diss., 187–89.

114. State v. Merritt, 37 Tenn. 67, 69–70 (1857). Only in the case of the most disastrous drafting errors—threatening to shut down a state's whole justice system—would courts consider falling back on the eighteenth-century common-law doctrines. Ripley v. Gifford, 11 Iowa 367, 370–71 (1860). And even *Ripley* was later repudiated. Howland v. Wright County, 47 N.W. 1086–87 (Iowa 1891).

115. E.g., Crittenden County v. Crump, 25 Ark. 235, 236 (1868); Town of Carlyle v. Sharp, 51 Ill. 71, 72 (1869); Crocker v. Supervisors of Brown County, 35 Wis. 284, 286 (1874); Montgomery H. Throop, *A Treatise on the Law Relating to Public Officers and Sureties in Official Bonds* (Chicago: T. H. Flood and Co., 1892), 432–33 (§§ 446–47), 457

(§ 478). Throop misstates the original common-law regime, missing *Veale* and *Ballard*. Ibid., 457 (§ 477).

116. People v. Green (1874), in *Reports of Cases Argued and Determined in the Court of Common Pleas for the City and County of New York*, ed. Charles P. Daly (New York: Baker, Voorhis and Co., 1876), 5:268–69. The case was reversed on other grounds. 58 N.Y. 295 (1874). The passage is quoted in Throop, *Treatise on the Law Relating to Public Officers*, 478 (§ 500), and in *Bates v. City of St. Louis*, 54 S.W. 439, 439–40 (Mo. 1899).

117. United States v. Shields, 153 U.S. 88, 91 (1894).

118. William D. Popkin, *Statutes in Court: The History and Theory of Statutory Interpretation* (Durham, NC: Duke University Press, 1999), 97–113.

119. "The Land Office," *Blackfoot (Idaho) Register*, June 25, 1881, p. 4.

120. For an opinion repudiating custom specifically, see *Smith v. Smith*, 1 Bail. 70 (S.C. 1828).

121. Lincoln v. Shaw, 17 Mass. 410, 412 (1821).

122. Shattuck v. Woods, 18 Mass. 171, 182 (1822).

123. Stow v. Converse, 3 Conn. 325, 346–47 (1820).

124. 1 Stat. 627, 661–62 (1799).

125. 1 Stat. 704, 706 (1799).

126. Ogden v. Maxwell, 18 F.Cas. 613, 614–15 (C.C.S.D.N.Y. 1855). For another unsuccessful attempt to invoke usage in federal court, see *Mattingly v. United States*, 16 F.Cas. 1144, 1144–46 (C.C.D.C. 1844).

127. Throop, *Treatise on the Law Relating to Public Officers*, 432 (§ 445). See also ibid., 432 (§ 446).

128. E.g., Carroll, Executor of Biscoe v. Tyler, 2 H. & G. 54, 57 (Md. 1827).

129. See also the reference to this issue in Prescott's impeachment trial, which I point out in note 69 to Chapter 1.

130. Hills v. Kernion, 7 Rob. 522 (La. 1844).

131. Kernion v. Hills, 1 La. Ann. 419 (1846).

132. On the complete turnover of the judges, see Mark Fernandez, "From Chaos to Continuity: Early Reforms of the Supreme Court of Louisiana, 1845–1852," *Louisiana History* 28 (1987): 19–36. Of the five judges on the old court, Henry Adams Bullard and Rice Garland both served in Congress as Whigs. And the chief justice, François-Xavier Martin, had written a very critical history of Andrew Jackson's exploits in Louisiana that was the object of controversy in the 1840s. Joseph G. Tregle Jr., "Andrew Jackson and the Continuing Battle of New Orleans," *Journal of the Early Republic* 1 (1981): 391. Of the four judges on the new court, all were appointed by Democratic governor Isaac Johnson. The chief was George Eustis, a prominent Jacksonian. See the entry for his son, George Eustis Jr., in *ANB*. And Thomas Slidell, who wrote the opinion in *Kernion v. Hills*, was identified with the Democrats and was the brother of the leading Jacksonian John Slidell. John M. Sacher, *A Perfect War of Politics: Parties, Politicians, and Democracy in Louisiana, 1824–1861* (Baton Rouge: Louisiana State University Press, 2003), 232.

133. *Hills*, 7 Rob. at 523–27; *Kernion*, 1 La. Ann. at 420.

134. There appears to have been some factual dispute on this point. For indications that the inspectors did sample and label up to 1836, see *Hills*, 7 Rob. at 526 ("previous to 1836, the inspectors furnished the samples without any additional charge"); ibid., 532n (dealers' petition for rehearing, which says, "The services for which the additional compensation was charged were such only as had been performed, under the same laws by all previous inspectors, and by the defendants themselves, from their appointment, until 1836."). For indications that they did not, see ibid., 527 ("Previous to 1836, this was not done, and the damaged tobacco has been classed since that time. At the time of the meeting [in 1836] there was a good deal of necessity for it, because the inspectors would not give any samples at all.").

135. Ibid., 526 ("in 1836, the buyers complained of the loss they sustained in the tare [i.e., the measurement of the weight of the packaging], &c."). See also ibid., 527 (noting that the extra fee had "given confidence to the [inspectors'] certificates of the samples," which suggests that their work in that area previously did not inspire confidence).

136. Ibid., 525–26.

137. Ibid., 523.

138. *Kernion*, 1 La. Ann. at 420 (the second lawsuit involves transactions "in the years 1842 and 1843"); ibid., 421 (in which the dealers agreed to pay the charges but did so under protest); ibid., 419–20 (dealers never actually paid, such that the inspectors are now suing the dealers).

139. *Hills*, 7 Rob. at 531.

140. Ibid., 528 (emphasis in original).

141. Ibid., 527.

142. Ibid., 530 (emphasis in original).

143. Ibid., 527.

144. Ibid., 531. The court was not invoking *quantum meruit* but a similar civil-law doctrine.

145. Ibid., 527–28 (emphasis in original). See also ibid., 530 (the now-complaining dealers "submitted to this charge for a certain number of years without complaint").

146. Ibid., 526–27. See also ibid., 531 (the extra charge was "better securing the interests of the dealers and of facilitating the operations of the trade").

147. Ibid., 527 ("The payment of forty cents has tended to better the trade, and has given confidence to the certificates of the samples.").

148. Ibid., 527 ("the regulations of 1836 have tended to make the tobacco stand higher [i.e., sell for higher prices] than it previously did").

149. Ibid., 528 (judges' paraphrase of dealers' argument). The court said there was "no proof" of this allegation. Ibid.

150. Ibid., 532n (dealers' petition for rehearing of the 1844 case).

151. *Kernion*, 1 La. Ann. at 420–21.

152. Ibid., 421 (emphasis in original). The court also assigned some significance to the fact that the statute said the officer, for inspection, was to receive sixty cents "and no more," though the court admitted that this could not be dispositive as to whether sampling and labeling were to be understood, to begin with, as part of the official duty for which "no more" than sixty cents was to be paid. Ibid., 420–21.

153. Evans v. City of Trenton, 24 N.J.L. 764, 767 (N.J. 1853). The opinion earlier refers to officers being on "fixed salary" but does not expressly contrast this with fees.

154. John F. Dillon, *Treatise on the Law of Municipal Corporations* (Chicago: J. Cockcroft, 1872), 206.

155. Throop, *Treatise on the Law Relating to Public Officers*, 464–72 (§§ 485–95). For other cases denying or permitting extra rewards, generally with a broad reading of official duty, see *Gilmore v. Lewis*, 12 Ohio 281, 286–87 (1843); *Pool v. City of Boston*, 59 Mass. 219, 221 (1849); *Kick v. Merry*, 23 Mo. 72 (1856); *Davies v. Burns*, 87 Mass. 349, 353 (1862); *Pilie v. City of New Orleans*, 19 La. Ann. 274 (1867); *In re Russell*, 51 Conn. 577 (Conn. Sup. Ct. 1884).

156. A few examples:

- An officer's geographic bailiwick could be defined narrowly. *Studley v. Ballard*, 47 N.W. 1000 (Mass. 1897).

- A person holding one office might be appointed simultaneously to a different one or to act in a separate (and less regulated) official capacity. Such was the case with U.S. consuls stationed in foreign ports. Fees for services they rendered under federal jurisdiction were brought under presidential regulation in 1856. 11 Stat. 52, 57 (1856). But in subsequent years, the State Department and the federal courts held that consuls could optionally render services that they were empowered to perform by state governments (e.g., administering estates) or by foreign sovereigns, without any federal regulation of their charges. *United States v. Badeau*, 33 F.Cas. 572, 576–77 (S.D.N.Y. 1886).

- Some federal judges appointed their court clerks as special commissioners for the purpose of naturalizing aliens, which allowed them to escape at least some statutory strictures on their total fee incomes, though the court rules do appear to have kept the amount per service fixed and uniform over many decades. See my discussion in note 87 to Chapter 4.

157. See my discussion in Chapter 1, text at notes 190–205.

158. David M. Fitzsimons, "Tom Paine's New World Order: Idealistic Internationalism in the Ideology of Early American Foreign Relations," *Diplomatic History* 19 (1995): 569–82, esp. 575; Felix Gilbert, *To the Farewell Address: Ideas of Early American Foreign Policy* (Princeton, NJ: Princeton University Press, 1961), 54–75; George C. Herring, *From Colony to Superpower: U.S. Foreign Relations since 1776* (Oxford: Oxford University Press, 2008), 14–15, 31, 36, 58.

159. On Americans' fear of foreign influence and their preference for limitations on alliances and diplomacy, see Gilbert, *To the Farewell Address*, 44–56, 73; Herring, *From Colony to Superpower*, 36.

160. "Draft Articles of Confederation, 12 July 1776," in *Documentary History of the Ratification of the Constitution*, ed. Merrill Jensen (Madison: State Historical Society of Wisconsin, 1976), 1:79 (art. 4).

161. *Journals of the Continental Congress, 1774–1789*, ed. Worthington Chauncey Ford (Washington, DC: GPO, 1907), 9:911 (art. 6).

162. See my discussion in Chapter 1, text at notes 197–205.

163. U.S. Constitution, art. 1, sec. 9, cl. 8. The convention records say only that the provision's sponsor, Charles Pinckney, "urged the necessity of preserving foreign ministers and other officers of the U.S. independent of external influence." *The Records of the Federal Convention of 1787*, ed. Max Farrand (New Haven, CT: Yale University Press, 1911), 2:389.

164. The occasion for making this policy was an inquiry from Thomas Pinckney, who had represented the United States at the Spanish and British courts, as to whether he could accept the customary presents. The Senate consented to let Pinckney accept, with seventeen in favor (mostly Federalists) and five opposed (all but one a Republican). 7 Annals of Congress 553 (1798). The question then went to the House, which refused to consent, by a vote of forty-nine (about three-quarters Republicans) to thirty-seven (nearly all Federalists). 8 Annals of Congress 1593 (1798). Soon after, the House "unanimously" adopted a resolution that its refusal to let Pinckney accept gifts arose "solely" from "motives of general policy." Ibid., 1775–76. According to the resolution's sponsor, the House meant to establish "an invariable rule precluding the acceptance of these presents." Ibid., 1775 (Rep. Bayard). It is unclear what, if anything, Congress had done with such inquiries between 1789 and 1798. Compare ibid., 1589 (1798) (Rep. R. Williams) (referring to Pinckney's inquiry as "the first application which had been made since the existence of the present Government"), with ibid., 1613 (Rep. Pinckney) (stating that "whenever [the privilege of accepting gifts] had heretofore been applied for, it had been invariably granted"). For overviews of these proceedings, see Robert Ralph Davis Jr., "Diplomatic Gifts and Emoluments: The Early National Experience," *Historian* 32 (1970): 378–79; John W. Foster, *The Practice of Diplomacy as Illustrated in the Foreign Relations of the United States* (Boston: Houghton, Mifflin and Co., 1906), 141–47.

165. 8 Annals of Congress 1591–1592 (1798) (Rep. Harper). On Harper's Federalism, see *ANB*.

166. 8 Annals of Congress 1587 (1798) (Rep. W. C. Claiborne).

167. Ibid., 1584 (Rep. W. C. Claiborne).

168. Ibid., 1589 (Rep. Lyon).

169. Ibid., 1587 (Rep. Venable).

170. Foster, *Practice of Diplomacy*, 148.

171. Middleton notes that Britain did not prohibit such gifts to its own diplomats until 1830, and it appears from his discussion that other powers were still permitting them at that time. Charles Ronald Middleton, *The Administration of British Foreign Policy, 1782–1846* (Durham, NC: Duke University Press, 1977), 184–85, 223.

172. Chapter 1, text at note 188.

173. James G. Lydon, *Pirates, Privateers, and Profits* (Upper Saddle River, NJ: Gregg Press, 1970), 118–19, 122–25; Carl E. Swanson, *Predators and Prizes: American Privateering and Imperial Warfare, 1739–1748* (Columbia: University of South Carolina Press, 1991), 45.

174. James E. Pfander, "Judicial Compensation and the Definition of Judicial Power in the Early Republic," *Michigan Law Review* 107 (2008): 14–19.

175. Pfander, "Judicial Compensation," 24–28. Pfander quotes a 1792 petition to the U.S. Senate complaining that the South Carolina federal judge was charging "the same enormous fees" as his colonial predecessor, which the South Carolina legislature had never regulated. Ibid., 25. Indeed, the colonial vice admiralty judge of South Carolina in 1764 had asserted the right to fees "established by long usage and custom." RFCC, 205.

176. "Brutus XI" (Jan. 31, 1788), in *Documentary History of the Ratification of the Constitution,* ed. John P. Kaminski et al. (Madison: State Historical Society of Wisconsin, 1984), 15:516. See also Pfander, "Judicial Compensation," 4–5.

177. In the English courts at Westminster, Parliament in 1799 took away the fees of all justices except the chiefs of King's Bench and Common Pleas. It took away the chiefs' fees in 1825. Daniel Klerman, "Jurisdictional Competition and the Evolution of the Common Law," *University of Chicago Law Review* 74 (2007): 1204.

178. There may have been other reasons for the reaction against federal judges' fees—reasons that applied at the state level, as well. At least some states prohibited fees for high-level judges during the revolutionary period, just as Congress did. Pfander, "Judicial Compensation," 11–13. Nobody has studied why the states made these changes. More broadly, we lack a comprehensive chronology of fee abolition for high-level state judges. Strikingly, judges in trial courts of general jurisdiction still made substantial fees across New York State up to 1846. D.D.F. [David Dudley Field], *Re-Organization of the Judiciary: Five Articles Originally Published in The Evening Post on That Subject* (New York: N.p., 1846), 2–3.

### CHAPTER 3: A REGULATORY NIGHTMARE

1. E.g., "Salaries and Fees—The County Clerk of the City of New York," *Law Reporter* 10 (Jan. 1848): 426 (noting argument of fee-system proponents "that a public officer will do his duty more promptly when paid for each act, by the piece, as it were, than when paid periodically"); "Abolish the Fee System," *Chicago Tribune,* Jan. 24, 1892, p. 12 (noting the pro-fee argument "that if an employee depends on fees he will hustle around and do something, while if he is paid regular wages he will do nothing").

2. Irwin v. Commissioners of Northumberland County, 1 Serg. & Rawle 505, 507 (Pa. 1815).

3. H.R. Rep. No. 32–50, at 6 (1852).

4. Crocker v. Supervisors of Brown County, 35 Wis. 284, 286 (1874).

5. Shattuck v. Woods, 18 Mass. 171, 177 (1822).

6. Hatch v. Mann, 15 Wend. 44, 47 (N.Y. 1835) (Walworth, Ch.).

7. People v. Green (1874), in *Reports of Cases Argued and Determined in the Court of Common Pleas for the City and County of New York,* ed. Charles P. Daly (New York: Baker, Voorhis and Co., 1876), 5:268. The case was reversed on other grounds. 58 N.Y. 295 (1874).

8. Evans v. City of Trenton, 24 N.J.L. 764, 767 (N.J. 1853). This case involved a salaried officer, but the analysis would clearly apply to a fee-paid officer.

9. People v. Green, in *Reports of Cases Argued and Determined in the Court of Common Pleas for the City and County of New York,* 5:268–69.

10. Curtis v. McNair, 68 N.Y. 198, 200 (1877).

11. AG Report 1883, p. 22. As late as 1932, a commentator in Texas noted that several factors, including "the great expansion of government activities and functions," had "brought about great discrepancies in the application and the structure of our fee system." S. B. McAlister, "The Fee System as a Method of Compensation for the Texas County Officials," *Southwestern Social Science Quarterly* 13 (1932): 26.

12. Thomas K. Urdahl, *The Fee-System in the United States* (Madison, WI: Democrat Printing Co., 1898), 148. He noted this was "especially" true for fees of "local officers."

13. "Civil Administration of Justice in the City of New-York," *Knickerbocker, or New York Monthly Magazine* 13 (Jan. 1839): 10.

14. Henry Bixby Hemenway, *Legal Principles of Public Health Administration* (Chicago: T. H. Flood and Co., 1914), 118.

15. "Mr. Gumbleton's Meeting," *New York Times*, Sept. 18, 1878, p. 2.

16. Anonymous letter to the editor, titled "Fraud of the Fee System," *New York Times*, Oct. 30, 1878, p. 3.

17. "Sheriff Reilly Accused," *New York Times*, Apr. 25, 1879, p. 5.

18. "Mr. Gumbleton's Defense," *New York Times*, Feb. 11, 1879, p. 5.

19. "The Gumbleton Case," *New York Times*, Mar. 18, 1879, p. 1. Compare "Decision in the Loew Case," *New York Times*, Mar. 18, 1879, p. 2, in which Robinson refrained from removing another officer accused of similar offenses, partly because they were committed by subordinates of whose conduct the officer had no knowledge, but also because the officer did not defend the charges once he knew about them.

20. "End of the Sheriff's Trial," *New York Times*, Oct. 3, 1879, p. 3 (stating that "Major Quincy, the head of the bureau, failed to tell the truth," but that Quincy's clerk, "Thomas J. Moore, did not hesitate to testify that he collected $11.75 over fifty times").

21. See "The Sheriff's Defense," *New York Times*, Sept. 20, 1879, p. 8; "Arguing for the Sheriff," *New York Times*, Sept. 30, 1879, p. 8; "End of the Sheriff's Trial," *New York Times*, Oct. 3, 1879, p. 3; "The Trial of the Sheriff," *New York Times*, Oct. 25, 1879, p. 2.

22. "The Health Officer's Income," *New York Times*, Oct. 16, 1881, p. 13.

23. "The Governor's Message," *New York Tribune*, Jan. 2, 1884, p. 2.

24. [Untitled editorial], *New York Times*, Nov. 18, 1881, p. 4.

25. See "The Health Officer's Income," *New York Times*, Oct. 16, 1881, p. 13; "B.," letter to the editor, *New York Times*, Feb. 12, 1884, p. 3; *Twenty-Eighth Annual Report of the Corporation of the Chamber of Commerce of the State of New-York for the Year 1885-'86* (New York: Press of the Chamber of Commerce, 1886), 107.

26. [Untitled editorial], *New York Times*, Nov. 18, 1881, p. 4.

27. "Current Topics," *Albany Law Journal* 4 (Dec. 23, 1871): 351.

28. H.R. Rep. No. 48–2164, at 10 (1884) (minority report by Rep. Milliken).

29. Frank J. Goodnow, *Comparative Administrative Law: An Analysis of the Administrative Systems, National and Local, of the United States, England, France and Germany* (New York: G. P. Putnam's Sons, 1893), 2:71.

30. E.g., "The Resolutions," *Colorado Springs Weekly Gazette*, Sept. 13, 1890, p. 4; E. B. Opdycke, letter to the editor, titled "Fees or Salaries—Which?" *Ohio Farmer* 105

(Jan. 23, 1904): 80; "A Good Measure," *Michigan Farmer* 31 (Mar. 13, 1897): 206; "The Demoralizing Fee System," *Michigan Farmer* 36 (Sept. 23, 1899): 226 (in part quoting the *Free Press*).

31. Commonwealth v. Mann, 31 A. 1003, 1005 (Pa. 1895) (Dean, J.).

32. Schuykill County v. Pepper, 37 A. 835, 836 (Pa. 1897) (Dean, J.).

33. Memorandum reproduced, approvingly, in the committee report on the ultimate bill, H.R. Rep. No. 65–960, at 2 (1919). See also I. Scott Messinger, *Order in the Courts: A History of the Federal Court Clerk's Office* (Washington, DC: Federal Judicial Center, 2002), 43–44.

34. Montesquieu, *The Spirit of the Laws* (1748), ed. Anne M. Cohler et al. (Cambridge: Cambridge University Press, 1989), 67.

35. For examples of these kinds of interpretations, see "Report of the Select Committee on Surrogates' Fees" (Mar. 21, 1844), compiled in *Documents of the Senate of the State of New-York, Sixty-Seventh Session, 1844* (Albany, NY: E. Mack, 1844), vol. 3, doc. no. 100.

36. *Md. Arch.* 63:203 (1771).

37. Herman Husband, "An Impartial Relation of the First Rise and Cause of the Present Difficulties in Public Affairs in the Province of North Carolina," in *Historical Sketches of North Carolina, from 1584 to 1851*, ed. John H. Wheeler (Philadelphia: Lippincott, Grambo & Co., 1851), 2:323. See also Marjoleine Kars, *Breaking Loose Together: The Regulator Rebellion in Pre-Revolutionary North Carolina* (Chapel Hill: University of North Carolina Press, 2002), 169.

38. *NC Recs* 8:388 (1771).

39. Coates v. Wallace, 17 Serg. & Rawle 75, 81 (Pa. 1827) (Gibson, C.J.).

40. E.g., Commonwealth v. Rodes, 45 Ky. 171, 191–92 (1845). Federal judges likewise did not closely check the charges of their clerks. AG Report 1890, p. xxi; H.R. Rep. No. 32–50, at 4 (1852). The accounts were mainly audited by clerks in Washington, DC. On that system, see my discussion in note 52 below.

41. Aechternacht v. Watmough, 8 Watts & Serg. 162, 164–65 (Pa. 1844).

42. "Report of the Select Committee on Surrogates' Fees" (Mar. 21, 1844), compiled in *Documents of the Senate of the State of New-York, Sixty-Seventh Session, 1844* (Albany, NY: E. Mack, 1844), vol. 3, doc. no. 100.

43. "Report of the Select Committee on the Reports of Surrogates" (May 1, 1845), compiled in *Documents of the Senate of the State of New-York, Sixty-Eighth Session, 1845* (Albany, NY: E. Mack, 1845), vol. 3, doc. no. 106, pp. 1–2.

44. H.R. Rep. No. 32–50, at 5–6 (1852).

45. Hearings (1892), 130. The words are those of the questioning congressman, with whom the witness judge agrees.

46. Hearings (1892), 134. The judge is referring to Stetson, the circuit clerk.

47. Buckley v. Brown, 4 F.Cas. 566, 567 (C.C.D. Pa. 1856) (Grier, Circuit Justice). He was referring not only to fee regulation but also to statutes on duties and penalties.

48. "Report of the Select Committee on So Much of the Governor's Message as Relates to the Fees of the Register, Assistant Register and Clerks in Chancery, and Clerks of the Supreme Court" (Feb. 9, 1839), compiled in *Documents of the Assembly of the State*

*of New-York, Sixty-Second Session, 1839* (Albany, NY: E. Crosswell, 1839), vol. 4, doc. no. 186, pp. 2–3.

49. GLO Report 1885, p. 233.

50. GLO Report 1877, p. 31.

51. E.g., New York customhouse officers continued to take customary tips even after they were banned. Hearings (1874), 227–29.

52. One might imagine that lawmakers, instead of replacing all fees with salaries, might have preserved the fee system by subjecting the officers' charges to careful auditing. In fact, this was tried and judged unsatisfactory. The attempts were made in the several federal agencies where officers provided services to recipients on a fee basis but had their fees paid out of the federal Treasury. Because the federal government was paying, it designated clerks in Washington, DC, to comb through the fee bills of the field officers. It turned out that the fee statutes were so manipulable, and the officers so ingenious, that auditors had to expend huge amounts of time to have any confidence they were checking abuse, and even then they feared they were missing a great deal. The high cost of this auditing became, in itself, an argument for converting the field officers to salaries. See Parrillo diss., 231–32.

53. Pennsylvania Constitution of 1776, sec. 36, echoed in Vermont Constitution of 1777, ch. 2, sec. 33.

54. Commonwealth v. Dennie (1827), in *Reports of Criminal Cases Tried in the Municipal Court of the City of Boston*, ed. Horatio Woodman (Boston: Little and Brown, 1845), 178.

55. Lynn L. Marshall, "The Strange Stillbirth of the Whig Party," *American Historical Review* 72 (1967): 467 (quoting the *Washington Globe* from 1831).

56. *Debates and Proceedings of the Constitutional Convention of the State of Illinois, Convened at the City of Springfield, Tuesday, September 13, 1869* (Springfield: E. L. Merritt and Brother, 1870), 2:1346.

57. For example, in New York City in the 1840s, nobody knew exactly how much the judges of the principal trial courts made in fees, and the illustrious law reformer David Dudley Field had to guess. D.D.F. [David Dudley Field], *Re-Organization of the Judiciary: Five Articles Published in the Evening Post on That Subject* (New York, 1846), 2. See also Urdahl, *Fee-System*, 224–25.

58. "System of Fees to Be Abolished," *Atlanta Constitution*, May 6, 1897, p. 5. See also Urdahl, *Fee-System*, 148–49, 228–29.

59. *Debates and Proceedings of the Constitutional Convention of the State of Illinois*, 2:1346. See also McAlister, "Fee System as a Method of Compensation," 26.

60. "A Good Measure," *Michigan Farmer* 31 (Mar. 13, 1897): 206. See also Urdahl, *Fee-System*, 229.

61. "A Heavy Salary," *Saturday Evening Post (Philadelphia)*, Sept. 29, 1849, p. 2 (sheriff of Philadelphia, $15,000 to $50,000); [Untitled editorial], *New York Daily Tribune*, Jan. 6, 1859, p. 4 (New York county clerk and register, $50,000).

62. Urdahl, *Fee-System*, 225nn1–2.

63. Ibid., 148–49.

64. "The Fee System," *Saturday Evening Post (Philadelphia)*, Mar. 24, 1849, p. 2.

65. *Debates and Proceedings of the Maryland Reform Convention to Revise the State Constitution* (Annapolis, MD: William M'Neir, 1851): 2:357.

66. Legler v. Paine, 45 N.E. 604, 610 (Ind. 1896).

67. "New-Jersey Legislature," *New York Times*, Feb. 20, 1879, p. 4.

68. Wallace McClure, *State Constitution-Making with Especial Reference to Tennessee* (Nashville, TN: Marshall and Bruce Co., 1916), 363.

69. "The Fee System," *Saturday Evening Post (Philadelphia)*, Mar. 24, 1849, p. 2. See also *Debates and Proceedings of the Constitutional Convention of the State of Illinois*, 2:1346.

70. "Payment by Fees," *New York Times*, Feb. 7, 1884, p. 4.

71. "Eaters of Taxes," *Galveston Daily News*, May 21, 1894, p. 6 (quoting speech of Barnett Gibbs). See also *Board of Commissioners of Converse County v. Burns*, 29 P. 894, 900 (Ariz. Terr. 1892).

72. John A. Fairlie, *Local Government in Counties, Towns and Villages* (New York: Century Co., 1906), 72. See also Urdahl, *Fee-System*, 227.

73. Allen Steinberg, *The Transformation of Criminal Justice: Philadelphia, 1800–1880* (Chapel Hill: University of North Carolina Press, 1989), 205; "The Health Officer's Income," *New York Times*, Oct. 16, 1881, p. 13; "The Brooklyn Investigation," *New York Times*, Mar. 8, 1887, p. 4; Urdahl, *Fee-System*, 225–26. For a general discussion of machine assessments, without specific reference to fees, see C. K. Yearley, *The Money Machines: The Breakdown and Reform of Governmental and Party Finance in the North, 1860–1920* (Albany: State University of New York Press, 1970), 109–10.

74. E.g., Conner v. Mayor of New York (1849), in *Reports of Cases Argued and Determined in the Superior Court of the City of New York*, ed. Lewis H. Sandford (New York: Banks, Gould and Co., 1851), 2:355, 377–78 (county clerk and others, in 1830s–40s); [Untitled editorial], *New York Times*, May 13, 1873, p. 4 (New York City marshals); Hoyt Landon Warner, *Progressivism in Ohio, 1897–1917* (Columbus: Ohio State University Press, 1964), 180 (county officers in large counties in 1906). Sometimes the high fee totals meant that the legislature had to compromise with the incumbents (or with the machine) by granting a high salary. Urdahl, *Fee-System*, 230.

75. Goodnow, *Comparative Administrative Law*, 2:73; Urdahl, *Fee-System*, 229.

76. E.g., James McQuade, Letter to the editor, titled "Gen. M'Quade and the Quarantine System," *New York Times*, Nov. 18, 1881, p. 8; Herman G. James, *Local Government in the United States* (New York: D. Appleton and Co., 1921), 146.

77. E.g., "Pittsburgh Moves to End Fee System," *New York Times*, Jan. 15, 1933, p. E6.

CHAPTER 4: A GOVERNMENT CAPABLE OF SAYING NO

1. For more on this point, see my discussion in the Introduction, text at notes 46–52, where I draw this interpretation of the general development of American politics from Richard L. McCormick, *The Party Period and Public Policy: American Politics from the Age of Jackson to the Progressive Era* (New York: Oxford University Press, 1986), 203–14, 223–27.

2. Secondary sources on the general operations of each system are cited throughout this chapter. I wish to acknowledge that I first learned of the importance of fees in

naturalization when Patrick Weil permitted me to read an early draft of part of his *The Sovereign Citizen: Denaturalization and the Origins of the American Republic* (Philadelphia: University of Pennsylvania Press, 2012).

3. For more on this point, see my discussion in the Introduction, text at notes 43–45.

4. Steinberg, *TCJ*, esp. 171–232 (quotation at 223).

5. *HSUS* series Aa33.

6. Reed Ueda, "Naturalization and Citizenship," in *Harvard Encyclopedia of American Ethnic Groups*, ed. Stephen Thernstrom (Cambridge, MA: Harvard University Press, 1980), 737.

7. Leon E. Aylsworth, "The Passing of Alien Suffrage," *American Political Science Review* 25 (1931): 114–15.

8. Alexander Keyssar, *The Right to Vote: The Contested History of Democracy in the United States* (New York: Basic Books, 2000), tables A.4 and A.12; U.S. Census Bureau, "Table 13: Nativity of the Population, for Regions, Divisions, and States: 1850 to 1990," http://www.census.gov/population/www/documentation/twps0029/tab13.html (last accessed Aug. 3, 2012).

9. Theda Skocpol, *Protecting Soldiers and Mothers: The Political Origins of Social Policy in the United States* (Cambridge, MA: Harvard University Press, 1992), 97–98, 100.

10. Purdy Report, 11. Later developments added further to citizenship's value. For example, state laws circa 1900 banned aliens from employment on public contracts. Ibid., 12–13.

11. On which courts can naturalize, see § 1, 2 Stat. 153, 153 (1802). For clarification, see § 3, 2 Stat. at 155.

12. Purdy Report, 22.

13. § 1, 2 Stat. at 153, codified in USRS § 2165.

14. Dorothee Schneider, *Crossing Borders: Migration and Citizenship in the Twentieth-Century United States* (Cambridge, MA: Harvard University Press, 2011), 202, 222–28.

15. Schneider, *Crossing Borders*, 196–97, 214–22.

16. Purdy Report, 58–62.

17. E.g., "The Naturalization Question," *New York Times*, June 13, 1892, p. 4; AG Report 1903, p. 396.

18. § 1, 2 Stat. 153, 153–54 (1802).

19. Purdy Report, 87. In the 1840s, New York City's three main naturalization courts required one. Hearings (1845), 16 (Marine Court), 12 (Superior Court), 56 (Common Pleas). In the 1880s, Boston's federal court required two. Hearings (1891), 382.

20. Courts sometimes asked the applicant to name the ship on which he arrived, which might be checked against the passenger records of the port. A New York judge ordered this kind of check in some cases, though not routinely. Hearings (1845), 50–51; see also Hearings (1892), 138. It does not appear that any court routinely ordered such checks. In Boston, at least, passenger records were not organized in such a way as to make these checks workable. Hearings (1892), 145.

21. § 4, 4 Stat. 69, 69 (1824). Before this 1824 statute, it had to be three years prior. § 1, 2 Stat. 153, 153 (1802).

22. H.R. Rep. No. 28–87, at 2 (1845); Alfred Conkling, *A Treatise on the Organization, Jurisdiction and Practice of the Courts of the United States in Suits at Law* (Albany, NY: W. C. Little, 1870), 742–43.

23. Courts apparently did little more than compare the applicant's signature with that on the court's copy of the declaration of the person he claimed to be. For examples in New York City, Philadelphia, and Boston, see Hearings (1845), 15–16, 51, 56, 103, 105; Hearings (1892), 171; 40 Cong. Rec. 7038 (1906) (quoting hearings).

24. § 1, 4 Stat. 69, 69 (1824), codified in USRS § 2167.

25. Conkling, *Treatise*, 745–46.

26. Purdy Report, 12.

27. Hearings (1891), 385; Hearings (1892), 128.

28. § 1, 2 Stat. 153, 154 (1802), codified in USRS § 2165.

29. E.g., Hearings (1845), 17, 20, 28, 49; Hearings (1891), 356, 372; "The Naturalization Question," *New York Times*, June 13, 1892, p. 4.

30. Conkling, *Treatise*, 747n1; C. C. Bonney, "Naturalization Laws and Their Enforcement," *New Englander and Yale Review* 13 (Nov. 1888): 309–10, 313. A few isolated courts expressed this view, as well, at least in the late 1800s. Noah Pickus, *True Faith and Allegiance: Immigration and American Civic Nationalism* (Princeton, NJ: Princeton University Press, 2005), 211n27.

31. Hearings (1845), 5–6, 20; Hearings (1891), 382; Hearings (1892), 128.

32. E.g., Hearings (1845), 42; Hearings (1892), 138.

33. John B. Scott, *An Appeal to the People from the Decision of the Senate in the Case of the Removal of the Justices of the Marine Court* (New York: Wm. G. Boggs, 1840), 12. See also Hearings (1845), 23.

34. Ueda, "Naturalization and Citizenship," 737, 740.

35. See Hearings (1845), 16 (Randell, justice of the New York City Marine Court), 20 (Sherman, judge of the New York City Marine Court), 53 (Smith, justice of the New York City Marine Court), 75 (Hoxie, former clerk of the New York Court of Common Pleas). Other judges gave some indication of a tighter process, though it was qualified either by the witness himself or by others. See Hearings (1845), 5 (Hammond, former justice of the New York City Marine Court), 27 (Vanderpoel, justice of the New York City Superior Court), 45 (Trenchard, the New York City marshal, recounting loose proceedings by Vanderpoel). Little had changed by the late nineteenth century. In Boston, U.S. District Court Judge Nelson admitted that "substantially all" the numerous applications to his court were granted. Hearings (1891), 382.

36. H.R. Rep. No. 25–1040, at 107 (1838) (letter from Chapin, editor); Hearings (1845), 29, 81, 86; Hearings (1891), 393; "The Naturalization Question," *New York Times*, June 13, 1892, p. 4.

37. This was the Marine Court. Hearings (1845), 53; Scott, *Appeal to the People*, 21–22, 24, 28.

38. Scott, *Appeal to the People*, 22 (reprinting attorney's affidavit).

39. For estimates of speed covering all three of New York City's main naturalization courts, see Hearings (1845), 10, 14, 20, 42, 53, 64, 75.

40. Hearings (1845), 56, 85. There were varying reasons why a person might serve as a repeat witness. Ibid., 53 (rabbi vouching for members of his religious community), 74 (profit seeker who charged fee for witnessing), 85 (party-machine agent seeking voters).
41. Schneider, *Crossing Borders*, 197–204; Ueda, "Naturalization and Citizenship," 737.
42. Purdy Report, 25, 90–91.
43. 1813 N.Y. Laws, vol. 2, pp. 342, 395. These fees pertain to the Justices' Courts of New York City. The Marine Court was one such court. For confirmation that the Marine Court's fee was $2.50, see Hearings (1845), 42. It also seems the Superior Court, prior to an 1844 statute, understood its "regular" fee to be $2.50. Ibid., 40. I presume the city's third major naturalization court (the Common Pleas) followed the same rule.
44. So stated a justice of the Marine Court. Hearings (1845), 50.
45. David Graham, *A Treatise on the Organization and Jurisdiction of the Courts of Law and Equity in the State of New York* (New York: Halsted and Voorhis, 1839), 48–52, 59.
46. Hearings (1845), 65.
47. Hearings (1845), 13, 28–29, 56. This testimony refers to the fee for granting naturalization as it was set for "clerks" by an 1844 statute, at a reduced rate (only fifty cents) from the 1813 statute ($2.50). 1844 N.Y. Laws 114, 114. The statute clearly applied to the clerks of the Superior Court and the Court of Common Pleas. Hearings (1845), 13, 56. But its reference to "clerks" rather than "judges" apparently made it doubtful whether it applied to the Marine Court (where fees went to judges). Still, the Marine Court voluntarily reduced its fees from $2.50 to $1. Ibid., 18.
48. A justice of the Marine Court noted the importance of an "expert clerk" to rapid proceedings. Hearings (1845), 53. A newspaper editor said, "[N]or it is singular," given fee incentives, "that the clerk . . . should hurry through the few ceremonies, without regard to particulars." H.R. Rep. No. 25–1040, at 108 (1838).
49. Hearings (1845), 12–13, 51, 55–56.
50. Some testimony suggested independent judicial scrutiny in the Superior Court and Common Pleas. Hearings (1845), 13 (Oakley, clerk of Superior Court), 27 (Vanderpoel, justice of Superior Court), 56 (Warner, clerk of Common Pleas). In nineteenth-century courts generally, though, it was a frequent pattern for judges to become rubber stamps for their clerks in naturalization matters. On rubber-stamping in the New York City Marine Court, see Scott, *Appeal to the People*, 17 (quoting state senator Verplanck in 1840). On rubber-stamping in Philadelphia courts in the 1840s, see Hearings (1845), 107 (Cohen, prothonotary of the Supreme Court of Pennsylvania for the Eastern District), 111 (Kline, clerk of several Philadelphia courts in succession); but see Hearings (1845), 117 (Francis E. Brady, deputy to prothonotary of District Court of Philadelphia). On rubber-stamping in federal courts later in the century, see H.R. Rep. No. 51–3808, at 8 (1891) (reprinting nativist memorial); Purdy Report, 85.
51. Hearings (1845), 15–16, 42.
52. H.R. Rep. No. 25–1040, at 108 (1838) (letter from Chapin).
53. Hearings (1845), 85.
54. Hearings (1845), 54. See also ibid., 22.
55. "From Philadelphia: Another View of the Election," *New York Tribune*, Oct. 16, 1856, p. 5 (emphasis added).

56. Hearings (1845), 71.

57. Hearings (1845), 34.

58. On the Superior Court, see Hearings (1845), 13, 28. On the Court of Common Pleas, see ibid., 43, 57. On the Marine Court, see ibid., 7–8. It appears the Marine Court began to disfavor such arrangements after 1840, though apparently with some exceptions. Ibid., 17–18, 20, 33, 51–52, 63–65.

59. One justice and one former justice of the Marine Court considered such discounts unfortunate but believed new legislation was needed to outlaw them. Hearings (1845), 6, 49.

60. Hearings (1845), 102, 108.

61. H.R. Rep. No. 25–1040, at 108 (1838) (letter from Chapin).

62. Hearings (1845), 42. On Riell's status, see Hearings (1845), 70, 73.

63. Jerome Mushkat, *Tammany: The Evolution of a Political Machine, 1789–1865* (Syracuse, NY: Syracuse University Press, 1971), 187.

64. H.R. Rep. No. 25–1040, at 107 (1838) (letter from Chapin).

65. Scott, *Appeal to the People*, 20–21 (printing affidavits); Hearings (1845), 33–34, 42, 74, 82.

66. On Philadelphia, see Hearings (1845), 102, 108. In New Orleans during the 1844 election, the Whigs and Democrats simultaneously agreed to volume discounts with one especially energetic fee-taking court, which proved so liberal as to spark a scandal. Hearings (1845), 160–61 (Report of Mr. Selby).

67. 1847 N.Y. Laws, vol. 2, pp. 560, 560–61 (clerk of Superior Court); 1854 N.Y. Laws 464, 464 (clerk of Common Pleas); David McAdam, *The Marine Court of the City of New York: Its Organization, Jurisdiction and Practice* (New York: Diossy and Co., 1872), 16 (Marine Court's loss of naturalization power by 1852 statute). On the continuing dominance of the Superior Court and Common Pleas in naturalization, see John I. Davenport, *The Election Frauds of New York City and Their Prevention* (New York: by the author, 1881) 1:118; "Courts Will No Longer Act," *New York Times*, June 8, 1895, p. 10.

68. Previously, judges had been appointed by the governor, who apparently deferred to the recommendations of the local members of his own party in the legislature. James Wilton Brooks, *History of the Court of Common Pleas of the City and County of New York* (New York: by subscription, 1896), 74. Since the Democrats did not have a lock on the governorship in this period, Tammany presumably had less control over local judges. But the state's new constitution of 1846 mandated that judges in cities be chosen by the local electorate, which the local Democratic machine was increasingly coming to dominate. *A Digest of the Charters, Statutes and Ordinances of, and Relating to, the Corporation of the City of New York* . . . , ed. Murray Hoffman (New York: Edmund Jones and Co., 1866), 2:382, 395–96.

69. Steven P. Erie, *Rainbow's End: Irish-Americans and the Dilemmas of Urban Machine Politics, 1840–1985* (Berkeley: University of California Press, 1988), 51; Davenport, *Election Frauds of New York City*, 1:118; "The Naturalization Question," *New York Times*, June 13, 1892, p. 4.

70. Up to the early 1900s, it was the conventional wisdom that naturalization was very loose. Purdy Report, 83; H.R. Rep. No. 59–1789, at 2 (1906); 40 Cong. Rec. 7049

(1906) (Rep. Hepburn); Ueda, "Naturalization and Citizenship," 740. The U.S. Department of Justice found that the liberality of state courts arose primarily from the political sympathy of the judges with the local machine, or (relatedly) from their concerns about their own electoral prospects in the local polity. AG Report 1903, p. 394; Purdy Report, 85. By that point, "a majority of the clerks of State courts" were "upon a salary basis," and "the general tendency in all States" was "to adopt the salary system" for those officers. Purdy Report, 91.

71. On such failed proposals, see Frank George Franklin, *The Legislative History of Naturalization in the United States: From the Revolutionary War to 1861* (Chicago: University of Chicago Press, 1906), 200, 203–05, 235–38, 243–46.

72. Scott, *Appeal to the People*, 13.

73. Cong. Globe, 41st Cong., 2d Sess., 4273 (1870) (Rep. Eldridge), quoted in John P. Roche, "Pre-Statutory Denaturalization," *Cornell Law Quarterly* 35 (1949): 128. On the modesty of the 1870 reforms, see Schneider, *Crossing Borders*, 202.

74. 40 Cong. Rec. 7042 (1906) (Rep. Smith).

75. H.R. Rep. No. 29–231, at 4 (1846).

76. Hearings (1845), 42.

77. Henry E. Riell, *An Appeal to the Voluntary Citizens of the United States from All Nations on the Exercise of their Elective Franchise, at the Approaching Presidential Election* (New York: Evening Post, 1840), 3.

78. H.R. Doc. No. 25–313, at 1 (1838) (emphasis added). See also the Massachusetts legislature's petition in H.R. Rep. No. 29–231, at 1 (1846).

79. Pickus, *True Faith and Allegiance*, 69–70.

80. Aylsworth, "The Passing of Alien Suffrage," 114–15.

81. "The Harm of Immigration," *Nation*, Jan. 19, 1893, p. 43.

82. Roche, "Pre-Statutory Denaturalization," 133.

83. Erie, *Rainbow's End*, 11–12, 51–53, 95.

84. Purdy Report, 11–12, 84.

85. "How Citizens Are Made," *Boston Daily Globe*, Nov. 4, 1876, p. 8.

86. United States v. Hill, 25 F. 375, 375 (C.C.D. Mass. 1885) (citing Massachusetts fee statute of 1879).

87. The origin and nature of federal clerks' fees for naturalization were a bit complicated. Congress neglected to establish by statute a fee for naturalization services. Yet federal clerks took fees for those services, the theory being that the clerks performed them not in their official capacity as clerks but instead as special commissioners for naturalization, appointed by the judge for that purpose. That is, their naturalization services were "unofficial," which made it lawful for them to take fees for those services without statutory authorization. In general, "unofficial" services were a disfavored and shrinking category during the nineteenth century (see Chapter 2), which made the clerks' naturalization fees exceptional. But it appears that everybody was comfortable with the exception, at least in the case of Massachusetts, presumably because the fees had been established and fixed by the illustrious Circuit Justice Joseph Story circa 1840 and had remained the same since that time. United States v. Hill, 25 F. 375, 379 (C.C.D. Mass. 1885); United States v. Hill, 120 U.S. 169, 181 (1887). Indeed, the U.S.

Circuit Court for the District of Massachusetts and the U.S. Supreme Court would both unanimously affirm the fees' lawfulness in the 1880s. *Hill*, 25 F. at 377–78; *Hill*, 120 U.S. at 179. See also Purdy Report, 25 (noting Congress never recognized or regulated the fees). Notably, the fees' "unofficial" status excepted them from Congress's $3,500 annual cap on clerks' official earnings, so clerks had an unlimited incentive to rack them up. For the cap, see 5 Stat. 475, 483 (1842). I further discuss the history of these fees in notes 106, 122, 128, and 132 below.

88. Circuit Court Clerk Stetson in 1892 testified about the "sharp competition" at the time of his arrival at the court in 1868, though he claimed to have put a stop to it as between the two federal courts. Hearings (1892), 118. See also the testimony of the U.S. District Court judge in Hearings (1892), 132.

89. "The Municipal Fight," *Boston Daily Globe*, Dec. 2, 1877, p. 8 (repeat witnesses); "Naturalization Laws," *Boston Daily Globe*, Jan. 21, 1880, p. 2 ("loose business" and "large sums"); "A Long Struggle," *Boston Daily Globe*, Mar. 22, 1883, p. 4 ("undignified rush").

90. Though their descriptions varied somewhat, the clerks and their deputies painted a picture of long-standing clerk dominance. They suggested that the judge would be involved only in three circumstances: especially close or contested cases, moments of nativist political agitation, or the lead-up to a major election. Hearings (1891), 345, 348, 350–51, 356, 363–64, 370; Hearings (1892), 113. The U.S. District Court judge declared that he and his predecessors had all considered it proper, indeed necessary, for clerks largely to handle naturalization decisions. Hearings (1891), 381. See also the testimony of John Lowell, a former district court and circuit court judge, in Hearings (1892), 137.

91. On the Superior Courts, see "How Citizens Are Made," *Boston Daily Globe*, Nov. 4, 1876, p. 8.

92. On the compromise, see "The New Law of Citizenship," *Boston Daily Globe*, Aug. 8, 1885, p. 2. On the potentially inconvenient procedures, which required applicants to make two trips to court and designate their witnesses far in advance, see 1885 Mass. Acts 802, 802–03; Hearings (1891), 357.

93. 1885 Mass. Acts 802, 803–04. It was not until three years later that these clerks were converted from fees to salaries for their general court business. 1888 Mass. Acts 207, 207–08.

94. H.R. Rep. No. 51–3823, at p. xxiii (1891). See also ibid., xxvii. For statistics showing federal-court dominance, see the nativist petition printed in Hearings (1892), 152.

95. Hearings (1891), 383. See also his comment in Hearings (1892), 131. U.S. Circuit Court Judge Colt agreed that the reform had a "tendency" to "drive" naturalizations "into the United States courts," since "the laws are stricter in the State courts than they are in the United States courts." Hearings (1892), 129 (partly questioner's words, with which witness agrees). At another point, Nelson somewhat contradicted his other statements and Colt's, saying that "before that act was passed [in 1885], substantially all the naturalization was [already] done in these [federal] courts and very few in the State courts, even in this vicinity." Hearings (1892), 132. I am skeptical that the federal courts' pre-1885 dominance was as total as this statement suggests. If it were,

hen it would mean that applications had become rapidly concentrated in the federal courts sometime after the late 1870s but prior to 1885, without an obvious cause. On substantial naturalization business in state superior courts in eastern Massachusetts in the late 1870s, see "How Citizens Are Made," *Boston Daily Globe*, Nov. 4, 1876, p. 8; "Lawrence," *Boston Daily Globe*, Oct. 20, 1878, p. 1.

96. Hearings (1891), 382.

97. Hearings (1891), 371. The circuit court clerk argued that repeat witnesses were often legitimate. Hearings (1892), 118.

98. Hearings (1891), 356. He added that he and his colleagues might infer the witnesses' veracity from their "general bearing." For similar statements by other clerks and deputies, see Hearings (1891), 372; Hearings (1892), 167. One said the officers might ask about an applicant's prior arrests. Hearings (1892), 171.

99. Hearings (1892), 152, 171.

100. Hearings (1891), 355–56, 363, 389.

101. Hearings (1891), 363.

102. Hearings (1892), 129. The words are the questioner's, with which the witness agrees. Presumably, he misspoke as to the state courts, where the clerks by now earned no fees and did little business.

103. Hearings (1891), 358–59.

104. Hearings (1892), 125.

105. Hearings (1892), 165. Some of the words are the questioner's, with which the witness agrees. The circuit court clerk himself took a different view: back in the 1860s, when he started, there had been "sharp competition" among the courts, but he had "at once put a stop to it," allowing the two courts to settle into a kind of cartel. Hearings (1892), 118.

106. Hearings (1891), 354–55, 359, 402. Recall that naturalization fees were considered "unofficial" and therefore were not subject to the $3,500 cap that applied to the clerk's "official" earnings. (I discuss this in note 87 above.) In September 1888, the district court judge phased in a new court rule whereby the district court clerk's naturalization fees were subjected to the $3,500 cap. Hearings (1891), 383; Hearings (1892), 131. But the circuit court judge said he doubted that this new rule blunted incentives: clerks still had reason to naturalize aliens to make sure they reached the cap. Hearings (1892), 127. The new rule apparently did not apply to the circuit court clerk.

107. "Local Fee System," *Boston Daily Journal*, Apr. 14, 1892, p. 2.

108. Hearings (1891), 363.

109. Hearings (1891), 372.

110. United States v. Hill, 25 F. 375, 377 (C.C.D. Mass. 1885); Hearings (1891), 362.

111. Hearings (1892), 117.

112. Hearings (1891), 372.

113. Erie, *Rainbow's End*, 40–42.

114. "Worcester Naturalization Frauds," *Boston Daily Globe*, Nov. 1, 1883, p. 1 (indicating that Democrats oppose Swedish voters).

115. Hearings (1891), 362. Massachusetts in 1890 included about 260,000 Irish-born and 76,000 English-born persons. *Report of the Population of the United States at the Eleventh Census: 1890, Part I* (Washington, DC: GPO, 1895), 606–07.

116. "Railroading Naturalization," *Boston Daily Globe*, Sept. 7, 1887, p. 4.

117. The district court clerk was always appointed by the district court judge. USRS § 555. The circuit court clerk was initially appointed (effectively) by the circuit justice (§ 2, 5 Stat. 321, 322 (1839)), then starting in 1869 by the circuit court judge (USRS § 619), then starting in 1878 by agreement of the circuit court judge and district court judge (20 Stat. 178, 204–05 (1878)). The appointing judges could apparently remove a clerk at pleasure. See *Federal Statutes Annotated*, ed. William M. McKinney and Peter Kemper Jr. (Northport, NY: Edward Thompson Co., 1904), 4:74–75 (citing *Ex parte Hennen*, 38 U.S. 225 (1839)).

118. Circuit Court Clerk Stetson was appointed in 1867. Hearings (1892), 95. This means that he must have been appointed by Circuit Justice Nathan Clifford, a Democrat. Philip Greely Clifford, *Nathan Clifford, Democrat (1803–1881)* (New York: G. P. Putnam's Sons, 1922), 270; Hearings (1891), 356. Stetson retained his office under three Republican-appointed circuit court judges (Shepley, Lowell, and Colt) and two Republican-appointed district court judges (Lowell and Nelson) up to 1891, when he ascended to the clerkship of the new U.S. Court of Appeals. Charles Warren, *History of the Harvard Law School and of Early Legal Conditions in America* (New York: Lewis Publishing Co., 1908), 3:90.

    At the district court, presided over by Republican appointees Lowell and Nelson from 1865 to 1897, one clerk (Edward Dexter) began service in 1869. Compare *The American Year Book and National Register for 1869: Astronomical, Historical, Political, Financial, Commercial, Agricultural, Educational, and Religions*, ed. David N. Camp (Hartford: O. D. Case and Co., 1869), 1:365 (noting Dexter's predecessor Sprague as clerk); with *The Boston Directory, Embracing the City Record, General Directory of the Citizens, and a Business Directory* (Boston: Sampson, Davenport and Co., 1869), 938 (listing Dexter as clerk). Dexter retired in 1879 and was replaced by Clement Hill. *Albany Law Journal*, Feb. 8, 1879, p. 120. Hill served till he came into an inheritance in 1887. *Proceedings of the Massachusetts Historical Society*, 2nd ser., 12 (1899): 375. He was succeeded by a subordinate (Elisha Bassett) who had worked at the court for fifty-two years. Hearings (1891), 368, 372; Hearings (1892), 170.

119. Hearings (1892), 119, 127, 131, 165–67.

120. "To Prevent Naturalization Abuses," *New York Times*, June 7, 1895, p. 4.

121. On clerk control in Brooklyn, see Purdy Report, 87.

122. "Brooklyn News: A Naturalization Mill," *New York Tribune*, Feb. 7, 1900, p. A1. According to the presentment, Morle was operating on the premise, approved by the judge of the court, that the $3,500 statutory cap on clerks' earnings did not apply to naturalization fees. On the judge's approbation, see "Judge Thomas Supports Morle," *New York Tribune*, Jan. 14, 1900, p. A5. For background on the cap and exceptions to it, see my discussion in note 87 above.

123. He was still clerk in 1908. See my discussion in this chapter, text at note 149.

124. William Anderson and Albert J. Lobb, *A History of the Constitution of Minnesota* (Minneapolis: University of Minnesota, 1921), 180.

125. "Bargain in Citizenship," *Minneapolis Journal*, Dec. 11, 1897, p. 4.

126. Purdy Report, 85–87.

127. AG Report 1903, p. 394; Purdy Report, 91.
128. 34 Stat. 596 (1906). Another congressional reform that may have lessened federal clerks' incentive to naturalize was the effort in 1898–1902 to bring the federal clerks' naturalization fees (which were supposedly "unofficial") under the $3,500 annual cap that generally covered all federal clerks' official fees. On the pre-reform refusal of many federal clerks and judges to treat naturalization fees as subject to the cap, see my discussion in notes 87 and 106 above, and see also H.R. Rep. No. 53–111, at 2 (1893). A congressional statute of 1898 attempted to place such fees under the cap. § 8, 30 Stat. 277, 317 (1898). But clerks (with judges' approval) dodged it by claiming to earn the fees in their capacity as ad hoc commissioners. E.g., "Judge Thomas Supports Morle," *New York Tribune,* Jan. 14, 1900, p. A5. Congress in 1902 declared that fees were subject to the cap even if earned "as commissioner, or in any other capacity." 32 Stat. 419, 475–76 (1902). Bringing naturalization fees under the cap presumably lessened federal clerks' energy in attracting and processing applicants, assuming they faced high-enough demand that they could easily make the maximum without effort, which in a few large urban districts they apparently did. See the fee totals (possibly not including naturalization fees) in H.R. Doc. No. 54–167, at 8–13 (1896). Still, the low cost of naturalization (if performed without much scrutiny) and the clerks' continuing power to draw the expenses of the process against the general receipts of their offices (compare my discussion in this chapter, text at notes 146–47) appears to have kept customer service alive in many districts as of 1905. Purdy Report, 85.
129. Rogers M. Smith, *Civic Ideals: Conflicting Visions of Citizenship in U.S. History* (New Haven, CT: Yale University Press, 1997), 446. See also Schneider, *Crossing Borders,* 204–05.
130. The vaunted federal registry, once it actually started operating, proved often faulty and incomplete. Schneider, *Crossing Borders,* 206.
131. § 4, 34 Stat. at 596–98; § 12, 34 Stat. at 599–600; 40 Cong. Rec. 3644, 3647 (1906) (Rep. Bonynge).
132. § 13, 34 Stat. at 600–01. For federal clerks, naturalization fees were subject only to this special new $3,000 cap, and they no longer counted toward the $3,500 cap on fees for general court business. "Accounting for Clerks' Fees in Naturalization Cases," *Decisions of the Comptroller of the Treasury* (Washington, DC: GPO, 1914), 20:765. For more on the $3,500 cap on fees for general court business, see my discussion in notes 87 and 128 above.
133. H.R. Rep. No. 59–1789, at 7 (1906).
134. "Emoluments of Clerks of United States Circuit Courts in Naturalization Cases," *Decisions of the Comptroller of the Treasury* (Washington, DC: GPO, 1912), 18:963.
135. 40 Cong. Rec. 7052 (1906) (Rep. Bonynge); Mulcrevy v. City of San Francisco, 231 U.S. 669 (1914).
136. § 3, 34 Stat. at 596.
137. For the original version, see H.R. Rep. No. 59–1789, at 7 (1906); 40 Cong. Rec. 3644, 3647 (1906) (Rep. Bonynge) (proposal for fees totaling $11). For the later change, see ibid., 7873 (Rep. Bonynge).
138. § 13, 34 Stat. at 600–01.

139. "Allowance for Additional Clerical Assistance to Clerks of Courts from Excess Naturalization Fees," *Decisions of the Comptroller of the Treasury* (Washington, DC: GPO, 1908), 14:71.

140. *Annual Report of the Chief of the Division of Naturalization to the Commissioner-General of Immigration for the Fiscal Year Ended June 30, 1910* (Washington, DC: GPO, 1910) 33; *Annual Report of the Commissioner of Naturalization to the Secretary of Labor, Fiscal Year Ended June 30, 1920* (Washington, DC: GPO, 1920), 19.

141. E.g., *Administration of the Office of Clerk of the Circuit Court, and of the Office of Clerk of the Superior Court of Cook County, Illinois* (Chicago: Bureau of Public Efficiency, 1911), 42.

142. H.R. Rep. No. 60–1361, at 1 (1908); S. Rep. No. 60–675, at 2 (1908).

143. *Hearings before the Subcommittee on Naturalization*, 60th Cong., 1st Sess. (Washington, DC: GPO, 1908), 20 (testimony of Morle).

144. John Palmer Gavit, *Americans by Choice* (New York: Harper, 1922), 164–65.

145. *Report of the Commission of Immigration of the State of New York* (Albany, NY: J. B. Lyon Co., 1909), 68–69. See also H.R. Rep. No. 60–1361, at 1 (1908).

146. Hearings (1892), 92–93.

147. This is evident from *Hearings before the Subcommittee on Naturalization*, 18 (testimony of Morle).

148. Ibid., 11, 13 (testimony of Director Campbell).

149. Ibid., 18 (testimony of Morle).

150. S. Rep. No. 60–675, at 2 (1908).

151. § 289, 36 Stat. 1087, 1167 (1911).

152. 40 Stat. 1182 (1919).

153. On the process by which examiners came to dominate decision-making, see *Annual Report of the Commissioner of Naturalization to the Secretary of Labor, Fiscal Year Ended June 30, 1917* (Washington, DC: GPO, 1917), 13; *Annual Report of the Commissioner of Naturalization to the Secretary of Labor, Fiscal Year Ended June 30, 1922* (Washington, DC: GPO, 1922), 10–12; Gavit, *Americans by Choice*, 194; Henry B. Hazard, "The Trend toward Administrative Naturalization," *American Political Science Review* 21 (1927): 342–49. In 1926, Congress endorsed the trend by authorizing federal courts to dispense with even the formality of a judicial hearing, if they first designated examiners to handle the business. 44 Stat. 709 (1926); H.R. Rep. No. 69–1328, at 1 (1926).

154. On how examiners generally raised standards, and how judges acquiesced, see Frank V. Thompson, *Schooling of the Immigrant* (New York: Harper, 1920), 333–34.

155. Hearings (1891), 382.

156. *HSUS* series Ad1030 (total naturalizations) and series Ad1037 (total denials of naturalization). See also Schneider, *Crossing Borders*, 209–10.

157. Gavit, *Americans by Choice*, 167–68.

158. Ibid., 171.

159. Pickus, *True Faith and Allegiance*, 92.

160. *Reports of the Department of Labor 1915* (Washington, DC: GPO, 1916), 85.

161. Gavit, *Americans by Choice*, 235; ibid., 176.

162. Schneider, *Crossing Borders*, 209. Soon after 1906 and increasingly in the subsequent years, civic organizations and the bureau itself mounted a campaign to educate immigrants, as a "direct result of resistance by naturalization examiners to the admission to citizenship of applicants ignorant of our form of government." *Reports of the Department of Labor 1915*, 85–86; see also Pickus, *True Faith and Allegiance*, 96–100.

163. Liav Orgad, "Creating New Americans: The Essence of Americanism under the Citizenship Test," *Houston Law Review* 47 (2011): 1237. See also Schneider, *Crossing Borders*, 206–07.

164. Thompson, *Schooling of the Immigrant*, 337.

165. Gavit, *Americans by Choice*, 155, 159, 173–77, 412–14, 417. The bureau encouraged local public schools and private institutions to offer courses in citizenship, but the instruction was decentralized and variable. Pickus, *True Faith and Allegiance*, 96–100. By 1920, a few courts would accept a diploma from such a course as sufficient to satisfy the English-speaking and attachment requirements if it were countersigned by an examiner, but the bureau would allow examiners to countersign only if they examined the applicant themselves. Thompson, *Schooling of the Immigrant*, 344–45. On the relatively small proportion of immigrants reached by these courses, see ibid. 59–62, 339–42. The bureau in 1918 issued a citizenship textbook that it hoped might impose uniformity on the numerous emerging courses, but it contained a large amount of useless and indigestible minutia, and few schools used it. The bureau did not even try to use the textbook as the basis for examiners' inquiries. Ibid., 347–49.

166. Gavit, *Americans by Choice*, 169.

167. Irene Bloemraad, "Citizenship Lessons from the Past: The Contours of Immigrant Naturalization in the Early 20th Century," *Social Science Quarterly* 87 (2006): 941. See also Erie, *Rainbow's End*, 92.

168. Ueda, "Naturalization and Citizenship," 744.

169. Dorothee Schneider, "Naturalization and United States Citizenship in Two Periods of Mass Migration: 1894–1930, 1965–2000," *Journal of American Ethnic History* 21 (2001): 57. There was also a general decline in political party mobilization. Bloemraad, "Citizenship Lessons from the Past," 946.

170. Bloemraad, "Citizenship Lessons from the Past," 942. Congress imposed a literacy requirement in 1917 as a condition of entering the country, rather than as a requirement for naturalization. The alien had to be literate in some language, not necessarily English. § 3, 39 Stat. 874, 877 (1917). This restriction "turned out to be ineffective due to the growing rate of literacy in Southern Europe." Orgad, "Creating New Americans," 1237.

171. See also Schneider, *Crossing Borders*, 210 (referring to the naturalization examiners' "unpredictable demands, their suspiciousness, and their disorganization and inertia").

172. Glasson, *FMP*, 266.

173. Skocpol, *Protecting Soldiers and Mothers*, 114, 117, 124–25.

174. On administration of widows' pensions, see Megan J. McClintock, "Civil War Pensions and the Reconstruction of Union Families," *Journal of American History* 83 (1996): 471–79.

175. Glasson, *FMP*, 123–38, esp. 136–38. There were also pensions for other, more specifically defined disabilities.

176. Ibid., 234–42, 271–72.

177. The description in this paragraph draws on Jerry L. Mashaw, "Federal Administration and Administrative Law in the Gilded Age," *Yale Law Journal* 119 (2010): 1422–24.

178. Mashaw, "Federal Administration," 1423, 1432. On majority voting, see H.R. Rep. No. 46–387, at 135 (1881).

179. Pension Bureau Report 1898, p. 78.

180. Dora L. Costa, *The Evolution of Retirement: An American Economic History, 1880–1990* (Chicago: University of Chicago Press, 1998), 211; H.R. Rep. No. 46–387, at 139 (1881).

181. Mashaw, "Federal Administration," 1429; Pension Bureau Report 1898, p. 75; Pension Bureau Report 1899, p. 100.

182. On rules, see Mashaw, "Federal Administration," 1430–31. On surgeons' neglect of them, see Pension Bureau Report 1902, p. 73; H.R. Rep. No. 46–387, at 574 (1881).

183. H.R. Rep. No. 46–387, at 154 (1881).

184. For the Washington office's frustrations on this point, see Pension Bureau Report 1898, p. 75; Pension Bureau Report 1899, p. 100; Pension Bureau Report 1901, p. 56.

185. On the critical importance of the surgeons' report, see Mashaw, "Federal Administration," 1428; Pension Bureau Report 1872, p. 331; Pension Bureau Report 1902, p. 73.

186. Glasson, *FMP*, 138, 153.

187. Mashaw, "Federal Administration," 1425.

188. Skocpol, *Protecting Soldiers and Mothers*, 107. See also Costa, *Evolution of Retirement*, 209.

189. H.R. Rep. No. 46–387, at 132–35 (1881).

190. S. N. Clark, "Some Weak Places in Our Pension System," *Forum* 26 (1898–99): 313.

191. Eugene V. Smalley, "The United States Pension Office," *Century Illustrated Monthly Magazine* 28 (1884): 430.

192. 4 Cong. Rec. 1082 (1876). On Ingalls and pensions, see Glasson, *FMP*, 162, 177n1, 186–87. For similar views of officials and politicians, see Glasson, *FMP*, 176 (citing pension commissioner in 1881); ibid., 211 (quoting President Cleveland); Smalley, "United States Pension Office," 430 (on "Washington" opinion).

193. A. B. Casselman, "An Inside View of the Pension Bureau," *Century* 46 (May 1893): 137. On Casselman's status, see ibid., 135n1.

194. R. P. C. Wilson, "How Shall the Pension List Be Revised?" *North American Review* 156 (1893): 419.

195. Skocpol, *Protecting Soldiers and Mothers*, 277.

196. Peter Blanck, "Civil War Pensions and Disability," *Ohio State Law Journal* 62 (2001): 135–48.

197. Hugh Rockoff, "Veterans," in chapter Ed of *HSUS*, 5–344. See also ibid., 5–346.

198. Skocpol, *Protecting Soldiers and Mothers*, 145.

199. Heywood T. Sanders, "Paying for the 'Bloody Shirt': The Politics of Civil War Pensions," in *Political Benefits: Empirical Studies of American Public Programs*, ed. Barry S. Rundquist (Lexington, MA: Lexington Books, 1980), 144–45. Another study

finds that pensions tended to be more concentrated in localities that were strongly Republican or especially competitive. Skocpol, *Protecting Soldiers and Mothers*, 147–48. It is not clear to me whether this effect would have resulted from surgeons' decisions or from the Washington office's manipulation. In any event, another study finds no such tendency in the period from the mid-1890s onward. Costa, *Evolution of Retirement*, 164.

200. For critiques by medical referees at the Washington office, see H.R. Rep. No. 46-387, at 574 (1881) (statement of Thomas Hood); Pension Bureau Report 1899, pp. 100, 102; J. F. Raub, "Defects in, and Suggestions for the Improvement of the Reports of Examining Surgeons," *Transactions of the National Association of United States Pension Examining Surgeons* 1 (1903): 74. For critiques in the press, see Smalley, "United States Pension Office," 429–30; "Sham and Fraud behind This Pension Giving," *New York Herald*, Nov. 17, 1890, p. 3.

201. Skocpol, *Protecting Soldiers and Mothers*, 145 (noting the importance of the "loose and locally rooted application system," the surgeons being the only local personnel). To be sure, the surgeons were not completely undiscriminating or irrational: a recent study found that their ratings correlated with veterans' age and subsequent mortality and inversely with their body-mass indices. Costa, *Evolution of Retirement*, 165, 209–11. But this does not refute the notion that surgeons were generous across the board, judged against the baseline of contemporary cultural assumptions. Applicants' success rates, as reported in another recent study, are not inconsistent with a common-sense characterization of the system as generous. For first-time claimants, surgeons found at least some compensable disability in 81 percent of cases, and when rating a disability, their ratings averaged 64 percent of the allowable maximum. Blanck, "Civil War Pensions and Disability," 193, 195.

202. *Report of the Secretary of the Interior [1869]* (Washington, DC: GPO, 1869), vii; Pension Bureau Report 1875, p. 442; Pension Bureau Report 1876, p. 701; S. Rep. No. 46-418, at 1 (1880); Smalley, "United States Pension Office," 430; "Sham and Fraud behind This Pension Giving," *New York Herald*, Nov. 17, 1890, p. 3; Casselman, "Inside View of the Pension Bureau," 139; 24 Cong. Rec. 1435 (1893) (Rep. Mutchler); "The Paying of Pensions," *Indiana State Journal*, Dec. 8, 1897, p. 8; Clark, "Some Weak Places in Our Pension System," 313.

203. Skocpol, *Protecting Soldiers and Mothers*, 118–20, 142–48. Skocpol also discusses partisan politics as a factor driving the system's liberality, but without linking it to the examining surgeons. Ibid., 147–48. It is conceivable that the surgeons' partisan ties might have rendered them more generous to members of their own party. They were, after all, patronage appointees. Pension Bureau Report 1905, p. 532. Yet there were efforts to ensure that each three-member board had at least one member from each party. Mashaw, "Gilded Age" 1432. Also, contemporaries hardly ever raised partisan politics as a reason for the surgeons' generosity. I have seen only one clear suggestion that examining surgeons made decisions with partisan motivation. Wilson, "How Shall the Pension List Be Revised?" 418 (referring to "examining-boards made up of the family physicians and personal and political friends of the persons examined").

Note he simultaneously cited doctor-patient ties and personal friendship. These were far more common accusations. See the sources I cite in note 202 above.

204. § 35, 17 Stat. 566, 576 (1873), codified in USRS § 4777.

205. § 4, 22 Stat. 174, 175 (1882).

206. Congress imposed this downward graduation through repeated provisions in annual appropriations acts, starting in 1885. Thomas P. Randolph and Edward P. Hall, *The Pension Attorney's Guide* (Washington, DC: John F. Sherry, 1892), 111. By 1908, Congress increased the fee for the initial exams to $3. 35 Stat. 418, 419 (1908). On the customary annual reenactment of this provision, see *Federal Statutes Annotated*, 2nd ed., ed. William M. McKinney (Northport, NY: Edward Thompson Co., 1918), 7:1107–08. Note the original provision of 1882 (not in an appropriations act) also remained on the books as a backstop to confirm surgeons' right to fees. Ibid., 7:1076.

207. Paul Starr, *The Social Transformation of American Medicine: The Rise of a Sovereign Profession and the Making of a Vast Industry* (New York: Basic Books, 1982), 84–85, 142–43.

208. To get this estimate, I averaged the annual "Fees for examining surgeons" from 1891 through 1900 in *Report of the Secretary of the Interior [1901]* (Washington, DC: GPO, 1901), lxxxix. The average was $1,050,543.19. I then calculated the average number of three-member boards by averaging the figures for four years during the 1890s for which I could find published data. Pension Bureau Report 1892, p. 35 (1,166 boards); Pension Bureau Report 1896, p. 12 (1,285 boards); Pension Bureau Report 1898, p. 78 (1,418 boards); Pension Bureau Report 1901, p. 68 (1,385 boards). The average was 1,313.5, which I multiplied by three for the number of surgeons.

209. "The Civil Service Law," *Minneapolis Journal*, Feb. 26, 1897, p. 7.

210. "Surgeons in Civil Service," *Washington Post*, Dec. 5, 1896, p. 4.

211. Casselman, "Inside View of the Pension Bureau," 139.

212. 22 Stat. 174, 175 (1882) (referring to claims "for pension or increased pension"), still in force in *Federal Statutes Annotated*, 2nd ed., 7:1076. There had originally been a requirement that every pensioner be reexamined biennially to confirm that his disability still existed, but that was dropped in 1879. Pension Bureau Report 1894, p. 18. See also Pension Bureau Report 1901, p. 55.

213. Pension Bureau Report 1875, pp. 440–41; Pension Bureau Report 1892, p. 104; *Report of the Secretary of the Interior [1901]*, lxxxi.

214. Casselman, "Inside View of the Pension Bureau," 136. See also ibid., 140.

215. Costa, *Evolution of Retirement*, 203.

216. Clark, "Some Weak Places in Our Pension System," 312.

217. Casselman, "Inside View of the Pension Bureau," 139; "Surgeons in Civil Service," *Washington Post*, Dec. 5, 1896, p. 4.

218. H.R. Exec. Doc. No. 48–172, at 1438–39 (1884) (bureau order stating that disappointed applicant is entitled to be reexamined by different surgeon); 24 Cong. Rec. 1699 (1893) (Rep. Taylor) ("if one examination is not satisfactory [the claimants] are given an opportunity of being examined by another board"); Pension Bureau Report 1899, p. 101 (common for disappointed claimants to "request examinations by some

other board," which they hope "may be more thorough"). The Washington office actually had some preference in favor of rotating an applicant or pensioner between multiple boards, since it thereby acquired the opinions of more surgeons. Randolph and Hall, *Pension Attorney's Guide*, 113 (order of 1876); Pension Bureau Report 1898, pp. 76–77. This may have mitigated forum-shopping, though presumably only by applicants themselves, not by attorneys. Also, presumably, a veteran seeking an increase, if sent before a new board and disappointed, could then ask to be examined by his old board. At a convention of examining surgeons, one gave a paper stating that the Washington office "in its leniency allows the applicant to appear before any Board he may select." E. M. Brown, "Some Observations from the Medical Examiner's End of the Pension Bureau," *Transactions of the National Association of United States Pension Examining Surgeons* 3 (1905): 47.

219. Pension Bureau Report 1901, pp. 55–56. On big-time pension attorneys in Buffalo, New York, and in Iowa, see Pension Bureau Report 1895, p. 15.

220. Peter Blanck and Chen Song, "Civil War Pension Attorneys and Disability Politics," *University of Michigan Journal of Law Reform* 35 (2001–02): 182.

221. Glasson, *FMP*, 179; Pension Bureau Report 1894, p. 37; Pension Bureau Report 1901, p. 56.

222. Except for a brief period from 1878 to 1884. See U.S. House Committee on Veterans' Affairs, 100th Cong., *Legislative History of the Ten Dollar Attorney Fee Limitation in Claims for Veterans' Benefits*, at 1–8, esp. 6 (Committee Print No. 8, 1987).

223. E.g., H.R. Exec. Doc. No. 48–172, at 23, 698 (1884).

224. Glasson, *FMP*, 245–46 (on Evans's forced resignation); "Jacob F. Raub, M.D.," *Transactions of the National Association of United States Pension Examining Surgeons* 4 (1906): 81 (on Raub's acceptance of demotion).

225. Pension Bureau Report 1898, pp. 76–77.

226. Pension Bureau Report 1901, p. 76 (emphasis added). For another example of forum-shopping, by (illegally) giving a false address for the claimant, see H.R. Exec. Doc. No. 48–172, at 1377 (1884).

227. Pension Bureau Report 1899, pp. 100–02 (emphasis added). See also Raub, "Defects in, and Suggestions for the Improvement of the Reports of Examining Surgeons," 61.

228. "Jacob F. Raub, M.D.," 80–81.

229. Brown, "Some Observations from the Medical Examiner's End," 47.

230. Pension Bureau Report 1877, pp. 731–32.

231. "Pension Frauds," *Minneapolis Journal*, Dec. 12, 1898, p. 1. The case occurred in Ohio. For a similar case, see Raub, "Defects in, and Suggestions for the Improvement of the Reports of Examining Surgeons," 62.

232. *Report of the Secretary of the Interior [1869]*, vii; Pension Bureau Report 1875, p. 442; S. Rep. No. 46–418, at 2 (1880).

233. S. Rep. No. 46–418 (1880) (favorably reporting S. 496); 11 Cong. Rec. index 478 (noting that S. 496 was never voted upon by the Senate).

234. Smalley, "United States Pension Office," 429.

235. For the offer of the amendment, see 24 Cong. Rec. 1653 (1893). Representative Mutchler said it would "abolish local boards of examining surgeons" and "substitute

in their place a single surgeon who is to be assisted by [salaried] surgeons detailed from the Pension Bureau." Ibid., 1434.

236. 24 Cong. Rec. 1646 (1893).

237. 24 Cong. Rec. 1690–91, 1704 (1893).

238. Glasson, *FMP*, 181. For Bentley's salarization proposals, see Pension Bureau Report 1875, p. 442; Pension Bureau Report 1877, p. 732.

239. Glasson 242–46. For Evans's echo of Bentley's salarization proposal, see Pension Bureau Report 1901, p. 72.

240. Glasson, *FMP*, 205–07, 229.

241. Casselman, "Inside View of the Pension Bureau," 138.

242. Glasson, *FMP*, 265–66.

243. Sanders, "Paying for the 'Bloody Shirt,'" 157.

244. Glasson, *FMP*, 211–14, 218–19.

245. Ibid., 269. See also Costa, *Evolution of Retirement*, 162.

246. Both quoted in Glasson, *FMP*, 187n2, 249.

247. For the system's gradual disappearance, see William Pyrle Dillingham, *Federal Aid to Veterans, 1917–1941* (Gainesville: University Press of Florida, 1952), 210–12.

248. Glasson, *FMP*, 269.

249. As indeed they were: veterans' benefits accounted for 17–21 percent of the federal budget from 1922 to 1932. William Pencak, *For God and Country: The American Legion, 1919–1941* (Boston: Northeastern University Press, 1989), 171–72.

250. On the transformation of federal taxation surrounding World War I, see W. Elliott Brownlee, *Federal Taxation in America: A Short History*, 2nd ed. (Cambridge: Cambridge University Press, 2004), 59–81.

251. § 312, 40 Stat. 398, 408 (1917).

252. Glasson, *FMP*, 283.

253. Karl Walter Hickel, "Entitling Citizens: World War I, Progressivism, and the Origins of the American Welfare State, 1917–1928" (Ph.D. diss., Columbia University, 1999), 111.

254. S. Doc. No. 65–75, at 9 (1917).

255. Hickel, "Entitling Citizens," 126; Rockoff, "Veterans," in chapter Ed of *HSUS*, 5–346.

256. § 302(2), 40 Stat. 398, 406 (1917); Hickel, "Entitling Citizens," 127.

257. Hickel, "Entitling Citizens," 128.

258. H.R. Rep. No. 65–130, pt. 3, at 2 (1917).

259. Even as it granted compensation to veterans, Congress did its best to reduce that compensation's importance by establishing simultaneously a system of subsidized disability insurance that soldiers could buy when they entered the military. Hickel, "Entitling Citizens," 129–30; S. Doc. No. 65–75, at 8 (1917). Despite the fond hopes of reformers, most soldiers who purchased the insurance soon let their policies lapse, and the scheme turned out to be far less important in the postwar years than outright compensation would be. Dillingham, *Federal Aid to Veterans*, 88, 101 (giving statistics); Pencak, *For God and Country*, 177.

260. Glasson, *FMP*, 273.

261. Pension Bureau Report 1917, pp. 306, 335. Though the number of boards was still on a par with the peak years circa 1900, their volume of business was much lower: only

about five thousand exams per year. Ibid., 335. The reason was that Congress in 1907 had declared that old age itself was a disability that entitled veterans to certain pension levels automatically. Glasson, *FMP*, 248–50. This greatly reduced the need for exams.

262. H.R. Rep. No. 65–130, pt. 2, at 9 (1917) (minority views); 59 Cong. Rec. 1090 (1920) (Sen. Smoot).

263. One committee tried to justify the approach by arguing that World War cash assistance was of a piece with the government's subsidized insurance program, so the WRIB should administer both. H.R. Rep. No. 65–130, pt. 3, at 6 (1917). This seems disingenuous. The reformers evidenced little concern for unified authority elsewhere. For example, they left the hospital-care and rehabilitation programs to two agencies that were separate from each other and from the WRIB, thus causing a disaster that was remedied only when President Harding combined all three agencies in the new Veterans' Bureau. On formation of the Veterans' Bureau, see my discussion in this chapter, text at note 281.

264. Brown, "Some Observations from the Medical Examiner's End," 46.

265. H.R. Rep. No. 65–130, pt. 2, at 7 (1917) (minority views).

266. H.R. Rep. No. 65–130, pt. 3, at 6 (1917) (emphasis added). This comment pertains specifically to the new system of purchasable insurance, which was supposed to reduce the importance of direct cash assistance but failed. See my discussion in note 259 above.

267. H.R. Rep. No. 65–130, pt. 3, at 2 (1917).

268. *War-Risk Insurance: Hearing before the Subcommittee of the Committee on Finance, United States Senate, Sixty-Fifth Congress, First Session, on H.R. 5723* (Washington, DC: GPO, 1917), 47 (Sen. Williams) (emphasis added).

269. See the views of Representative Parker, member of the Pension Committee, in H.R. Rep. No. 65–130, pt. 2, at 2 (1917) (minority views); Hickel, "Entitling Citizens," 123–24.

270. H.R. Rep. No. 66–277, at 1–3, 7 (1919).

271. 58 Cong. Rec. 9722 (1919) (index entry for H.R. 2022 in first session); 59 Cong. Rec. 9710 (1920) (no index entry for H.R. 2022 in second session); 60 Cong. Rec. 4932 (1921) (no index entry for H.R. 2022 in third session).

272. S. Doc. No. 65–75, at 9 (1917).

273. Quoted in Pencak, *For God and Country*, 177.

274. H.R. Rep. No. 65–130, pt. 3, at 5 (1917). Other key players made the same point. *War-Risk Insurance: Hearing before the Subcommittee of the Committee on Finance, United States Senate, Sixty-Fifth Congress, First Session, on H.R. 5723*, 18 (statement of Senator Williams); ibid., 47 (statement of Judge Julian Mack).

275. Hearings (1923), 1425.

276. Hickel, "Entitling Citizens," 138.

277. § 303, 40 Stat. 398, 406 (1917).

278. PHS Report 1920, pp. 232–33; *Bureau of Veteran Reestablishment: Hearing before the Committee on Interstate and Foreign Commerce of the House of Representatives, Sixty-Sixth Congress, Third Session, on H.R. 14961* (Washington, DC: GPO, 1921), 76.

279. By July 1919, PHS had a plan to assign one salaried doctor (full-time or part-time) to every U.S. city of ten thousand people or more. For lower-population areas not provided with salaried doctors, PHS planned to hire physicians "on a fee basis." *Second Deficiency Appropriation Bill, Fiscal Year 1920: Hearing before Subcommittee of House Committee on Appropriations in Charge of Deficiency Appropriations for the Fiscal Year 1920 and Prior Fiscal Years*, 66th Cong., 2d Sess. (Washington, DC: GPO, 1920), 840. For the date of the plan, see ibid., 849. At this time, cities of ten thousand people or more numbered 746. *Fourteenth Census of the United States Taken in the Year 1920: Population 1920: Number and Distribution of Inhabitants* (Washington, DC: GPO, 1921), 320–31. By mid-1920, the salaried PHS doctors, performing exams across the nation, numbered more than 1,500. PHS Report 1920, pp. 254, 291; *Annual Report of the Director of the Bureau of War Risk Insurance* (Washington, DC: GPO, 1920), 67.

280. *Consolidation of Government Soldier Compensation Bureaus: Hearings before a Subcommittee of the Committee on Interstate and Foreign Commerce of the House of Representatives, Sixty-Sixth Congress, Third Session, on H.R. 14677 and H.R. 14961* (Washington, DC: GPO, 1921), 20 (statement of C. H. Lavinder, assistant surgeon general).

281. Treasury Report 1921, p. 101; PHS Report 1921, pp. 269–70, 276.

282. Veterans' Bureau Report 1922, p. 64.

283. Veterans' Bureau Report 1925, p. 30.

284. Quoted in Hickel, "Entitling Citizens," 151–52. The next director in 1923 raised a distinct issue, writing that outside physicians too often permitted "personal equations [to] enter into consideration [of disability claims]," particularly the claimant's "reputation in the community." Quoted in ibid., 151.

285. H.R. Rep. No. 65–471, at 1 (1918).

286. 40 Stat. 555, 555–56 (1918). There were narrow exceptions for litigation over purchased insurance policies and the rote preparation of papers, for which the fee was capped at $3. Later that year, McAdoo cited the attorneys' expulsion as "[o]ne of the most striking features" of the new system. Treasury Report 1918, p. 91.

287. On the incompetence and delay in early World War benefits adjudication, see Pencak, *For God and Country*, 177–79, 182.

288. It should be noted that statistics on claims are too limited to make much of a contribution to my analysis. For the Civil War, we have actual data on examining surgeons' recommendations (gathered through laborious archival research). E.g., Blanck, "Civil War Pensions and Disability"; Larry M. Logue and Peter Blanck, "'Benefit of the Doubt': African-American Civil War Veterans and Pensions," *Journal of Interdisciplinary History* 38 (2008): 377–99. But there seems to be nothing comparable for World War I. For that war, the published data reflect only the final decisions of the Washington office, which must have varied from those of doctors in the field, though by how much we cannot be certain. Even a comparison of Washington-office behavior between the Civil War and World War I is difficult, since the World War data are often unclear or inconsistent as to whether they include claims for increase of compensation by reason of worsened disability and claims for death benefits, which,

if included, make it hard to isolate disability determinations. Treasury Report 1920, pp. 611–12, 617–18, 620; Treasury Report 1921, p. 422; Veterans' Bureau Report 1922, p. 426; Hearings (1923), 1732–33; Veterans' Bureau Report 1923, p. 537; Veterans' Bureau Report 1924, p. 14; Hickel, "Entitling Citizens," 137. What the data do suggest (in a very rough way) is that denials of World War applications were extremely common, something on the order of half of all applications. See particularly Veterans' Bureau Report 1924, p. 14. Compare Mashaw's statement about the Washington office's behavior in the Civil War system: "[W]hile acceptance rates are difficult to compute, they seem to have hovered between seventy and eighty percent." "Federal Administration," 1424.

289. Samuel McCune Lindsay, "Soldiers' Insurance versus Pensions," *American Review of Reviews* 54 (1917): 403. See also Hickel, "Entitling Citizens," 116.

290. Quoted in Hickel, "Entitling Citizens," 153.

291. Hickel, "Entitling Citizens," 134–35.

292. Ibid., 144.

293. To be sure, the Veterans' Bureau hired "clean-up squads" of salaried officers to encourage veterans to apply for benefits. Hickel, "Entitling Citizens," 131–32; Pencak, *For God and Country*, 182. But congressional investigators suggested that the bureau tended to give "clean-up" work to its lowest-quality personnel, with the result that they did not greatly help claimants navigate the process. Hearings (1923), 1435–40.

294. E.g., 24 Cong. Rec. 1699 (1893) (Rep. Taylor).

295. Hearings (1923), 1513.

296. Ibid., 1557–59.

297. Ibid., 1557, 1559–61.

298. Ibid., 1440. To be sure, not everybody took this view of the World War system. Senate committee counsel John F. O'Ryan, a National Guard general, thought the system overly generous. Without quantifying, he said that there were numerous "excessive ratings unjustified by the evidence," particularly in cases where the applicant stood near the borderline of 10 percent loss of earning power (which had to be met to receive any benefit at all, whether cash or vocational rehabilitation). S. Rep. No. 68–103, pt. 2, at 26 (1924). (On borderline cases, see also the testimony of an investigating doctor in Hearings (1923), 585.) Yet even O'Ryan admitted there was some (smaller) number of cases, still numbering in the "thousands" and dating especially from the disorganized "early days" just after the war, where the claim was improperly disallowed or not given a high enough rating, and the claimant gave up by reason of "the attitude of indifference or the supposed hostility of the bureau." S. Rep. No. 68–103, pt. 2, at 26 (1924). See also Hearings (1923), 266, 1465–66. It should also be noted that O'Ryan was ideologically hostile to welfare benefits, which may have affected his assessment. S. Rep. No. 68–103, pt. 2, at 26 (1924).

299. Pencak, *For God and Country*, 177–79, 182.

300. Ibid., 178; Marquis James, *A History of the American Legion* (New York: William Green, 1923), 97–99; *Charges against the Federal Board for Vocational Education: Hearings and Report of the Committee on Education, House of Representatives, Sixty-*

*Sixth Congress, Second Session* (Washington, DC: GPO, 1920), 1:849 (letter from director of WRIB citing Legion support).

301. Pencak, *For God and Country*, 172, 175. For the Legion's role in later debates on veterans' benefits, in which it was generally a force for moderation and compromise (though not entirely consistent), see ibid., 189–90, 196–97, 200, 203–05.

302. § 19, 43 Stat. 607, 612–13 (1924); Pencak, *For God and Country*, 185–86.

303. A prominent example was tuberculosis in 1921. Hickel, "Entitling Citizens," 143–44; Pencak, *For God and Country*, 185.

304. The same point—that administrators' independence and alienation from veterans forced those veterans to go to Congress and get their demands written into legislation—can be made about the campaign for benefits resting simply on service rather than disability (known as "The Bonus," or "adjusted compensation"). World War disability benefits would never come near to being de facto service-based benefits as the Civil War pensions had. In part because of this, World War veterans and their lobbyists made strong collective demands for the bonus, and congressmen ultimately reached a compromise in 1924 that promised all veterans a lump-sum payment twenty-one years in the future, thus mitigating the concerns of anti-tax interests by allowing the revenue to be raised gradually. (Later, amid the changed political climate of the Depression, Congress in 1936 would mandate immediate payment of the bonus.) On the political battle over the bonus in 1924, see Anne L. Alstott and Ben Novick, "War, Taxes, and Income Redistribution in the Twenties: The 1924 Veterans' Bonus and the Defeat of the Mellon Plan," *New York University Tax Law Review* 59 (2006): 373–438.

305. Pencak, *For God and Country*, 195–96.

306. Eric Kades, "The Dark Side of Efficiency: *Johnson v. M'Intosh* and the Expropriation of Indian Lands," *University of Pennsylvania Law Review* 148 (2000): 1065–1190.

307. On the work of the military and especially the Bureau of Indian Affairs in removal and containment of Indians, see Stephen J. Rockwell, *Indian Affairs and the Administrative State in the Nineteenth Century* (Cambridge: Cambridge University Press, 2010). As Rockwell notes, the bureau also carried out programs to "civilize" the Indians, but these were usually a far second to the primary goals of physically removing and containing them. E.g., ibid., 200, 208, 256, 262, 268–69, 270, 273. And even if "civilization" had been a top priority, many Indians were likely to experience it as an imposition, not an honoring of their preferences. Ibid., 271–72.

308. For a comprehensive survey of the distribution of federal land, see E. Louise Peffer, *The Closing of the Public Domain: Disposal and Reservation Policies, 1900–50* (Stanford, CA: Stanford University Press, 1951), appendix. Generally, Indian land had to pass through federal ownership before it could go to nonfederal recipients like state governments or white individuals. That said, the transfer was at times nearly direct, as when whites illegally settled on Indian land and then had their ownership confirmed when the federal government succeeded in extinguishing title. Markku Henriksson, *The Indian on Capitol Hill: Indian Legislation and the United States Congress, 1862–1907* (Helsinki: SHS, 1988), 123.

309. This interpretation of the settlement laws generally follows the work of Paul W. Gates, particularly his *History of Public Land Law Development* (Washington, DC: GPO, 1968).

310. See generally Milton Conover, *The General Land Office: Its History, Activities, and Organization* (Baltimore: Johns Hopkins University Press, 1923).

311. Gates, *History*, 220.

312. Ibid., 236, 243, 246.

313. Ibid., 221–24.

314. Ibid., 225, 229–30, 235.

315. On the difficulty of these adjudications and the role of the officers therein, see Gates, *History*, 223, 232–33; Malcolm J. Rohrbough, *The Land Office Business: The Settlement and Administration of American Public Lands, 1789–1837* (New York: Oxford University Press, 1968), 205–06, 209.

316. Gates, "Homestead Act," 28.

317. §§ 10–15, 5 Stat. 453, 455–57 (1841); Gates, *History*, 236–40.

318. On laborers' wages, see *HSUS* series Ba4253 through series Ba4257. I have annualized assuming a six-day workweek.

319. § 10, 5 Stat. at 455–56.

320. § 15, 5 Stat. at 457.

321. § 12, 5 Stat. at 456.

322. § 10, 5 Stat. at 455.

323. § 13, 5 Stat. at 456.

324. 12 Stat. 392 (1862); Gates, *History*, 393–95.

325. § 2, 12 Stat. at 392. On the fees, see my discussion in note 355 below.

326. § 5, 12 Stat. at 393.

327. § 6, 12 Stat. at 393. See also Gates, *History*, 462, 484.

328. Gates, *History*, 395.

329. § 8, 12 Stat. at 393; Gates, *History*, 395.

330. E.g., the Timber Culture Act of 1873 (repealed 1891), discussed in Gates, *History*, 399–400, 462, 484–85.

331. Gates, *History*, 395 (noting government after 1862 shifted about fifteen million acres, compared with a prior stock of more than eighty-three million acres). See also ibid., 417–18, 435–40.

332. Gates, "Homestead Act," 31. See also Gates, *History*, 247.

333. Gates, *History*, 448–49, 461–62, 484.

334. Gates, "Homestead Act," 33–35.

335. Lisi Krall, "US Land Policy and the Commodification of Arid Land (1862–1920)," *Journal of Economic Issues* 35 (2001): 659–60.

336. Ibid., 660–61, 672; Gates, "Homesteading," 121. Congress recognized this problem in the early 1900s, authorizing somewhat larger homesteads, though still not large enough. It was too little, too late. Gates, "Homesteading," 122; Gates, *History*, 498–501, 504–08.

337. Thomas Donaldson, "The Public Lands of the United States," *North American Review* 133 (1881): 206.

338. Under the Preemption Act, the initial application had to state an intent to comply with the criteria for final application. § 15, 5 Stat. at 457. These criteria, in turn, required only that the applicant "inhabit and improve the [land]" and "erect a dwelling thereon." § 10, 5 Stat. at 455. Under the Homestead Act, the initial application had to declare that the "entry is made for the purpose of actual settlement and cultivation," while the final stage required proof that the applicant had "resided upon or cultivated the [land]" and had not "actually changed" his or her "residency" or "abandoned the said land for more than six months at a time." § 2, 12 Stat. at 392; § 5, 12 Stat. at 393. Apart from the Homestead Act's mention of "six months" absence, there was nothing in either statute to flesh out the vague terms *inhabit, improve, dwelling, settlement, cultivation, residency,* or *abandonment.* See Peffer, *Closing of the Public Domain,* 147–48.

339. The Preemption Act again said the initial application had to state an intent to meet the requirements of the final application. § 15, 5 Stat. at 457. These criteria, in turn, said the applicant must swear that (1) the settlement was for his or her own use, not speculation, and that (2) the applicant had made no agreement whereby title would go to someone else. § 13, 5 Stat. at 456. The Homestead Act made the applicant swear to essentially the same two points at the initial stage. § 2, 12 Stat. at 392. And it was construed to require those points to obtain at the final stage, as well. Fain v. United States, 209 F. 525, 529 (8th Cir. 1913).

340. The most radical Jeffersonians proposed to prohibit homesteaders from ever selling the lands they acquired. But Congress did not adopt such proposals. Gates, *History,* 395.

341. *Hearings before the Subcommittee of House Committee on Appropriations . . . in Charge of Sundry Civil Appropriation Bill for 1910* (Washington, DC: GPO, 1909), 471 (statement of H. H. Schwartz, chief of General Land Office Field Service Division).

342. GLO Report 1885, p. 50, quoted in Gates, *History,* 472.

343. E.g., Leonard D. White, *The Republican Era, 1869–1901: A Study in Administrative History* (New York: Macmillan, 1958), 205.

344. Gates, *History,* 477–78; ibid., 454.

345. Krall, "US Land Policy," 658; Gates, "Homestead Act," 29, 33–34.

346. Gates, "Homestead Act," 36.

347. Gates appears to say that selling a relinquishment was illegal. *History,* 400, 425. That is too broad. It was illegal to make an initial application in bad faith, that is, with intent to sell the relinquishment. But it was not illegal to make an initial application, then change one's mind, and then sell the relinquishment. Fain v. United States, 209 F. 525, 529–30 (8th Cir. 1913) (citing cases). For the exact steps in the sale of a relinquishment, see Yasuo Okada, *Public Lands and Pioneer Farms: Gage County, Nebraska, 1850–1900* (Tokyo: Keio Economic Society, 1971), 56–60. See also Gates, *History,* 240, 469; Gates, "Homesteading," 113.

348. Gates, "Homestead Act," 34–35; Gates, *History,* 400.

349. Gates, "Homestead Act," 35. See also ibid., 31; Gates, *History,* 472; Gates, "Homesteading," 110, 112.

350. Gates, *History,* 485n63.

351. This was especially problematic given the registers' and receivers' myriad other responsibilities (e.g., keeping records, deciding contests) and the vast acreage and slow transportation of some districts. Gates, *History*, 240, 468, 488; Gates, "Homesteading," 109; Gates, "Homestead Act," 32; White, *Republican Era*, 205. On the rough scale of the manpower shortage and ways in which officers might have tried to overcome it, see Parrillo diss., 326n363.

352. 3 Stat. 466 (1818), codified in USRS § 2238 item 2.

353. § 12, 5 Stat. at 456, amended by § 4, 13 Stat. 35, 35 (1864), codified in USRS § 2238 item 1. Note that fees were increased by 50 percent in certain far-western states. USRS § 2238 item 12.

354. Each officer was entitled to 1 percent of all money received. 3 Stat. 466 (1818), codified in USRS § 2238 item 2. For a typical homestead (160 acres), the cash price would be $1.25 per acre, or $200 total, of which 1 percent is $2.

355. The 1862 provision that initially set the officers' fees (§ 6, 12 Stat. at 393) was replaced in 1864 by a different one that remained in place into the twentieth century. The 1864 provision granted each officer, "at the time of entry, one per centum upon the cash price as fixed by law, of the land applied for, and like commission when the claim is finally established and the certificate therefore issued as the basis of a patent." § 2, 13 Stat. 35, 35 (1864), codified in USRS § 2238 item 3. For a typical homestead (160 acres), the cash price, had it been purchased, would be $1.25 per acre, or $200 total, so each officer's 1 percent commission would be $2. Thus, the applicant paid $2 to the register and $2 to the receiver at the initial stage, then $2 to the register and $2 to the receiver at the final stage, for a total of $8. There was also a $10 fee to the public Treasury. § 2, 12 Stat. at 392. This yields a grand total of $18, which matches the figure in Thomas Donaldson, *The Public Domain: Its History, with Statistics* (Washington, DC: GPO, 1884), 412, and in Gates, *History*, 394.

356. On fees for the Timber Culture Act, see USRS § 2238 item 4.

357. See the nationwide annual fee totals for the period 1880–83 in Donaldson, *Public Domain*, 517–18. The sum for "sales of public lands" should be multiplied by 1 percent for each officer. For "fees and commissions" on homestead claims, we can assume very conservatively that the figure includes both the fee to the public Treasury ($10 per claim) and the fees to each officer (totaling $8 per claim), which means that we should multiply the figure by eight-eighteenths to determine the officers' earnings. Calculated in this way, their earnings are still more than double those for commissions on sales. And these calculations do not even count fees and commissions for other settlement-law claims, such as timber culture or preemption. Statistics for 1906 likewise indicate that settlement-law fees were officers' biggest income source. GLO Report 1906, p. 344.

358. White, *Republican Era*, 205.

359. Gates, *History*, 478.

360. Ibid., 524. For an additional brief reference to this issue, see Gary D. Libecap, "Bureaucratic Opposition to Assignment of Property Rights: Overgrazing on the Western Range," *Journal of Economic History* 41 (1981): 153.

361. GLO Report 1885, p. 233.

362. "Changes Likely in Land Offices," *Idaho Statesman*, Mar. 28, 1906, p. 2.

363. *Report of the Secretary of the Interior [1887]* (Washington: GPO, 1887), 6–7.

364. Gates, *History*, 485.

365. GLO Report 1887, p. 134; Gates, *History*, 477–78.

366. § 3, 13 Stat. 35, 35 (1864) (requiring "distance" or "good cause" preventing applicant from attending the federal office), codified in USRS § 2294.

367. §§ 1–2, 19 Stat. 403, 403–04 (1877), codified in USRS § 2291.

368. GLO Report 1887, p. 172.

369. USRS § 2240.

370. The proportion reaching the maximum are as follows: GLO Report 1885, pp. 377–80 (48 / 108 = 44 percent); GLO Report 1890, pp. 259–60 (53 / 107 = 50 percent); GLO Report 1895, pp. 322–25 (34 / 113 = 30 percent); GLO Report 1900, pp. 363–65 (53 / 115 = 46 percent); GLO Report 1905, pp. 494–95 (54 / 115 = 47 percent); GLO Report 1910, pp. 133–36 (64 / 102 = 63 percent); GLO Report 1915, pp. 308–11 (48 / 99 = 48 percent).

371. Note that the cap on registers' and receivers' fees did not operate like the 1906 cap on naturalization fees for court clerks. Land officers could draw their expenses against the general fee incomes of their offices without limit; they could then pocket up to $2,500 of those fees once all expenses were paid. By contrast, court clerks doing naturalization could draw their expenses only against the fees that came in under the $3,000 cap. Thus, the naturalization cap limited the portion of fees that could be spent for customer service. The land-office cap did not.

372. Gates, *History*, 451.

373. Gates, *History*, 473–77; Gates, "Homestead Act," 32.

374. Gates, *History*, 482, 486. For more on Western congressmen's success in maintaining administrative laxity, see ibid., 484–85, 488; Gates, "Homestead Act," 29; White, *Republican Era*, 196.

375. Quoted in Gates, *History*, 471.

376. Arthur A. Ekirch Jr., *Man and Nature in America* (New York: Columbia University Press, 1963), 81–82.

377. William Cronon, "Landscapes of Abundance and Scarcity," in *The Oxford History of the American West*, ed. Clyde A. Milner II et al. (New York: Oxford University Press, 1994), 606.

378. Gates, *History*, 416–19. Another option was the preemption-like Timber and Stone Act. Ibid., 534–61.

379. Ibid., 462, 464, 565–66.

380. I infer this from ibid., 567–68.

381. Ibid., 488, 572–73.

382. Ibid., 567–68, 579–80, 771; Cronon, "Landscapes," 610–11.

383. Gates, *History*, 573, 579.

384. Ibid., 567, 581.

385. Roosevelt considered the Forest Service a model for all public-land management. Peffer, *Closing of the Public Domain*, 84.

386. Cronon, "Landscapes," 612.

387. Ibid., 610.
388. *Report of the Secretary of the Interior [1907]* (Washington, DC: GPO, 1907), 13.
389. S. Doc. No. 59–310, at 8 (1907).
390. Theodore Roosevelt, *Theodore Roosevelt: An Autobiography* (New York: Macmillan, 1913), 451.
391. On their salaried status, see the Interior Department regulations printed in S. Doc. No. 59–396, pt. 3, at 816 (1907) (giving salary classes); 33 Stat. 1156, 1184 (1905) (providing for per diem).
392. On their establishment via appropriations acts, see *United States v. Schlierholz*, 133 F. 333, 335 (E.D. Mo. 1904); S. Doc. No. 59–396, pt. 3, at 816 (1907). In the mid-1890s, special agents numbered only twenty-two full-time equivalents. GLO Report 1895, p. 399.
393. One factor was the forest-policy debate. Peffer, *Closing of the Public Domain*, 42. Another was a new irrigation program in 1902 that encouraged applications. Ibid., 43. A third was a land-fraud scandal. John Messing, "Public Lands, Politics, and Progressives: The Oregon Land Fraud Trials, 1903–1910," *Pacific Historical Review* 35 (1966): 35–66; Roosevelt, *Theodore Roosevelt: An Autobiography*, 448.
394. S. Doc. No. 59–141, at 2 (1906).
395. S. Doc. No. 59–310, at 6 (1907).
396. The appropriation is the one for protection of the public lands. For the nominal amounts in fiscal 1885, 1890, 1895, 1900, 1910, and each year thereafter, see Conover, *General Land Office*, 159–64. For 1905 (on which Conover's number is wrong), see 33 Stat. 452, 482 (1904). For 1906, see 33 Stat. 1156, 1184 (1905). For 1907 through 1909, see H.R. Doc. No. 60–1333, at 4 (1909). I adjusted the nominal amounts for inflation using *HSUS* series Cc2. For the number of final homestead entries for all years, see GLO Report 1915, p. 287.
397. S. Doc. No. 59–310, at 6 (1907). The first appropriation after Roosevelt's demand came with strings attached restricting enforcement. 34 Stat. 1295, 1332 (1907); Gates, *History*, 492. But in the next one, the restrictions disappeared. 35 Stat. 317, 345–46 (1908).
398. The number in service at the close of the fiscal year steadily rose from fifty-five in 1903 to ninety-one in 1908. *Hearings before the Subcommittee of House Committee on Appropriations . . . in Charge of Sundry Civil Appropriation Bill for 1910* (Washington, DC: GPO, 1909), 465–66 (James Garfield, interior secretary). Late in 1908, the secretary, armed with the big new appropriation, reported adding a large number. *Report of the Secretary of the Interior [1908]* (Washington, DC: GPO, 1908), 9. The average number of agents employed per month was 141 in fiscal 1908–09. GLO Report 1909, p. 63. It was 216 in fiscal 1909–10, 155 in fiscal 1910–11, and 147 in fiscal 1911–12. GLO Report 1912, pp. 113–14.
399. *Report of the Secretary of the Interior [1908]*, 9; GLO Report 1912, p. 113; GLO Report 1913, p. 123; GLO Report 1914, p. 130.
400. S. Doc. No. 62–728, at 4 (1912).
401. See the instructions to special agents printed in S. Doc. No. 59–396, pt. 3, at 855 (1907).

402. GLO Report 1911, p. 107; GLO Report 1913, p. 123; GLO Report 1914, p. 130. Such rates are probably more meaningful evidence of adjudicator stringency for settlement-law applications than for naturalization or pension applications, since a settlement law applicant had to incur greater costs.

403. S. Doc. No. 62–728, at 5, 16 (1912).

404. It seems disputes between applicants and special agents were assimilated to the more general model of land-office contests. S. Doc. No. 62–728, at 12, 17 (1912). For registers' and receivers' fees for hearing contests, see USRS § 2238 item 10. For an example of a district land office in which contest fees were more important than other kinds, see "Shrinking Receipts Menace Jobs of Land Office Attaches," *Oregonian*, Feb. 12, 1911, p. 9.

405. Gates, "Homesteading," 122.

406. Peffer, *Closing of the Public Domain*, 147–48.

407. Gates, *History*, 500.

408. Peffer, *Closing of the Public Domain*, 53, 148–49.

409. Quoted in Peffer, *Closing of the Public Domain*, 149.

410. Peffer, *Closing of the Public Domain*, 154. See also Gates, "Homesteading," 122; Gates, *History*, 507.

411. Gates, *History*, 507.

412. H.R. Doc. No. 60–1333, at 2–3 (1909).

413. For the first quote, see *Report of the Secretary of the Interior [1908]*, 10. For the second quote, from the chief of the General Land Office field service, see H.R. Doc. No. 60–1333, at 12 (1909).

414. Peffer, *Closing of the Public Domain*, 167. This is the total of homestead and stock-raising entries. See also Libecap, "Bureaucratic Opposition," 157.

415. GLO Report 1915, pp. 308–11 (ninety-nine offices); Gates, *History*, 127 (in 1921, ninety-four offices); S. Rep. No. 74–508, at 2 (1935) (twenty-three offices).

416. Special agents were effective in checking final applications, which presumably suppressed techniques like the use of dummy applicants. But the sale of relinquishments was harder to suppress. Because good-faith settlers might legitimately change their minds and relinquish their claims before proving up, these bad-faith initial applications were hard to identify. GLO Report 1911, p. 122. In 1920, the commissioner found the "large number of relinquishments" to be "indicative of the extent of 'trading' in unperfected homestead entries." GLO Report 1920, p. 36. But as applications themselves fell in the 1920s, relinquishments went with them.

417. Gates, *History*, 489.

418. Libecap, "Bureaucratic Opposition," 151.

419. On the use of land as a commons, see Libecap, "Bureaucratic Opposition," 151; Gates, *History*, 489. On dummy applicants, see Gates, *History*, 466–67.

420. Gates, *History*, 515, 523, 527.

421. Gates, "Homesteading," 128; Gates, *History*, 512–19, esp. 517.

422. On the danger of breakup, see Gates, *History*, 519.

423. 48 Stat. 1269 (1934).

424. Gates, "Homesteading," 133.

425. Philip O. Foss, *Politics and Grass: The Administration of Grazing on the Public Do-main* (Seattle: University of Washington Press, 1960), 73–87; Christopher McGrory Klyza, *Who Controls Public Lands? Mining, Forestry, and Grazing Policies, 1870–1990* (Chapel Hill: University of North Carolina Press, 1996), 100–16.

426. S. Rep. No. 74–508 (1935) (noting registers still receive some homestead fees); Reor-ganization Plan No. 3, § 403, 60 Stat. 1097, 1100 (1946) (abolishing registers).

CHAPTER 5: STATE AND LOCAL TAXATION

1. The latest discussion of more than passing length is Jens Peter Jensen, *Property Taxa-tion in the United States* (Chicago: University of Chicago Press, 1931), 353–57.

2. C. K. Yearley, *The Money Machines: The Breakdown and Reform of Governmental and Party Finance in the North, 1860–1920* (Albany: State University of New York Press, 1970), 46–47, 56, 73.

3. Robin L. Einhorn vividly describes this regime in the North during the colonial period and early republic. She points out that the development of a well-functioning process of localized negotiation—fostered by election of local officials—made it feasible for Northern polities to tax property on the basis of value. *American Taxation, American Slavery* (Chicago: University of Chicago Press, 2006), 53–78, esp. 55, 63, 71, 74–75, 78 (on Massachusetts); ibid., 83–92, esp. 92 (on Pennsylvania); ibid., 81–82, 209–10 (on the North generally).

   The development of taxation in the Southern colonies and early Southern states was somewhat more complex. In those jurisdictions, local officials were not elected but were appointed from the ranks of local oligarchs. Einhorn argues that, because of this lesser level of political participation, the Southern jurisdictions failed to develop the kind of localized political negotiation found in Northern taxation and therefore had to tax property by cruder means that left less discretion to localities and their of-ficers (e.g., a flat sum for every acre or slave). Ibid., 29–52, esp. 39 (on Virginia), 79–83 (on the South generally). Though this early Southern system was less participatory, its tendency toward crude and simple methods of taxation was apparently in the service of keeping the tax burden low. Ibid., 220–21 (noting that, in the antebellum period, taxes were much lower in the South at the state level and probably the local level). I therefore think the early Southern system is best understood as aimed at diminishing imposition of any kind (familiar or alien). We might call it *non-imposition*.

   In any event, most Southern states by the 1840s shifted toward the Northern model of familiar imposition: electing local officers and taxing land and some other forms of property, sometimes even slaves, by value (though Southern statutes were admittedly more particular about rates on various tax bases). Ibid., 105, 219, 223, 227–28, 230. By the time Southern states began to consider using tax ferrets after the Civil War, they generally had locally elected assessors, just like in the North. See my documentation of the elected status of assessors in tax-ferret states, in note 126 below. See also *Report of the Special Tax Commission of the State of Kentucky 1912–14* (Frankfort, KY: State Journal Co., 1914), 77 (stating the Kentucky local assessor is "controlled politically by the very persons" he is "expected to assess"); M. C. Rhodes, *History of Taxation in Mississippi (1798–1929)* (Nashville, TN: George Peabody College for Teachers, 1930), 83 (stating Mississippi local assessor is selected through "'hand-shaking politics'"). On Northern assessors in the mid-1800s—including their elected status, decentralization, wide discretion, and enmeshment in local politics—see Yearley, *Money Machines*, 52–55, 66–74.

4. Up to 1775, taxes at the colony level were extremely low. The Revolutionary War increased that burden, causing friction and dysfunction until the new federal government in 1789 assumed the debt and sank it through the invisible and painless method of customs duties, thus allowing states to return to their low-tax norm. Max M. Edling and Mark D. Kaplanoff, "Alexander Hamilton's Fiscal Reform: Transforming the Structure of Taxation in the Early Republic," *William and Mary Quarterly*, 3rd ser., 61 (2004): 713–44; see also H. James Henderson, "Taxation and Political Culture: Massachusetts and Virginia, 1760–1800," *William and Mary Quarterly*, 3rd ser., 47 (1990): 90–114.

For the nineteenth century, the starting place is the work of John Joseph Wallis, who sets forth estimates of revenue (not taxes) for the state and local levels. These indicate a large, lasting increase in state revenue around the middle of the century. For the nation as a whole, real state revenue per capita more than doubled in 1800–40 and more than doubled again in 1840–60. "American Government Finance in the Long Run: 1790 to 1990," *Journal of Economic Perspectives* 14 (2000): 65. Also, Wallis estimates that real local revenue per capita nearly doubled in 1840–60 and more than doubled in 1860–70. Ibid.

To be sure, Wallis's estimates do not give us a complete picture: they cover revenue, not taxes, and they say nothing at all about local revenue (or taxes) prior to 1840. Still, there are fragments of data suggesting that the combined burden of state and local taxation rose greatly in 1800–40 (and thereafter). Consider Ohio. It appears that that state's real state and local tax dollars per capita rose substantially in 1826–30, doubled in the 1830s, doubled in the 1840s, and doubled in the 1850s. For Ohio's nominal statewide totals for the state and local levels in 1826–60, see Richard T. Ely, *Taxation in American States and Cities* (New York: Thomas Y. Crowell and Co., 1888), 456. For price-level adjustment, see *HSUS* series Cc2. For state population, see U.S. Census Bureau, "Table 16: Population: 1790 to 1990," http://www.census.gov/population/www/censusdata/files/table-16.pdf (last accessed Aug. 3, 2012). Also, consider Massachusetts. That state's real state and local tax dollars per capita were apparently more than four times higher in 1861 than in the mid-1790s. For estimates of Massachusetts's annual nominal state and local tax dollars per capita in 1794–96, see Henderson, "Taxation and Political Culture," 112 ($0.35 + $1.71 = $2.06). For Massachusetts's nominal statewide totals for the state and local levels in 1861, see *Reports of the Commissioners Appointed to Inquire into the Expediency of Revising and Amending the Laws Relating to Taxation and Exemption Therefrom* (Boston: Wright and Potter, 1875), 551. For price-level adjustment and population, see the same sources used for Ohio. (For Massachusetts, I used the 1860 population.)

To gauge these tax trends against economic growth, compare the two states' rates of increase in real per capita tax dollars with Thomas Weiss's estimate that American real per capita income did not even double between 1800 and 1860. "U.S. Labor Force Estimates and Economic Growth, 1800–1860," in *American Economic Growth and Standards of Living before the Civil War*, ed. Robert E. Gallman and John J. Wallis (Chicago: University of Chicago Press, 1992), 27.

5. Wallis, "American Government Finance," 66–69; Glenn W. Fisher, *The Worst Tax? A History of the Property Tax in America* (Lawrence: University Press of Kansas, 1996), 46–49.

6. Henderson, "Taxation and Political Culture," 106–07 (on 1780s); Sumner Benson, "A History of the General Property Tax," in *The American Property Tax: Its History, Administration, and Economic Impact*, ed. George C. S. Benson et al. (Claremont, CA: Institute for Studies in Federalism, 1965), 37 (on first half of 1800s).

7. James Bryce, *The American Commonwealth* (London: Macmillan, 1888), 1:493. On the difficulty of discovering personalty, see Benson, "History of the General Property Tax," 58; Edwin R. A. Seligman, "The General Property Tax," in *Essays in Taxation*, 9th ed. (New York: Macmillan, 1921), 23. On the difficulty of finding intangibles in particular, see Benson, "History of the General Property Tax," 55; Yearley, *Money Machines*, 16.

8. See, e.g., Charles J. Bullock, "The Taxation of Property and Income in Massachusetts," *Quarterly Journal of Economics* 31 (1916): 33–34 (referring, as of 1916, to the recent "growth of private agencies for collecting and distributing information concerning the ownership of corporation stocks"). I further address this informational issue later in this chapter, in text at notes 141, 145–47, and 257.

9. On credits, see Ajay K. Mehrotra, "Forging Fiscal Reform: Constitutional Change, Public Policy, and the Creation of Administrative Capacity in Wisconsin, 1880–1920," *Journal of Policy History* 20 (2008): 98. On the transition to intangibles more generally, see Yearley, *Money Machines*, 39.

10. Wallis, "American Government Finance," 69–70.

11. See note 4 above.

12. Benson, "History of the General Property Tax," 48; Wallis, "American Government Finance," 65; Yearley, *Money Machines*, 3–13, 104.

13. Benson, "History of the General Property Tax," 31–34; John Joseph Wallis, "A History of Property Taxation in America," in *Property Taxation and Local Government Finance: Essays in Honor of C. Lowell Harriss*, ed. Wallace E. Oates (Cambridge, MA: Lincoln Institute of Land Policy, 2001), 137–38; Yearley, *Money Machines*, 77–78.

14. Benson, "History of the General Property Tax," 31, 37–44; Wallis, "American Government Finance," 69–71; Wallis, "History of Property Taxation," 127. Though liberal equality was the driving force behind the general property tax in the Northern states, its original impetus in the Southern states was to protect slave property against discriminatory taxation. Einhorn, *American Taxation*, 230–44.

15. Yearley, *Money Machines*, 27. In 1890, it accounted for 72 percent of state revenue and 92 percent of local revenue. Benson, "History of the General Property Tax," 48.

16. For characteristics of the local assessor's office, see Jensen, *Property Taxation in the United States*, 353; Harley Leist Lutz, *The State Tax Commission: A Study of the Development and Results of State Control over the Assessment of Property for Taxation* (Cambridge, MA: Harvard University Press, 1918), 574; Mehrotra, "Forging Fiscal Reform," 98; F. J. Meier, "The Iowa 'Tax Ferret' Law as Illustrated by the Experience of Polk County" (M.A. thesis, Drake University, 1910), 17; Jon C. Teaford, *The Rise of the States: Evolution of American State Government* (Baltimore: Johns Hopkins University Press, 2002), 45. Assessors sometimes had broad power to compel testimony, but they did not exercise it. *Report of the Special Tax Commission of the State of Kentucky 1912–14*, 77; Ely, *Taxation in American States and Cities*, 155.

17. On elected and decentralized status, see Yearley, *Money Machines*, 52–55, 66–74. In a few states, the assessor was appointed by locally elected officials, which meant that his political and social situation, incentives, and behavior were little different than if he were himself elected. See Lutz, *State Tax Commission*, 575 (taking example of North Carolina). For state-by-state confirmation of the elected status of assessors, see my discussion in note 126 below.

18. *Report of the Special Tax Commission of the State of Kentucky 1912–14*, 77.

19. Yearley, *Money Machines*, 88–92; Wisconsin Manufacturers' Association, *Wisconsin Should Not Introduce Non-Resident Tax Ferrets, Addressed to the Members of the Wisconsin Legislature* (no place or publisher, 1911), 1.

20. "The Taxation Question," *Ohio Farmer* 89 (Mar. 19, 1896): 248.

21. Teaford, *Rise of the States*, 45, 51, 54; Yearley, *Money Machines*, 72, 143–44, 180–81, 194–96.

22. Simeon E. Leland, *The Classified Property Tax in the United States* (Boston: Houghton Mifflin Co., 1928), 29; *Report of the Honorary Commission Appointed by the Governor to Investigate the Tax System of Ohio and Recommend Improvements Therein* (no place or publisher, 1908), 26.

23. *The Government of Kentucky: Report of the Efficiency Commission of Kentucky* (Frankfort, KY: State Journal Co., 1924), 1:234–35.

24. Rhodes, *History of Taxation in Mississippi*, 83.

25. Ely, *Taxation in American States and Cities*, 155.

26. Nelson W. Evans, *The Assessment of Personal Property for Taxation in Ohio* (Columbus: Ohio State Board of Commerce, 1904), 24. See also *Report of the Special Tax Commission of the State of Kentucky 1912–14*, 77; Meier, "Iowa 'Tax Ferret' Law," 3; Yearley, *Money Machines*, 88. Even in states where the assessor was term limited, it was common for him to run for another local office (like sheriff or county clerk), such that he still had the incentive not to make enemies. *Report of the Special Tax Commission of the State of Kentucky 1912–14*, 37–38.

27. Yearley, *Money Machines*, 41.

28. Ely, *Taxation in American States and Cities*, 159. These were Ely's words, to which the official replied, "It is true." See also Yearley, *Money Machines*, 66; *Report of the Honorary Commission . . . to Investigate the Tax System of Ohio*, 28.

29. Benson, "History of the General Property Tax," 54.

30. *HSUS* series Ca10. On implausible mismatches between realty and personalty assessment in many individual cities, see Benson, "History of the General Property Tax," 57; Yearley, *Money Machines*, 42–43, 46.

31. *Report of the Honorary Commission . . . to Investigate the Tax System of Ohio*, 58, 61. For more on noncompliance for intangibles, see Benson, "History of the General Property Tax," 51–52, 56–57, 64; Teaford, *Rise of the States*, 46.

32. Ely, *Taxation in American States and Cities*, 158; Seligman, "General Property Tax," 23.

33. Thomas M. Cooley, *A Treatise of the Law of Taxation, including the Law of Local Assessments* (Chicago: Callaghan and Co., 1881), 512.

34. State ex rel. Coleman v. Fry, 95 P. 392, 394 (Kan. 1908).

35. Evans, *Assessment of Personal Property for Taxation in Ohio*, 18–19.

36. Ely, *Taxation in American States and Cities*, 231.

37. Yearley, *Money Machines*, 39–41.

38. Teaford, *Rise of the States*, 44.

39. Yearley, *Money Machines*, 151–52, 157. Farmers were generally the strongest interest group in support of tax-ferreting. E.g., "Just and Equal Taxation," *Ohio Farmer* 85 (Mar. 1, 1894): 170; "Ohio Legislature News," *Ohio Farmer* 109 (Mar. 17, 1906): 299. See also Association of Iowa Tax Ferrets, *Facts with Reference to the Tax Ferret Law, Prepared for the Use of Members of the Thirtieth General Assembly and Others Who May Be Interested in the Subject* (no place or publisher, 1904), 16 (quoting *Dubuque Telegraph*).

40. State v. Cappeller, 39 Ohio St. 207, 211 (1883).

41. 1880 Ohio Laws 205, 205–06; 1885 Ohio Laws 152; 1888 Ohio Laws 170; T. N. Carver, "The Ohio Tax Inquisitor Law," *Economic Studies* 3 (1898): 178–80.

42. Carver, "Ohio Tax Inquisitor Law," 198.

43. "Resolutions," *Ohio Farmer* 85 (Mar. 1, 1894): 172.

44. E.g., State ex rel. Wilson v. Lewis, 78 N.E. 523, 526 (Ohio 1906).

45. Carver, "Ohio Tax Inquisitor Law," 193.

46. "Law Reports," *Indianapolis Sentinel*, Dec. 6, 1878, p. 3; "The Tax Ferret," *Indianapolis Sentinel*, Mar. 16, 1880, p. 3.

47. 1879 Ind. Acts Special Sess. 130, 142–43.

48. 1881 Ind. Acts Special Sess. 611, 661–62.

49. 1891 Ind. Acts 199, 257 (codifying the above-cited section of the 1881 act but omitting the final sentence banning ferret contracts).

50. City of Richmond v. Dickinson, 58 N.E. 260, 261–62 (Ind. 1900).

51. "'Tax Ferrets' in Indiana," *New York Tribune*, Jan. 29, 1902, p. 5.

52. *Report of the Commission on Taxation to the Governor [of Indiana]* (N.p.: Fort Wayne Printing Co., 1916), xiv.

53. *The General Statutes of Kentucky* (Frankfort, KY: Major, Johnston, and Barret, 1881), 753–56 (statute of 1880).

54. E.g., Simeon E. Leland, *Taxation in Kentucky* (Lexington: University of Kentucky, 1920), 59; *Government of Kentucky*, 1:260; "State News," *Southern Economic Journal* 3

(1937): 480. For analogy to Ohio, see *Report of the Special Tax Commission of the State of Kentucky 1912–14,* 79–80.

55. This office was established in 1875; its power to have persons and property assessed was made clear in an 1894 statute. Rhodes, *History of Taxation in Mississippi,* 107–08.

56. 1895 Tenn. Pub. Acts 203, 244–45.

57. 1896–97 Ala. Laws 521.

58. On Mississippi, see Institute for Government Research of the Brookings Institution, *Report on a Survey of the Organization and Administration of State and County Government in Mississippi* (no place or publisher, 1932), 281 [hereinafter Brookings Institution, *Report on a Survey of . . . Government in Mississippi*]. On Alabama, see Lutz, *State Tax Commission,* 558.

59. [No headline], *Chicago Daily Tribune,* May 22, 1884, p. 4; "Tax-Ferreting," *Chicago Daily Tribune,* Aug. 21, 1884, p. 8.

60. "The Day at Springfield," *Chicago Daily Tribune,* Apr. 19, 1885, p. 8.

61. "President Busse Urges Taxes Bill," *Chicago Daily Tribune,* Apr. 1, 1909, p. 4.

62. Stevens v. Henry County, 75 N.E. 1024 (Ill. 1905). See also *Gannaway v. McFall,* 109 Ill.App. 23 (1902).

63. "Mayor Approves the 'Tax Ferret' Plan to Council," *Chicago Daily Tribune,* Aug. 15, 1918, p. 4.

64. John E. Brindley, *History of Taxation in Iowa* (Iowa City: State Historical Society of Iowa, 1911), 1:311, 313.

65. Brindley, *History of Taxation in Iowa,* 1:344–55.

66. Ibid., 1:315–17, 327–29; "Tax Ferrets Get Busy," *Cedar Rapids (IA) Evening Gazette,* Dec. 16, 1910, p. 8. See also the association's own pamphlet, *Facts with Reference to the Tax Ferret Law.*

67. Grannis v. Board of Commissioners of Blue Earth County, 83 N.W. 495 (Minn. 1900); "'Tax Ferret,'" *Minneapolis Journal,* Nov. 24, 1899, p. 3.

68. "Tax Ferret Forestalled," *Aberdeen (SD) Daily News,* Nov. 2, 1903, p. 1.

69. On the 1890s, see "Costly Collections," *Topeka Weekly Capital,* Sept. 27, 1898, p. 7. For the quotation, see "How Taxes Are Collected in Kansas," *Aberdeen (SD) Daily News,* Feb. 29, 1904, p. 7 (drawing upon the *Kansas City Journal*). For the court decision, see *State ex rel. Coleman v. Fry,* 95 P. 392 (Kan. 1908).

70. Pierson v. Minnehaha County, 134 N.W. 212 (S.D. 1912).

71. "Fant's Contract with County Ended," *Colorado Springs Gazette,* Jan. 19, 1899, p. 5; Chase v. Board of Commissioners of Boulder County, 86 P. 1011 (Colo. 1906).

72. "Notice to the Public," *Colorado Springs Gazette,* Nov. 27, 1913, p. 9.

73. "To Fight Tax Ferret Law," *Kansas City (MO) Times,* Sept. 22, 1908, p. 11.

74. 2004 Oklahoma Attorney General Opinion 24 ¶ 7.

75. On Fort Worth, see "Tax Ferret Plan Is Up to City Board," *Fort Worth Star-Telegram,* Apr. 12, 1910, p. 2; "Opinion Declares Tax Contract Legal," *Fort Worth Star-Telegram,* Apr. 16, 1910, p. 1; "Order May Stop Tax Collections," *Fort Worth Star-Telegram,* Jan. 9, 1914, p. 1. On Austin, see "Holds against Tax Ferrets," *Dallas Morning News,* Jan. 8, 1914, p. 5.

76. White v. McGill, 114 S.W.2d 860, 862 (Tex. 1938). This case discusses the practice prior to the statutes of 1930–31, citing *Von Rosenberg v. Lovett*, 173 S.W. 508 (Tex.Civ. App. 1915), and subsequent cases.

77. 1930 Tex. Gen. Laws 4th and 5th Called Sessions 9; 1931 Tex. Gen. Laws 383, 383–84.

78. "City Employs Tax Ferrets," *Kansas City (MO) Star*, Oct. 17, 1911, p. 1; "Tax Ferrets' Work Limited," *Kansas City (MO) Star*, Oct. 17, 1911, p. 6; "Tax Ferret Order in Doubt," *Kansas City (MO) Star*, Oct. 21, 1911, p. 2; "Enjoins the Tax Ferrets," *Kansas City (MO) Star*, Mar. 7, 1912, p. 1.

79. On Milwaukee, see "Impressive Failure of Socialism in City Government of Milwaukee," *Los Angeles Times*, Apr. 23, 1911, p. 7; "Tax Law Will Bring Business," *Duluth (MN) News-Tribune*, Oct. 26, 1912, p. 11. On the legislature, see Wisconsin Manufacturers' Association, *Wisconsin Should Not Introduce Non-Resident Tax Ferrets*, 3; "'Tax Ferret' Bill Killed," *Duluth (MN) News-Tribune*, June 22, 1911, p. 7; "Wisconsin Kills Tax Ferret Bill," *Cedar Rapids (IA) Evening Gazette*, Mar. 14, 1911, p. 12. On both together, see Harold M. Groves and A. Bristol Goodman, "A Pattern of Successful Property Tax Administration: The Wisconsin Experience — III. Local Assessment and Its Results," *Journal of Land and Public Utility Economics* 19 (1943): 418–19.

80. 1913 Ga. Laws 123, 126–27.

81. L. B. Raisty, *The Intangible Tax of Georgia* (Athens: University of Georgia, 1940), 8–9.

82. "Big Fees in Sight for Senator Long," *New York Times*, May 26, 1935, p. E6.

83. Murphy v. Swanson, 198 N.W. 116, 120 (N.D. 1924).

84. Simpson v. Silver Bow County, 285 P. 195 (Mont. 1930).

85. The first ten were Alabama, Georgia, Indiana, Iowa, Kentucky, Mississippi, Ohio, Oklahoma, Tennessee, and Texas. The other ten were Colorado, Illinois, Kansas, Louisiana, Minnesota, Missouri, Montana, North Dakota, South Dakota, and Wisconsin. For populations, see U.S. Census Bureau, "Table 16: Population: 1790 to 1990," available at http://www.census.gov/population/www/censusdata/files/table-16.pdf (last accessed Aug. 3, 2012).

86. 11 A.L.R. 913 (1921), revised in 32 A.L.R. 88 (1924).

87. 1888 Ohio Laws 170, 170–71 (stating ferrets can furnish information on any omission, but then stating they are to be paid only from 20 percent of taxes on "moneys, credits, investments in bonds, stocks, joint-stocks, annuities or other valuable interests"). But note that the Ohio statutes were interpreted also to permit counties to contract for correction of the omission or undervaluation of realty. State ex rel. Deckebach v. Hagerty, 3 Ohio C.D. 161 (Ohio Cir. 1891); State ex rel. Seymour v. Gilfillan, 19 Ohio C.D. 709 (Ohio Cir. 1905).

88. E. A. Angell, *The Tax Inquisitor System in Ohio* (no place or publisher, 1897), 8. This is a printing, under separate cover, of an article that appeared in the *Yale Review* in February 1897.

89. The key statute was 1891 Ind. Acts 199, 257 (referring to omitted property and deleting prohibition on ferreting that had appeared in 1881 Ind. Acts 611, 661–62).

90. Both the majority and minority reports of the 1916 tax commission, while disagreeing about whether ferreting was good or bad, discussed it solely in relation to intangibles. *Report of the Commission on Taxation to the Governor [of Indiana]*, xii, xvi.

91. 1900 Iowa Acts 33, 33–34; Brindley, *History of Taxation in Iowa*, 1:310; 1913 Ga. Laws 123, 126; Raisty, *Intangible Tax of Georgia*, 10–12; 2004 Oklahoma Attorney General Opinion 24 ¶ 7 (discussing statutes on omitted property); "Would Drive Out Tax Ferret," *Kansas City (MO) Star*, Apr. 9, 1916, p. 5A (saying "specialty" of Oklahoma County ferret is "Mortgages").

92. On the early period, see "Opinion Declares Tax Contract Legal," *Fort Worth Star-Telegram*, Apr. 16, 1910, p. 1; "Order May Stop Tax Collections," *Fort Worth Star-Telegram*, Jan. 9, 1914, p. 1. On the later period, see "Await Approval of Taxation Plan," *El Paso Herald-Post*, July 17, 1937, p. 2.

93. On intangibles, see "Fant's Contract with County Ended," *Colorado Springs Gazette*, Jan. 19, 1899, p. 5. On omitted property generally, see *Chase v. Board of Commissioners of Boulder County*, 86 P. 1011 (Colo. 1906); "Notice to the Public," *Colorado Springs Gazette*, Nov. 27, 1913, p. 9.

94. On intangibles, see "Tax-Ferreting," *Chicago Daily Tribune*, Aug. 21, 1884, p. 8; "Hits Education Board Raise," *Chicago Daily Tribune*, May 12, 1909, p. 2. On omitted property generally, see *Stevens v. Henry County*, 75 N.E. 1024, 1024 (Ill. 1905).

95. On intangibles, see "May Employ 'Tax Ferrets,'" *Kansas City (MO) Star*, July 6, 1906, p. 2. On omitted property generally, see "Costly Collections," *Topeka Weekly Capital*, Sept. 27, 1898, p. 7.

96. "City Employs Tax Ferrets," *Kansas City (MO) Star*, Oct. 17, 1911, p. 1; "Tax Ferrets' Work Limited," *Kansas City (MO) Star*, Oct. 17, 1911, p. 6.

97. Pierson v. Minnehaha County, 134 N.W. 212 (S.D. 1912).

98. "Milwaukee Socialists Have Been Unable to Carry Out Their Glittering Promises," *Los Angeles Times*, Nov. 12, 1911, p. 7. On Minnesota and North Dakota, my sources refer only to omitted property without specifying that intangibles were the focus, though it seems entirely possible they were. E.g., Grannis v. Board of Commissioners of Blue Earth County, 83 N.W. 495 (Minn. 1900); Murphy v. Swanson, 198 N.W. 116, 120 (N.D. 1924).

99. On Kentucky, see Leland, *Taxation in Kentucky*, 57–59; *Government of Kentucky*, 1:260; Kentucky State Tax Commission, *Sixth Annual Report* (Frankfort, KY: State Journal Co., 1923), 10; "Makes Defense of Back Tax Suits," *Lexington (KY) Herald*, July 24, 1905, p. 4; "Six Residents Sued for Delinquent Tax: Actions Taken to Recover on Out of State Stocks," *Lexington Herald*, Dec. 31, 1913, p. 4. On Alabama, see Lutz, *State Tax Commission*, 556; "Back Tax Report," *Montgomery Advertiser*, Nov. 15, 1906, p. 2. On Mississippi, see Brookings Institution, *Report on a Survey of . . . Government in Mississippi*, 280–82; Rhodes, *History of Taxation in Mississippi*, 107–08. In some Tennessee cases, the court and parties appeared to assume that it was generally ordinary for the revenue agent to seek the back-assessment of omitted intangibles, though with certain exceptions. Southern Express Co. v. Patterson, 123 S.W. 353 (Tenn. 1909); Tennessee Fertilizer Co. v. McFall, 163 S.W. 806 (Tenn. 1912). For Tennessee cases going beyond intangibles taxation, see *Swift & Co. v. Hailey*, 219 S.W. 1039, 1040 (Tenn. 1920); *Eastland v. Sneed*, 185 S.W. 717 (Tenn. 1916).

100. 1913 Ga. Laws 123, 126–27 (capped 10 percent); 1896–97 Ala. Laws 521, 525 (set at 10 percent); 1900 Iowa Acts 33, 33–34 (capped 15 percent); 2004 Oklahoma Attorney

General Opinion 24 ¶ 7 (capped 15 percent); 1895 Tenn. Pub. Acts 203, 245 (set by comptroller, not more than 15 percent); White v. McGill, 114 S.W.2d 860, 862 (Tex. 1938) (capped 15 percent); *Government of Kentucky*, 1:260 (set at 75 percent of 20 percent penalty); *The Mississippi Code of 1906* (Nashville, TN: Brandon Printing Co., 1906), 1283 (set at 20 percent); 1888 Ohio Laws 170, 170–71 (capped at 20 percent for some counties).

101. E.g., "Costly Collections," *Topeka Weekly Capital*, Sept. 27, 1898, p. 7 (Harvey County, Kansas, 50 percent); Grannis v. Board of Commissioners of Blue Earth County, 83 N.W. 495 (Minn. 1900) (Blue Earth County, 50 percent).

102. Compensation might be a certain per diem, or it might be in the discretion of the county or town board, capped at a certain per diem. E.g., *Burns' Annotated Indiana Statutes*, ed. Harrison Burns (Indianapolis: Bowen-Merrill Co., 1901), 3:1139–40, 1149–50; *Annotated Code of the State of Iowa* (Des Moines, IA: F. R. Conway, 1897), 1:267; *The Verified Revised Statutes of the State of Ohio*, ed. Rufus B. Smith (Cincinnati: Ohio Valley Co., 1890), 1:391; *Wisconsin Statutes of 1898* (Chicago: Callaghan and Co., 1898), 1:580, 593. See also *Annotated Statutes of the State of Illinois* (Chicago: Callaghan and Co., 1885), 2:2056 (compensation set by town or county board "for the time necessarily employed").

It should be noted that a few states set the local assessor's pay as a percentage of taxes arising from his assessments or occasionally as a percentage of the value of the property he assessed, but it appears this practice did not result in more aggressive assessment and was not intended to.

First of all, governments often set the total revenue they needed as a fixed amount and used the initial ordinary assessment merely to apportion that amount. In such cases, a percentage-paid assessor would make the same income no matter what he did, so long as the basis for his compensation was actual tax dollars (though not if it were total valuation). Jackson Lumber Co. v. McCrimmon, 164 F. 759, 764 (C.C.N.D. Fla. 1908). And even if the revenue was not fixed, lawmakers blunted any incentive by keeping the assessor's percentage low and graduating it downward with rising assessments. *The Code of Alabama* (Nashville, TN: Marshall and Bruce Co., 1907), 1:864–65 (statute of 1897); James W. Martin and Glenn D. Morrow, "Organization of Kentucky Local Tax Assessments," *Bulletin of the Bureau of Business Research, College of Commerce* 2, no. 4 (1941): 59; Freeman v. Terrell, 284 S.W. 946, 947 (Tex. 1926); *Compiled Statutes of Oklahoma, 1921* (Ardmore, OK: Bunn Publishing Co., 1922), 3:3195 (statute of 1911). Though the Mississippi assessor's commission was not graduated downward, it was capped. *The Mississippi Code of 1906* (Nashville, TN: Brandon Printing Co., 1906), 682 (statute of 1898). Though the Tennessee assessor's commission was ungraduated and uncapped under an 1889 statute, the officer was converted to a pure salary only six years later. 1889 Tenn. Pub. Acts 145, 163; compare *Public and Permanent Statutes of a General Nature, Being an Annotated Code of Tennessee* (Nashville, TN: Marshall and Bruce Co., 1896), 1:291 (statute of 1895 converting officer to pure salary).

Low commissions and downward graduation (or capping) apparently blunted any incentive effect. Observations of pervasive assessor laxity were as easy to find in the states just cited as in all the others. Lutz, *State Tax Commission*, 559 (on Alabama); ibid., 562 (on Texas); *Report of the Special Tax Commission of the State of Kentucky 1912–14*, 35–39; Rhodes, *History of Taxation in Mississippi*, 83–87. Indeed, commission-based compensation of assessors probably was not even intended to incentivize higher assessment. More likely, it served as a rough-and-ready way to calibrate the pay of part-time officers to the amount of their labor, which varied significantly between localities. The tax ferrets' compensation was far different and provided a much stronger incentive. It was calculated on the basis of taxes unpaid in the initial round, was generally set at a much higher percentage (ranging from 10 percent to 50 percent), and was never graduated downward.

103. E.g., *Public and Permanent Statutes of a General Nature, Being an Annotated Code of Tennessee* (Nashville, TN: Marshall and Bruce Co., 1896), 1:291.

104. E.g., *Report of Committee to Investigate Assessment and Taxation, State of Tennessee, 1915* (Nashville, TN: McQuiddy Printing Co., 1915), 9.

105. "Martin's Ferry," *Wheeling (WV) Register*, Sept. 18, 1888, p. 3.

106. C. L. Poorman, "Reply to the Letter of Hon. Thomas McDougall," *Cincinnati Commercial Tribune*, Feb. 19, 1888, p. 14.

107. Auditor's letter quoted in ibid. See also Carver, "Ohio Tax Inquisitor Law," 182; "Current Comment," *Ohio Farmer* 101 (Mar. 27, 1902): 296.

108. "Governor's Message," in *Journal of the House of Representatives of the State of Mississippi at a Regular Session Thereof in the City of Jackson Commencing Tuesday, January 8, 1924, Ending Saturday, April 12, 1924* (Jackson, MS: Hederman Bros., 1924), 101–02.

109. Carver, "Ohio Tax Inquisitor Law," 181.

110. Ibid., 200. Note that even a ferret working in his own county in Ohio would be less local than the assessors, who were elected by their respective towns, which were even smaller than counties. Several states had assessors elected by the town. See my discussion in note 126 below.

111. Carver, "Ohio Tax Inquisitor Law," 200–01.

112. "Current Comment," *Ohio Farmer* 110 (July 14, 1906): 22.

113. Brindley's categorization and description of Iowa tax ferrets indicates that most were nonlocal. *History of Taxation in Iowa*, 1:312, 344–55. For newspaper references to individual ferrets or ferret firms each holding contracts with many counties, see "Shows Work of Tax Ferret Law," *Cedar Rapids (IA) Evening Gazette*, Jan. 31, 1911, p. 12 (McCoy, thirty counties); "Tax Ferret Tangle," *Omaha World Herald*, June 9, 1901, p. 1 (Fleener-Carnahan, twenty-three counties); "Here and There in Iowa," *Sioux City Journal*, Aug. 11, 1900, p. 4 ("One firm," twenty counties); "After Bank Depositors," *Omaha World Herald*, Nov. 17, 1900, p. 3 (F. M. Cunningham, eleven counties).

114. "County Contract with Tax Prober Declared Illegal," *Atlanta Constitution*, Jan. 16, 1925, p. 5.

115. The tax-ferret firm of Fleener and Carnahan surfaced in litigation in Jasper County and faraway Parke County. Fleener v. Litsey, 66 N.E. 82, 83 (Ind. App. 1903); Board of Commissioners of Jasper County v. Marion, 58 N.E. 1095, 1095 (Ind. 1900). The same firm worked many counties in Iowa. See my discussion in note 113 above.

116. "To Fight Tax Ferret Law," *Kansas City (MO) Times*, Sept. 22, 1908, p. 11; "Denies Fraud in Ferret Contract," *Ada (OK) Evening News*, Apr. 22, 1928, p. 5.

117. Marquart v. Harris County, 117 S.W.2d 494, 495n1 (Tex. Civ. App. 1938).

118. Chase v. Board of Commissioners of Boulder County, 86 P. 1011, 1011 (Colo. 1906) (noting that ferret is resident of El Paso County but has contract with Boulder County).

119. Wisconsin Manufacturers' Association, *Wisconsin Should Not Introduce Non-Resident Tax Ferrets*, 1.

120. "Object to 'Tax Ferrets,'" *Kansas City (MO) Star*, Aug. 3, 1911, p. 5.

121. "Great Chance for Graft," *Kansas City (MO) Star*, Aug. 5, 1911, p. 9.

122. Wisconsin Manufacturers' Association, *Wisconsin Should Not Introduce Non-Resident Tax Ferrets*, 10.

123. Ibid., 10.

124. Brindley, *History of Taxation in Iowa*, 1:313–14.

125. This was true of most of the states where county contracts were recognized by legislation. 2004 Oklahoma Attorney General Opinion 24 ¶ 7; 1891 Ind. Acts 199, 257, as construed in City of Richmond v. Dickinson, 58 N.E. 260, 261–62 (Ind. 1900); 1900 Iowa Acts 33, 33–34; Von Rosenberg v. Lovett, 173 S.W. 508 (Tex. Civ. App. 1915); White v. McGill, 114 S.W.2d 860, 862 (Tex. 1938). The only exceptions were Georgia and Ohio. In Georgia, contracts were with a special county tax board, though this board was itself appointed by the commissioners. 1913 Ga. Acts 123, 126–27. In Ohio, the decision lay with the commissioners (of whom there were three), the elected county auditor, and the elected county treasurer, or any majority of these five officers. Carver, "Ohio Tax Inquisitor Law," 180. Although the auditor and treasurer lacked the commissioners' political stake in the level of county revenue, the legislature had granted them shares, of 4 percent and 5 percent, respectively, of all taxes arising from newly discovered omitted personalty, literally allowing them a cut of the profits of ferreting. 1868 Ohio Laws Adjourned Sess. 122, 122–23; Nelson W. Evans, *A History of Taxation in Ohio* (Cincinnati, OH: Robert Clarke Co., 1906), 157. A survey of Ohio county auditors in the 1890s found that the large majority supported the use of ferrets. Carver, "Ohio Tax Inquisitor Law," 198. In states where tax ferrets did not receive legislative authorization, contracts with counties were likewise generally made with county boards:

- Colorado: Chase v. Board of Commissioners of Boulder County, 86 P. 1011 (Colo. 1906); but see "Notice to the Public," *Colorado Springs Gazette*, Nov. 27, 1913, p. 9 (statement of county treasurer that he, not commissioners, employed ferret).

- Illinois: "The Day at Springfield," *Chicago Daily Tribune*, Apr. 19, 1885, p. 8.

- Kansas: "Costly Collections," *Topeka Weekly Capital*, Sept. 27, 1898, p. 7; State ex rel. Coleman v. Fry, 95 P. 392 (Kan. 1908).

- Minnesota: Grannis v. Board of Commissioners of Blue Earth County, 83 N.W. 495 (Minn. 1900); "Tax Ferret Forestalled," *Aberdeen (SD) Daily News*, Nov. 2, 1903, p. 1.

- Montana: Simpson v. Silver Bow County, 285 P. 195 (Montana 1930).

- North Dakota: Murphy v. Swanson, 198 N.W. 116, 120 (N.D. 1924).

- South Dakota: Pierson v. Minnehaha County, 134 N.W. 212 (S.D. 1912).

126. Of the ten states in which the legislature authorized tax-ferreting, three elected their assessors at the town level. *The Revised Statutes and Other Acts of a General Nature of the State of Ohio* (Columbus, OH: H. W. Derby and Co., 1879), 1:477; *Annotated Code of the State of Iowa* (Des Moines, IA: P. R. Conway, 1897), 1:404; *General Statutes of Oklahoma 1908* (Kansas City, MO: Pipes-Reed Book Co., 1908), 1010 (town trustee elected), 1014 (town trustee is assessor). Five elected their assessors at the county level. *The Code of Alabama* (Nashville, TN: Marshall and Bruce Co., 1887), 1:152; Kentucky Constitution of 1891, sec. 99; *The Annotated Code of the General Statute Laws of Mississippi* (Nashville, TN: Marshall and Bruce Co., 1892), 808; *Public and Permanent Statutes of a General Nature, Being an Annotated Code of Tennessee* (Nashville, TN: Marshall and Bruce Co., 1896), 1:290–91; *Revised Civil Statutes of the State of Texas* (Austin: Eugene Von Boeckmann, 1895), 1037. One state elected assessors at both the county and town level. *Annotated Statutes of the State of Indiana* (Indianapolis: Bowen-Merrill Co., 1894), 3:794, 802–03. The statutes of Georgia are unclear on this point.

127. Lutz, *State Tax Commission*, 556, 559–60 (on Alabama); Leland, *Taxation in Kentucky*, 57–59; 1895 Tenn. Pub. Acts 203, 244.

128. *The Mississippi Code of 1906* (Nashville, TN: Brandon Printing Co., 1906), 1279.

129. Leland, *Taxation in Kentucky*, 59; 1895 Tenn. Pub. Acts 203, 244–45. Though the Tennessee law contemplated that each of the state's five agents would have a geographic area, this would be far larger than any one of the state's ninety-five counties.

130. "Governor's Message," in *Journal of the Senate of the State of Alabama. Session of 1907* (Montgomery: Brown Printing Co., 1907), 25. For more on their laxity, see Lutz, *State Tax Commission*, 559; "Back Tax Report," *Montgomery Advertiser*, Nov. 15, 1906, p. 2.

131. C. L. Poorman, "Reply to the Letter of Hon. Thomas McDougall," *Cincinnati Commercial Tribune*, Feb. 19, 1888, p. 14.

132. Quoted in ibid.

133. Evans, *History of Taxation in Ohio*, 159.

134. "Starbeams," *Kansas City (MO) Star*, Aug. 8, 1911, p. 6.

135. James C. Scott, *Seeing Like a State: How Certain Schemes to Improve the Human Condition Have Failed* (New Haven, CT: Yale University Press, 1998).

136. Quoted in Carver, "Ohio Tax Inquisitor Law," 201.

137. Brindley, *History of Taxation in Iowa*, 1:347, 350–51.

138. "Tax Investigator Engaged by City," *Atlanta Constitution*, May 8, 1924, p. 1.

139. *Report of the Special Tax Commission of the State of Kentucky 1912–14*, 71; "Tax Dodgers Rounded Up," *Minneapolis Journal*, Sept. 5, 1900, p. 9.

140. E.g., "Sick of Its Bargain: County Board Would Get Out of Cunningham Contract If It Could," *Omaha World Herald*, Nov. 29, 1900, p. 3 (on Iowa); "Cunningham's Antiquarian Search," *Omaha World Herald*, Dec. 17, 1900, p. 3 (on Iowa); "$100,000

Due in Back Taxes," *Minneapolis Journal*, Dec. 21, 1900, p. 20; "South Dakota News," *Aberdeen (SD) Daily News*, June 11, 1909, p. 2.

141. Carver, "Ohio Tax Inquisitor Law," 181; "Martin's Ferry," *Wheeling (WV) Register*, Sept. 18, 1888, p. 3; "Iowa Tax Ferret Is Here," *Aberdeen (SD) Daily News*, Jan. 13, 1910, p. 4; Board of Commissioners of Wayne County v. Dickinson, 53 N.E. 929, 929 (Ind. 1899); Von Rosenberg v. Lovett, 173 S.W. 508, 513 (Tex. Civ. App. 1915). But see "Our Columbus Letter," *Ohio Farmer* 85 (Mar. 29, 1894): 258 (noting recent statute requiring auditors of Ohio counties to report mortgages to each other).

142. "Cunnigham's Antiquarian Search," *Omaha World Herald*, Dec. 17, 1900, p. 3 (on Iowa). But states sometimes required those courts to report property directly to the local tax authorities, cutting the ferret out of the loop. Carver, "Ohio Tax Inquisitor Law," 188.

143. "Outcome of Divorce Case," *Omaha World Herald*, Jan. 19, 1903, p. 2 (on Iowa).

144. "After Bank Depositors," *Omaha World Herald*, Nov. 17, 1900, p. 3; "Council Bluffs Expects to Get In Much Money," *Omaha World Herald*, Dec. 27, 1904, p. 3.

145. "Tax Ferrets Get Busy," *Cedar Rapids (IA) Evening Gazette*, Dec. 16, 1910, p. 8; Wisconsin Manufacturers' Association, *Wisconsin Should Not Introduce Non-Resident Tax Ferrets*, 9; Raisty, *Intangible Tax of Georgia*, 22.

146. For Iowa, this is clear from "Tax Ferrets Get Busy," *Cedar Rapids (IA) Evening Gazette*, Dec. 16, 1910, p. 8. On Ohio, see Oliver C. Lockhart, "Recent Developments in Taxation in Ohio," *Quarterly Journal of Economics* 29 (1915): 515.

147. Angell, *Tax Inquisitor System*, 3n1.

148. *Twenty-Third Annual Conference of [Indiana] State Board of Tax Commissioners and County Assessors* (Indianapolis: William B. Burford, 1924), 113. This discussion is of state agencies, not tax ferrets, but the point holds just the same. See also John E. Brindley, "Five Mill Tax on Moneys and Credits in Iowa," *Quarterly Journal of Economics* 30 (1916): 595.

149. M. E. Ingalls, *Tax Inquisition: Argument before the Committee on Taxation of the General Assembly of Ohio* (Cincinnati, OH: Robert Clarke Co., 1896), 11–12.

150. Article from *Cleveland Plain Dealer*, Dec. 17, 1903, quoted in Ernest Ludlow Bogart, *Financial History of Ohio* (Urbana-Champaign: University of Illinois, 1912), 242.

151. Bullock, "Taxation of Property and Income in Massachusetts," 33–34. This is a discussion of tax investigation generally, not of tax ferrets, but it is entirely possible that ferrets did this.

152. Northwestern Mutual Life Insurance Co. v. Suttles, 38 S.E.2d 786, 794 (Ga. 1946).

153. "Tax Ferrets May Be Hired," *Fort Wayne (IN) News Sentinel*, Jan. 6, 1922, p. 17; "Tax Ferrets' Work Limited," *Kansas City (MO) Star*, Oct. 17, 1911, p. 6. On the growth of a private market in information about securities ownership generally, see Bullock, "Taxation of Property and Income in Massachusetts," 33–34.

154. They invoked this expense to justify their high commissions. E.g., C. L. Poorman, "Reply to the Letter of Hon. Thomas McDougall," *Cincinnati Commercial Tribune*, Feb. 19, 1888, p. 14; Angell, *Tax Inquisitor System*, 20.

155. Some said settlement pressure arose from the expense of litigation. "Tax Ferrets Condemned," *Dallas Morning News*, Apr. 9, 1916, p. 11. Others said it arose from

the prospect of bad publicity. "Tax-Ferreting," *Chicago Daily Tribune*, Aug. 21, 1884, p. 8; State ex rel. Coleman v. Fry, 95 P. 392, 394 (Kansas 1908). Yet others said ferrets inflated their initial claims to intimidate the taxpayer. "Exit the Tax Ferret," *Colorado Springs Gazette-Telegraph*, Nov. 29, 1913, p. 8; "Inaugural Address of Gov. Theo. G. Bilbo," in *Journal of the House of Representatives of the State of Mississippi at a Regular Session Thereof in the City of Jackson Commencing Tuesday, January 4, 1916, Ending Saturday, April 8, 1916* (Memphis, TN: Dixon-Paul, n.d.), 185–86.

156. For invocations of procedural safeguards, see Carver, "Ohio Tax Inquisitor Law," 198–99; C. L. Poorman, "Reply to the Letter of Hon. Thomas McDougall," *Cincinnati Commercial Tribune*, Feb. 19, 1888, p. 14; Meier, "Iowa 'Tax Ferret' Law," 19. For details on such safeguards across several states, see Parrillo diss., 384.

157. Brindley, *History of Taxation in Iowa*, 1:315–17, 332; "Iowa May Get Rid of Its Tax Ferret Law," *Omaha World Herald*, Feb. 23, 1904, p. 3; "Great Chance for Graft," *Kansas City (MO) Star*, Aug. 5, 1911, p. 9; "A Tax of 84 Per Cent!" *Kansas City (MO) Star*, Aug. 8, 1911, p. 6.

158. Quoted in Brindley, *History of Taxation in Iowa*, 1:333. See also *Facts with Reference to the Tax Ferret Law*, 19 (quoting *Sloan Star*); Angell, *Tax Inquisitor System*, 12.

159. *Government of Kentucky*, 1:311, 338; Lutz, *State Tax Commission*, 557, 560 (on Alabama); "Poorman and Morgenthaler," *Cincinnati Commercial Tribune*, Feb. 16, 1888, p. 7 (quoting report of anti-ferret group). The Ohio legislature, when it extended the authorization of tax-ferret contracts to all counties in 1888, recognized this danger and provided for criminal penalties against any ordinary tax officers who "wilfully" kept property off the rolls. 1888 Ohio Laws 170, 171. Later, the state supreme court seemed to indicate that prosecutions under this law had not been sufficiently vigorous. State v. Lewis, 78 N.E. 523, 525 (Ohio 1906).

160. S. H. Ellis, "The Morgenthaler Law," *Ohio Farmer* 89 (Apr. 23, 1896): 360.

161. Leland, *Taxation in Kentucky*, 59.

162. "The Fight Is On," *Ohio Farmer* 89 (Feb. 20, 1896): 152.

163. "Figures Show Tax Ferrets Beneficial," *Des Moines (IA) Daily News*, Feb. 5, 1911, p. 10. For further assertions that there would be little or no compliance without tax-ferret coercion, see "Shows Work of Tax Ferret Law," *Cedar Rapids (IA) Evening Gazette*, Jan. 31, 1911, p. 12; Meier, "Iowa 'Tax Ferret' Law," 19, 29; *Facts with Reference to the Tax Ferret Law*, 13 (quoting *Sloan Star*); ibid., 16–17 (quoting *Odebolt Chronicle*).

164. For arguments of ferret effectiveness, see, e.g., C. L. Poorman, "Reply to the Letter of Hon. Thomas McDougall," *Cincinnati Commercial Tribune*, Feb. 19, 1888, p. 14; "Morgenthaler's Figures," *Ohio Farmer* 89 (Apr. 16, 1896): 338 (asserting that Cincinnati and Cleveland have per capita tax duplicate more than double that of Chicago); Gov. Lee Russell, "Governor's Message," in *Journal of the House of Representatives of the State of Mississippi at a Regular Session Thereof in the City of Jackson Commencing Tuesday, January 8, 1924, Ending Saturday, April 12, 1924* (Jackson: Hederman Bros., 1924), 101. For arguments of ferret failure, see Angell, *Tax Inquisitor System*, 11; *Report of the Special Tax Commission of the State of Kentucky 1912–14*, 81; Allen R. Foote, "Taxation Work and Experience in Ohio," in *State and Local Taxation: Fourth Annual Conference, under the Auspices of the International Tax Association, Held at*

*Milwaukee, Wisconsin, August 30 to September 2, 1910: Address and Proceedings* (Columbus, OH: International Tax Association, 1911), 218.

165. Carver, "Ohio Tax Inquisitor Law," 211–12. He did believe the tax was far more effective in Ohio than in other states, which suffered "humiliating failures" to list personalty. Ibid.

166. Brindley, *History of Taxation in Iowa*, 1:344–54, 355.

167. On moving investments to non-ferret jurisdictions, see "South Dakota News," *Aberdeen (SD) Daily News*, June 11, 1909, p. 2. Wisconsin Governor Francis McGovern noted that an unreasonably high personal property tax caused taxpayers, even when they remained in the state, to put their money in investments outside the state, since these were less easily discoverable. "Tax Law Will Bring Business," *Duluth (MN) News-Tribune*, Oct. 26, 1912, p. 11.

168. Harley L. Lutz, *The Georgia System of Revenue: Its Problems and Their Remedies* (Atlanta: Foote and Davies Co., 1930), 46; Raisty, *Intangible Tax of Georgia*, 10; "Public Offices," *Daily Inter Ocean (Chicago)*, Oct. 8, 1886, p. 12; *Report of the Commission on Taxation to the Governor [of Indiana]*, xvi (minority report of economist William W. Rawles); "Taxing Moneys and Credits," *Waterloo (IA) Times-Tribune*, Nov. 12, 1910, p. 4; "Why People Leave Iowa," *Waterloo (IA) Evening Reporter*, Dec. 23, 1910, p. 4; *Report of the Special Tax Commission of the State of Kentucky 1912–14*, 80; "The Revenue Agent Must Go," *Lexington (KY) Herald*, Nov. 21, 1911, p. 4; "Inaugural Address of Gov. Theo. G. Bilbo," in *Journal of the House of Representatives of the State of Mississippi* (1916), 185–86; Angell, *Tax Inquisitor System*, 15, 23 (on Ohio); Evans, *History of Taxation in Ohio*, 159; "Would Drive Out Tax Ferret," *Kansas City (MO) Star*, Apr. 9, 1916, p. 5A (on Oklahoma); "Tax Ferret Plan Is Up to City Board," *Fort Worth Star-Telegram*, Apr. 12, 1910, p. 2.

169. Benson, "History of the General Property Tax," 64. See also Teaford, *Rise of the States*, 47–48.

170. Charles J. Bullock, "A Classified Property Tax," in *State and Local Taxation: Third International Conference, under the Auspices of the International Tax Association, Held at Louisville, Kentucky, September 21–24, 1909: Addresses and Proceedings* (Columbus, OH: International Tax Association, 1910), 100–05. See also Institute for Government Research of the Brookings Institution, *Report on a Survey of Administration in Iowa: The Revenue System* (Des Moines: State of Iowa, 1933), 73 [hereinafter Brookings Institution, *Report on a Survey of Administration in Iowa*].

171. Leland, *Classified Property Tax*, 335.

172. Benson, "History of the General Property Tax," 64.

173. Brookings Institution, *Report on a Survey of Administration in Iowa*, 73.

174. "More of Moneys and Credits," *Waterloo (IA) Reporter*, Dec. 28, 1910, p. 4 (quoting *Dubuque (IA) Times-Journal*).

175. *Third Biennial Report of the Minnesota Tax Commission* (Minneapolis: Syndicate Printing Co., 1913), 585.

176. *Report of the Special Tax Commission of the State of Kentucky 1912–14*, 91–94.

177. Evans, *History of Taxation in Ohio*, 160–61.

178. Ibid., 159.

179. Brookings Institution, *Report on a Survey of . . . Government in Mississippi*, 282–83. The legislature in 1924 had capped the earnings of the State Revenue Agent himself (later renamed state tax collector) at $5,000, plus a similar $5,000 cap on the earnings of each of his appointed deputies. Ibid., 280 (citing 1924 Miss. Laws 578). One commentator characterized this measure as "placing the revenue agent on a salary basis." Rhodes, *History of Taxation in Mississippi*, 108. But the law still mandated that "the compensation of any deputy shall only be paid out of the amounts collected as a result of the services of the said deputy." 1924 Miss. Laws 578. This may well have kept the profit motive alive for the deputies. That provision was not changed until 1942 Miss. Laws 362, 362–63.

180. Seligman added this sentence to the revision of his essay "The General Property Tax," in *Essays in Taxation*, 8th ed. (New York: Macmillan, 1913), 27.

181. Ingalls, *Tax Inquisition*, 9–10. Ingalls was unaware of Chicago's brief experiments with tax ferrets.

182. James Rudolph Garfield, "Listing and Valuation," in *National Conference on Taxation under the Auspices of the National Civic Federation* (no place or publisher, 1901), 13.

183. *Report of the Honorary Commission . . . to Investigate the Tax System of Ohio*, 26.

184. Wisconsin Manufacturers' Association, *Wisconsin Should Not Introduce Non-Resident Tax Ferrets*, 3.

185. Lutz, *Georgia System of Revenue*, 46.

186. Walter Wolfgang Heller, "State Income Tax Administration" (Ph.D. diss., University of Wisconsin, 1941), 86. See also Clara Penniman and Walter W. Heller, *State Income Tax Administration* (Chicago: Public Administration Service, 1959), 84 (similar passage).

187. John E. Brindley, "Recent Tax Legislation in Iowa," *Quarterly Journal of Economics* 26 (1911): 180; "Report of the State Board of Tax Commissioners" (1933–34), in *Year Book of the State of Indiana for the Year 1934* (Indianapolis: William B. Burford Printing Co., 1934), 351. On the Alabama ferrets' more general stake in maintaining evasion, see Lutz, *State Tax Commission*, 558.

188. John O. Stark, "The Establishment of Wisconsin's Income Tax," *Wisconsin Magazine of History* 71 (1987): 27. Congress had enacted a federal income tax to help finance the Civil War. Compliance depended heavily on wartime patriotism, and there was little interest in making it permanent after the emergency ended. W. Elliott Brownlee, *Federal Taxation in America: A Short History*, 2nd ed. (Cambridge: Cambridge University Press, 2004), 33–37.

189. For a discussion of those early experiments along these lines, see *Report of the Special Tax Commission of the State of Kentucky 1912–14*, 91–94.

190. On annual town election of assessors, see *Annotated Statutes of Wisconsin, Containing the General Laws in Force October 1, 1889* (Chicago: Callaghan and Co., 1889), 1:480–81.

191. Brindley, *History of Taxation in Iowa*, 1:313–14.

192. "Taxing Moneys and Credits," *Waterloo (IA) Times-Tribune*, Nov. 12, 1910, p. 4; "More of Moneys and Credits," *Waterloo (IA) Reporter*, Dec. 28, 1910, p. 4; "Tax Legislation

Interest Center," *Muscatine (IA) Journal*, Jan. 18, 1911, p. 1; Brindley, "Recent Tax Legislation," 179.

193. The reformers had the anti-ferret statute (1911 Iowa Acts 48) passed first, to knock out the ferrets as lobbyists against the classification measure. See Brindley, "Recent Tax Legislation in Iowa," 180. On the anti-ferret measure, see *Journal of the House of Representatives of the Thirty-Fourth General Assembly of the State of Iowa* (Des Moines, IA: Emory H. English, 1911), 268–69 [hereinafter *Journal of the [Iowa] House (1911)*] (passes house 83–18); *Journal of the Senate of the Thirty-Fourth General Assembly of the State of Iowa* (Des Moines, IA: Emory H. English, 1911), 456 [hereinafter *Journal of the [Iowa] Senate (1911)*] (passes Senate 34–11). On the low-rate tax on intangibles, see *Journal of the [Iowa] House (1911)*, 1313 (passes house 90–8); *Journal of the [Iowa] Senate (1911)*, 1063 (passes Senate 42–5); *Journal of the [Iowa] House (1911)*, 1525 (passes house after senate's recall and return, 68–7); *Journal of the [Iowa] Senate (1911)*, 1327 (passes senate 44–0).

194. For articles stating that the one reform logically necessitated the other, see "Cart before Horse" [Editorial], *Iowa City Citizen*, Jan. 27, 1911, p. 2; "At the State Capital," *Bedford (IA) Times-Republican*, Apr. 6, 1911, p. 3. For articles presenting the two as a pair under the heading "tax reform," see "Tax Ferrets Get Busy," *Cedar Rapids (IA) Evening Gazette*, Dec. 16, 1910, p. 8; "Would Repeal Tax Ferret Law," *Bedford (IA) Times-Republican*, Feb. 2, 1911, p. 7.

195. "Many New Laws Important," *Waterloo (IA) Evening Courier*, Apr. 12, 1911, p. 4; see also "The Farmer and Population," *Oelwein (IA) Register*, Mar. 1, 1911, p. 4 (quoting *Davenport (IA) Democrat*).

196. "Bring Back Your Money," *Iowa City Citizen*, Apr. 8, 1911, p. 2.

197. "Repeal Ferret Law," *Waterloo (IA) Evening Courier*, Dec. 20, 1910, p. 6 (quoting outgoing state senator); "Cart before Horse" [Editorial], *Iowa City Citizen*, Jan. 27, 1911, p. 2; "Would Repeal Tax Ferret Law," *Bedford (IA) Times-Republican*, Feb. 2, 1911, p. 7; "Good By, Mr. Tax Ferret," *Williamsburg (IA) Journal-Tribune*, Feb. 2, 1911, p. 4; "At the State Capital," *Bedford (IA) Times-Republican*, Mar. 2, 1911, p. 7.

198. "Sentiment Growing for Revision of Tax Laws," *Cedar Rapids (IA) Evening Gazette*, Jan. 24, 1911, p. 4 (quoting state senator); "Half a Loaf in Sight," *Cedar Rapids (IA) Evening Gazette*, Mar. 18, 1911, p. 4.

199. "The Case of John Jones," *Iowa Recorder*, Jan. 25, 1911, p. 1 (quoting *Sioux City (IA) Journal*).

200. "Money and Credits," *Humeston (IA) New Era*, Mar. 22, 1911, p. 3 (noting that the proposed commission would have "supervision over all tax collectors and assessors in the state, has the power to direct movements to collect taxes, . . . and, in fact is the head tax body of the state"). One critic bemoaned "the folly of taxpayers voting the power of taxing their property into a bureau of officials not directly elected by them." "The Tax Commission," *Marble Rock (IA) Journal*, Mar. 30, 1911, p. 1.

201. *Journal of the [Iowa] Senate (1911)*, 1138 (defeated by Senate, 22–18); "Spaulding Bill Went Too Far," *Cedar Rapids (IA) Evening Gazette*, Mar. 30, 1911.

202. The fourteen were Allen (of Pocahontas), Ames, Bennett, Brown, Chapman, Chase, Crow, Gates, Hunter, Jewell, Schrup, Sullivan, White, and Wilson. The other five were Legel, McColl, McManus, Saunders, and Smith (of Shelby). See *Journal of the*

[*Iowa*] *Senate*, 456 (ferret abolition vote), 1063 (intangibles classification vote), 1138 (tax commission vote).

203. Brookings Institution, *Report on a Survey of Administration in Iowa*, 74. The Brookings Institution considered the reform a disappointment, as did Brindley in "Five Mill Tax." For a somewhat more positive view, see Leland, *Classified Property Tax*, 348–51; Benson, "History of the General Property Tax," 64.

204. Leland, *Classified Property Tax*, 350.

205. Brindley, "Five Mill Tax," 591–93; Leland, *Classified Property Tax*, 348.

206. Brindley, "Five Mill Tax," 593–94; Brookings Institution, *Report on a Survey of Administration in Iowa*, 76–77.

207. Brookings Institution, *Report on a Survey of Administration in Iowa*, 74–75; Leland, *Classified Property Tax*, 348.

208. In 1924 it authorized county boards to hire contractors to discover omitted property, but only for a "reasonable salary or per diem," not a percentage of proceeds. *Code of Iowa 1924* (Des Moines: State of Iowa, 1924), 908 (statute of 1923–24).

209. "Gov. Hammill Appoints Tax Commissioners," *Oelwein (IA) Daily Register*, July 13, 1929, p. 1. On the incremental increase in intangibles assessment achieved by the agency in its early days, see Brookings Institution, *Report on a Survey of Administration in Iowa*, 74–75.

210. Penniman and Heller, *State Income Tax Administration*, 89–90.

211. "Current Comment," *Ohio Farmer* 109 (May 5, 1906): 488. Lawmakers at the session did manage to repeal the fee system for compensating county officers across the state, thus terminating the commissions enjoyed by county auditors and treasurers on inquisitor discoveries. 1906 Ohio Laws 89, 89–90; Hoyt Landon Warner, *Progressivism in Ohio, 1897–1917* (N.p.: Ohio State University Press, 1964), 180, 204n18.

212. See my discussion in this chapter, text at note 41.

213. Ohio Constitution of 1851, art. 2, sec. 26.

214. State ex rel. Wirsch v. Spellmire, 65 N.E. 619 (Ohio 1902); Warner, *Progressivism in Ohio*, 105–08; "Current Comment," *Ohio Farmer* 110 (July 14, 1906): 22.

215. State ex rel. Wilson v. Lewis, 78 N.E. 523, 525 (Ohio 1906). This holding was a departure. Back in 1883, the court had decided that an 1880 statute retroactively legalizing tax-inquisitor contracts was not of a general nature. State v. Cappeller, 39 Ohio St. 207, 215 (1883). See also *Thomas v. State ex rel. Gilbert*, 81 N.E. 437 (Ohio 1907) (admitting that *Lewis* was unforeseeable).

216. "Ohio State Journal Wins Its Great Fight against the System of Tax Inquisitors; Graft Knocked Out by Supreme Court," *Ohio State Journal*, June 27, 1906, p. 1. The anti-inquisitor lawsuit trumpeted by the *Ohio State Journal* was from Columbus (Franklin County). See State ex rel. Seymour v. Gilfillan, 15 Ohio Dec. 756 (Ohio Com. Pl. 1905), *reversed in part*, State ex rel. Seymour v. Gilfillan, 19 Ohio C.D. 709 (Ohio Cir. 1905). The two cases decided in *Lewis* were separate from this Franklin County case; they were from Hamilton and Allen Counties. The *Lewis* opinion arguably endorsed some of the criticisms of inquisitors made by the *Ohio State Journal*, but it did so in very oblique language, and such charges were logically irrelevant to its decision. *Lewis*, 78 N.E. at 525.

217. "County Saves Half Million," *Cleveland Plain Dealer*, June 27, 1906, p. 3.
218. "Current Comment," *Ohio Farmer* 110 (July 14, 1906): 22; "Current Comment," *Ohio Farmer* 110 (July 7, 1906): 6.
219. On the timing of legislative sessions, see Warner, *Progressivism in Ohio*, 192. On the upcoming fight, see John C. Hale, "Annual Address," in *Ohio State Bar Association*, vol. 28, *Proceedings of the Twenty-Eighth Annual Session of the Association* (Columbus, OH: Berlin Printing Co., 1907), 96; "Current Comment," *Ohio Farmer* 110 (July 7, 1906): 6.
220. The story of the Ohio legislature's rejection of tax inquisitors at the 1908 session is as follows: A pro-inquisitor house member, James Welker, adopted a "stealth" strategy to achieve his goal. He introduced a bill to restructure the uncontroversial system for contractor collection of already-assessed taxes so as to reinstate the inquisitors in an indirect but effective way. It had long been the practice in Ohio for commission-paid contractors to collect tax debts in cases in which liability had already been determined. Historically, such contractors became involved only after a tax had been assessed and collection attempted in the ordinary course. But Welker's bill would have authorized county officials to place newly discovered taxable property on the delinquent list from which these contractors made collections. This would effectively allow the tax inquisitors, in the guise of ordinary debt collectors, to resume their work of discovering omitted property, though technically they would be paid their commissions not for their labor in discovering the property but for their labor in collecting the consequent tax debts. Practically, the business would be much the same. For the bill, see H.B. 954, 77th General Assembly, 2nd Reg. Sess. (Ohio 1908). For its introduction, see *Journal of the House of Representatives, Second Regular Session, Seventh-Seventh General Assembly of Ohio* (Columbus, OH: F. J. Heer, 1908), 116 [hereinafter *Journal of the [Ohio] House* (1908)]. For explanations of how it could resurrect the tax-inquisitor system, see "Guaranteed Banks," *Newark (OH) Advocate*, Mar. 9, 1908, p. 5; "Shuler Finds Sleeper in Welker's Tax Bill," *Ohio State Journal*, Feb. 9, 1908, p. 1.

    Welker deceptively explained his bill as a mere codification or strengthening of existing law, and the house passed it without anybody raising the issue of tax inquisitors. *Journal of the [Ohio] House* (1908), 154–55; "Shuler Finds Sleeper in Welker's Tax Bill," *Ohio State Journal*, Feb. 9, 1908, p. 1; "Find 'Sleeper' in Welker Bill," *Hamilton (OH) Daily Republican-News*, Feb. 8, 1908, p. 1; "Tax Inquisitor Still Dead," *Ohio State Journal*, May 2, 1908, p. 2. But when it reached the senate, members realized that it could be a Trojan horse to smuggle the inquisition back into Ohio. "Guaranteed Banks," *Newark (OH) Advocate*, Mar. 9, 1908, p. 5; "Shuler Finds Sleeper in Welker's Tax Bill," *Ohio State Journal*, Feb. 9, 1908, p. 1.

    One newspaper predicted that the discovery would "no doubt kill the bill in the senate." "Find 'Sleeper' in Welker Bill," *Hamilton (OH) Daily Republican-News*, Feb. 8, 1908, p. 1. Indeed, the senate instantly delayed proceedings on it. "Taft Victory Is Complete," *Richwood (OH) Gazette*, Feb. 20, 1908, p. 6. A few months later, though, the senate passed a completely revised bill, allowing the county auditor reimbursement for itemized expenses in discovering taxable property, capped at 5 percent of the taxes arising therefrom. (To be exact, the bill was initially changed to one that allowed the county auditor "such reasonable expense" as was necessary to discover unlisted property, then further changed to cap those expenses at 5 percent, in which form it passed the senate 20–13.) *The Journal of the Senate of the State of Ohio, for the Second Regular Session of the Seventy-Seventh General Assembly* (Columbus, OH: F. J. Heer, 1908), 737–38, 762 [hereinafter *Journal of the [Ohio] Senate* (1908)]; see also *Journal of the [Ohio] House* (1908), 918–19 (giving text of the bill as passed by the senate). Some observers interpreted the senate-passed bill as a complete rejection of the tax inquisitors. "New Prison in Sight for Ohio," *Ohio State Journal*, May 1, 1908, p. 1. It is easy to see why they thought this: the 5 percent cap would likely keep anybody from bidding for the job, since it was much lower than the maximum or mandatory compensation of tax ferrets anyplace else in America. But other lawmakers, while acknowledging that the bill was greatly watered down compared to the pre-1906 regime, still feared that it might lead to reinstatement of the inquisitors. "Tax Inquisitor Still Dead," *Ohio State Journal*, May 2, 1908, p. 2 (quoting Chamberlain's later speech on the bill, stating that it "seeks to resurrect the tax inquisitor system").

The house, now confronting the issue self-consciously for the first time during the session, rejected the senate-passed bill, 52–9. The majority apparently included some representatives who disliked the bill because they thought it too likely to revive the inquisition (e.g., Chamberlain), but also some who disliked it because they thought it not likely enough to revive it (e.g., Welker). For the house vote, see *Journal of the [Ohio] House* (1908), 919–20. On Chamberlain and Welker's views about tax inquisitors, see "Tax Inquisitor Still Dead," *Ohio State Journal*, May 2, 1908, p. 2.

The house vote resulted in the original "stealth" bill—which would have resurrected the tax inquisitors in full—going back to the senate. In a testament to the depth of opposition to a full-blown return to the system, the senate rejected that version 34–0. *Journal of the [Ohio] Senate* (1908), 787–88; see also "New Prison in Sight for Ohio," *Ohio State Journal*, May 1, 1908, p. 1 (stating that "the senate refused to recede from its stand against the inquisitors").

Those who hoped for a compromise made a last-ditch effort by setting up a conference committee. *Journal of the [Ohio] House* (1908), 930, 936; *Journal of the [Ohio] Senate* (1908), 797. That committee proposed increasing the cap on commissions from 5 percent to 10 percent, but the senate rejected this measure, by a vote of 18–13. *Journal of the [Ohio] Senate* (1908), 828. For the report of this result to the house, see *Journal of the [Ohio] House* (1908), 966. Given the range of options on the table, it is hard to discern the strategic considerations motivating the yes and no votes.

Back in the house, Welker moved that the chamber reconsider its rejection of the 5 percent bill. The "only speech in opposition" to Welker's motion, reported one newspaper, was "brief but effectual": an anti-inquisitor representative conceded that the 5 percent bill was "better" than the stealth bill that would have fully restored the inquisitors, "but even the better bill seeks to resurrect the tax inquisitor system" and therefore had to be defeated. "A chorus of 'noes' killed the motion . . . , and the tax inquisitor system is still dead in Ohio." "Tax Inquisitor Still Dead," *Ohio State Journal*, May 2, 1908, p. 2. (It appears that such motions were not recorded in the house's journal.)

221. Warner, *Progressivism in Ohio*, 198.
222. This is evident from the commentary of the commission that drew up the amendment and reported at the start of the session. *Report of the Honorary Commission . . . to Investigate the Tax System of Ohio*, 37.
223. Warner, *Progressivism in Ohio*, 209n75. On the difficulty of amending the Ohio constitution, see "The Proposed Amendments to the State Constitution," *Ohio Farmer* 83 (May 25, 1893): 416.
224. Warner, *Progressivism in Ohio*, 227–28.
225. For a narrative of the conference, see Clair Wilcox, *Rate Limitation and the General Property Tax in Ohio* (Columbus: Ohio State University, 1922), 26–27. For Harmon's promise (including the quotation), see "Appraisers Ask for Change in Tax System," *Coshocton (OH) Daily Age*, Dec. 16, 1909, p. 1. Contrary to Wilcox, the conference was not called by the State Tax Commission (which did not yet exist) but by the state auditor. "Over One Thousand," *Mansfield (OH) News*, Dec. 15, 1909, p. 1.
226. Localities could go up to a higher maximum limit by way of local referenda, but the total rate could never go above fifteen mills. On the Ohio rate-limit statute (replaced by a revised version in 1911), see Lockhart, "Recent Developments in Taxation in Ohio," 490–91; Lutz, *State Tax Commission*, 486–87; Warner, *Progressivism in Ohio*, 228, 280–81. On how rate limitation was "practically an administration measure," see Lockhart, "Recent Developments in Taxation in Ohio," 490.
227. Wilcox, *Rate Limitation*, 29 (House unanimity); Foote, "Taxation Work and Experience in Ohio," 200 (party platforms).
228. Harmon, "Governor's Message to the 78th General Assembly" (1910), in *Ohio Legislative History, 1909–1913*, ed. James K. Mercer (Columbus, OH: Edward T. Miller Co., 1914), 31; Lockhart, "Recent Developments in Taxation in Ohio," 489.
229. Lockhart, "Recent Developments in Taxation in Ohio," 489. See also ibid., 498.
230. Harley L. Lutz, "The Operation of the Ohio Tax System, as Illustrated by the Experience of Cleveland," in *The Reform of the Ohio Tax System*, ed. Harley L. Lutz and Edwin S. Tood (Columbus: Ohio State University, 1917), 20.
231. Wilcox, *Rate Limitation*, 27–28.
232. Harmon, "Governor's Message," 30. See also Lutz, *State Tax Commission*, 487.
233. On Foote's activities, see Foote, "Taxation Work and Experience in Ohio," 200, 205–06.
234. On Foote and the National Tax Association, see Ajay K. Mehrotra and Joseph J. Thorndike, "From Programmatic Reform to Social Science Research: The National Tax Association and the Promise and Perils of Disciplinary Encounters," *Law and Society Review* 45 (2011): 601–04.
235. Foote, "Taxation Work and Experience in Ohio," 202 (emphasis added). For his condemnation of the inquisitors, see ibid., 192 (quoting Garfield). For his praise of rate limitation, see ibid., 198–201.
236. Ibid., 222.
237. Lockhart, "Recent Developments in Taxation in Ohio," 518. On the sameness of leadership between classification and rate limitation, see ibid., 489.

238. § 81, 1910 Ohio Laws 399, 420–21. See also §§ 111–12, 1910 Ohio Laws at 427–28 (setting forth penalties for disobedience). Under section 81, the commission also had power to "order a re-assessment of the real or personal property in any taxing district, when in the judgment of said commission such property has not been assessed at its true value in money," and it could appoint its own appraisers to do so, though only at the wages of local assessors. It does not seem that this power was used much or at all with respect to personalty; the economists' analyses do not mention it. In addition, section 81 said the commission was to "require county auditors to place upon the tax duplicate any property which may be found to have, for any reason, escaped assessment and taxation," but the auditors were already required to do this, and it does not seem that the commission had any particular capacity to monitor what personalty was going unassessed.

239. Warner, *Progressivism in Ohio*, 229–31; Lockhart, "Recent Developments in Taxation in Ohio," 496; Lutz, *State Tax Commission*, 482, 490.

240. When Ohio Governor James M. Cox in 1914 discussed the (ultimately short-lived) 1913 legislation to centralize personalty assessment, he said: "When the present administration came into power [in 1913] the personal property of individuals and the property of incorporated companies were the only classes of property in this State that were not listed by the Tax Commission, or under its supervision." He added that new legislation in 1913 had been "enacted primarily to extend the jurisdiction of the Tax Commission to the assessment of the two classes of property which had theretofore been inadequately assessed," that is, individual and corporate personalty. See Cox's untitled message, printed in *Journal of the Senate of the Eightieth General Assembly of the State of Ohio: Second Extraordinary Session, Monday July 20, 1914* (Columbus, OH: F. J. Heer Printing Co., 1914), 7–8 [hereinafter Cox Message]. Cox's words clearly indicate that the commission in 1910–13 exercised no control over personalty assessment. Consistent with this, Lutz wrote in 1917 that, although the commission in 1910 had been "given general supervision over the local assessors," in the period 1910–13 "[c]omparatively little use was made of the original supervisory powers by the state tax commission except in connection with the reappraisal and equalization of real estate." Lutz, "Operation of the Ohio Tax System," 18–19. Further, Lutz stated in 1918 that the "equalization of 1910 was confined to real estate, and the commission made no attempt to readjust the personal property returns. Since 1910 no formal equalization of the personalty assessment has been made, and such changes as the commission has ordered have come as the result of appeals." Lutz, *State Tax Commission*, 490. Admittedly, Lutz did speak of how "[m]ore influence has been exerted through the commission's supervision over the original assessment" and said that "[i]n 1911 and again in 1912 the commission brought strong pressure to bear upon the local assessors for a more complete listing and assessment of personal property." Lutz, *State Tax Commission*, 490, 502. But Lutz gave no specifics as to what kind of "pressure" the commission exerted. Given Cox's view that it exercised no control in this period, it seems unlikely that it did more than moral exhortation of the assessors. On this point, Lockhart spoke of how rising personalty assessments after 1910 might

have resulted not only from the rate limitation but also from "the agitation in favor of more honest returns and truer valuations of property," which "affected assessing officials as well as taxpayers." Lockhart, "Recent Developments in Taxation in Ohio," 494. This "agitation," which Lockhart does not link to any bureaucratic accountability structures, may suggest some kind of moral suasion effort.

241. Wilcox, *Rate Limitation*, 31.

242. Ibid., 27; Lockhart, "Recent Developments in Taxation in Ohio," 498.

243. Lockhart, "Recent Developments in Taxation in Ohio," 500–01; see also Lutz, *State Tax Commission*, 487.

244. It was fifteen mills, compared to Iowa's five mills. Brindley, "Five Mill Tax," 588; Lockhart, "Recent Developments in Taxation in Ohio," 490–91. For arguments that the high rate was reducing effectiveness in coaxing returns, see Lutz, "Operation of the Ohio Tax System," 20, 29; Lockhart, "Recent Developments in Taxation in Ohio," 498.

245. 1913 Ohio Laws 786, 786–804. On the system's operation, see Cox Message, 8 (cited in note 240 above). See also Lockhart, "Recent Developments in Taxation in Ohio," 508–09; Warner, *Progressivism in Ohio*, 429–30; Wilcox, *Rate Limitation*, 55.

246. Cox Message, 6–10 (cited in note 240 above).

247. Lutz announced that the new Ohio system was "the most radical administrative change in taxation that has yet been undertaken in the United States." *State Tax Commission*, 503.

248. *Taxation in Ohio: Report of the Civic League of Cleveland 1915* (Cleveland, OH: Civic League of Cleveland, 1915), 7–9. See also Lutz, *State Tax Commission*, 506–07; Warner, *Progressivism in Ohio*, 430–31, 438n21; Lutz, "Operation of the Ohio Tax System," 27.

249. *Report of the Commission on Taxation to the Governor [of Indiana]*, xvi (minority report).

250. 1915 Ohio Laws 246.

251. Oliver C. Lockhart, "The Ohio Tax Situation," *Bulletin of the National Tax Association* 2 (1917): 164.

252. Wilcox, *Rate Limitation*, 55.

253. Lutz, *State Tax Commission*, 504, 517.

254. For these developments, see 1917 Ohio Laws 29; Lutz, "Operation of the Ohio Tax System," 19; Lockhart, "Ohio Tax Situation," 164–65.

255. On Ohio county auditors' softness, see Carver, "Ohio Tax Inquisitor Law," 182, 204, 212. In states like Indiana and Wisconsin, moving assessment from the township to the county level had done little to alter elected administrators' accommodationist attitudes. Mehrotra, "Forging Fiscal Reform," 98.

256. *Report of the Ohio Tax and Revenue Commission* (Columbus, OH: F. J. Heer Printing Co., 1940), 54–55; Heller, "State Income Tax Administration," 13. Rate limitation had remained an official watchword through the 1920s, although the legislature had faced strong demands to create exceptions, and it had begun doing so for broad subjects starting about 1919 (e.g., highway improvement). Wilcox, *Rate Limitation*,

39–42. On Ohio's history of attempts at classification amendments in 1909–1929, see Leland, *Classified Property Tax*, 106–10.

257. On the post-1929 regime's use of banks for assessment and collection, see *Report of the Ohio Tax and Revenue Commission [1940]*, 54–55. On Ohio banks' support for classification up to 1929, see Leland, *Classified Property Tax*, 113. On banks' success in lobbying against disclosure requirements prior to the 1929 classification measure, see Lockhart, "Recent Developments in Taxation in Ohio," 515.

258. The new power of the commission was granted in 1931 Ohio Laws 714, 738. On the overall approach to intangibles assessment, see *Report of the Ohio Tax and Revenue Commission [1940]*, 83.

259. See my discussion in this chapter, text at note 79.

260. Wisconsin Manufacturers' Association, *Wisconsin Should Not Introduce Non-Resident Tax Ferrets*, 4.

261. "Milwaukee Socialists Have Been Unable to Carry Out Their Glittering Promises," *Los Angeles Times*, Nov. 12, 1911, p. 7.

262. On the adoption of the income tax as the preferred alternative to tax-ferreting, see Groves and Goodman, "A Pattern of Successful Property Tax Administration," 419.

263. See my discussion in this chapter, text at note 188 (including discussion in the note itself).

264. T. S. Adams, "The Wisconsin Income Tax," *American Economic Review* 1 (1911): 906–07. See also Mehrotra, "Forging Fiscal Reform," 106.

265. Benson, "History of the General Property Tax," 64; Bullock, "Taxation of Property and Income in Massachusetts," 51.

266. To be exact, it was 1.96 percent. The rate was uniform through all localities, but we need to calculate an average rate to account for progressivity. Note this was the rate on individuals. The rate on corporations was higher, averaging 5.4 percent. T. S. Adams, "The Significance of the Wisconsin Income Tax," *Political Science Quarterly* 28 (1913): 571.

267. *Sixth Biennial Report of the Wisconsin Tax Commission to the Governor and Legislature* (Madison: n.p., 1912), 19 (citing 1910 rate).

268. Charles J. Bullock assumed such a 6 percent rate in his income-tax analysis. "The Operation of the Massachusetts Income Tax," *Quarterly Journal of Economics* 32 (1918): 531.

269. For the Iowa and Ohio rates, see note 244 above.

270. "Tax Law Will Bring Business," *Duluth (MN) News-Tribune*, Oct. 26, 1912, p. 11 (quoting McGovern).

271. Teaford, *Rise of the States*, 56–57; Adams, "Wisconsin Income Tax," 908–09; Adams, "Significance of the Wisconsin Income Tax," 572–73.

272. Adams, "Significance of the Wisconsin Income Tax," 574.

273. Mehrotra, "Forging Fiscal Reform," 106–07, Teaford, *Rise of the States*, 56–57; Adams, "Significance of the Wisconsin Income Tax," 577.

274. Heller, "State Income Tax Administration," 139; Penniman and Heller, *State Income Tax Administration*, 129.

275. Adams, "Significance of the Wisconsin Income Tax," 577. For a similar point about Ohio in 1913–15, see Lockhart, "Recent Developments in Taxation in Ohio," 514 (on the commission's effort to procure "lists of stockholders in foreign corporations").

276. "Tax Law Will Bring Business," *Duluth (MN) News-Tribune*, Oct. 26, 1912, p. 11 (quoting McGovern).

277. Penniman and Heller, *State Income Tax Administration*, 137.

278. Brownlee, *Federal Taxation in America*, 70.

279. Penniman and Heller, *State Income Tax Administration*, 217–22. Heller found in interviews in 1940 that "a couple of states" had received access informally before 1925. Ibid., 217.

280. Dixwell L. Pierce, "The Use by State Authorities of Federal Income Tax Returns," *Taxes* 17 (Nov. 1939): 637.

281. Penniman and Heller, *State Income Tax Administration*, 245–46.

282. *Sixth Biennial Report of the Wisconsin State Tax Commission* (Madison: n.p., 1912), 18–20.

283. Teaford, *Rise of the States*, 56–57; Mehrotra, "Forging Fiscal Reform," 102–07.

284. Adams, "Significance of the Wisconsin Income Tax," 575–77.

285. *Sixth Biennial Report of the Wisconsin State Tax Commission*, 41.

286. Teaford, *Rise of the States*, 51 (citing Harley Lutz); *Report of the Commission on Taxation to the Governor [of Indiana]*, xxv (minority report of economist William W. Rawles); Leland, *Classified Property Tax*, 132.

287. Harley L. Lutz, "The Progress of State Income Taxation since 1911," *American Economic Review* 10 (1920): 81.

288. Mark Graves, "Administration of State Taxes as Viewed by an Administrator," *Annals of the American Academy of Political and Social Science* 183 (1936): 195.

289. Heller, "State Income Tax Administration," 132. See also Penniman and Heller, *State Income Tax Administration*, 119.

290. Heller, "State Income Tax Administration," 86–87. See also ibid., 86n2 (quoting top Indiana tax official on need for tax officers to act as "salesmen"); Penniman and Heller, *State Income Tax Administration*, 84 (similar passage).

291. For additional information on the eventual decline of tax ferrets in other states, see Parrillo diss., 729–41.

CHAPTER 6: FEDERAL TAXATION

1. For estimates covering the federal level and states and localities nationwide for 1840 through 1890, see John Joseph Wallis, "American Government Finance in the Long Run: 1790 to 1990," *Journal of Economic Perspectives* 14 (2000): 65. For estimates covering the federal level plus two states and the localities therein for 1794–96, see H. James Henderson, "Taxation and Political Culture: Massachusetts and Virginia, 1760–1800," *William and Mary Quarterly*, 3rd ser., 47 (1990): 112.

2. Public-land sales and other nontax receipts accounted for more than 20 percent of federal revenue in only eleven years from 1801 through 1900. *HSUS* series Ea588 through series Ea592.

3. For relative proportions of customs and internal revenue over time, see *HSUS* series Ea588 through series Ea593. See generally W. Elliott Brownlee, *Federal Taxation in America: A Short History*, 2nd ed. (Cambridge: Cambridge University Press, 2004).

4. For the nickname, see S. Rep. No. 42–227, at 228 (1872); 2 Cong. Rec. 4808 (1874) (Sen. Alcorn); ibid., 4813 (Sen. Edmunds); David A. Wells, *Congress and Phelps, Dodge & Co.: An Extraordinary History* (New York: n.p., 1875), 137 (quoting the *Dubuque (IA) Telegram*); "The President's One-Term Pledge and Civil-Service Reform," *Nation* 24 (June 7, 1877): 333.

5. Proponents of abolishing moieties for customs officers in 1874 invoked, as an analogy, the abolition of such rewards for internal-revenue officers in 1872. Hearings (1874), 53, 59–60, 64; 2 Cong. Rec. 4038 (1874) (Rep. Beck); ibid., 5228 (Rep. Roberts).

6. The most extensive discussion is in R. Elberton Smith, *Customs Valuation in the United States: A Study in Tariff Administration* (Chicago: University of Chicago Press, 1948), 104–17, which briefly cites the 1874 hearings (ibid., 116), though not the debates. Smith rightly identifies certain developments of the 1860s—new investigatory powers and the assignment of special agents—as factors driving overzealous enforcement, but he unfairly attributes these developments to the greedy machinations and lobbying of the officers themselves, slighting the very real enforcement problems that arose from Congress's demand for wartime revenue and protection. Smith pays almost no attention to the problem of distinguishing intentional underpayments from mistaken ones, nor does he address the question of what kind of institutions are necessary to make that distinction. He misses key issues like mistakes of law and the advent of the "whole invoice" rule. And he ignores the tension between adversarialism and voluntary compliance. Overall, his treatment is a fairly literal recital of the key statutes and the main conclusions of the various investigations. As to the Phelps Dodge case, Smith excuses the company too easily, adopting (ibid., 114) the overly indulgent view that the firm conformed to the spirit of the customs laws. See my discussion in this chapter, text at notes 31–33 (including discussion in the notes themselves).

   For briefer treatments of the story, often narrated superficially in terms of corruption, see John Dean Goss, *The History of Tariff Administration in the United States*, 2nd ed. (New York: Columbia University, 1897), 69–71; William J. Hartman, "Politics and Patronage: The New York Custom House, 1852–1902" (Ph.D. diss., Columbia University, 1952), 186–91; Ari Hoogenboom, *Outlawing the Spoils: A History of the Civil Service Reform Movement, 1865–1883* (Urbana: University of Illinois Press, 1961), 104–05, 130–32; David M. Jordan, *Roscoe Conkling of New York: Voice in the Senate* (Ithaca, NY: Cornell University Press, 1971), 210–11; Richard Lowitt, *A Merchant Prince of the Nineteenth Century: William E. Dodge* (New York: Columbia University Press, 1954), 275–83; Thomas C. Reeves, *Gentleman Boss: The Life of Chester Alan Arthur* (New York: Knopf, 1975), 59, 81–84; Mark Wahlgren Summers, *The Era of Good Stealings* (New York: Oxford University Press, 1993), 175, 244; Leonard D. White, *The Republican Era, 1869–1901: A Study in Administrative History* (New York: Macmillan, 1958), 123–26.

7. Perhaps the only scholar who accords adequate respect to the mid-nineteenth-century customhouse as a site of modern state power—and to the bounty as an instrument of

that power—is Andrew Wender Cohen, in a brief but important discussion in a recent article, though he does not recognize bounty abolition itself as an attempt (by an alternative route) at state-building. "Smuggling, Globalization, and America's Outward State, 1870–1909," *Journal of American History* 97 (2010): 380–82, 393–94. Gautham Rao analyzes customhouses as important sites of state power, but his focus is confined to the early republic, and his rendition of the officers during that period—which I find convincing—is as local notables, engaged in what I would term *familiar imposition.* "The Creation of the American State: Customhouses, Law, and Commerce in the Age of Revolution" (Ph.D. diss., University of Chicago, 2008).

8. Referring to the most notorious of the moiety-seeking enforcers, one witness declared that "his harshness, his severity, his injustice, is the legitimate, the necessary product and result of the law. Indeed I believe the same law, carried out to its full extent . . . will make a hundred men just like him." Hearings (1874), 89. Other advocates for the merchants made this same distinction between individuals and institutions. Ibid., 45, 113, 125, 154. "It is not pretended," explained the floor manager for the abolition bill in the House, "that [the officers' enforcement actions] have not been made in accordance with the letter of the law." Rather, "[t]he system works the mischief." 2 Cong. Rec. 4030 (1874) (Rep. Roberts). Other congressmen concurred. Ibid., 4036 (Rep. Beck), 4046 (Rep. Kasson), 4807 (Sen. Alcorn), 4822 (Sen. Edmunds), 5238 (Rep. Tremain). To be sure, bounty-seeking had some critics who couched the matter in terms of crime or venality. The strongest accusation came from the merchant lobbyist John Hopper. Hearings (1874), 139. But even Hopper recognized that there was some argument about the matter. Quoting a petition he authored, he referred to "a forced construction of the loosely-drawn statutes in revenue-matters" by which "these practices would seem in some measure authorized." Ibid., 135. Also, two congressmen made statements in tension with their other statements (cited above) that the officers had not acted illegally. 2 Cong. Rec. 3667 (1874) (Sen. Edmunds) ("evils . . . chiefly grow out of administration instead of out of law"); ibid., 4306 (Beck) ("corrupt espionage and robbery"). Rep. Fernando Wood was ambiguous about whether official conduct had been illegal, or merely venal and exploitative of the law's imperfections. 2 Cong. Rec. 4043 (1874) (referring to "the legal justification which exists in favor of these corrupt officials and which gives them legal sanction in their wrongdoing"). See also ibid., 2056, 4041.

9. H.R. Exec. Doc. No. 27–212, at 212 (1842).

10. For receipts of the New York customhouse in fiscal 1856–57, see Treasury Report 1860, p. 119. For nationwide customs receipts, see *HSUS* series Ea589.

11. Calculations based on Treasury Report 1873, pp. 371–72.

12. In terms of fines, penalties, and forfeitures (from which moieties came), Boston was the only customhouse that came close to New York. Even then, it never exceeded about two-thirds of the New York total and usually had far less. E.g., Treasury Report 1869, p. 72; S. Misc. Doc. No. 43–114, at 2–5 (1874); H.R. Exec. Doc. No. 43–124, at 90, 110 (1874); Treasury Report 1875, p. 602.

13. Treasury Report 1877, pp. xxix–xxx. For contrasts between the 1870s and the early republic, when smuggling had been more prevalent, see 2 Cong. Rec. 2055–56 (1874) (Rep. Wood); Hearings (1874), 141.

14. During the early republic, ad valorem duties accounted for about 30–50 percent of customs receipts. See the figures reported throughout *American State Papers, Finance* (Washington, DC: Gales and Seaton, 1832–58). E.g., ibid., 2:375–76 (about 29 percent in 1809); ibid., 4:378 (about 48 percent in 1822). Congress in 1846 committed itself to ad valorem duties exclusively, but in 1861 it reintroduced specific duties on several goods, though keeping ad valorem duties on numerous others. Smith, *Customs Valuation*, 95, 102, 121n28. This mixed regime remained in place into the 1900s.

15. On the respective treatment of purchased and nonpurchased goods, see Hearings (1874), 9–11. On confusion and frequent change in the realm of additional charges, see ibid., 106–07, 119; S. Misc. Doc. No. 43–36, at 4 (1874). On the rule that purchased goods must pay on the basis of purchase price or market value, whichever is higher, see Smith, *Customs Valuation*, 63, 95–96, 113, 132–35. For more on that rule, see Hearings (1874), 28–29, 102, 121, 160, 201, 239–40.

16. H.R. Exec. Doc. No. 27–212, at 211 (1842) (stating that the real check on undervaluation ought to be the appraisement system).

17. Hearings (1874), 112; Hearings (1865), 4, 5, 80.

18. Hearings (1865), 5, 100.

19. S. Misc. Doc. No. 43–36, at 4 (1874); Hearings (1865), 73, 81, 85.

20. Hearings (1874), 276; Hearings (1865), 5, 72, 100.

21. Smith, *Customs Valuation*, 118–20; Hearings (1874), 239; Hearings (1865), 4.

22. Smith, *Customs Valuation*, 128–32.

23. Observe the continuing importance of invoices in the investigations of 1909–13. See my discussion in this chapter, text at notes 224–28.

24. Apart from these civil sanctions, the fact that importers had to swear to their invoices meant that intentional inaccuracy made them criminally liable for perjury under some circumstances, though they were rarely prosecuted for that. Hearings (1874), 222–23.

25. Importers with invoices reflecting submarket purchases could avoid the penalty if, when filling out their entry forms, they "marked up" the prices to match market value and paid duty thereon. E.g., Smith, *Customs Valuation*, 95.

26. On the penalty-forfeiture distinction, see Hearings (1874), 201. On the requirement of fraudulent intent for forfeiture, see § 22, 1 Stat. 29, 42 (1789) ("with design to defraud"); § 66, 1 Stat. 627, 677 (1799) ("with design to evade"). The new collection statute of 1863 imposed forfeiture for "knowingly" making entry of goods by a "false" document. § 1, 12 Stat. 737, 738 (1863). The courts construed it to impose the same requirement of fraudulent intent as before. Cliquot's Champagne, 70 U.S. 114, 144 (1865) (approving the trial judge's instruction, reprinted in ibid., 126–27); In re Twelve Hundred & Nine Quarter Casks, etc., of Wine, 24 F. Cas. 398, 406–07 (S.D.N.Y. 1868).

27. On the "goods or their value" option, in both the 1799 and 1863 statutes, see *United States v. Baker*, 24 F. Cas. 953, 954 (S.D.N.Y. 1871).

28. Ring v. Maxwell, 58 U.S. 147 (1851), construing § 3, 9 Stat. 3, 3–4 (1846).

29. For a compilation of newspaper commentary, see Wells, *Congress and Phelps, Dodge & Co.*

30. Congressmen referred to the case as "the capital on which the enterprise of this [reform] bill proceeds," 2 Cong. Rec. 4819 (1874) (Sen. Edmunds), "the pivotal case,"

ibid., 4033 (Rep. Beck), and "the ground-work" for the reform bill, ibid., 5221 (Rep. Butler).

31. The clearest description of the irregularity was by former U.S. attorney Noah Davis. Hearings (1874), 239–40. Still, in my view, Davis gave the firm too much credit. He disagreed strongly, as a matter of policy and morals, with the rule that purchased goods were to be taxed on the higher of either the purchase price or the market price. This normative view led Davis to state (too generously) that the firm was obeying the "spirit" of the law, obscuring what is otherwise the clear gravamen of his testimony— that Phelps Dodge paid less than it legally owed. The same goes for Smith, who tracks Davis's explanation. *Customs Valuation*, 113–14. For Dodge's own explanation of the irregularity, see Hearings (1874), 21. See also ibid., 30 (admitting "we erred; we should have been more correct").

32. For Dodge's overpayment claim, see Hearings (1874), 26, 29. For repetition of it, see 2 Cong. Rec. 4036 (1874) (Rep. Beck), 4682 (Sen. Scott), 4712 (Sen. Bayard).

33. For the amounts, see Bliss's letter, printed in Wells, *Congress and Phelps, Dodge & Co.*, appendix, p. 80; Hearings (1874), 23–24. On the changing legal doctrines regarding the extent of forfeiture, see my discussion in this chapter, text at notes 77–83.

34. The figures are mostly drawn from H.R. Exec. Doc. No. 43–124, at 78–79 (1874). Note that Jayne's share would be the informer's share, of which he actually pocketed one-third. Hearings (1874), 192. Also, the U.S. attorney was entitled to 2 percent of the gross total. § 11, 12 Stat. 737, 741 (1863).

35. U.S. Attorney Davis and Treasury Secretary Boutwell (neither of whom received any moieties in the case) both thought the case superficially bore this red flag when they first encountered it, even if there turned out to be no fraud in the end. Hearings (1874), 235–36; 2 Cong. Rec. 4684–85 (1874) (Sen. Boutwell).

36. Hearings (1874), 171, 175, 248–49. There seems to be no evidence for the assertion of one congressman that the officers knew of the overpayments and deliberately concealed them. 2 Cong. Rec. 4033 (1874) (Rep. Beck).

37. Hearings (1874), 20, 23. Dodge said the smallness of the lost duties was kept "from us purposely." Ibid., 24.

38. Special Agent Jayne admitted that knowledge of the overpayment might have changed his mind as to intent. Hearings (1874), 171, 175.

39. Hearings (1874), 223; 2 Cong. Rec. 4718 (1874) (Sen. Stockton).

40. Customs statutes imposed forfeiture for many kinds of irregularities, one of which was undervaluation. In *Barlow v. United States*, 32 U.S. 404, 410–11 (1832), a case regarding an irregularity besides undervaluation, the Supreme Court found that a mistake of law was no defense. The provision imposing forfeiture for the irregularity in *Barlow*, § 84, 1 Stat. 627, 694 (1799), required intent even more clearly than did the undervaluation provisions of 1799 or 1863 (on which see note 26 above). Clearly, therefore, the undervaluation provisions also would recognize no such defense. This was confirmed by two opinions of Supreme Court justices riding circuit and construing the 1863 provision. 146,650 Clapboards, 27 F. Cas. 274, 276 (C.C.D.R.I. 1874) (Clifford, J.); Sinn v. United States, 22 F. Cas. 226, 227 (C.C.S.D.N.Y. 1878) (Waite, C.J.). See also Hearings (1874), 239–41.

41. For the relevant statutory provision, including citations to its many prior versions, see USRS § 5292. Though it was not obvious from the statutory language, the provision was understood to empower the secretary to remit or mitigate not only for mistakes of fact but also for mistakes of law. Morris v. United States, 23 U.S. 246, 297 (1825) (Johnson, J., concurring); Hearings (1874), 240–41.

42. When asked to remit or mitigate, the secretary had great discretion. If the merchant had violated the law by mistake, the secretary would "have power to mitigate or remit" the punishment, or "any part thereof," "upon such terms or conditions [as] he may deem reasonable and just." USRS § 5292. His decision was unreviewable. *Morris*, 23 U.S. at 284–85. In making this highly discretionary decision, the secretary and his subordinates in Washington were in the habit of relying on information from moiety-seeking officers at the port, such as the special agents, which they were not inclined to second-guess. Hearings (1874), 45, 50. But see ibid., 218–19 (witness asserting that at least some of these officers are not, in fact, involved in the proceedings). Officers were in a position to control (and, potentially, to manipulate) information the secretary received about the case. Treasury Report 1869, p. vi; Treasury Report 1874, p. 222. Further, officers sometimes engaged Republican bosses as counsel or advisers. In the Phelps Dodge case, Special Agent Jayne had Representative Benjamin Butler as his advocate. Hearings (1874), 23–24, 173. And the officers were informally advised by Senator Roscoe Conkling. Hearings (1874), 226, 233, 247. Given all this, merchants lost confidence that the remission and mitigation process could protect them. Ibid., 29, 48, 124, 233; 2 Cong. Rec. 4033 (1874) (Rep. Beck). It should be noted this was not a simple matter of Republican politicians mistreating Democratic merchants. Dodge and his top ally Jackson Schultz were both Republicans. Hearings (1874), 233; 2 Cong. Rec. 4035 (1874) (Rep. Beck).

43. E.g., 2 Cong. Rec. 4038 (1874) (Rep. Beck); S. Misc. Doc. No. 43–36, at 3 (1874); Treasury Report 1874, p. 222; Hearings (1874), 84.

44. Hearings (1874), 43, 50.

45. E.g., ibid., 84, 108, 114, 130; 2 Cong. Rec. 4042 (1874) (Rep. Wood). Virtually alone, U.S. Attorney Bliss defended rigid enforcement on the ground that it caused merchants to invest more in correcting mistakes. Hearings (1874), 202.

46. Former U.S. Attorney Davis testified before Congress that Phelps Dodge was "led into the error which they committed, (and which was a plain, palpable violation of the statute,) by the idea which their foreign correspondent had, which they did not know enough of the law to be able to correct," and probably also by a U.S. consul's erroneous suggestion that the firm was "doing what the law required." Hearings (1874), 240. Davis further told Congress that he warned the officers that the smallness of the duties lost was likely to convince a jury that Phelps Dodge did not deserve to be punished, meaning that—although the mistake of law was no legal defense—the jury was likely to defy the law and let the firm off. Since the only way to prevent such jury nullification was to convince the judge to direct a verdict in favor of forfeiture, Davis advised the officers to settle the case rather than take the risk. Ibid., 238, 248.

47. Hearings (1874), 25, 226.

48. 2 Cong. Rec. 4682 (1874) (Sen. Scott). For similar complaints about other cases, see Hearings (1867), 279–80; Hearings (1874), 267–70, 276–77.

49. The judge of New York City's U.S. District Court instructed his juries that the size of the undervaluation, though not legally dispositive, was probative evidence of the merchant's intent. In re Twelve Hundred & Nine Quarter Casks, etc., of Wine, 24 F. Cas. 398, 406–07 (S.D.N.Y. 1868). Others agreed. Hearings (1874), 32–33, 115–16, 217–18.

50. Hearings (1874), 274–75. Also, a small undervaluation could move goods into a different class, which might dramatically affect duty. Ibid.

51. Hearings (1874), 55, 103, 167, 214; 2 Cong. Rec. 4681 (1874) (Sen. Sherman); ibid., 4818 (Sen. Conkling, quoting A. T. Stewart); Treasury Report 1874, p. xxvii.

52. 2 Cong. Rec. 4822 (1874) (Sen. Edmunds).

53. Hearings (1874), 50. See also ibid., 33–34.

54. Ibid., 208. To be exact, moieties had been in place since 1789 "except a brief period" from 1846 to 1849. Ibid. The Treasury Department had construed a poorly drafted statute of 1846 to take away moiety rights from customs officers, but a U.S. District Court ruled (persuasively, I think) that this was a drafting error and should be ignored. Hooper v. Fifty-One Casks of Brandy, 12 F. Cas. 465, 468 (D. Maine 1848). The department followed the judge's construction from 1849 on.

55. Hearings (1874), 63–64. See also ibid., 58–59.

56. Rao, "Creation of the American State," esp. 1–22, 119–44.

57. Gautham Rao, "Customhouses, Coercion, and Consent: Collecting Revenue in the Early American Republic" (*Journal of Policy History* Conference, Columbus, OH, June 3–6, 2010). This research will appear in Rao's book *At the Water's Edge: Customhouses, Governance and the Origins of the Early American State* (University of Chicago Press, forthcoming).

58. Goss, *History of Tariff Administration in the United States*, 88–89.

59. See my discussion in this chapter, text at notes 119–26 and at figure 6.1.

60. Rao, "The Creation of the American State," 74–86. The law against customs officers being financially concerned with imports was not enforced. Ibid., 141. On the theoretical concept of a regime of notables, focusing on the justices of the peace in England, see Weber, *ES*, 2:1059–64.

61. Jerry L. Mashaw, *Creating the Administrative Constitution: The Lost One Hundred Years of American Administrative Law* (New Haven, CT: Yale University Press, 2012), 297 (citing Rao). On notable rule generally in America during this period, see also William E. Nelson, "Officeholding and Powerwielding: An Analysis of the Relationship between Structure and Style in American Administrative History," *Law and Society Review* 10 (1976): 191–99.

62. For background, see Nelson, "Officeholding and Powerwielding," 206–20; Martin Shefter, "Party, Bureaucracy, and Political Change in the United States," in *Political Parties and the State: The American Historical Experience* (Princeton, NJ: Princeton University Press, 1994), 63–72.

63. The data are as follows:

- John Lamb (1789–97), merchant. *ANB*.

- Joshua Sands (1797–1802), merchant. Leonard Benardo and Jennifer Weiss, *Brooklyn by Name: How the Neighborhoods, Streets, Parks, and More Got Their Names* (New York: New York University Press, 2006), 51.

- David Gelston (1802–21), merchant. James Monroe to Thomas Jefferson, Mar. 23, 1801, in *The Writings of James Monroe*, ed. Stanislaus Murray Hamilton (New York: G. P. Putnam's Sons, 1900), 3:274.

- Jonathan Thompson (1821–30), merchant. *The Memorial History of the City of New-York*, ed. James Grant Wilson (New York: New York History Co., 1893), 4:540.

- Samuel Swartwout (1830–38), "soldier, merchant, speculator, and politician." *Dictionary of American Biography*, ed. Dumas Malone (New York: Charles Scribner's Sons, 1936), 9:238–39. Swartwout's preappointment career was too various to categorize him as a merchant.

- Jesse Hoyt (1838–41), lawyer. William L. MacKenzie, *The Lives and Opinions of Benj'n Franklin Butler . . . and Jesse Hoyt* (Boston: Cook and Co., 1845), 13.

- Edward Curtis (1841–44), lawyer. "Biographical Directory of the United States Congress," http://bioguide.congress.gov/biosearch/biosearch.asp (last accessed Aug. 3, 2012).

- Cornelius P. Van Ness (1844–46), lawyer. *The Twentieth Century Biographical Dictionary of Notable Americans*, ed. Rossiter Johnson (Boston: Biographical Society, 1904), vol. 10. No page numbers; see alphabetical entry.

- Cornelius W. Lawrence (1846–50), merchant. "Biographical Directory of the United States Congress."

- Hugh Maxwell (1850–53) lawyer. Marian Gouverneur, *As I Remember: Recollections of American Society during the Nineteenth Century* (New York: D. Appleton and Co., 1911), 44.

- Greene C. Bronson (1853–54), lawyer. Hartman, "Politics and Patronage," 40. For the full cite to this source, see note 6 above.

- Heman J. Redfield (1854–58), lawyer. Ibid., 50–51.

- Augustus Schell (1858–61), lawyer. Ibid., 62–63.

- Hiram Barney (1861–65), lawyer. Ibid., 88–89.

- Simeon Draper (1865), merchant; auctioneer. Ibid., 113.

- Preston King (1865), lawyer. Ibid., 119–20.

- Charles P. Clinch (1865–66), career customs officer. Ibid., 125.

- Henry A. Smythe (1866–69), manufacturing, dry goods, and banking. Ibid., 127–28.

- Moses H. Grinnell (1869–70), merchant. Ibid., 150–51.

- Thomas Murphy (1870–71), manufacturing; war contractor. Ibid., 159.

- Chester A. Arthur (1871–78), lawyer. ANB.

64. Hearings (1874), 116.

65. This is an example of how the Jacksonian patronage system—though usually conceived as the exact opposite of rational bureaucracy—actually furthered some of the classic features of bureaucracy, in this case the separation between person and office.

See Matthew A. Crenson, *The Federal Machine: Beginnings of Bureaucracy in Jacksonian America* (Baltimore: Johns Hopkins University Press, 1975).

66. H.R. Exec. Doc. No. 27–212, at 57, 216, 225, 231–32, 244, 250, 270 (1842); see also the separately paginated supplement appended to this document, pp. 29, 32, 36–37.
67. One investigator concluded there was a conspiracy between Hoyt and the manufacturers. H.R. Exec. Doc. No. 27–212, at 212–24, 243 (1842). Two other investigators said the manufacturers did nothing improper, but they did not deny that Hoyt acted in the manufacturers' interests. Ibid., 57–58.
68. Printed in H.R. Exec. Doc. No. 27–212, at 21 (1842). See also ibid., 244, 260 (quoting Hoyt's complaints about lack of support in the trading classes and among juries, which often included merchants).
69. H.R. Exec. Doc. No. 27–212, at 57, 224–26 (1842).
70. Sidney Ratner, *The Tariff in American History* (New York: Van Nostrand, 1972), 13 (rate in 1816), 15 (1824), 19 (1832), 20–21 (1833–42), 22 (1842), 24 (1846), 26 (1857). For most of the rates he gives, Ratner says he is referring to ad valorem rates. The *HSUS* ratio of total duties to total dutiable imports (which covers not only ad valorem but also specific duties) varies somewhat from Ratner's figures. See *HSUS* series Ee430. Since ad valorem duties were much harder to enforce and were therefore associated with moieties, I rely on Ratner's numbers.
71. Ratner, *Tariff*, 17.
72. On enforcement difficulty in New York, see F. W. Taussig, *The Tariff History of the United States* (New York: G. P. Putnam's Sons, 1888), 103–04.
73. Ratner, *Tariff*, 30, 33–35.
74. White, *Republican Era*, 123.
75. Ratner, *Tariff*, 21, 22, 24, 26.
76. Note also the temporary unavailability of moieties from about 1846 to 1849. See my discussion in note 54 above.
77. § 66, 1 Stat. 627, 677 (1799) ("if any goods . . . shall not be invoiced according to the actual cost thereof . . . with design . . . all such goods . . . shall be forfeited").
78. § 4, 4 Stat. 409, 410 (1830) ("if such package or invoice be made up with intent . . . to evade . . . the same shall be forfeited"); Buckley v. United States, 45 U.S. 251, 262 (1846); United States v. Sixty-Seven Packages of Dry Goods, 58 U.S. 85, 94 (1854) (Campbell, J., dissenting).
79. § 1, 12 Stat. 737, 738 (1863).
80. Two Hundred and Fifty Barrels of Molasses v. United States, 24 F. Cas. 437, 443 (C.C.D.S.C. 1869) (Chase, C.J.).
81. Six Cases of Silk Ribbons, 22 F. Cas. 247, 252 (S.D.N.Y. 1869). See also Hearings (1874), 212.
82. Calculated from the data in Hearings (1874), 50–51.
83. Regarding Phelps Dodge, see 2 Cong. Rec. 4039 (1874) (Rep. Beck); ibid., 4042 (Rep. Wood); ibid., 4682 (Sen. Scott); ibid., 4712 (Sen. Morrill); ibid., 4712 (Sen. Bayard); ibid., 5236 (Rep. Tremain). Regarding other cases, see Hearings (1874), 115, 119, 138, 259–66; Hearings (1867), 300–02. Draconian though it was, there was at least an arguable rationale for this approach. As the U.S. attorney for New York City

contended, it was easier to conceal the undervaluation of certain items by including them in an invoice with many other correctly valued items. Hearings (1874), 213. This meant the forfeiture of the whole invoice made sense, in that an evader faced an ever-worse punishment the more he tried to camouflage his wrongdoing.

84. The concept of legibility, developed in James C. Scott, *Seeing Like a State: How Certain Schemes to Improve the Human Condition Have Failed* (New Haven, CT: Yale University Press, 1998), is applied to federal investigatory power in the late 1800s and early 1900s in Ken I. Kersch, "The Reconstruction of Constitutional Privacy Rights and the New American State," *Studies in American Political Development* 16 (2002): 61–87. See particularly ibid., 66 (discussing customs statutes of the 1860s and 1870s).

85. §§ 24–27, 1 Stat. 29, 43–44 (1789); §§ 68–71, 1 Stat. 627, 677–78 (1799).

86. § 8, 4 Stat. 583, 592 (1832) (imposing penalty of $50). A penalty would remain in force at least through the reforms of 1890. Goss, *History of Tariff Administration*, 83 (referring to $100 fine).

87. Clifton v. United States, 45 U.S. 242, 245–48 (1846), construing § 71, 1 Stat. 627, 678 (1799), discussed in 2 Cong. Rec. 4683 (1874) (Sen. Bayard).

88. § 7, 12 Stat. 737, 740 (1863). See also Hearings (1874), 197 (noting the judge "ordinarily" grants the warrant).

89. § 2, 14 Stat. 546, 547 (1867).

90. He referred to the bill's "[p]rovisions designed to facilitate the procurement of proof of fraudulent practices" among the "measures" "requiring legislation." H.R. Misc. Doc. No. 37–18, at 8 (1863).

91. E.g., Stockwell v. United States, 23 F. Cas. 116, 120–22 (C.C.D. Maine 1870); In re Twelve Hundred & Nine Quarter Casks, etc., of Wine, 24 F. Cas. 398, 412 (S.D.N.Y. 1868); Hearings (1874), 59, 74; 2 Cong. Rec. 4035 (1874) (Rep. Beck). Goss says seizures of papers were allowed since 1789. *History of Tariff Administration*, 60, 66. But Smith corrects this error. *Customs Valuation*, 107n8. The erroneous view was also set forth by Special Agent Jayne, who said that, prior to 1863, one could obtain a warrant from a mere justice of the peace to seize papers. Hearings (1874), 7; see also ibid., 160–61. Sen. Scott quoted Jayne's statement and called it implausible, since such a legal landscape would have occasioned numerous complaints. 2 Cong. Rec. 4682–83 (1874). Sen. Bayard noted that Jayne was no authority on the law prior to 1863, since he only started doing customs work in 1869. 2 Cong. Rec. 4683 (1874). The erroneous justice-of-the-peace story was repeated in Treasury Report 1885, vol. 2, page lii.

92. Boyd v. United States, 116 U.S. 616, 621–23 (1886).

93. Hearings (1874), 82. See also ibid., 87.

94. Hearings (1874), 85. There may have been stronger safeguards imposed by the U.S. District Court judge in Boston, though apparently not in New York. Ibid., 171, 201.

95. For evidence that officers did this, see Hearings (1874), 93 (quoting Special Agent Jayne's testimony at an 1872 hearing); see also Hearings (1874), 83, 119–20.

96. E.g., Hearings (1864), 78, 82, 265; Hearings (1867), 14–15, 275–76, 296–97, 300, 303–04; Hearings (1874), 155–57.

97. It was common for a seizure of papers to take place in conjunction with a seizure of goods and of the store. For references to such triple seizures, see Hearings (1867),

15, 270, 273, 289, 296, 300, 302–03. The 1863 statute said simply that the government could keep the books as long as necessary, so long as it had the approval of the solicitor of the Treasury at Washington. § 7, 12 Stat. 737, 740 (1863). The solicitor's power was later transferred to the U.S. District Court judge. § 2, 14 Stat. 546, 547 (1867).

98. Hearings (1874), 199.

99. E.g., 2 Cong. Rec. 4029 (1874) (Rep. Roberts) (ten months); S. Rep. No. 42–227, at xcix (1872) (six weeks); ibid., cxiii (about eight months).

100. Hearings (1867) 15, 298; S. Rep. No. 42–227, at xcix (1872); Hearings (1874), 114, 175; 2 Cong. Rec. 4806 (1874) (Sen. Wadleigh).

101. See generally *A History of Enforcement in the United States Customs Service, 1789–1875* (San Francisco: U.S. Customs Service, 1988), 83–102.

102. Smith, *Customs Valuation*, 105–12.

103. The Treasury solicitor first proposed their employment in this vein, abroad and at home, in 1862. Treasury Report 1862, p. 133. By 1869, there were several assigned to fraud prevention, who raked in substantial forfeitures. Treasury Report 1869, p. 71. One congressman said the assignment of special agents to customs fraud began with the Grant administration in 1869. 2 Cong. Rec. 4047 (1874) (Rep. Niblack). By the early 1870s, there were four to seven special agents in New York. Hearings (1874), 180.

104. Hearings (1874), 19, 88, 114, 166.

105. Ibid., 59, 61, 65, 89, 154, 226.

106. "Mr. Boutwell's Exhibit," *New York Tribune*, Dec. 6, 1871, p. 4.

107. Regarding the powers and activities of the three principal officers: The collector could decide whether a firm was suspicious enough for the customhouse to seize and examine its books. Though he might delegate this decision to a deputy, he frequently made it himself. Hearings (1874), 7, 180, 185, 197, 221; Hearings (1864), 34. Because there was little supervision from Washington, noted one congressional committee, "the importer is at the mercy of the collector." Hearings (1867), 12. The naval officer could likewise play a big role. One incumbent of the office, George Denison, asked in 1861 to be put in charge of the seizure business, which he then ran in conjunction with a deputy collector. Hearings (1864), 34. Denison gathered evidence on firms and directed his staff in seizing their books, sometimes personally accompanying them on raids, or examining the books himself. Hearings (1864), 72–74, 240. Collector Barney feared that Denison might be "severe in his judgment of the conduct and motives of importers" and "too anxious to make money out of their alleged delinquencies." Hearings (1864), 34. But Denison won plaudits from several other observers, including a congressional committee that commended his "indefatigable patience and industry in ferreting out and exposing . . . systematized villainies" of undervaluation. Hearings (1865), 4. There is evidence that Denison's successors in the naval office were also active in investigations. Hearings (1867), 279; Hearings (1874), 221, 234–35. Both the naval officer and collector could hear merchants' challenges to allegedly improper seizures by other officers. Hearings (1864), 275; Hearings (1867), 289. Finally, the surveyor, in charge of the customhouse's outdoor business, "generally attend[ed] to the seizures on board ships." Hearings (1864), 240. See also Hearings (1874), 221. This

presumably focused on the concealment of goods in passenger baggage and perhaps misdescription of cargoes by invoice.

The collector, naval officer, and surveyor sometimes acted together: in the case of a firm suspected of false invoicing, once the examination of its books was complete, the three would, as a rule, form a "council" to decide whether to bring a forfeiture suit, consulting with the U.S. attorney in questionable cases. Hearings (1874), 186. During trial, the collector would be consulted regarding "evidence and witnesses." Hearings (1874), 221. In settlement negotiations, the collector was always consulted, and he sometimes did the bargaining himself. Hearings (1867), 76; Hearings (1874), 205, 221.

I do not assign much weight to the statement of former U.S. Attorney Davis that the principal officers left all enforcement work to their subordinates and that moieties therefore had no effect on the principals' behavior. Hearings (1874), 250. A few other observers made similar statements to Davis, but more equivocal than his. Hearings (1874), 45 ("[g]enerally the collector has no personal knowledge of the case"), 65 ("may have had no connection with the matter"); Treasury Report 1871, p. x ("in most of the cases" of enforcement, principals do not perform "special services"). The notion that principals did nothing is flatly contradicted by the evidence I cited earlier in this note. See also 2 Cong. Rec. 4030 (1874) (Rep. Roberts) ("The chief customs officers construe laws, administer them, direct prosecutions, receive propositions for compromise and settlement"). The principals were the gatekeepers of enforcement, deciding which cases went forward. As Davis admitted, the collector had to decide "whether he will order the [U.S.] district attorney to sue," so the collector was "in a great degree a judicial officer." Hearings (1874), 250. Others also referred to the principals (or the collector particularly) as having judgelike power. Hearings (1874), 65, 275; 2 Cong. Rec. 4051 (1874) (Rep. Dawes). More broadly, the principal officers ran the customhouse and had much autonomy in hiring and firing personnel. Hartman, "Politics and Patronage," 16–17. This presumably gave them leverage in setting the tone for the subordinate officers doing the legwork of enforcement. And though the special agents were technically excepted from the principals' control, their instructions said they were to act "in concert with, and under the direction of" the principals, and Special Agent Jayne always consulted the principals before acting. Hearings (1874), 180. To be sure, Collector Chester A. Arthur refused to testify at the Phelps Dodge hearings, claiming to have "no personal knowledge of any of the cases before the committee." Hearings (1874), 179. But he was lying. In fact he had been quite involved. Hearings (1874), 221; Reeves, *Gentleman Boss*, 83. Arthur's true reason for refusing to testify was presumably to avoid public association with a case that had drawn wide criticism. Reeves, *Gentleman Boss*, 83.

108. § 38, 1 Stat. 29, 48 (1789), superseded by the similar § 91, 1 Stat. 627, 697 (1799), which remained in force up to modification in 1867.

109. For examples of nonprincipal officers taking part in enforcement, see Hearings (1865), 4 (deputies to collector and naval officer); *Hooper v. Fifty-One Casks of Brandy*, 12 F. Cas. 465, 466 (D. Maine 1848) (inspectors); and my discussion in this chapter, text at notes 101–03 (special agents).

110. It seems that up to 1867 the distribution of proceeds of forfeitures was a decentralized process conducted by individual courts and collectors in particular ports. Hearings (1874), 12; 2 Cong. Rec. 4030, 4052 (Rep. Roberts) (1874). This may have allowed for variation between ports, depending on the judge or collector, except insofar as the Treasury Department attempted to impose a uniform policy. As of 1848 the Treasury Department said that only private tipsters, not subordinate officers, could present themselves as informers to win moieties. Hooper v. Fifty-One Casks of Brandy, 12 F. Cas. 465, 466 (D. Maine 1848). In that year, however, a U.S. District Court judge in Maine rejected this interpretation of the law. Ibid., 466. Did the Treasury Department follow this ruling? We know that it did so with respect to a separate issue in the same case. Treasury Report 1853, p. 12; see also Hearings (1874), 208–09. But it is not clear whether it did so with respect to subordinate officers' eligibility for informers' shares. For suggestions that the department did allow subordinate officers to share during the period 1848–67, see "The Internal Revenue Law," *New York Times,* May 8, 1869, p. 4; *United States v. One Hundred Barrels of Distilled Spirits,* 27 F. Cas. 300, 302 (D. Mass. 1868); Hearings (1867), 185–87. For suggestions that it did not, see Cong. Globe, 39th Cong., 2nd Sess. 1820 (1867) (Sen. Edmunds); Hearings (1874), 11; Hearings (1864), 77.

111. Up to 1863, the U.S. attorney had no monetary interest in forfeitures, except the modest flat fee that he received for winning any judgment. In 1863, Congress granted him a 2 percent commission on all judgments (including settlements) collected in revenue cases. § 11, 12 Stat. 737, 741 (1863), codified in USRS § 825; Hearings (1874), 215. Sen. Fessenden, shepherding the bill through Congress, said the commission would give the U.S. attorney a salutary "inducement" to make collections. Cong. Globe, 37th Cong., 3rd Sess. 905 (1863). At New York, the U.S. attorney was normally consulted when officers sought a warrant to search a firm's premises or books, and he had to approve before an enforcement suit was discontinued or settled. Hearings (1874), 5, 7, 124–25, 185–86, 197, 210, 215.

112. Cong. Globe, 39th Cong., 2nd Sess. 1819–20 (1867).

113. Cong. Globe, 39th Cong., 2nd Sess. 1820 (1867) (Sen. Edmunds).

114. § 1, 14 Stat. 546, 546 (1867).

115. Cong. Globe, 39th Cong., 2nd Sess. 1820 (1867) (Sen. Edmunds). Edmunds's short speech specifically discussed smuggling rather than undervaluation, but his amendment applied to an officer "making the seizure," and seizures were common in cases of undervaluation. E.g., Twenty-Eight Cases of Wine, 24 F. Cas. 415, 415 (S.D.N.Y. 1867). It is clear from Special Agent Jayne's testimony that, as an officer, he served as informer in undervaluation cases in the 1870s. Hearings (1874), 192, 194; see also ibid., 23.

116. On the Senate, see Cong. Globe, 39th Cong., 2nd Sess. 1820 (1867). In the House, Representative Ross questioned whether moieties were a good idea, but Representative Hooper responded that they were already established, that their "object" was "to make [the officers] more zealous," and that the bill slightly moderated them by ordering that duties be deducted first, not mentioning the clarification about allowing subordinate officers to share. For this colloquy and House passage, see Cong. Globe,

39th Cong., 2nd Sess. 1783 (1867). We can infer a voice vote because the *Congressional Record* lists no division.

117. On the channeling of moieties to officers, with only limited cuts for private informers, see Hearings (1874), 43, 57. See also ibid., 192, 194.
118. Hearings (1874), 33–34.
119. 2 Cong. Rec. 4051 (1874) (Rep. Dawes).
120. Hearings (1874), 130.
121. Ibid., 56.
122. Ibid., 58–59.
123. Ibid., 19. See also 2 Cong. Rec. 2055 (1874) (Rep. Wood).
124. Hearings (1864), 81–82, 86, 264–67. See also ibid., 8, 72–74.
125. Ibid., 277. On Stewart, see *ANB*.
126. Hearings (1867), 13.
127. Calculations based on figures in 2 Cong. Rec. 4030 (1874). Technically the figures are for the collector, but the law awarded identical earnings to the naval officer and surveyor.
128. Hearings (1874), 192.
129. USRS § 160.
130. The name was used in, e.g., *Keck v. United States*, 172 U.S. 434, 459 (1899).
131. Hoogenboom, *Outlawing the Spoils*, 167–74.
132. Ratner, *Tariff*, 33–35.
133. See the reports of these agents throughout Treasury Report 1885, vol. 2.
134. Smith, *Customs Valuation*, 122 (stating penalties were "still a rigorous proposition" after 1874).
135. § 12, 18 Stat. 186, 188 (1874).
136. 2 Cong. Rec. 4824 (1874) (Sherman).
137. 2 Cong. Rec. 4824 (1874) (Sherman).
138. Similar fines and jail terms had previously been available for *forged* invoices. § 19, 5 Stat. 548, 565 (1842) (codified in USRS § 2865); United States v. Sixty-Seven Packages of Dry Goods, 58 U.S. 85, 92–93 (1854). But the 1874 statute covered the much broader category of fraudulent invoices. Fines and jail had also been available prior to 1874 for perjury, but the 1874 statute covered all kinds of fraudulent statements, some of which did not meet perjury's technical definition. Hearings (1874), 222–23.
139. § 13, 18 Stat. at 188–89. The merchant could alternatively give bond for the fines, if satisfactory to the court.
140. 2 Cong. Rec. 4032 (1874) (Rep. Roberts, quoting letter from merchant lobbyist Schultz).
141. § 5, 18 Stat. at 187.
142. 2 Cong. Rec. 4047 (1874) (Rep. Niblack).
143. Brief for the United States at 6, *Boyd v. United States* 116 U.S. 616 (1886) (No. 983).
144. Hearings (1874), 7.
145. This is noted in Brief for the United States at 6, *Boyd v. United States* 116 U.S. 616 (1886) (No. 983).

146. 2 Cong. Rec. 4817 (1874) (Sen. Conkling); ibid., 4825 (Sen. Howe); ibid., 4827 (Sen. Stewart).

147. 2 Cong. Rec. 4828 (1874) (Sen. Bayard).

148. E.g., United States v. Three Tons of Coal, 28 F. Cas. 149, 158 (E.D. Wis. 1875) (ordering production of all a firm's books kept for "spirits and liquors" between certain dates).

149. Compare § 2, 14 Stat. 546, 547 (1867), with § 5, 18 Stat. 186, 187 (1874). See also 2 Cong. Rec. 4684 (1874) (Sen. Scott).

150. *Boyd*, 116 U.S. at 622.

151. *Boyd*, 116 U.S. at 639 (Miller, J., concurring).

152. For the House bill, see 2 Cong. Rec. 4027 (1874). For the very similar Senate bill, see ibid., 4711. On the noncriminal nature of the sanction in the Senate bill, see ibid., 4681 (Sen. Sherman), 4809 (Sen. Stewart), 4810 (Sen. Sargent).

153. 2 Cong. Rec. 4827 (1874).

154. This is consistent with the dicta in *United States v. Auffmordt*, 19 F. 893, 899 (S.D.N.Y. 1884).

155. The relevant statute was 15 Stat. 37 (1868). See John F. Witt, "Making the Fifth: The Constitutionalization of American Self-Incrimination Doctrine, 1791–1903," *Texas Law Review* 77 (1999): 886–87, 904–06.

156. This hypothetical was raised, in a crude and exaggerated manner that would have violated the 1868 statute, in 2 Cong. Rec. 4035 (1874) (Rep. Beck). The scenario may have actually occurred in the *Boyd* case. The account of the government's behavior in Samuel Dash, *The Intruders: Unreasonable Searches and Seizures from King John to John Ashcroft* (New Brunswick, NJ: Rutgers University Press, 2004), 50–56, seems to fly in the face of the 1868 statute but would be lawful if one assumes the government at the criminal stage of the case used other evidence than that obtained by the production order.

157. § 16, 18 Stat. 186, 189 (1874).

158. The Ways and Means Committee apparently got the idea for this provision from Davis, who understood it to establish a mistake-of-law defense. Hearings (1874), 239–41. As the Phelps Dodge case involved a mistake of law, it is understandable that Congress's reform would do this. See also 2 Cong. Rec. 4719 (1874) (Sen. Thurman). Just such a reading of the provision was suggested in *Sinn v. United States*, 22 F. Cas. 226, 227 (C.C.S.D.N.Y. 1878) (Waite, C.J.), and expressly set forth in *United States v. Three Trunks*, 8 F. 583, 585–86 (D. Cal. 1881).

159. One Senator predicted this exact effect. 2 Cong. Rec. 5137 (1874) (Sen. Carpenter). See also ibid., 4718–19 (Sen. Carpenter), 4723 (Sen. Howe). Enforcers after 1874 felt the requirement greatly favored the accused. Treasury Report 1885, vol. 2, pp. 373, 391, 420, 430, 437, 591.

160. § 2, 18 Stat. at 186. The provision took away the moieties of all officers. This included the 2 percent commission of the U.S. attorney. To be sure, a U.S. District Court would later read the statute to leave the U.S. attorney's commission in place. *One Horse*, 27 F. Cas. 266 (S.D.N.Y. 1874). But that decision clearly went against Congress's intent. The statute's moiety-abolishing section 2 was sweeping and surely covered the

commission. Further, the bill's House floor manager declared that, under the bill, "the [U.S.] district attorney has not even a commission to impel him" to overreach. 2 Cong. Rec. 4032 (1874) (Rep. Roberts). Two other members of the Ways and Means Committee, in describing the *existing* enforcement system, expressly criticized the U.S. attorney's 2 percent share but did not criticize the bill for failing to abolish that share, indicating they assumed the bill did abolish it. Ibid., 4042 (Rep. Wood), 4051 (Rep. Dawes). The debate contains nothing to support *One Horse*.

161. Hearings (1874), 34.

162. John C. Hopper, *Examine!!! All Who Are Interested, and Who Is Not? Administration of Customs Collection and National Banking Laws* (New York: J. W. Amerman, 1873), 25–26 (quoting "Regulations of the Treasury Department, instructing the [special] agents"). It should be noted that the act did include a provision denying discretion to customs officers to refrain from enforcing the law "upon detection of any violation." § 15, 18 Stat. at 189. Of course, the predicate of detecting a violation meant that every officer would have to make an initial determination as to whether an undervaluation was intentional, so the provision did not relieve the officers of the need to exercise subjective judgment. Sen. Edmunds, an eminent lawyer with an interest in the customs laws, called the provision "very inconsequential." 2 Cong. Rec. 4718 (1874).

163. 2 Cong. Rec. 4030 (1874).

164. 2 Cong. Rec. 4047 (1874). There were additional calls for a more understanding and less adversarial official attitude toward technical violations, mistakes, and the like. E.g., 2 Cong. Rec. 4037 (1874) (Rep. Beck); ibid., 4051 (Rep. Dawes); Hearings (1874), 43, 124, 130, 135.

165. For the definition of "smuggling," see § 4, 18 Stat. 186, 186 (1874). The amount of a reward was in the Treasury secretary's discretion, capped at one-half the recovery. §§ 3–4, 18 Stat. at 186. Rewards had to come from a dedicated appropriation, which Congress kept very low. Treasury Report 1874, p. xxvii; Treasury Report 1878, p. xxx.

166. As originally reported in the House, the bill repealed the existing power to seize papers (from the 1867 statute), and this repeal was never amended. So the baseline throughout the floor debates was a complete absence of evidence-gathering power. On top of this baseline, the bill initially included the production-order provision. 2 Cong. Rec. 4026 (1874). The bill was then amended to soften the sanction for nonproduction from "confession" of the allegation to a mere jury instruction that nonproduction could be weighed as evidence against the party. Ibid., 4048 (1874) (amendment proposed), 4052 (amendment adopted). Then the entire production-order provision was simply stricken out (by a vote of 97–43). Ibid., 4052. Then the bill passed the House. Ibid., 4052. In the Senate, the Finance Committee restored the production-order provision. Ibid., 4679. But the full Senate struck it out (by a vote of 26–21). Ibid., 4685. The Senate then reinserted the provision (without a recorded vote). Ibid., 4827 (amendment proposed, "a little changed in phraseology"), 4829 (amendment adopted). The House, at the recommendation of the Ways and Means Committee, disagreed to the Senate's reinsertion of the provision. Ibid., 4956. But a five-member conference committee—including Representatives Roberts and

Wood—agreed to the reinsertion, with a slight modification. Ibid., 5132–33. Both chambers agreed to the conference report. Ibid., 5138, 5168.

167. 2 Cong. Rec. 4044 (1874).

168. § 13, 18 Stat. 186, 188–89 (1874).

169. Schultz letter, quoted in 2 Cong. Rec. 4032 (1874) (Rep. Roberts). He was actually understating, since the statute allowed seizure of goods valued at *double* the claimed sum.

170. 2 Cong. Rec. 4032 (1874).

171. Hearings (1874), 141.

172. On Wood's position in the House and his effort to attract reformers and merchants, see Jerome Mushkat, *Fernando Wood: A Political Biography* (Kent, OH: Kent State University Press, 1990), 190, 193–94, 199–203, 205–06.

173. 2 Cong. Rec. 4040–41 (1874).

174. 2 Cong. Rec. 4028–29 (1874). It should be noted that Roberts supported the removal of the production-order provision from the bill. Ibid., 4030. But his concern about that provision likely still drove his desire to temper officers' incentives, since (at the time he made the above remarks), he probably could not predict whether the proposal to remove the provision would succeed, and even if it succeeded, the Senate might reinsert the provision, as indeed it did—a change which the conference committee (of which Roberts was a member) ultimately approved, with a slight modification. Ibid., 4956 (referring to the eighth amendment by the Senate), 5167–68 (conference report).

175. Hearings (1874), 104.

176. Treasury Report 1874, p. 222.

177. 2 Cong. Rec. 4042 (1874).

178. S. Misc. Doc. No. 43–36, at 1 (1874).

179. Hearings (1874), 63.

180. See my discussion in the Introduction, text at notes 110–13.

181. 2 Cong. Rec. 4041 (1874).

182. Hearings (1874), 88.

183. Ibid., 106.

184. S. Misc. Doc. No. 43–36, at 4 (1874).

185. Hearings (1874), 100.

186. S. Misc. Doc. No. 43–36, at 7 (1874).

187. Treasury Report 1874, pp. 222–23. See also 2 Cong. Rec. 4050 (1874) (Rep. Dawes) ("the informer in every position of society, . . . is an odious and despised being"); ibid., 4052 (Rep. Dawes) (referring to Special Agent Jayne as one of the "informers").

188. Treasury Report 1874, p. 224.

189. Hearings (1874), 64.

190. 2 Cong. Rec. 4038 (1874).

191. 2 Cong. Rec. 4029 (1874).

192. 2 Cong. Rec. 4804 (1874). Sargent attacked the bill and predicted bad consequences from its passage. He strongly defended bounties for private informers (saying nothing definitive on bounties for officers). Ibid., 4804–05. He ultimately voted in favor

of the bill, having won (what he believed to be) a strengthening amendment. Ibid., 4827–29.

193. Hearings (1874), 211.

194. Ibid., 208. See also ibid., 5220 (Rep. Butler).

195. 2 Cong. Rec. 4804 (1874). See also ibid., 5138 (Sen. Stewart).

196. For the House vote, see 2 Cong. Rec. 4052 (1874). We can infer a voice vote because the *Congressional Record* lists no division. For the Senate vote, see ibid., 4829. It should be noted that, although the bill passed the Senate by a vote of 39–3 (all three nays being Republicans), a much higher fraction of Republicans (twenty-seven of fifty-two) were recorded as absent than were Democrats (two of nineteen). 2 Cong. Rec. 4829 (1874). (This count excludes the two Liberal Republicans, Orris Ferry and Morgan Hamilton.) How to interpret the absences? As the Senate operated on a quorum of a majority of members (see the U.S. Constitution, art. 1, sec. 5), one cannot view the absences as equivalent to nays. Indeed, at least one absent Republican (the reformist Carl Schurz) was surely in favor of the bill. Absenteeism was generally very high in the Senate during this period. See Richard Forgette and Brian R. Sala, "Conditional Party Government and Member Turnout on Senate Recorded Votes, 1873–1935," *Journal of Politics* 61 (1999): 470–71, 482. And the vote was taken late in the evening, shortly before the Senate adjourned at 8:50 p.m. 2 Cong. Rec. 4829 (1874). It may be that Democrats were more eager than Republicans to be recorded in favor of the bill, since the much-maligned "moiety men" at the time were Republican officeholders.

197. On Roberts, see *ANB*. On Dawes, see *ANB*; Ida M. Tarbell, *The Tariff in Our Times* (New York: Macmillan, 1911), 71–79. On Kasson, see Tarbell, *Tariff in Our Times*, 35–37, 51, 88, 255–56. On Wood, see *ANB*; Tarbell, *Tariff in Our Times*, 84–92. On Beck, see Tarbell, *Tariff in Our Times*, 112, 117, 128. For Dawes speaking in favor of moiety abolition, see, e.g., 2 Cong. Rec. 4051 (1874).

198. See the comments of Roberts and Wood that I cite in this chapter, text at notes 173, 174, 177, 181, 191. To be sure, Roberts and Wood did get into a partisan spat toward the end of the debate, but this did not alter their basic agreement on the bill; it pertained only to the question of which party deserved more credit for it. 2 Cong. Rec. 4052 (1874).

199. 2 Cong. Rec. 4029 (1874).

200. On Simon Cameron's protectionism, see *ANB*. Skepticism was also expressed by Senator William Stewart, a Nevada Republican. 2 Cong. Rec. 5138 (1874). On Stewart's protectionism (more expedient than consistent), see Russell R. Elliott, *Servant of Power: A Political Biography of Senator William M. Stewart* (Reno: University of Nevada Press, 1983), 110, 138, 170, 186. George Edmunds, too, was both a protectionist (see *ANB*) and a skeptic of moiety abolition (see my discussion in note 201 below). On Sherman's protectionism, see Tarbell, *Tariff in Our Times*, 4–5, 114–15, 118.

201. On civil service reformers' support of moiety abolition, see Hoogenboom, *Outlawing the Spoils*, 130. However, Sen. Edmunds, a friend of civil service reformers (see ibid., 59, 101), spoke skeptically about the 1874 bill and absented himself from the vote. 2 Cong. Rec. 4721, 4811–14, 4819–22 (1874).

202. 2 Cong. Rec. 4052 (1874) (passes House without division); ibid., 4829 (passes Senate by a vote of 39–3, with thirty-one absent).

203. Hoogenboom, *Outlawing the Spoils*, 130, 133.
204. For example, Senator John Logan, then a leading opponent of civil service reform, Hoogenboom, *Outlawing the Spoils*, 57, 87, 155, voted for the anti-moiety bill, 2 Cong. Rec. 4829 (1874).
205. Hoogenboom, *Outlawing the Spoils*, 167–74, 254–55; Ronald N. Johnson and Gary D. Libecap, *The Federal Civil Service System and the Problem of Bureaucracy: The Economics and Politics of Institutional Change* (Chicago: University of Chicago Press, 1994), 33–34.
206. On the continued importance of collectors and special agents in anti-fraud enforcement, see Hearings (1911), 184, 192–93.
207. "No Federal Spoils in Murphy's Gift," *New York Times*, Nov. 15, 1912, p. 3.
208. On the exception of special agents from civil service up to 1889, see Treasury Report 1890, p. 880. On the advent of noncompetitive examination for special agents in 1889, see "Evils of the Spoils Plan," *New York Times*, Aug. 22, 1889, p. 1; Treasury Report 1889, p. 827.
209. *Twenty-Sixth Annual Report of the United States Civil Service Commission for the Year Ended June 30, 1909* (Washington, DC: GPO, 1910), 17–18; Treasury Report 1892, p. 830.
210. S. Exec. Doc. No. 53–157 (1894) (listing twenty-eight special agents with dates of appointment; twenty-four having been appointed since Mar. 8, 1885). I use March 8, 1885, as the starting date, because on that date there was a full complement of twenty-eight special agents. Treasury Report 1885, vol. 2, p. xxxviii. For confirmation that the number of agents remained constant at twenty-eight for this period, see 19 Stat. 143, 152 (1876) (setting number at twenty); 20 Stat. 178, 187–88 (1878) (adding eight, raising total to twenty-eight); 26 Stat. 948, 968 (1891) (confirming the total at twenty-eight).
211. *Hearings before Subcommittee of House Committee on Appropriations . . . in Charge of Sundry Civil Appropriation Bill for 1913*, pt. 1 (Washington, DC: GPO, 1912), 449.
212. Treasury Report 1875, p. xxxiii (noting the immediate drop); Goss, *History of Tariff Administration*, 70 (noting that, in Southern District of New York, there were 957 suits producing $3,696,232.53 in 1864–74, but only 254 suits producing $393,774.72 in 1874–84).
213. *HSUS* series Ea589.
214. Treasury Report 1877, pp. xxviii–xxx.
215. Treasury Report 1885, vol. 2, p. lvi. On his trade views, see *ANB*.
216. See his letters to the editor: "The Undervaluation-Scandals," *New York Times*, June 20, 1885, p. 5; "More Facts about Reappraisements," *New York Times*, July 8, 1885, p. 5.
217. Boyd v. United States, 116 U.S. 616 (1886).
218. *Boyd*, 116 U.S. at 623–24. On the public status of distillers' books under the internal revenue laws, see *United States v. Distillery at Petersburg*, 25 F. Cas. 853 (C.C. E.D. Va. 1876) (Waite, C.J.). In *United States v. Mason*, 26 F. Cas. 1189 (N.D. Ill. 1876), a U.S. district court judge held that, if a distiller were to keep a private set of books, the government had just as much right to inspect them as to inspect the ones he submitted to meet the record-keeping requirements. Ibid., 1190–91. *Mason* was repu-

diated in *Boyd*, see 116 U.S. at 637, but only with respect to a separate point (the civil status of forfeiture proceedings), not with respect to the point about private books. Further, *Mason* was cited with respect to private books, with no contrary cases, in *United States Compiled Statutes Annotated 1916*, ed. John A. Mallory (St. Paul, MN: West, 1917), 6:7118. There is a strange absence of reported cases on the applicability of *Boyd* and its required-record exception to the realm of internal revenue. Bernard D. Meltzer, "Required Records, the McCarran Act, and the Privilege against Self-Incrimination," *University of Chicago Law Review* 18 (1951): 715. But it seems from newspaper coverage that internal revenue officers' surveillance of distillers and tobacco-product manufacturers continued to be highly intrusive despite *Boyd*. "An Objectionable Ruling," *Baltimore Sun*, Aug. 28, 1899, p. 8; "Seeing Rum Made," *Boston Daily Globe*, Nov. 10, 1901, p. 25; "New Tobacco Rules," *Baltimore Sun*, July 14, 1907, p. 2.

219. Wilson v. United States, 221 U.S. 361, 380 (1911). For articulation of this broad exception by a state supreme court shortly after *Boyd*, see *State v. Davis*, 108 S.W. 894, 895 (Mo. 1892). For a review of cases on the matter, see the Brief for the United States, at 50–61, in *United States v. Sullivan*, 274 U.S. 259 (1927) (October Term, 1926, No. 851).

220. Hale v. Henkel, 201 U.S. 43 (1906).

221. Kersch, "Reconstruction of Constitutional Privacy Rights," 70–73, 78–85; "The Life and Times of *Boyd v. United States* (1886–1976)," *Michigan Law Review* 76 (1977): 184.

222. § 17, 26 Stat. 131, 139 (1890); § 28, 36 Stat. 100, 104–05 (1909); 38 Stat. 114, 189–90 (1913).

223. *1923 Supplement to United States Compiled Statutes Annotated* (St. Paul, MN: West, 1923), 2:1661–62 (listing no decisions up to 1922, when these provisions were repealed in the 1922 tariff). It may be that the failure to test the statute judicially from 1890 to 1911 reflected the authorities' unwillingness to enforce it. See Hearings (1911), 184–85. However, even after the aggressive campaign of 1909–13 (on which see my discussion in this chapter, text at notes 224–28), its constitutionality was still apparently never tested in a reported case.

   In 1921, Congress dropped the fine per day and instead punished noncompliant importers by barring them from making importations until they complied. § 405, 42 Stat. 9, 18 (1921). This law remained in force for the following fifty years, and no reported case ever held it unconstitutional. The provision was reenacted in § 511, 42 Stat. 858, 969 (1922); and in § 511, 46 Stat. 590, 733 (1930). It survived intact as 19 U.S.C. § 1511 (1976). It was discussed, with no mention of being unconstitutional, in *United States v. Molt*, 444 F. Supp. 491, 494–95 (E.D. Pa. 1978).

224. "William Loeb, 70, Executive, Is Dead," *New York Times*, Sept. 20, 1937, p. 23.

225. I. Newton Hoffmann, "Customs Administration under the 1913 Tariff Act," *Journal of Political Economy* 22 (1914): 852–54.

226. Hearings (1911), 184.

227. Hoffmann, "Customs Administration under the 1913 Tariff Act," 852–54.

228. On the raid, the books, and related legal issues, see "Raid Duveens, Partners Held," *New York Times*, Oct. 14, 1910, p. 1; "Form New Charges against Duveens," *New York Times*, Oct. 15, 1910, p. 6; "Sue the Duveens for Appeasing Wise," *New York Times*,

Apr. 26, 1912, p. 9. For details of the civil settlement, see "Duveens Pay $1,180,000," *New York Times*, May 4, 1911, p. 10. On the guilty plea and fine of the top dealer, see "H. J. Duveen Let Off with a $15,000 Fine," *New York Times*, May 25, 1911, p. 3.

229. Hearings (1911), 193.

### CHAPTER 7: CRIMINAL PROSECUTION

1. On the limited role of English public officials in prosecuting ordinary crime, without any real parallel to the American public prosecutor, see John H. Langbein, *The Origins of Adversary Criminal Trial* (Oxford: Oxford University Press, 2003), 40–47, 51. For English officials' role in prosecuting extraordinary cases, see ibid., 84–86, 98–99, 113–22. On early American public prosecutors and their murky origins, see Jack M. Kress, "Progress and Prosecution," *Annals of the American Academy of Political and Social Science* 423 (1976): 100–04.

2. Steinberg, *TCJ*; Steinberg, "FPP." Besides Steinberg, the most extensive discussions (still brief) are Dirk G. Christensen, "Incentives vs. Nonpartisanship: The Prosecutorial Dilemma in an Adversary System," *Duke Law Journal* 1981 (1981): 323n94, 325–28; Tracey L. Meares, "Rewards for Good Behavior: Influencing Prosecutorial Discretion and Conduct with Financial Incentives," *Fordham Law Review* 64 (1995): 880–82. On fee compensation of federal law enforcement officers (including U.S. attorneys but also many other officials), see Stephen Cresswell, *Mormons & Cowboys, Moonshiners & Klansmen: Federal Law Enforcement in the South and West, 1870–1893* (Tuscaloosa: University of Alabama Press, 1991), 118, 166–71, 223–24, 248, 252–54; Wilbur Miller, *Revenuers and Moonshiners: Enforcing Federal Liquor Law in the Mountain South, 1865–1900* (Chapel Hill: University of North Carolina Press, 1991), 117–25, 183–85.

3. Julius Goebel Jr. and T. Raymond Naughton, *Law Enforcement in Colonial New York: A Study in Criminal Procedure* (New York: Commonwealth Fund, 1944), 732.

4. E.g., ibid., 737–41; *Stat. of Penn. (1682–1801)*, 5:165 (statute of 1752, differentiating between true and ignored bills but not between conviction and acquittal). It was also the initial practice in New Jersey, before the legislature condemned and altered it in a statute of 1728. *Laws of the Royal Colony of New Jersey*, ed. Bernard Bush (Trenton: New Jersey State Library, 1977), 2:378 (statute of 1728).

5. This is from the recital in *Laws of the Royal Colony of New Jersey*, 2:378 (statute of 1728). Also, the New York legislature tried to halt the practice in 1708, only to be thwarted by the Privy Council. Goebel and Naughton, *Law Enforcement*, 741.

6. On financing, see *Acts and Laws of the Commonwealth of Massachusetts* (Boston: Wright and Potter, 1890), volume for 1782–83, p. 139. On fee structure, see *Acts and Laws of the Commonwealth of Massachusetts* (Boston: Adams and Larkin, 1896), volume for 1794–95, p. 399.

7. On financing, see 1811 Conn. Pub. Acts (May Session) 62, 62, modifying *The Public Statute Laws of the State of Connecticut, Book I* (Hartford, CT: Hudson and Goodwin, 1808), 230–33. On fee structure, see *The Public Statute Laws of the State of Connecticut* (Hartford, CT: S. G. Goodrich, Huntington and Hopkins, 1821), 395–96.

8. On financing, see *The Public Laws of the State of Rhode-Island and Providence Plantations* (Providence, RI: Carter and Wilkinson, 1798), 171. On fee structure, see ibid., 214.

9. *Laws of the State of New York Passed at the Sessions of the Legislature Held in the Years [1789–1796]* (Albany, NY: Weed, Parsons and Co., 1887), 3:644–45 (statute of 1796).

10. On financing, see *The Laws of Vermont of a Publick and Permanent Nature* (Windsor, VT: Simeon Ide, 1825), 556–57, 559 (statute of 1797). On fee structure, see 1798 Vt. Laws 3, 9.

11. On financing, see *The Statutes at Large of Pennsylvania from 1682 to 1801*, ed. James T. Mitchell and Henry Flanders (Harrisburg, PA: C. E. Aughinbaugh, 1911), 15:501 (statute of 1797). On fee structure, see 1813 Pa. Laws 352, 353–54.

12. *The First Laws of the State of Delaware* (Wilmington, DE: M. Glazier, 1981), 2:1103 (statute of 1793).

13. On financing, see *The Laws of Maryland*, ed. William Kilty (Annapolis, MD: Frederick Green, 1799), vol. 1; this volume has no page numbers; the statute appears in the section for November 1781 and is designated chapter 11. On fee structure, see *The Laws of Maryland* (Baltimore: Philip H. Nicklin and Co., 1811), 1:131 (statute of 1715).

14. *The Statutes at Large of South Carolina*, ed. Thomas Cooper (Columbia, SC: A. S. Johnston, 1839), 5:152, 154 (statute of 1791) (referring to the practice up to the time of enactment, which the statute alters).

15. *The Laws of the Territory of Louisiana* (St. Louis, MO: Joseph Charless, 1808), 184–85 (statute of 1807). Here the structure was a little different from the other states: a publicly financed fee of $6 for noncapital acquittals and an $8 fee collectible only from the defendant for noncapital convictions.

16. See my discussion in this chapter, text at notes 51 and 60.

17. *Laws of the State of Maine* (Hallowell, ME: Calvin Spaulding, 1822), 299, 349 (statutes of 1821).

18. *Ordinances and Decrees of the Consultation, Provisional Government of Texas and the Convention, Which Assembled at Washington March 1, 1836* (Houston, TX: National Banner Office, 1838), 141.

19. 1846 Iowa Acts 41, 42 (session went into 1847).

20. On fee structure, see 1855 Neb. Laws 2nd Sess. 167, 170. I infer that the legislature meant to follow the public-financing provisions of Iowa law (see my citation in note 19 above), which was Nebraska territory's default. 1855 Neb. Laws 1st Sess. 55, 56.

21. *The Revised Codes of the Territory of Dakota, A.D. 1877*, ed. George H. Hand (Yankton, Dakota Territory: Bowen and Kingsbury, 1880), 164–65.

22. Steinberg, *TCJ*, 80–83, 149, 185–86, 205, 222, 224–25, 228.

23. Steinberg, "FPP."

24. On assault and battery, see Steinberg, *TCJ*, 50, 59, 61, 63, 71. On theft (larceny), see ibid., 50, 59, 61, 72.

25. Steinberg, "FPP," 572–73; and see generally Steinberg, *TCJ*, 13–78.

26. Steinberg, *TCJ*, 25, 28, 39.

27. Ibid., 146 (noting that the grand jury sometimes performed investigations at the urging of the court, without result).

28. Steinberg, "FPP," 575–76 (citing treatise stating that grand jury's role was to limit private prosecutions).

29. Ibid., 577. See also Steinberg, *TCJ*, 82.

30. Steinberg, "FPP," 577–79.
31. Ibid., 581–82 (citing 1860 fee schedule).
32. Ibid., 577.
33. Ibid., 578; see also ibid., 580–82; Steinberg, *TCJ*, 185–86.
34. Steinberg, *TCJ*, 38, 68–69, 231; Steinberg, "FPP," 574–75. Also there is "considerable evidence" that African Americans accessed the system. Steinberg, *TCJ*, 258n31. See also ibid., 37–38.
35. Steinberg, *TCJ*, 65 (referring to pretrial confinement and bail).
36. Ibid., 56–57, 63–65. In prosecutions for property crimes, there was somewhat less discretion and harsher treatment of defendants, but only to a limited extent. Ibid., 72–74, 77. The use of criminal prosecutions by private accusers to obtain monetary compensation for injuries was also common in England. Norma Landau, "Indictment for Fun and Profit: A Prosecutor's Reward at Eighteenth-Century Quarter Sessions," *Law and History Review* 17 (1999): 507–36.
37. Steinberg, *TCJ*, 59. See also ibid., 71, 77; Steinberg, "FPP," 581.
38. Steinberg, *TCJ*, 68–69.
39. Ibid., 74.
40. Ibid., 71–72, 77, 230. See also ibid., 54–55, 78, 91, 201; Steinberg, "FPP," 583.
41. Steinberg, *TCJ*, 50, 53–54, 87–90, 131–33. For quotation, see ibid., 49–50.
42. Steinberg, "FPP," 582.
43. Steinberg, *TCJ*, 220–22, 224–25.
44. Also, in terms of case initiation, private accusers faded in importance compared to the salaried police, who were established in the 1850s. Steinberg, "FPP," 582; Steinberg, *TCJ*, 222.
45. Steinberg, *TCJ*, 229.
46. Steinberg, "FPP," 587. See also Steinberg, *TCJ*, 225.
47. Steinberg, *TCJ*, 223.
48. Steinberg, "FPP," 582–83.
49. Steinberg, *TCJ*, 226.
50. *Laws of the Royal Colony of New Jersey*, 2:169 (statute of 1714); ibid., 5:428 (statute of 1748).
51. *Statutes at Large of South Carolina*, 5:152, 154 (statute of 1791). This was made permanent by a statute of 1795. Ibid., 5:265.
52. *The Laws of Indiana Territory 1801–1809*, ed. Francis S. Philbrick (Springfield: Illinois State Historical Library, 1930), 561–62 (statute of 1807); *The Laws of Indiana Territory 1809–1816*, ed. Louis B. Ewbank and Dorothy L. Riker (Indianapolis: Indiana Historical Bureau, 1934), 164–65 (statute of 1810).
53. 1819 Ill. Laws 204, 204–05. For trials ending in acquittal, this statute granted fees, but lower ones, and even these were soon abolished. 1820 Ill. Laws 7, 7–8.
54. *Statutes of the Mississippi Territory* (Natchez, MS: Peter Isler, 1816), 63 (statute of 1810), 454 (statute of 1816); *The Revised Code of the Laws of Mississippi* (Natchez, MS: Francis Baker, 1824), 242–44 (statute of 1822); 1818 Ala. Laws 98, 98–100.
55. 1819 Ala. Laws 46, 46–47.

56. *Code of Mississippi*, ed. A. Hutchinson (Jackson, MS: Price and Fall, 1848), 411 (statute of 1848).

57. 1832 Tenn. Pub. Acts 15, 16–17.

58. 1850 Fla. Laws 119, 119 (session went into 1851).

59. *The Laws of the Territory of Louisiana* (St. Louis, MO: Joseph Charless, 1808), 184–85 (statute of 1807). A few of the fees were slightly lower for acquittal than for conviction.

60. 1820 La. Acts 32, 32.

61. *Laws of the State of Missouri; Revised and Digested by Authority of the General Assembly* (St. Louis, MO: E. Charless, 1825), 1:373–74 (statute of 1825).

62. *Revised Statutes of the State of Arkansas* (Boston: Weeks, Jordan and Co., 1838), 387.

63. *A Digest of the General Statute Laws of the State of Texas*, ed. Williamson S. Oldham and George W. White (Austin, TX: John Marshall and Co., 1859), 209–10 (statute of 1848).

64. *Revised Statutes and Laws of the Territory of New Mexico* (St. Louis, MO: R. P. Studley and Co., 1865), 290, 294 (Kearny Code of 1846).

65. *The Statutes of Oregon, Enacted and Continued in Force by the Legislative Assembly* (Oregon: Asahel Bush, 1854), 435 (statute of 1853).

66. *Statutes of the Territory of Washington* (Olympia, WA: George B. Goudy, 1855), 418 (statute of 1854).

67. *The General Laws of the State of California, from 1850 to 1864, Inclusive*, ed. Theodore H. Hittell (San Francisco: H. H. Bancroft and Co., 1865), 1:316 (statute of 1856).

68. 1861 Colo. Sess. Laws 387, 392–93.

69. *The Howell Code: Adopted by the First Legislative Assembly of the Territory of Arizona* (Prescott: Office of the Arizona Miner, 1865), 428–29. See also 1873 Ariz. Sess. Laws 71, 72.

70. *The Code of West Virginia: Comprising Legislation to the Year 1870* (Wheeling, WV: John Frew, 1868 [*sic*]), 664, 725.

71. 1873–74 N.C. Sess. Laws 253, 253–54. On the state's odd fee structure prior to 1874, see my discussion in this chapter, text at note 112.

72. 1857 Ky. Acts, vol. 1, pp. 41, 41 (session went into 1858). This act granted a share of all judgments, which would include fines.

73. Formally, Georgia had case-based fees. But from at least 1823 onward, each public prosecutor was to take them out of the fines and forfeitures collected in the court where he practiced. *Digest of the Laws of the State of Georgia*, 2nd ed., ed. Oliver H. Prince (Athens, GA: By the author, 1837), 659 (statute of 1823); *The Code of the State of Georgia* (Atlanta: Harrison and Co., 1882), § 4631. This led judges to impose fines on convicted defendants simply to ensure the payment of fees. "Give Salaries to Solicitors," *Atlanta Constitution*, July 16, 1905, p. A6. The public prosecutor was therefore dependent on convictions for his income, as contemporaries confirmed. "O'Neill Retires from the Race," *Atlanta Constitution*, Apr. 26, 1900, p. 7.

74. § 3, 1 Stat. 275, 277 (1792).

75. H.R. Exec. Doc. No. 32–93, at 20–26 (1852).

76. § 1, 10 Stat. 161, 161–62 (1853).

77. In many of the Western states, explained one U.S. District Court judge, "the courts feel that they should be liberal in awarding the allowances of a counsel fee in case of conviction," since it would otherwise be hard to attract good lawyers for the job. Weed v. United States, 65 F. 399, 401 (D. Mont. 1894). The U.S. attorney in Massachusetts, testifying in 1890, spoke of a $30 conviction fee as if it were routine. Hearings (1891), 339, 342 (referring to the $50 sum of $20 trial fee and $30 conviction fee). Rep. James Connolly, formerly a U.S. attorney in Illinois, spoke similarly. 28 Cong. Rec. 2412 (1896).

78. H.R. Rep. No. 53–931, at 1 (1894). It should be noted that Congress capped each U.S. attorney's annual fees at $6,000 after expenses. § 1, 5 Stat. 421, 428 (1841); § 1, 5 Stat. 475, 483 (1842); § 3, 10 Stat. 161, 166 (1853). This might have turned the U.S. attorneys into de facto salaried officers, but in fact it did not. In all district-years for the period 1873–82, only 11 percent of U.S. attorneys had fee totals exceeding the cap, and most did not come close. H.R. Exec. Doc. No. 48–92, at 2–10 (1884). The proportion reached 37 percent by the time of salarization in 1896. H.R. Doc. No. 54–167 (1896). But "as a general rule [the U.S. attorneys] are apt to agonize until that maximum is reached." 28 Cong. Rec. 836 (1896) (Rep. Cannon). And while some U.S. attorneys acquired salaried assistants, the behavior of those assistants was strongly influenced by the fee-maximizing wishes of their bosses. 28 Cong. Rec. 846 (1896) (Rep. Lacey).

79. *Messages of the Governors of Tennessee*, ed. Robert H. White (Nashville, TN: State Historical Commission, 1952), 3:255 (message of Governor Newton Cannon, 1837).

80. *Twenty-Fifth Annual Report of the Executive Committee of the Prison Association of New York, and Accompanying Documents, for the Year 1869* (Albany, NY: Argus Co., 1870), 41.

81. Miller, *Revenuers and Moonshiners*, 119, 215n46.

82. H.R. Rep. No. 48–2509, at 3 (1885).

83. "Secrets of Fee System," *Chicago Daily Tribune*, Feb. 1, 1897, p. 4.

84. Excerpted in *Eighteenth Biennial Report of the Attorney-General of Kansas, 1911–1912* (Topeka: State Printing Office, 1912), 20. For more on the incentive rationale for conviction fees, see AG Report 1871, p. 2; 15 Cong. Rec. 6125 (1884) (Rep. Bayne); *Messages of the Governors of Tennessee*, 7:648 (message of Governor Robert Love Taylor, 1897).

85. David Rossman, "'Were There No Appeal': The History of Review in American Criminal Courts," *Journal of Criminal Law and Criminology* 81 (1990): 546–47 (quoting *Lavett v. People*, 7 Cow. 339, 343 (N.Y. 1827)).

86. Shelton v. State, 1 Stew & P. 208, 211 (Ala. 1831).

87. Robert M. Ireland, "Privately Funded Prosecution of Crime in the Nineteenth-Century United States," *American Journal of Legal History* 39 (1995): 43–46.

88. *Shelton*, 1 Stew. & P. at 211 ("the fact is well known that prisoners usually employ [lawyers] of the strongest talents, and the more important the case, the more distinguished the defending counsel generally are"). See also Mike McConville and Chester Mirsky, "The Rise of Guilty Pleas: New York, 1800–1865," *Journal of Law and Society* 22 (1995): 454–55.

89. See David J. Bodenhamer, *The Pursuit of Justice: Crime and Law in Antebellum Indiana* (New York: Garland, 1986), 97 (briefly surmising that conviction fees for Indiana district attorneys were attractive because they would give "no inducement to prosecute dubious cases," so the district attorney would "hold a tighter rein on grand juries," easing "crowded dockets").

90. State v. Henley, 41 S.W. 352, 360 (Tenn. 1897).

91. "Cortlandt Parker Dead," *New York Times*, July 31, 1907, p. 7.

92. Printed in E. C. Wines and Theodore W. Dwight, *Report on the Prisons and Reformatories of the United States and Canada, Made to the Legislature of New York, January, 1867* (Albany, NY: Van Benthuysen and Son's, 1867), 517.

93. 28 Cong. Rec. 2457 (1896).

94. 1873–74 N.C. Sess. Laws 253, 253–54.

95. Nicholas Parrillo, "The Rise of Non-Profit Government in America: An Overview and a Case Study" (unpublished paper, on file at Yale Law Library, 2008), 51–69. The public prosecutor's means of dominating the grand jury likely included (1) leveraging his monopoly of legal knowledge—particularly as the legal profession's authority increased—in such tasks as drawing up indictments, and (2) convincing judges to prohibit the grand jurors from investigating accusations not channeled through the public prosecutor. Ibid., 63–64.

96. As to Kansas, see my discussion of liquor prosecutions in this chapter, text at notes 132–38. As to Illinois, Louisiana, and Texas, in the bulleted list immediately below, I provide the following data for each of those three states: (1) the date when the state adopted conviction fees, on which see my discussion in this chapter, text at notes 50–73; (2) the date when the state converted to salaries, on which see this book's Appendix; and (3) the citation(s) for the statute(s) in which the legislature authorized the public prosecutor to prosecute by "information," that is, without the grand jury. Note, for each state, the overlap in time between the public prosecutor's right to conviction fees and his power to prosecute by information.

   - *Illinois:* (1) 1819; (2) 1913; (3) *The Revised Statutes of the State of Illinois*, ed. Harvey B. Hurd (Springfield: Illinois Journal Co., 1874), 343 (statute of 1874). The information covered all offenses cognizable in county courts, which meant all nonpenitentiary offenses. On jurisdiction of county courts, see 1871 Ill. Laws 325, 326–27.

   - *Louisiana:* (1) 1820; (2) New Orleans 1916; rest of state 1924–50; (3) 1841 La. Acts 1st Sess. 59 (covering New Orleans district attorney, for all minor crimes), explained in *State v. McLane*, 4 La. Ann. 435 (1849); 1855 La. Acts 151, 151 (covering whole state, for all noncapital crimes). The information required approval of the judge, but judges granted it "as a matter of course." State v. Anderson, 30 La. Ann. 557 (1878).

   - *Texas:* (1) 1848; (2) after 1900; (3) *A Digest of the General Statute Laws of the State of Texas*, ed. Williamson S. Oldham and George W. White (Austin, TX: John Marshall and Co., 1859), 614–15 (statute of 1856) (covering all misdemeanors).

97. Generally, all the conviction-fee states that I cataloged earlier in this chapter (in text at notes 50–73) had a scheme along these lines, with the exception of the many states that adopted public financing for conviction fees (which I catalog in text at notes 98–109).

98. 1812 N.J. Laws 2nd Sitting 39, 39–40 (session went into 1813).

99. 1813 Tenn. Pub. Acts 185, 185–86 (public financing); 1832 Tenn. Pub. Acts 15, 16–17 (conviction fees).

100. On public financing of criminal costs, see *The Revised Statutes of the State of Missouri* (St. Louis, MO: J. W. Dougherty, 1845), 248–49. On the conviction-based nature of public prosecutors' fees, see ibid., 490.

101. A *Digest of the General Statute Laws of the State of Texas*, ed. Williamson S. Oldham and George W. White (Austin, TX: John Marshall and Co., 1859), 209–10 (statute of 1848 instituting conviction fees); ibid., 675 (statute of 1858 instituting public financing in cases of felony).

102. The state initially instituted conviction fees with public financing. 1850 Fla. Laws 119, 119 (session went into 1851). Then it granted salaries, with no fees. 1854 Fla. Laws 69, 69–70 (session went into 1855). Then it instituted conviction fees, apparently without public financing. 1865 Fla. Laws 70, 70–71. Then it switched to conviction fees with public financing. 1883 Fla. Laws 72, 72–73. Last, it converted to salaries, with no fees. 1895 Fla. Laws 122.

103. *The Statutes of Oregon, Enacted and Continued in Force by the Legislative Assembly* (Oregon: Asahel Bush, 1854), 435 (statute of 1853).

104. *Statutes of the Territory of Washington* (Olympia, WA: George B. Goudy, 1855), 418 (statute of 1854).

105. *The General Laws of the State of California, from 1850 to 1864, Inclusive*, ed. Theodore H. Hittell (San Francisco: H. H. Bancroft and Co., 1865), 1:316. Public financing started in 1856, and the legislature made exceptions for three counties in 1857. Ibid., 1:316n. In later years, the number of counties excepted from public financing would grow. See *The Codes and Statutes of California*, ed. F. P. Deering (San Francisco: Bancroft-Whitney Co., 1886), 4:520 (about half excepted).

106. 1861 Colo. Sess. Laws 290, 334 (public financing); 1861 Colo. Sess. Laws 387, 392–93 (conviction fees).

107. 1884 La. Acts 47, 47.

108. North Carolina in 1874 provided public financing for half the fee when the defendant was insolvent. 1873–74 N.C. Sess. Laws 253, 253–54. And it would ultimately grant full public financing for capital crimes, forgery, and conspiracy. *Consolidated Statutes of North Carolina* (Raleigh, NC: Commercial Printing Co., 1920) 1:1585–86 (collecting statutes).

109. 1873 Ariz. Sess. Laws 71, 72–73 (public financing in felony cases).

110. § 4, 1 Stat. 275, 277 (1792).

111. "Fees of District Attorneys, Marshals, and Clerks" (1877), in *Official Opinions of the Attorneys-General of the United States*, ed. A. J. Bentley (Washington, DC: W. H. and O. H. Morrison, 1880), 15:386–88.

112. *The Revised Statutes of the State of North Carolina* (Raleigh, NC: Turner and Hughes, 1837), 1:551–52 (statutes of 1818 and 1820).
113. See the statutes cited in note 112 above.
114. 1873–74 N.C. Sess. Laws 253, 253–54.
115. *The General Statutes of the State of Kansas* (Lawrence, KS: John Speer, 1868), 284–85 (granting fees whenever "prosecutor," that is, prosecuting witness, is adjudged to pay costs); ibid., 872 (criteria for when prosecuting witness must pay costs).
116. A complaining witness had a complete defense to an action for malicious prosecution if he pressed charges on the advice of the public prosecutor. Doble v. Norton, 22 Kan. 101 (1879). Perhaps this meant that if the public prosecutor advised accusers to press frivolous charges, he would not get paid.
117. Georgia had a provision that was similar on its face to those of North Carolina and Kansas. *Digest of the Laws of the State of Georgia*, 2nd ed., ed. Oliver H. Prince (Athens, GA: By the author, 1837), 659 (statute of 1823); *The Code of the State of Georgia* (Atlanta: Harrison and Co., 1882), § 4630. But apparently the provision for fees in frivolous cases was not frequently invoked, since contemporaries said the officer's pay depended on conviction. See my discussion in note 73 above. Also, Utah Territory in 1859 adopted a similar provision, but the county was authorized to pay up to 50 percent of the public prosecutor's fee if not collectible from defendant or complainant, which brought the fee structure closer to a simple case-based scheme. *Acts, Resolutions, and Memorials Passed at the Several Sessions of the Legislative Assembly of the Territory of Utah* (Great Salt Lake City, UT: Henry McEwan, 1866), 74–75 (statute of 1859).
118. E.g., *The Revised Code of the Statute Laws of the State of Mississippi* (Jackson, MS: E. Barksdale, 1857), 631; 1861 Colo. Sess. Laws 387, 392.
119. 1819 Ala. Laws 46, 46–47.
120. 1840 Ala. Laws 103, 156 (session went into 1841).
121. For the gambling fees, see *The General Laws of the State of California, from 1850 to 1864, Inclusive*, ed. Theodore H. Hittell (San Francisco: H. H. Bancroft and Co., 1865), § 3327 (statute of 1855); ibid., § 3331 (statute of 1857); ibid., § 3335 (statute of 1860). On the fees for capital offenses and other felonies, see ibid., § 2279.
122. New Mexico offered $50 for a conviction of housing or financing gambling operations when a capital conviction paid only $20. *Revised Statutes and Laws of the Territory of New Mexico* (St. Louis, MO: R. P. Studley and Co., 1865), 84 (statute of 1859 on gambling); ibid., 294 (Kearny Code of 1846 on capital crimes). Gambling convictions were later reduced to only $10–$15. 1875–76 N.M. Laws 65, 66. Nevada offered $250 for conviction of any gaming offense. 1869 Nev. Stat. 119, 120. At that time, public prosecutors were otherwise salaried, at $750–$2,000 per year. 1866 Nev. Stat. 126, 126.
123. 1842–43 Ark. Acts 27, 27; *A Digest of the General Statute Laws of the State of Texas*, ed. Williamson S. Oldham and George W. White (Austin, TX: John Marshall and Co., 1859), 209 (statute of 1848); *The Revised Code of the Statute Laws of the State of Mississippi* (Jackson, MS: E. Barksdale, 1857), 598, 631.

124. 1835–36 Tenn. Pub. Acts 152, 152 ($20 for illegal lottery conviction); 1832 Tenn. Pub. Acts 15, 16–17 ($20 for capital conviction).

125. 1840 Ala. Laws 103, 144–45 (session went into 1841). On the extraordinary nature of this power, see G.J.C., annotation, "Matters within Investigating Powers of Grand Jury," 22 A.L.R. 1356, 1364 (1923).

126. State v. Blocker, 14 Ala. 450, 452 (1848) (emphasis omitted).

127. William Church Osborn, "Liquor Statutes in the United States," *Harvard Law Review* 2 (1888): 125–38.

128. *Code of Mississippi*, ed. A. Hutchinson (Jackson, MS: Price and Fall, 1848), 269–70 (statute of 1839).

129. *The Revised Statutes of Kentucky, Approved and Adopted by the General Assembly, 1851 and 1852, and in Force from July 1, 1852*, ed. Richard H. Stanton (Cincinnati, OH: Robert Clarke and Co., 1860), 1:375 (statute of 1852).

130. 1852 Mass. Acts 257. For background, see William J. Novak, *The People's Welfare: Law and Regulation in Nineteenth-Century America* (Chapel Hill: University of North Carolina Press, 1996), 178–83.

131. 1855 Mass. Acts 623, 630–31. The fee was repealed four years later. 1859 Mass. Acts 1st Sess. 357.

132. See my discussion in this chapter, text at note 115.

133. Robert Smith Bader, *Prohibition in Kansas: A History* (Lawrence: University Press of Kansas, 1986), 63–65.

134. 1885 Kansas Sess. Laws 236, 242–43.

135. *General Statutes of the State of Kansas*, ed. W. C. Webb (Topeka, KS: W. C. Webb, 1897), 2:317. I reached the $15 amount by adding the fee for indictment or information in a felony case ($5) to the trial fee ($10).

136. "Kansas Legislation," *Kansas City (MO) Evening Star*, Mar. 11, 1885, p. 2.

137. 1864 Kansas Sess. Laws 111.

138. For the exception, see *General Statutes of Kansas 1901*, ed. C. F. W. Dassler (Topeka, KS: Crane and Co., 1901), § 2475; 1913 Kansas Laws 314, 318.

139. Franklin G. Davidson, "The Prosecuting Attorney's Office — Do Modern Conditions Create New Duties for This Office?" *Indiana Law Journal* 4 (1929): 333.

140. Tennessee offered $20 for a conviction of carrying a concealed bowie knife, punishable by up to six months' imprisonment. 1837–38 Tenn. Pub. Acts 200, 200–01. Its fee for a capital conviction was the same. 1832 Tenn. Pub. Acts 15, 16–17. Meanwhile, Alabama offered $20 for conviction of carrying a concealed gun or bowie knife, punishable by fine only. *The Code of Alabama* (Montgomery, AL: Brittain and De Wolf, 1852), § 3996 (referring to §§ 3273–74). Its fee for a general felony conviction was $10. Ibid., § 3996.

141. For all cited anti-Klan provisions, see 1868 Tenn. Pub. Acts 18, 21–22. For the capital crime fee, see *A Compilation of the Statute Laws of the State of Tennessee* (St. Louis, MO: W. J. Gilbert, 1873), § 4542.

142. 1868–69 Ark. Acts 63, 67.

143. "Urges Trust Legislation," *Charlotte (NC) Daily Observer*, Feb. 11, 1909, p. 1, 3.

144. Quote from *State v. Brady*, 118 S.W. 128, 130 (Tex. Civ. 1909). 1889 Mo. Laws 96, 97–98 (fine up to $5,000; fee equaling 20 percent of fine); 1889 Tenn. Pub. Acts 475, 475–76 (50 percent of fine); Jonathan W. Singer, *Broken Trusts: The Texas Attorney General versus the Oil Industry, 1889–1909* (College Station: Texas A&M University Press, 2002), 49–50 (10 percent of fine in 1889, then 25 percent in 1899); 1899 N.C. Sess. Laws 852, 854 (flat fee for charter forfeiture action).

145. The congressional discussions I cite in this case study sometimes refer not only to U.S. attorneys but also to other fee-paid officers in federal law enforcement (e.g., U.S. marshals, their deputies), or to federal law enforcement generally. I think it appropriate to cite such statements in my analysis of U.S. attorneys, since informed observers viewed U.S. attorneys as the dominant actors in federal law enforcement, with the most control over who was prosecuted. See the comments of Representative Connolly, former U.S. attorney, in 28 Cong. Rec. 2408–09, 2411 (1896), and of Rep. Brown, a former state-level prosecutor, in 28 Cong. Rec. 2396–97 (1896). See also 28 Cong. Rec. 2512 (1896) (Rep. Tracey). Congressmen sometimes stated that other classes of officers were also important, but they indicated that the U.S. attorneys were at least equally so. H.R. Rep. No. 54–544, at 1 (1896); 28 Cong. Rec. 2303 (1896) (Rep. Henderson). Notably, in the U.S. attorney general's frequent recommendations to reform the compensation and incentives of various federal law enforcement officers, U.S. attorneys were the only officials who were always included. AG Report 1873, p. 17; AG Report 1877, pp. 10–12; AG Report 1879, pp. 12–14; AG Report 1880, pp. 12–14; AG Report 1881, pp. 11–13; AG Report 1883, p. 22; AG Report 1884, p. 17; AG Report 1890, p. xix; AG Report 1893, pp. xxiii–xxv; AG Report 1894, p. xxix; AG Report 1895, pp. 5–6. That said, two congressmen rejected the idea that U.S. attorneys and marshals could effectively control deputy marshals (who made arrests for fees) and therefore argued that stopping the abuse required salarizing those deputies, as well. 28 Cong. Rec. 2510 (1896) (Rep. Swanson); ibid., 2524 (Rep. Tate). But the 1896 statute powerfully answered this concern by guaranteeing the control of the newly salaried U.S. attorneys over deputies in internal-revenue enforcement: it required advance approval by the U.S. attorney for an arrest warrant in internal-revenue prosecutions. § 19, 29 Stat. 140, 184 (1896); see also 28 Cong. Rec. 2394 (1896) (Rep. Brown); ibid., 2522 (adoption of provision). It may be that such prior approval was already required before 1896, at least on a regional or temporary basis. 28 Cong. Rec. 2396–97 (1896) (Rep. Brown); Hearings (1891), 305, 336; Cresswell, *Mormons & Cowboys*, 167. In any event, the steep fall in prosecutions that occurred just after the salarization of U.S. attorneys and U.S. marshals (and not deputies) in 1896 suggests that these more senior officers did effectively control federal prosecution. See my discussion in this chapter, text at notes 182–85.

146. §§ 6–7, 29 Stat. 140, 179–81 (1896).

147. 28 Cong. Rec. 2408 (1896) (Rep. Connolly) ("none of these troubles about frivolous prosecutions were ever complained of . . . until we had an internal revenue law [starting in the 1860s]"). On the indirectness of federal governance in the early republic, see Brian Balogh, *A Government Out of Sight: The Mystery of National Authority in Nineteenth-Century America* (Cambridge: Cambridge University Press, 2009).

148. W. Elliott Brownlee, *Federal Taxation in America: A Short History*, 2nd ed. (Cambridge: Cambridge University Press, 2004), 37–38.
149. USRS §§ 3258–3260; see also § 3247 (defining "distiller").
150. USRS § 3279. See also Hearings (1884), 234–35.
151. USRS §§ 3232, 3233, 3242; see also § 3244 ¶ 4 (defining "retail dealer in liquors").
152. On big distillers, see Miller, *Revenuers and Moonshiners*, 68. On small, see ibid., 27–30, 40.
153. 28 Cong. Rec. 838 (1896) (Representative Settle, inserting remarks of Judge Robert P. Dick). See also 15 Cong. Rec. 6123 (1884); Hearings (1891), 43, 295.
154. Aleck Boarman, "Correspondence," *Central Law Journal* 41 (1895): 277–78; Hearings (1884), 332.
155. USRS §§ 3363, 3366.
156. 28 Cong. Rec. 2396–97 (1896) (Rep. Brown); Hearings (1884), 229–31, 331–32.
157. USRS §§ 3324, 3376, 3406; United States v. Ulrici, 28 F.Cas. 328, 331–32 (C.C. E.D. Mo. 1875).
158. *Ulrici*, 28 F.Cas. at 331 (Miller, J.).
159. Grover Cleveland, First Annual Message (Dec. 8, 1885), in *A Compilation of the Messages and Papers of the Presidents*, ed. James D. Richardson (New York: Bureau of National Literature, 1897), 11:4939.
160. I base this calculation on population figures in *HSUS* series Aa7 and on criminal justice figures in the following sources:

   - For the 1820s: I rely on the number of annual indictments reported in Dwight F. Henderson, *Congress, Courts, and Criminals: The Development of Federal Criminal Law, 1801–1829* (Westport, CT: Greenwood Press, 1985), 214; see also ibid., 47–48. The totals drawn from Henderson are an undercount, but probably not much. Henderson says that he covers "circuit courts." Ibid., 47–48, 214. These were the only federal courts that tried criminal cases, except for those district courts situated outside any circuit. Ibid., 7, 209–10. In several instances, Henderson's charts contain nonzero data for a judicial district during a period when that district was outside any circuit: Tennessee 1801–07, Ohio 1804–07, Louisiana 1805–28, Kentucky 1801–07, Indiana 1817–28, and Illinois 1818–28. This indicates that Henderson counted indictments in most of the district courts that had circuit-court-like jurisdiction in criminal matters. See also ibid., 53n94 (noting he compiled data from "records of circuit *and* district courts"). That said, he completely omits Missouri, Alabama, and Mississippi, which omission (we may presume) modestly reduces the national total. In addition, Henderson believes *state* courts in this period could try federal crimes. But he admits we know little about their involvement. Ibid., 37–38, 211. And another study argues there is little evidence for such involvement. Michael G. Collins and Jonathan Remy Nash, "Prosecuting Federal Crimes in State Court," *Virginia Law Review* 97 (2011): 266–78. On which district courts were situated within circuits, see Federal Judicial Center, "History of the Federal Judiciary," http://www.fjc.gov/history/home.nsf/page/index.html (last accessed Aug. 3, 2012).

- For the 1870s and 1890s, I relied on the number of criminal cases terminated postindictment per year, as reported in the AG Reports for those years, nearly always in "Exhibit B" of the report. Data in the AG Reports give separate numbers for the District of Columbia, which I excluded, since federal prosecution in that district covered ordinary crimes that, anywhere else, would be under state law.

161. Calculations based on the number of criminal cases terminated postindictment per year, as reported in the AG Reports for those years, nearly always in "Exhibit B" of the report. I excluded the District of Columbia, for the reason I stated in note 160 above.

162. Robert M. Goldman, "The 'Weakened Spring of Government' and the Executive Branch: The Department of Justice in the Late 19th Century," *Congress and the Presidency* 11 (1984): 172.

163. Miller, *Revenuers and Moonshiners*, 16; 28 Cong. Rec. 2392, 2394 (1896) (Rep. Brown).

164. 28 Cong. Rec. 2394 (1896) (Rep. Brown).

165. 28 Cong. Rec. 3172 (1896) (Sen. Allison of Iowa); ibid., 2461 (Rep. Tawney of Minnesota); ibid., 3183, 3209 (Sen. Hoar of Massachusetts).

166. Miller, *Revenuers and Moonshiners*, 50–59 (quote at 55).

167. Quoted in Miller, *Revenuers and Moonshiners*, 45.

168. 18 Cong. Rec. 1502 (1887). He had made the same argument earlier. 15 Cong. Rec. 6124 (1884).

169. 28 Cong. Rec. 1649 (1896) (Sen. Chandler) ("fictitious and useless and unnecessary prosecutions"); ibid., 1684 (Sen. Vest) (prosecution of "miserable, trivial, little offenses"); ibid., 2390–91 (Rep. Updegraff) ("multitude of frivolous convictions, prosecutions, and expensive litigations"; "frivolous and vexatious cases of prosecution"); ibid., 2392 (Rep. Little) ("useless and frivolous prosecutions"); ibid., 2394–96 (Rep. Brown) ("frivolous and useless prosecutions"; "frivolous indictments and unnecessary prosecutions"; "frivolous prosecutions and technical violations of the laws"; "unnecessary and frivolous prosecutions"); ibid., 2397–99 (Rep. Burton) ("frivolous and unnecessary, and in many cases pernicious and malicious, prosecutions"; "unnecessary, frivolous, pernicious, and malicious suits"); ibid., 2401 (Rep. Tracey) ("frivolous prosecutions"; "Technical violations"; "prosecutions for trivial offenses"); ibid., 2402 (Rep. Underwood) ("technical violation of the law"); ibid., 2408 (Rep. Connolly) ("frivolous prosecutions"); ibid., 2447 (Rep. Bailey) ("frivolous and vexatious prosecutions"); ibid., 2459 (Rep. Dockery) ("frivolous indictments and petty persecutions"); ibid., 4427 (Rep. Dockery) ("petty persecutions and prosecutions of honest citizens"); ibid., 2460 (Rep. Strode) ("trivial violations of the internal-revenue laws"); ibid., 2461 (Rep. Tawney) (referring to "technical conviction"); ibid., 2506 (Rep. McMillin) ("vexatious prosecutions"; "petty and frivolous prosecutions"); ibid., 2507 (Rep. Allen of Utah) ("frivolous prosecutions"); ibid., 2524 (Rep. Tate) ("frivolous prosecutions"; "petty offenses"); ibid., 3229 (Sen. Hoar) ("small and vexatious causes"; "trifling offenses"; "little vexatious suits"); ibid., 3263 (Sen. Vilas) ("vexatious litigation . . . in the way particularly of prosecutions for minor offenses"); ibid., 5643 (Rep. McRae)

("petty prosecutions"; "frivolous, groundless, and vexatious prosecutions"); 28 Cong. Rec. Appendix 78 (1896) (Rep. Swanson) ("petty and frivolous suits").

170. The only such reference I can find, which appears in debate on the related but distinct issue of appropriations for rewards to private informers, is 28 Cong. Rec. Appendix 321 (1896) (Rep. Swanson) ("Many an innocent man has been convicted upon such suborned and perjured testimony.").

171. 28 Cong. Rec. 2393 (1896) (Rep. McRae) (stating that "too often frivolous and utterly groundless prosecutions" resulted in "trial among strangers" for numerous defendants who were ultimately acquitted or discharged); ibid., 2397 (1896) (Rep. Burton) (stating that one evil "inherent in the fee system" is "the frivolous and unnecessary, and in many cases pernicious and malicious, prosecutions that are instituted and maintained in the Federal courts"); ibid., 2403 (Rep. Underwood) (invoking the plight of "innocent people who are persecuted" and referencing only the number of cases on the docket, not mentioning the number of convictions), 2529 ("hundreds of innocent people are dragged before the courts . . . and prosecuted"). Though Representative Swanson was the sole congressman to make an express reference to conviction of the innocent in 1896 (see my discussion in note 170 above), his other remarks are consistent with a focus on preverdict process. 28 Cong. Rec. Appendix 78–79 (1896). For a present-day analysis of the importance of process costs in the adjudication of minor offenses, see Malcolm M. Feeley, *The Process Is the Punishment: Handling Cases in a Lower Criminal Court* (New York: Russell Sage Foundation, 1992).

172. 28 Cong. Rec. 2397 (1896) (statement of Rep. Brown) (quoting letter from U.S. District Judge C. D. Clark); ibid., 2526 (Rep. Tate); 28 Cong. Rec. Appendix 79 (1896) (Rep. Swanson). For references to imprisonment that is unmistakably pretrial, see 28 Cong. Rec. 2393 (1896) (Rep. McRae). See also Cleveland, First Annual Message (1885), in *A Compilation of the Messages and Papers of the Presidents*, 11:4940.

173. See my discussion in this chapter, text at note 77 (and also my discussion in note 77 itself).

174. § 1, 10 Stat. 161, 161–62 (1853).

175. John P. Altgeld, *Our Penal Machinery and Its Victims*, rev. ed. (Chicago: A. C. McClurg and Co., 1886), 50–51; Hearings (1884), 331–32; Hearings (1891), 338, 375–76.

176. Hearings (1884), 229.

177. 15 Cong. Rec. 6123–24 (1884) (Rep. White).

178. In the House debate on the merits of salarization (as opposed to particular salary levels), the four longest speeches, by far, were by Judiciary Committee members Updegraff, Brown, Burton, and Connolly. 28 Cong. Rec. 2390–2412 (1896).

179. 28 Cong. Rec. 2396 (1896) (Rep. Brown). The judge found the case so outrageous that he dismissed it, despite legal guilt.

180. 28 Cong. Rec. 2398 (1896).

181. Near the start of the session, Representative Claude Swanson, the Virginia Democrat, gave a speech that helped put salarization on the agenda for the session, complaining that too many federal convictions "were convictions where no benefits could accrue to the Government." 28 Cong. Rec. Appendix 79 (1896). Rising in support of Swanson, Thomas Settle, a North Carolina Republican, submitted a testimonial from a

federal judge complaining about "strict and rigid enforcement" against small-time liquor sales: "I can see no public good that can result from the prosecution of every person who sells or offers for sale without payment of the [legally required] special tax," even though, in such cases, "[t]he evidence generally makes out a clear case of violation of law, and honest juries convict." 28 Cong. Rec. 838 (1896). Later in the session, John Tracey, a Missouri Republican, declared that "[t]echnical violations of the internal-revenue laws have been prosecuted to conviction with no possible resulting benefit either to the Government or to the people" — "no benefit to society." 28 Cong. Rec. 2401 (1896). Note that Tracy had helped the Judiciary Committee draft the salarization bill. H.R. Rep. No. 54–544, at 2 (1896). Alabama Democrat Oscar Underwood declared it improper to prosecute men "who might have violated the law to a slight extent, who might have been guilty of a mere technical violation of the law" and who were "probably" just "selling a pint of whisky or a plug of tobacco." 28 Cong. Rec. 2402 (1896). (Underwood was specifically discussing how U.S. commissioners and deputy marshals furthered these unjust prosecutions, not U.S. attorneys, but his comment demonstrates his support for deliberate underenforcement of the internal revenue laws.) Over in the Senate, Missouri Democrat George Vest called it "a cruelty" to prosecute a man merely because he "happens to have gone across the line to get two or three sticks of timber on Government land." 28 Cong. Rec. 1685 (1896). Senator George Hoar, the Massachusetts Republican and chairman of the Judiciary Committee, complained of the "multiplication of small and vexatious causes" against "men who are guilty of trifling offenses." He cited a rigid statute making it a crime to put a handwritten message on a printed document and mail it at less than the letter rate. A person would do this, "innocent that it is a violation of the postal law of the United States, and some official gets up a prosecution against that person." 28 Cong. Rec. 3229 (1896); USRS § 3887.

182. The measure became law on May 28, 1896, and it mandated that all fees that otherwise would have gone into the pockets of U.S. attorneys and U.S. marshals should begin going into the Treasury on the first day of fiscal 1896–97 (i.e., July 1, 1896), and it contained no exception for cases that were pending at the time of passage. § 6, 29 Stat. 140, 179–80 (1896). Salarization took away the incentive of the affected officers to maximize fees. Therefore, they presumably began pushing prosecutions toward indictment at a lower rate, certainly by July 1, 1896, but probably on May 28 or a bit earlier, anticipating that some or all of the fees in pending cases would not accrue until after the cutoff date. The change in behavior would explain the much-reduced termination total for fiscal 1896–97 and the similarly low totals for the subsequent years. I am assuming, of course, that it would take less than a year for an (unobserved) decrease in pushing cases toward indictment to manifest itself in the (observed) postindictment termination totals, which in turn rests on the assumption that the average length of a case was relatively short (somewhat less than a year). This seems a fair assumption, for contemporaries spoke of case lengths in terms of "months." Cleveland, First Annual Message (1885), in *A Compilation of the Messages and Papers of the Presidents*, 11:4940; 28 Cong. Rec. 2393 (1896) (Rep. McRae).

183. 28 Cong. Rec. 2399 (1896); AG Report 1896, pp. vii–x.

184. The 1896 statute salarizing the U.S. attorneys and marshals included a distinct provision that authorized the Washington office of the Justice Department to review and reduce the number of (still fee-paid) deputies appointed by each U.S. marshal. § 11, 29 Stat. 140, 182–83 (1896). With the Washington office playing a supervisory role, the number of these deputies did indeed drop substantially between fiscal 1895–96 and fiscal 1896–97.

However, the exact size of the decrease is not clear. The attorney general reported that the number of "field" deputies (as opposed to the "office" deputies, who performed clerical duties) had been "greatly decreased" between May and November 1896. AG Report 1896, p. x. The list of the names of all deputies (both field and office) who served at some point in the course of fiscal 1896–97 totaled about 1,300. AG Report 1897, pp. 234–95. The nearest thing to a comparable figure for the pre-reform period comes from a list of the number of "[d]eputy marshals reported to the Department of Justice by the United States marshals" in each district, dated December 23, 1895, and reported to Congress, which gives a national total of 1,905. H.R. Doc. No. 54–167, at 30 (1896). But there are several problems with comparing the 1895 figures to the 1896–97 figures. First, it is not clear whether the 1895 figures refer to the deputies employed on a given day or to the number employed over some period of time. Second, the 1895 figures do not distinguish between field deputies and office deputies as the 1896–97 figures do. Third, deputies were often part-time, and both sets of figures measure only the number of officers, not the man-hours expended.

The new supervision over hiring deputies probably contributed to the reduction in prosecutions, since deputies were important detectors of federal crime. But they were hardly the only ones: for example, the agents of the Internal Revenue Bureau played a very important role in detection. See generally Miller, *Revenuers and Moonshiners*. Further, there is much reason to think the salarization provision by itself would have greatly curtailed prosecutions even if there had been no supervision of hiring deputies. For one thing, general debate on the 1896 reform measure focused overwhelmingly on salarization as the remedy for excessive prosecution, with much less discussion of personnel reduction. 28 Cong. Rec. 2302–04, 2390–2412 (1896); 28 Cong. Rec. Appendix 288–90 (1896). The brief references to reduction in the number of deputy marshals during the general debate appear in 28 Cong. Rec. 2390 (Rep. Updegraff), 2396 (Rep. Brown); 28 Cong. Rec. Appendix 289 (Reps. Swanson and Brown), 290 (Rep. Swanson). Further, salarization of the U.S. marshal and of the U.S. attorney was probably sufficient, by itself, to curtail greatly the appointment of deputies, even without any provision for supervision by the Washington office. Consider:

- As to the U.S. marshal, this officer was—under the pre-1896 regime—lawfully entitled to a share of his deputies' fees, so he tended to appoint lots of deputies, to maximize his own income. Thus, placing the marshal on salary meant he would no longer feel the need to make so many appointments. Many observers suggested this. 28 Cong. Rec. 846 (1896) (Rep. Lacey); ibid., 2395–97 (Rep. Brown, at times quoting U.S. District Judge Clark); ibid., 2510 (Rep. Swanson);

"Criminal Costs: Something of Pressing Interest to Tennessee Tax-Payers," *Knoxville (TN) Journal*, Aug. 17, 1896, p. 6 (quoting report of Tennessee Bar Association committee).

- As to the U.S. attorney, this officer had long exercised important controls over the fee-earning tasks that deputies could perform (e.g., by authorizing them to make arrests, which power was confirmed in 1896, on which see my discussion in note 145 above). Thus, placing the U.S. attorney on salary meant that he would no longer have the incentive to maximize the sorts of business that justified the employment of lots of deputies. Representative Connolly, a former U.S. attorney, argued that, if you "take away" the "inducement from the [U.S.] attorney" to "multiply cases frivolously, for the mere sake of making fees," then "the marshal and deputy marshal drop their fees," since the U.S. attorney is the "main spoke in the wheel" of the criminal process. "When the motive is taken away from the [U.S.] attorney to authorize unnecessary writs, the field deputies will have no unnecessary writs to serve." 28 Cong. Rec. 2409, 2411 (1896). See also ibid., 2397 (Representative Brown, quoting Judge Clark's statement that U.S. attorneys control the "issuance of warrants" from which marshals and deputies can make fees).

185. The incoming McKinley administration reduced the number of internal revenue agents, but Congress then increased it. Miller, *Revenuers and Moonshiners*, 186. In any event, neither of these changes occurred until after McKinley's inauguration in March 1897 (nine months into the fiscal year), and the plunge in prosecutions was noticeable in summer and fall 1896. AG Report 1896, pp. vii–x.

186. Figure 7.2 shows a small, transient dip in the first year of the reform, probably because U.S. attorneys used the nolle prosequi to clear their dockets of cases that had already entered the pipeline under the fee system but that, under the salary system, could no longer earn them money. Consistent with this, the nolle prosequi in fiscal 1896–97 accounted for a higher percentage of nonconviction terminations (73 percent) than it had in any of the previous ten years.

187. AG Report 1878, p. 11; AG Report 1890, p. xix; Hearings (1884), 234–35; 15 Cong. Rec. 6123 (1884) (Rep. White); Cresswell, *Mormons & Cowboys*, 254.

188. Hearings (1891), 142, 182.

189. This pattern is articulated, with respect to suspended sentences, in H.R. Rep. No. 51–3823, at vi–ix (1891). For illustrations of light punishment coupled with guilty pleas, see Hearings (1891), 26–27, 46.

190. For the fee schedule, see USRS § 824. The $10 fee for a judgment rendered without a jury covered a guilty plea. Waters v. United States, 31 Ct. Cl. 307, 311–13 (1896); H.R. Rep. No. 53–931, at 1 (1894). Unfortunately, statistics on federal convictions do not differentiate between guilty pleas and trial convictions until after 1900.

191. Hearings (1891), 138, 173.

192. There was no discussion directly on this point in 1896. One congressmen said he had seen "the accused, after a trial and technical conviction . . . sentenced to imprisonment in the custody of the United States marshal until sundown, the sentence

being imposed about 4 in the afternoon." 28 Cong. Rec. 2461 (1896) (Rep. Tawney).
Another read one anecdote about a scheme of outright collusion between defendants
and prosecution witnesses, to get witness fees. Ibid., 2412 (Rep. Connolly).

193. Miller, *Revenuers and Moonshiners*, 1–14.

194. Ibid., 7.

195. Ibid., 10–12.

196. Ibid., 117–25, 161–63, 183–85. On the 1896 reform, see ibid., 185.

197. Ibid., 97–126.

198. H.R. Exec. Doc. No. 47–131, at 1–2 (1882). For testimonials from other officials along
the same lines, see ibid., 6; Hearings (1884), 31.

199. On the investigation, see Goldman, "'Weakened Spring,'" 170–71; Eugene Coleman
Savidge, *Life of Benjamin Harris Brewster with Discourses and Addresses* (Philadelphia: J. B. Lippincott Co., 1891), 204–11; and the entry on Brewster in *ANB*.

200. The quotations are from Brewster Cameron's report, printed in Hearings (1884), 2,
and from his oral remarks, printed in ibid., 10. On Cameron's background, see Jane
Wayland Brewster, "The San Rafael Cattle Company: A Pennsylvania Enterprise in
Arizona," *Arizona and the West* 8 (1966): 138.

201. H.R. Rep. No. 48–1779, at 1–2 (1884). On the bipartisan origins of this measure, see
also 15 Cong. Rec. 6121–22 (1884) (Rep. Springer).

202. 15 Cong. Rec. 6121–22 (1884) (Rep. Springer). Brewster's full message is in H.R. Rep.
No. 48–1779, at 2–5 (1884).

203. 15 Cong. Rec. 6123–25 (1884); 18 Cong. Rec. 1501–02 (1887). The only hint of a substantive argument by lawmakers in favor of U.S. attorney incentive fees after 1887 is
one cryptic sentence in H.R. Rep. No. 51–541, at 1 (1890).

204. In 1896, the House included the salarization measure as an amendment to an appropriations bill. It adopted the amendment and passed the bill itself by voice votes.
28 Cong. Rec. 2531 (1896). (We can infer voice votes because the *Congressional
Record* lists no divisions.) It adopted the conference report by voice vote. Ibid., 5643.
(Same inference.) House deliberations were devoid of any opposition to salarization
of U.S. attorneys in principle. Ibid., 835–38, 846–48, 2302–05, 2359–61, 2390–2412,
2444–66, 2492–2514, 2521–31, 3958–63, 4422–28, 5638–44; 28 Cong. Rec. Appendix
78–79, 288–90. See also 28 Cong. Rec. 2407 (Rep. Gillett) ("there seems to be a general recognition by the House that [the bill's] principle is sound"). The absence of
vocal opposition was not the result of time limits on the debate, which was quite open
ended. See the procedural comments and steps in ibid., 2302, 2360, 2392, 2397, 2408,
2409. See also William A. Robinson, *Thomas B. Reed: Parliamentarian* (New York:
Dodd, Mead 1930), 326 (noting this was a "quiet session" in the House).
    The Senate considered a proposal to strike the salarization measure from the ap-
propriations bill on the procedural ground that it was not a proper subject for that
kind of bill. It defeated this proposal by a vote of 30–18, with forty-one not voting.
28 Cong. Rec. 3266 (1896). It then passed the appropriations bill without a recorded
vote. Ibid., 3279. It likewise adopted the conference report without a recorded vote.
Ibid., 5736. The division on the procedural vote did not indicate a division on the
substantive merits of salarization. Freighting an appropriations bill with substantive

legislation was a weighty matter in itself, for the pressure to vote yes on appropriations bills was much greater than for other bills. For example, George Hoar spoke against the salarization measure on the procedural ground but discussed it favorably as a substantive matter. Ibid., 3229. The Judiciary Committee, which he chaired, had reported a separate, freestanding bill in favor of salarization. Ibid., 2813. Hoar stated that the Senate favored salarization, in substance, "with substantial unanimity." Ibid., 3229. See also ibid., 3167 (Sen. Cullom), 3265 (Sen. Allison). Overall, Senate deliberations on salarization of U.S. attorneys contained no opposition to it in principle (see ibid., 1647–52, 1681–86, 3166–87, 3227–33, 3262–66, 3894–98, 4765–67, 5732–36), with one exception. That exception — to which I think we should assign no weight — was the grumbling of John Sherman, the famous but aging Ohio Republican. Ibid., 3227–28, 3265. Sherman was then the longest-serving senator in U.S. history, and one suspects that the root of his animus to the measure was procedural, involving the protection of the Senate from House coercion. Admittedly, Sherman did suggest that salarization would be problematic, but his objection — that it would weaken officers' incentives to collect fees from litigants in private cases — was uninformed, incoherent, and irrelevant. Even Sherman's admiring biographer admits he was suffering memory loss and confusion, due to advanced age, around this time. Theodore E. Burton, *John Sherman* (Boston: Houghton Mifflin Co., 1906), 403–04. During Sherman's grumbling, other Senators tried gently to correct his confusion.

205. 28 Cong. Rec. 846 (1896) (Rep. Lacey); ibid., 2400 (Rep. Tracey); ibid., 2409 (Rep. Connolly).

206. See the report by the Reed-controlled Rules Committee of a resolution to let the salarization measure come to the floor as an amendment to the appropriations bill. 28 Cong. Rec. 2302 (1896).

207. The House tacked Springer's proposal onto a larger appropriations bill. Springer believed this necessary, since salarization affected government expenditures. 15 Cong. Rec. 5507 (1884). But when the bill went to conference, the Senate conferees felt that an appropriations bill was not a proper vehicle for salarization, since it was really substantive legislation. The matter returned to the House, where it came up very late at night during a marathon proceeding at the end of the session. Springer asked the House to back him against the Senate. A majority of members present voted to let the matter drop, but the members present were not enough for a quorum. Springer, under pressure to keep things moving, gave up and let the vote stand, promising to fight another day. Ibid., 6119–25. That these proceedings occurred late at night is evident from the fact that the House had been in session twenty hours (see ibid., 6125) and the session had begun at 9:00 a.m. (see ibid., 6086).

208. 18 Cong. Rec. 1549 (1887) (Rep. Gibson).

209. 28 Cong. Rec. 2408 (1896) (Rep. Gillett).

210. H.R. Rep. No. 53–931, at 4 (1894). See also 17 Cong. Rec. 2897 (1886) (Rep. Gibson); 17 Cong. Rec. 2919 (1886) (Reps. Warner and Gibson); 17 Cong. Rec. 2920 (1886) (Rep. Gibson); 28 Cong. Rec. 2399 (1896) (Rep. Burton); 28 Cong. Rec. 2407 (1896) (Rep. Gardner).

211. 18 Cong. Rec. 1548–54 (1887).

212. 28 Cong. Rec. 1651 (1896) (Sen. Vest), recalling the proceedings in 23 Cong. Rec. 4477–79 (1892).

213. On Democratic acceptance of the excise, see Miller, *Revenuers and Moonshiners*, 6, 9–10, 13, 145, 148–50. On moonshiners' lack of strong identification with one political party, see ibid., 41–45, 59.

214. § 48, 28 Stat. 509, 563 (1894); H.R. Rep. No. 53–276 (1894); Miller, *Revenuers and Moonshiners*, 166.

215. Miller, *Revenuers and Moonshiners*, 164–67.

216. See figure 7.1.

217. For claims of savings from salarization, see H.R. Rep. No. 54–544, at 1–2 (1896); 28 Cong. Rec. 2392 (1896) (Rep. McRae); 28 Cong. Rec. 2401 (1896) (Rep. Tracey); 28 Cong. Rec. Appendix 78 (1896) (Rep. Swanson).

218. For evidence of the continued difficulty of overcoming those differences, see the bickering in 28 Cong. Rec. 2444–66, 2492–2514 (1896).

219. On the political environment of the session, see Robinson, *Thomas B. Reed*, 324–26. On the absence of dissent, see my discussion in note 204 above.

220. 28 Cong. Rec. 835–38, 846–48 (1896); H.R. Rep. No. 54–544 (1896).

221. H.R. Rep. No. 54–544 (1896); 28 Cong. Rec. 2302 (1896) (Rep. Henderson); ibid., 3264–65 (Sen. Allison). Also, the arguments of Rep. Updegraff were largely (though not entirely) fiscal. Ibid., 2360, 2390–92.

222. 28 Cong. Rec. 2397–98 (1896) (Rep. Burton); ibid., 2393 (Rep. McRae); ibid., 2397 (Representative Brown, quoting Judge C. D. Clark); ibid., 2401 (Rep. Tracey); ibid., 2398 (Representative Burton, quoting anonymous federal judge). See also ibid., 2403 (Rep. Underwood).

223. On East Tennessee, see Cresswell, *Mormons & Cowboys*, 133–80.

224. 28 Cong. Rec. 2396 (1896).

225. Kenneth C. Martis, *The Historical Atlas of United States Congressional Districts, 1789–1983* (New York: Free Press, 1982), 128–29.

226. Miller, *Revenuers and Moonshiners*, 12–13, 138–39, 142, 144–46.

227. *Herringshaw's Encyclopedia of American Biography of the Nineteenth Century*, ed. Thomas William Herringshaw (Chicago: American Publishers' Association, 1901), 156.

228. Miller, *Revenuers and Moonshiners*, 220n38; Henry M. Wiltse, *The Moonshiners* (Chattanooga, TN: Times Printing Co., 1895), 124–25.

229. 28 Cong. Rec. 2396 (emphasis added).

230. Martis, *Historical Atlas of United States Congressional Districts*, 128–29.

231. 28 Cong. Rec. 2398 (1896). Contrary to Brown and Burton, another of the engaged members of the committee characterized the salarization bill as "one step in the direction of finally getting rid of the internal-revenue law," which he considered a good thing, though he immediately added: "But while we have that internal-revenue law it must be enforced." 28 Cong. Rec. 2408 (1896) (Rep. Connolly).

232. For a map of the district, overlapping the Blue Ridge Mountains, see Henry C. Ferrell Jr., *Claude A. Swanson of Virginia: A Political Biography* (Lexington: University Press of Kentucky, 1985), 10.

233. 26 Cong. Rec. Appendix 369 (1894).

234. For Swanson's votes, see 26 Cong. Rec. 1795–96, 1796–97, 8482 (1894).

235. 28 Cong. Rec. Appendix 78–79, 290 (1896). For a similar argument by a congressman in a similar political situation, see 28 Cong. Rec. 2524–26 (1896) (Rep. Tate).

236. On Dick, Settle's father, and the Republican Party, see Jeffrey J. Crow, "Thomas Settle Jr., Reconstruction, and the Memory of the Civil War," *Journal of Southern History* 62 (1996): 689–726.

237. Miller, *Revenuers and Moonshiners*, 120–21.

238. 28 Cong. Rec. 838 (1896) (emphasis added). Note Dick's proposed remedy for over-prosecution was not salarization (which he did not mention either way) but a revision of the statute so that it would only prohibit selling as a regular business. Still, Settle submitted Dick's statement in the context of a debate about the fee system. (Note that Dick had expressed support for the fee system many years earlier, in 1881. Miller, *Revenuers and Moonshiners*, 119.)

239. As one U.S. attorney testified: "It is very hard to draw the line as to what amounts to [liquor] retailing." Hearings (1891), 43.

240. Compare Miller, *Revenuers and Moonshiners*, 124.

241. The phrase is from William J. Stuntz's seminal article, "The Pathological Politics of Criminal Law," *Michigan Law Review* 100 (2001): 506.

242. 28 Cong. Rec. 2457 (1896). See also 28 Cong. Rec. Appendix 79 (1896) (Rep. Swanson).

243. The U.S. attorneys were not even formally united in a Department of Justice until 1870, and even then, the department's Washington office lacked the resources (and often the inclination) to set nationwide policy on criminal law enforcement, which was only one of many items on its plate. On the department's lack of direction for its field service during its early decades, see Cresswell, *Mormons & Cowboys*, 249–51; see also ibid., 5, 112–13, 128, 148, 159–60, 177–78, 180. The attorney general, in his first report after salarization, trumpeted the instant plunge in prosecutorial business as a joyous triumph, with no suggestion that his office was telling the now-salaried U.S. attorneys how to select among cases. AG Report 1896, pp. vii–x. No general substantive guidelines on criminal prosecution appear in the department's volume of circulars for the period 1896–1903. "Department of Justice Circular Book No. 3, Beginning February 5, 1896, Ending October 20, 1903," Record Group 60, Entry 121-A, Administrative Orders, Circulars, and Memorandums, 1856–1977, National Archives and Records Administration, College Park, MD. The department's published manual for U.S. attorneys, in its editions of 1898 and 1904, said nothing specific about prosecutorial decisions or enforcement priorities, except to note, without elaboration, that "frivolous and unnecessary" cases were to be avoided. *Instructions to United States Marshals, Attorneys, Clerks, and Commissioners* (Washington, DC: GPO, 1898), 118; *Instructions to United States Marshals, Attorneys, Clerks, and Commissioners* (Washington, DC: GPO, 1904), 175. Goldman's study of the department in the 1880s and 1890s confirms that it underwent no administrative changes having much substantive impact on law enforcement, except for fee abolition itself, which he discusses briefly. "'Weakened Spring,'" 172, 174–75. A Brookings Institution study in 1927 found

that the department had never sought "to control the action of [U.S.] attorneys in criminal cases by general regulation." Albert Langeluttig, *The Department of Justice of the United States* (Baltimore: Johns Hopkins Press, 1927), 76. Admittedly, the department did institute a requirement that the Washington office preapprove a U.S. attorney's decision to enter a nolle prosequi (i.e., to drop a case), but that requirement did not come into being until decades after salarization, and even then, it included no substantive guidelines and excepted "petty offenses" of the kind that had been central to the 1896 debate. *Instructions to United States Marshals, Attorneys, Clerks, and Commissioners* (Washington, DC: GPO, 1916), 142. (The "petty offenses" exception was dropped in 1925. *Instructions to United States Marshals, Attorneys, Clerks, and Commissioners* (Washington, DC: GPO, 1925), 178.) Even today, U.S. attorneys' offices are very far from being under centralized control. James Eisenstein, *Counsel for the United States: U.S. Attorneys in the Political and Legal Systems* (Baltimore: Johns Hopkins University Press, 1978), 11, 120–22. Finally, one might perhaps argue that other federal agencies outside the Justice Department (particularly the Internal Revenue Bureau) imposed central control on the U.S. attorneys' decision-making at the time of salarization in 1896, but the evidence for that is not persuasive. See Parrillo diss., 583n258.

244. 28 Cong. Rec. 2408 (1896) (Rep. Gillett); 17 Cong. Rec. 2897 (1886) (Rep. Gibson).

245. Eisenstein, *Counsel for the United States*, 9.

246. See also Goldman, "Weakened Spring," 173–74 (noting that the Civil Service Reform Act of 1883 had "minimal impact" on the Justice Department).

247. Earl H. De Long, "Powers and Duties of the State Attorney-General in Criminal Prosecution," *Journal of Criminal Law and Criminology* 25 (1934): 395.

248. Michael J. Ellis, "The Origins of the Elected Prosecutor," *Yale Law Journal* 121 (2012): 1528–69.

249. Kress, "Progress and Prosecution," 105–06; Duane R. Nedrud, "The Career Prosecutor: Prosecutors of Forty-Eight States," *Journal of Criminal Law, Criminology, and Political Science* 51 (1960): 344–45.

250. People v. Wabash, St. Louis & Pacific Railway Co., 12 Ill.App. 263 (1882); Clara Foltz, "Duties of District Attorneys in Prosecutions," *Criminal Law Magazine and Reporter* 18 (1896): 415–16; "Report of Committee on Criminal Cost Reform," in *Proceedings of the Sixteenth Annual Meeting of the Bar Association of Tennessee, Held at Nashville, Tenn., July 28, 29, 30, 1897* (Nashville, TN: Marshall and Bruce Co., 1897), 46; "Stop the State's-Attorney's Fees," *Chicago Daily Tribune*, Jan. 6, 1897, p. 6; George W. Warvelle, *Essays in Legal Ethics* (Chicago: Callaghan and Co., 1902), 140; "Praises Wayman and Burke," *Chicago Daily Tribune*, June 2, 1910, p. 2 (quoting speaker at Illinois State's Attorneys' Association).

251. On the press, see Carolyn B. Ramsey, "The Discretionary Power of 'Public' Prosecutors in Historical Perspective," *American Criminal Law Review* 39 (2002): 1321–22, 1342–47, 1349, 1391–93. For judicial views, see, e.g., *Keyes v. State*, 23 N.E. 1097, 1097 (Ind. 1890); *State v. Kent*, 62 N.W. 631, 634 (N.D. 1895); *Wyatt v. State*, 16 S.W.2d 231 (Tex. Crim. App. 1929).

252. E.g., Fout v. State, 4 Tenn. 98 (1816); State v. Fields, 7 Tenn. 140 (1823); Ireland, "Privately Funded Prosecution," 47–48 (on John Rowan speech of 1839); Rush v. Cavenaugh, 2 Pa. 187, 189–90 (1845) (Gibson, C.J.).

253. By the late 1800s, Americans were apparently losing faith in the jury's accuracy, but part of their anxiety (perhaps their main anxiety) was that jurors were too willing to *acquit.* For a sense of the criticisms, see Henry C. Caldwell, "The American Jury System," *American Law Review* 22 (1888): 853, 870; Elizabeth Dale, "*People v. Coughlin* and Criticisms of the Criminal Jury in Late Nineteenth-Century Chicago," *Northern Illinois University Law Review* 28 (2008): 503–36.

254. "The Administration of Criminal Law in New Orleans," *New Orleans Monthly Review* 1 (Apr. 1874): 37.

255. "Salaries for Solicitors General," *Columbus (GA) Daily Enquirer*, July 20, 1888, p. 2. See also "Salaries for Solicitors," *Macon (GA) Telegraph*, Aug. 30, 1888, p. 4.

256. Lawrence M. Friedman, *A History of American Law*, 3rd ed. (London: Touchstone, 2005), 216–19, 442–49, 452–53.

257. Edward L. Ayers, *The Promise of the New South: Life after Reconstruction*, 15th anniversary ed. (Oxford: Oxford University Press, 2007), 136–46.

258. "The State Needs Peace," *Fort Worth Star-Telegram*, Aug. 3, 1909, p. 6.

259. "Criminal Costs: Something of Pressing Interest to Tennessee Tax-Payers," *Knoxville (TN) Journal*, Aug. 17, 1896, p. 6 (quoting report of Tennessee Bar Association committee).

260. *Messages of the Governors of Tennessee*, 7:593–94 (message of Governor Peter Turney).

261. See entries in this book's Appendix for California, Indiana, Louisiana, and Oregon.

262. *Messages of the Governors of Tennessee*, 7:593–94 (message of Governor Peter Turney).

263. "Municipal Government of Tulsa Most Modern," *Tulsa (OK) World*, Feb. 26, 1911, p. 47.

264. State ex rel. Griffith v. Baird, 231 P. 1021 (Kansas 1925).

265. On elected prosecutors' accommodation of local preferences, see Herman G. James, *Local Government in the United States* (New York: D. Appleton and Co., 1921), 148.

266. "Governor's Message," *Clarion (Jackson, MS)*, Jan. 11, 1888, supplement, p. 1; *Messages of the Governors of Tennessee*, 7:648 (message of Governor Robert Love Taylor); "Vote to Abolish Fee System," *Atlanta Constitution*, Oct. 26, 1916, p. 6.

267. 1885 Kansas Sess. Laws 236, 242–43.

268. Bader, *Prohibition in Kansas*, 80, 82, 114; *Sixth Biennial Report of the Attorney General of the State of Kansas* (Topeka: Kansas Publishing House, 1888), 9.

269. Bader, *Prohibition in Kansas*, 118, 162–68.

270. *Eighteenth Biennial Report of the Attorney-General of Kansas, 1911–1912* (Topeka, KS: State Printing Office, 1912), 19.

271. *Seventeenth Biennial Report of the Attorney-General of Kansas, 1909–1910* (Topeka, KS: State Printing Office, 1911), ix.

272. "House Issues a Statement," *Iola (KS) Daily Register*, July 20, 1911, p. 9. On House, see Bader, *Prohibition in Kansas*, 171, 181.

273. On the veto, see *Eighteenth Biennial Report of the Attorney-General of Kansas, 1911–1912*, 20. On Stubbs and Dawson, see Bader, *Prohibition in Kansas*, 170.

274. Bader, *Prohibition in Kansas*, 168–72; Patrick G. O'Brien and Kenneth J. Peak, *Kansas Bootleggers* (Manhattan, KS: Sunflower University Press, 1991), 32–40.

275. "Graft in the Raids — Sapp," *Kansas City (MO) Star*, July 14, 1911, p. 1. On Sapp's wet sympathies, see O'Brien and Peak, *Kansas Bootleggers*, 38–39.

276. Bader, *Prohibition in Kansas*, 169–70.

277. "Graft in the Raids — Sapp," *Kansas City (MO) Star*, July 14, 1911, p. 1. Bizarrely, there is a paragraph of another, separate story, on page 2 of the *Star* that day, titled "Senate Fixes a Voting Day," which clearly belongs in the story about Sapp. Dawson's statement appears in this separate paragraph.

278. 1913 Kansas Sess. Laws 538, 538–39. For Dawson's support of this bill and a previous one, see *Eighteenth Biennial Report of the Attorney-General of Kansas, 1911–1912* (Topeka: State Printing Office, 1912), 19–21. On the new governor, see O'Brien and Peak, *Kansas Bootleggers*, 40–41.

279. 1915 Kansas Sess. Laws 7. The same provision appeared in nearly every biennial appropriations act for more than thirty years thereafter (with the odd exception of 1927). For citations, see Parrillo diss., 593n294. Note, however, that Dawson's successors may have made arrangements with some assistants whereby the assistant received compensation from the contingent fund that was similar in form to conviction fees. "Split in Bone Dry Pact," *Kansas City (MO) Star*, May 3, 1918, p. 11; "A Fight for Fees," *Kansas City (MO) Star*, Jan. 28, 1919, p. 1; "Mayor Warns a Fee Grabber," *Kansas City (MO) Star*, Jan. 30, 1919, p. 8; "Hubbard Gets Commission," *Kansas City (MO) Star*, Jan. 31, 1919, p. 7. Liquor conviction fees remained in place for the county attorneys. Heinz v. Larimer, 241 P. 241 (Kansas 1925).

280. E.g., "The State Needs Peace," *Fort Worth Star-Telegram*, Aug. 3, 1909, p. 6; Robert B. Mayes, "Annual Address of the President of the Mississippi State Bar Association," in *Minutes of the Ninth Annual Meeting of the Mississippi State Bar Association . . . Held at Gulfport, Mississippi, April 30–May 1, 1914* (Jackson, MS: Hederman Brothers, 1914), 51; Frank Backus Williams, "The Administration of the Law for the Prevention of Cruelty to Animals," in *Legislation for the Protection of Animals and Children* (New York: Columbia University, 1914), 21–22; "Solicitors on Salary," *Statesville (NC) Landmark*, Mar. 8, 1923, p. 4.

## CHAPTER 8: INCARCERATION

1. Rebecca M. McLennan, *The Crisis of Imprisonment: Protest, Politics, and the Making of the American Penal State, 1776–1941* (Cambridge: Cambridge University Press, 2008).

2. On Southern convict leasing, see especially Douglas A. Blackmon, *Slavery by Another Name: The Re-Enslavement of Black Americans from the Civil War to World War II* (New York: Anchor Books, 2009); Alex Lichtenstein, *Twice the Work of Free Labor: The Political Economy of Convict Labor in the New South* (London: Verso, 1996); Matthew J. Mancini, *One Dies, Get Another: Convict Leasing in the American South,*

*1866–1928* (Columbia: University of South Carolina Press, 1996); Robert Perkinson, *Texas Tough: The Rise of America's Prison Empire* (New York: Metropolitan Books, 2010), 83–176. A deep question about the South that demands further examination is whether we should understand the arrangements that replaced outright convict-leasing (particularly road-building chain gangs and prison farms) as "profit-seeking" even though the benefits went to the state or taxpayer. On this issue, see particularly Perkinson, *Texas Tough*, 151–53, 160, 179, 320. Relatedly, Perkinson's account suggests that the Southern prison has *never* achieved legitimacy. Ibid., 10–11, 366–70. (It should be noted that McLennan gives some attention to the South, but it is not her main focus. McLennan, *Crisis of Imprisonment*, 90, 101–02, 116–18, 157–60, 164–65, 186–87.)

3. McLennan, *Crisis of Imprisonment*, 23.
4. This is evident from *Lyon v. Ide*, N. Chip. 49 (Vt. 1790).
5. Michael Ignatieff, *A Just Measure of Pain: The Penitentiary and the Industrial Revolution, 1750–1850* (New York: Pantheon, 1978), 29–35.
6. Ignatieff, *Just Measure of Pain*, 30, 36–37 (on England); Michael Meranze, *Laboratories of Virtue: Punishment, Revolution, and Authority in Pennsylvania, 1760–1835* (Chapel Hill: University of North Carolina Press, 1996), 175 (on Pennsylvania).
7. Sidney Webb and Beatrice Webb, *English Prisons under Local Government* (New York: Longmans, Green and Co., 1922), 5n2.
8. On waves of experimentation with incarcerated labor in England prior to the advent of the penitentiary in the late 1700s, which provided limited precedent for that institution, see Ignatieff, *A Just Measure of Pain*, 11–14, 31–32.
9. Ibid., 38–39.
10. Ibid., 40; McLennan, *Crisis of Imprisonment*, 46, 59–60.
11. McLennan, *Crisis of Imprisonment*, 36–38.
12. Mark E. Kann, *Punishment, Prisons, and Patriarchy: Liberty and Power in the Early American Republic* (New York: New York University Press, 2005), 159–65.
13. McLennan, *Crisis of Imprisonment*, 39–40.
14. Ibid., 37–38.
15. Meranze, *Laboratories of Virtue*, 181.
16. *Laws of the State of New York Passed at the Sessions of the Legislature Held in the Years [1789–1796]* (Albany, NY: Weed, Parsons and Co., 1887), 3:669, 673 (statute of 1796).
17. McLennan, *Crisis of Imprisonment*, 43–48.
18. Ibid., 56–61.
19. Ibid., 65.
20. Ibid., 60, 67. The first significant New York riots since the 1820s were in the 1850s, and they arose from the *restriction* of the contract regime. Ibid., 82.
21. Ibid., 53, 63–65, 67. An alternative scheme, whereby inmates labored individually in their cells, was ill suited to the kind of factory production in which contractors engaged, and it never spread far. Ibid., 61–64.
22. Ibid., 69–71.
23. For this reason, the original New York prison disciplinarian, Elam Lynds, was suspicious of the contract system. Ibid., 60.

24. W. David Lewis, *From Newgate to Dannemora: The Rise of the Penitentiary in New York, 1796–1848* (Ithaca, NY: Cornell University Press, 1965), 251.

25. McLennan, *Crisis of Imprisonment*, 97–101, 134. On the short-lived movement to ameliorate the contract system prior to the Depression, see ibid., 90–97.

26. Ibid., 106–07, 131–34.

27. Ibid., 125.

28. Ibid., 126–27, 131.

29. Ibid., 120. McLennan appears to qualify this by later stating, in passing, that officers "ceased to enforce rules prohibiting instructors and officers from giving prisoners 'gifts' or trading with or selling anything to prisoners." Ibid., 127. But she says nothing else along these lines.

30. Ibid., 135.

31. Ibid.

32. Ibid., 137–46, 167–68.

33. Ibid., 142.

34. Ibid. See also ibid., 144.

35. Ibid., 147–48 (emphasis in original).

36. Ibid., 139, 143n7.

37. Ibid., 149. See also ibid., 172–73.

38. Ibid., 149, 155, 160–65.

39. Ibid., 152n36, 172–73, 182, 231, 235–37.

40. Ibid., 171.

41. Ibid., 144–45, 166–68.

42. Ibid., 168–69. All quotes are McLennan's paraphrase, except "wiped out."

43. Ibid., 172–73.

44. Ibid., 189.

45. Ibid., 173. See also ibid., 192.

46. Ibid., 187–88, 189, 185.

47. Ibid., 201–02, 208–09.

48. Ibid., 262–65.

49. Ibid., 222–28.

50. Ibid., 214, 228–29, 254–55, 276–77 (quote at 214).

51. Ibid., 211–18.

52. Ibid., 209, 213–15.

53. Ibid., 219, 254.

54. Ibid., 269–70.

55. Ibid., 271–72.

56. Ibid., 257.

57. Ibid., 254–55.

58. Ibid., 258–59.

59. See generally ibid., 319–416, and especially ibid., 408–09 (analyzing the anti-bureaucratic nature of Osborne's management).

60. Ibid., 417–67.

CHAPTER 9: NAVAL WARFARE

1. Prior treatments of the U.S. abolition of prize money and head money are brief and do not seriously attempt to explain why it happened when it did. Robert W. Daly, "Pay and Prize Money in the Old Navy, 1776–1899, *United States Naval Institute Proceedings* 74 (Aug. 1948): 967–71; Harold D. Langley, "Dewey, Sampson, and the Courts: The Rise and Fall of Prize and Bounty Money," in *New Interpretations in Naval History: Selected Papers of the Thirteenth Annual Symposium Held at Annapolis, Maryland, 2–4 October 1997*, ed. William M. McBride (Annapolis, MD: Naval Institute Press, 1998), 91–107. In a previous article, focused mainly on U.S. privateering rather than the U.S. Navy, I offered a brief discussion of the abolition of prize money within the U.S. Navy. Nicholas Parrillo, "The De-Privatization of American Warfare: How the U.S. Government Used, Regulated, and Ultimately Abandoned Privateering in the Nineteenth Century," *Yale Journal of Law and the Humanities* 19 (2007): 91–94. In this book, I adopt a different interpretation of abolition within the navy, in light of research I have done since that article was published.

2. This view was best articulated by Thomas Paine. David M. Fitzsimons, "Tom Paine's New World Order: Idealistic Internationalism in the Ideology of Early American Foreign Relations," *Diplomatic History* 19 (1995): 569–82.

3. See my discussion in this chapter, text at notes 143–45.

4. Members of the militia during the eighteenth and early nineteenth centuries could often take property as a result of success, particularly in conflicts with Indians. E.g., James Grenier, *The First Way of War: American War Making on the Frontier, 1607–1814* (Cambridge: Cambridge University Press, 2005), 189, 196, 208 (referring to pillaging). Militia members and volunteers who fought the Indian Wars of the nineteenth century often expected to take Indian lands. E.g., ibid., 216. There were also rewards from the public treasury. For example, in the French and Indian War (1754–63), the four largest colonies all offered scalp bounties, typically to small, semiregular units of "rangers," usually for the scalps of enemy Indians, though sometimes for those of whites. See Alan Taylor, "'A Kind of Warr': The Contest for Land on the Northeastern Frontier, 1750–1820," *William and Mary Quarterly*, 3rd ser., 46 (1989): 15 (Massachusetts); Peter Silver, *Our Savage Neighbors: How Indian War Transformed Early America* (2007), 161–72, 360n2 (Pennsylvania); *Md. Arch.* 52:651–52 (1756) (Maryland); *The Statutes at Large, Being a Collection of All the Laws of Virginia, from the First Session of the Legislature, in the Year 1619*, ed. William Waller Hening (Richmond, VA: W. W. Gray, 1819), 6:550–52 (statute of 1755). On ranger units and scalp bounties, see Grenier, *First Way of War*, 64–65, 125–26, 158, 167. As late as the Revolutionary War, Pennsylvania and South Carolina made such offers. Colin G. Calloway, *The American Revolution in Indian Country: Crisis and Diversity in Native American Communities* (Cambridge: Cambridge University Press, 1995), 49. A general in the regular U.S. Army offered scalp bounties to scouts in the 1790s. Walter R. Hoberg, "A Tory in the Northwest," *Pennsylvania Magazine of History and Biography* 59 (1935): 38.

5. During the Second Seminole War in 1841, one U.S. Army colonel, with the support of his fellow officers, placed his ranger units under an "unofficial bounty system, by

which soldiers were paid $100 for every warrior captured or killed." William B. Skelton, *An American Profession of Arms: The Army Officer Corps, 1784–1861* (Lawrence: University Press of Kansas, 1992), 321. (I thank John Fabian Witt for this reference.) In the Civil War, when General William T. Sherman and his associates ordered massive foraging and property destruction in the South, their policy practically resulted in some level of self-enrichment by Union soldiers, beyond the necessity of war. But it is hard to say how much of this occurred, or how much Sherman and other commanders approved. Mark Grimsley, *The Hard Hand of War: Union Military Policy toward Southern Civilians, 1861–1865* (Cambridge: Cambridge University Press, 1995), 96–111, 151–62, 190–204. There was also bounty-seeking in state and local forces. As late as 1862, Minnesota's adjutant general, facing the Sioux uprising, offered $200 for every scalp. Edward D. Neill, *History of Hennepin County and the City of Minneapolis* (Minneapolis: North Star Publishing Co., 1881), 153. As late as the 1880s, there were reports of local governments in the West offering scalp bounties. E.g., "Indian Extermination," *Worcester (MA) Daily Spy*, Oct. 13, 1885, p. 1 (Arizona counties); Robert McElroy, *Grover Cleveland: The Man and the Statesman: An Authorized Biography* (New York: Harper and Brothers, 1923), 1:229–30 (Grant County, New Mexico, citing the *Southwest Sentinel* of Silver City, New Mexico).

6.  This and the next paragraph rely on John A. Lynn II, *Women, Armies, and Warfare in Early Modern Europe* (Cambridge: Cambridge University Press, 2008), 24–33, 145–51, 221–28; John A. Lynn, "How War Fed War: The Tax of Violence and Contributions during the *Grand Siècle*," *Journal of Modern History* 65 (1993): 286–310; Fritz Redlich, *De Praeda Militari: Looting and Booty, 1500–1815* (Wiesbaden, Germany: F. Steiner, 1956).

7.  On the importance of calibrating extraction to avoid sparking resistance in land warfare, see Julian S. Corbett, "The Capture of Private Property at Sea," *Some Neglected Aspects of War* (Boston: Little, Brown and Co., 1907), 123, 126, 132. Lynn notes that Louis XIV sought to curtail soldiers' taking of property largely because his troops often imposed their demands on France's own population—a practice that became intolerable as the army grew. Lynn, "How War Fed War."

8.  Janice E. Thomson, *Mercenaries, Pirates, and Sovereigns: State-Building and Extraterritorial Violence in Early Modern Europe* (Princeton, NJ: Princeton University Press, 1994), 22.

9.  David Loades, *The Tudor Navy: An Administrative, Political and Military History* (Aldershot, UK: Scolar Press, 1992), 11.

10. Loades, *Tudor Navy*, 33–34. Both also received wages.

11. P. K. Kemp, *Prize Money: A Survey of the History and Distribution of the Naval Prize Fund* (Aldershot, UK: Wellington Press, 1946), 10.

12. "A Proclamation Appointing the Distribution of Prizes . . ." (1708), in *English Historical Documents, 1660–1714*, ed. Andrew Browning (London: Eyre and Spottiswoode, 1953), 834.

13. Daniel A. Baugh, *British Naval Administration in the Age of Walpole* (Princeton, NJ: Princeton University Press, 1965), 112.

14. James Stephen, *War in Disguise; Or, The Frauds of the Neutral Flags*, 3rd ed. (London: C. Whittingham, 1806), 129.

15. For this paragraph and the next, see the literature on prize law and the Declaration of Paris, especially Olive Anderson, "Some Further Light on the Inner History of the Declaration of Paris," *Law Quarterly Review* 76 (1960): 379–85; Henry J. Bourguignon, *Sir William Scott, Lord Stowell: Judge of the High Court of Admiralty, 1798–1828* (Cambridge: Cambridge University Press, 1987); C. I. Hamilton, "Anglo-French Seapower and the Declaration of Paris," *International History Review* 4 (1982): 166–90; Richard Hill, *The Prizes of War: The Naval Prize System in the Napoleonic Wars, 1793–1815* (Portsmouth, UK: Royal Naval Museum Publications, 1998); H. W. Malkin, "The Inner History of the Declaration of Paris," *British Yearbook of International Law* 8 (1927): 1–44; Parrillo, "De-Privatization of American Warfare"; Donald A. Petrie: *The Prize Game: Lawful Looting on the High Seas in the Days of Fighting Sail* (Annapolis, MD: Naval Institute Press, 1999); Bernard Semmel, *Liberalism and Naval Strategy: Ideology, Interest, and Sea Power during the Pax Britannica* (Boston: Allen and Unwin, 1986); Warren F. Spencer, "The Mason Memorandum and the Diplomatic Origins of the Declaration of Paris," in *Diplomacy in an Age of Nationalism: Essays in Honor of Lynn Marshall Case*, ed. Nancy N. Barker and Marvin L. Brown Jr. (The Hague: Martinus Nijhoff, 1971); Francis R. Stark, *Abolition of Privateering and the Declaration of Paris* (New York: Columbia University, 1897).

16. Baugh, *British Naval Administration*, 113–15; Brian Lavery, *Nelson's Navy: The Ships, Men, and Organization, 1793–1815* (London: Conway Maritime Press, 1989), 116.

17. "A Proclamation Appointing the Distribution of Prizes . . . ," 834; Kemp, *Prize Money*, 24–25; Lavery, *Nelson's Navy*, 116. On the "blood money" nickname, see Michael Lewis, *The Navy in Transition, 1814–1864: A Social History* (London: Hodder and Stoughton, 1965), 232.

18. Lavery, *Nelson's Navy*, 116, 318.

19. Lewis, *Navy in Transition*, 212–13.

20. See generally H. Richard Uviller and William G. Merkel, *The Militia and the Right to Arms; or, How the Second Amendment Fell Silent* (Durham, NC: Duke University Press, 2002), 109–32. On the locally oriented, nonprofessional, and democratic organization of Civil War army units, see Christopher J. Olsen, *The American Civil War: A Hands-On History* (New York: Hill and Wang, 2006), 88–89; Gerald J. Prokopowicz, *All for the Regiment: The Army of the Ohio, 1861–1862* (Chapel Hill: University of North Carolina Press, 2001), 18–19.

21. HSUS series Ed28. Ira Katznelson notes that the War of 1812 and Mexican War had "virtually no 'ratchet effect'" on the size of the permanent military. "Flexible Capacity: The Military and Early American Statebuilding," in *Shaped by War and Trade: International Influences on American Political Development*, ed. Ira Katznelson and Martin Shefter (Princeton, NJ: Princeton University Press, 2002), 98.

22. E.g., Robert M. Utley, *Frontiersmen in Blue: The United States Army and the Indian, 1848–1865* (New York: Macmillan, 1967), 14–15, 21, 101–02, 210.

23. Cong. Globe, 34th Cong., 1st Sess., Appendix 902 (1856) (Rep. Davis).

24. Parrillo, "De-Privatization of American Warfare," 3–4.
25. Akhil Reed Amar, *The Bill of Rights: Creation and Reconstruction* (New Haven, CT: Yale University Press, 1998), 50–59.
26. Mlada Bukovansky, "American Identity and Neutral Rights from Independence to the War of 1812," *International Organization* 51 (1997): 234.
27. On England's formidable "fiscal-military state," see John Brewer, *The Sinews of Power: War, Money, and the English State, 1688–1783* (Cambridge, MA: Harvard University Press, 1988). On the fear and suspicion of this apparatus among Englishmen themselves, see ibid., 155–62.
28. William P. Leeman, *The Long Road to Annapolis: The Founding of the Naval Academy and the Emerging American Republic* (Chapel Hill: University of North Carolina Press, 2010), 20–21.
29. Ibid., 110–11.
30. Craig L. Symonds, *Navalists and Antinavalists: The Naval Policy Debate in the United States, 1785–1827* (Newark: University of Delaware Press, 1980), 12–14, 233–35.
31. George Washington, "Farewell Address," in *George Washington: Writings*, ed. John Rhodehamel (New York: Library of America, 1997), 974.
32. Walter Russell Mead, *Special Providence: American Foreign Policy and How It Changed the World* (New York: Routledge, 2002), 195.
33. [Tench Coxe], *Thoughts on the Subject of Naval Power in the United States of America* (Philadelphia, 1806), 10.
34. Leeman, *Long Road to Annapolis*, 21. See also ibid., 47.
35. Except where otherwise noted, this section relies on Parrillo, "De-Privatization of American Warfare," 15–50, 64–70.
36. Wade G. Dudley, *Splintering the Wooden Wall: The British Blockade of the United States, 1812–1815* (Annapolis, MD: Naval Institute Press, 2003), 10–13.
37. See my discussion in note 107 below.
38. Christopher McKee, *A Gentlemanly and Honorable Profession: The Creation of the U.S. Naval Officer Corps, 1794–1815* (Annapolis, MD: Naval Institute Press, 1991), 214–15.
39. §§ 6–7, 2 Stat. 45, 52–53 (1800).
40. McKee, *Gentlemanly and Honorable Profession*, 341.
41. Parrillo, "De-Privatization of American Warfare," 26.
42. McKee, *Gentlemanly and Honorable Profession*, 346–47 (prizes), 490–91 (salary).
43. H.R. Rep. No. 47–144, at 4–6 (1882) (documenting practice of the early republic).
44. McKee, *Gentlemanly and Honorable Profession*, 345–47 (Decatur's award), 490–91 (highest possible captain's salary).
45. Semmel, *Liberalism and Naval Strategy*, 14–15; Bukovansky, "American Identity," 222.
46. Semmel, *Liberalism and Naval Strategy*, 152. See also ibid., 19; Bukovansky, "American Identity," 238.
47. Semmel, *Liberalism and Naval Strategy*, 18. See also Bukovansky, "American Identity," 222, 233, 237.
48. Bukovansky, "American Identity," 224, 227–28.
49. Stark, *Abolition of Privateering*, 13–45.

50. Adams to Richard Rush (July 28, 1823), in *Policy of the United States toward Maritime Commerce in War*, ed. Carlton Savage (Washington, DC: GPO, 1934), 1:309 (emphasis omitted).

51. On trade as promoter of peace and cosmopolitanism, see Semmel, *Liberalism and Naval Strategy*, 4.

52. On the connection between privateering and the mercantilist outlook, see Carl E. Swanson, *Predators and Prizes: American Privateering and Imperial Warfare, 1739–1748* (Columbia: University of South Carolina Press, 1991), 16–21.

53. "Application to Abolish Privateering in Time of War" (1821), in *American State Papers: Naval Affairs* (Washington, DC: Gales and Seaton, 1834), 1:723.

54. On postmillennialism and the mitigation of war, see Semmel, *Liberalism and Naval Strategy*, 69.

55. E.g., Adams to Richard Rush (July 28, 1823), in *Policy of the United States toward Maritime Commerce*, 1:307.

56. Ibid., 1:304, 307. See also "Application to Abolish Privateering in Time of War" (1820), in *American State Papers: Naval Affairs*, 1:628.

57. Message of President Monroe to Congress (Dec. 2, 1823), in *Policy of the United States toward Maritime Commerce*, 1:321. John Quincy Adams endorsed the same policy as president in 1826. Message of President John Quincy Adams to the House of Representatives (Mar. 15, 1826), in *Policy of the United States toward Maritime Commerce*, 1:324.

58. *Policy of the United States toward Maritime Commerce*, 1:56–64.

59. Clay to the Appointed Delegates to the Congress at Panama (May 8, 1826), in *Policy of the United States toward Maritime Commerce*, 1:329.

60. Bukovansky, "American Identity," 223, 234.

61. Parrillo, "De-Privatization of American Warfare," 54–57.

62. Marcy to the French Minister (Sartiges) (July 28, 1856), in *Policy of the United States toward Maritime Commerce*, 1:388. See also Message of President Pierce to Congress (Dec. 4, 1854), in *Policy of the United States toward Maritime Commerce*, 1:380.

63. Cong. Globe, 34th Cong., 1st Sess., Appendix 898, 902 (1856) (Rep. Davis).

64. Parrillo, "De-Privatization of American Warfare," 61.

65. "Philosophy of Privateering—Shall the Practice Be Abandoned?" *New York Times*, Aug. 5, 1858, p. 4.

66. Stark, *Abolition of Privateering*, 150; Semmel, *Liberalism and Naval Strategy*, 71.

67. Cong. Globe, 37th Cong., 3d Sess. 1023 (1863) (Sen. Collamer).

68. George T. Davis, *A Navy Second to None: The Development of Modern American Naval Policy* (New York: Harcourt, Brace and Co., 1940), 11.

69. HSUS series Ed38.

70. Lance E. Davis and Stanley L. Engerman, *Naval Blockades in Peace and War: An Economic History since 1750* (Cambridge: Cambridge University Press, 2006), 151–58.

71. HSUS series Ed38.

72. Harold Sprout and Margaret Sprout, *The Rise of American Naval Power, 1776–1918* (Princeton, NJ: Princeton University Press, 1939), 165–67.

73. Sprout and Sprout, *Rise of American Naval Power*, 171, 174.

74. Davis, *Navy Second to None*, 32.

75. "Jackie's Chance for Affluence," *Minneapolis Journal*, May 18, 1898, p. 13.

76. As of about May 1, 1866, the Treasury since 1861 had paid more than $10,100,000 in prize money to officers and seamen, about half going to officers. H.R. Exec. Doc. No. 39–114, at 2 (1866). For later years, see Treasury Report 1867, p. 123 (fiscal year 1866–67: more than $1,142,000); Treasury Report 1868, p. 129 (fiscal year 1867–68: more than $438,000); Treasury Report 1869, p. 136 (fiscal year 1868–69: more than $235,000); Treasury Report 1870, p. 123 (fiscal year 1869–70: more than $158,000).

77. I estimate wartime officer man-years by adding the total number of officers on active duty for 1862, 1863, 1864, and 1865, for a total of 19,871. *HSUS* series Ed39.

78. Donald Chisholm, *Waiting for Dead Men's Shoes: Origins and Development of the U.S. Navy's Officer Personnel System, 1793–1941* (Stanford, CA: Stanford University Press, 2001), 292.

79. § 6, 2 Stat. 45, 52 (1800) (granting 5 percent of prize money to squadron commander). Since half the proceeds of seizure went to the government, the commander's 5 percent of the prize money was 2.5 percent of the total proceeds.

80. For Lee's actions and his own estimate of his prize money ($110,000), see Dudley Taylor Cornish and Virginia Jean Laas, *Lincoln's Lee: The Life of Samuel Phillips Lee, United States Navy, 1812–1897* (Lawrence: University Press of Kansas, 1986), 114–15, 119–23. For a higher estimate (of $129,000), see *Washington Star*, reprinted in "Many Large Sums of Naval Prize Money," *State (Columbia, SC)*, Oct. 25, 1898, p. 5. For an admiral's salary, see Chisholm, *Waiting for Dead Men's Shoes*, 292.

81. *Washington Star*, reprinted in "Many Large Sums of Naval Prize Money," *State (Columbia, SC)*, Oct. 25, 1898, p. 5.

82. E.g., § 3, 12 Stat. 600, 606 (1862); 12 Stat. 759 (1863); 13 Stat. 306 (1864). Though comfortable with prize money at sea, Congress rejected the navy's effort to expand the rewards into the realm of cotton seizures on inland rivers. § 7, 13 Stat. 375, 377 (1864); Cong. Globe, 38th Cong., 1st Sess. 2822 (1864) (Sen. Morrill) (noting the measure does not affect captures at sea); Craig L. Symonds, *Lincoln and His Admirals: Abraham Lincoln, the U.S. Navy, and the Civil War* (New York: Oxford University Press, 2008), 283–84, 295, 305.

83. John Niven, *Gideon Welles: Lincoln's Secretary of the Navy* (New York: Oxford University Press, 1973), 447.

84. Robert M. Browning Jr., *From Cape Charles to Cape Fear: The North Atlantic Blockading Squadron during the Civil War* (Tuscaloosa: University of Alabama Press, 1993), 215.

85. Cong. Globe, 40th Cong., 2nd Sess. 1721 (1868) (Sen. Hendricks).

86. § 11, 13 Stat. 306, 310 (1864).

87. 17 Stat. 53 (1872).

88. S. Rep. No. 41–250, at 1 (1870).

89. The captain's share was 10 percent. § 10, 13 Stat. 306, 309–10 (1864).

90. For key procedural steps in the various iterations of the *Kearsarge* bill, see Cong. Globe, 38th Cong., 1st Sess. 1210–11 (1865); Cong. Globe, 39th Cong., 2d Sess. 1403 (1867) (passes House without division, which implies voice vote); Cong. Globe, 39th Cong., 2nd Sess. 1992–93 (1867); Cong. Globe, 40th Cong., 3rd Sess. 1143 (1869)

(passes House by division of 85–25 without roll call); ibid., 1365–66 (1869) (reduced to $50,000, passes Senate without recorded vote); ibid., 1782, 1783, 1874 (1869); Cong. Globe, 41st Cong., 2nd Sess. 3637 (1870) (passes House without division, which implies voice vote); ibid., 5400 (1870); Cong. Globe, 42nd Cong., 2d Sess. 1784 (1872) (passes Senate without recorded vote); ibid., 2211 (1872) (passes House by roll call of 90–58). On how the bill repeatedly failed for "want of time" at session's end, see Cong. Globe, 41st Cong., 2nd Sess. 3458 (1870) (Rep. Hale).

91.  S. Rep. No. 42–40, at 2 (1872).

92.  Cong. Globe, 42nd Cong., 1st Sess. 2210 (1872) (Rep. Cox). Rep. Banks voiced agreement with Cox on army-navy equity but still voted for the *Kearsarge* award. Ibid., 2211. For previous criticism of prize money by Cox, see Cong. Globe, 38th Cong., 2nd Sess. 1210 (1865).

93.  Cong. Globe, 37th Cong., 2nd Sess. 3009 (1862) (Sen. Sumner).

94.  "Why Not Prize Money for the Army?" *Round Table* (NY), Jan. 13, 1866, p. 25; Letter to the editor, "Navy Pay, Prize Money, and Pensions," *Army and Navy Journal*, Feb. 17, 1866, p. 409.

95.  "Why Not Prize Money for the Army?" *Round Table*, Jan. 13, 1866, p. 25; "Prize Money and the Navy," *Springfield (MA) Republican*, Dec. 26, 1868, p. 2. In fact, congressmen were quite aware of the army-navy difference, and several expressly justified it on the ground that naval prize money made up for enlistment bounties, which were available in the army but not the navy. Cong. Globe, 38th Cong., 1st Sess. 533 (1864) (Rep. Schenk); ibid., 726 (Rep. Conness); ibid., 1997 (Rep. Kelley).

96.  Letter to the editor, "Navy Pay, Prize Money, and Pensions," *Army and Navy Journal*, Feb. 17, 1866, p. 409; "Prize Money and the Navy," *Springfield (MA) Republican*, Dec. 26, 1868, p. 2. For the same complaint in the 1700s, see Baugh, *British Naval Administration*, 114–15.

97.  H.R. Rep. No. 47–1008, at 3 (1882).

98.  Ibid.

99.  13 Cong. Rec. Index 675 (Morse's introduction of H.R. 5096).

100.  H.R. Rep. No. 47–1008, at 2 (1882).

101.  Letter to the editor, "Navy Pay, Prize Money, and Pensions," *Army and Navy Journal*, Feb. 17, 1866, p. 409.

102.  H.R. Rep. No. 47–1008, at 2–3 (1882).

103.  Index entry for H.R. 5906 in 13 Cong. Rec. 675 (1882).

104.  In 1884, the Senate passed a resolution asking the navy secretary for his opinion regarding abolition of prize money. The sponsor was not clear about the query's motivation, though he apparently had some concern about the increasingly fine division of labor among navy ships, with only a subset doing the fighting. 15 Cong. Rec. 2677–78 (1884) (Sen. Beck). I have been unable to find a published response to the resolution. No published congressional deliberations or statutory changes resulted.

105.  See my discussion in this chapter, text at notes 143–45.

106.  § 13, 30 Stat. 1004, 1007 (1899).

107.  For the ranking of the world's navies, see George Edmund Foss, "The American Navy.—The Old and the New," *Our Day* 17 (June 1898): 257 (citing U.S. Office of

Naval Intelligence). For the dates at which the world powers abolished naval profit-seeking, see the following sources:

- On Britain, see my discussion in this chapter, text at notes 260–79.

- On France, see James Wilford Garner, Prize Law during the World War: A Study of the Jurisprudence of the Prize Courts, 1914–1924 (New York: Macmillan, 1927), 35n2 (prize money awarded up to 1916, then collectivized to pay benefits to the wounded, widows, and the like); C. John Colombos, A Treatise on the Law of Prize, 3rd ed. (London: Longmans, Green, 1949), 341 (prize money restored in 1939, not clear for how long).

- On Russia, see Maxwell H. Anderson, The Navy and Prize: An Essay (Portsmouth, UK: Gieves Publishing Co., 1916), 56 (prize money abolished shortly before Russo-Japanese War of 1904–05); but see Colombos, Treatise on the Law of Prize, 340 (suggesting that Russia did not abolish until 1915).

- On Italy, see Anderson, Navy and Prize, 56 (prize money awarded as of 1916); Garner, Prize Law during the World War, 35n2 (prize money collectivized in 1917, but government could still reward captors in "special circumstances").

- On Germany, the sources are not clear or consistent. It is possible the government abolished profit-seeking before World War I but reinstated it during that war. See these works: Lawrence Sondhaus, Preparing for Weltpolitik: German Sea Power before the Tirpitz Era (Annapolis, MD: Naval Institute Press, 2004), 265n112 (noting that, after making captures in the Franco-Prussian War, one commanding officer and crew "were still asking for their prize money" in 1872 "and apparently never received it"); Hans Wehberg, Capture in War on Land and Sea, with introduction by John M. Robertson (London: P. S. King and Son, 1911), 17 ("the prize regulations of all Powers except Germany and North America [i.e., the United States] assign the prize-money to the crews, or at least a reward for the seizure of the vessels"); Garner, Prize Law during the World War, 35n2 ("Germany . . . never adopted the practice of awarding the captors a share of the prize, but during the World War liberal bounties appear to have been accorded naval commanders or seamen, especially of submarines."); "Prize Money," U.S. Naval Institute Proceedings 43 (Aug. 1917): 1787 (reporting that the British Admiralty had acquired a schedule of prize and bounty awards available to German warships, including U-boats, for capturing and sinking Allied and neutral ships).

- On Japan, see 32 Parl. Deb., H.C. (5th Ser.) (1911) 1661 (statement of Roberts) (stating that Japan abolished prize money at start of war against China in 1894); Colombos, Treatise on the Law of Prize, 341 (stating that Japan has abolished prize money, citing regulations of 1894 and 1904).

108. E.g., "Reform It Altogether," Washington Post, Aug. 2, 1898, p. 6 (stating that "the most advanced nations" still award prize money); Detroit Free Press, reprinted in "The Prize Money System," Washington Post, Aug. 9, 1898, p. 6 (asserting that con-

gressional abolition of prize money would place the United States on a "higher plane of military principle and practice than any nation has yet taken").

109. Davis, *Navy Second to None*, 37–55; Sprout and Sprout, *Rise of American Naval Power*, 182–201.

110. Parrillo, "De-Privatization of American Warfare," 74–84.

111. Ibid., 84–87.

112. Davis, *Navy Second to None*, 86–89, 94; Parrillo, "De-Privatization of American Warfare," 85.

113. Sprout and Sprout, *Rise of American Naval Power*, 217.

114. Parrillo, "De-Privatization of American Warfare," 87; ibid., 87n537.

115. Foss, "The American Navy," 257.

116. David F. Trask, *The War with Spain in 1898* (New York: Macmillan, 1981), 8–9, 21–22, 26.

117. Ibid., 24–25, 28–31, 35–36.

118. Gerald F. Linderman, *Mirror of War: American Society and the Spanish-American War* (Ann Arbor: University of Michigan Press, 1974), 58.

119. Trask, *War with Spain*, 52–56.

120. For examples of the board's role, see ibid., 92, 115, 121, 172–73, 187, 280–82, 292, 339–40, 374. On Mahan, see ibid., 88–90; John A. S. Grenville and George Berkeley Young, *Politics, Strategy, and American Diplomacy: Studies in Foreign Policy, 1873–1917* (New Haven, CT: Yale University Press, 1966), 291.

121. See generally Sprout and Sprout, *Rise of American Naval Power*, 233–37; Warren Zimmermann, *First Great Triumph: How Five Americans Made Their Country a World Power* (New York: Farrar, Straus and Giroux, 2002), 277–83. On the commercial blockade of Cuba, see Trask, *War with Spain*, 89–90, 109–11. On refraining from privateering, see telegram from Secretary of State Sherman to Diplomatic Representatives (Apr. 22, 1898), in *Policy of the United States toward Maritime Commerce*, 1:486. On the objective of attacking the Philippines, see Trask, *War with Spain*, 78. On Puerto Rico, see Trask, *War with Spain*, 367–68; Zimmermann, *First Great Triumph*, 294–95. On Guam, see Zimmermann, *First Great Triumph*, 301.

122. Zimmermann, *First Great Triumph*, 288–92.

123. Ibid., 7, 294–95, 313–14, 316, 368–70.

124. The terms of Cuba's "independence" limited its capacity to make treaties and empowered the U.S. military to intervene in Cuban affairs. Zimmermann, *First Great Triumph*, 378–86.

125. Robert Seager II, *Alfred Thayer Mahan: The Man and His Letters* (Annapolis, MD: Naval Institute Press, 1977), 416.

126. Trask, *War with Spain*, 42–43.

127. Grenville and Young, *Politics, Strategy, and American Diplomacy*, 268–69.

128. Mike Sewell, "Humanitarian Intervention, Democracy, and Imperialism: The American War with Spain, 1898, and After," in *Humanitarian Intervention: A History*, ed. Brendan Simms and D. J. B. Trim (Cambridge: Cambridge University Press, 2011), 314–15.

129. Frank Freidel, "Dissent in the Spanish-American War and the Philippine Insurrection," in *Dissent in Three American Wars* (Cambridge, MA: Harvard University Press, 1970), 77–78.

130. Richard F. Hamilton, *President McKinley, War, and Empire* (New Brunswick, NJ: Transaction, 2007), 2:83.

131. Sewell, "Humanitarian Intervention," 313.

132. Davis, *Navy Second to None*, 153–56.

133. Ibid., 154.

134. The nominal figures are from ibid., 473 (totals, including deficiencies). I adjusted the nominal amounts for inflation using *HSUS* series Cc2.

135. For the 1898 ranking, see Foss, "The American Navy," 257. For the later increase, see Davis, *Navy Second to None*, 169–72; George Modelski and William R. Thompson, *Seapower in Global Politics, 1494–1993* (Houndmills, UK: Macmillan, 1988), 76.

136. Peter Karsten, *The Naval Aristocracy: The Golden Age of Annapolis and the Emergence of Modern American Navalism* (New York: Free Press, 1972), 149–50, 221, 226–27, 231. On Mahan particularly, see Seager, *Alfred Thayer Mahan*, 391–94.

137. Theodore Roosevelt, "The Genesis of the Personnel Bill," *North American Review* 167 (Dec. 1898): 651–57. For confirmation that salary equalization was in the original bill, see "Bill Proposed by the Personnel Board," *Army and Navy Journal*, Jan. 1, 1898, p. 332.

138. On combat promotion in the War of 1812, see McKee, *Gentlemanly and Honorable Profession*, 275–78, 292–95, 297–302. On the Civil War, see Symonds, *Lincoln and His Admirals*, 306–09. On the regime as structured toward the end of the Civil War and for decades afterward, see Chisholm, *Waiting for Dead Men's Shoes*, 291, 305–06; USRS §§ 1506, 1508 (conferring promotion authority on the president, with approval of Congress or the Senate).

139. The report is H.R. Rep. No. 55–1375 (1898), with the hearings appended. On the process, see George Edmund Foss, "From the Standpoint of the People," *North American Review* 167 (Dec. 1898): 677.

140. *Annual Reports of the Navy Department for the Year 1898: Report of the Secretary of the Navy, Miscellaneous Reports* (Washington, DC: GPO, 1898), 57–58. The cited pages discuss promotion, with nothing on prize money or head money.

141. Foss, "The American Navy," esp. 259.

142. 32 Cong. Rec. 660 (1899). On the dearth of legislative history for the measure, see Arnold W. Knauth, "Prize Law Reconsidered," *Columbia Law Review* 48 (1946): 73. The only other substantive comment in the legislative record, by Representative Albert Berry, a Kentucky Democrat, was a passing invocation of the army-navy distinction: "[T]he men [of the army] who made that magnificent charge at San Jan Hill . . . are as much entitled to take [the city of] Santiago as a reward for their services as the men who sank [Spanish Admiral] Cervera's ships." This tells us little. The army-navy distinction had been well known in the Civil War, yet Congress had not considered it a reason to end naval rewards. Note that Berry's words are reported in "The Naval Personnel Bill," *New York Times*, Jan. 14, 1899, p. 4. His remarks are completely omitted from the *Congressional Record*, which says they were printed in the Appendix. 32 Cong. Rec. 669 (1899). But they are not.

143. For the amendment's adoption, see 32 Cong. Rec. 718 (1899). We can infer a voice vote because the *Congressional Record* lists no division. For the report that the House's action was "without debate, and by a unanimous vote," see "A Victorious Crusade," *Washington Post*, Jan. 23, 1899, p. 6.

144. 32 Cong. Rec. 726 (1899). We can infer a voice vote because the *Congressional Record* lists no division.

145. 32 Cong. Rec. 1982 (1899). See also "The Navy Personnel Bill," *New York Times*, Feb. 18, 1899, p. 4 (noting that the version passed by the Senate "kept the clause abolishing prize money").

146. This is based on the figures listed in Treasury Report 1901, p. 3; Treasury Report 1902, p. 3; Treasury Report 1903, p. 3; Treasury Report 1904, p. 3. The figures in the reports are the total from captures, which was then divided equally between government and captors. Compare Treasury Report 1901, p. 1, with p. 3.

147. Parrillo, "De-Privatization of American Warfare," 92n571.

148. J. G. Carlisle, "Our Future Policy," *Harper's New Monthly Magazine* 97 (Oct. 1898): 726. See also Carl Schurz, "American Imperialism," in *ROE*, 332, 342; Schurz, "Thoughts on American Imperialism," in *Schurz Papers*, 5:509–10; Andrew Carnegie, "Should the United States Expand?" in *ROE*, 93–94, 96; Adlai E. Stevenson, "A Republic Can Have No Subjects," in *ROE*, 268; Charles A. Towne, "Lest We Forget," in *ROE*, 320; Henry Van Dyke, "The American Birthright and the Philippine Pottage," in *ROE*, 440–43.

149. Carl Schurz, "Thoughts on American Imperialism," in *Schurz Papers*, 5:509–10. See also Carlisle, "Our Future Policy," 726; Carnegie, "Should the United States Expand?" in *ROE*, 93; Stephen M. White, "The Passing of Constitutional Restraints," in *ROE*, 202; Van Dyke, "The American Birthright and the Philippine Pottage," in *ROE*, 440–43; Henry U. Johnson, "Imperial Splendor and Imperial Mistakes," in *ROE*, 646; William G. Sumner, *The Conquest of the United States by Spain: A Lecture before the Phi Beta Kappa Society of Yale University, January 16, 1899* (Boston: Dana Estes and Co., 1899), 25.

150. Carlisle, "Our Future Policy," 726–27.

151. Stevenson, "A Republic Can Have No Subjects," in *ROE*, 266; John W. Daniel, "The Effect of Annexation of the Philippines on American Labor," in *ROE*, 419.

152. Seager, *Alfred Thayer Mahan*, 388.

153. Carnegie, "Should the United States Expand?" in *ROE*, 95.

154. Schurz, "American Imperialism," in *ROE*, 345.

155. William Jennings Bryan, "First Speech against Imperialism," in *ROE*, 12. See also Stevenson, "A Republic Can Have No Subjects," in *ROE*, 269–70; Schurz, "Thoughts on American Imperialism," *Schurz Papers*, 5:500–03.

156. Towne, "Lest We Forget," in *ROE*, 320. See also Carl Schurz, "Our Future Foreign Policy," in *Schurz Papers*, 5:487–88; Schurz, "American Imperialism," in *ROE*, 343; Daniel, "The Effect of Annexation," in *ROE*, 419; Van Dyke, "The American Birthright and the Philippine Pottage," in *ROE*, 443–44; John L. McLaurin, "Our New Colonial Policy," in *ROE*, 586.

157. Augustus O. Bacon, "Independence for the Philippines," in *ROE*, 540.

158. Schurz, "American Imperialism," in *ROE*, 348.

159. William McAdoo, "Reorganization of the Personnel of the Navy," *North American Review* 159 (1894): 463. See also David D. Porter, "Discipline in the Navy," *North American Review* 150 (1890): 417.

160. Carlisle, "Our Future Policy," 725. See also White, "Passing of Constitutional Restraints," in *ROE*, 203.

161. Johnson, "Imperial Splendor and Imperial Mistakes," in *ROE*, 628. See also Carl Schurz, "Militarism and Democracy," in *Schurz Papers*, 6:66.

162. David Starr Jordan, "Imperial Democracy," *The New World: A Quarterly Review of Religion, Ethics and Theology* 7 (Dec. 1898): 615.

163. Freidel, "Dissent in the Spanish-American War," 75; Trask, *War with Spain*, 55, 58; Louis A. Perez, "Incurring a Debt of Gratitude: 1898 and the Moral Sources of United States Hegemony in Cuba," *American Historical Review* 104 (1999): 357–58; Sewell, "Humanitarian Intervention," 306–09.

164. William McKinley, [Untitled message to Senate] (Apr. 11, 1898), in *A Compilation of the Messages and Papers of the Presidents* (New York: Bureau of National Literature, n.d.), 13:6286; ibid., 13:6282.

165. Zimmermann, *First Great Triumph*, 262.

166. Quoted in Perez, "Incurring a Debt of Gratitude," 357.

167. 31 Cong. Rec. 3835 (1898). See also Trask, *War with Spain*, 36.

168. Letter from Schurz to McKinley (June 1, 1898), in *Schurz Papers*, 5:474 (emphasis omitted).

169. Schurz, "Thoughts on American Imperialism," in *Schurz Papers*, 5:499.

170. William McKinley, "Address at the Trans-Missouri Exposition at Omaha, Nebraska, October 12, 1898," in *Speeches and Addresses of William McKinley, from March 1, 1897, to May 30, 1900* (New York: Doubleday and McClure Co., 1900), 104.

171. On this issue, see Ephraim K. Smith, "'A Question from Which We Could Not Escape': William McKinley and the Decision to Acquire the Philippine Islands," *Diplomatic History* 9 (1985): 374; Sewell, "Humanitarian Intervention," 312–13.

172. Sewell, "Humanitarian Intervention," 316. See also Trask, *War with Spain*, 454.

173. William McKinley, "Speech at Dinner of the Home Market Club, Boston, February 16, 1899," in *Speeches and Addresses of William McKinley*, 188–89, 192.

174. Towne, "Lest We Forget," in *ROE*, 308.

175. Ibid., 325–26.

176. Stevenson, "A Republic Can Have No Subjects," in *ROE*, 271–72.

177. Schurz, "American Imperialism," in *ROE*, 351.

178. Johnson, "Imperial Splendor and Imperial Mistakes," in *ROE*, 636.

179. Hoar's speech is printed in "Our New Foreign Relations," *Springfield (MA) Republican*, Nov. 2, 1898, p. 6.

180. Bryan, "First Speech against Imperialism," in *ROE*, 11–12.

181. Schurz, "Thoughts on American Imperialism," in *Schurz Papers*, 5:500. See also Schurz, "Our Future Foreign Policy," in *Schurz Papers*, 5:479–80, 492; Carlisle, "Our Future Policy," 721; White, "The Passing of Constitutional Restraints," in *ROE*, 187; Daniel, "The Effect of Annexation," in *ROE*, 418–19; Bacon, "Independence for

the Philippines," in *ROE*, 527; "Opposition to Imperialism," *Springfield (MA) Republican*, June 16, 1898, p. 5 (reprinting speech of Gamaliel Bradford: "humanity" has been "played upon for other purposes" including commercial gain and "naval glory").

182. [Untitled item], *City and State: Commonwealth above Party* 4, no. 30 (Apr. 28, 1898): 524.

183. "An Inglorious Occupation," *New York Times*, Apr. 26, 1898, p. 6.

184. [Editorial in unidentified New York newspaper], quoted in "The Government Is Responsible," *Springfield (MA) Daily Republican*, Apr. 28, 1898, p. 6.

185. "Prize Money," *Washington Post*, July 26, 1898, p. 6.

186. "Reform It Altogether," *Washington Post*, Aug. 2, 1898, p. 6. See also "Amend the Blockade," *Washington Post*, Aug. 13, 1898, p. 6.

187. *Detroit Free Press*, reprinted in "The Prize Money System," *Washington Post*, Aug. 9, 1898, p. 6.

188. "The Head Money Evil," *New Haven (CT) Register*, July 15, 1898, p. 6.

189. Frank H. Lamson, "The Evolution of Our Army and Navy," *National Magazine*, 8 (June 1898): 263 (referring to head money by its other common label, "bounty").

190. For a rare editorial defense of prize money in 1898–99 (and a very qualified one at that), see [No title], *Los Angeles Times*, May 1, 1898, p. 2. For a rare post-1899 defense, see Henry B. Brown, "Address of Mr. Henry B. Brown, of Washington, D.C.," *American Society of International Law Proceedings* 3 (1909): 183.

191. On the *Post*'s support of annexation, see "Blundering History and False Analogy," *Washington Post*, Jan. 1, 1899, p. 6; "The Problem in the Philippines," *Washington Post*, Jan. 8, 1899, p. 6; "Danger in the Philippines," *Washington Post*, Jan. 10, 1899, p. 6.

192. "Shafter and Sampson," *Washington Post*, Dec. 3, 1898, p. 6. See also "Prize Money," *Washington Post*, July 26, 1898, p. 6; "A Victorious Crusade," *Washington Post*, Jan. 23, 1899, p. 6.

193. "The Prize Money," *Washington Post*, Sept. 21, 1898, p. 6. See also "Prize Money and Bounty," *Washington Post*, Sept. 13, 1898, p. 6.

194. "Prize and Booty in Santiago," *Springfield (MA) Republican*, July 22, 1898, p. 6.

195. *Syracuse Post*, reprinted in "The Prize Money System," *Washington Post*, Aug. 21, 1898, p. 6.

196. *Philadelphia North American*, reprinted in "The Post's Reform Movement," *Washington Post*, Jan. 26, 1899, p. 6.

197. "Naval Prize Money," *Omaha World Herald*, Sept. 17, 1898, p. 4.

198. "Minimize the Spoliation of War," *Dallas Morning News*, Apr. 28, 1898, p. 4.

199. "The Head Money Evil," *New Haven (CT) Register*, July 15, 1898, p. 6.

200. "The Captured Merchantmen," *Hartford (CT) Courant*, Apr. 29, 1898, p. 8.

201. "Prize Money Injustice," *New York Tribune*, Aug. 5, 1898, p. 4.

202. [Untitled], *Atlanta Constitution*, Aug. 15, 1898, p. 4.

203. *Atlanta Journal*, reprinted in "Why Prize Money?" *Washington Post*, Aug. 1, 1898, p. 6; "Reform It Altogether," *Washington Post*, Aug. 2, 1898, p. 6; *Louisville (KY) Courier-Journal*, quoted in "Reform It Altogether," *Washington Post*, Aug. 2, 1898, p. 6; *Detroit Free Press*, reprinted in "The Prize Money System," *Washington Post*,

Aug. 9, 1898, p. 6; "Battle of the Orators," *Chicago Daily Tribune*, Aug. 18, 1898, p. 12; "Where a Change Should Be Made," *Atlanta Constitution*, Aug. 24, 1898, p. 4; "National Capital Topics," *New York Times*, Aug. 28, 1898, p. 11; "Prize Money," *Trenton (NJ) State Gazette*, Aug. 4, 1898, p. 4; "The Abolition of Prize Money," *Pawtucket (RI) Times*, Jan. 20, 1899, p. 6. For similar comments, see "Navy Prize Money," *Minneapolis Journal*, Jan. 21, 1899, p. 4 ("days of the buccaneers"); [Untitled], *Tacoma (WA) Daily News*, Aug. 24, 1898, p. 6 ("piratical in its nature").

204. "Attorney-General Griggs on Advances in Jurisprudence in the Nineteenth Century," *Law Notes* 3 (Aug. 1899): 91.

205. On the *Press*, see the entry in *ANB* on its editor, Charles Emory Smith.

206. *Philadelphia Press*, block-quoted in "A Victorious Crusade," *Washington Post*, Jan. 23, 1899, p. 6.

207. "A Victorious Crusade," *Washington Post*, Jan. 23, 1899, p. 6.

208. *Philadelphia North American*, reprinted in "The Post's Reform Movement," *Washington Post*, Jan. 26, 1899, p. 6.

209. Foss, "From the Standpoint of the People," 679.

210. 33 Cong. Rec. 4231 (1900).

211. *International Law Association: Report of the Twenty-Third Conference Held at Berlin, October 1st–5th, 1906* (London: West, Newman and Co., 1907), 156.

212. Brown, "Address of Mr. Henry B. Brown, of Washington, D.C.," 183.

213. 32 Cong. Rec. 660 (1899) (Rep. Foss); Roosevelt, "Genesis of the Personnel Bill," 657; *Proceedings of the American Society of International Law at Its First Annual Meeting Held at Washington, D.C., April 19 and 20, 1907* (New York: Baker, Voorhis and Co., 1908), 86 (remarks of former Representative Barrows); ibid., 87 (remarks of War College President Stockton); Samuel J. Barrows, "The Bulwarks of Peace," *Advocate of Peace* 69 (June 1907): 133.

214. Caspar F. Goodrich, "Naval Education," *Journal of Social Science, Containing the Transactions of the American Association*, no. 33 (Boston: Damrell and Upham, 1895), 29.

215. Quoted in Grenville and Young, *Politics, Strategy, and American Diplomacy*, 276–78.

216. Samuel J. Barrows, "The Abolition by the United States of Naval Prize Money," *Report of the Ninth Annual Meeting of the Lake Mohonk Conference on International Arbitration* (N.p.: Lake Mohonk Arbitration Conference, 1903), 60.

217. This point is raised but too quickly discounted in Knauth, "Prize Law Reconsidered," 71.

218. John W. Coogan, *The End of Neutrality: The United States, Britain, and Maritime Rights, 1899–1915* (Ithaca, NY: Cornell University Press, 1981), 237. See also ibid., 26.

219. Ibid., 28.

220. 31 Cong. Rec. 5785 (1898). For another example of this misinterpretation, see the 1907 speech of Joseph Choate in *Proceedings of the Hague Peace Conferences: Translation of the Official Texts*, ed. James Brown Scott (New York: Oxford University Press, 1921), 3:753–54.

221. 31 Cong. Rec. 5784 (1898).

222. Charles Henry Butler, *A Letter Addressed to Captain A. T. Mahan in Regard to Freedom of Private Property on the Sea from Capture during War* (Washington: n.p., 1898), 5. The latter two quotations were taken by Butler from McKinley's own proclamation.

223. 31 Cong. Rec. 5785 (1898).

224. "Report of the Committee on International Law," *Annual Reports of the American Bar Association* 21 (1898): 430.

225. Henry M. Hoyt, "Recent Developments and Tendency of the Law of Prize," *Yale Law Journal* 12 (1903): 317.

226. Charles Henry Butler, "Position of the United States in Regard to Freedom of Private Property on the Sea from Capture during War," in *Report of the Eighteenth Conference Held at Buffalo, U.S.A. August 31st–September 2nd, 1899*, by International Law Association (London: William Clowes and Sons, 1899), 79.

227. Charles Chauncey Binney, "The Latest Chapter of the American Law of Prize and Capture," *American Law Register* 54 (1906): 537. For similar linkages between prize-money abolition and immunity, see [Untitled], *Tacoma (WA) Daily News*, Aug. 24, 1898, p. 2; "A Good Movement," *Washington Post*, Nov. 6, 1898, p. 6; "A Victorious Crusade," *Washington Post*, Jan. 23, 1899, p. 6; "To Abolish Prize Money," *Philadelphia Inquirer*, Feb. 26, 1899, p. 8; "Privateers and Men-of-War," *The Critic: An Illustrated Monthly Review of Literature, Art and Life*, 36 (Apr. 1900): 360–61; *International Law Association: Report of the Twenty-Third Conference Held at Berlin, October 1st–5th, 1906* (London: West, Newman and Co., 1907), 155–56 (comment of Benjamin F. Trueblood); "The Abolition of 'Prize-Money'" [Untitled Editorial], *American Journal of International Law* 1 (1907): 484; Speech of Joseph Choate in *Proceedings of the Hague Peace Conferences: Translation of the Official Texts*, 3:753; "Private Property on the High Seas," *American Lawyer* 15 (1907): 381.

228. Coogan, *End of Neutrality*, 113. On the broader informality and (often) incoherence of institutional U.S. naval policymaking in this period, see ibid., 69, 121–22.

229. Ibid., 242. On naval officers' more general aversion to limits on war, see Karsten, *Naval Aristocracy*, 218–21.

230. Semmel, *Liberalism and Naval Strategy*, 92–94, 98.

231. There are intimations of this in Alfred T. Mahan, "Possibilities of an Anglo-American Reunion," *North American Review* 159 (Nov. 1894): 561–63. And the warning is clear in Alfred T. Mahan, "The War on the Sea and Its Lessons," *McClure's Magazine*, 12 (Dec. 1898): 357; A. T. Mahan, *Sea Power in Its Relations to the War of 1812* (Boston: Little, Brown and Co., 1905), 1:287; Alfred T. Mahan, "The Hague Conference: The Question of Immunity for Belligerent Merchant Shipping," in *Some Neglected Aspects of War* (Boston: Little, Brown and Co., 1907), 174. On other observers' awareness of the point, see Semmel, *Liberalism and Naval Strategy*, 78, 87, 158.

232. On Britain's distant blockade in World War I, see Eric W. Osborne, *Britain's Economic Blockade of Germany, 1914–1919* (London: Frank Cass, 2004), 44–114, esp. 67–68, 73–74, 84, 99–100. On the increasing strategic attractiveness of distant blockade prior to 1914 and the perceived legal issues with it, see Semmel, *Liberalism and Naval Strategy*, 113, 143, 162; Charles H. Stockton, "The Capture of Enemy Merchant Vessels at Sea," *North American Review* 168 (Feb. 1899): 210; letter from Mahan to

Theodore Roosevelt (July 20, 1906), in *Letters and Papers of Alfred Thayer Mahan*, ed. Robert Seager II and Doris D. Maguire (Annapolis, MD: Naval Institute Press, 1975), 3:164–65; Julian S. Corbett, "The Capture of Private Property at Sea," in *Some Neglected Aspects of War*, 136–37.

233. Mahan, "Possibilities of an Anglo-American Reunion," 563.

234. Mahan to the editor of the *New York Times* (Nov. 15, 1898), in *Letters and Papers of Alfred Thayer Mahan*, 2:611.

235. On Stockton's association with Mahan, see John Hattendorf, "Rear Admiral Charles H. Stockton, the Naval War College, and the Law of Naval Warfare," in *The Law of Armed Conflict: Into the Next Millennium*, International Law Studies, no. 71, ed. Michael N. Schmitt and Leslie C. Green (Newport, RI: Naval War College, 1998), xxxiii.

236. Stockton, "The Capture of Enemy Merchant Vessels at Sea." Stockton announced that he wrote the article "at the suggestion of Captain Mahan." Ibid., 206.

237. Ibid., 207–08, 210.

238. Stockton wrote privately in 1898 that the "north Pacific is our sphere of influence by divine right." Quoted in Hattendorf, "Rear Admiral Charles H. Stockton," xxxviii.

239. Stockton, "The Capture of Enemy Merchant Vessels at Sea," 207.

240. Ibid., 206, 211.

241. "The Right of Marine Capture," *Nation* 68 (Feb. 16, 1899): 122. In a discussion years later, Stockton took offense at suggestions that naval high-seas captures resembled piracy and invoked prize money's 1899 abolition to refute the comparison. *Proceedings of the American Society of International Law at Its First Annual Meeting Held at Washington, D.C., April 19 and 20, 1907* (New York: Baker, Voorhis and Co., 1908), 87. For a similar effort to legitimate the right of capture by ensuring that "all thought of gain" be removed "from the minds of the agents of the State," see the 1907 remarks of the French delegate Louis Renault in *Proceedings of the Hague Peace Conferences: Translation of the Official Texts*, 3:784.

242. Coogan, *End of Neutrality*, 28.

243. The conference concluded that "[i]nnocent enemy goods and ships" should be immune on the high seas, but with a major exception for "vessels propelled by machinery and capable of keeping the high seas." U.S. Naval War College, *International Law Topics and Discussions 1905* (Washington, DC: GPO, 1906), 9, 20. The right to capture all seagoing enemy steamships had potentially far-reaching effects, for it meant that all neutral-owned cargo on such ships could be prevented from reaching the enemy nation. Stockton himself had pointed this out. "The Capture of Enemy Merchant Vessels at Sea," 209–10. Furthermore, the conference poked another hole in immunity by noting that "an extension of the list of contraband" would "probably" be necessary. *International Law Topics*, 19. It should be noted that the preface to the conference's report was written by then-Captain Charles Sperry. Ibid., 3. Sperry in fact strongly opposed high-seas immunity and worked to defeat the U.S. proposal for it at The Hague in 1907. Coogan, *End of Neutrality*, 60, 69, 241.

244. Coogan, *End of Neutrality*, 56–62, 69, 92, 102–03, 241; Semmel, *Liberalism and Naval Strategy*, 154–58.

245. Coogan suggests this but qualifies it a good deal. *End of Neutrality*, 127, 243. On the same issue, see Semmel, *Liberalism and Naval Strategy*, 153–54.

246. Coogan, *End of Neutrality*, 169–256; Ross A. Kennedy, *The Will to Believe: Woodrow Wilson, World War I, and America's Strategy for Peace and Security* (Kent, OH: Kent State University Press, 2009), 65–103. Legally, Britain justified its starvation approach largely (1) by defining contraband to include food and (2) as retaliation for German submarine warfare. Kennedy, *Will to Believe*, 66–67; Semmel, *Liberalism and Naval Strategy*, 162. On German civilian deaths, see Kennedy, *Will to Believe*, 249n55.

247. Semmel, *Liberalism and Naval Strategy*, 165–68.

248. "Comments on the Seizure of Private Property at Sea" (Feb.–Mar. 1906), in *Letters and Papers of Alfred Thayer Mahan*, 3:623.

249. Mahan, "The Hague Conference," in *Some Neglected Aspects of War*, 162.

250. E.g., Leeman, *Long Road to Annapolis*, 146–47. In a sample of Annapolis graduates commissioned between 1865 and 1880, 70 percent served ten years or more. Karsten, *Naval Aristocracy*, 281–82.

251. "Who Will Defend It?" *Washington Post*, Aug. 16, 1898, p. 6. See also *Syracuse (NY) Post*, reprinted in "The Prize Money System," *Washington Post*, Aug. 21, 1898, p. 6; "The Prize System," *Army and Navy Register*, Sept. 24, 1898, p. 184; 31 Cong. Rec. 5785 (1898) (Rep. Gillett). Apart from humanitarian legitimation and rationality, the most common line of argument against prize money was to invoke the army-navy difference. But this was usually just a way of restating the humanitarian argument: the army was already civilized, and the navy should catch up to it. E.g., "The Head Money Evil," *New Haven (CT) Register*, July 15, 1898, p. 6; "Prize and Booty in Santiago," *Springfield (MA) Republican*, July 22, 1898, p. 6; "Prize Money," *Washington Post*, July 26, 1898, p. 6; "Prize Money," *Trenton (NJ) State Gazette*, Aug. 4, 1898, p. 4; "To Abolish Prize Money," *Philadelphia Inquirer*, Feb. 26, 1899, p. 8. Occasionally, persons invoking the army-navy difference seem to have been genuinely interested in interservice equity and indifferent as to whether prize money was abolished in the navy or booty reestablished in the army. "Prize System in the Navy," *Los Angeles Times*, Sept. 20, 1898, p. 8; "Navy Prize Money," *Minneapolis Journal*, Jan. 21, 1899, p. 4.

252. In a previous article, focused mainly on U.S. privateering rather than the U.S. Navy, I offered a brief discussion of the abolition of prize money within the U.S. Navy. Parrillo, "De-Privatization of American Warfare," 91–94. There I invoked rationality as the reason for abolition within the navy, but I now reject that interpretation in light of research I have done since.

253. Stephen, *War in Disguise*, 129.

254. Baugh, *British Naval Administration*, 112–15; G. J. Marcus, *Heart of Oak: A Survey of British Sea Power in the Georgian Era* (London: Oxford University Press, 1975), 124.

255. For discussions of the British blockade in the War of 1812 finding it highly effective, see Brian Arthur, *How Britain Won the War of 1812: The Royal Navy's Blockades of the United States, 1812–1815* (Woodbridge, UK: Boydell Press, 2011); Davis and Engerman, *Naval Blockades in Peace and War*, 94–108. For a more skeptical view, see Dudley, *Splintering the Wooden Wall*, 131–60. On the British blockade in the Crimean War, see Andrew D. Lambert, "The Crimean War Blockade, 1854–56," in *Naval*

*Blockades and Seapower: Strategies and Counter-Strategies, 1805–2005*, ed. Bruce A. Ellman and S. C. M. Paine (London: Routledge, 2005), 46–59. Lewis asserts that, at the start of the Crimean War, the British government collectivized all prize money into a navy-wide fund and ceased making awards to individual ships. *Navy in Transition*, 237. He is mistaken. The British government continued to award a share to each individual ship that was "in sight" of prize and captor, so as to intimidate the former and encourage the latter. *Second Supplement to the London Gazette of Tuesday the 28th of March*, Mar. 29, 1854, No. 21537, pp. 1010–12; Naval Pay and Prize Act, 1854, 17 Vict., c. 19. For an example of such an award, see *London Gazette*, Feb. 17, 1857, p. 542. On the Union blockade in the Civil War, see my discussion in this chapter, text at notes 68–70. On the U.S. blockade of Cuba in 1898, see Trask, *War with Spain*, 89–90, 109–11. On wireless telegraphy, see my discussion in this chapter, text at note 264.

256. There is evidence that prize money sometimes caused an individual ship to refrain from cooperating with its fellow blockaders, in hope of winning a whole prize for itself, but navies had effective mechanisms for combating that kind of misbehavior, such as court-martial. Browning, *From Cape Charles to Cape Fear*, 259. In any event, I have seen no mention of this issue in the discourse of 1898–99, except one vague, passing assertion that prize money "tends to the disorganization of discipline and reduces the efficiency of the service." "The Abolition of Prize Money," *Pawtucket (RI) Times*, Jan. 20, 1899, p. 6.

257. The hearings (242 pages) are appended to H.R. Rep. 55–1375 (1899). The sole reference to prize money is purely incidental, in a written statement giving the history of the warrant officer corps. Ibid., 192.

258. There is a reference to "rewards" for officers, but this refers to promotion practices. *Annual Reports of the Navy Department for the Year 1898: Report of the Secretary of the Navy, Miscellaneous Reports* (Washington, DC: GPO, 1898), 57–58.

259. See my discussion in note 107 above.

260. Modelski and Thompson, *Seapower in Global Politics*, 76.

261. Kemp, *Prize Money*, 18.

262. *London Gazette*, Sept. 21, 1900, No. 27231, pp. 5823–26.

263. *Proceedings of the Hague Peace Conferences: Translation of the Official Texts*, 3:898, 900.

264. Nicholas A. Lambert, "Strategic Command and Control for Maneuver Warfare: Creation of the Royal Navy's 'War Room' System, 1905–1915," *Journal of Military History* 69 (2005): 361–410. On the U.S. Navy and the radio, see Susan J. Douglas, "Technological Innovation and Organizational Change: The Navy's Adoption of Radio 1899–1919," *Military Enterprise and Technological Change: Perspectives on the American Experience*, ed. Merritt Roe Smith (Cambridge, MA: MIT Press, 1985), 117–74.

265. Osborne, *Britain's Economic Blockade of Germany*, 44–49. See also my discussion in this chapter, text at note 232.

266. 32 Parl. Deb., H.C. (5th Ser.) (1911) 1664–67 (statements of Macnamara).

267. *Supplement to the London Gazette of Friday the 28th of August*, 1914, No. 28882, pp. 6873–74. This was confirmed by the Naval Prize Act of 1918, 8 & 9 Geo. 5, c. 30.

268. 69 Parl. Deb., H.C. (5th Ser.) (1915) 1020 (statement of Macnamara).

269. 31 Parl. Deb., H.L. (5th Ser.) (1918) 69 (statement of Desart).

270. C. S. Goldingham, "Naval Prize Money," *Royal United Service Institution Journal* 63 (1919): 98.

271. Kemp, *Prize Money*, 29.

272. 29 Parl. Deb., H.L. (5th Ser.) 643 (1918) (statement of Beresford).

273. For shares, see Kemp, *Prize Money*, 30. For seamen's wages, see Richard Compton-Hall, *Submarines and the War at Sea, 1914–18* (London: Macmillan, 1991), 162.

274. *London Gazette*, Mar. 2, 1915, No. 29086, p. 2081; *London Gazette*, Feb. 29, 1916, No. 29492, pp. 2234–35; 69 Parl. Deb., H.C. (5th Ser.) (1915) 1020 (statement of Macnamara). Note the British sometimes referred to "head money" by the alternative name "prize bounty."

275. Admiral [pseud.], "The Navy and the War," *United Service Magazine* (Dec. 1914), reprinted in *Journal of the Military Service Institution of the United States* 56 (Mar.–Apr. 1915): 274.

276. 27 Parl. Deb., H.C. (5th Ser.) (1911) 659–61 (statement of Roberts).

277. This was reported years later in 353 Parl. Deb., H.C. (5th Ser.) (1939) 692 (statement of Shakespeare).

278. 159 Parl. Deb., H.C. (5th Ser.) (1922) 1735 (statement of Eyres-Monsell); Compton-Hall, *Submarines and the War at Sea*, 162, 322n3.

279. For defenses of head money by Vice-Admiral Taylor and Captain Marsden, see 457 Parl. Deb., H.C. (5th Ser.) (1948) 1878–79, 1888–89; 458 Parl. Deb., H.C. (5th Ser.) (1948) 969. For a critical view of head money by a former navy commander, see 457 Parl. Deb., H.C. (5th Ser.) (1948) 1875 (statement of Pursey).

280. *The Independent*, reprinted in "Our Unfair Naval Rewards," *Springfield (MA) Republican*, Sept. 7, 1898, p. 5.

## EPILOGUE

1. Desmond King and Robert C. Lieberman, "Ironies of State Building: A Comparative Perspective on the American State," *World Politics* 61 (2009): 571. For a survey of the literature on America's divergence from the Weberian type, see my discussion in note 22 to the Introduction.

2. Elisabeth S. Clemens, "Lineages of the Rube Goldberg State: Building and Blurring Public Programs, 1900–1940," in *Rethinking Political Institutions: The Art of the State*, ed. Ian Shapiro et al. (New York: New York University Press, 2006), 188.

3. David Osborne and Ted Gaebler, *Reinventing Government: How the Entrepreneurial Spirit Is Transforming the Public Sector* (New York: Plume, 1992), 12–16, 124–30, 195–205, 209–11, 253, 268–69, 324.

4. Ibid., 15.

5. Weber, *ES*, 1:221.

6. John D. Donahue, *The Privatization Decision: Public Ends, Private Means* (New York: Basic Books, 1989). See also Steven J. Kelman, "Achieving Contracting Goals and Recognizing Public Law Concerns: A Contracting Management Perspective," in *Government by Contract: Outsourcing and American Democracy*, ed. Jody Freeman and Martha Minow (Cambridge, MA: Harvard University Press, 2009).

APPENDIX

1. 1886–87 Ala. Laws 161.

2. Individual counties: 1885 Ariz. Sess. Laws 117, 120 (Cochise); ibid., 122, 125 (Mohave); ibid., 178, 181 (Pima); ibid., 265, 267–68 (Apache); ibid., 281, 281–82 (Maricopa); ibid., 293, 296 (Yavapai); ibid., 299, 302 (Graham). Rest of territory: 1893 Ariz. Sess. Laws 120, 125.

3. 1937 Ark. Acts 790.

4. On San Francisco, see 1856 Cal. Stat. 145, 148–49. In the years after 1856, the legislature salarized officers (including district attorneys) of several individual counties by special acts. Contemporaries described these acts as numerous and extraordinarily confusing. *The Codes and Statutes of the State of California*, ed. Theodore H. Hittell (San Francisco: A. L. Bancroft and Co., 1876), 2:1440 (editor's note). In 1907, the legislature enacted a general county government statute. 1907 Cal. Stat. 354. It provided that the salaries and fees enumerated therein for each officer were to be the full compensation for that officer's services unless otherwise provided in the statute itself. Ibid., 545–56. The statute's catalog of all counties included no fees for any district attorney.

5. Capped: 1891 Colo. Sess. Laws 307, 308, discussed in *Airy v. People*, 40 P. 362, 362 (Colo. 1895). Fully converted: 1919 Colo. Sess. Laws 388.

6. 1895 Fla. Laws 122.

7. A constitutional amendment of 1916 made it easier for the legislature to salarize public prosecutors. 1916 Ga. Laws 24, amending the Georgia Constitution of 1877, art. 6, sec. 13, para. 2. Between 1916 and 1933, the legislature converted public prosecutors to salaries in most of the judicial circuits. *The Code of Georgia of 1933* (Atlanta: Harrison, 1935), § 24–2904n. On later developments, see Duane R. Nedrud, "The Career Prosecutor: Prosecutors of Forty-Eight States," *Journal of Criminal Law, Criminology, and Political Science* 51 (1960): 348–49.

8. 1913 Ill. Laws 360.

9. 1907 Ind. Acts 330 (salarizing circuits consisting of one county and having population 71,000 to 150,000 in 1900 census, meaning Allen and Vanderburg); 1911 Ind. Acts 491, amended by 1913 Ind. Acts 259 (salarizing circuits consisting of one county and having population 84,000 to 150,000 in 1910 census, meaning St. Joseph and Vigo); 1921 Ind. Acts 851 (salarizing counties having population more than 300,000, meaning Marion); 1931 Ind. Acts 607 (salarizing all others). For the counties within each circuit, see *Burns' Annotated Indiana Statutes* (Indianapolis: Bobbs-Merrill, 1914), § 1461.

10. 1891–92 Ky. Acts 258, 265; Nedrud, "The Career Prosecutor," 348 (officers reach maximum "without effort" as of 1960); 1976 Ky. Acts Extraordinary Sess. 183, 185.

11. On New Orleans, see Louisiana Constitution of 1913, art. 148 (amendment ratified 1916). The Constitution of 1921 said the district attorney of each parish would no longer receive fees once the legislature set his salary. Louisiana Constitution of 1921, art. 7, secs. 59, 64. Over the next several years, the legislature set salaries for many parishes by local acts, cataloged in *Louisiana Revised Statutes of 1950* (St. Paul, MN: West, 1950–59), Title 16, §§ 191, 241, 281, 321, 351, 381, 401, 421, 451, 481, 511, 541, 571, 601, 621. The last were salarized in 1950 La. Acts 362.

12. Mississippi Constitution of 1890, art. 6, sec. 174.
13. On St. Louis misdemeanors, see 1865 Mo. Laws 77, 79–80. On St. Louis felonies, see *Folk v. City of St. Louis*, 157 S.W. 71, 73 (Mo. 1913) (discussing change of 1869). On subsequent developments, see 1893 Mo. Laws 168 (salarizing counties with population 100,000 to 300,000, meaning Jackson); 1907 Mo. Laws 274 (salarizing counties of population 32,000–50,000, meaning Macon); 1913 Mo. Laws 709 (salarizing counties of population 80,000–150,000, meaning Buchanan, Jackson, and Marion); 1919 Mo. Laws 672 (greatly increasing salaries, thus reducing fees' importance); 1945–46 Mo. Laws 1535 (salarizing third- and fourth-class counties); 1945–46 Mo. Laws 1566 (salarizing first-class counties); *Revised Statutes of the State of Missouri, 1949* (Jefferson City, MO: Mid-State Printing Co., 1950), § 56.340 (salarizing second-class counties).
14. For the initial wave of county-specific acts, see 1874 N.J. Laws 411; 1874 N.J. Laws 487; 1875 N.J. Laws 283, 283–84; 1875 N.J. Laws 287; 1875 N.J. Laws 288; 1875 N.J. Laws 324; 1875 N.J. Laws 411; 1875 N.J. Laws 411; 1875 N.J. Laws 412; 1875 N.J. Laws 438; 1875 N.J. Laws 462; 1875 N.J. Laws 629; 1880 N.J. Laws 321. For the court's decision, see *Passaic County v. Stevenson*, 46 N.J.L. 173 (1884). For the later acts, see the catalogue in *Revised Statutes of New Jersey, 1937* (Newark, NJ: Soney and Sage Co., 1938–39), Title 2, § 182–11 note. All were on salary in 1919 N.J. Laws 344.
15. 1913 N.M. Laws 65.
16. 1923 N.C. Sess. Laws. 453, 453–54.
17. 1898 Or. Laws Special Sess. 7 (fourth judicial district, including Multnomah County, containing Portland); 1899 Or. Laws 184, 184–85 (rest of state).
18. 1877 S.C. Acts Extra Sess. 246, 247. This statute is poorly drafted and might be read to apply only to the first circuit, but I think it applied to all circuits, as confirmed by its rendering in *The Revised Statutes of South Carolina* (Columbia, SC: Charles A. Calvo Jr., 1894), vol. 1, § 568.
19. 1897 Tenn. Pub. Acts 170.
20. On the initial cap, see 1897 Tex. Gen. Laws Special Sess. 42, 42–43. On the loosening of caps for some counties, see, e.g., 1911 Tex. Gen. Laws 111, 116 (permitting district attorney of Harris County, containing Houston, to retain 25 percent of fees above cap). The provisions in force for various districts as of 1928 can be found in *1928 Complete Texas Statutes* (Kansas City, MO: Vernon Law Book Co., 1928), §§ 3882–92. As for the eventual local acts converting all district attorneys to salaries, I shall not enumerate them (they are numerous). See the index entries for "District Attorneys" in the Texas session laws for the 1920s to the 1940s. For confirmation that all were eventually on salary, see 1949 Tex. Gen. Laws 112.
21. *Code of Washington Containing All Acts of a General Nature* (Olympia, WA: C. B. Bagley, 1881), §§ 2147, 2151, 2158–59.
22. 1908 W.Va. Acts Extra Session 72; 1915 W.Va. Acts 454, 456.
23. 1879 Conn. Pub. Acts 458.
24. *The Annotated Revised Codes of the Territory of Dakota, 1883*, 2nd ed., ed. A. B. Levisee and L. Levisee (St. Paul, MN: West Publishing Co., 1885), 539–40 (statute of 1883).
25. 1871 Del. Laws 50.

26. 1886 Iowa Acts 91, 93.

27. 1839 Maine Laws 582, 583.

28. In 1864–66, the Baltimore state's attorney was earning fees somewhat less than $3,000 per annum. "Reports of the Clerks of Co. Commissioners and Circuit Courts," p. 4, appended as Document B to *Proceedings of the State Convention, of Maryland, to Frame a New Constitution, Commenced at Annapolis, May 8, 1867* (Annapolis, MD: George Colton, 1867). The Maryland constitution of 1867 capped state's attorneys' earnings at $3,000 per annum. Art. 15, sec. 1. This cap presumably converted the Baltimore state's attorney to salary de facto, as the city's population grew. On Cecil County, see 1892 Md. Laws 150. For the later local acts, see the entry "State's Attorney" for each county in *Code of the Public Local Laws of Maryland*, ed. Horace E. Flack (Baltimore: King Brothers, 1930).

29. 1822 Mass. Acts January Sess. 720; 1832 Mass. Acts 396, 404–07.

30. 1867 Neb. Laws 48, 49.

31. On New York City, see 1820 N.Y. Laws November Sess. 91 (session went into 1821). In 1838–52, the legislature salarized district attorneys in several counties by local acts. E.g., 1838 N.Y. Laws 83, 84 (Erie County). In 1852, it authorized each county to decide the form of its district attorney's compensation. 1852 N.Y. Laws 447. By 1884, "most, if not all" counties paid their district attorney by salary. Clinton A. Moon, *A Digest of Fees of Town and County Officers of the State of New York*, 5th ed. (Rochester, NY: Williamson and Higbie, 1884), 36.

32. Salarization of the first three counties was mandated by the Pennsylvania Constitution of 1874, art. 14, sec. 5, implemented through 1876 Pa. Laws 13. On the rest of the state, see 1905 Pa. Laws 170.

33. 1852 R.I. Acts & Resolves (June Session) 119.

34. 1859 Vt. Acts & Resolves 11, 12–14.

35. 1874 Idaho Sess. Laws 579, 580; 1880 Idaho Sess. Laws 250, 253 (session went into 1881); *The Revised Statutes of Idaho Territory* (Boise: n.p., 1887), 269, 277, 280 (statute of 1887).

36. On the conversion of all fees to salaries (except in liquor cases), see 1899 Kansas Sess. Laws 285, 287–88. On the Kansas fee structure and its evolution, see my discussion in Chapter 7, text at notes 115–16, 132–38, 267–79.

37. For boards' power, see *The Revised Statutes of the State of Michigan* (Detroit: John S. Bagg, 1838), 44. On how boards favored salaries, see E. C. Wines and Theodore W. Dwight, *Report on the Prisons and Reformatories of the United States and Canada, Made to the Legislature of New York, January, 1867* (Albany, NY: Van Benthuysen and Son's, 1867), 518 (comment of H. K. Clark).

38. When Congress created the Minnesota Territory, it said Wisconsin law was to remain in place unless changed. § 12, 9 Stat. 403, 407 (1849). At the time, Wisconsin compensated public prosecutors purely by salary. *The Revised Statutes of the State of Wisconsin* (Southport, WI: C. Latham Sholes, 1849), 102. See also 1859–60 Minn. Laws 94, 95–96.

39. 1885 Mont. Laws 59, 60; 1889 Mont. Laws 147, 150; 1891 Mont. Laws 235, 236–37.

40. On initial salaries, see 1866 Nev. Stat. 126. On conviction fees for selected offenses, see 1869 Nev. Stat. 119, 120 (gambling); 1873 Nev. Stat. 189, 190 (vagrancy); 1901 Nev. Stat. 23, 23 (slot-machine law). For eventual county-specific salarization acts, see, e.g., 1885 Nev. Stat. 85, 85–86 (Washoe), 91 (Douglas); 1907 Nev. Stat. 137, 138 (Elko).

41. *The Laws of the State of New Hampshire* (Hopkinton, NH: Isaac Long Jr., 1830), 70 (statute of 1789); ibid., 71 (statute of 1829); *The Revised Statutes of the State of New Hampshire* (Concord, NH: Carroll and Baker, 1843), 468.

42. The earliest statute I can locate on public prosecutors' compensation is 1815 Ohio Laws 118, 120, which says that each officer is to receive "such sum as shall be allowed by the court of common pleas of the proper county, to be paid out of the county treasury." This probably means a salary. A search of Ohio statutes throughout the nineteenth century yields no reference to any fees for the public prosecutor.

43. *The Statutes of Oklahoma 1890*, ed. Will T. Little et al. (Guthrie, OK: State Capital Printing Co., 1891), 395–96.

44. *Acts, Resolutions, and Memorials Passed at the Several Sessions of the Legislative Assembly of the Territory of Utah* (Great Salt Lake City, UT: Henry McEwan, 1866), 74–75 (statute of 1859); 1874 Utah Laws 37, 47.

45. *The Revised Statutes of the State of Wisconsin* (Southport, WI: C. Latham Sholes, 1849), 102.

46. For initial scheme, see 1869 Wyo. Sess. Laws 373, 376. For salarization, see 1877 Wyo. Sess. Laws 98, 98–99 (Laramie County); ibid., 101, 101–02 (Albany); ibid., 108, 108 (Carbon); ibid., 112, 112–13 (Uinta); 1879 Wyo. Sess. Laws 74, 77 (rest of state).

# INDEX

accusers. *See* victims of crime, as accusers

acquittal, fees in cases of, 258–59, 267–69

Adams, John, 79

Adams, John Quincy, 322–23, 329, 347, 523n57

Adams, T. S., 216–19

administration as subsequent to legislation, 15–16, 93

admiralty and vice-admiralty courts, 59–60, 67–68, 109–10, 398n82, 400n102, 401n116, 402n134, 419n175

African Americans: convict leasing, 295; fugitive slaves, 37; Jim Crow South, 44–45, 291; Ku Klux Klan, 271; naturalization of, 128; and urbanization, 291–92; use of Philadelphia criminal justice system by, 127. *See also* slaves

agriculture, 163–69, 177, 187–88, 191, 200, 274–75, 282. *See also* public lands

Alabama: arrest fees in, 44, 392n136; conviction fees in, 263, 265, 269–71, 291, 363, 502n140; as moonshine region, 283; tax ferrets in, 192, 194, 197

*Albany Law Journal*, 117

alcohol. *See* liquor

aldermen (criminal-law magistrates in Philadelphia), 127, 259–61

alienation of service recipients (by abolition of facilitative payments): in general, 23; in naturalization, 142–45; settlement laws, 173–79; World War I veterans' benefits, 159–62

alien imposition: in criminal prosecution, 28, 43, 262–89, 291–94; in customs duty collections, 41–42, 232–39, 241–54; defined, 24–26, 384n54; initial promise of bounties to effectuate, 26–28, 31–33; legitimation of, difficult to achieve with bounties, 28–30, 36–37; and navy/ military, 46–47, 315–25, 336–52; in penitentiaries, 46, 298–306; in *qui tam* statutes, 26–28; spread of, in mid-1800s to early 1900s, 31; in state and local property taxation, 38–39, 187–220; unbearable in absence of discretionary nonenforcement, 39–40. *See also* discretionary nonenforcement and forbearance; informers; legitimacy; positivism; surveillance; technical violations of law; trust; victimless crimes

alien suffrage, 128, 136

alliances, fear of international, 47, 79, 108–9, 308–10, 317–18, 337

American exceptionalism (and Weber's ideal type of bureaucracy), 6–8, 360–62

*American Law Reports*, 194

American Legion, 161–62. *See also* veterans' lobby